Mystics, Monarchs, and Messiahs

HARVARD MIDDLE EASTERN MONOGRAPHS
XXXV

Mystics, Monarchs, and Messiahs

Cultural Landscapes of Early Modern Iran

Kathryn Babayan

DISTRIBUTED FOR THE
CENTER FOR MIDDLE EASTERN STUDIES
OF HARVARD UNIVERSITY BY
HARVARD UNIVERSITY PRESS
CAMBRIDGE, MASSACHUSETTS
LONDON, ENGLAND

For my teacher, the late Martin B. Dickson,
and for my family

Contents

Note on Transliteration and Usage

The system of transliteration adoped for Persian, Turkish, and Arabic is that used by the *International Journal for Middle Eastern Studies* with a few modifications. Terms and names that commonly appear in scholarship on Islamdom are rendered without diacritical marks; hence *'ulamā'* and *Isfāhān* appear as *ulama* and *Isfahan*. Technical terms shared in Persian, Turkish, and Arabic are transliterated according to the original language; hence *raj'a* rather than *raj'at*. All terms are transcribed, indicating long vowels (ā, ī, ū) as well as diphthongs (ay, aw). In the body of this monograph, however, proper names are not transcribed.

Acknowledgments

Many people participated in the making of this book. Martin Dickson first revealed the Safavi world to me, relating its vibrancy through literature and art. He planted the seed of my fascination with the *ghulāt* and left me wondering about the religiosity of the Qizilbash. This book is the product of his inspiration and is enlivened by his teachings, which engaged with and imagined the Safavis and their times. I wish that he had lived to read it.

During the trajectory of my life as a historian, I have been fortunate to encounter several true scholars and human beings *(javānmard)*. I deeply appreciate their guidance, their willingness to share ideas, and the generosity of spirit with which they perform these roles. Peter Brown graciously took me on at a time in the writing of my dissertation when Martin Dickson's death left me orphaned. Peter Brown alerted me to the "massiveness" of the phenomenon of the maintenance of historical memory in the Persian world, and the questions he asked shaped the conceptual frame of this book. His own work as a renegade medievalist provided an alternative method for the study of religious history in the Mediterranean world of late antiquity and helped me situate Islam and the *ghulāt* within broader cultural maps as well as coherent and enduring mindsets. Afsaneh

Najmabadi also has given freely of her time and thought; the questions she posed about my work prodded me toward critical rethinking of key points. Her own intriguing readings of gender and sexuality in modern Iran have encouraged me to view Safavi society from multiple horizons. Without her encouragement and efforts, this book would have taken much longer to be published, and we all know what that means when we are up for tenure. I am grateful for her friendship.

Thanks to Sayyid Husayn Mudarresi's vast knowledge of the sources and familiarity with the culture of the *ulama*, I have acquired a sensibility for the tensions that infused Safavi religious culture. Questioning my renderings of Qizilbash Islam, he probed me to strengthen my assumptions and to imagine what it might have been like for a mystic turned messiah accused of heresy. From the beginning of my studies, Cemal Kafadar has been a refreshing presence—always curious and willing to play with ideas. His work on Anatolian culture, which complicates life on the frontiers, has served as an example of how we can productively use literary works such as epics or hagiographies for the study of popular culture. I would also like to thank Roy Mottahedeh for his kind support and his writing of social history. So much of my understanding of Iranian history is due to his sharp elucidation of the ways in which constructs such as loyalty and authority are expressed through language to represent social networks and ethical bonds that generate particular associations in the medieval Persianate world.

Without the boundless love, generosity, and encouragement of my family, this book would have never been written. My passion and spirit are indeed the gift of their nurturing. As this book came into being, many friends showered me with love and receptive attention, enduring both my tribulations with writing and academia and my obsession with *ghuluww*. They carefully read the various pieces that went into this book and responded with thoughtful comments that helped me refine my ideas and words to describe the multiplicity of processes of change considered in this book. All of those friends are part of this project:

Katy Ansari, Begonia Aretxaga, Azar and Ahmad Ashraf, Sussan Babaie, Ina Baghdiantz McCabe, Carol Bardenstein, Gary Beckman, Michael Bonner, Robert Cohanim, Michael Cook, Dick Davis, Kobra Eghtedary, Massumeh Farhad, Cornell Fleischer, Daniela Gobetti, Robert McChesney, Charles Melville, Parvaneh Pourshariati, Yopie Prins, Helmut Puff, Setareh Sabety, Anton Shammas, Sanjay Subrahmanyam, Ismael Velasco, Teresa Verdera, Gernot Windfuhr, Davida Wood, Jamilé Woods, and Norman Yoffee.

In working on this project, I was fortunate to have been awarded two Humanities Institute fellowships. The first, at the Robert Penn Warren Center for the Humanities at Vanderbilt University (1995–1996), was conceived around the theme of "The Apocalypse: Fin de Siècle Millennium, and Other Transitions." At Vanderbilt, I began to think in megahistorical terms about tensions between cyclical time and Abrahamic senses of endings. Thanks to Margaret Doody, Mona Frederick, and David Wood, I came to appreciate the pervasiveness of time and apocalyptic thinking in Western art, literary works, and philosophy. There we sat in Nashville, imagining what could replace the image of a mushroom cloud over Hiroshima with the coming of the new millennium; little did we know that it would be the image of two jetliners colliding with the World Trade Center towers on September 11, 2001. I spent the 1999 to 2000 academic year as a visiting fellow in the Institute for the Humanities at the University of Michigan. I would like to thank Tom Trautmann and Eliza Woodford for creating a warm space where the fellows could exchange ideas, read, and write, free from the pressures of academic responsibilities. Anne Carson's presence among us that year was a special gift that infused the discussions with fresh words and thoughts: her individuality and creativity were contagious. I would also like to thank my graduate students, Belgin Eraydin, Stuart Goldberg, Layla Hourani, Erik Ohlander, and Madina Zainullina-Goldberg, who participated with such enthusiasm and insight in the seminar I taught at the Institute that year on Cultural Memory, Cyclical Time and the

Writing of History in Early Modern Iran. They too are part of this book.

I am grateful for the generous assistance of Filiz Cagman, director of the Topkapi Palace Museum and Library; Massumeh Farhad, curator of Islamic art at the Arthur M. Sackler and Freer Gallery; Sophie Macariou, curator of Islamic art at the Department of Oriental Antiquities in the Louvre; Mary MacWilliams, curator of Islamic and Indian art at Harvard University's Arthur M. Sackler Museum; Marilyn Palmeri, photography and rights manager at the Pierpont Morgan Library; and the photo reproduction staff at the Library of Congress for granting me the permission to reproduce the images in this book. I would like to single out the copious efforts of Massumeh Farhad in waiving fees and contacting publishers to arrange for the speedy processing of many of these permissions.

Sections from two of my articles, "The Safavi Synthesis: From Qizilbash Islam to Imamite Shi'ism," *Iranian Studies,* 27 (1994): 135–161, and "Sufis, Darvishes, and Mullas: The Controversy over Spiritual and Temporal Dominion in Seventeenth-Century Safavi Iran," in *Safavid Persia,* edited by Charles Melville (London: Tauris, 1996), have been used in this book. I would like to thank the editors of *Iranian Studies* and I. B. Tauris for their permission to reprint several revised selections from those articles.

Last but not least, I would like to acknowledge the professionalism and assistance of Habib Ladjevardi, chair of the Editorial Board of the Harvard Middle Eastern Monographs. He made the process of publishing easy and pleasurable. I would also like to recognize the editorial assistance of Müge Galin, Anne Marie Oliver, Eileen Pollack, and Rosemary Winfield, who helped me craft this narrative and gave it its final shape. Erik Ohlander compiled the index and drew the chart mapping out the early Alid Ghulat. His meticulous temperament and efficiency are much appreciated. Layla Hourani helped me with my bibliography. And Rob Haug and Karl Longstreth at the Map Library of the University of Michigan were kind enough to draw me the map of the Safavi empire at the peak of centralization.

Preface

This book is about idealists and visionaries who believed that justice can reign in this world. It is about the sense of immediacy inherent in the desire to experience utopia on earth. Reluctant to await another existence following death, individuals with *ghuluww,* or "exaggeration,"[1] emerged at the advent of Islam, expecting to approach the apocalyptic horizon of truth. In their minds, Muhammad's prophecy represented one such cosmic moment of transformation.

Because time is imagined as cyclical, change and renewal have no limits for the *ghulāt* (exaggerators). History is lived as a story of successive struggles to achieve paradise on earth. The *ghulāt* do not see the universe in the linear terms of a beginning and an end but as successive cycles in which the end of one era spontaneously flows into another. By *cyclical* I do not intend to convey a conception of repetitive same-times because some *ghulāt* believe in reincarnation *(tanāsukh)* and see death as the end of one physical form leading to metamorphosis, with the spirit enhanced each time it incarnates into new and purer forms. In this alchemical sense, for most *ghulāt* the final apocalypse is not their end as it is for the more mainstream Jews, Christians, and Muslims. They fathom time and being as eternal. What distinguishes each cycle is a new prophetic vision, with each cycle unveiling layers of the mystery of the universe. And because the cosmos is understood to be alive, different dimensions endlessly unraveling in such a way that renders ultimate truth inexplicable, there are no bounds to new imaginings.

The *ghulāt* envisaged divinity as incarnated *(hulūl)* in humans, with each believer an earthly god who is able to connect with the holy personally through prophetic inspiration, illumination, or permeation. They believed in the dual and yet integrated existence of spirit and matter and in the human potential to transcend matter and access the divine while on earth. In fact, *transcenders* might be a more appropriate term for them. Instead, they are branded as *heretics,* resisting as they do the separation between heaven and earth posited by Muhammad's monotheistic vision—thus, the contemptuous cast of *ghulāt* in Muslim discourse.

Even into the early modern period, some denizens of Islamdom continued to hope for a utopia despite numerous aborted promises and expectations. In a moment of enthusiasm, one group called the Qizilbash (Red Heads), the subject of this book, took up arms at the turn of the sixteenth century to fight for Shaykh Isma'il Safavi, their divinely inspired leader, a veritable godhead in their eyes, to establish truth and justice on earth. Half a century earlier, these predominately Turkmen tribesmen from Anatolia and Syria had been spiritual adepts of the Safavi mystical order; within two generations they had conquered Iran and Iraq and become the soldiers, generals, governors, and courtiers of Shah Isma'il (r. 1501–1524), who ruled what they believed to be the just kingdom. The Qizilbash enjoyed multidimensional roles in the space of what they perceived as an eon, marked by a new dispensation of Safavi universal rule (1501–1722). But theirs is a story of betrayal and of human frailty when confronted with the task of using spiritual and temporal power.

This work attempts to understand how basic issues with which human beings have been preoccupied throughout recorded history—questions such as where we come from, what our purpose is in the world, and where we travel from here—animated the spiritual landscape of the Qizilbash. What myths did the Qizilbash create in their attempt to make sense of existence? What were the particular cultural (social, religious, and political) conditions under which such tendencies were expressed in the agrarianate age and in the geographical and historical settings of early modern Iran, Iraq, Syria, and Anatolia?

It is my hope that this study will shed light on one cultural variety—on a particular option, synthesis, and paradigm born out of the eclecticism of the Hellenistic age, a product of interaction between Irano-Semitic, Hellenic, and Indic tectonic plates. For I understand the cultural landscape of Qizilbash Islam, in particular, and *ghuluww*, in general, as a distinct mixture of myths and beliefs disseminated by the spiritual revolution of the late antique world, which in its apocalyptic mode pondered good and evil, holy and human, spirit and matter, and gave birth to new visions of prophets like Jesus, Mani, and Muhammad.

Ghuluww is a treasure trove for understanding the gnostics born out of Mazdean, Jewish, Christian, or pagan communities in Mesopotamia, Iran, and Asia Minor, who maintained an older sense of time, which monotheisms like Islam with their emphasis on end-time rejected.[2] The *ghulāt* imagined time as analogous to the change of seasons and the cyclical motion of the stars and planets around the ceiling of the earth. The pervasiveness of time affects the way we narrate the past, the way we write history—a history in which we ourselves are agents of change and continuity. Different languages and memories of past times lived on into the Islamic era, finding new lives and crafting new narratives. These recollections represent a variety of competing strands, some of which maintained to lesser or greater degrees vestiges of their dualist pasts.

I narrate the ways in which a Persianate ethos participated in the making of new Muslim (Alid and sufi) identities and cultural systems.[3] It is a story of conversion and intercultural translation, of attempts made to apply traditional patterns of thought against a novel phenomenon, and of the rise of a new revelation

(Islam) and the predominance of Arab rule in the Iranian world. Some Persianate practices and modes of consciousness continued to exist despite prevalent Muslim (Sunni) hegemonies, breathing life into heterogeneous spaces of opposition amongst the *ghulāt* and Alid loyalists. And some others adapted to and survived in "legitimate" Muslim arenas shaping new forms of religiosity (Shi'ism and Persianate sufism). Such processes of cultural change over time lie at the core of this book's inquiry. Transformation will be studied at a particular historical junction of conversion, as Islam was consolidating its cultural dominance eastward and northward into Mesopotamia, Iran, and Anatolia. These were landscapes in which Persianate systems of belief had been entrenched for generations. Three sites in which their "survival" is most pronounced are explored: *ghuluww,* Alid loyalty, and sufism (mysticism). In the case of the Safavis, Alid loyalty and sufism mingled with *ghuluww.* I isolate the symbolic resources that allowed for continuities and provided creative spaces for the generation of new forms of Muslim sensibilities within these three arenas. Rather than resort to the type of textual analysis that is more common, I emphasize the ways in which such spaces allowed for the maintenance of different memories of past times in daily practice.

I have contextualized the actors of this book within their particular cultural, political, and social settings, weaving such forces together with characters who acted with or against them. Yet to maintain a sense of dynamic change in time, I have concentrated on transformations through the long process of conversion of the Iranian lands to Islam. Comparing medieval manifestations of what are represented in official sources as "exaggerated" impulses to their early modern counterparts (Qizilbash, Nuqtavi), I explore how in the writing of history dominant discourses came to dismiss these messianic movements, limiting and silencing entire cosmologies, histories, and oppositional practices in the process. These oppressive discourses illuminate endeavors to marginalize practices that I consider to be a form of resistance. In the process of canonizing one "unified language" of Qur'anic truth, they succeed in supplanting a multiplicity of expression—social and religious dialects operating in the midst of a Bakhtian heteroglossia.[4] Ironically, just as the Safavis attempt a rationalization of religion, they come to reject the very language with which they led a successful revolution in early modern Iran.

The Safavi case serves as an example of the ways in which a particular expression of "exaggeration" practiced in Alid mystical circles succeeded in fomenting a revolution and was subsequently exposed to attempts at erasure and expulsion into the realms of heresy. The social settings (*futuvvat* and *tarīqat*) in which such beliefs were performed in Safavi Iran are highlighted to explore the relationship between discourse and practice. Given our limited knowledge of the socioeconomic systems of early modern Iran, I privilege culture and politics here, not only because I am a historian drawn to such forms of human expression but also because these dimensions are so much more accessible through extant Safavi sources.[5] Yet some kind of materialism is presumed when analyzing Safavi subjects and their sociocultural practices.

I am assuming that culture affects the way people act—the way they talk, revolt, choose their lifestyles, and enact their rituals. Geertz's interpretation of "culture" as a web of meanings encoded in symbols that are publicly expressed so that we can comprehend them (language, artifacts, rituals, calendars) has inspired my reading of the Safavi world.[6] People make and write history. And when they write, they reveal their attempts to make sense or give meaning to their experiences. I hope to capture the ways in which Persianate and Alid idioms mediated Safavi actions and narratives through cultural constructs of authority, loyalty, honor, and piety. More particularly, I seek to incorporate human experiences of temporality in a reconstruction of history. Ricoeur points out the pervasiveness of time.[7] He relates temporal conceptions to the way we act and the way we narrate history or give meaning to actions and experiences that become embedded in a variety of literary (history, poetry, epics), visual (painting, architecture), or symbolic productions (rituals, commemoration). Cyclical time, so central to *ghulāt* cosmologies, marks these cultural productions.

Memory is vital to an inscription of the past. It affects the way we come to narrate a present and anticipate a future through this pastness. Memory links the present to the past as memory making relates Persianate and Alid pasts to their experiences in the Safavi present.[8] I delineate the sites (*futuvvat, Abū Muslimnāme, Shāhnāme,* solar calendar, Persian language) through which this past was memorized and performed. Features of these Persianate and Alid idioms are drawn from particular symbolic forms that clustered together repeatedly in Ricoeur's sense of "texts." Sufism, Alid loyalty, and *ghuluww* are repositories from which these different pasts could be recalled and modified in the present. I understand these cultural arenas as channels through which continuities were maintained through narrative memory, creating bridges between aporia of past and present times.[9] But were these memories habitual memories (*milieux de mémoire*), unconsciously mediating channels through which "older" cultural systems continued to live on different modes and shapes?[10] In other words, were these memories part of a Safavi habitus?[11] Or were these conscious memories, evoked and appropriated in a circumstance in which there was a sense of rupture with the past, a fear that this past was being forgotten and hence that gave rise to the need to create a *lieu de mémoire* in which they would be remembered?[12] Could these consciously narrated memories become routine as they were ritualized or dramatized?

To probe these issues in the spirit of Geertz, I have privileged symbols within these three sites (*ghuluww,* Alid loyalty, and sufism) and then explored the different ways in which these signs were imbued with meaning. How are they encoded in the text to shape particular significations that manifest older readings? By comparing the multitude of emplotments, I hope to distinguish different identities. An ethos may be inferred from icons embedded in such narratives allowing for an identification of an

Alid and a Persianate variety that often overlap. Although different mediums *(Shāhnāme, Abū Muslimnāme)* were used to preserve and ritualize such memories, they were part of everyday practice. I have tried to contextualize these symbols to uncover meanings and texture, layer by layer, recreating and imagining the landscapes in and about which these memory texts were recorded in the past and performed in the Safavi present. How are these webs of meanings represented to reflect particular attitudes or behaviors? Where were they performed? Do they resonate with the motivations that then led some *ghulāt* (Qizilbash, Nuqtavis) to revolt, taking up arms to return to a pre-Islamic Persian past or to an ideal Muslim (Alid) utopia?

I find Geertz's understanding of semiotic systems and the tight fit he observes between clusters of symbols and the moods, motivations, and behaviors that these symbols shape insightful. Memory is a cultural phenomenon that speaks through signs and influences behavior as well.[13] Culture, however, is mutable. Geertz's methods are essentially synchronic—that is, they tend to help us understand one face of history as a temporal complex. But the other face of history as transformation, the diachronic aspect, remains untapped in his notion of culture.[14] Here is where Yuri Lotman's meditations on culture help to make sense of change in time.[15] Lotman and Uspenskii's work on the semiotics of Russian culture in the light of history focuses on sites of conflict, dialogue, and change within cultures that speak different languages. They conceptualize cultural differences at the intrasociety level. Although Geertz tends to emphasize differences between societies, writing comparatively about "the Javanese" or "the Berbers," Lotman troubles this "single functioning whole" by proposing a "semiotic physiology" that posits a dynamic between different languages embedded in the whole (semiosphere), privileging heterogeneity within Russian culture. Lotman opens an analytical space to think about how cultural systems are transformed within complex or, as he calls them, "collective" cultures, raising the possibilities for disjunctions or continuities.[16] The Bakhtian trope of heteroglossia permits a refinement of such processes of change—sensitive to the diversity of social voices uttered through language. For Bakhtin language is alive; it dwells in the process of becoming. Its transcription is not only a product of its context but is subject to multiple refractions and meanings that encompass a variety of worldviews, group behaviors, and fleeting tendencies. Such stratification and heteroglossia highlight a dynamic between cultural systems and the particular language of social groups. The life and development of language can thus be explored as an expressive system born of social, religious, and political milieus in perpetual dialogue and movement.

I tend to see both continuities and discontinuities in the fragments from the Irano-Islamic past that I study, and I am fascinated by the ways in which this Iranian past blends with the Islamic present in different forms and shapes as well as in degrees of transmutations. The problematic of trying to explain cultural continuities amid change lies at the core of my study. To conceptualize such a dynamic process without losing a sense of multiplicity within an ever-evolving system is difficult. Lotman's binary model of change, based on his reading of medieval and early modern Russian history, is useful when looking at the Iranian case where a similar transformation from a dualist past to a monotheist present was occurring. I wonder whether patterns of change are contextually specific, in that they pertain to similar historical moments, or whether a deeper structural affinity must exist for such paradigms to be pertinent. Conceptual formulations derived from one cultural system may be more relevant if compared to another culture that possesses similar blueprints or templates. Lotman's meditations may be telling us about those cultural landscapes that tend to be rooted in a binary worldview. Both Russian and Iranian culture share a structural binary that permeates the ways in which they gave meaning to their universe and the ways in which they constructed their social and political realities. Lotman is suggesting that we apply a binary framework to explore cultures according to their own terms of cognizance by searching out and analyzing the symbolic forms—words, images, institutions, and memories by which people represent themselves to themselves and to one another.

How are we to understand the persistent rhetoric in some Irano-Islamic religious movements (heresies) of a return to an Iranian past—to a time before the advent of Islam? Vivid memories of this past are preserved in texts, and memories continue to be evoked and performed up to a millennium after the Islamic conquests of the Iranian plateau. The massiveness of the phenomenon of the maintenance of historical memory in Iran is striking. The historian R. G. Collingwood coined the term *encapsulated history* in his *Philosophy of History* to refer to European attitudes to the past—to large tracts of history that were known and preserved and yet were seen as forbidden alternatives to the dominant values of the present.[17] The problem of how these come to form a symbolic resource that can be brought back into the present is fascinating. The Renaissance is one example, but it is not nearly as drastic as the Iranian case. Lotman and Uspenskii's work on the role of dualist models in the dynamics of Russian cultural change depicts a similar sense of a total reversal much more so than the gentler leverage of an *encapsulated past* on the present exercised by Judaism and paganism in Western culture.

Ghuluww is a belief system that played a central role in the (trans)formation of Islamic identities. It was a repository for different traditions that with the cultural project of Islam came to be marginalized and cast as heretical. The book asks why this occurred and attempts to delineate how it happened. In the pages to come, I hope to illuminate aspects of a gnostic way of being and cyclical sense of time alien to modern minds and sensibilities. The reader must be prepared to take an imaginative leap into a way of life and thought very different from his or her own. This narrative, I hope, will facilitate the plunge into another world and another way of experiencing history.

GHULUWW IN DISCOURSE AND PRACTICE

Safavi Islam may have been a mixture of many different currents and tendencies in Islamdom, but *ghuluww,* Alid loyalty, and sufism (mysticism) are its predominant features. *Ghuluww* is the most ambiguous and problematic characteristic of Safavi religiosity.[18] To begin with, it is a pejorative term coined by Muslim heresiographers emerging in the tenth century initially among Imami Shi'i circles to distinguish themselves from a series of Alid movements that had risen in the first centuries of Islam. Sunnis then adopted this early category in their literature on heresy, and the concept of *ghuluww* evolved to designate a particular kind of other.[19] Muslim heresiographer's definitions were, of course, ideologically motivated and were meant to alienate conceptually groups so designated from their own particular mainstream or orthodoxy. As such, the term erroneously suggests an anachronistic impression of marginality. Attacks by so-called orthodoxy on such movements are indeed often indications of the seriousness of their threat to the identity of the norm, and for a Muslim scholar to condemn a group as *ghulāt* is to promote a self-fulfilling aim, not merely noting a particular belief system as falling outside the boundaries of orthodoxy but actively seeking to push it thither. Although those Muslims who came in time to represent an orthodoxy have historically labeled the *ghulāt* as heretics and beyond the pale of Islam, I hope to demonstrate in the pages to come that *ghuluww* does represent an interpretation, a particular fusing of old traditions familiar to the syncretic cultures of Asia Minor, the Fertile Crescent, Mesopotamia, and the Iranian plateau—those core lands in which Islam came to spread its visionary seeds and articulate its divine mission.

The term *ghuluww* immediately posits a dichotomy between a mainstream and a margin at a time when the mainstream was still in the process of self-definition and exaggerated visions held serious possibilities for mainstream development. However, because the term has already been crystallized in Muslim discourse, we have little choice but to use it. Despite the ambiguity and irreverence surrounding the term *ghuluww,* in this study I hope to render the concept more specific for the historian of Islamdom. Aware that its use may create an artificial sense of homogeneity, I am mindful of the variety of "exaggerated" expressions in time and space. At once aware of these expressions' multiplicities and perceptive of their similarities, I study *ghuluww* as one of the numerous simultaneous and divergent choices, visions, and interpretations of Islam, some of which were destined to attain hegemonic status, temporarily or permanently.

Ghuluww symbolizes one worldview against which Islam came to define itself, as well as one among many interpretations and adaptations of Islam. The verb *ghalā* (to exceed or overdo) appears twice in the Qur'an (3:171, 4:71) in the context of condemning those "People of the Book" (Christians) who raise the station of Jesus above that of the human being, deifying him.[20] Indeed, this denunciation represents a chapter in the evolution of Muslim identity and a special one at that, for it played a pivotal role from its genesis all the way to the early modern period, particularly within the Alid idiom in the lands of Anatolia, Iraq, and Iran. *Ghuluww* should be understood in relation to Abrahamic monotheisms, particularly the monotheism of Muhammad as interpreted from the Qur'an. "Exaggeration" signals a different sense of time and being; it is more cyclical and gnostic than mainstream monotheisms.[21] The predominant feature distinguishing it from Abrahamic monotheisms is its exaggerated sense of continuous prophetic unveilings merging heaven with earth and spirit with matter. Peter Brown in *The Making of Late Antiquity* captures this cultural spirit of the Mediterranean world in late antiquity (150–750 C.E.).[22] Brown sees Muhammad and the rise of Islam as a turning point in Mediterranean and Mesopotamian history, when a shift in sensibilities gave way to new styles of cultural and social life that came to shape the medieval world. The late antique debate about the holy arrived at a decisive turn, coinciding with the evolution of early Christianity and the rise of Muhammad, their shared at-

tempts to separate heaven from earth and to define the holy and
the human, and their success in achieving those goals.

The belief in one omniscient and transcendental God is key to
this transformation. The Qur'an is filled with chapters *(sura)*
that emphasize that God is the only one who creates all beings
and endows them with life, the only one who never dies, the
only one who has knowledge of the unseen. Various chapters
also insist that the prophets were ordinary people who lived and
died like everyone else; Muhammad, in particular, is referred to
as an ordinary man who distinguished himself in his role as
spokesman for God. When he was asked to perform miracles
and refused to do so, it was his human limitations that were emphasized.[23] We should also understand the Muslim preoccupation with outlining a typology of the supernatural, distinguishing miracles from magic, trickery, and divinations in this light:
"The hour of doom is drawing near, and the moon is cleft in
two. Yet when they see a sign, the unbelievers turn their backs
and say 'the same old magic'" (Qur'an 54:2).[24] In this quote
from the Qur'an, Peter Brown senses Muhammad's frustration
with the dualist tradition that prevailed in the Mediterranean.
Some denizens of the Mediterranean world, in their binary
imagination of the supernatural, had the choice of selecting their
demons and angels on earth.[25] Muhammad's monotheistic vision, which must have represented a current in late antique Arabia, defined itself, in part, against a more prevalent, older mode
that sensed time cyclically and saw supernatural power represented on earth through human agents who were either good or
evil. A gnostic sense that an enlightened elite had access through
special knowledge to universal secrets impinged on the essence
of monotheistic prophecy and revelation.

Although this esotericism would persist to animate the spiritual landscapes of some *ghulāt,* Shi'is (Isma'ilis, Imamis), and
mystics (sufi), it continued to be a point of contention, polariz-
ing Muslims down to modern times. For some Muslims, Islam is
represented in the Qur'an as other than *ghuluww.* In the process
of labeling *ghuluww* as other from the outset, some Muslims

continued to imagine themselves in relation to it and so in time came to develop aspects of this other, internalizing it. Yet other Muslims came to read exaggeration in the Qur'an. Hence, from its very inception, a distinct belief system held on more firmly to its old worldview and way of being and understood Muhammad and his revelation as one among many who have and shall come forth in the ever-unfolding cycles of illuminating emergence.

The prophets Abraham, Moses, Jesus, and Muhammad, the figure of Ali, and the anticipated messiah (Mahdi) are just as much part of the traditions of some Alid *ghulāt* as they are for most Muslims. Differences emerged in time with normative Islam, in regard to the way in which the *ghulāt* understood the missions of such men, what membership in the family of the Prophet meant as far as divine inheritance was concerned, and which other holy figures from the past shared in this genealogy. Modern scholars, with a few exceptions, have neglected the *ghulāt*. They have either rejected them, without analyzing the rhetoric of the heresiographers, or they have been uninterested in them entirely due to their unorthodox views and marginalization in time. Perhaps they are dubious with regard to the diversity of names and movements that have appeared under the rubric of *ghuluww* in Islamic literature. It is true that the variety of men and groups who espoused such tendencies enjoyed only brief moments of power and hegemony. They were either defeated in battle, were persecuted by the court with the sanction of the clergy, or, as in the case of the Abbasids, Fatimids, and Safavis, betrayed their revolutionary ideals to (re)invent normative Islam once they had attained temporal power. In this process, they aided in the consolidation of a mainstream, making it a legitimizing program of Muslim authority.

This renders the task of a historian more formidable, for official Muslim sources are normally sparing in words and tainted in attitude when it comes to *ghuluww*. And as for literature written by the *ghulāt*, little remains. Nevertheless, this problematic provides the historian with a creative challenge to use as many types of texts as possible—whether revolts, reli-

gious polemics, chronicles, epics, poetry, or miniatures—to gain
an understanding of the spiritual landscape of the *ghulât*. In this
book, I make use of all these forms of "texts" to focus the lens
on the cultural landscape of the Safavis in the hope of illuminating the particularities of an orientation that has been part of the
living tradition of Islam, hence gaining a glimpse of the complex
processes through which *ghuluww* played a role in the formation and unfolding of Islamic identities. In so doing, I hope
to unearth one variety among a multiplicity of exaggerated expressions.

   This narrative attempts to penetrate the cosmos of Safavi devotees. Why did some Qizilbash (Red Heads) enter the battlefield
unarmed, believing that the miraculous powers of their spiritual
guide *(pīr)*, Isma'il, would shield them?[26] What medley of beliefs
and myths inspired some Qizilbash to devour men alive in submission and devotion to a man whom they saw as a living god?[27]
This book explores the Safavi world (1501–1722), an esoteric
chapter in the history of early modern Iran, where the Qizilbash
lived and for a century ruled. Theirs was an age that witnessed
the joining of the spheres of the temporal and the spiritual with
the royal enthronement (in 1501) of a charismatic, red-haired
master named Isma'il. Shah Isma'il fused the dual meaning of
the title *shah* current in the political and religious cultures of the
central and eastern lands of Islamdom.[28] The roles of king and
holy man converge in Isma'il, and he was also a hero on the battlefield and crusader *(ghāzī)* for the faith. These three stock characters—king, warrior, and saint—enjoy a resonance of sanctity
in the beliefs of those Muslims, like the Turkmen Qizilbash, who
had acquired a taste for Persianate culture. Mystics or monarchs
who entered the battlefield and proved themselves as chivalrous
warriors could access prophecy and attain the paradigmatic station of Messiah.

   As Isma'il together with his Qizilbash conquered Iran and
Iraq (1501), he composed poetry *(divan)* in Turkish in which he
claimed to be the reincarnation of a host of Abrahamic prophets
(Adam, Noah, Abraham, Moses, Jesus, and Muhammad) and

Mazdean kings (Jamshid, Zahhak, Feraydun, Khusraw, and Alexander) from Iran's cultural past. Core Islamic texts, like the Qur'an, as well as famous Persian literary works, such as the *Shāhnāme,* formed the repertoire from which Isma'il drew his image.[29] The self-image of Isma'il illuminates the ways in which a Persianate ethos participated in the making of hybrid Muslim identities. Through a study of the Safavis, I hope to delineate the content and meanings of such syncretic forms of conversion to Islam.

The Persian classical epic of kings, the *Shāhnāme* of Ferdowsi, one of the earliest recorded voices of Iranian culture in its Islamicate mode, preserves for future generations a core of Persianate views on humanity and ethics, as well as a particular sense of history and cosmology.[30] In the *Shāhnāme,* the late tenth-century poet Ferdowsi crystallized an image of an Iranian past that lived on in the imaginations of those who came to embrace Persianate culture, from the rulers and courtiers of Ottoman, Safavi, and Mughal courts, to the Turk or Iranian (Tajik) perfume seller who participated in the culture of storytelling in the coffee houses of larger cities and towns in central and eastern Islamdom. The *Shāhnāme* narrates Iranian mythohistory as a cosmic battle between the forces of good, embodied in Iran, and those of evil, personified by their Turanian (non-Iranian) enemies. For Mazdeans, who were adherents of diverse forms of Zoroastrian dualisms, the physical world was created as one such battleground, where history provided humanity with the challenge of truth, for the force of good (Ahura Mazda) had created man and the world to help him fight evil and lies *(drug).* Zoroaster had conceived a cosmology that explained the existence of good and evil in universal terms, relating the physical world to the human dimensions of ethics, spirituality, and even psychology. In this *Epic of Kings,* Jamshid (Yim of the Zoroastrian Avesta) initially fulfills the role of an ideal king, teaching his people the different crafts and organizing society into three classical Indo-Iranian functions (priests, warriors, and artisans).[31] But at the height of his power, he orders demons to build him a carriage in which he rises to the skies. Seduced by evil (Ahriman), he proclaims himself God, at which moment his divine glory *(farr/khwarnah)* departs, leaving Iran open to invasion (evil). It is Jamshid whom Isma'il, not so haphazardly, evokes in his *Divan.* Iran's sovereignty is wholly dependent on the nature of the king, and so long as the king is virtuous and wise, he will maintain his role and his glory, ruling by means of justice and securing his frontiers with a strong army.

But temporal power can be corrupting, and kingship, supreme power on earth, symbolizes the archetypical human struggle between good and evil. Jamshid loses his divine glory *(farr),* and so Iran falls prey to the evil Arab oppressor Zahhak, who literally creates a brain drain in Iran with his need to use the heads of Iranian boys to satiate the appetite of the snakes he has grown from his shoulders. In his *Divan,* Isma'il maintains that he had been Zahhak as well as Feraydun, who succeeded in overthrowing him, binding Zahhak to the mountain range (Alburz) that flanked the northern frontier of Iran (Caspian Sea). Isma'il imagines himself to have lived through one full cycle of history that saw the initial glory, subjugation, and eventual rebirth of Iranian universal rule.

It is interesting that Isma'il also chooses another Iranian (Kayani) king, Kay Khusraw, as one of his former incarnations. Like Isma'il, Kay Khusraw was of mixed Iranian and Turanian (Turk) descent. He was famous for his wisdom and nobility and defeated the Turanian enemy, Afrasiab. Instead of this victory going to his head, at the pinnacle of power, Kay Khusraw relinquished his throne to embark on the spiritual journey of an ascetic. This binary struggle between man's temporal and spiritual existence permeates mystical poetry and informs the topos of the prince turned mystic in Muslim literature. In the *Shāhnāme,* Iranian kings and warriors, descended from noble bloodlines of charismatic rulers and fearless heroes, are constantly challenged to balance the temporal with the spiritual, rather than succumb to the temptations of power and arrogance it can nurture. And the king is summoned to rule his subjects with justice. But the just sovereignty of the king is invariably linked to his character. To rule justly, the king must be a peerless human being, the perfect man.[32]

As a Muslim, Isma'il places himself within the Abrahamic era that traced its genealogy to prophets, beginning with Adam. Noah, Abraham, Moses, and Jesus became part of a prophetic chain in the Qur'an, Muhammad's divine message from Allah. But for Isma'il, this chain did not begin with Adam; nor was it sealed with the advent of the prophet Muhammad, for prophecy continues in every age. As a certain type of Muslim, Isma'il asserts even more: "Know for certain that Khata'i [Isma'il's pen name, which means "the culpable"] is of divine nature, that he is related to Muhammad Mustafa. He is issued from Safi, he is the scion of Junayd and Haydar [Isma'il's grandfather and father], he is related to Ali Murtaza [Muhammad's cousin and son-in-law]."[33]

Isma'il's charismatic persona and the particular cultural roles he came to assert were also laced with two distinct sacred Muslim genealogies, one real and the other fictional. Such a pedigree allowed Isma'il to demand and command unquestioned loyalty. Invoking his "fictitious" lineage that originates with Muhammad and Ali, Isma'il partook in the veneration that some Muslims (Alids) came to focus on the figure of Ali, whom they deified.[34] Isma'il claimed to have inherited the divine spark of the prophet that passed through Ali to his grandchildren, the immaculate Imams. And through the intermediary of his ancestor, the fourteenth-century mystic-saint (sufi) Shaykh Safi al-din (d. 1334), from whom the eponym *Safavi* was derived, Isma'il's "real" pedigree was hallowed with the spiritual sanctity that had come to encircle sufi masters in Islamdom.

Embedded in Qizilbash devotion lay a particular mystical flavor of love for Ali, who appears as the divine beloved in Isma'il's poetry: "Oh my beautiful Shah [Ali] my moon, the fulfillment of my desires, the beloved of my heart. Oh Thou, in whose beauty God manifests himself."[35] As sufis often did in their poetry, Isma'il utilized the metaphor of the beloved to sym-

bolize God himself. For the Qizilbash, this meant more than just
a poetic convention. As Ali had become the object of devotion
through whom the divine could be encountered, and since
Isma'il claimed to possess Ali's blood, the Safavis partook in an
active Alid charisma and in the whole drama that came to surround the story of the betrayal of Muhammad's descendants in
the first century following the prophet's death (632 C.E.). In the
continuation of this drama that was history, the Qizilbash took
on the role of avengers of the family of the prophet, redressers of
truth and justice. Isma'il captures, or perhaps defines, the intensity of their allegiance: "No one can become a Qizilbash," he
writes, "until his heart is a-burning and his breast a-bleeding
like a ruby."[36]

What was this web of beliefs that burned the Qizilbash so as
to bleed for their Safavi masters and the Alid cause—beliefs historians have vaguely termed "Qizilbash Shi'ism" or "extreme
Shi'ism"?[37] Are the cultural ingredients of Qizilbash Islam
identifiable? What is to be made of the mystical origins of the
Safavis (1301) and their transformation into a mystical brotherhood *(tarīqat)* with messianic aspirations (1447) and finally into
an empire (1501)? What was the relationship of the Safavi masters to metaphysics? Was it based on the respectability of the so-
called high sufi tradition or on the religious and political radical-
ism of the so-called low tradition? In this book I contend that
both elements were present. Was one a mask? Was there a hypo-
critical plot involved? In the language of sufi metaphysics, which
is the contingent form and which the necessary essence? I do not
claim to be able to answer all of these complex questions but
merely aspire to present clues to new directions in which answers may be sought.

The cosmology and the particular sense of time and being embedded in most *ghuluww*-tempered landscapes differentiates
them from normative Islam and from the eschatological faiths
that have become hegemonic in our modern technical age. Most
"exaggerators" do not believe in an end time, in a judgment day,
or in bodily resurrection *(ma'ād)*. Their cosmos is devoid of a

hell, and human beings are believed to die but to be reincarnated *(naskh)*—returning *(raj'a)* to this world in a different form. Heaven is conceived of as a potential paradise on earth.[38] For the *ghulāt,* then, history was the story of humanity's successive struggles for the establishment of truth and justice in this world. Depending on the choice narrative of history (Alid or Mazdean), each age was to uncover its particular revelations, each time cycle unveiling different layers of cosmic secrets of existence. The *ghulāt* imagined a cosmic union between heaven and earth in which the individual was in palpable and perceptible contact with the divine. Although human beings were deemed capable of transcendence, some special men were regarded as being more privy, more deserving, and perhaps most capable of succeeding in this holy quest. Revered as models, these men were blessed with a sacred aura, and they were expected to be paragons of truth and justice. Here lies a distinct feature of Mazdean idiosyncrasy active in *ghuluww.* In the cyclical sense of time and in the particular functions and lineages of those agents of the divine, those loci of divinity on earth *(farr),* the distinctively Persianate idiom is apparent, where kings, warriors, and mystics are crowned with haloes and with access to cosmic secrets.[39] For those Safavi devotees like the Qizilbash who imagined themselves within an Alid narrative, ultimate truth would be unveiled once the messiah (Mahdi) manifested himself to the world.

Movements referred to pejoratively by Islamic heresiographers as *ghuluww* share a conception of cyclical history—the notion that prophetic revelation never ceases and that history is a succession of dispensations, one replacing another. As we shall see with the case of the Nuqtavis, a messianic group, some *ghulāt* voice their Iranian identity and lineage more explicitly. The Nuqtavis will serve as a foil for the Qizilbash, revealing two distinct yet overlapping varieties of *ghuluww,* one Persianate and the other Alid. "Exaggerative" circles seem to have provided a space for Mazdean and Shi'i beliefs to intermingle free from hegemonic impulses to normalize Islam. Their geographic location on the eastern frontiers of Islam reveals the Indo-

Iranian cultural landscapes in which some Alid opposition took refuge from the ruling Abbasid caliphs centered in Baghdad. Alid loyalty was nurtured and matured in Persianate landscapes, whether through conversion or mere immersion in the culture. As we shall see with the creation of Alid memories recalling an early Islamic past where Ali's son, Husayn, married the daughter (Shahrbanu) of the last Iranian monarch (the Sasanid Yazdgird III), these two cultures are bound together in conversion narrative memories transmitted orally through popular epics like the *Abū Muslimnāme*. Alongside this mix of Alid and Persianate languages stands another more consciously Iranian identity—that of the Nuqtavis.

Nearly a century after the rise of Shah Isma'il, his great-grandson Shah Abbas I (1587–1629) began to centralize the Safavi domains and seize the reins of power, taming the *ghulāt* in the process. Consequently, some Qizilbash and craftsmen abandoned the Safavis and embraced a new spiritual master of the Nuqtavi order who imagined a different scenario for the future turn of events. The Nuqtavis represent one response to the Safavi move away from *ghuluww*. Nuqtavi cosmology divided the history of humanity (sixty-four thousand years) into four cycles of sixteen thousand years each, with eight thousand years of Arab domination followed by an era of Iranian rule. Each cycle was to bring forth a succession of eight Arab and eight Iranian prophets.[40] The founder of the Nuqtavis, Mahmud Pasikhani (d. 1427), believed that the final cycle during which all of humanity would attain truth belonged to the Iranians: "The cycle of the Ajam (Iranians) will prevail. . . . the religion of Muhammad is abrogated [*mansūkh*]; now the religion is the religion of Mahmud":

> The turn of the final praiseworthy sufis *(rind)* has arrived.
> That which the Arabs taunted the Iranians with has passed.[41]

On such beliefs the Nuqtavis claimed that a member of their order would overthrow the Safavis a millennium after the rise of Islam. Some *ghulāt* like the Nuqtavis and Isma'ilis seem to have envisaged a final era of unveiled truths. What is more particular to the *ghuluww* of the Nuqtavis is that for them, truth is linked to a restoration of Iranian universal sovereignty. Nevertheless, the advent of the personification of the holy, bearing glad tidings of a new reign of justice, is set in the here and now—not at the end of linear time as envisioned by Abrahamic monotheists.

Two temporal modes and their related conceptions of history, one Abrahamic and the other Persianate, converge at moments of grand transformation—of revolution, conflict, and fear—for they share the paradigm of an imminent messiah. The same astronomical conjunctions of Saturn and Jupiter are presented as astrological forecasts of cosmic change and hence the advent of the messiah, the perceived inevitability of which drove some *ghulāt* into armed rebellion.[42]

The construction of Persianate and Abrahamic imaginations of the cosmos, of time and being, had been inspired by at least a millennium of encounters between ancient belief systems that animated the physical and spiritual landscapes of inhabitants from the shores of the eastern Mediterranean to the Indus Valley. With the rise to dominance of the Persian empire of the Achaemenids (559–331 B.C.E.) and the subsequent conquests of Alexander (r. 334–323 B.C.E.), Irano-Semitic, Indic, and Hellenic cultures faced each other under the shadows of Persian and Hellenic rule. Egyptians, Greeks, Jews, Mazdeans, Hindus, Buddhists, and pagans mingled in an unprecedented closeness that seems to have rekindled an exploration of the meanings and interrelationship of good and evil, heaven and earth, holy and human, spirit and matter—a pondering that would reach its peak of creativity in the realm of cosmic imagination in the age of late antiquity (150–750 C.E.) with the visions of Jesus, Mani, Zardusht (founder of Mazdakis), and Muhammad.[43] And it was in Mesopotamia, where the bulk of our *ghulāt*, Alids, and Sufis first appear at the advent of Islam, that the creativity was most eclectic.

As modern historians, we have been too purist in our approach when tracing the cultural heritage of Islamdom, either overemphasizing its Hellenic past or reacting against an "orientalist" bias, as Henry Corbin does, seeing gnostic philosophers like Yahya Suhrawardi (d. 1191) or Isma'ili cosmology through purely Persian (Mazdean) lenses. But if we put such politics aside, there is no doubt that the influence of the Indo-Iranian world on the formation of Islam was substantial, at least in its core eastern lands from Mesopotamia to Anatolia and Central Asia. Although Persian influences in the realm of political and administrative practices have been recognized, cultural influences have been neglected. It is the Judeo-Christian influences that are emphasized instead, something the early Muslim sources themselves acknowledged as they incorporated Biblical narratives *(Isra'iliyyat)* into their traditions. These early Muslim sources are silent about Mazdean religious influences, which we also continue to ignore.

This silence, however, is telling. In an era of monotheism, pagan or dualist pasts were erased, as they continue to be to this day. But those who persisted in identifying themselves with an Iranian past continued to speak and write in the Persian language despite three centuries of silence and in spite of the language's transformation through the Arab encounter (alphabet and vocabulary). This is enough to confirm the existence of a resilient Persianate ethos and worldview in all its multiplicities and new incarnations. And this is why Hodgson's term *Persianate* is so useful: with some *ghulāt* there is a clear substratum of Mazdean ideas that are distinguishable, although they had already been transmuted through their synthesis with Semitic, Hellenic, and Indic cultural motifs and were now merging into new Muslim identities.

Muhammad and the Qur'an were ambiguous about the continued role of prophecy—the possibility of human agents of the supernatural providing access to the divine for each believer. Referring to a multitude of prophets, the Qur'an gave no clear indication that Muhammad was to be the last of them. It is later Islamic tradition that defines Muhammad as "the seal of the prophets," a phrase originally coined by the neo-Mazdean prophet Mani (d. 274 C.E.).[44] Although Muhammad never claimed to be divine, some who shared the temperament of the "exaggerators" came to view him and his descendants, the Imams, as such. The *ghulāt* insisted on the continuation of prophecy and saw Muhammad as one prophet in a chain of prophets, expecting each age to yield its own, so that this world would never be devoid of divine presence and illumination. They also shared a common apocalyptic language and astronomical moments of cataclysmic change. For some Muslims, who in time would be distinguished as Shi'is, the Imams after the death of Muhammad had continued to bless the world with their holy presence. "Exaggerating" temperaments refused to separate heaven from earth; in fact, for some, heaven exists on earth, and it is to earth, they believed, that we keep returning in different forms; thus Muhammad, Ali, Jesus, or Moses could be reincarnated in an individual at any given historical time. This cosmology and ontology embedded in *ghuluww* represents their essential difference from normative Islam and accounts for their being considered heretics by Muslim orthodoxy.

I hope to demonstrate, however, that a core of beliefs held by the early *ghulāt* does survive in Islamdom, shaping a variety of Muslim symbolic forms (Shi'ism and sufism). Traces of this cluster embraced by the Qizilbash in the sixteenth century continue to survive into the nineteenth century, as manifest in the Babi movement (1844–50).[45] We must not forget that the *ghulāt* still exist today and that some, like the Shabak of northern Iraq, continue to treat Shah Isma'il's poetry as revelation.[46] Naturally, this nucleus of beliefs has in time incorporated, generated and rejected a variety of motifs, as in the case of the Safavis where Alid loyalty and sufism mingled with *ghuluww*. Inasmuch as *ghuluww* was never institutionalized as a belief system, its doctrines did not undergo the process of canonization that is natural to normative religions. They also did not enjoy a centralized organization through time to unify doctrine.[47] This partially accounts for the absence of homogeneity, for the fluidity and the variety of doctrinal mixtures, languages, and names we find under the rubric of *ghuluww* in the heresiographies.[48] Moreover, the Muslim orthodoxy, Shi'i and Sunni, came to apply the designation rather loosely in different historical contexts to label a variety of dissenters.[49] Nevertheless, a corpus of identifiable doctrine—beliefs particular to many groups labeled in Muslim literature as *ghulât*—continued to live on. Marshall Hodgson has isolated that core, and Wilferd Madelung's meticulous study of early *ghuluww* (Kaysaniyya and Khurramdiniyya) confirms that this corpus lived on into the twelfth century.[50] Through an exploration of the Qizilbash and the Nuqtavis, I hope to capture their distinctive forms of *ghuluww* and isolate some of the mediums through which such a system of beliefs was filtered and kept alive into the fifteenth and sixteenth centuries.

In this introduction, my concern has been to place the *ghulât* within their historical context, viewing them as an alternative way in which Muhammad's vision was understood, just as we comprehend Sunnis, Imami, or Isma'ili Shi'is, and Kharijis. In the Islamic era, *ghuluww* became one choice among several, against which a section of Islam destined to become dominant defined itself. The predominance of this latter competing vision, however, was not at that time a fait accompli, and if *ghuluww* interpretations had attained preeminence, we would have been tempted to see this "exaggerated" version of Islam as mainstream. *Ghuluww,* therefore, seems to me to represent not only a mentality Islam rejected, but one of the choices Islam made from among a multitude of competing choices—a choice that did not attain, in a later epoch, normative status, although it remained alive in a minority, often persecuted and sometimes disguised. Studying such movements in this light is to study not simply a marginal group on the fringes of Islam but, more important, a chapter in the evolution of Islamic identity, which in its own time was anything but fixed. That it did not attain normative status, while other alternatives did, poses questions that may potentially illuminate whole areas of Islamic history.

SAFAVI HISTORIOGRAPHY

Contemporary historians writing about the Safavi world have focused on the Qizilbash as political actors because in the imperial age (1501–1722) they came to form the military and administrative backbone of the empire. During the revolutionary phase (1447–1501), the Qizilbash, composed mainly of Turkmen converts to the Safavi cause, had organized themselves militarily into *oymaqs*, a Mongol term loosely translated as "tribe." Members of particular tribes or localities in Anatolia and Syria had been converted to Qizilbash Islam by Isma'il's grandfather (Junayd) and father (Haydar); tribes, however, had not converted en masse. Qizilbash religiosity created the structure around which individuals coalesced into a single group, like the Shamlu, Rumlu, or Takkalu. A system of beliefs then entered into the dynamics of a set of Turco-Mongol kinship ties in the process of reformulation.

In the imperial era, the Safavis attempted to contain the revolutionary fervor that had won them temporal rule. An individual could no longer convert to Qizilbash Islam; to become a Qizilbash, one now had to be born into the *oymaq* that had originally associated themselves with the Safavi house.[51] Blood ties were to solidify the spiritual bonds that had formerly brought the *oymaq* together, and Qizilbash Islam was to be channeled to Ottoman Anatolia for export only. The significance and implications of this shift in Safavi policy of membership in the order has been generally ignored. I intend to incorporate it into my reading of Safavi history.

As for the religious affiliation of the Qizilbash, the adopted imperial religion of Imami Shi'ism (Twelver) has received scholarly attention, for once Isma'il conquered Iran, he began to temper his revolutionary rhetoric.[52] In the course of the reigns of Isma'il (r. 1501–1524) and his successor Tahmasb (r. 1524–1576), the Safavis came to emphasize the political aspect of the title of *shah*, drawn from the Iranian tradition of kingship. They backed away from Messianic claims that played with the cultural (Imami) paradigm of the emergence *(khurûj)* of the hidden Imam (Mahdi) before the end of time. Safavi historians have assumed that conversion ensued with Isma'il's proclamation of Shi'ism as the religion of his imperium.[53] This study troubles such a static and homogeneous picture and instead focuses on tensions and the various ways of embracing Shi'ism.

As far as sufism is concerned, only its manifestation in poetry or in the philosophic writings of intellectuals *(ulama)* in the Safavi realm has received attention. What sufism may have meant for the early Safavis and what it came to mean in the imperial era remain ambiguous. Moreover, our knowledge of the relationship between sufism and Alid loyalty, embedded in the role of Ali as the perfect individual *(insān-i kāmil)*, among some sufi circles, continues to be vague and ahistorical. The confluence of Alid and mystical idioms in post-Mongol messianic movements (Sarbidars, Mush'ash'a, Hurufis, Nurbakhshis), in which the sword is raised in the name of Ali and his progeny, has not been explored.[54] And so the religiosity of the Qizilbash, beginning with our seduction by the late sixteenth-century Safavi chronicles presenting an already rewritten history of the revolution, has anachronistically been regarded as an anomaly and characterized by the term *militant* Shi'ism or by the pejorative and equally nebulous label *extremist*. No attempt has been made to understand the complex nature of Safavi Islam or its historical affinity with earlier Alid movements in general and with Shi'ism (Imami) in particular. In fact, Qizilbash Islam has been denigrated and relegated to the realm of the low, the folk, the degenerate. I regard this spiritual landscape seriously as a broader phenomenon in Islamdom, for a series of similar messianic movements manifested themselves between the fourteenth and sixteenth centuries in the eastern Mediterranean world, Mesopotamia, Iran, Transoxiana, and India, our understanding of which remains just as vacuous.[55]

Urban members of the Safavi order based in Ardabil (in northwest Iran) have also been neglected. After all, Ardabil, site of the tomb of Shaykh Safi (d. 1334), was the center of Safavi commercial, religious, and political power long before the rise of Isma'il. Thanks to a recent study of Kishwar Rizvi on the architectural transformation of the Shrine of Shaykh Safi, which she places within this nexus, we can finally understand the extent of Safavi local and regional power extending from Azerbaijan to the Caspian Sea region and into the Iranian plateau.[56] Through a study of endowment deeds *(sarīh al-milk)* delineating properties bequeathed to this shrine, we now have a picture of the social, economic, and geographical basis of Safavi power. The importance of artisans and craftsmen *(futuvvat)* in the membership of the Safavi order is key to understanding the nature of Safavi religiosity and social power. But the question arises whether all the members of the Safavi order were *ghulāt*. Surely, heterogeneity prevailed among the Safavi devotees (Qizilbash and artisans). As I sketch the different tendencies among Safavi disciples, I hope to elucidate the way in which the cult of Ali and his family (Imam) created a common culture, which bound them in solidarity.

Thanks to the pioneering work of a generation of Safavi scholars in realms of religious thought as well as political and institutional history, we can now begin to imagine a less fragmented picture while delving into nuances and layers that have come into focus.[57] Now that we have a sense of Safavi political and religious history, we need to focus on the points at which these two realms intersect. To understand Safavi society, religion and politics must be studied as two complementary spheres interacting within a cultural system. A dichotomy between these two domains did not exist, for the Qizilbash were spiritual devotees of their masters as well as his armed companions on the battlefield and his imperial administrators. Religion and politics in classical Safavi society were components of a system that embodied behavior and attitudes as well as ideology. We will examine the Qizilbash in the imperial era of Safavi "absolutist" rule when these lines are just beginning to harden. As the Qizilbash respond to the Safavi betrayal of their revolutionary call *(da'wa)*, the distinct flavors of their Islam emerge.

In exploring *ghuluww* expression, this book focuses on tensions that were kindled as Qizilbash Islam confronted the more rational currents of imperial Shi'ism (Imami). Frictions surfaced from the inception of Safavi rule and are key to an understanding of the classical Safavi idiom. Here I attempt to capture the explosive encounter between what would consolidate itself in the Iranian world as mainstream Imami Shi'ism and what would finally be relegated to the marginal realm of the heterodox. I am assuming that there was a turning point in the history of the Persianate "semiosphere" where boundaries were being (re)drawn, distinguishing previously overlapping linguistic spheres.[58] At this moment, Alid loyalty, sufism, and *ghuluww* are distinguished. Unfortunately, except for Shah Isma'il's poetry, we do not possess Qizilbash writings illuminating their beliefs. For the Safavis went through a process of redefining themselves once they were able to discipline the Qizilbash. They rewrote their own history and purged it of exaggeration.[59]

So it is the Qizilbash and Nuqtavi response to change that concerns us. The way in which change was faced will serve as a mirror reflecting the traits of the face itself. Once the instruments of the erosion of Qizilbash Islam were being institutionalized, responses were verbalized. The political and religious ramifications of the centralizing reforms the Safavis set in motion to tame the Qizilbash shall be reconstructed. The worldview of the Qizilbash, then, is examined at a time when their waning was becoming an institutional reality and when the Imami orthodoxy was receiving political support to redraw the map of Shi'ism in Safavi Iran. Sufism and *ghuluww*, tendencies so embedded in the classical Safavi idiom, were cast as heretical and once again pushed beyond the boundaries of legitimacy. At this point, some obedient Qizilbash disciples revolted against their mystical master, who had turned into a full-fledged temporal king *(shah)*. The language of rebellion both at court and in the provinces—the motifs and symbols evoked in reaction to this betrayal—are revealing aspects of the original nature of Safavi Islam.

The writing of an oppressive discourse was undertaken by a current of Imami Shi'i clerics destined to become dominant. The rejection of *ghuluww* and sufism in Safavi Iran was voiced through a genre of religious disputations *(rudūd)*, targeting sufis in general and an Alid hero by the name of Abu Muslim (d. 755).[60] These polemics highlight the differences between syncretic *(mufawwida)* and rationalist *(muqassira)* tendencies in Imamism, between the use of song, mystical poetry, and dance or of prescribed ritual prayer in the path of communion with God; between guidance of a mystic or of clerics *(ulama)* and between reciting Rumi's poetry *(masnavi)* or cursing him. These refutations encapsulate the debates about the locus of the holy on earth, about spirit and matter, chaos and order. The particularities of Safavi heteroglossia emerge with the variety of religious groups categorized under the rubric of sufis, as well as the doctrinal contentions between them and the rationalist *(shari'a-minded)* authors of this discourse. A unified language of Shi'ism was being canonized, claiming legitimacy as divine truth. But with this ideological unification, so linked to cultural and sociopolitical processes of centralization, the realities of heteroglossia continued to impinge on this project.

In fact, mysticism, theology, and philosophy had in many respects become inseparable during the fourteenth and fifteenth centuries, when the Safavi movement was incubating. Technically, mysticism, with its esoteric experience of the godhead, should be contrasted in Islam with theology, which emphasizes the revealed knowledge of the one transcendent God, and with philosophy, which seeks a reasoned understanding of his essence. One of the truly grand intellectual efforts to merge all three approaches into a single gnostic view of truth was underway during this period. The effort was to continue through the early Safavi age to reach its climax with the philosophizing mystic Mulla Sadra (d. 1650) of the Isfahan school (Illuminationist) in the first half of the seventeenth century.[61] This gnostic language of plurality threatened the livelihood of those scholars who spoke a single dialect based on a rationalized reading of Islam.

A thread that ties the *ghulāt* together with the sufis was their common belief in unitive fusion *(ittihād)* and incarnation of part or all of the divine in humans *(hulūl)*. The connection lies in questions concerning the soul, the individual, the divine, and their interrelationship—issues that preoccupied the *ghulāt* and were later taken up by some sufis and philosophers. The meaning that the *ghulāt* and sufis ascribed to the relationship between the individual and the divine was tinged by gnostic attitudes, for some disciples saw their spiritual guides as divine, just as some Alids venerated their Imams. The exaggerated sensibilities of some believers, which led them to seek constant guidance and communication with a living god or prophet, were being channeled to dervishes as well as to religious scholars. This role, just like the one dervishes played in the religious cosmology of believers, had repercussions for rationalist, *shari'a*-minded clerics, who were attempting to reserve that role for the awaited Mahdi and those interpreters of the divine law *(shari'a)*, the jurisconsults *(mujtahid)*. Among the Shi'is, earlier debates were revived concerning the divine or human nature of the Imams that had been articulated during the period of the Imams' presence and the lesser occultation (632–930 C.E.)—an era in which *ghuluww* and Imamism had once before come into close contact.[62] This time, they centered on the divine qualities of other intermediaries between God and the believer—spiritual masters, dervishes, *ulama*, and philosophers.

Special human "friends of God" *(awliyā')* were perceived as holy and venerated. Such individuals were deemed capable of attaining the status of "perfect individual," and here is where sufism, philosophy, Shi'ism, and *ghuluww* merge. Each current had its particular path and understanding of how transcendence, unity with God, saintliness, and earthly utopias could be attained. And each had its distinct sense of who could attain it.

For Alid *ghulāt,* the prophet Muhammad (d. 632), the figure of Ali (d. 661), and the Imams possessed an intrinsic divinity inherited through blood. For some gnostic philosophers (Ishraqi), it was the spiritually and intellectually illuminated elite, those singular "perfect individuals" who could combine experience and reason together with the knowledge of God's words to encounter him. And for some sufis, it was through experience and intuition alone, guided by an already illuminated master, that one could transcend material existence and attain communion with God. Moreover, temporal and spiritual authority continued to be viewed as twins by some sufiesque *ghulāt* like the Qizilbash, indeed, there lay their hope of a just kingdom on earth.

The particular historical moment of conversion to Shi'i Islam in which Safavi devotees found themselves in the sixteenth century will allow us to study the very tensions, processes, and adaptations of "exaggeration" and "rationalist" Islam in the complex history of the evolution of Islamic identities. At this very junction, a religious orthodoxy (Imami) was defining and distinguishing itself from *ghuluww.* The way in which change was faced in the Safavi court, religious seminaries, coffeehouses, dervish circles (*futuvvat* and *tarīqat*), and public squares of Isfahan will serve as texts that illuminate our understanding of the different dimensions of what it may have meant to be a devotee of the Safavi order. In the pages to come, change is detailed in all these arenas and levels of society, as I attempt to trace the shifting paradigms and loci of authority in Safavi cultural and social life. The way in which the old was inscribed into the new will illuminate processes that generated a maintenance, reshaping, or revival of the old. Contextualizing the (re)creation of the category of *ghuluww* in Shi'i discourse reveals how Shi'ism can be read through a binary paradigm of change. In the process of self-description, there is a need for a unified structuring and canonizing of some texts and the exclusion of others. These texts (content and code) form one of the repositories for cultural memory—a pool of symbolic resources that can be brought back into the present but only for that particular cultural group that can recognize and speak the code. Lotman sees each of these texts as preserving a memory of past readings of itself (preserving a context in which the text was read) and accords the reader the ability to remember these past readings.[63] Moreover, this heteroglossia allows for multiple and overlapping readings of the same text by different "language groups," which for me is useful because the movements (Alid and Persianate) that I study consider the same sacred Muslim texts (Qur'an and hadith) but interpret them in very different ways.

Let me take you into this Persianate world whose denizens spoke in signs that were intelligible to a larger Muslim (Alid) community. Some of these signs overlapped. Some were read differently. And yet others remained untranslatable. These came to be categorized as *ghuluww,* and in time their custodians retreated into the eastern refuges of Islamdom, continuing to speak in codes.

NOTES

1. The word *ghuluww* (n.) is derived from the Arabic root *gh.l.w,* literally meaning "to exceed the proper boundary"; *ghālī* (s.)/*ghulāt* (pl.) is rendered often and incorrectly as "extremist." "Exaggerator" is more accurate.

2. I use the term *Mazdean* to refer to the variety of interpretations of Zoroaster's visions that place Ahura Mazda (Lord Wisdom) at the center of their cosmology.

3. For the coining of the term *Persianate,* see Marshall Hodgson, *The Venture of Islam: Conscience and History in a World Civilization* (Chicago: University of Chicago Press, 1974), vol. 2, 293–294. Hodgson uses the term to signify a whole cultural orientation within Islamdom that was inspired by Persian traditions and used the Persian language as a vehicle of expression. Unlike Hodgson, I do not limit the Persianate ethos to the spheres of "high" literate culture.

4. M. M. Bakhtin, "Discourse in the Novel," *The Dialogic Imagination: Four Essays* (Austin: University of Texas Press, 1981).

5. For recent contributions to the nascent field of Safavi economic history, see the works of Ina Baghdiantz-McCabe, *The Shah's Silk*

for Europe's Silver: The Eurasian Trade of the Julfa Armenians in Safavid Iran and India (1530–1750 (Atlanta: Scholars Press, 1999); Rudolph P. Matthee, *The Politics of Trade in Safavid Iran: Silk for Silver 1600–1730* (Cambridge: Cambridge University Press, 2000); Edmund Herzig, "The Armenian Merchants of New Julfa: A Study in Premodern Asian Trade," Ph.D. diss., Oxford University, 1991.

6. See Clifford Geertz, "Religion as a Cultural System," *The Interpretation of Cultures: Selected Essays* (New York: Basic Books, 1973).

7. Paul Ricoeur, *Time and Narrative,* trans. Kathleen McLaughlin, 3 vols. (Chicago: University of Chicago, 1984). Also see David Wood's introduction to *On Paul Ricoeur: Narrative and Interpretation* (London: Routledge, 1991).

8. See Mieke Bal, Jonathan V. Crewe, and Leo Spitzer, eds., *Acts of Memory: Cultural Recall in the Present* (Hanover, NH: Dartmouth College, University Press of New England, 1999), for an elaboration of this approach to memory.

9. I am referring to Paul Ricoeur's *Time and Narrative,* where he delineates the ways in which narratives heal aporia and make them productive. Here I am adding the aspect of memory.

10. Ibid. See introduction for a distinction between habitual, or routine, memory and narrative memory.

11. See Pierre Bourdieu, *Outline of a Theory of Practice* (Cambridge: Cambridge University Press, 1977), for his coining of the term *habitus.* Habitus, according to Bourdieu, is a system of durable dispositions transportable through each individual. It is a largely unconscious vector of unity and permanence. Habitus explains why individuals act in society according to preexistent schema that tend to reproduce social relations of domination of some groups over others.

12. Pierre Nora, *Realms of Memory: Rethinking the French Past,* trans. Arthur Goldhammer, *Conflicts and Divisions* (New York: Columbia University Press, 1996), vol. 1, Introduction.

13. Bal et al., Introduction, *Acts of Memory.*

14. William Sewell makes this point in "Geertz, Cultural Systems, and History: From Synchrony to Transformation," in Sherry Ortner, ed., *The Fate of "Culture": Geertz and Beyond* (Berkeley: University of California Press, 1999). This issue had already been raised

by Natalie Zemon Davis in "Anthropology and History in the 1980s: The Possibilities of the Past," *Journal of Interdisciplinary History* 11 (1981): 267–276; and discussed by Suzanne Desan in *The New Cultural History,* ed. Lynn Hunt (Berkeley: University of California Press, 1989), 52–53.

15. I would like to thank Peter Brown for having introduced me to Yuri M. Lotman and Boris A. Uspenskii, *The Semiotics of Russian Culture,* trans. Ann Shukman (Ann Arbor: University of Michigan, 1984).

16. See William Sewell's chapter in *The Fate of "Culture": Geertz and Beyond,* 46, for his discussions on the paucity of social theory dealing with the problem of historical change. "The overriding problem posed by most social theory has been accounting for social order or structure. This is true, for example, not only of Geertz's work but of nearly all of anthropology before 1980. And even those theorists who have made the explanation of change a central problematic—principally, Karl Marx, Max Weber, and such successors as Louis Althusser, Jurgen Habermas, or Immanuel Wallerstein—have usually employed such teleological notions of temporality that their concepts must be extensively revised to be useful to historians."

17. Once again, I am grateful to Peter Brown for pointing out R. G. Collingwood's *Essays in the Philosophy of History* (Austin: University of Texas Press, 1965) and for his generous comments on the differences between European attitudes to the past and the "massiveness" of memory in the Iranian world.

18. I would like to thank Ismael Velasco, whose perceptive questions and speculations on a paper on "Persianate Flavor of Qizilbash Islam: Alid 'Ghuluww' and Sufism" that I presented at the School of Oriental and African Studies, University of London, have refined my understanding of *ghuluww.*

19. See Wadad al-Qadi, "The Development of the Term *Ghulāt* in Muslim Literature with Special Reference to the Kaysaniyya," *Akten des VII. Kongresses für Arabistik und Islamwissenschaft* 98 (1976): 295–316.

20. al-Qadi, "The Development of the Term *Ghulāt* in Muslim Literature," 298–299.

21. Fully developed orthodox Zoroastrianism reckons time in four periods of three thousand years each. The attack of evil (Ahriman) is

situated in the middle of time, in the year 6000, which inaugurates historical time as matter and spirit mix for three thousand years until the coming of the religion of Zoroaster in the year 9000. His posthumous sons are thought to manifest themselves at the end of each subsequent millennium (i.e., 10000, 11000). A savior (Astavatrta) was expected to appear finally in the year 12000. There exist alternative year schemes for the duration of each cycle. Mary Boyce, *A History of Zoroastrianism* (Leiden: Brill, 1975), vol. 1, 284–293, posits an original tradition of six thousand years. Windfuhr notes the prevalence of the number 9 (hence 9000) in the Iranian tradition, including temple structures that may predate the duodecimal Mesopotamia/Hellenic patterns. In addition, a seven-thousand-year scheme appears in the late Bahman Yasht, which corresponds to planets and mixed ages of metals. Windfuhr suggests that the earliest evidence for the millennial speculations already exists in the Avesta (Yasht 19, 9–97). Yasht 19 deals with the owners of the divine and royal glory *(khwarnah)*. See Gernot Windfuhr, "References to Zoroaster and Zoroastrian Time Reckoning in Rumi's Masnavi," *Proceedings of the Third International Congress,* K. R. Cama Oriental Institute, Bombay, January 6–9, 2000. Although scholars of Zoroastrian cosmology have not used the term *cyclical* to describe their notions of time, R. C. Zaehner in *Zurvan: A Zoroastrian Dilemma* (Oxford: Clarendon Press, 1955, 106–107), states that the "Iranian theory of Time is seen to have little or no affinity with ever recurring Kalpas of the Hindu or Hellenistic aeons. At a given moment, finite Time [the cosmic period of twelve thousand years] comes into existence out of Infinite Time, moves in a circle until it returns to its beginning, and then merges into Infinite time, that is Timelessness. The process is never renewed." For the Persianate *ghulāt,* however, cyclical recurrences are mixed with a sense of a circular return or in some cases, an eventual end time (Fatimid-Ismail'is). Mazdean notions of time were not monolithic; syncretic mixtures with Hindu, Hellenistic, and Abrahamic systems must have been active. I would like to thank Gernot Windfur for graciously providing me with this information and with detailed bibliographical references on the scholarship and original sources of Zoroastrian cosmology. Henry Corbin first signaled out the affinities between cyclical time among Mazdeans and Isma'ilis. See his *Cyclical Time and*

Ismai'ili Gnosis: Islamic Texts and Contexts (London: Kegan Paul, 1983).

22. See Peter Brown, *The Making of Late Antiquity* (Cambridge: Harvard University Press, 1978), and Brown, *The World of Late Antiquity: From Marcus Aurelius to Muhammad* (London: Thames and Hudson, 1971). Brown does not speak of the idea of cyclical time, which seems to have been alive farther east in Mesopotamia among Mazdeans who were more influenced by Indo-Iranian thought.

23. For this discussion, see Sayyid Husayn Modarresi-Tabātabā'ī, *Crisis and Consolidation in the Formative Period of Shi'ite Islam* (Princeton: Darwin Press, 1993), 19, where he cites the Qur'an— 6:102, 27:64, 30:40, 35:3, 17:111, 34:22, 28:88, 27:65, 6:57, 12:40, 67, 39:3, 5:75, 14:38, 25:20, 18:110, 17:90–94.

24. The Arabic reads *sihrun mustamirrun*, which means "uninterrupted or continuing magic." I would like to thank Sherman Jackson for this translation.

25. Brown, *The Making of Late Antiquity*, 19.

26. In his introduction to the *Tazkirat al-mulūk* (London: Gibb Memorial Series, 1989), 13, Vladimir Minorsky quotes an anonymous Venetian merchant who was in Tabriz (in northwest Iran) in 1518: "This Sophy is loved and reverenced by his people as a God and especially by his soldiers, many of whom enter into battle without armour, expecting their master Ishmael to watch over them in fight." Hans Roemer quotes a Qizilbash battle cry without citing a source: "My spiritual leader and master, for whom I sacrifice myself *(Qurbān oldïgïm pirüm mürshidim)*." *Cambridge History of Iran,* ed. Ihsan Yarshater (Cambridge: Cambridge University Press, 1983), vol. 6, 214.

27. About the cannibalistic tendencies of the Qizilbash, see Nasrallah Falsafi, *Zindigānī-yi Shah 'Abbas-i Avval* Tehran: Chāp-i Kayvān, 1955) vol. 2, 125–127. Falsafi is quoting from the *Ahsan al-tavārīkh,* the *Khulāsat al-tavārīikh,* the *Tarīkh-i 'Abbasī/Jalālī,* and the *Rawzat al-safaviyya.* These sources speak of a practice of "live-eating" *(zindahkhwarī)* during the reigns of Isma'il I (1501–1524), Muhammad Khudabandah (1577–1587), and Abbas I (1587–1629).

28. Thackston in his analysis of the religious aspects of Shah Isma'il's

poetry observes, "As became customary with the Safavis, a liberal mixture of terminology from both the royal and spiritual spheres is applied to the shah." Wheeler Thackston, "The Diṣan of Khatā'ī: Pictures for the Poetry of Shah Isma'il," *Asian Art* (Fall 1988): 54. For Isma'il, whose pen name was Khatā'ī, see *Il Canzoniere di Shah Isma'il*, ed. Tourkhan Gandjei (Naples: Instituto Universitario Orientale, 1959); Vladimir Minorsky, "The Poetry of Shah Isma'il I," *Bulletin of the School of Oriental and African Studies* 10 (1942): 1006–1053; Sadeddin Nūzhet Ergun, *Hatayi Divāni: Shah Isma'il Safevi Edebi Hayati ve Nefesleri* (Istanbul: Maarif Kitaphanesi, 1956).

29. It is not clear whether Isma'il was active in this image making or if it was his entourage who crafted it. I am assuming here that Isma'il did play a role in the shaping of his public persona.

30. Marshall Hodgson, *The Venture of Islam: Conscience and History in a World Civilization* (Chicago: University of Chicago Press, 1974), vol. 2, 293–294. Also see Ihsan Yarshater, "Iranian Common Beliefs and Worldviews," in *Cambridge History of Iran*, ed. Ihsan Yarshater (Cambridge: Cambridge University Press, 1983), vol. 3, ch. 10a.

31. This information about Jamshid appears only in the early Leiden Manuscript. Ferdowsi chose not to incorporate all the stories about Jamshid in circulation during the tenth century into his narrative. I would like to thank Dick Davis for bringing this to my attention.

32. Dick Davis in his recent work entitled *Epic and Sedition: The Case of Ferdowsi's Shāhnāme* (Fayetteville: University of Arkansas Press, 1992), 26, has dared to rethink Ferdowsi's *Shāhnāme* as a critique of kingship "constantly calling into question the validity of the very political and social assumptions that it appears to celebrate."

33. Khatā'ī, *Il Canzoniere di Shah Ismā'il*, verse 22/1–3.

34. The term *Alid* is used here to denote all those who regarded descent in the male line from Ali, not primarily from Fatima, as legitimate. For those who gave precedence to the whole family of Ali, any descendant of Abu Talib (Ali's father) could be revered as Imams.

35. Khatā'ī, *Il Canzoniere di Shah Ismā'il*, verse 249/9.

36. Ibid., verse 211/3.
37. Other designations have also been utilized, such as extremist Shi'ism and folk Islam.
38. See Marshal Hodgson, "Ghulāt," *EI2;* Wilferd Madelung's *Religious Trends in Early Islamic Iran* (Albany, N.Y.: Persian Heritage Foundation, 1988), and his articles "Ismā'īliyya," "Imāma," "Kaysaniyya," "Khodja," and "Khurramiyya" in *EI 2.* Entries on the *ghulāt* in books on heresy (Nawbakhti or Shahrastani, for example) include this cluster of precepts. These early Persianate messiahs shared an adherence to certain key precepts: (1) *tanāsukh* transmigration of the soul in humans, animals, and angelic bodies; (2) the notion that prophetic revelation never ceases; (3) a dualist cosmology of the world (light and dark); (4) Imams as a recourse in legal matters only because the *shari'a* is not eternal and everything is licit; (5) the *mahdī* will reappear *(raj'a)* to make the cause prevail; (6) God's nature is anthropomorphic; and (7) *qiyāmat,* rejection of the body in favor of the soul/spirit.
39. When I speak of an Iranian or Persian idiom, I do not intend to convey an image of purity. In fact, by the age of late antiquity, Mazdeanism embodied an admixture of Irano-Semitic, Indic, and Hellenic elements.
40. Mobed Shah, *Dabistān al-mazāhib,* ed. Rahīm Rezāzādah-yi Malik (Tehran: Kitābkhānah-ī Tahūrī, 1983–1984), vol. 1, 275.
41. Ibid., vol. 1, 276.
42. The Nuqtavis understood the conjunction of Saturn and Jupiter as a sign of the fall of the Safavis and the end of Muslim rule. Although the greatest conjunction of Saturn and Jupiter occurred in 1582/990 as calculated by Mahmud Pasikhani, the effects of the conjunction had been extended to coincide with the end of the first Muslim millennium. Some Muslims followed a tradition where Muhammad confirmed that in the beginning of each century, God would send a descendent of his family to elucidate and reinvigorate the true tenets of Islam *(mujaddid).* See E. van Donzel, "Mudjaddid," *EI2.*
43. For such interpretations of late antiquity, see Brown, *The Making of Late Antiquity,* and Hodgson, *The Venture of Islam,* vol. 1.
44. Although the term "seal of the prophets" *(khātim al-nabiyin)* does appear in the Qur'an (33:40), its reference to Muhammad as the last prophet is ambiguous.

45. Abbas Amanat, *Resurrection and Renewal: The Making of the Bābī Movement in Iran, 1844–1850* (Ithaca: Cornell University Press, 1989). See especially his introduction and his discussion on "Prophets and Prophesies: Sufism and Popular Religion," 70–105. Also see Juan Ricardo Cole, *Modernity and the Millennium: The Genesis of the Baha'i Faith in the Nineteenth-Century Middle East* (New York: Columbia University Press, 1998).

46. Matti Moosa, *Extremist Shi'ites: The Ghulāt Sects* (Syracuse, NY: Syracuse University Press, 1987), 156–158, where he discusses al-Shabak and the *Kitab al-manāqib,*, or the *Buyruk*, which consists of a discussion between Shaykh Safi and his son Shaykh Sadr al-din. For the *ghuluww* of the Ahl-i Haqq, Nusayris, Shabak and Bektashis. For the Marāghi(s) in Iran, see Ihsan Yarshater, "Mazdakism," in *Cambridge History of Iran*.

47. The Qarmatis, the Nizaris, and the Fatimids are an exception, for they were more centralized and localized in Bahrayn, Alamut, and Cairo, respectively. See Wilferd Madelung, "Isma'ilism: The Old and the New Da'wa," in his *Religious Trends in Early Islamic Iran*, and Farhad Daftary, *The Isma'ilis: Their History and Doctrines* (Cambridge: Cambridge University Press, 1990).

48. This has led scholars like Said Arjomand to deny any continuity and instead to highlight their antidogmatic stance against Islam—a characteristic they all share, of course. Because these movements opposed the status quo, they often raised nonconformist banners. At times, they were antisocial; at others, anti-intellectual or antinomian. This does not preclude the fact, however, that they shared a cluster of beliefs and that these realms could provide openings for change. Said Arjomand, "Religion, Political Action, and Legitimate Domination in Shi'ite Iran: Fourteenth to Eighteenth Centuries A.D.," *European Journal of Sociology* 20 (1979): 76 n. 79.

49. See Wadad al-Qadi, "The Development of the Term *Ghulāt* in Muslim Literature with Special Reference to the Kaysaniyya," in *Aktendes VII. Kongresses für Arabistik und Islamwiss-enschaft Göttingen*, ed. Albert Dietrich (Göttingen: Vandenhoeck & Ruprecht, 1976) for an historical reconstruction of this lumping.

50. Hodgson, "Ghulāt," *EI2*; Wilferd Madelung's *Religious Trends in Early Islamic Iran* and his articles, "Ismā'īliyya," "Imāma," "Kaysaniyya," "Khodja," and "Khurramiyya" in *EI2*. Madelung

speaks of the Mubayida sect surviving into the twelfth century, as well as the neo-Mazdaki group called the Pārsiyān (1141–1142).

51. Martin B. Dickson, "Shah Tahmasb and the Uzbeks: The Duel for Khurasan with Ubayd Khan, 930–46/1524–40," Ph.D. diss., Princeton University, 1958, 8.

52. Said Arjomand, *The Shadow of God and the Hidden Imam: Religion, Political Order, and Societal Change in Shi'ite Iran from the Beginning to 1890* (Chicago: University of Chicago Press, 1984); Arjomand, "Religion, Political Action and Legitimate Domination in Shi'ite Iran"; Andrew Newman, "Towards a Reconsideration of the Isfahan School of Philosophy: Shaykh Baha'i and the Role of the Safavid Ulama," *Studia Iranica* 15 (1986): 165–199; Newman, "The Myth of the Clerical Migration to Safavid Iran," *Die Welt des Islams* 33 (1993): 66–112.

53. Albeit with some resistance epitomized by the Sunni episode of Isma'il II's (1576–1577) year-long reign. See Michel Mazzaoui, "The Religious Policy of Safavid Shah Isma'il II," in Michel Mazzaoui and Vera B. Moreen, eds., *Intellectual Studies on Islam: Essays Written in Honor of Martin B. Dickson* (Salt Lake City: University of Utah Press, 1990); Shohreh Golsorkhi, "Isma'il II and Mirza Makhdum Sharifi: An Interlude in Safavid History," *International Journal of Middle East Studies* 26 (1994): 477–488; Rosemary Stansfield-Johnson, "Sunni Survival in Safavid Iran: Anti-Sunni Activities during the Reign of Tahmasb I," *Iranian Studies* 27 (1994): 123–133.

54. For an attempt at investigating this phenomenon, see Shahzad Bashir's dissertation on Muhammd Nurbakhsh, "Between Mysticism and Messianism: The Life and Thought of Muhammad Nurbakhsh (d. 1464)," Ph.D. diss., Yale University, 1997.

55. Cornell Fleischer's forthcoming book on the *Mediterranean Apocalypse* (Princeton: Princeton University Press) will certainly fill this vacuum.

56. Kishwar Rizvi, "Transformation in Early Safavi Architecture: The Shrine of Shaykh Safi al-Din Ardabili in Iran," Ph.D. diss., Massachusetts Institute of Technology, 2000.

57. For political and institutional history, see the works of Vladimir Minorsky, the "father of Safavi history," Martin Dickson's works on Shah Tahmasb, and the perceptive works of Jean Aubin. For religious and philosophical studies, see Said Arjomand, Henry

Corbin, Husayn Modarresi, James Morris, Husayn Nasr, and Andrew Newman. All works are cited in the bibliography.

58. Yuri M. Lotman, *The Universe of the Mind: A Semiotic Theory of Culture* (London: Tauris, 1990), pt. 2, on his concept of "semiosphere."

59. Sholeh Alysia Quinn, *Historical Writing during the Reign of Shah 'Abbas: Ideology, Imitation, and Legitimacy in Safavid Chronicles* (Salt Lake City: University of Utah Press, 2000), examines Safavi historiography and demonstrates how the gradual move toward orthodoxy translates itself onto official dynastic histories. Of particular interest for my work is the shifting version emphasizing the spiritual and miraculous nature of the early Safavi guides—Shaykh Safi al-din, in particular. By the age of Abbas I (1587–1629), once the *ghuluww* of the Qizilbash had been toned down, the official chroniclers omit passages from Safi al-din's earlier biographies in which he was portrayed as a holy man who aspired to join spiritual and temporal dominion.

60. Wilferd Madelung in his *Religious Trends in Early Islamic Iran,* 77, notes that the *Abū Muslimnāme* romance "provoked an angry reaction among the Persian Imami Shi'ite *ulama* (in the seventeenth century), who had no sympathy for this ideological deviation." Madelung is making use of Ghulam Husayn Yusufi, "Abu Muslim Khorasani," in *EI2.* Martin Dickson pointed me in this direction of research.

61. For scholarship on the Isfahan school of philosophy, see Sayyid Husayn Nasr, "The School of Isfahan," in *A History of Muslim Philosophy,* ed. M. M. Sharif (Wiesbaden: Harrassowitz, 1966); Henry Corbin, *En Islam Iranien, Aspects Spirituels et Philosophiques* (Paris: Gallimard, 1971), vol. 4; Fazlur Rahman, *The Philosophy of Mulla Sadra* (Albany: State University of New York Press, 1975); and James Winston Morris, *The Wisdom of the Throne An Introduction to the Philosophy of Mulla* (Princeton: Princeton University Press, 1981; For early examples of the intermingling of *ghuluww* with Imami Shi'ism, see Modarresi-Tabātabā'ī, *Crisis and Consolidation,* 49; and Mohammad Ali Amir-Moezzi, *The Divine Guide in Early Shi'ism The Sources of Esotericism in Islam* (Albany: State University of New York Press, 1994).

62. On these early tendencies and debates, see Sayyid Husayn

Modarresi Ṭabāṭabā'ī, *An Introduction to Shi'i Law: A Bibliographical Study* (London: Ithaca Press, 1984), 27. On the continuation of these debates, see ibid., 19–51. Also see his *Crisis and Consolidation*.

63. Lotman, *Universe of the Mind*, ch. 1 on the "Three Functions of the Text."

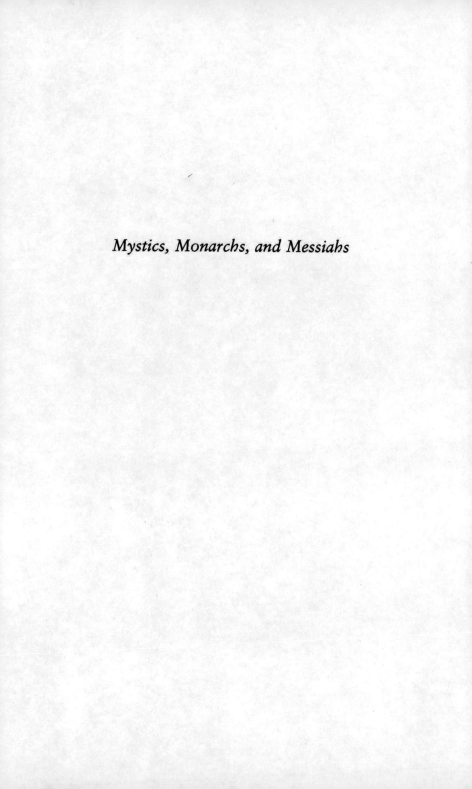

Mystics, Monarchs, and Messiahs

Part I

PERSIANATE WAYS OF BEING AND SENSING TIME

ONE

New Safavi Beginnings: Breaking with the "Way of Metempsychosis"

Every 960 years, Saturn and Jupiter face each other in the same position as observed from the vantage point of the earth, having traveled the full course of the zodiac. This recurring astronomical phenomenon, referred to as the "greatest conjunction," formed the apocalyptic text from which an astrological reading forecasting a shift in terrestrial and celestial hegemony signaled the emergence of a new and final era of Persian rule. Indeed, the Nuqtavis predicted that with the completion of the first millennium of Muhammadan rule, a Persian (Ajami) dispensation would reemerge, displacing Arab (Muslim) rule. This Persian cycle of rule was to be inaugurated by a Nuqtavi master who had attained truth and would conjoin his spiritual authority with temporal sovereignty. Seemingly fulfilling all predictions, Shah Abbas I (r. 1587–1629) abdicated the Safavi throne on Thursday, 5 August 1593 (1001 A.H.) for a period of three days in favor of a rival Nuqtavi disciple, Ustad Yusufi Tarkishduz (the quiver maker), who had unveiled "secret" Nuqtavi beliefs, divulging their "big claims" and "corrupt ideas" to the king.[1] There is a history to the development of intimacy and trust between the Safavi monarch, Shah Abbas I, and Ustad Yusufi, which I explore later in this book. The Shah's response is said to

3

have been based on the verification of Ustad Yusufi's verbal claims with Nuqtavi writings as well as through consultation with his own court astrologer (Jalal al-din Munajjim Yazdi) about the meaning of the trajectory of the stars in the skies above.[2]

The spiritual master of the Nuqtavis (Dervish Khusraw) in Qazvin, along with his close trustees and devotees, were then captured, and Ustad Yusufi Tarkishduz, the master quiver maker who had trusted the king with Nuqtavi "secrets," was brought to court. Shah Abbas I signaled for his attendants to bring him a kingly attire *(chārqab)* with a crown *(tāj)* and an inlaid belt along with other kingly accoutrements. In an act of royal and perhaps spiritual investiture, Shah Abbas I proceeded to personally adorn Yusufi as monarch. He placed the kingly tuft *(jīghah)* on Yusufi's head, sat him on the throne, and bowed down to him in a gesture of reverence worthy of kings.[3] To further authenticate this ritual coronation, Shah Abbas I stood guard, holding an inlaid cane, in accordance with the custom of the master of ceremonies (Ishik Aqasi Bashi).[4] High-ranking officials and notables of the empire were called in to pay their respects to the new king, each poised in accordance to their individual rank and position. For three days, the grand generals and noble viziers held court in that manner.[5] A court panegyrist (Hakim Rukn al-Dawlah) writes of this occasion:

> From all over the world they came to him (Yusufi) in prostration, the very moment that your command (Abbas I) made him Shah of Iran.
>
> Despite God's command Satan did not pander to Adam but to your command mankind prostrated before Satan.[6]

This theater of Safavi history was played out for three consecutive days. And as the poet implied, Shah Abbas I composed and directed a drama through which he was able to achieve something even God fell short of. On 8 August 1593, Abbas I ordered that a high scaffold be built, and they carried the master quiver maker outside the palace. Ustad Yusufi was shot by a firing squad, and his body was hung on the scaffold in full public view.[7] On the same day at an auspicious hour determined by the court astrologer, Shah Abbas I reclaimed his throne. And thus began a new era of Safavi rule with Isfahan (1590–1722), an anticipated site of the emergence of a messiah in Zoroastrian and Shi'i (Imami) eschatology, as the capital city mirroring paradise. Shah Abbas I appropriated and (re)inverted such millenarian expectations while he began to unfold a novel message and program as Shi'i monarch of Safavi Iran. The Nuqtavi coronation and subsequent suppression of the movement marked the official Safavi disavowal of a worldview that had brought them to power a century earlier. The court chroniclers frame Shah Abbas I's actions in religious terms, stating that the king "considered it among the necessities of religion to suppress those apostates of imaginary religion [*dīn*] and politics [*dawlat*]."[8]

Suppression entailed the massacre of all of those who had been suspected of Nuqtavi beliefs—poets, artists, storytellers, even his Qizilbash courtiers. The punishment of Dervish Khusraw, one of the spiritual leaders of the movement, echoed the dramatic tenor of Yusufi's mock coronation and subsequent execution. He was first brought to his heresy trial by the Imami *ulama* with the shah in attendance.[9] The presence of these men of religion would signal the prominent role they came to play in the seventeenth-century repression of a variety of gnostic currents active in Safavi landscapes. The interrogation was to have been conducted by religious authorities, who asked Dervish Khusraw questions, "the majority of which he responded to unrespondingly."[10] The shah then ordered that Khusraw be evicted and in an act of humiliation "his long beard, which resembled the tail of a dog," was chopped off. He was seated backward on a donkey and paraded around the bazaar and the districts of the capital city, Qazvin: "Men and women, at home and in the street, came out and threw sticks and rocks and dirt at him. The following day he was tied up from head to foot with a rope and placed on a camel. Again, he was paraded around town, and every passerby is said to have inflicted a different punishment on him. With such honor and prestige, he was taken to the gibbet."[11] To teach the "heretics" *(mulhid)* a lesson, the shah decreed that Dervish Khusraw's body remain on the stake, in full public view, for a week. And as for the other Nuqtavi devotees, Iskandar Bek Munshi Turkman, the official chronicler of the reign of Shah Abbas I, asserts that "if anyone escaped punishment, they either fled to India or found themselves a corner and remained anonymous, so that in Iran the way of metempsychosis [*shīvah-yi tanāsukh*] was abolished."[12] What was this way that so threatened the authority of Shah Abbas I? What were the "secrets" disclosed to the shah by Yusufi the quiver maker? And what was this worldview that linked stars to cycles of Persian and Arab authority, to new kings, to revelations, and to incarnations? Finally, what meaning could Yusufi's theatrical coronation have held for the new directions of Safavi rule?

NOTES

1. Iskandar Bek Munshī Turkmān, *Tārīkh-i 'Ālam Ārā-yi 'Abbāsī*, 2 vols. (Tehran: Amir Kabir, 1971), vol. 1, 474. For a similar horoscope ascribed to Ardavan see the *Kārnāmak* of Ardashir as well as the *Shāhnāme*.

2. Jalāl al-dīn Munajjim Yazdī, *Tārīkh-i 'Abbāsī* (Tehran: Intishārāt-i Vahīd, 1987), 121.

3. Afushtah-yi Natanzī, *Naqāvat al-āsār fī zikr al-akhyār* (Tehran: Intishārāt-i Ilmī va Farhāngī, 1971), 522.

4. The Ishik Aqasi Bashi of the Harem's abode *(kashīk-khānah)* was strategically located at its threshold. There he stood guard, night and day, except on Fridays. He supervised the activities of his subordinates, the *Qapuchis* (gatekeepers) and the Ishik Aqasi(s) of the harem as well. He represented the channel through which the harem communicated with the Outer Court *(bīrūn)*, and vice versa.

5. Afushtah-yi Natanzī, *Naqāvat al-āsār*, 522–523. Although the *Naqāvat* describes the three-day reign of Yusufi as occurring in Qazvin and talks of Shah Abbas taking on the role of the Ishik Aqasi Bashi at the palace in Qazvin, Turkmān, *Tārīkh-i 'Ālam Ārā-yi 'Abbāsī*, 474–476, states that the shah crowned Yusufi in

Luristan, where he stayed behind riding for a few days, not attending to the affairs of state, while Yusufi was escorted along with generals, functionaries, and troops to the divankhanah (court at Qazvin).

6. Hakīm Rukn al-Dawlah, whose pen name was Masīh or Masīhā; see Muhammad Tāhir Nasrābādi's *Tazkirah-yi Nasrābādī*, ed. V. Dastgirdi, under Hakim Ruknā-yi Kāshī (Tehran: Chāpkhānah-yi Armaghān, 1973), 214–217.

7. Ibid.

8. Afushtah-yi Natanzī, *Naqāvat al-āsār fī zikr al-akhyār*, 519.

9. According to Turkmān, *Tārīkh-i 'Ālam Ārā-yi 'Abbāsī*, vol. 1, 476, Dervish Khusraw was tried after the shah returned from his Luristan campaign in 1001/1593. Also in Natanzī, *Naqāvat al-āsār*, 523.

10. Afushtah-yi Natanzī, *Naqāvat al-āsār*, 523. The *Tārīkh-i 'Ālam Ārā-yi 'Abbāsī*, vol. 1, 476, states that men of religion *(ulama)* were summoned to look into the state of Dervish Khusraw. Jugs of wine were found in his cloister *(takkiya)*, and when it became obvious from the extent of his drinking and disbelief that he did not follow the principles of the *shari'a*, his execution was ordered.

11. Afushtah-yi Natanzī, *Naqāvat al-āsār*, 524.

12. Turkmān, *Tārīkh-i 'Ālam Ārā-yi 'Abbāsī*, vol. 1, 477.

TWO

Cycles of Time and Rhythms of Change:
Persianate Imaginations of History

An Era means a definite space of time, reckoned from the beginning of some
past year, in which either a prophet, with signs and wonders, and with a
proof of his divine mission, was sent, or a great and powerful king arose, or
in which a nation perished by a universal destructive deluge, or by a violent
earthquake and sinking of the earth, or a sweeping pestilence, or by intense
drought, or in which a change of dynasty or religion took place, or any
grand event of the celestial and the famous tellurian miraculous occurrences,
which did not happen save at long intervals and at times far distant from
each other.[1]

Abu Rayhan Biruni (d. 1050), the medieval scientist and historian, includes this definition of an epoch in his chronicle *(al-
Āthār al-bāqiyah)* of the different ways in which ancient peoples
(Indians, Persians, Greeks) and religious traditions (Zoroastrians, Christians, Jews) reckoned time. A variety of calendars are
represented, whether lunar, solar, or luni-solar, from Greece
eastward through Iran to India and Central Asia. These calendars related a compendium of diverse calculations and attitudes
of time practiced and preserved by Hellenistic cultures recorded
for future generations, "the memory and splendor of which will
last," Biruni hoped, as his "heirloom in posterity through the
flood of ages."[2] The particular dating systems and computations
marking sacred cultural moments like beginnings and ruptures
are delineated by Biruni, through whose mathematical and as-

tronomic elaborations we can sense a deep understanding of the
sciences involved in such calculation. Biruni's definition of an
era is a synopsis of the different ways in which Greeks, Babylonians, Persians, Indians, and Khwarazmians understood fixed
moments of time (epochs) and settings of change, abstractions
that allowed for a coherent universe. The Babylonians marked
the beginning of an epoch with a flood that did not reach Iran
and India, according to Biruni, but the idea was adopted by the
Jews, Christians, and Muslims. Jews and Christians saw the rise
of prophets unveiling divine revelation in the form of a holy
book as symbolic of a new era. The Persians, according to
Biruni, interpreted the rise of their kings as the originators of a
new cycle.

Biruni, describing the early debates between Muslims when
selecting their calendrical system and determining the beginning
of the new Muslim era with the migration of Muhammad and
his followers *(muhājirūn)* to Medina (622 A.H.), states that Muslims decided not to use the dating system of the Greeks, who inaugurated their era with the rise of Alexander. Muslims chose as
well not to follow the solar Persian calendar for "as soon as a
new king arises among the Persians he abolishes the era of his
predecessor."[3] The lunar calendar would be adopted by the
Muslims, some Muslims continued to observe ancient cosmological beliefs from a Persian past in the myths and lore that surround a solar basis for the calculation of time as their concept of
time shaped their model of the world.[4] With the imaginations of
some Persianate Muslims like the Nuqtavis, the solar *(khurshīdī/
Jalālī)* calendar, with the sun as its focal symbol, represented a
Persian pre-Islamic past. Astronomy, along with its particular
astrological implications, was one channel through which components of a Persianate universe survived as well. Such notions
of time and history were associated with a distinctive sense of
being in this universe that related the celestial to the terrestrial
world. "Representations of time are essential components of social and cultural consciousness, whose structure reflects the
rhythm and cadences which mark the evolution of society and

culture," writes Aron Gurevitch in *Time as a Problem of Cultural History.*[5]

Notions of "grand celestial events with miraculous terrestrial repercussion that occurred at long intervals and at times far distant from each other" have a Persianate lineage to them, according to Biruni, who preserves myths on the transmission of ancient Persian knowledge in his chronicle. These legends depict the ancient Iranian mythical king Tahmurath depositing manuscripts of various scientific works written on the bark of khadank trees called *tuz* in a fort he had built in Isfahan (Sarawiya) to preserve them from warnings of the flood.[6] One of these manuscripts, ascribed to an ancient Persian sage, contained calculations determining the behavior of planets: "The people of the time of Tahmurath and the more ancient Persians called these the 'cycles of the thousands'; and the wise men of India and their kings, the ancient kings of Persia, and even the ancient Chaldeans who lived in Babylon determined the mean longitudes of the seven planets by means of them, preferring them over others because of their accuracy and brevity."[7] Through the Famous astrologer Abu Ma'shar (d. 886 C.E.), renowned even in early modern Europe (as Albumasar) for his elaboration on the "cycles of conjunctions and triplicities," we hear one version of this transmission myth.[8] The contents of an ancient Persian body of knowledge, hidden by the order of Persian kings to protect it from a forecasted flood and then recorded in the early Muslim era (Abbasid era, eighth century), became the narrative memory through which some Iranians could transcend their domination by the Arabs and hope for a renewal of a lost age of Iranian glory.[9] Memory of a Persian past that came to envision hidden secrets rediscovered at a later stage was key to a sense of revival. For Christians in Europe, Abu Ma'shar's theory of the rise and fall of dynasties in accordance with a timetable set by the occurrence of certain types of conjunctions of planets (Saturn/Jupiter) was understood in the sixteenth century to signal Christian eschatological expectations of the coming of the antichrist.[10] This same conjunction of Saturn and Jupiter was fathomed by the Nuqtavis, a thousand years after the rise of Muhammad, as a sign of the end of Arab rule and the return of Persian sovereignty. Another version of this narrative memory of secret Persian knowledge is preserved by Abu Sahl al-Fazl b. Nawbakhti, the late eighth-century court astrologer of Harun al-Rashid (r. 786–809), in his *Kitāb al-nahmatan*.[11] Abu Sahl b. Nawbakht directly links two Mazdean prophets, Zarathustra and Jamasp, to these divinations. It was thanks to the advice of these two Iranian prophets that pre-Islamic Persian kings were said to have concealed copies of texts on astronomy and astrology in India and China, until Ardashir I (r. 225–240 C.E.), the founder of the Sasani dynasty, recovered them.[12] Abu Sahl b. Nawbakht, a Persian convert to Islam, had learned astronomy from his Zoroastrian father, who had also been employed as court astrologer to the Abbasids (Mansur, r. 754–775). Members of this Persian notable family (Nawbakhti) would act as court astrologers for their Muslim patrons and would also engage in the translation projects of rendering Pahlavi texts into Arabic. Members of the Nawbakhti family would go on to fill important bureaucratic *(kuttāb, munshī)* functions at the Abbasid court and produce noteworthy Imami Shi'i scholars *(mutakalim)*.[13] Indeed, an entire series of translations from Middle Persian (Pahlavi) to Arabic was undertaken in this period, and these were not only philosophical works, for Ibn al-Muqaffa' (d. 756) translated the Indo-Iranian political fable the *Kalilah va Dimna,* as well as the Sasani *Book of Kings (Khwadaynamag)* and the Buddhist Jataka stories on Budhasaf.[14] Assuming that these texts would help shape an Irano-Islamic cultural idiom and that first-generation Persian converts to Islam would carry into their understanding and expression of Islam their own Mazdean perceptions of the cosmos, I explore in the first two parts of this book a variety of ways in which a Persianate ethos participated in the shaping of Shi'i and Irano-Islamic cultural systems.

The Iranian convert to Islam Abu Sahl Nawbakhti, who served as court astrologer to the Abbasids, recorded a narrative

memory using Zoroastrian apocalyptic literature that validated
the prophet Jamasp as the source of such secret predictions. Zoroastrians living and practicing their beliefs as a protected religious minority *(ahl-i kitāb)* in the Irano-Islamic lands possessed
a book of prophecies *(Jamāspnāme)* narrated as a dialogue between Jamasp and the mythical Iranian king Gushtasp, who is
said to have been the first to convert to Zoroastrianism. Jamasp
was thought to have been a contemporary of Zarathustra and
his successor as chief priest *(mobed-i mobedān)*. In this work,
Zarathustra confirms Jamasp before King Gushtasp (Vishtasp):
"By the command of God, I have made Jamasp wise. He knows
everything."[15] As priest and astrologer, part of Jamasp's knowledge entailed "how many stars (there are in) the sky, what is (the
time of) the falling of each star, and what is the good of that!
What a knowledge is this!"[16] The *Jamāspnāme* explicitly forecasts an end to Arab rule. After the last Sasani kings, "there
come Arabs who bring up their seeds from the branch of
Hashem. They take the country of Iran with violence and force,
for ten hundred and eighty-two years, nine months, seven days,
and four hours." A millennium of Arab rule (1082 years), if
calculated from the migration of Muhammad to Medina
(622 C.E.), is to end in the early eighteenth century (1704 C.E.).

This millenarian hope embedded in the *Jamāspnāme* is integrated in the narratives around the story of Abu Muslim
(d. 755), the Alid hero who succeeded in overthrowing the oppressors of the family of Muhammad, the Umayyads. As is
shown in part 2, the *Abū Muslimnāme* recorded in the eleventh
century is both a narrative constructing an Alid memory and
also a record of conversion from an Iranian past to a Muslim
present. The *Jamāspnāme* appears in the *Abū Muslimnāme* as
an Iranian vizier (Khwaja Muhammad Nihavandi) confirms the
Shi'i Imam's (Muhammad Baqir) prediction concerning the
apocalyptic rise of Abu Muslim by introducing the *Jamāspnāme*
as a proof text. The Iranian Vazir assures his Khwarazmian patron king, who is contemplating whether he should join the
ranks of rebellion with Abu Muslim, that it is recorded in the

Jamāspnāme that "on the day of judgment, when they martyr Imam Husayn, there will occur the revolt of the seventy-two. At the end of the line of these there will appear a chivalric warrior [*javānmard*]. His name is Abu Muslim. . . . Whether you aid him or not, he will be triumphant with the help of God Almighty. And he will cleanse this curse from the house of the Prophet." This episode creates a memory of a past, conjoining Iranian and Alid apocalyptic beliefs. It speaks of a hope for change that fuses Mazdean prophets like Jamasp with Shi'i Imams like Muhammad Baqir and holy Alid heroes like Abu Muslim. It also provides a narrative for those imbued with a Persianate ethos to merge a sense of an Iranian past with an Alid present. I emphasize that those ensconced in a Persianate ethos are not necessarily of Iranian blood, for the Khwarazmians were Persian-speaking Turks living in Central Asia where Mazdean belief systems (Manichaeans and Zoroastrians) had been hegemonic centuries before the rise of Islam.

Jamasp's narrative of creation and of history finds echoes in Ferdowsi's rendering of the Iranian past as well. Although Ferdowsi uses other sources and does not include Jamasp in his epic, pre-Islamic sources like the *Jamāspnāme* used by Ferdowsi had Mazdean notions of time and change emplotted in their narratives. Ferdowsi himself mentions that he has collected oral and written accounts of Iranian history. Naturally, Ferdowsi presents his version of history in the way he chose to emphasize the injustice of kings, for example. But the material he incorporates into his epic preserves a cyclical rhythm of change that permeates the *Shāhnāme*. Ferdowsi finishes his history with the prophecy by the Sasani commander Rustam Pur-i Hormozd, who was an astrologer as well, foretelling the imminent invasion of the Arabs. Ferdowsi does not explicitly introduce a future scenario of change. I say "explicitly" because I think that due to the way change is imagined cyclically in Ferdowsi's narrative, the possibility of a return to a purer time for the lands of Iran is left open, a point to which I return. I am suggesting as well another channel, astronomy, through which the Persianate ethos flourished.

Perhaps astronomy was an ambiguous medium through which Mazdean ideas could be expressed within a Muslim context.

Gernot Windfuhr unravels the cosmological logic of Zarathustra that astronomically links three cosmic dimensions of the human, rational, and ethical worlds.[17] Embedded in the understanding of the assembly of stars lies a hidden set of laws that rule the entire universe, interlacing the terrestrial and celestial spheres, which permeated the way in which the Nuqtavis understood their position and role in history. Along with a written legacy of astronomy, an oral knowledge seems to have been transmitted as well, all of which constructed a memory of a Persian past and predicted future celestial events that saw an inevitable return to a time before the Arabs and before Islam.

Abu Ma'shar in his astrological works attempts to separate and distance religion from "the science of the stars." Why else in a work on astrology would he insist on the preferability of monotheism in contrast to the "evil worshipping of idols" unless that connection had been an integral part the astral knowledge of the Persians he was recounting? Abu Ma'shar instead emphasizes the basic unity of the sciences of all the civilized nations of the world.[18] For some, like the Nuqtavis (Persianate *ghuluww*), astronomy and human history remained closely intertwined in their cosmology. In their cyclical imagination of history these groups shared similar worldviews with the Isma'ilis (Alid *ghuluww*), yet in seeing history in terms of an ultimate victory of the Persians over the Arabs, the Nuqtavis did intend to break with Islamic law and rituals, which reflected the very essence of their cultural life. Some Irano-Muslims merged the Persian and Arab cycles in their conception of history, thus shaping their identity. But unlike the Nuqtavis, they did not desire a future return of Persian hegemony because they expected the apocalyptic Alid messiah (Mahdi). It was perhaps due to the opaque nature of these awaited messiahs in Mazdean and Abrahamic traditions that apocalyptic movements tended to attract a wide spectrum of believers from within both traditions.

The Nuqtavis were not the first in the Islamic era to see in the conjunction of Saturn and Jupiter a sign of hope and an invitation to armed rebellion against Arab hegemony. In the tenth century, the Qarmati-Isma'ilis, a group of Alid devotees, had also interpreted this conjunction (27 October 928 C.E.) in the language of Persianate messianism and had established an utopian enclave in Southern Arabia (Bahrayn, 899 C.E.).[19] Their emergence marked a breach with Islam, as they sacked Mecca during the Hajj season (930), slaughtering the pilgrims and throwing their corpses into the holy well of Zamzam and carrying off the sacred black stone (said to be given by the angel Gabriel to Abraham) from the Ka'ba, the locus of circumbulation at the holiest shrine of Islam.[20]

The History of the Qarmatis and of Islam interprets this tenth-century (316/928) planetary conjunction of Saturn and Jupiter differently than does the history of the Nuqtavis. Yet both Qarmatis and Nuqtavis share a sense of cyclical rhythms that fashioned their parallel conceptions of change. Some Qarmatis in Bahrayn anticipated a Persian messiah who would restore the rule of justice and truth. Groups such as the Isma'ilis (Alid *ghulāt*) originally adopted Persianate notions of cyclical time without invoking the Iranian genealogies in which these precepts had converged. Some, like the Qarmatis, however, continued to imagine themselves within the last Muhammadan cycle and in the tenth century awaited the return of the seventh Imam (Muhammad b. Isma'il), when Islamic law was to be abrogated with a complete revelation of past hidden esoteric truths. What exactly this truth would be seems to have been understood in different ways by various Qarmati followers. Not all Qarmatis approved of the sacrilegious massacre at Mecca, especially when two years later (931 C.E.) a Persian from Isfahan was designated as their new ruler. Announcing that he was the Mahdi (messiah), this Isfahani messiah claimed that Moses, Jesus, Muhammad, Ali, and the Imams were impostors and that the true religion was that of "our father Adam." He abolished the *shari'a* and sanctioned the worship of fire and the cursing of Muhammad and his family. For some Qarmatis, finding the truth was predicated on a return to Mazdean religious practice. Other devotees expected an Alid revealer of deeper truths as foretold in Jewish, Christian, and Muslim scriptures, but for the Persianate *ghulât* the cycle of Muslim prophets (Muhammad) and "silent ones" (Ali) represented just an intermediary epoch in historical imagination. Heteroglossia allowed not only for a multitude of visionary languages but also for shared apocalyptic symbols to render different meanings and narratives.

Astrologers, key actors in the transmission of memory and Persianate prophecy, had associated Isfahan with the rise of a Persian dynasty that would overthrow the Muslim caliphate.[21] Links may have existed with some Zoroastrian circles, for the chief priest *(mobed)* Isfandiyar b. Adharbad was accused and executed for complicity with the Qarmatis.[22] Zoroastrians living in Irano-Muslim landscapes were protected as a religious community by Islamic law and continued to practice their faith, expecting their messiah *(saoshyant)* into the early modern period, as we have seen with the *Jamāspnāme*. These texts transgressed confessional boundaries as they were translated into Muslim dialects. Biruni associates the choice of the date of 928 C.E. the conjunction of Saturn and Jupiter, for the emergence of a Persian messiah with the passing of fifteen hundred years from the death of Zarathustra, when according to both Zarathustra and the prophet Jamasp, the Mazdeans would restore their rule, and Islam would be abolished.[23] Although Biruni rejects the validity of predictions of a Mazdean restoration, he speculates on the astronomical logic behind the choice of Qarmati's timing for their emergence. He speaks of a book of cycles and conjunctions written by another astrologer—Abu Abdullah Al'adi—who calculated that the eighteenth conjunction after the birth of Muhammad would coincide with the tenth millennium of the Hijra, "whence a man will come forth and restore Mazdean rule and will occupy the whole world and do away with the rule of the Arabs and others. He will unite mankind in one religion and under one rule, he will do away with evil."[24] This sounds like an idea the Nuqtavis may have been familiar with. Biruni records such an active conception in the late tenth century and questions the rationale of Persians associating the "fiery conjunction" with an era of Persian hegemony, simply because they claimed the Sasanis ruled during the "fiery conjunction." In the same century some Iranians are reported to have believed that a Muslim dynasty (Buyids, 945–1055) had also come to power in Iraq and Iran during a fiery conjunction. And, again, Biruni wonders why "people [Iranians] used to promise each other the restoration of Persian rule, given that the actions of the Buyid family were not like those of ancient [Persian] kings."[25] The Buyids were of Persian (Daylamis) descent, and they were the first Irano-Muslim rulers to take the Persian regal title of *shahanshah* (king of kings) in the Islamic era, but they were Muslims. Some Iranians in medieval Islam did not distinguish between aspects of cultural exchange that were being synthesized in a transgressive mix that shaped the Irano-Muslim idiom.

I am interested not in origins and in "pure" continuities in my exploration of Persianate cultures but in the ways in which Persian symbols mingled with Islam, the strategies employed in the construction of "identity," and the ways in which these symbols are represented and remembered as possessing Persian lineages. Although Biruni questions the absurdity of a number of floating beliefs regarding the Buyids as Persian kings, he points to a dynamic dialogue in oral culture that links planetary conjunctions to a Persian past and to a future return of a past style of sovereignty. Once the Buyids (Rukn al-Dawla in 962) took on the Persian title of shahanshah, Biruni points out, they were wishfully perceived by some as restorers of Persian glory because they were from the Persian Caspian Sea region. The Nuqtavi conjunction in the sixteenth century was also entering the fiery conjunction associated with Persian dominion.

Nuqtavi cosmology envisioned universal history, thought to consist of sixty-four thousand years, as four cycles of sixteen thousand years each. The first cycle of history was conceived as one in which minerals, plants, and animals evolved with time until Adam came into being—literally when the Adam form appeared—marking the beginning of human history.[26] It is not clear within which of the following three cycles of human history the Nuqtavis placed themselves in the fifteenth century. They did ground themselves, however, within their historical context, imagining their lives in a cycle that had been inaugurated by the Arabs (Muhammad) and would in the near future be consummated by the Persians (Mahmud). Yet the rise of a Persian era is expressed in terms of a return to an "old" age that had passed but that would finally be revived in the form of a final and eternal victory. The Nuqtavis manifest a Persian recollection of the Arab conquests that acknowledged the temporary victory of Islam but maintained the hope of a return to a pre-Islamic past. What is notable about the Nuqtavi construction of Irano-Islamic history is that it does not cast the age of Arab/Muslim conquests as an evil age of oppression; Nuqtavi cosmology simply envisions a gradual purification of humanity leading to an initial age of harmony associated with Iranian hegemony.[27] One would assume, then, that the Nuqtavis were placing themselves as well as the Arabs in the third and final cycle of world history. However, in Nuqtavi texts recorded a century before the Nuqtavi actual emergence *(khurūj)* onto the religious and political landscapes of Safavi Iran, they do speak of recurring cycles of eight thousand years of Arab domination followed by that of Iranian rule, as though there might be a repetition of this scenario in the future.

These historical patterns are construed as fixed, and so such a future outcome is considered as universally determined and inevitable. Each cycle was to bring forth a succession of eight Arab prophets *(mursil-i mukammil)* and eight Iranian manifestations *(mubīn-i mukammil)*.[28] The Arab prophets are termed "messengers of God," while the Persians are called "manifestations of the divine." Abu Ma'shar's notion of a regeneration of spiritual and temporal rule recurring approximately every thousand years at the time of the greatest conjunction of Jupiter and Saturn and ultimately leading to a revival of Iranian dominion is embedded in Nuqtavi cosmology. Eras are perceived in the same way as Biruni six centuries earlier in terms of cyclical change in religious or dynastic dispensations with one cosmic king prophet replacing another. Mahmud predicts that eight hundred years following the advent of Muhammad, the last person *(shakhs-i ākhir)* will appear up to an hour, a day, a week, or a year until one thousand years have passed and the millennial person will be the possessor of that century.[29] The theory of triplicities and of the "great year" mark Nuqtavi reckonings of time. The Nuqtavi conception of cyclical history, successive revelations, and two forms of illumination—revelation followed by divine manifestation—resonates with some Shi'i (Isma'ili and early Imami) views of history and prophecy. In fact, the Safavi historian Natanzi includes one group of Persianate Isma'ilis (Nizari) in the satanic Nuqtavi genealogy as precursors of demonic movements in the Islamic era, following those of Mani and Mazdak. What differentiates the Nuqtavis from the Isma'ilis is exactly what differentiated those Qarmatis who embraced the Isfahani Mahdi from the rest the Isma'ili community. Their final truth did not entail enlightenment or a deeper understanding of Abrahamic revelations but rather an unveiling of an older truth associated with the Persians. Yet that did not prevent them from sharing a familiar cosmology and raise the banner of revolt together.

In the Gathas composed by Zarathustra, knowledge of the truth and of order *(asha),* of the skies and of time, is hidden *(guzra)* from all except the one in the know *(widwah).*[30] Zarathustra taught that the battle between the forces of good and evil could be won only with the knowledge of a cosmic order that entails an understanding of the associations between the material and spiritual world, with the earth at its center and patterns of stars above. Ultimate victory, which is what *saoshyant* means, lies with the possessor of such knowledge, who will be able to save the world.[31] The "one in the know" must comprehend the order governing this world and its synchronicity with universal ethics. Embedded in this holistic system lay the mysteries of the end of worldly time and the return to eternity at which time every believer would recover his original spiritual state. The end was imagined as a return to a former age of purity. Zoroastrian cosmic drama understood good and evil as two separate and contrary forces in perpetual struggle with each other. Although the origin of evil was obscure, it was thought to have existed prior to all cause, emanating out of a dark abyss, invading light and ravaging material existence. But in the end, light (Ahura Mazda) would triumph over dark (Ahriman), truth over untruth. Evil was then not perceived as eternal, nor was it deemed as powerful as the force of good, which was personified in the supreme God of light, wisdom, or Ahura Mazda. Humankind was located in the last three millennia of a universal history lasting twelve millennia, in which individuals actively engaged in combating Ahriman, the spirit of darkness (evil, lies, envy, greed), along with his demonic agents. Ahura Mazda challenges the human being, whether king, priest, warrior, or herdsman, to attain the divine glory *(farr)*, as angels and demons aid or obstruct mankind in this endeavor. At the apocalyptic conclusion of the war against untruth, the savior Saoyoshant—rising from the depths of lake Frazdan, where the seed of Zarathustra is said to have been preserved will usher in the final triumph over evil.[32] Good thoughts, good deeds, and good words are the weapons with which individuals will have to fight. A set cast of characters, each personifying a permanent role within the cosmic drama, returns to earth cyclically during the three millennia of worldly existence in which good and evil had intermingled. In every age, this was the challenge laid before a Zoroastrian believer who lived in eastern Muslim landscapes.

Mazdean cosmologies shape the narrative themes and structure of Ferdowsi's epic on Iranian history. In the composition of the *Shāhnāme,* Ferdowsi, who wondered about Iran's past and present era of subjugation by Muslim Arabs and Turks (Ghaznavids) wove together both written and oral stories in circulation three centuries after the rise of Islam to create a meaningful story of the Iranian past. As mentioned, he probably used the *Jamāspnāme* as a source for his project. A Mazdean cosmology is inherent in the intertwining cycle of the epics of kings and warriors that Ferdowsi brings together in the *Shāhnāme*. We should not forget that Ferdowsi names the Zoroastrian *mobed* as a source for his epic: "There was a book from ancient times in which there was an abundance of stories. It was dispersed into the hands of every *mobed*. Every wise one possessed a portion of it." Priests were a source of religion as well as history; for the Zoroastrians the two disciplines were intertwined. Mythic, cosmic, and historical time all ticked together. Although it is clear that Ferdowsi was not a Zoroastrian—in fact, he is even critical of Zoroastrian orthodoxy in his epic—the *Shāhnāme* continued to be associated in the Muslim era with the Zoroastrians (Gabr) because it embodied Mazdean ethics and cosmology.[33]

Ferdowsi crystallized a history of Iran in the *Shāhnāme*, which became a classic in the shaping of an Iranian collective memory for generations following him. Ferdowsi must have sensed that this might happen, for he was conscious of the importance of a recorded narrative to bring together an Iranian history and culture that before Islam was predominantly oral. He makes a point of mentioning in the *Shāhnāme* that during the years he spent writing the epic, he had been deprived of material comforts, a deprivation for which he had not been remunerated. Rather, this was a labor of love with a vision of the magnanimity of its import. Dick Davis observes that Ferdowsi was self-consciously marking the end of an era.[34] Ferdowsi was writing to ensure that Iranians would remember the particularities of their past, despite the fading of memory through the passage of time. Ferdowsi concludes his book with the hope that the *Shāhnāme* will echo this past throughout time, "Henceforth, I cannot die for I live having broadcast the seeds of my verse."

Such consciousness of the urgency to preserve the past points to a context in which such a memory may have been in danger of being lost, a historical moment in which there was a rupture with the past. To avoid that rupture, Ferdowsi wrote the *Shāhnāme* as a *lieu de mémoire*—what Pierre Nora characterizes as a setting in which that memory was no longer a part of everyday life, where only a residual sense of community remained, and so sites were crystallized in commemoration.[35] Ferdowsi reveals this sense of dispossession in his nostalgic reflections on memory and past knowledge, the key to which is the wise old man: "From the speech of the old man of learned heart, listen to his words and learn them bit by bit." Through oral transmission of stories, Iranian history circulated from mouth to mouth. At least six generations of Iranians had lived and died since the advent of Islam, but still there was an awareness of a "time that goes far back in the memory of human beings. A son learned it from his father, and told about it in every detail."

Ferdowsi, however, seems to question whether young boys remember any more. He has Piran, the wise advisor of Iran's archenemy, Afrasiab the Turk (Turan), say, "A young boy: what memory has he of things past, what knowledge has he?" To which Kay Khusraw, the model king for Ferdowsi, responds with the cryptic remark "A caravan dog [*kārivānī*] cannot bring down a roaming lion."[36] The reference to the Arab Bedouins as caravan dogs is clear, but is Ferdowsi voicing sedition through his ideal king Kay Khusraw? Are Iranian youth being reminded that they are lions not to be defeated by Arabs?

Reiterated by virtuous characters throughout the poem (Zal, Isfandiyar, Gordiyeh) is an appeal to the past that is seen as nobler than the present but that no longer has any binding force.[37] Davis's reading of the *Shāhnāme* detects a nostalgia for an older order that is idealized but has little effect on the way father's treat their sons or kings their subjects. Such past notions of loyalty, honor, and authority shape the Persianate ethos that Ferdowsi commemorates in the *Shāhnāme*.

Pierre Nora remarks perceptively that a break with the past enables the observer to question a tradition, however venerable, for the rift permits perspective. Distance allowed Ferdowsi to separate himself from a received Iranian tradition and critique it, since Iran had been conquered by Arabs *(tāziyān)* three centuries earlier and now the Turks (Turan) were the new masters.

Dick Davis reads the *Shāhnāme* as an epic of sedition—a book
that does not celebrate and glorify Iranian monarchy but in fact
questions it, while also embracing it as a tradition. Despite its injustice and incomprehensibility, Ferdowsi seems to suggest that
preserving custom is better than other evils. Were there a subtitle
to the *Epic of Kings,* it might read "A History of Betrayal of
Sons, Warriors, and Subjects," for such is the nature of
Ferdowsi's pondering of an Iranian past. The patron who commissions him to compile the book wants Ferdowsi to write
about how the Iranians "held on to the world in the beginning
and why is it that it has been left to us in such a sorry state?" As
Davis points out, there is a "sense of belatedness, of living irre-
trievably after the golden age" in the *Shāhnāme*.[38] In the hope
that "all our labors will [not] be in vain," Ferdowsi constructs a
self-image of and for Iranians, one that comes to shape what I
have called a Persianate ethos.

It is important to remember the cultural context in which
Ferdowsi conceived his project. The literary debates of the
Shu'ubiyya (eighth and ninth centuries) were one expression of
Iranians who had assimilated into elite circles of Irano-Muslim
society and who debated their right to be equal with all Muslims. This cultural assimilation of Arabs and Persians can be
witnessed in Tabari's (d. 930) writing of history. As a Persian
and a Muslim, Tabari includes in his famous *History* both an
Abrahamic record of prophets and an Iranian story of kings.
The long and continuous history of the kings of Iran had come
to an end for Tabari with the rise of Islam, which inaugurated a
superior religious and political order. This Muslim era was a
golden age. Although Abrahamic and Mazdean historical memories are synchronized in Tabari, the ultimate truth lay within
the Qur'an. Thus, for example, where the Iranians had no record of a flood, Qur'anic narratives that mention the flood were
deemed as truth and hence as factual history. As Tarif Khalidi
states, "Islam and history are coeval."[39] Yet not all Muslims
would embrace this coexistence.

In the recording of official Muslim history, Tavakoli-Targhi has shown the variety of ways in which Iranian history is Islamicized, as the first Persian man king Gayumars is assimilated with Adam or as his androgyny is transformed into virility, marrying thirty women and fathering many offspring.[40] As a contemporary of Ferdowsi, Balami translates Tabari's history into Persian and (re)writes Islamic history from the perspective of an eastern Iranian (Khurasanian). According to Meisami, Balami is more interested than Tabari in coordinating the history of Abrahamic prophets with Iranian kings.[41] Whereas Tabari presents a disjointed narrative of kings and prophets, placing the two side by side, Balami smoothens the narrative into a continuous and united flow, linking this dual Irano-Semitic heritage to his Samanid patron Mansur b. Nuh (961–976).[42] Tabari's and Balami's narratives illustrate different symbiotic mergings of Persian and Muslim identities, each reflecting the distinct remembrance and construction of a group.[43]

Much like some *ghulāt* among the Qarmatis who sacked Mecca and willed to return to a pre-Islamic Iranian past, Ferdowsi, in contrast to Tabari and Balami, refuses to see any merging of identities. The atmosphere that allowed Arabs to look back to their pre-Islamic Arabian past and discover the purity of the Arabic language reflects an era in which the Islamic venture is secure enough for the revisiting of pagan pasts. As Arabs rediscovered their *jahaliyya* history, Persians in the eastern lands of Islam began writing in a Persian language transformed by its Arabic experience. The political settings that allowed for such an articulation were significant in creating a space where Iranian culture could find "official" expression. After all, Persian had been the lingua franca in eastern Iran long before Islam, and, clearly, the Arab conquests did not alter that. People continued communicating in Persian, though not when writing history or poetry. By the tenth century, the decentralization of Abbasid rule had allowed for the rise of Persian local dynasties in central (Buyid) and eastern Iran (Tahirid, Saffarid, Samanid), all of which came to draw their genealogies from Iranian kings or warrior generals. In fact, the Saffarids and

Samanids even came to patronize Persian literature and history, leading to what has been called the Persian Renaissance, from which the *Shāhnāme* emanates. Depending on the degree to which they were grounded in the Persianate ethos, audiences must have received and understood the *Shāhnāme* in different ways. Although Ferdowsi preserves a Persianate idiom in his emplottment of Iranian history, one had to be familiar with the cultural code to recognize and understand its Mazdean worldview. But the *Shāhnāme* with its wide circulation came to organize a worldview for its listeners—a particularly Persianate sense of time and being.

The history of Iran as represented by Ferdowsi in the *Shāhnāme* describes cycles of change alternating between ages of wisdom and justice, when Iran was prosperous, and dark eras, in which tyranny and chaos reigned and virtue was humiliated. The *Shāhnāme's* cyclical structure does not lie in "the basic historical paradigm of the rise and fall of states and the transfer of rule from one group to another," as Meisami maintains.[44] Such a trite understanding of the cyclicity that pervades Mazdean cosmology tends to blur the distinctions between Ferdowsi's notions of cyclical history and that of, say, Ghazali or Ibn Khaldun. Dick Davis perceives a gradual deterioration in the affairs of the world depicted in the *Shāhnāme* with Iran as its center. Personal, public, and cosmic degeneration are intertwined, just as in Mazdean cosmology. Often, familial betrayals (fathers of sons) reflect a broader imperial decline (kings and subjects). This decay "generates a great many of the historical incidents that make up the poem's overt narrative."[45] But evil flourished in cycles of violence, and those who are in authority—that is, kings—are repeatedly the source of Iran's decadence. Seduced by the demons of power, envy, false pride, and greed, they lose Iran's divinely bestowed splendor *(farr)*. The injustice of Iranian monarchs, whose oppression begins in their own households and spreads beyond their courts, leaves Iran vulnerable to the foreign invasions that regularly punctuate history.

From the beginning of Iranian history, when the first king man Gayumars reigned benevolently until the advent of the Arab invasions, Iran experienced recurring eras of evil dominion interspersed with moments of justice. An original period of brilliance, however, marks an Iranian glorified past as it evolves technologically and socially and ritualizes its identity.[46] But evil gradually invades Iran from the first demonic act of the killing of Gayumars's son Siamak to the vanity of Jamshid, who after having orchestrated the civilizing process of Iran, stopped paying homage to God and uttered blasphemy, recognizing no lord but himself. Just as in the Zoroastrian Avesta, Jamshid's (Yim) vanity marks the end of an initial era of Iranian justice and glory. And it is because of his pride that the world becomes full of discord and the evil millennium of Zahhak, recognized as an Arab *(tāzī)* invader, ravishes Iran. After a thousand years of oppression and cruelty, Feraydun rebels with the help of the blacksmith Kaveh, who had personally suffered from Zahhak's repression, losing seventeen of his eighteen sons, and restores the rule of justice to Iran. It is Kaveh who reminds the prince Feraydun of the monarch's role in Iranian tradition: "Your duty as king is to let me have justice." Ferdowsi does not hide his disdain for the Arabs. He, in fact, endorses this rebellion; it is "the one insurrection against a ruling monarch that is presented as wholly justified."[47] That Ferdowsi legitimizes rebellion against Zahhak in a meditation on Iranian sovereignty that he questions and yet invariably supports signals an invitation to rebellion for Iranians listening to his epic. Zahhak is represented allegorically as the avatar of the Zoroastrian Ahriman. Subsequently, as unjust and tyrannical rule befalls Iran in cycles, every evil king would be associated with Zahhak's serpent demons. Evil is often foreseen by a prophetic character like the Sasani commander Rustam, who foretells the Arab invasion of Iran. The apocalyptic horizon of truth is also often divined through the channel of dreams, where ideal kings like Feraydun and Kay Khusrow are recognized as recapturing Iran's divine glory. Change in the *Shāhnāme* is represented in such rhythmic modes where avatars of justice ironically are rare and where when they do appear on the stage of Iranian history they relinquish temporal rule. Alongside these cycles of change, Ferdowsi chooses to focus his narrative on the recurrence of morally inept kings, according to Davis (Kavus fills six volumes of nine). Here is where Ferdowsi is emplotting himself and his meditations on the state of Iran in an Islamic age. Davis captures the tone of Ferdowsi's reflection on the Iranian legacy of sovereignty: "The man best fitted to be King by that very fact will not want to be King."[48]

Just as Mazdean cosmology imagined an initial state of purity before evil invaded the universe, Ferdowsi reproduces a picture of an initial era of Iran's justice and wisdom. It is noteworthy that Ferdowsi's ideal king ruled before the advent of Zarathustra. Kay Khusraw at the height of his temporal power had experienced a crisis of consciousness as he withdrew from society and eventually vanished into the mountains in a snowstorm: "With a lamp of wisdom," writes Ferdowsi, "he sought the path of God." Kay Khusraw's contemplation of life and power leads him to a spiritual awakening: "Creator of Heaven, Giver of Light to Virtue, Justice and Love, for me there lies no profit in empire if Thou, O Lord, is discontented with me. . . . give me a place in Paradise," Ferdowsi has him say. Such is the content of a secret knowledge Kay Khusraw becomes conscious of, revealing Ferdowsi's conception of wisdom to which he pays homage at the introduction of his work. Ferdowsi holds Kay Khusraw in greater veneration than Feraydun, who defeats Zahhak thanks to his military prowess. Feraydun's chivalry encompasses physical strength, whereas Kay Khusraw conjoins physical potency with ethical substance. Even Anushiravan, the ideal Sasani monarch who maintains his status in Muslim historiography, is no Kay Khusraw for Ferdowsi. Here Davis provides us with a clue as to why. After Goshtasp, the first Iranian king to embrace Zarathustra, kingship is depicted as more absolute. In fact, this dynasty of kings destroys its loyal clients (house of Nariman), who have fought for Iranian kings for generations. The king Goshtasp contrives the hero Rustam's death. Although the association of the king with God's divine will further cement loyalty to the crown, this association did not necessarily nurture a sense of mutual obligation on the part of the king to treat his subjects righteously. Now that it was a religious dictate to be loyal and just, kings and fathers were even more abusive.

Perhaps Ferdowsi was attempting to distance himself in a Muslim era from any associations with Zoroastrianism. And perhaps, as Davis sees it, Ferdowsi was being critical of the way Iranian kings embraced Zoroastrianism for the pragmatic reason of consolidating their power upholding the authority of God, king, and father at the expense of man, subject, and son.[49] The rigidity of this ethic in all three spheres—cosmos, empire, and family—is what Ferdowsi seems to be critical of. He provides no simple answer for the ambiguities of power and the unjust state of the world, as these are incomprehensible from the perspective of this poet historian. But is there hope for Iran in Ferdowsi's narrative to return to its initial stage of righteousness?

Although there is a degeneration in the integrity of post-Zoroastrian kings, who invariably give in to the corrupting influence of absolute power, thus drawing a sense of linear decline, cyclical time marks the rhythm of Ferdowsi's narrative in the way Iranian society is portrayed as encountering similar ethical dilemmas in different ages. In each era, kings are confronted with analogous situations as they attempt to rule their dominion with justice and to deal with political realities and ethical choices regarding their sons, warriors, subjects, and neighbors (Turan, Hind, Rum). In the struggle between truth and untruth, Iran embodies the good, and thus Iranian kings as well as warriors had to mirror such an image whose purity was visualized in the quality of light, in the potent rays of the sun and flames of fire whose beauty was likened to a cypress tree. The values embraced in the *Shāhnāme* are Mazdean, drawn from a set of ethical codes binding the chivalric army of good together in combat against Ahriman and his forces of evil, which manifest themselves in humans in the form of envy, greed, and false pride. The expectations voiced of the king and of his champion warriors in the *Shāhnāme* involve abstaining from these vices, exercising instead generosity and compassion as well as bravery and the courage to remain faithful to the grave. These expectations are mutual and hence necessitate a social hierarchy of authority and obligation. Loyalty and respect for social superiors is the cement that binds the realms together. Once this social order is transgressed, cosmic chaos ensues. Even when Davis senses Ferdowsi's consistent sympathy toward subjects (sons, warriors, villagers) who are more moral than their kingly superiors, as in the episode of Mazdak's egalitarian revolt, Ferdowsi opts for preserving order. Although Mazdak spoke with "knowledge, wisdom, and perfection" and acted with justice, look at his fate. Living in a reality of absolutist kingship, Mazdak and his like will be killed.

Kings, princes, and warriors were expected to be archetypes in the cosmic battle that is history. These characters held positions of power where the personal, imperial, and universal crossed paths, creating in the process complex entanglements that particularized each episode of the *Shāhnāme*. What creates symmetry between them is the motif of authority, which is the most potent and ambiguous theme running through Ferdowsi's narrative. Although stories of kings and warriors are differentiated, there is a regularity in the repetition of scenarios that Davis has masterfully delineated with the intertwining motif of filicide (Rustam and Suhrab/Kavus and Siyavush), with superiors betraying their inferiors (kings and subjects). Characters resemble each other not in a linear doubling but in a recurrent sharing of traits, choices, or fates. The treatment of recurring motifs does not take the same form every time. Ferdowsi presents them each in different guises and with new subtleties. Jamshid is not Zahhak's double, but both share their rebellion against authority, the former against God and the latter against his father. For Jamshid, false pride leads him into a pact with demons; for Zahhak, greed (literally, his carnivorous habits) leads him astray.

Ferdowsi does create certain characters (Rustam and Isfandiyar/Siyavush and Kay Khusraw) and scenarios (Rustam and Suhrab/Kavus and Siyavush) that are virtually identical with each other. And with this repetition, he suggests the cyclical nature of the cosmic order. Some characters, like Rustam and Isfandiyar, are even rebirths of each other, according to Davis. Isfandiyar is a new Rustam in the age of Zoroastrianism: "The essence of Rustam's character is a kind of careless freedom of action, an instinctive rallying to the righteous cause. The essence of Isfandiyar's is a concern for legality, for the precise observance of the letter of the law. Though they are presented as two avatars of the same chivalric spirit, and though their fundamental kinship of role is emphasized (Rustam as a defender of Iran and its monarchy, Isfandiyar as a defender of the new faith of Zoroastrianism), the spirit that unites them is shaped by the eras to which they belong. Rustam is part of a heroic and freebootingly individualistic age, and Isfandiyar part of the more authoritarian, prescriptive court of Goshtasp."[50] Here, Ferdowsi is voicing his critique of Zoroastrianism, perhaps couched in a commentary on Islam as well, for his criticism sounds very much like Hafez's reproach of the rigidity of the market inspector's *(muhtasib)* superficial enforcement of Islamic law. Although the notions of righteousness and loyalty espoused by Rustam and Isfanidyar are identical, once Isfandiyar's father Goshtasp enforces Zoroastrianism as the imperial religion, such ideals lose their meaning. They become legal and mechanical.

In the cosmic battle that unites the forces of good against evil, each individual can choose to take on this challenge as one in a cast of characters who continuously return to fight this paradigmatic struggle. But every age has its particularities, and each character returns to the point where each left off. So in the continuous line of the chivalric knights in the Sasani period, Bahram-i Chubineh, regarded as a messianic figure from whom the Samanids claimed descent, revolts against his king and takes power. But Ferdowsi has Bahram's sister articulating the female voice that has preserved tradition, remind Bahram of his position of submission. Ferdowsi embraces the tradition of loyalty, which is the embodiment of the past that must be preserved despite its injustice.[51]

Ferdowsi leaves the end of his narrative open, perhaps to allow room to return to the pure age of Persian glory when Gayumars, Houshang, and Jamshid ruled at the opening of his history. The way these stories were heard over and over again orally could add to the cyclical sense of the epic's conception. And so Ferdowsi chooses to end his history with the apocalyptic advent of Islam as foretold in a dream by the Iranian soldier Rustam, who till the end, despite his doubts about the king, remains on the battlefield and becomes a martyr, while Yazdgird, the last Sasani king, flees like a coward. That Ferdowsi chooses to ignore the history and cosmology of Iranians living under Islam in the *Shāhnāme* is an important silence. If we are to understand the structure of the *Shāhnāme* as cyclical, then the Arab episode of Zahhak and Feraydun's apocalyptic rebellion and restoration of Iranian rule may be seen as a possibility open to revisitation but this time with hindsight.

The camel-herding conquerors are associated with the Arabs. Ferdowsi places the apocalyptic moment at the beginning of Iranian history so that there should be little reason to think that he might have been referring to the rise of Muhammad. The scenario of Zahhak's rule has close affinity with the advent and spread of Islam. Zahhak's father (read Muhammad) was a good man. But his children (read the Umayyads) were seduced by the devil, who is represented as a cook tempting Zahhak with delicious dishes (read "pleasure"). Zahhak ruled for a thousand years of injustice while Iran lost its youth to the appetite of a ravenous Arab. Remember what Ferdowsi has Kay Khusraw tell us that youths should remember: "A caravan dog cannot bring down a roaming lion." And remember that Ferdowsi was writing at a time when prophecies foretelling the fall of the Arabs after a millennium of rule were in circulation in both Zoroastrian and Muslim circles.

Early modern messianic revolts like that of the Qizilbash

emerged from within this medley of Mazdean (Persianate) and Abrahamic (Alid) apocalyptics. Differences as well as similarities between these worldviews allowed for a confluence of interest among the Nuqtavis and the Qizilbash at a particular junction of history (1592 C.E.) marking a thousand years of Muslim rule. Some millenarian movements even used the same text *(Zīj al-hizārāt)* of Abu Ma'shar on which the Nuqtavis had based their expectations for future change. Millenarianism was a global phenomenon. The early modern (990/1582) conjunction of Saturn and Jupiter was read as an apocalyptic symbol not only in Islamdom but in Christendom as well. A variety of religious movements used Abu Ma'shar's theory to construct their universe, their history, their present and future. And some tendencies continued to reveal the underlying affinity between time and being that such apocalyptic visions of change assumed.

Across the Asian continent in Europe, Queen Elizabeth was faced with prophetic forecasts similar to those that Shah Abbas I had encountered, for these apocalyptic symbols were part of a shared Hellenistic repertoire of Jews, Zoroastrians, Christians, and Muslims. Abu Ma'shar's (d. 886) *Zīj al-hazārāt* was introduced into Europe through Muslim Spain, a medieval arena of active cultural dialogue among the three Abrahamic belief systems (Judaism, Christianity, and Islam). John of Spain had translated Abu Ma'shar's work in the twelfth century; Roger Bacon had referred to it in his *Opus Magnum*. Based on Abu Ma'shar's theory of conjunctions and triplicities, Queen Elizabeth had been warned that in the fatal year 1588 the world would be destroyed and the Lord would appear triumphant.[52] The physiognomy of future imaginations based on the conjuncture of Saturn and Jupiter varied according to particular apocalyptic languages and historical lineages. For some Christians of Europe, who viewed Abu Ma'shar's theory of conjunctions in terms of Christian eschatology, the conjunction signaled the arrival of the antichrist. Similarly, for Sunni Muslims, it signaled the end of time, the coming of the Muslim antichrist *(dajjāl)* and the arrival of the messiah. The genealogy of this messiah was particular to Sunni Muslims, for he was not of the house of David but a descendant of Muhammad. For some Shi'i Muslims, based on their own particular cosmogony, the apocalyptic messiah was termed the hidden Imam. The Mahdi had gone into occultation *(ghayba)* and would return *(raj'a)* at the end of time, but he too was a descendant of Muhammad. Whether this hidden Imam would be the seventh (Muhammad b. Isma'il) descendant of Muhammad (beginning with Ali, his paternal cousin and son-in-law) or the twelfth (Muhammad b. Abul Hasan) depended on the specific Shi'i group—Isma'ili or Imami. However, for some early modern millenarianists like the Nuqtavis, the conjunction of Saturn and Jupiter signaled a return to Iranian traditions—to the future of an imagined Mazdean past.

Although the very same conjunctions of Saturn and Jupiter punctuate timings of cosmic emergences in Abrahamic and Mazdean history, the way in which each made room for new emergences within its own particular scenarios of history differed. How messiahs imagined the past varied in terms of creation, the length of history, the number of cycles, the nature of epochs, genealogies of holy men and symbols, as well as their sense of a future either as an end, a return to the past, or a new cycle in the continuity of eternal cycles of time. Each genealogy (Abrahamic/Persianate) accompanied different conceptions of time and being as reflected in the language of unveiled truths, preserving traces of complex processes of change and yet sharing motifs that reveal a common Hellenistic cultural past from which these symbols are drawn and with which new meanings are ascribed.

The experiences of Jews and Zoroastrians during the Hellenistic age (330 B.C.E.–150 C.E.) of Alexandrian rule had stimulated a flowering of apocalyptic literature that reflects a sense of crisis, of an imminent climax and an unveiling of truths that would fulfill the dream of a time beyond this time when absolute justice would prevail. These Jewish and Zoroastrian responses, perhaps to Hellenic dominance, were expressed apocalyptically. They have engraved an image of a catastrophic end to human history that maintains its hegemony today. A few centuries before the advent of Alexander (323 B.C.E.), Zarathustra had propounded a sense of an end to historical time, yet his eschatology was not conceived as a catastrophic symbol, for the end was comprehended as an auspicious time when the cosmic battle between good and evil would finally transpire with the ultimate victory of good and the return to an eternal kingdom of justice on earth.[53] The end was a separation of good from evil—an expiration of evil and the dawn of the supremacy of good. There would be no more darkness, only light. Some Mazdeans believed that with each age *(asvan)*, history would witness a steady weakening of evil, from the time that the force of evil Ahriman had invaded the universe, marking the dawn of human history. If in every age each individual fulfilled her or his particular role within a cast of human characters, if she or he fought for truth and conquered lies, thought good thoughts, spoke good words, and performed good deeds, the world would gradually regain its original purity. The notion of an end time that Zarathustra had posited before the rise of the Achaemenids (559–331 B.C.E.) came to be more intimately linked by Jews and Zoroastrians in their Hellenistic context to a holocaust.[54] And here lie the seeds of a conception of a disastrous end to the world that continues to color the apocalyptic imagination of modern man, even the most postmodern of philosophers like Maurice Blanchot *(L'ecriture du desastre)*. Blanchot imagines the end, however, as a void—a gradual fading out through indifference rather than an apocalyptic moment:

> All the way, that is, to the end of history: the world completely known and totally transformed, in the unity of the knowledge which knows itself (and this is to say that the world has forever become, or that it is dead, like man, who was its temporary representation, like the subject whose sage identity is no longer anything but indifference to life's immobile vacancy).[55]

The shared cultural forms and complex processes through which such ideas have been engraved in human (Mazdean and Abrahamic) consciousness remain elusive, given that modern scholarship has paid much attention to the syncretic interplay between Hellenism and Judaism, but little to the intermingling of Judaisms, Zoroastrianisms, and Indic thought, or, for that matter, Mazdean influences on Judaism, Christianity, and Islam.[56] Some parallels have been delineated, but their historical connections and dynamic interactions have been neglected.[57] Nevertheless, I am tentatively assuming, in accordance with Boyce's analysis, that dominance and a sense of injustice and lost glory may have inspired both Zoroastrians and Jews living together in Mesopotamia and Iran to rethink and explain their contexts, questioning their own practices and ideas. And through this process, the sense of an end imbued in Zoroastrian cosmology began to merge with the memory of a cataclysmic deluge preserved in ancient Mesopotamian myths—hope for change was expressed in the language of apocalyptic messianism.

Zoroastrian apocalyptic writings unveil a conception of a world-year of twelve months, a thousand years each. Zarathustra was thought to have lived in the beginning of the tenth month. The end of his millennium would give rise to the coming of the Saoshyant or world savior (Middle Persian Usedar), who was to make righteousness flourish. Zarathustra had prophesied the coming of a messiah born of his seed at the end of the millennium after Zarathustra's death. But in time, to make room for history and the continued expectation of this worldly savior, two sons of Zarathustra came to be expected at the end of each millennium. Boyce argues that once the tenth millennium had come to be perceived as an age of evil (the millennium of Ahriman), subjugated Zoroastrians came to associate it with the age of the Greeks, the Romans, the Turks, and, later, the Arab conquerors, all of whom were cast as agents of the evil ones *(dev)*. The *Zand* texts of Vahman Yasht, commentaries on the *Avesta* compiled during the early Islamic era, indicate that the Zoroastrians continued to anticipate the emergence of the Saoshyant and that they continued to interpret contemporaneous events as signs that would lead to his coming. And so in late antiquity, Zoroastrian expectations came to date the beginning of the apocalyptic age to their current era, designating the year 631 (the enthronement of the last Sasani king) as the year of the advent of their world savior.[58] Muhammad rose as a prophet in this period, and perhaps some Mazdeans may have embraced Muhammad, initially thinking that he was their expected messiah. This apocalyptic mood in late antiquity was shared by Jews, Mazdeans, Christians, and some pagan Arabs alike, who articulated it in different languages.

Jews expected an apocalyptic messiah king to appear at an imminent end of time, ushering in God's rule and the restoration of Israel to the Jews.[59] Jews with messianic expectations awaited the return of Elijah as a precursor of the Messiah (Mal. 4:5), "to lead aright the coming ages," restore the purity of families, bring peace, settle disputes and questions of ritual, and explain difficult passages of the scripture."[60] Rabbi Beroka of Khuzistan claimed Elijah appeared to him frequently in the marketplace of Jundishapur. A Jew who had served in the Sasani army a century before the Muslim conquests is said to have found a scroll in the Persian archives that forecast that the end of the world would begin in 531 C.E.[61] Both Jews and Zoroastrians had heightened their apocalyptic expectations with Hellenistic rule and throughout the rise of Islam; they continued to share in this apocalyptic mood even up to the sixteenth century in the Ottoman empire and in the lands of eastern Islamdom, until the coming millennium was once again expected by Jew, Muslim, Zoroastrian, and Christian. Zoroastrians expected their Saoashyant in 1632, and some Jews embraced Sabatai Zvi in Iran as well. This is why the rhetoric of justice takes on such a central role in the messages of messiahs like Jesus, Muhammad, and the *ghulāt.* Justice becomes central to the language of prophecy as well as kingship, and so kings like the Sasani Anushirvan (r. 531–579 C.E.), who defeated the Mazdakis and appropriated their egalitarian language, was idolized as the just king (Anushirvan-i 'ādil) in the Muslim era. In this eclectic language of inspiration, prophets unraveled new ways of making sense of existence and of historical circumstances in universal terms. Jesus, Mani, Zaradusht (founder of Mazdakism), Muhammad, Isma'il, Mahmud Pasikhani, and many others who have not made it into the annals of history were products of this syncretic discourse, questioning, and breaking old paradigms, synthesizing and revealing new ones.

Shi'i Muslims construed history as a road to salvation in which the mysteries of creation had been unveiled by a succession of Abrahamic prophets, Muhammad being the seal, and his descendants, the Imams, the divine interpreters of secret knowledge. It is this special role allotted to the descendants of the prophet as Imams that distinguishes the Shi'a from the Sunni. In accordance with an Abrahamic sense of rectilinear time, the Shi'a posited an end to history, which was to culminate in the emergence of the eschatological messiah. The Shi'is designate their messiah as the hidden Imam, who will reveal the essence of the future by establishing the last just kingdom on earth. What is particularly Shi'i about their beliefs is that resurrection is intimately tied to the return of the hidden Imam at the end of time and to his final mission of conquering the forces of ignorance, avenging the oppressed as an act of revenge against the betrayal of Ali and the murder of Imam Husayn (d. 680 C.E.), Ali's son and Muhammad's grandson.[62] At such a time beyond the present, when time itself would expire, resurrection would ensue, and each individual would be judged according to his or her loyalty and love for the Imams. A future eternal paradise was promised for the loyal, God's sovereignty would be restored, and, finally, justice and knowledge would prevail. Fear of the day of judgment and hope for a better existence were integral to the construction of such a cosmos. This fear permeates the Qur'an.[63] Some early sufis are known to have focused on the fear of judgment in their piety. But love of God, later associated with the early female mystic Rabi'a, came to be the dominant devotional emphasis for mystics. The sufi's will to break eschatology and commune with God came to be articulated in a language of love rather than fear. Mystics and *ghulât* share the urge to break eschatology, to experience the holy. The desire to experience the divine directly is expressed in a variety of ontologies, all of which center on the encounter between the believer and the divine being.[64] The locus of divinity, the holy site of devotion on earth, varies for a sufi or a Shi'i, from a romantic lover to Ali, respectively, although at times both symbolized the same thing. What clearly differentiated the sufi or the Shi'i from the *ghulât* was the belief in an end to history, for the *ghulât* hold that human life on earth is to be forever cyclical.

The cosmic imagination of denizens of the Safavi domains, sufis, and dervishes with an Alid or Persianate *ghuluww* temperament blurred the boundaries between heaven and earth, the temporal and the spiritual, the holy and the human. Safavi devotees expected encounters with the divine during their lifetime on earth. Justice and knowledge were claimed in the here and now. The Nuqtavis present us with one expression, one language laden with meanings and significations from amid such a late antique gnostic worldview. They speak of the hope that believers should maintain in the coming of the millennial messiah during their lifetimes.[65] Although they use the designation *mahdi* to refer to their messiah, it is but one of his titles, the most singular of which is the "Western Sun." Nuqtavi cosmology pivots around the sun, and from their earthly vistas Nuqtavi devotees see neither beginning nor end to the eternal sunrise.[66] What is cast as the last is in reality the first and is understood as a return to an original purity and truth.

NOTES

1. Muhammad b. Ahmad al-Bīrūnī, *The Chronology of Ancient Nations (al-Āthār al-bāqiyah)* (1879), trans. and ed. Edward Sachau (London: Allen, 1993), 16.

2. Ibid., 3.

3. Ibid., 34.
4. Aron Gurevich, *Time as a Problem of Cultural History: Cultures and Time* (Paris: n.p., 1976), 229.
5. Ibid., 229.
6. Ibn al-Nadīm, *Fihrist* (Cairo, N.D.), 348–350, as cited in David Edwin Pingree, *The Thousands of Abū Ma'shar* (London: Warburg Institute, 1968), 3–4. Ibn al-Nadīm is citing from Abū Ma'shar's *Kitāb ikhtilāf al-zījāt*.
7. Ibid.
8. Abū Ma'shar (d. 272/886 in his *Zīj al-hazārāt* discusses the conjunction of two superior planets, Saturn and Jupiter, which occurs every twenty years in a cycle of trigons (a set of three signs of the zodiac, each 120 degrees from one another) or triplicities into which the zodiac is divided (referred to as "the great conjunction"). Every 240 years, the (greater) conjuncion moves into a new triplicity and every 960 years (greatest conjunction) it makes a full cycle of all four trigons. This theory of great conjunctions was elaborated by a (Balkhi) scholar by the name of Abū Ma'shar, who in his *Zīj al-hazārāt* interpreted these conjunctions as symbolizing the advent of a prophet and a change in religion. Abū Ma'shar combines Indian, Sasani, and Greek astronomical traditions, claiming to have used an ancient Persian text from antediluvian times written in the reign of Tahmurath. I would like to thank Gernot Windfuhr for his insights into the Zoroastrian logic of astronomy, astrology and cosmology. Abū Ma'shar's work was translated by John of Spain (twelfth century) and is referred to by Roger Bacon in his *Opus Magus*. See Margaret Aston, "The Fiery Trigon Conjunction: An Elizabethan Astrological Prediction," *ISIS* (1970): 177.
9. Pingree, *The Thousands*, 14–15 (from Ibn Juljul, *Kitāb al-ulūf*). This legend of Gayumarth (the Persian Adam) narrated in verse *(qasīda)* included a warning about the flood. Pingree understood this as connected to Abū Ma'shar's observation of the conjunction of Saturn and Jupiter, which marked the shift of the conjunctions from the airy to the watery triplicity (indicating the flood).
10. John David North and Roy Porter, *The Norton History of Astronomy and Cosmology* (New York: Norton, 1994), 184.
11. Pingree, *The Thousands*, 9 (citing Ibn al-Nadīm in his *Fihrist*, 345–348).

12. Pingree, *The Thousands*, 10. Pingree includes other versions of this myth from the Zoroastrian *Dinkard*, which claims that with the conquests of Alexander, Zoroastrian texts were hidden in China and India and rediscovered at a later age (*Dinkard*, V. IV). Shahpur b. Ardashir is said to have collected writings from India and Byzantium on medicine, astronomy, movement, time, space, substance, creation, becoming, passing away, and change in qualities. Pingree is citing R. C. Zaehner's translation from his *Zurvan: A Zoroastrian Dilemma* (Oxford: Clarendon Press, 1955), 7–9.

13. Abbas Iqbal, *Khāndān-i Nawbakhtī*, 1–4, 11–14.

14. Louise Marlow, *Hierarchy and Egalitarianism in Islamic Thought* (Cambridge: Cambridge University Press, 1997), 76–90.

15. Jamasp Namak or "The Book of Jamaspi," translated by Jivanji Jamshedji Modi (1903), 1, available on the Web at http://www.avesta.org/pahlavi/jamaspi.htm. I would like to thank Parvaneh Pourshariati for providing me with a copy of this text.

16. Ibid.

17. Gernot Windfuhr, "The Gates of Mithra, the Nocturnal Sun, and the Dates of Zarathushtra," Paper presented at the First North American International Avesta Conference, Framingham, MA, November 1997.

18. Pingree, *The Thousands*, 18, 58.

19. The Fatimid caliph 'Ubaydullah al-Mahdi (d. 322/934) had claimed the Imamate of the anticipated Isma'ili Mahdi (Muhammad b. Ismā'īl) for himself. The Qarmatis broke away from the Fatimid Isma'ili's (297–567/909–1171), reaffirming their belief in the imminent return of their anticipated messiah from the family of the Prophet (Muhammad b. Isma'il). For a detailed history of the Isma'ilis, is Farhad Daftary, *The Isma'ilis: Their History and Doctrines* (Cambridge: Cambridge University Press, 1990); Heinz Halm, *The Empire of the Mahdi: The Rise of the Fatimids*, trans. M. Bonner (Leiden: Brill, 1996).

20. Wilferd Madelung, *Religious Trends in Early Islamic Iran* (Albany, NY: Persian Heritage Foundation, 1988), 96–97.

21. Ibid., 97. See part 2 for more on the Kaysānī-Tayyārī messiah, Abdullah b. Mu'awiyah, whose followers expected his return in Isfahan.

22. Madelung, *Religious Trends*, 104–105, citing Ali b. al-Husayn Mas'ūdī, *Kitāb al-tanbīh wa al-ishrāf*.

23. Madelung, *Religious Trends,* 97 (citing Muhammad b. Ahmad al-Bīrunī, *The Chronology of Ancient Nations,* 196).

24. al-Bīrunī, *The Chronology of Ancient Nations,* 196–197.

25. Ibid., 197.

26. Mobed Shah, *Dabistān al-mazāhib,* ed. Rahim Rezāzādah-yi Malik (Tehran: Kitābkhānah-ī Tahūrī 1983–1984), vol. 1, 275.

27. See Muhammad Tavakoli-Targhi on the Azar Kayvanis, an early modern esoteric Zoroastrian school of thought that cast the Arabs as ruthless conquerors and did not include Muhammad or Ali in their spiritual genealogies as did the Nuqtavis. "Contested Memories: Narrative Structures and Allegorical Meanings of Iran's Pre-Islamic History," *Iranian Studies* 29, no. 1–2 (1996): 149–175.

28. Shah, *Dabistān al-mazāhib,* vol. 1, 275, quoting from sayings of Mahmud recorded in his *Mīzān.*

29. Sādiq Kiyā, "Nuqtaviyān yā Pasikhāniyān," *Iran Kudeh* 13 (1941): 90.

30. Windfuhr, "The Gates of Mithra."

31. Ibid.

32. Three millennia were imagined with one son of Zoroaster emerging at the end of each millennium.

33. Alid eulogists like Kāshī complain about the popularity of stories of kings and heroes, wishing that stories about Muhammad and Ali would be recounted instead. I will return to the point of Ferdowsi's critique of Zoroastrian orthodoxy. Let me just note here that this may be the poet Daqiqi's influence, given that the segment on Zoroaster and the king Gushtāsp was written by Daqiqi and incorporated by Ferdowsi into his narrative.

34. Dick Davis, "Introduction," in Reuben Levy, trans., *The Epic of the Kings: Shāhnāme, the National Epic of Persia* (New York: (Mazda, 1980), xxvi.

35. See the general introduction to Pierre Nora, *Realms of Memory: Rethinking the French Past,* trans. Arthur Goldhammer (New York: Columbia University Press, 1996), 1.

36. The reading *kārivānī* (caravan dog) dates probably to the Safavi period. All significant manuscripts of the *Shāhnāme* consulted in the Khaleghi Motlagh edition that date up to the 1498 manuscript give the reading *kārizārī* (wild/fierce). This indicates that post-Safavi recensions discreetly alter the text to create a commentary

on Persian-Arab rivalries. I would like to thank Dick Davis for this comment.

37. Dick Davis, *Epic and Sedition: The Case of Ferdowski's Shāhnāme* (Fayetteville: University of Arkansas Press, 1992), 83. Davis speaks of Ferdowsi using Gordiyeh as his mouthpiece to represent tradition, for she is the one who preserves memory "from the old sayings." Ferdowsi, *Shāhnāme*, vol. 8, ed. A.Y. Bertel et al. (Moscow, 1966–1971), 409, 1552.

38. Davis, "Introduction," in Levy, *The Epic of the Kings*, xxvi.

39. Tarif Khalidi, *Arabic Historical Thought in the Classical Period* (Cambridge: Cambridge University Press, 1994), 8.

40. Tavakoli-Targhi, "Contested Memories," 155. The author is citing the "Bundahish or the Original Creation," in *Pahlavi Texts* (Oxford: Clarendon Press, 1880) 53; *Bundahish*, 155.

41. Julie Scott-Meisami, *Persian Historiography to the End of the Twelfth Century* (Edinburgh: Edinburgh University Press, 1999), 29.

42. Ibid., 25.

43. Scott-Meisami makes a similar point in her recent book, *Persian Historiography*, viewing the *Shāhnāme* and Balami's translation of Tabari as different versions of history targeted to a Samanid audience, whether the landed aristocracy of *dihqān* from Khurasan and Transoxiana, Arab conquerors and emigrants, Iranian converts to Islam, or Turkish slaves. I tend to see these productions of history not so much as a courtly enterprise targeted at a clientele but as one expressing a particular group identity and hence a particular construction of memory.

44. Scott-Meisami, *Persian Historiography*, 41.

45. Davis, *Epic and Sedition*, 18.

46. I am referring to Houshang, who separates rock from iron and invents fire and irrigation, and Jamshid, who makes weapons, spins and weaves and creates a threefold division of society into priest kings, warriors, and farmer craftsmen. As far as cultural identity being forged through ritual, Houshang's fire (Sade) festival and Jamshid's New Year celebration come to mark Persian identity.

47. Davis, *Epic and Sedition*, 32.

48. Ibid., 51.

49. Davis, *Epic and Sedition*, 134.

50. Ibid., 154–155.

51. I refer the reader to Dick Davis's book *Epic and Sedition* for the nuances of such cyclical dilemmas of authority and loyalty faced by kings, sons, and heroes in the *Shāhnāme*. Here I have greatly benefited from the clarity with which Davis presents Ferdowsi's complexities of values and ethics invoked by the dynamics of Iranian history.

52. See Aston, "The Fiery Trigon Conjunction," 177. For the Islamic context, see Jalāl al-din al-Suyūtī (d. 911/1505) in his *Kashf'an mudjāwaza hadhihi 'l-umma*, where he refers to and criticizes a belief held in some circles that Islam would not outlive a thousand years. Conceptions that the tenth century of Islam was the last days were alive in Yemen too in this era. Shihab al-dīn Ahmad b. 'Abd al-Qādir, *Futūh al-habasha* (written shortly after 967/1559–1560).

53. Mary Boyce, *Zoroastrianism: Its Antiquity and Constant Vigor* (Costa Mesa: Mazda, 1992), ch. 4; Boyce, *Textual Sources for the Study of Zoroastrianism* (Chicago: University of Chicago, 1984).

54. Mary Boyce, *A History of Zoroastrianism*, Vol. 3, *Under Macedonian and Roman Rule* (Leiden: Brill, 1991); Norman Rufus Colin Cohn, *Cosmos, Chaos, and the World to Come: The Ancient Roots of Apocalyptic Faith* (New Haven: Yale University Press, 1993).

55. Maurice Blanchot, *The Writing of the Disaster*, trans. Ann Smock (Nebraska, 1995), 73.

56. Cohn, *Cosmos, Chaos and the World to Come*, is an exception.

57. Boyce, *A History of Zoroastrianism*, vol. 3, "Under Macedonian and Roman Rule."

58. Ibid.

59. For the diversity of ideas on messiahs in Judaisms, see Jacob Neusner, "Passing the Rabbinic Canon with the History of an Idea: The Messiah," *Formative Judaism: Religious, Historical, and Literary Studies* (Chico, CA: Scholars Press, 1983), 173–193.

60. Michael G. Morony, *Iraq after the Muslim Conquest* (Princeton: Princeton University Press, 1984), 326.

61. Ibid., 326.

62. Muhammad Ali Amir-Moezzi, *The Divine Guide in Early Shi'ism: The Sources of Esotericism in Islam* (Albany: State University of New York Press, 1994), 10–12. In Amir-Moezzi's innovative inquiry into the predominant structures of early Imamism, he dem-

onstrates an esoteric substratum rooted in Imami thought, shared with the Isma'ili Shi'is, *ghulât,* and sufis, that later on by the ninth century becomes overshadowed by a rationalist tendency that is more attuned to the dialectical and logical modes of theological and juridical discourse in Sunni *kalâm* (Muta'zilite and Ashari). Early conceptions of *'aql* involved cosmogonic, mystic, esoteric, even magical and occult elements—namely, nonrational elements. But by the ninth century, Amir-Moezzi demonstrates how *'aql* is rationalized and humanized "in a culture where reason and man cannot be conceived of except through their relation with God."

63. See, for example, Qur'an 82, 56:1–95, 69:13–37, 78:17–31, 83:10–26, and 88:1–16.

64. For such shared spirituality in early Imamism and sufism, see Amir-Moezzi, *The Divine Guide,* 54–55. For Iranian gnostic influences in sufism and *ghulāt,* see Bernd Radtke, "Iranian and Gnostic Elements in Early Tasawwuf Observations Concerning the Umm al-kitāb," *Proceedings of the First European Conference of Iranian Studies,* ed. G. Gnoli and A. Panaino (Rome: Instituto Italiano Per il Media Ed Estremo Oriente, 1990).

65. Untitled Nuqtavi text cited in Kiyā, "Nuqtaviyān yā Pasikhāniyān," 90: "keh sāhib-i qarn-i miyah dar hāl-i hayāt-i khwīsh āmadah ast umīd bāyad dāsht."

66. Ibid., 85. Kiyā is quoting from an untitled Nuqtavi text.

THREE

Mani's Image:
Genealogies of Heretics in
Persianate Historiography

When introducing Dervish Khusraw's Nuqtavi movement, Afushtah-yi Natanzi, a contemporaneous chronicler of the reign of Shah Abbas I *(Naqāvat al-āsār fī zikr al-akhyār)*, provides a mythohistorical genealogy of Nuqtavi beliefs. He casts the Nuqtavis as representatives of "satanic" forces, devils in disguise, that have from the beginning of creation deceived Adam and his descendants, leading them astray from the path of religion *(tarīq-i dīn)*. Masked through jugglery *(shu'badah)* and tricks *(farīb)*, they open the doors of rebellion and corruption *(fitna va fisād)* with their myths *(afsānah)*, spells *(afsūn)*, magic *(nayrang)*, and arts *(funūn)*.[1] As a Muslim, Natanzi uses Qur'anic descriptions of Satan to illustrate the role of evil in this world and so engages in the debate over the holy by defining what is licit and illicit, distinguishing between acting through the agency of God versus acting through the agency of Satan. He casts Nuqtavi leaders as demons masquerading in ascetic clothes who attract superstitious "common" folk through magic. Natanzi locates the Nuqtavis within the binary opposition between good and evil, fashioning their ways as ignorant and irrational.

47

Natanzi elaborates on Nuqtavi demonic lineage by naming two pre-Islamic parallels to historicize his analysis—Mani (d. 277 C.E.) and Mazdak (sixth century C.E.).[2] The way in which Natanzi remembers these two gnostic reformers of Zoroastrianism is revealing, for it provides us not only with a particular mythology that links the Nuqtavis to an Iranian past but with a sense of the author's Irano-Islamic identity, as well. Whether real or imaginary, these linkages were alive and embedded within the consciousness of literate denizens like Natanzi in Safavi Iran. Natanzi's characterization of Mani and Mazdak leads him to epitomize them as satanic and provides us with a dichotomy, revealing the two extreme poles that were in tension in Safavi Iran a thousand years after the Muslim conquests. For Natanzi, Mani represents a magician acting through the auspices of the devil. Natanzi situates Mani within the monotheistic tradition that separates the dual forces of good and evil and attributes to God the supreme position of good, while allocating evil to God's rebellious angel, Satan, in accordance with Islamic tradition. The atheism *(ilhād)* of the Nuqtavis is associated with Zoroastrianism: "In every day and age these people are known by a certain name and title, and in the Islamic era they are known as atheists [*malāhidah*]."[3] For Natanzi, people like Ustad Yusufi, "that antiquated Zoroastrian atheist master [*pīr-i gabr-i kuhnah-yi mulhid*]," are old believers who continue to cling to dualism. *Mazdean (zindīq)* and *atheist (mulhid)* are used as synonyms to designate the abject Nuqtavis.[4]

Natanzi's narrative linking Mani and Mazdak with Dervish Khusraw and Yusufi Tarkishduz will also allow us to focus on the extent to which these memories were derived from popular literary sources, like the *Shāhnāme*. An analysis of Nuqtavi writings and aspirations will illuminate those aspects that could have been understood as vestiges of Manichee or Mazdaki beliefs. As a forerunner of Nuqtavi-like movements from the Islamic era, the chronicler cites the example of the Ismai'lis (Nizari), Hasan-i Sabbah, renowned in the West as the leader of the Assassins in Alamut. A historical sense of recurring

Persianate gnosticism into the Islamic era is represented, each cycle bringing forth its Mani-like heretic. These continuities permeate medieval Muslim heresiographical condemnations of the *ghulāt*, and a strand among Safavi intellectuals does the same. But modern historians have continued to view these statements as mere slander bearing no historical reality, even as constructs coloring the imaginations of some denizens of the early modern Persianate world. I do not take the derogatory remarks of heresiarchs or polemicists at face value, but neither do I ignore them. Rather, I explore this discourse as a source that reveals aspects of cultural (re)production and the dynamics of conversion to Islam.

Natanzi characterizes Mani as a painter *(naqqāsh)* and shaper of images *(taswīr)*, making use of terminology that dates back to Hellenistic depictions of Mani as calligrapher and painter. Historically, Mani developed a calligraphic script of his own through which his doctrines were recorded and personally illuminated his writings.[5] He composed a pictorial illustration of his cosmological teachings called the Ardahang that is thought to have survived into the eleventh century in Ghazna.[6] Mani is reported to have incorporated painting, calligraphy, and music into his religious rituals. Gnostic tendencies seem to have drawn on all sensual and sensory mediums in the process of illumination, requiring a more interactive and intuitive role on behalf of their devotees. In the Islamic era, however, Mani's association with the arts in general survives only as painter, the designation used by Ferdowsi, who in his *Shāhnāme* speaks of Mani the painter *(musawwir)*. As we shall see, Natanzi's narrative on Mani closely follows Ferdowsi's.[7]

There is little doubt that Natanzi and other literate members of Safavi society would have been aware of Ferdowsi's famous epic history, which by the early modern period was patronized by Persianate kings to mark their reigns with ornately illuminated manuscripts that have been passed down to us. Stories from the *Shāhnāme* were not only depicted in miniatures but recited by professional *Shāhnāme* tellers in coffeehouses, bazaars, and court assemblies. The lore around Mani's art of painting would continue to be embellished in famous medieval Persian poetry like that of Nizami's *Iskandarnāme* (Alexander Romance) and his *Khusraw and Shirin*. Both these poems would be the subject of many illuminated miniatures in the medieval and early modern Persianate realms.[8] But the meaning of a painter, as miniaturist or illustrator, was but one dimension of this art: we are told by Ferdowsi as well as by Natanzi that it was through his painting that Mani claimed prophethood. His dexterity in creating highly realistic images is what led him to claim proof of his miracles and prophecy. Mani's story as framed in the *Shāhnāme* depicts a peerless *musawwir* of his age coming to the court of the Sasanian king Shahpur I (r. 240–272 C.E.) from China, considered by medieval Muslim aesthetic tastes as the abode where the art of portraiture had attained perfection.[9] Claiming to be a prophet due to his ability to create images, Mani went so far as to assert that he was the best of all the prophets the world had yet encountered *(bi-surat garī guft payghambaram ze dīn āvarān-i jihān bartaram)*. The notion of a succession of prophets each revealing a portion or layer of truth existed in Manichee thought, and Mani was believed to be the seal of such a chain of prophets. It is Muhammad, however, who would be named "the seal of the prophets" by the Muslims. And as for the high esteem in which calligraphy was held by the Manichees as a secret gnostic script to be used in conjunction with visual and aural aids, that too would later be disassociated from a Manichee taint to become the highest form of sacred art in Islam. In modern terminology, the gnostic multimedia approach to revelation was being limited in the Islamic era to the word.

In the Sasani parallel to the Nuqtavi story recounted by Ferdowsi, the king invites Mani to court and is enchanted by his eloquence and dexterity. An inquiry is ordered by the Sasani king, and as a result the Zoroastrian *mobed* divulges the "suspicious" *(sukhan-i badgumān)* beliefs of Mani. His wisdom discloses the idol-worshiping *(suratparast)* nature of Mani's beliefs, and he emphasizes that there is but one God *(keh gūyandah gūyad keh yazdān yekīst juzz as bandagī kardanat chārah nīst)*. The Zoroastrian priest is said to have criticized Mani for claiming proof of prophecy through created images: "If you can make this image move, then it is worthy to consider the mover as proof *[burhān surat chera nigaravī sizad gar ze-junbandah burhān kunī]*."[10] Once the Zoroastrian priest's words of wisdom unveil the "crazy" views of Mani, he is removed from court, skinned to death, stuffed with hay, and displayed in full public view on the Shah's command. In the Muslim era, Ferdowsi, like many other Zoroastrians, was attempting to emphasize the monotheistic nature of Zoroastrian dualism and separate it from Mazdean heresies like that of the Manichees.

Natanzi's narrative on the Nuqtavi master quiver maker Yusufi echoes Ferdowsi's story of Mani preserved in the *Shāhnāme*. Natanzi used the *Shāhnāme* as a source on Mani and as a narrative model for his own composition, or perhaps Shah Abbas I had been inspired by Mani's story in the *Shāhnāme*. Natanzi provides some background information preserved in the *Shāhnāme* on Mani, but what he emphasizes is Mani's art of image making and the various ways in which Mani used that craft *(hunar)* to fool the "simple folk" through tricks, illusions, and false perceptions. The deft hand that could create images so real was feared due to its potential for generating life in matter. Natanzi, like Ferdowsi, condemns Mani and Ustad Yusufi for taking on the role of creator and fashioner of forms; in their universe, there was but one fashioner, and he was Allah. There are prophetic sayings that have Muhammad denounce the makers of images as wrongdoers for they try to imitate the creation of God.[11] These men are associated with magic, witchcraft, and idol worship. But there was a strand within vernacular Islam that expressed itself in alchemical texts and in some sufi/Shi'i writings that asserted that *insān-i kāmil*, perfect individuals, did possess the power to create life—by the grace of God, of course. These writings also offered the Qur'anic examples of Solomon commanding the spirits *(jinn)* to make representations *(tamthīl)*

and help him build the temple in Jerusalem, as well as Jesus raising the dead and giving life to birds, to legitimate their beliefs. In
the Qur'an, *musawwir* refers to God as the ultimate image
maker. The "creator, the former, and fashioner" is one of God's
name.[12] Although the root of this term *s.w.r* in its second form is
used in the Qur'an to denote divine creation, it is later used for
human creation as well, and that is where the meaning of
painter is derived. *Musawwir* is also a self-designation used by
alchemists in their medieval treatises to denote the aspect of
their craft that has to do with bringing material substance to life
through physical, verbal, and mental action, hence imitating the
role of divine fashioner *(al-musawwir)*.[13] An association between the alchemical process of the artificial generation of life
(takwīn) and the making of images permeates alchemical treatises, in general, and Nuqtavi writings, in particular. The theme
is also played on in the topos of painter as creator in mystical
poetry.

In Nizami's *Khusraw and Shirin,* an epic love story between
the Sasanian emperor Khusraw Parviz (r. 591–628) and the Armenian princess Shirin, images constructed through words and
paint initially create the aura of love between the two souls who
have not yet met. Shapur, a painter and friend of the Sasani king,
boasts of his ability to draw, and, of course, it is Mani, the
model messiah painter, and his illuminated cosmological works
that he compares himself with:

> When I make a pen-drawing and put colors on it,
> Mani strikes out his pictures in the gallery of Arzhang.
> The person whose head I paint moves.
> The bird whose wings I paint flies.[14]

Here, we recall the criticism of Mani that Ferdowsi utters
through his foil, the Zoroastrian priest, concerning Mani's inability to give life to his inanimate images. Now Nizami has
Shahpur claim that, indeed, not only can he draw objects to perfection, but he can also animate them by making them move and
fly, just like Jesus who fashioned a bird out of clay and made it

fly, according to the Qur'an. There are many levels to this poetry, but one underlying dimension pertinent to our discussion is
the visual power of the art of painting and image making, its se-
ductiveness, its imaginative ability to create something concrete
and tangible, and hence, its association with the act of divine
creation. The transformative power of words and images as in-
cantations and spells is an aspect of gnostic thought embedded
in alchemy that permeates mystical poetic discourse. Rumi, for
example, describes God's actions in his *Masnavi* in terms of the
arts and crafts of a tailor, weaver, calligrapher, and painter.[15]
Rumi draws from a language of magic and alchemy when describing the act of creation and the experience of love that unites
the human with the divine:

When I write my friend's [Shams-i Tabrizi] name upon earth,
Each piece of clay is turned into a *hurī* (angel) in paradise.
When I recite a spell of his upon fire,
The burning fire turns into limpid water.
In short, even non-existence, when I come to it with his name,
    turns into thriving existence.[16]

The late antique debate over the holy is central to the Nuqtavi
episode of Safavi history. Differences between what is understood to be Mani's "satanic" vision by Muslims like Ferdowsi
and Natanzi (six centuries apart) and how mystically inclined
Muslims like Nizami and Rumi who were immersed in alchemy
are blurred.[17] These debates have an entire history prior to the
Safavi period. They largely concern the prerogatives of the
creator and hence attempt to define the distinction between
the creation of animate and inanimate objects, human and divine creation, miracles and charlatanry, reason and intuition, as
well as licit and illicit magic. It is this clash between two polar
understandings of the divine and the human that we are entering
with the Nuqtavi episode. Ferdowsi's and Natanzi's stance on
Mani is clear: he abused his talent to create illusions, which
fooled ignorant and led the mindless astray. Mani as painter is
recast as Mani the fake miracle worker *(mu'jiza)*, idol wor-

shiper, and Satan in disguise. For Rumi, in contrast God's creation is framed in the language of magic and conjuration. Through his words and music, the perfect individual can engage in rituals that mimic creation.

NOTES

1. Afushtah-yi Natanzī, *Naqāvat al-āsār fī zikr al-akhyār* (Tehran: Intishārāt-i Ilmī va Farhangī, 1971) 509.
2. The founder of the Mazdaki movement was the third-century Zarādusht of Fasā. On their doctrines, see Ihsan Yarshater, "Mazdakism," *Cambridge History of Iran,* ed. Ihsan Yarshater, vol. 3 (Cambridge: Cambridge University Press, 1983); Mansour Shaki, "The Social Doctrine of Mazdak in the Light of Middle Persian Evidence," *Archive Orientálni* 46 (1978): 289–306; and the more recent revisionist interpretation of Mazdak, Patricia Crone, "Kavad's Heresy and Mazdak's Revolt," *Iran: Journal of the British Institute of Persian Studies* 29 (1991): 21–42.
3. Afushtah-yi Natanzī, *Naqāvat al-āsār,* 514.
4. Ibid., 517.
5. Hans-Joachim Klimkeit, *Manichaean Art and Calligraphy* (Leiden: Brill, 1982), 15. I would like to thank Gernot Windfuhr for kindly providing me with this reference.
6. Ibid., 15. For example, the Parthian Turfan Fragment M35 depicts the fire at the end of time. Al-'Alavī, Abū Ma'āli, the author of the *Bayan al-adyān* (Tehran: Sipihr, 1997), writing in the eleventh century in Ghazna, speaks of the Arzhang (Ardahang) housed among the treasures of Ghazna (42).
7. Most information on Mani in Natanzi corroborates Ferdowsi. He adds, however, three miracle stories (from Nizami) around Mani and his art of painting that Ferdowsi does not include. Natanzi quotes as well another tradition that has Mani entering Iran under the reign of the Ashkānī (Seleucid) king Firuz ibn Bahram. He says that there are two traditions (Shahpur I, as in the *Shāhnāme*), but he seems to embrace the former. Finally Natanzi deemphasizes the fact that in the *Shāhnāme,* the king is enchanted by Mani's ideas. Instead, Natanzi says Mani's fame grew to such a degree in Iran that finally the king called him to court and had him questioned by Zoroastrian priests *(mobed)* and philosophers *(hakīm).*

8. Priscilla Soucek, "Nizami on Painters and Painting," *Islamic Art in the Metropolitan Museum of Art*, ed. Richard Ettinghausen (New York: Metropolitan Museum of Art, 1972). I would like to thank Sussan Babaie for this reference.

9. Ibn Batuta (1304–1377), as cited in Johann Christoph Bürgel, *The Feather of Simurgh: The "Licit Magic" of the Arts in Medieval Islam* (New York: New York University Press, 1988), 120.

10. Ferdowsi, *Shāhnāme*, ed. Jules Mohl (Tehran: Intishārāt-i Ilmī va Farhangī, 1995), Book 5, vol. 3, 1558.

11. Ahmad b. Muhammad al Barqī, *al-mahāsin*, ed. Jalāl al-Dīn Husaynī Muhaddis Urmavī, (Tehran: Dār al-Kutūb al-Islāmīyah, 1950–1951), vol. 1, 244. In the most inflexible Shi'i tradition, Ali claims that whoever makes images will not be considered Muslim. al Barqī, *al-mahāsin*, vol. 2, 612; Muhammad b. al-Hazan al-Hurr al-'Amilī, *Wasā'il al-shī'āh ilā Tahsīl Masā'il al-sharī'a*, ed. Abd al-Rahīm Rabbānī, Muhammad b. Alī Sharīf al-Rāzī, and Abū al-Hasan Sha'rānī (Tehran: Maktabat al-Islāmīyah, 1961), vol. 3, 562. For Sunni traditions on *timthal rajūl*, see Ibn Hanbal, vol. 2, 305.

12. Qur'an 59:24

13. See Kathleen O'Connor's excellent dissertation on alchemy in medieval Muslim tradition, "The Alchemical Creation of Life (Takwīn) and Other Concepts of Genesis in Medieval Islam," Ph.D. diss., University of Pennsylvania, 1994, 40, citing the *Kitāb al-tibb al-ruhāni* by Muhammad b. Zakariya al-Rāzī, in P. Kraus, *Abi Bakr Mohammadi filii Zachariae Raghensis Opera Philosophica* (Cairo: Imprimerie de l'Institut Français d'archeologie Orientale, 1939), vol. 1, 86 n. 10.

14. Nizami, *Khusraw u Shirin*, 59, line 5, cited in Bürgel, *The Feather of Simurgh*, 130.

15. Ibid., 18.

16. Ibid., 18–19, quoting Rumi, *Divan*, ed. Furuzanfar (Tehran: Tehran University Press, 1957–1968), Ruba'i, n. 512.

17. I do not claim that the Nuqtavi cosmos was perceived and experienced in the same way as that of Rumi, Nizami, or other alchemists and cabalists. Although *shari'a*-minded attacks in the seventeenth century would attempt to paint all mystically inclined tendencies with one brush, claiming they were all heretics, this book attempts to comprehend the particulars of Nuqtavi and

Qizilbash ways of being and sensing time, which overlapped with mystical, philosophic, and alchemical dimensions of Islam. I hope that through the course of this narrative, the reader will be able to gain a sense of the spectrum of mystical beliefs that impinged on monotheism.

FOUR

The Cosmos of the Nuqtavis in Early Modern Iran

Whatever you are, you are Mahmud, and Mahmud is water, earth, air, and fire, and they are all one *(vāhid)*, a single human *(ādam)*, and Adam is Muhammad, and Muhammad is the truth, and the truth is God *(Allah)*, and God is one, and one is water, air, fire, and earth.[1]

The Nuqtavis are a rare case because there is enough material written by them as well as about them to offer a glimpse into their universe. In this reconstruction, I have distinguished among Nuqtavi writings, defamatory accounts, and what seem to be sympathetic descriptions. This exploration of the Nuqtavi universe is based primarily on Nuqtavi self-portrayals. Where such writings corroborate images provided by "outsiders," whether hostile sources such as the official Safavi chroniclers or the less pejorative representations found in the biographies of poets, these outside sources are used as supplemental material. What the Nuqtavis define as Ajami (Persian), using mixed Mazdean and Muslim cultural symbols, are read as constructions of themselves in relation to what they term *other* and *Arab*. Where there is dissonance between Nuqtavi writings and those of their detractors, I have used the material as a way to understand the operations of meaning by which the "rationalist" tendency was attempting to invent the norm as it defined an old worldview. We are here entering a contest for religious space and authority as categories such as *ghuluww,* sufi, and Shi'i (Imami) are being hardened.

The writings of Mahmud Pasikhani (d. 1427), the founder of the Nuqtavi movement, recorded a century before the Nuqtavis' sortie as a millenarian movement in Safavi Iran, reveal an alchemical conception of creation and evolution linked to the four elements of nature—fire, water, air, earth.[2] The Nuqtavi cosmos *(aflak)* is composed of these four elements, and cosmic order is understood to permeate every level of reality.[3] Associations between stars, planets, and human beings of all spiritual ranks—prophets, kings, mystics, and devotees—are drawn on the elemental level. We are all different transmutations of the same substance, and everything is in the process of perpetual generation, growth, death, and regeneration. Human beings are imagined to be evolving within this process as they gradually become conscious of their assimilation into the cosmos on many levels, from the imaginary to the sensory and the quantifiable. Such a cosmic affinity is deemed to be measurable mathematically through arithmetic, geometry, or algebra, or ritually, using the physical patterns of nature as models, just as the fixed backdrop of recurring astral patterns that reveal the trajectory of planets circulating above us. Nuqtavi theurgy recognized the individual as an active participant in "genesis" as she fathomed and mimicked these patterns.[4]

Even though the Qur'an speaks of "stages of creation" and of man being created "from the earth like a plant," the Nuqtavi mode of thinking posed a problem for the Muslim monotheist who saw creation as an act of the grace of God—a classic problem that philosophers encounter with monotheist theologies. The issue was treated by some Muslim philosophers like Ibn-i Sina (d. 1037), who drew on the necessity of the Aristotelian first cause, using contingency and necessary existence to confirm the abyss between creator and creation. Muslim mystics like Rumi (d. 1273) understood stages of creation from mineral to plant to animal and human metaphysically. Nuqtavi gnosis, however, understood it spiritually as well as materially; its followers did not distinguish between creator and creation. Why the Nuqtavis came to question and utter their views aloud in the form of an organized movement at this particular junction of Safavi history is fascinating, for such tensions between gnostic and rationalist worldviews were present throughout medieval Islam. Exploring these contexts may shed light beyond the Safavi world to illuminate other such impulses that emerged simultaneously in Ottoman and Mughal landscapes.

Because the Nuqtavis believed in the unity of all existence, each individual was deemed to have the potential to recognize his or her own divinity. This is a feature that the Nuqtavis share with monist sufis *(wahdat-i wujūdī)*, philosophers, and Shi'is. Philosophers like Ibn-i Arabi or Mulla Sadra believed that only saints like themselves could attain God, and some Imami Shi'a *mufawidda* believed that Ali and his eleven descendants, the Imams, shared in God's divinity. The loci of divinity for such groups and intellectuals were either "the family of the Prophet" *(ahl-i bayt)*, elite philosophers, or special sufi saints, all of whom were considered "lovers of God." It is no surprise, then, that Nuqtavis and other *ghulāt* groups were depicted as demons by those who wanted to separate heaven and earth and relegate communion with the divine to the day of resurrection. As we shall see, seventeenth-century proponents of this antimonist program went on to attack and ostracize famous Illuminationist philosophers like Mulla Sadra, as well as a variety of sufi groups, for such beliefs, however limited their sense of divinity might have been. The ontology of being was being debated here; whether the individual could engage in creation and partake in divinity was critical to the debate. There were some Muslims (Sunni/Shi'i) who imagined their creativity as secondary to that of God; they acted through his agency and his grace as representatives of the divine. Philosophers acting through nature used reason and proof to understand the difference between God and human. And some mystics who believed in a more direct role imagined that the human being had the potential to see and experience the divine. Each current created its own divine icons, imagined either as incarnated *(hulūl)*, delegated *(tafwīd)*, or unified *(ittihād)* in the form of Imams, kings, mystics, philosophers, or messiahs. Following the Nuqtavi suppression in the seventeenth century, all these nuances of difference were blurred by a group of Imami Shi'a, *muqassira*—defined as "shortcomers" by the *ghulāt*, for they tended to separate the human and the holy in a rigid ontology of being.

Believing that Adam, Muhammad, Ali, Mahmud, and God himself were made of the same elements in spirit as well as in matter reveals the Nuqtavi reincarnationist conception of the life cycle. Mahmud Pasikhani terms the cyclical and alchemical manner in which they perceived the unity of being as Ajami knowledge *(ta'līm)*.[4] This knowledge is said to have been fathomed by the one who with his soul *(nafs)* has recognized the first and the last knowledge, a concept referred to by the Nuqtavis using Muslim parlance as *lawh-i mahfūz*, or the "hidden eternal tablet."[5] And so Mahmud describes himself as both Adam and the *shakhs-i ākhir*, the "last individual"—that is, as both first and last, the original and the eternal. As Muhammad and the *kāmilān-i mursil*, or "the complete messengers," are considered to be those who come into this world, observe, become conscious of the absolute forms *(suwar-i kul)*, study their occult *(ghayb)* dimension, and come to realize that all is one and whose "recto and verso" are the same in terms of human and holy and in terms of cosmic knowledge. Today we might call the Nuqtavis "essentialist" and "universalist." This is perhaps why Nuqtavi doctrines appealed to the Mughal ruler Akbar (r. 1556–1605), who attempted to promulgate a new universal religion *(dīn-i ilāhī)* that would encompass the cultural diversity of Indian landscapes. One recalls Abū Ma'shar's insistence eight centuries earlier that science (astronomy) has no ethnicity or religious affiliation but is universal and ubiquitous.

You may ask, then, if the Nuqtavis considered knowledge to be universal, what was "Persian" about their sense of identity? Whatever the mixtures of Nuqtavi beliefs, they do reveal a consciousness centered on symbols remembered as Persian, if articulated from within a Muslim vocabulary. Nuqtavi ideas are products of an eclectic Hellenistic atmosphere in Mesopotamia and Iran in late antiquity that continued to exist, merge, and regenerate, shaping Muslim cultures in the process. Less than a century after the Nuqtavi revolt, a Muslim observer, Muhammad Baqir b. Muhammad Taqi Lahiji, considered the Nuqtavis as Hermetics, who embraced a genealogy of Abrahamic prophets and Hellenic philosophers (Moses, Jesus, Muhammad, Hermes, Plato, Socrates, and Aristotle).[6] Again in the seventeenth century, a Jewish rabbi, Yehuda Ben El'Azar from Kashan, a stronghold of the Nuqtavis, characterizes Nuqtavi metempsychosis as Pythagorean *(mazhab-i pitâghurs hakîm)* and notes their similarities with the Kabbalists.[7] He encapsulates these tensions with an allegorical reference to Exodus (19:12), where Moses has climbed Mt. Sinai and is instructed by God to set limits on his people, warning them against "going up to the mountain and (or) touching the borders of it."[8] Such boundaries between the divine and the human were nonexistent for gnostics like the Nuqtavis, hermetics, and kabbalists.

The complex ways in which Mazdean worldviews merged and reemerged in different shapes within Islam is interesting and revealing of Nuqtavi historical processes. Although Nuqtavi theurgy exhibits Pythagorean and Hermetic motifs, a Mazdean substratum is discernible in the Nuqtavi language of understanding the cosmos, their sense of time and being. That is what I term *Persianate* in this book. Moreover, it is significant that the Nuqtavis themselves seem to have recognized one such layer and therefore specified their own ideas as Ajami (Persian). Iamblicus (240–325 c.e.), the late antique Syrian Platonist, anticipated many aspects of Hermetic and Nuqtavi theurgy, yet he chose to identify his neo-Pythagorean philosophy with the "old ways" of the Egyptians.[9] The reasons behind Iamblicus's choice of an Egyptian identification for his philosophy have much to do with the late antique Roman context in which he lived, with the decline of traditional pagan culture, and with the end of a way of life that "severed contact with the gods, threatened their society, and distributed the order of nature."[10] In his *De Mysteriis*, Iamblichus reproached the "Hellenes" for having abandoned their religious heritage, blaming them for the loss of sanctity in his age.[11] His anti-Hellenic criticism led him to embrace the Egyptians, who had stayed loyal to "old ways" of being that preserved humanity's contact with the gods.[12] As we go on to explore what the Nuqtavis considered to be the content of this Ajami knowledge, we shall question why in the early modern period they invoked the Iranian idiom and wanted to restore it. Muslim nomenclature was also utilized by the Nuqtavis not just because they wanted to make themselves more palatable to their Muslim audience but because terms like *mahdi* or prophets like Muhammad, whom they invoke, are part of their own vocabulary, history, and consciousness:

> Because a certain power *(quvvatī)* comes together in elements that by mingling attains a mineral form, and its potential *(isti'dād)* increases until it puts on the robe *(khil'at)* of vegetation, and it increases in ability *(tavānā'ī)* and worthiness *(shāyistagī)* until it takes on the shape of animals so that the elements that cause the composition of humans to attain a splendor from which a complete human arises and in that fashion since the appearance of the human body in Adam, humans have been progressing *(taraqī)* until they attained the Muhammadan rank *(rutbah-yi Muhammadī)*, that is, his ascension *(mi'rāj)*. At this time since it had become more complete *(akmal)* and more pure *(asfā')*, Mahmud arose.[13]

Nuqtavi evolutionary organicism imagined the human being dying, decomposing, and mixing with the earth. Bodily parts were believed to reappear in the form of inanimate *(jamādī)* objects or vegetal *(nabātī)* life until that vegetation became food for animals or for human beings and so in the process was transformed again into human. Through this transmutation, this mixing of older human essences into new ones, knowledge and experience were deemed transferable as well. The dispersed parts of the body consolidated into one form, avoiding fragmentation of human essences, preventing what modern psychology would term *schizophrenia*.[14] There is an underlying alchemical notion concerning the intrinsic power *(quvvat)* rooted in the four natural elements to purify themselves through transmutations, ultimately arriving at their purest form. The paradigm of evolution is reflected in the spiritual growth of humans toward divinity. According to the Nuqtavis, Muhammad's body attained a more complete form in the shape of Mahmud.[15]

Withdraw from Muhammad into Mahmud
For from the former was reduced and into the latter was augmented.[16]

This sense of the generation of life is in tune with a variety of gnostic beliefs that hold that each individual has the potential to improve himself through stages of perfection. The Nuqtavi emphasis on power *(quvvat)*, potential *(isti'dād)*, ability *(tavānā'ī)*, and worthiness *(shāyistagī)* is what endows the human being with the capability to attain purity, designated as the "original solid essence" *(zāt-i murabba')*—that is, the human spirit *(rūh)*. Through the acquisition of a special, hidden knowledge that is predicated on consciousness of self, on locating one's position both spiritually and materially within the cosmic order, each devotee is able to participate directly in the divine, in what is metaphysically invisible.[17] As in Zoroastrian esoteric thought, cosmology is intimately linked to transcendence. Such a conception of the alchemy of the soul corresponds as well with the sufi notion that the human being must pass through different levels and stages on its transcendental path to the divine. Both Nuqtavis and sufis make use of the same concepts to explain human gradations in essential abilities *(isti'dād-i zātī)* and characteristic potentialities *(qābiliyāt-i sifatī)*. Each individual is thought to have the ability to observe "the beautiful light."[18] Sufi language for expressing the "subtleties of being" through a spectrum of five or seven different colors of light is also a feature shared by early Imami (Shi'i) esotericism. Again, the vocabulary used to refer to these transcendental stages is distinct. The early Imamis spoke in a mythological language referring to the five stages of union with the divine in terms of the sun, the throne *('arsh)*, the seat *(kursī)*, the veil, and the curtain.[19] Although these gnostic vocabularies are different, they all speak in the same language of union with the divine.

Despite the confluence of spirit and matter in Nuqtavi alchemy, Manichaean dualism, which thought that matter was corrupt, tarnishing the pure spirit within, subsists in Nuqtavi practice. Through stages of spiritual perfection and elevation, the initiate must lead the ascetic life of a devout *(pārsā)* dervish, and the one who can successfully practice celibacy is granted the special title of *vāhid*, or "the singular one." Celibacy was a visible sign that marked the elite of Nuqtavi saints. Sex, considered a carnal desire to be disciplined if the individual willed to evolve, was to be avoided. The Nuqtavis, however, recognized that there would be some who could limit themselves to one sexual encounter during their lifetime; others would need to engage in sex once a year, every forty days, once a month, once a week, or once a day. Noncelibates are granted the title of the "truthful" *(amīn)*, but the celibate *(vāhid)* who spent his life in devotion, separating himself from all but the most basic material needs for survival, was seen to be progressing *(taraqī)* through a hierarchy that envisions the evolution of humans from the rank of Adam to that of rank of Muhammad.[20] Finally, through Mahmudian status, the individual would attain the station of Allah *(martabah-yi allah)*—that is, the pure composite *(murakkab-i mubīn)*.[21] The continuity of illumination after Muhammad is emphasized by Mahmud, who voices uncertainty as to the precise nature of this manifestation *(zuhūr)* and yet does recognize these material representations and situates them temporally as old and eternal. Knowledge, truth, and illumination are understood as symbols embedded in basic material objects that are visible, tangible, and palpable to the one who seeks them out. What are these Nuqtavi symbols, and what hidden meanings do they convey?

Whatever I may be, I do not know what this manifestation *(zuhūr)* is upon me, but the compound forms *(suwar-i murakkabah)* are eternal *(qadīm)*. And you have not found that singular compound soul *(nafs-i vāhid-i murakkab)* until you have sought the image *(sūrat)* of the possessor of the end time *(sāhib-i zamān-i ākhar)*.[22]

The reader may recall that in Nuqtavi cosmology, Adam is understood to be the embodiment of the four elements (water, fire, earth, air). He inaugurated the recurring cycles of Persian and Arab rule in world history. Adam, Muhammad, and Ali were part of a history of consciousness that would see its completion in Mahmud. And Mahmud was a symbol of all past illuminations. Certain human beings in their roles as prophets, kings, mystics, or warriors were revered in Iranian tradition along with a spectrum of holy representations, such as stars, images in Mani's paintings, or ritual relics. All these objects came to be defined as "pagan idols" in the Muslim era. It is, of course, the particular significations that such signs embodied in Mazdean culture that led Muslims to cast these forms as idols, associating them with a past bereft of Qur'anic revelation, an age of ignorance, superstition, and magic. That kings, messiahs, mystics, and warriors continued to be associated with the holy in Persianate circles into the medieval period is attested by messianic *(ghulāt)* movements that venerated their leaders as divine in a cult of saints and in stories about heroes like Rustam and kings like Kay Khusraw in the *Shāhnāme* that played on their affinity with a divine universal order.[23]

For Muslims, these idols referred to a variety of forms of "image worship," one of which was the human being who continued to represent the divine on earth in the minds of some Persianate gnostics. The variety, layers, and features of meanings remain one dimensional in Muslim rhetoric: they are "satanic." Among the Nuqtavis, for example, it was not enough to contemplate God: the believer had to experience him theurgically. Like the Pythagoreans, the Nuqtavis made use of mathematics "for the recollection (anamnesis) of the divine principle," and so they consecrated numbers and geometric shapes to the divine.[24] Whether in geometric figures symbolized by the circular sun that appeared in the heaven at particular moments or in numerical associations with the Persian alphabet, the Nuqtavis created mathematical visualizations of the divine. These functioned as contemplative icons for the Nuqtavis, ways of remembering a past and understanding the knowledge it engendered. In the seventeenth century, with the Safavi endeavor to control these gnostic tendencies, the official language of discipline expressed itself in terms of "breaking the idols of ignorance."[25]

According to Mobed Shah, a Zoroastrian priest who had met some Nuqtavi exiles in India, in his *Dabistān al-mazāhib*, the Nuqtavis believed that idols representing Persians (Ajami) served as a means of remembering this past and maintaining its vitality during the cycle of the Arabs: "When the cycle [*dawr*] of the Ajam comes to an end and the Arabs take over, people begin to realize that those whom they used to venerate are of a higher rank [*rutbah-yi fawq*] than these present ones [Arabs], so they go and build idols [*but*] resembling the people [*bar mānand-i mardum*] and venerate them until the cycle of the Ajam arrives.[26] We already know that the Nuqtavis considered Ajami knowledge to be the purest form of truth, but their building of idols "resembling the people (Ajami)" verifies the heresiographers' accusation that images *(suwar)* were part of their religious rituals. What gets blurred in rationalist attacks is the question of how these images were understood—whether they were worshiped as divine representations of God, whether an indwelling of divinity was imagined in all of creation, or whether certain images were seen as reminders to the pious gaze of the existence of the divine.

Idol worship lay at the core of an Arab pagan past that Muhammad's monotheistic vision rejected. Biruni in his work on comparative religions attempts to explain that Hinduism was not idol worship to a biased Muslim mind. He recounts a Hindu story relative to Nuqtavi myths a tale about the god Indra who appears to king Ambarish: "If you are overpowered by human forgetfulness, make to yourself an image like that in which you see me; offer to it perfumes and flowers and make it a memorial of me, so that you may not forget me. If you are in sorrow, think of me, if you speak, speak my name; if you act, act for me."[27] Biruni goes on to discuss a similar Greek attitude and practice in order to sanction Hindus in Muslim eyes. He recounts a Greek fable recorded by Galen concerning a sculptor who builds a statue of Hermes. Biruni explains that the statue was a memorial to Hermes but was not the god himself. He writes that "the ancient Greeks also considered idols as mediators between themselves and the first cause, and they worshiped them under the name of stars and the highest substance. For they described the first cause not with positive but only with negative predicates, since they considered it too high to be described by human qualities, and since they wanted to describe it as free from any imperfection. Therefore, they could not address it directly in worship."[28] Biruni is here referring to Neoplatonist and Pythagorean attitudes that are part of a shared late antique culture alive among gnostics in Mesopotamia who continued to express themselves in currents such as the Ikhwan al-Safa, reemerging within new vocabularies of Islam. At times, depending on the cultural contexts, their "pagan" lineage was associated with the Greeks, with the Iranians, or with the Indians.

The Zoroastrian priest Mobed Shah, writing his comparative volume on religious beliefs current in seventeenth-century Mughal India, asserts that for the Nuqtavis these idols were not only statues or stars but humans themselves: "They venerate the human being [*insān rā parastand*] . . . and believe that his essence [*zāt*] is truth."[29] Men like Mahmud Pasikhani and Ustad Yusufi were considered divine representations; they were manifestations of truth on earth. Of all the stars, the sun was singled out by the Nuqtavis as an Ajami symbol. The Zoroastrian priest seems to cast their reverence for the sun as idol worship: "And they bow down to the sun and say some prayers as they face the sun." Yet the sun for the Nuqtavis, like the direction of prayer *(qibla)* for the Muslims, represented their cosmic orientation, situating the believer in the orbit of the universe. The sun for the Nuqtavis lay at the center of their cosmos, and its contemplation was much more nuanced than mere idolatry. As we shall see, the sun and the letters of the Persian alphabet encoded for the Nuqtavis their sense of difference, a particular way of being and experiencing time that was key to Nuqtavi enlightenment.

Roy Mottahedeh speaks of the ways in which Muslims—from the ninth-century Arab poet al-Buhturi to the eleventh-century Persian poet Khaqani—contemplated the ruins of Ctesiphon, the ancient palace of Sasani kings in Mesopotamia. Mottahedeh adduces from poetry that "perhaps the pre-Islamic past was most significant as a locus of poignancy, for the consolation, the moral warning, and the amazement at the world's mutability."[30] For some Nuqtavis, the ruins of Ctesiphon and Persepolis represented icons of a lost Iranian splendor and also a symbol for its return. Others may have understood Khaqani's metaphors invoking the enduring existence of this pre-Islamic past in the Islamic present figuratively:

> If you say, "Where did those crowned heads go?" Lo,
> The earth's belly is eternally pregnant with them
> That wine which the vine gives is the blood of Shirin;
> The pitcher which the vintner sets out is made of the clay of [King]
>   Parviz.[31]

There are Alid elements in Nuqtavi thought as well. We should recall that the Nuqtavi founder Mahmud Pasikhani had been a follower of an Alid movement (Hurufi). Nuqtavi and Hurufi texts need to be compared more closely to explore the affinities between the two, but they do share an understanding of the cosmos and time.[32] For the Nuqtavis, however, the figure of Ali took on a different emphasis: he was one among a succession of Illuminati and not central to Nuqtavi cosmology as the Imams are in Alid circles. But the fact that Mahmud had been a Hurufi and that the Qizilbash would join the Nuqtavi movement highlights the porous boundaries between these two circles. Using an oft-quoted Shi'i tradition in which Muhammad is said to have told Ali, "I and Ali are of a single light [*nūr*], and your flesh [*lahm*] is my flesh and your body [*jism*] is my body,"

Mahmud Pasikhani confirms his belief in the unity of being.[33] This hadith was utilized by some Shi'is to argue that Ali was the legitimate successor of Muhammad. Shah Tahmasb (r. 1524–1576) uses it in his *Memoire* (Tazkire) to confirm his esoteric brand of Shi'a identity that sees divine knowledge passed down from Muhammad to Ali and his progeny, the Imams, all manifestations of the same divine light on earth.[34] The Nuqtavis, however, understood this very same tradition alchemically, arguing that it substantiated their belief that the characteristics *(sifāt)* and power *(quvvat)* of all prophets *(anbiyā')* and saints *(awliyā')* merge together as the bodies of Muhammad and Ali are leavened *(mukhamir)*. In this fashion, elements *(guzidah)* of Muhammad's and Ali's body *(jasad)* were mixed together and thus generate Mahmud.[35] Here is an example of the different ways in which Alid loyalty and its repertoire of sacred texts *(hadith)* were understood by a range of movements that incorporated Muhammad, Ali, and the Imams in their genealogies. This is an Ajami commentary *(tafsīr)* among several Shi'a interpretations that understood Muhammad and the Arabs as belonging to two separate but consecutive cycles of rule, integrated into a Mazdean framework of history that has as its conclusion a cyclical return to the pure truth as originally fathomed by Iranians (Ajami). The veneration of Ali as divine shapes a common ground, but the way in which this union is conceived highlights the topographical particularities of Nuqtavi and Alid landscapes.

Although there is a merging of Alid and Mazdean elements in Nuqtavi thought that reveals a complex process of shared histories and experiences, a sense of difference is nevertheless maintained. This blending of Arab and Persian identity is termed "Ajami knowledge" and is expressed through both linguistic and symbolic differences. According to the Nuqtavis, Ali spoke a Persian version of Arabic. Should we understand this shared construction of Ali as a symbol of opposition to mainstream Sunnism *(jamā'ah)*, embraced by disenfranchised movements, whether Shi'i or Mazdean? Or can it also be assumed that there

was an early modern conception among the Nuqtavis that Alid
loyalty embodied Mazdean symbols, so that when the Nuqtavis
distinguish between Arab and Persian, they are pointing to the
differences between an Arab Muslim and one variety of Persian
Muslim? Modern scholars have explored and traced some of the
"unconscious" yet visible traces of Mazdean cosmology in
sufism and Shi'ism. What is fascinating about the Nuqtavis is
the ostensible consciousness of its merging of Iranian and Shi'i
cultures.

Nuqtavi portrayals of the end-time savior delineate what they
remembered as Persianate in the early modern period, a thousand years after the advent of the Arabs and the defeat of
Zoroastrianism by Islam. Mahmud called himself the "millennial king" *(pādishah-i hizārah)* as well as the expected Mahdi
(mahdi-yi maw'ūd), drawing perhaps on the similarity between
these two loci of divinity in Persian and Muslim cultures.
Pasikhani was also trying to legitimize his views by drawing on
traditional Muslim proof texts, for he uses the Qur'an and the
hadith throughout his writings and argues that Muhammad anticipated his manifestation.[36] Moreover, Mahmud constructs a
binary opposition, not only in his choice of the Persian and
Muslim titles for the messiah but in his reference to solar verses,
lunar calendars, and an alchemical versus creationist theory
of the universe. Mahmud explains: "In Ajami, I am water, fire,
air, earth; in Arabic, I am the sole creator [*makhlūq-i
mutlaqam*]."[37] Mahmud is constantly translating for the Muslim
imagination whatever is Ajami and is similar to Islam but at the
same time distinct. In the process of defining one in relation to
the other, he defines Ajami as opposed to Arab. I would venture
to argue that he is defining and distinguishing one tendency
within Persianate Islam that is different from Arab Islam.

Mahmud shapes himself as the millennial king *(pādishah-i
hizārah)*, using the Persian regal title *pādishah*. Along with this
image of a millennial king, he terms himself the "western sun."
The sun and the king appear as Iranian twin symbols, evoking
both spiritual and temporal sovereignty. As we have seen, in Ira-

nian tradition monarchs enjoyed a holy status. Their cosmic power is reflected in architecture through the conception of circular cities with the king's throne at the center, the axis of the world revolving together with the sun in Medean, Parthian, and Sassani capitals and even in the Abbasid capital city of Baghdad.[38] This representation can be seen in other artifacts as well. In Achaemenid seals, coins, and rock reliefs on royal tombs in Persepolis, the sun and the moon are juxtaposed symbols of the universal role of kings. Sasani silver plates, textiles, and royal iconography continue to draw on the symbol of the sun and the crescent moon[39] (see figure 1). And the brilliant halo that appears around the Sasani king Khusraw II's (591–628) head on the rock relief at the Taq-i Bustan represents his divinity. Iranian kings are presented both in Greco-Roman and Persian sources as brothers of the sun and of the moon.[40] Whether by late antiquity their divinity was understood as real or merely symbolic is a matter of debate in modern scholarship, but in some Persianate circles, the sun, the king, and the divine were intimately associated during the Islamic era. The holy aspect of kingly rule in Iranian tradition must have been alive in medieval Islam, for when the Persian Buyid ruler Jalal al-Dawla (r. 1025–1044) requests permission from the Abbasid caliph to adopt the Persian kingly title of shahanshah, the Hanafi scholar Abu 'Abdullah al-Saymari, who is consulted by the caliph (al-Qa'im, r. 1031–1074), allows the title to be granted, so long as the intent *(al-qasd wa-l-niyya)* is to refer to someone on earth who is ruling temporally.[41]

The sun was an icon of divine rule. Biruni reports on Sasani legends concerning the king and his cosmic role at the New Year festivities, during which the monarch is seated on a golden throne resting on the shoulders of his officials and is raised toward the sun, just as Jamshid was raised in Zoroastrian mythology: "When the rays of sun fell on him and people saw him, . . . he rose that day like the sun, the light beaming forth from him as though he shone like the sun. Now people were astonished with the rising of the two suns."[42] Medieval Mazdean rebels who rose

up against Muslim subjugation held onto the sun, defined by
Muslim sources as their direction of prayer *(qibla)*, refusing to
face Mecca, for the sun was their direction of worship, the point
that centered them within their cosmos. The "heretic" Muqanna
is said to have veiled his face like some Sasani kings may have
done, for their faces were said to mirror their divinity, blazing
like fire with such intensity that human eyes were deemed unable to withstand their brilliance. In Irano-Muslim astrological
traditions, the zodiacal sign of Leo also came to be associated
with kingship and was often represented as the sun emerging
from behind the Lion's torso[43] (see figure 2).

The sun and moon are also juxtaposed in Nuqtavi writings,
and here the calendrical association between the Muslim lunar
reckoning of time and the Persian solar calendar informs their
binary worldview. Muhammad is cast as the moon and
Mahmud as the sun, so Persians were associated with the day
and Arabs with the night. What the Nuqtavis seem to have done
in the process of translating elements of Iranian cosmology onto
a Muslim context was to transfer notions of aggressive moon
kings onto the Arab conquerors who adopted the lunar calendar, delegating the role of the peaceful sun king to an awaited
Iranian messiah.[44] Iranian kingship continued to imply both
temporal and spiritual authority, with an expectation that monarchs would fulfill their prophetic functions as conservers of the
just order *(asha)*, reestablishing it once it had been distributed.
The function of kings as protectors of the cosmic order necessitated collaboration with warriors and mystics to discover the
nature of that order and to acquire the military capability to establish it temporally. Some like Isma'il played the role of mystic
and warrior, finally assuming the position of monarch of Safavi
Iran.

Nuqtavi associations between the moon Arabs (Muhammad)
and sun Persians (Mahmud) are based on particular calendars of
the two groups—on the different ways in which they measured
time. Arabs computed time according to the phases of the moon,
and the Persians according to the houses of the sun. A remem-

brance of the solar calendar as Persian and the lunar calendar as an Arab innovation is preserved in Nuqtavi thought. As we shall see, the Nuqtavis reveal a sense of superiority linked to the solar calendar, measured by way of ethical, moral, and temperamental criteria. This shows us ways in which time and being were connected in Nuqtavi thought and practice. Both solar and lunar calendars were used by the Safavis. The court chronicler of Abbas I's reign (Iskandar Bek Munshi Turkman) provides a detailed account of the Nuqtavi episode, explaining his usage of the mixed Turki-Hijri calendar: "And I reflected to myself that if I adopt the Hijri [lunar] year, which according to Arab usage begins on the first of Muharram, most of the people of Iran will not understand it; for among Turks and Persians the beginning of the year is the Now Ruz (vernal equinox), which is the first day of spring, and [for them] the year is then completed at the end of the four seasons, when it becomes New Year again."[45] That most denizens of Safavi Iran, including Persians and Turks, continued to follow the seasonal rhythms of the solar calendar may have contributed to the vitality of a whole system of myths and lore associated with the sun in Mazdean cosmology. And that Persian as well as Turks partook in this way of being and sensing time is confirmed by the ethnically mixed composition of the Nuqtavis. It is the multi-dimensional meanings (numerology, astronomy, alchemy, and psychology) that the Nuqtavis attach to the solar and lunar calendars that are particularly illuminating of the Nuqtavi ethos:

> So whatever is the sun is old [qadīm]
> and whatever is the moon is new [jadīd].[46]

The moon was understood to represent Muhammad in the astrological sense of the moon presiding over the horoscope of Muhammad and in the sense of Muhammad and the moon as sharing an affinity of being. In Nuqtavi cosmic history, occurrences in Muhammad's life were believed to be synchronic with lunar phases; thus, Muhammad's rise occurred on the fourteenth of the lunar month, which corresponds to the full moon.

According to Mahmud, this is why Muhammad did not claim to be the circular sun.[47] There is a whole body of significations in Nuqtavi writings on the sun and the moon that reflect their understanding of change and of human psychology. A mathematical dimension lies at the core of these ideas, for there is a Pythagorean effort to measure physical phenomena numerically and to comprehend these numbers that delineate patterns metaphysically. Everything is seen to be rooted in mathematics, which illuminates the corresponding place of each form within the structure of the universe. There seems to have been a sense that the complexity of the universe was a result of simple rules, models, or algorithms (recipes), which were termed in Nuqtavi vocabulary the "pure compound," the first living organism that shared a self-similarity with Adam. Only when the individual came to comprehend the mechanisms behind the generation of life could she feel and experience it. And so the craft of an artist or a mathematician was deemed analogous to the creativity they exercised to depict ways to see the invisible, artistic forms of generation with the precision of a brush stroke or a mathematical equation.

Mahmud is questioned by one of his followers about his reasons for considering Persian months to be old.[48] He responds that the western sun, which he equates with the last person *(shakhs-i ākhir)*, is eternal; it does not change *(taghyir u tabdīl)*: "The Sun has not come like the Moon, moody [*mughayir al-hāl*]."[49] What makes the sun singular and superior in the eyes of the Nuqtavis is its consistency, its ever-presence at the leavening of Adam, as well as at the end time of the last person. The particular position, the role and function, of the sun in the universe, affirms its superior rank. The number twelve is what Mahmud understands to be the mathematical description of the unique sun as well as those forms that correspond to it. Mahmud names the twelve Persian months to draw on the connection between the sun and the twelvefold Persian structuring of time (calendar).

And Mahmud links the twenty-eighth-day lunar month with

the Arabs, whose alphabet is comprised of twenty-eight letters. The number twelve is deemed to have been even more deeply rooted in Persian culture, not only in the way Persians calculated time but in the way they expressed themselves through language (being). The Persian language itself, particularly the four singular letters of the Persian alphabet, were key to this cosmic self-similarity with the sun. The twelve-month Persian solar calendar is associated with the variance in their alphabet that possesses four extra letters differentiating Persian from Arabic. The number twelve is embodied in the three dots *(nuqta)* that distinguish the four singular Persian letters *p, ch, zh, geh* (گ, ژ, چ, پ) The first three letters are all written in the Arabic alphabet literally with three dots. The fourth letter, geh (گ), however, is written with a line, equivalent to three dots. Four singular Persian letters, comprised of three dots each, if multiplied give the numerical value of twelve. And here lies the basic mechanism, the mathematical equation, behind the Nuqtavi science of dots, for which they received their epithet, Nuqtavi (pointillists). What is peculiar to their system is that dots are associated with particular Persian letters, visual and sonic reminders to every Persian speaker and reader that the Persians are culturally different from the Arabs, that they speak a different language, although expressed through a shared alphabet. This consciousness of a Persian past symbolized in language and calendar have had reverberations into the modern period, whether in the pan-Iranist endeavors of intellectuals like Ahmad Kasravi to purify the Persian language or in attempts of the last king of Iran (Muhammad Reza Pahlavi) to revive a pre-Islamic Persian glory as he reformed the Iranian solar calendar that reckoned time from the rise of Islam to a solar calendar that began its history a millennium earlier with the rise of the Achaemenid dynasty:

> What in Ajami we say twelve thousand [*ithnā 'ashar alfī*] is the right [*haqq*] of the Ajami Sun who is the last Sāhib Qirān [Master of the auspicious conjunction] and the seal of manifestation [*khātam al-zuhūr*] and laws [*ahkām*] and is the complete manifestation [*mubīn-i kul*].[50]

Here, Mahmud is associating Mazdean apocalyptics with Muslim eschatology. Mazdean cosmology envisioned a "world year" of twelve millennia (twelve x one thousand), corresponding with the twelve-month calendar. Mazdeans divided human history into three millennia "ushered in successively by Zarathustra and the first two World Saviors."[51] The Mazdean third savior, Saoshyant, is here equated with the Muslim apocalyptic world conqueror of the auspicious conjunction (associated in early modern Islam with Alexander and Timur) as well as the Mahdi (hidden Imam) and the Persian sun. Alid, Turco-Mongol, and Mazdean apocalyptic symbols and cosmological views exist in symbiosis within Nuqtavi discourse. Mahmud is cast as the twelver (Shi'i), for his soul is manifest in the twelve Imams.[52] The twelve solar months, twelve Persian dots, and twelve Imams are all identical: "they are the Persian soul [*nafs-i 'Ajami*] and the manifestation of which is the sun, and the manifestation of twelve is from the sun."[53] There is a circularity in Nuqtavi logic, for they claim that "the sun has twelve houses and the twelfth Imam implies him [Mahmud], who is the manifestation of *p, ch, zh, g*."[54]

The language used to express the Nuqtavi worldview integrates Muslim cultural terms and canons as the devotees draw parallel meanings, creating their own Persianate cultural memories and icons. Language and calendars are emphasized as the two distinguishing markers that differentiate Persian and Arab identity. Both are vehicles through which a sense of difference is actualized, and cultural texts like the *Shāhnāme* and astrological works like Abū Ma'shar's *Zīj-i Hizārāt* form the repositories of these memory narratives. But there is also a notion that Persian and Arab are two sides of one circle that complete each other, as reflected in the Nuqtavi conception of history and in their designations of cycles, both Arab and Persian.

A conception of a relationship between anthropology, astronomy, ethics, and psychology permeates Nuqtavi thought. Stars are designated as friends *(ashāb)* of God; they are the Imams and the caliphs, just like Muhammad is the moon. And they travel and work together and rise and set together, as the sun rises; they all turn black and become hidden along with the sun's soul *(nafs)*.[55] All the major Muslim historical figures are believed to have had astral and planetary counterparts. Ali holds a prominent role as the propitious planet Jupiter as well as the morning star, "who is the loyal announcer [*mukhbir*] and precursor of the sun."[56] The other planets are seen to symbolize the successors of Muhammad (caliphs) as well as the first generation of the founding fathers of Muslim schools of law.[57] The superiority of the Persian solar calendar to the Arab lunar one is expressed in Nuqtavi writings, not in terms of precise calculations of time but in terms of human qualities. The Nuqtavis deem valuable the permanence of the sun—the fact that it is unchangeable and indestructible. The moon, in contradistinction, is constantly altering its shape, waxing and waning. Consistency and stability, both in terms of form *(hāl)* and ability *(majāl)*, mark the sun's superiority as a model. In a cyclical imagination of repetitive patterns the element that is deemed eternal and invariable is the sun, rising every morning, setting every night, only to be encountered the next day in the same way. Immutability in the midst of predictable patterns of change lies at the conceptual core of the Nuqtavi cosmos.[58]

The peerless and unique sun is associated with a warm spirit *(garm anfās)*, pleasant *(khush liqā)* and sweet *(shīrīn navā)*.[59] Once again, it is contrasted to the characteristics of the moon, which is seen as cool *(khunuk)*, weeping *(giryān)*, weary *(malūl)*, and sad *(mahzūn)*. Moods are ascribed to the moon and to the sun and by association to Persian and to Arabs.[60] Thus, the holistic worldview of the Nuqtavis linked universal phenomena to human temperaments. As we enter into the cultural and political landscapes of Safavi Iran, we shall attempt to explore other aspects, social and political, that are integrated as well into a complex and interconnected Nuqtavi reality. Here I have isolated a couple of "hooks" on which Nuqtavi memory of an Iranian past fastened itself—the solar calendar and the Persian language, particularly four letters not used in Arabic: *p, zh, ch, g*. These are visual and aural reminders to every Persian speaker and reader that they are different from the Arabs, that they speak a different language although expressed through a shared alphabet. I have tried to delineate the ways in which this memory of past times was maintained in a practical manner. Now let us explore the communicative channels through which such ideas were experienced.

HETEROGLOSSIA IN SIXTEENTH-CENTURY IRAN

Mahmud Pasikhani (d. 1427), a native of Gilan (northwestern Iran), founded the Nuqtavi movement after having broken from his Hurufi spiritual master, Sayyid Fazlullah Astarabadi (d. 1394). Both Pasikhani and Astarabadi (northeastern Iran) were natives of the Caspian Sea region populated predominantly by Persian speakers who have preserved their distinct dialects (Gilaki, Mazandarani, Astarabadi) up to the modern age. Astarabadi, however, claimed Alid (Musavi) descent, symbolized in his title of *sayyid*. Astarabadi's sacred lineage linked him to the family of the prophet Muhammad and distinguished his millenarian language from that of his Nuqtavi former disciple Mahmud Pasikhani. Although Fazlullah wrote poetry in the Persian dialect of Astarabad, as well as in Arabic and Turkish, he claimed to be the awaited Mahdi anticipated in the Alid tradition. A mixed Irano-Islamic idiom is embedded in Hurufi beliefs. Astarabadi's gnostic understanding of cosmic secrets encoded in letters *(huruf)* and their corresponding numerical values, incorporated both the Arabic (28) and the Persian (32) alphabets.[61] Pasikhani, however, emphasized the singularity of the Persian alphabet through four distinct letters not shared with Arabic. Differences rather than similitudes, dots rather than letters, mark Nuqtavi language.

When I use the word *language,* I am referring to a self-contained system of signs whose meanings are determined by their relations to each other. What distinguishes the Nuqtavis is a whole substratum of Persianate referents associated with these dots. Yet what characterizes both the Nuqtavis and the Hurufis as Muslims is their use of a Muslim genealogy and their employment of the Qur'an as a collection of cultural proof texts from which their gnostic interpretations emanate or are at least corroborated and legitimized. Both Astarabadi and Pasikhani were engaging in a form of Qur'anic interpretation *(ta'wil)*, and their works are examples of symbolic readings of the Qur'an produced by a range of Muslim esoterics *(bātinī)*. Nuqtavi interpretations of sacred axioms of the Qur'an and hadith are examples of how differently each tendency reads these core texts. In the Muslim era, the Qur'an became the sacred center from which creative impulses emerged. Heteroglossia issued from the accompanying texts appropriated as vestiges, through which these worldviews were shaped, expressed, and experienced. The case of the Nuqtavis reveals how a particular older worldview, alive in oral accounts or encoded in ancient written texts, came to shape the way in which a new text, like the Qur'an, was (re)read and given meaning.

Socially, Pasikhani sought to curtail the prestige of descendants of Muhammad's family *(sayyid)*. Unlike the moon Arabs, says Pasikhani, the sun Persians have not come boasting about the Prophet's tribe and clan (Quraysh).[62] He argued that the distinction between Arab *(sayyid)* and Ajam *(sādah)* was superficial, given that one is but the transmutation (reincarnation) of the other. The Nuqtavis should be understood in the larger context of Irano-Arab acculturation as well as in the more immediate historical context of Alid millenarian rebellions, for in the early modern, period movements like that of the Hurufis claiming authority through the Shi'i messianic paradigm and lineage of the Prophet were widespread. If, indeed, Persianate movements like the Nuqtavis were numerous in early modern Iran, they have not been recorded in extant annals of Irano-Muslim history. The Safavis emerged in the sixteenth century from within one such Alid discourse.

In the fourteenth and fifteenth centuries, as the lands of Iran, Mesopotamia, and Asia Minor were experiencing a period of decentralization after the fall of the Mongols (Ilkhanid, 1258–1335), Alid millenarian movements attempted to gain regional control in all corners of the Iranian plateau. They formed a territorial circle around the central desert, amid the inhabitable regions of the Iranian plateau. From the northern Caspian Sea region of Mazandaran (Mar'ashis/Mir-i Buzurg, d. 1379), to eastern Iran (Sarbidars, 1336–1381, and Nurbakhshis/Muhammad Nurbakhsh, d. 1464), and into the southwest (Musha'sha'/Muhammad b. Falah, d. 1462), Alid claimants emerged from within sufi circles as apocalyptic messiahs. I do not wish to imply that these movements were all identical; each maintained particularities that remain to be studied.[63] But clearly, there was an Alid revival in this period, and the impulses behind such a rekindling remain ambiguous. It is probable that with the Mongol conquests of the central and eastern lands of Islamdom, when the core lands of Islam came under the control of non-Muslim rulers for the first time, a greater number of Muslims placed their hopes in the betrayed family of the Prophet (Alids), who had from the beginning of the expansion of Islam contested the worldly ways of Muslim caliphs (Umayyads and Abbasids, 650–1258). It is from within such Alid landscapes that the Nuqtavis emerge as different. There are some important parallels, of course, for they share components of Alid *ghuluww* that color their notions of time, history, and being. (The particulars of Alid circles are analyzed in part 2.) The case of the Nuqtavis we are dealing with here is unique, for it shares many features with Alid *ghuluww* and yet is distinguished by its Persianate rhetorical emphasis.

The Nuqtavis share with the Shu'ubiyah the will to establish equality *(taswiyah)* between Arabs and Persians, an aspiration that had been voiced by an Irano-Muslim literary elite (Shu'ubiyah) in medieval Islamic Iran.[64] Mottahedeh argues that the Shu'ubiyah controversy over the position of Arabs and Iranians was not an anti-Islamic movement but rather a literary expression by a group of Persian Muslim elites who coveted an equal status with their Arab Muslim peers.[65] As we shall see, however, the Nuqtavis emerge from diverse social milieus and so voice their demands for equality not only in the social terms of equal status and prestige but also in the religiopolitical terms of apocalyptic change with anti-Islamic overtones that envisioned a utopia for all, whether dispossessed Persians or betrayed Qizilbash Turks. Unlike the Shu'ubis, the Nuqtavis took up arms and harbored political aspirations as well. Yet Nuqtavi and Shu'ubi critiques advocating the equality of Persians and Arabs share in their imagination of human parity. They point out as well a tension that persisted. Mottahedeh quotes Ibn 'Abd Rabbih (d. 940) on the arguments of the Shu'ubis: "You are all from Adam, and Adam was from the dust. The Arab has no superiority to the non-Arab [Ajamis] except by virtue of righteousness [taqw].[66] Both the Nuqtavis and Shu'ubis were invoking the egalitarian Qur'anic ideal that all Muslims were equal before God, despite their status, wealth, or social and ethnic backgrounds.

For some Irano-Muslim imaginations, it was not enough to engage in a literary controversy to voice their discontent against Arab exclusivity; their sense of cultural superiority was based on their remembrance of an "older" and "purer" revelation that they cast as a lost utopia and willed to recover. Both Hurufis (Alid *ghuluww*) and Nuqtavis (Mazdean *ghuluww*) shared the belief that history was cyclical and revelation continuous, yet Pasikhani believed that the final cycle when all of humanity would attain truth belonged to the Iranians. According to the Nuqtavis, "the cycle of the Ajam [Iranians] will prevail, the religion of Muhammad is abrogated [*mansūkh*]; now the religion is the religion of Mahmud." As Islam grew from an Arabian cult to a universal religion that successfully spread its monotheistic vision from Spain eastward to central Asia and northern India, new converts articulated different renderings. Some syncretic gnostics, whether exhibiting Jewish (Isawiyya), Mazdean (Khurramiyya), or Christian (Mughiriyya) traits, resisted Muslim rule and revolted, using the language of messianic opposition.[67] Such pious opposition from within the Muslim community continued to punctuate the history of early and medieval Islam as the cultural bearings of Islam were debated and negotiated between a variety of new and potential converts. And egalitarianism lay at the core, at least in the discourse of those Alid and Persianate groups that took up arms to fight for their ideals. Belief in reincarnation *(tanāsukh)* and in the possible incarnation of all or part of the divine in certain men *(hulūl)* had allowed some Alid *ghulāt*, like the Mubayyads who arose in Transoxiana twenty years after Abū Muslim's death (755), to claim that Abū Muslim had been the incarnation of a succession of prophets from Adam, Moses, and Jesus to Muhammad. Abū Muslim, himself probably a Persian convert to Islam, had succeeded in mustering much support from among the nonelite Persian population of Khurasan. Whatever the religious proclivities of Abū Muslim may have been, some of his newly converted followers regarded him as a restorer of Mazdean rule. His appearance in Khurasan with his famous black banners enters into Zoroastrian eschatological texts as an apocalyptic sign of the coming of the Saoshyant, recorded two centuries after Abū Muslim's revolt, which secured the success of the Abbasid revolution, itself a conglomerate of Alid movements.

Persianate aspirations and fantasies continued to be articulated in the form of rebellions into the twelfth century, with some like the Parsis (Parsiyan), remnants of the Khurramiyya (neo-Mazdakis) who traced their spiritual lineage back to ancient mythical kings of Iran, beginning with Jamshid. The Parsis believed that the prophetic chain had been passed from the mythical Kayani dynasty of Persian kings, to the Arabs with Muhammad, and then back to the Iranians with Abū Muslim.[68] Although Abū Muslim's "heroic effort to break the Arab domination and restore justice" had failed, his grandson Gawhar "would complete his work and restore the Iranian religion and the dominance of the mahdi."[69] This Persianate reading of history saw the dispensation of Mazdean kings and Muslim religions figures (Prophet and Imams) as forming a single lineage that linked these cycles of rule. And the epic hero of the Abbasid revolution, Abū Muslim, is cast as the restorer of Persian rule in the Muslim era. For some Persianate Muslims, Abū Muslim stood as a symbolic savior of the Iranians from Arab dominance.

Such movements continued to threaten Muslim rule (Abbasids, Fatimids, Saljuks), whether as restorers of Iranian traditions or as Alid revealers of true Islam. Groups in formation often embody multiple voices and aspirations; once they have attained power, however, a more singular definition takes shape as centrifugal impulses to dominate gradually eliminate heterogeneity. In the early modern world of Asia Minor, Iran, and Central Asia, it was only when the identity of the messiah had been unveiled that we see a spectrum of emerging offshoots. Some Qarmatis rejected the Isfahani Mahdi, and some Isma'ilis rejected Budayl only after the Isfahani Mahdi and Budayl had unveiled the particulars of their cosmic secrets. A member of the elite like Ustad Yusufi among the Nuqtavis was also privy to secret knowledge. All the devotees of the Nuqtavis, however, may not have been aware of their Persianate aspirations.

As we have seen, the intermingling of Islamic and Persianate belief systems permeates Nuqtavi thought. The Nuqtavis understood both the sun and the Ka'ba as their direction of prayer *(qibla)*. Mahmud Pasikhani claimed to be a mixed incarnation of Muhammad and Ali, a more complete form of Muhammad.[70] Just as he claimed to be the Mahdi, he was also the western sun.[71] Although Persianate movements were less common in early modern Islamdom, the Nuqtavis were able to amass popular support in the Iranian heartland and threatened to overthrow the Safavis. Some Nuqtavis may have even joined the Safavi revolution. And as we shall see, some Qizilbash disciples of the Safavi Alid movement would in the late sixteenth century break away from the Safavis and enter the ranks of the Nuqtavis. Lines between *ghulāt* movements, whether Alid or Persianate, seem to have been quite fluid, for they shared a cosmic view that allowed for believers to switch from one to another without having to change their worldviews. The secretive nature of these movements also meant that some dimensions of their visions remained hidden to many devotees. And here, material gains and a will to attain a more equitable social status must have played a role in the attraction of followers to the Nuqtavi cause.

An element that distinguishes medieval *ghulāt* movements, whether Persianate or Alid, from early modern ones, is the degree to which mysticism played a role in their practice and expression. The medieval history of the interplay and merging of sufi and Alid circles is yet to be written. In the next part, I outline this fusion in the sixteenth century.[72] We must assume that there were many different meanings and expressions of mysticism and Alid loyalty in the late medieval and early modern periods and that these forms of Muslim piety and visions of ideal societies existed together harmoniously at times. Sufism is an element that the Nuqtavis shared with Alid movements like the Safavis. Mysticism was an arena in which the Nuqtavi movement crystallized in Safavi Iran. Toward the middle of the sixteenth century, Dervish Khusraw, a future trustee *(amīn)* of the Nuqtavis, was born into a poor family from the district of Darb-i Kush in Qazvin. Refusing to follow in the footsteps of his ancestors, who had engaged in digging wells and irrigation canals *(qamshī)*, he chose the path of an ascetic and "donned the clothes of the qalandars and dervishes."[73] Nuqtavi writings identify their form of mysticism with those independent ascetics, the roaming *qalandars* and *rinds*. Mahmud Pasikhani writes:

> The turn of the final praiseworthy *rinds* [*sufis*] has arrived.
> What the Arabs taunted the Iranians with has passed.

The Nuqtavis differentiated themselves from the commercial turn that the sufism of the brotherhoods (sufism) had taken since the late medieval period.[74] The institutionalization of spirituality within individual orders, each possessing its particular genealogies of past and present ascetics, transformed early sufism from a religious impulse into a trend. What had been a spontaneous expression of pious opposition against the "worldly" turn Islamic culture had taken was now ritualized and codified into a detailed discipline. Devout men in the early centuries of the expansion of Islam into a universal and imperial religion had been recalled by their honesty in speaking out, either verbally or through acts of social defiance, against the worldliness of the caliphs, the Muslim successors of Muhammad. Some pious men like Ibrahim b. Adham (d. 777–778) had chosen to live on the Byzantine frontier of Islam and came to be venerated in the medieval period as holy warriors who led lives of strict abstinence that Muslims should emulate.[75] And by the early modern period, Ibrahim b. Adham would be recast as a "prince turned ascetic" to accentuate this break with materiality. Centuries later, a spiritual elite of sufi masters would make use of the genealogies of dead men whom they sanctified and whose pious acts and thoughts they consolidated into organized movements with detailed liturgies. Spiritual genealogies and rituals came to distinguish brotherhoods from one another, and sufis were identified according to a semiotics of clothing they wore, whether they chanted aloud or quietly, or whether they preferred silence to music and dance as they communed with the divine. As an ideal form of religiosity, sufism became an alternate dimension of Muslim devotion and piety, emphasizing the inner thoughts and feelings of the believer rather than his outward social and religious comportment. Piety and spiritual knowledge, rather than wealth, rank, and social status, were considered by sufis as marks of nobility. They honored the Qur'an as enshrining God's message to Muhammad but devoted themselves not to the letter of its words but instead "to repeat in their own lives something of the inspirational experiences of Muhammad."[76] They were concerned with the spirit of the Qur'an. Other pious Muslims felt that believers should be guided by God's revealed laws, and so they worked out another program *(shari'a)* to shape the private and public lives of Muslims. For the *shar'ia*-minded, the divine words of the Qur'an were to act as frameworks for social and personal order.

The mystical dimension of Islam practiced through the guidance of peerless masters *(pīr)* in cloisters and hospices *(khāniqah)* provided spaces of religious life alongside mosques. Or rather, the mystics had their own type of mosques located at the threshold of the tombs of their holy founders. Sufi metaphysics and philosophy even penetrated the curriculum of theological seminaries *(madrasah)*. These two predominant faces of Islam—the *shari'a*-minded and the mystical-minded, as Hodgson coins them—were embraced by some Muslims comfortably but were mistrusted by others, creating an undercurrent of tensions that reemerge at particle junctions in the history of Islamdom. The Safavi age is one junction where these different meanings and understandings of Muslim piety clashed openly. One should question why such tensions arose, persisted, and collapsed with the victory, albeit temporary, of the *shari'a*-minded in early modern Iran and in Safavi-specific sociocultural contexts. Some sufi orders like the Safavis enjoyed enough social, economic, and political power locally as well as regionally to mobilize themselves militarily and conquer Iran and Iraq at the turn of the sixteenth century. Unlike some of those early sufi saints who rejected the worldliness of the caliphs and refused to use their power and prestige politically, some mystic guides of the early modern orders came to exercise that power, making use of the rhetoric of a just and egalitarian society in the Qur'an. And here is where the ideals of the *ghulāt* (Alid or Mazdean) and the sufis merge, social and religious equality remaining an integral aspect of their aspirations. This desire seems to have been impinged on by the monotheistic will to distance the holy from the human. In the cosmologies of the *ghulāt* and the sufis, individual access to the divine was connected to the sense of equality. Muhammad had voiced God's words, which emphasized the equality of all Muslims before the divine. Not only did the conquering Muslims come to distinguish between new converts to Islam, whether Persian, Greek, Armenian, or Jew; such egalitarian visions also became idealized and tamed in didactic courtly literature, rarely to be actualized.[77] And so a variety of gnostic movements in early Islam took on the role of redressers of the truth and justice, whether as avengers of the betrayed family of the Prophet (Alids), as restorers of Iranian rule, or as Jewish and Christian messiahs.

Sufi disciples, regardless of their social rank as bakers or bureaucrats, were considered spiritually equal before God. But hierarchies of power and financial interests tended to taint such ideals, especially as sufism began to be institutionalized. By the early modern period, the spontaneity and individuality of sufism became mere mimesis in brotherhood circles. Now sufi practice was formalized through orders, defined and controlled through detailed ritual. Some independent-minded sufis like the Malamatis (the blameworthy) rejected this form of piety that for them had lost its essence. They felt that sufis had begun to place undue emphasis on being recognized as pious; it was no longer for the love of God that they embarked on the ascetic path. Malamatis strove to incur blame so that they would be certain that it was not for recognition that they were being devout. They shaved their hair, even their eyebrow, mutilated themselves, and went around naked, like savages belittled in the eyes of a cultured sedentary society in formation. Malamatis refused to follow and give public recognition to the rationalist urbanizing Muslim culture that was taking shape. And it was in social arenas of the sufi cloister *(khāniqah)* and chivalric brotherhoods *(futuvvat)* that sentiments like those of the Malamatis found many devotees.

The Nuqtavis considered themselves carefree *(lā ubālī)* dervishes, who unlike entrepreneurial *(jā dar pardāz)* sufis, were "single riders" *(yek savārah)*.[78] They did not follow one particular spiritual master of an order and would not wear the sufi cloak of initiation *(khil'at)* that indicated membership in a particular brotherhood.[79] Instead, the Nuqtavis were styled as "singular naked Ajami Qalandars."[80] They rejected systematic and homogeneous spirituality and deemed it against the very nature of mystical piety. The famous Persian poet Sa'di (d. 1291–1292), who wrote as the Mongols were conquering the Iranian domains, captures this mood in his *Gulistān:*

Someone asked a Shaykh: "What is the essence of sufis?" He responded: "In the past they [sufis] were a dispersed group in the
world, but in reality they were united. Today, they are a people
who in appearance are united, but in their hearts they are dispersed."[81]

A new type of ascetic movement emerged with the institutionalization of mystical orders (sufism), giving birth to dervish
groups like the Qalandariyya and the Haydariyya.[82] Distinct
from the mysticism of brotherhoods, these mystics rejected the
very social and cultural forms that impinged on their notion of
piety. Moving from place to place, they rejected stability and
material comfort and expressed this attitude through a language
of social deviance and a strict interpretation of poverty. Celibacy, sodomy, mendicancy, starvation, and self-mutilation were
their responses to the crystallization of social and cultural forms
that valued heterosexual marriage, opulence, and attention to
physical appearance. Although the term *qalandar* referred to a
wandering dervish who was not linked to one particular order
or genealogy *(silsila)* and to the customs and rituals of the cloister, some form of cohesion and network did take shape among
them.[83] A Qalandariyya movement crystallized under the leadership of a Persian named Jamal al-din (d. 1232–1233), from
Saveh in central Iran. The leadership of the Qalandariyya who
established communities of believers through hospices in the
Fertile Crescent (Damascus, Damietta, Jerusalem) and Egypt
was ethnically Persian. Iran lay at the crossroads between India
and the eastern Mediterranean world, Jamal al-din Savi's disciple and Shirazi biographer Khatib Farisi (b. 696/1297) wrote
about his master in the Persian language. Both detractors and
sympathizers of the Qalandariyya speak of them dressing in the
manner of the Iranians and the Magi *(al-majūz wa al-'ajam)*, as
well as learning their beliefs from Iranian shaykhs *(fuqarā al-
'Ajam)*.[84] Whether speaking in Persian, as Ibn Taymiyya accuses
the *qalandars,* or begging in Persian, as a Qalandari poet describes his fellows, the vehicle is the Persian language, distinguished in dress and in words. Language is the medium through

which cultures breathe and speak. As we have seen with Nuqtavi beliefs, the Persian language, whether expressed through the symbol of the sun or by the four additional letters of the Persian alphabet, represented Nuqtavi sense of a Persian (Ajami) identity. These signs distinguished the Nuqtavis from other Muslims like the Hurufiyya (Alid *ghulāt*), from whom they had broken away. And there must have been a range of understandings of Ajami identities as well. Let us turn to another Persianate language communicated by Hafez.

Mystically minded poets like Hafez (d. 1389), a contemporary of Mahmud Pasikhani appropriated by some later Nuqtavis is an adherent, writes of the hypocrisy of the sufis in his poetry.[85] Zarrinkub, in his perceptive study on Hafez, attempts to place this mystic poet of Shiraz in his cultural context. He understands Hafez as one who questions the various forms of religiosity available to a pious Muslim in his native Shiraz, where he encountered Qalandars. Mistrust and doubt of current piety pervade Hafez's poetry *(divan)*, and this leads him according to Zarrinkub to the "street of the *rinds*":

Will I find union with a shah like you?
Me, the ill famed "I do not care" rogue [*rind*]?[86]

Hafez prefers to be guided by the metaphoric *pīr-i Mughān* (Magi priest) than by the opportunist sufi, the rational philosopher who seeks God's proof in creation, or the judge *(qāzī)* and market inspector *(muhtasib)* who enforce only the exoteric aspects of God's message through scrutinizing public conduct. The Magi priest does not represent Mazdean religiosity for Hafez but objectifies the untainted religious man, righteous because he truly believes and not because he is proselytizing or participating in a trend. Like the *rind*, he was not attached to a particular school or genealogy. And like the insignificant Magi priest in the Muslim era, the *rind* did not seek power and so was beyond scorn and disgrace. Hafez's religiosity veers toward the road of the *rinds*, the nonconformist carefree ascetic who breaks from all societal norms and formulates his own way of living as a pious Iranian Muslim.

Zarrinkub understands Hafez's religiosity as entailing a certainty that could not be acquired through reasoning, or argumentation. Belief for Hafez, as for many other Muslim mystics, emerges through seeing rather than knowing, or understanding intellectually and logically. Intuition and perception were linked to the ability to imagine the divine through inspiration and revelations that each believer had to experience on his own. This type of experience was imagined in different languages by a variety of mystics, whether Hafez, Dervish Khusraw, or Mulla Sadra. The particular ontological forms and significations of these experiences of union were being debated, and hostile attacks tended to paint the diversity and spectrum of sufism in early modern Iran with one brush, despite the many layers that came to coat sufi landscapes.

NUQTAVI MYSTICS AND SAFAVI MONARCHS

Some religious men who joined the Nuqtavis, like Dervish Khusraw, may have been in search of something other than the conformist turn that the institution of sufi brotherhoods had embarked on. While Dervish Khusraw traveled from place to place in search of a new life, he came across some Nuqtavis, whose doctrines he found attractive. *Siyāhat* (traveling) is a verb used in Islamicate discourse to describe the metaphysical journey of an individual into consciousness and union. It entailed leaving one's homeland to discover new landscapes, understanding oneself in the context of the other as one engages in comparison. We are not informed of the geographic direction in which Dervish Khusraw's travels took him when he left his native Qazvin. But we can assume from the later centers of Nuqtavi uprisings and persecutions that he must have either traveled north to the Caspian Sea region or directly south to central Iran (Iraqi-i Ajam), where Nuqtavi ideas had spread since the death of the founder Pasikhani. We are told that Dervish Khusraw spent time with the Nuqtavis and learned their ways *(shīvah)* and teachings. On his return to Qazvin, during the reign of Shah Tahmasb (1524–1576), he began living beside a mosque. There he attracted a group of dervishes, and in the pejorative language of chronicler Iskandar Bek Munshi Turkman, he opened a stall *(dukkān)* of theosophy *(ma'rifat)*.[87] Iskandar Bek remarks that this dervish was well known for his ability to mingle with all types of people.[88] His charisma and social skills aside, the environment seemed ripe for seekers of this path, for his fame grew to such an extent that Shi'i religious scholars became wary of his popularity. Along with the market inspector *(muhtasib)*, they denied Dervish Khusraw's teachings and forbade him to linger around the mosque.

Despite the threatening words of the *ulama*, Dervish Khusraw continued to reside by the mosque and attract Qazvinis to his company. The *ulama* must have voiced their complaints to Shah Tahmasb, who then summoned Dervish Khusraw and questioned him about his state *(ahvāl)*.[89] Once the dervish communicated the ordinances of Islam and the principles of the Imami faith, we are told, all accusations were repudiated. Since the Shah could not detect any outward deviation from the *shari'a*, the dervish was exonerated. Yet Shah Tahmasb heeded the demands of the men of religion and ordered that the dervish no longer "set up shop" by the mosque and that he refrain from attracting "half-witted folk." At this point, Shah Tahmasb did not perceive Dervish Khusraw as a political threat; otherwise, he would have executed him. This allows us to speculate that up until the last quarter of the sixteenth century, the Nuqtavis had not yet infiltrated the ranks of the Qizilbash, or at least Shah Tahmasb was not aware of such infiltration.[90] Moreover, it tells us that local dervish cults were not yet officially the target of attacks, as they would be a century later.[91]

It is true that Shah Tahmasb broke away from the image of his father Isma'il as messiah. But he did not abandon his mystical heritage. Shah Tahmasb left for us his *Memoir,* in which he attempts to portray his singularity through the medium of a first-person narrative in prose. This *Memoir* was a vehicle for Tahmasb to chisel a new image as pious Shi'i mystic king, distinct from that of his godlike father, Isma'il. Unlike his father, who claimed to be the messiah/God, Tahmasb positions himself within that comfortable distance of dreams that had become a recognized mystical medium of communicating with the divine, an accepted distance between the holy and the human. In limiting the universality of cosmic potentialities after the prophet Muhammad to particular revelatory mediums like dreams and to loci like the Imams and sufi masters, Tahmasb is also affirming the monotheistic position of one transcendent divinity as well as the centrality and finality of prophethood. As Tahmasb was breaking away from the *ghulāt* heritage of his father, he was taking yet a few more steps in the long process of the Islamization of Iranian world. He was also placing himself within the ontological debates of his age.

Tensions between these two faces of Islam (mystic versus rational) in which Tahmasb positioned himself were rife in the sixteenth century. The Nuqtavi Dervish Khusraw had been judged by his outward adherence to the *shari'a* (divine law) and his conformity to its prescribed norms. The "men of religion" *(ulama al-dīn)* in this period were attempting to enforce proper Islamic *(shar'i)* behavior through the office of the market inspector, with the support and patronage of the shah.[92] Dervish Khusraw's semblance of outer conformity seems to have been adequate. For some *ulama*, however, the fact that Dervish Khusraw had operated alongside a mosque, the domain reserved for the propagation of Imami rituals, was perceived as threatening. They had already begun to voice their discomfort with the often interchangeable paths of *shari'a* and *tarīqa*. The attraction of followers to an alternative quest toward God, presented by the dervish, jeopardized the endeavors of some clerics to convert the masses to a more legalistic (*shari'a*-minded) style of Imamism. Dervish Khusraw was conscious of the fact that to survive, he needed to conform outwardly to the norms established by the Imami theologians. "In order to allay their suspicions, he [Dervish

Khusraw] began to visit the *ulama,* studied jurisprudence *(fiqh),* and attended the Friday prayers at the Masjid-i Jami': nobody had any business with him any longer"[93]

But outer conformity to the *shari'a* did not protect all Nuqtavi devotees in this period. A famous poet of Shah Tahmasb's court, Abul Qasim Amiri, in 1565, was suspected of being a Nuqtavi and blinded on the order of Shah Tahmasb. The fate of rebelling members of the Safavi household, if they were not imprisoned or killed, was that of losing their eyesight, a symbolic punishment that disqualified an individual from temporal rule. Islamic norms of sovereignty dictated that the ruler be healthy, both ethically and physically, and the inability to see was deemed a physical handicap. Abul Qasim Amiri belonged to a landed family of Iranian notables from the vicinity of Isfahan (Virkupay). His older brother, Mowlana Abū Turab, was a famous calligrapher at the court of Shah Tahmasb. We are informed that on his brother's death (1565 or 1566) Shah Tahmasb blinded Abul Qasim.[94]

Shaykh Abul Qasim was a religious man, a philosopher poet.[95] He was trained in some of the "religious sciences" like mathematics, mysticism, and the occult *('ulūm-i gharībah, jafr, 'adad, harf va nuqta).*[96] His studies did not include those sciences necessary to become a jurisconsult, however. What seems to have been threatening about Shaykh Abul Qasim was his religious style, which impinged on a rationalist school of thought. But despite Shaykh Abul Qasim's emphasis on mysticism, philosophy, and alchemy, he had a large following among a variety of religious men *(fuzala va ulama).* Poets and dervishes respected him and would visit him, seeking insight and companionship *(suhbat).*[97] In a sympathetic biography of poets—'*Urafat al-'ashiqīn*—Shaykh Abul Qasim is said to have been falsely accused by "evil" ones who "exaggerated" *(gazāfah)* about him to Shah Tahmasb, accusing him of planning a rebellion *(khurūj)* and aspiring to rule politically. Once there is the threat of conjoining the temporal and the spiritual, Safavi dominion is threatened and hence the suppression of these types of movements.

But what is also at issue here is the tension between the two faces of Islam, the mystically minded and the *shari'a*-minded tendencies. As the *shari'a*-minded are tempted to restrict the variety of possibilities of experiencing Islam, particular acts of meaning production unfold, revealing the attitudes of these image makers and the heterogeneous nature of what is being negotiated.

The case of Shaykh Abul Qasim demonstrates that the Nuqtavis were loosely organized; there was not one single spiritual guide, for he was a contemporary of Dervish Khusraw. Nor was there one variety of Nuqtavi experience and meaning. It also shows that literate men, learned in a variety of sciences and respected by the *ulama*, were attracted to the Nuqtavi worldview. It is not as the chroniclers would like us to believe—that only the ignorant and the illiterate *(avvām va jāhil)* were captivated by Nuqtavi ways. After all, Shah Abbas I himself seems to have been fascinated by them. The famous Mughal courtier, Abul Fazl 'Allami, had also been enchanted by Nuqtavi cosmology, which inspired his patron king Akbar's (r. 1556–1605) universalist religiosity *(dīn-i ilāhī)*. Whom the chroniclers identified as "illiterate" and what they came to label as "magic" had nothing to do with literacy. It had to do rather with a different style of piety. Some pious Muslims like Shaykh Abul Qasim combined mysticism, philosophy, and alchemy and expressed their devotion through their poetry. Moreover, local and regional authorities were closely linked through informal networks of mystical circles and spiritual guides deemed repositories of temporal authority.

The Safavi case falls into this category. A variety of believers from diverse social milieus were attracted to the *mentalité* of the Nuqtavis. Abul Qasim Amiri seems to be closer to a Nizami, the poet prophet who through his poetry reveals knowledge of the unseen as prophets reveal scripture. But there is a fine line here between being perceived as acting through God and acting independently and some Nuqtavis, like Yusufi the quiver maker, seem to have claimed. Amiri tries to explain this difference to the shah. From his retreat in his native *(vatan-i asli)* village near Isfahan, he writes a poem addressed to Shah Tahmasb about this incident:

> The one who calls me a poet and a magician does so out of ignorance.
> He cannot distinguish God from our Iranian kings [*Kayanis*].
> What does philosophy of unity [*'ilm-i tawhīd*] have to do with magic [*sihr*] and numbers [*a'dād*]?
> What is the connection between the sand from Kashan and kohl from Isfahan?[98]

In the enduring debate over the holy a classification of licit and illicit magic was being forged. An affinity between poetry and magic (alchemy) is revealed in this process of canonization. The creative act is central to this discussion, whether it entailed fashioning the universe, a beautiful poem, a painting, or a song. Medieval Islamdom viewed the arts as emulating creation, each through particular sensory mediums that stimulated sensual responses. Artists were believed to be endowed with a special power and ability to perform miracles in the way that they could mirror the magnificence of creation. The ability to capture that splendor was deemed to be magic, through words strung together in poetry that aroused emotions or colored images that constructed realities. Power to stimulate imagination, motion, and life through words, paint, or sound (vocal and instrumental) elevated the artist in the eyes of Muslims to the status of a prophet or a saint. Nizami considered himself a prophet poet: "The magic of my speech is so accomplished that I am called 'mirror of the invisible.'"[99] But Nizami only claimed to be the mirror that acted as a reflection of God's beauty. Some mystics like Rumi used an alchemical epistemology to describe man's experience along the path of communion with God:[100]

> From myself I am copper, through you, gold.
> From myself I am a stone, through you, a pearl.[101]

Other poet mystics, like Shah Isma'il, proclaimed that they were divine—not acting through God or through his divine manifestation but partaking directly in God's divinity:

> I am God's eye [or "God himself"]; come now,
> O blind man gone astray, to behold truth [God]
> I am the absolute doer of whom they speak.
> Sun and moon are in my power.[102]

What Abul Qasim Amiri is responding to is a conflation between these different ontologies and epistemologies of union with God and to a diversity of equations in which human and holy were related to one another. Amiri was also responding to the conflation of the philosopher's view of the unity of being *(tawhīd)* with magic *(sihr)*. The poetry of Nizami came to be considered as licit magic, primarily because Nizami was a Muslim monotheist who believed that it was through the grace of God that he composed such ingenious verse. But even the legitimacy of Rumi would be questioned in the oppressive discourse produced in the seventeenth century. Amiri was also a monotheist; in his poem he reproaches his ignorant detractors for confusing magic with the neoplatonic philosophy of emanation and unity of being (Ibn-i 'Arabi). It was God's beauty reflected in nature that some poets and painters were attempting to imitate. Amiri was striving to separate those like himself who believed that they were working through God and those "magicians" who believed that they were acting independently through nature. Amiri, like Natanzi the Safavi chronicler, viewed this latter group as heretics and as satanic beings. But unlike Natanzi and the "evil" ones who had accused Amiri of magic, Amiri did not view all alchemists as magicians. Abul Qasim Amiri had a more nuanced view of licit and illicit magic.

In Arabic, the word *sihr,* or "magic," denotes a form of exposing or unveiling of true nature. And here is where *sihr* shares with gnosticism the metaphor of a hidden knowledge, of cosmic secrets that the individual hopes to attain and then to unveil as universal truths. For philosophers *(hukamā)* and alchemists, nature was composed of four elements—fire, water, air, earth. Whether the human body, a plant, or a metal, all matter was seen as a different mixture of these four basic elements. The purest compounds were those that came closest to a harmonious combination of these elements. Harmony was central to this worldview, in which universal and human euphony were believed to reflect one another: the purest compound was analogous to the perfect individual. Chemical and spiritual transformations were understood as following parallel patterns of change, and so basic ruling principles underlying the repetitive circular motions of cosmic objects were understood to have an effect on human fate and history. Astronomy, geometry, algebra, and alchemy were used as mathematical tools to calculate these celestial patterns, adducing an ontological rationality of the universe that allowed for the building of a cohesive science of the cosmos.[103] The circular motions of heavenly objects and the fourfold nature of elements were used as frameworks through which harmony could be created on earth. Geometric principles of dimension and proportion together with astronomic patterns reflected themselves in the structure of poetry, architecture, painting, and music—arts in which a harmonious equilibrium of proportions *(tanāsub)* and symmetry *(i'tidāl)* are central.[104]

The alchemist, the artist, and the philosopher all share the wisdom of cosmic principles. What seems to differentiate them is the way in which knowledge of proportions, symmetry, and pattern is applied and awarded different signification. Some alchemists actually put this knowledge into practice, whereas others used this knowledge symbolically, as metaphors in their poetry, as proportions that informed their designs of mosques, or as artistry in their miniature paintings. Here we are reminded of Hafez's criticism of philosophers who limit their understanding of creation to knowledge and proof of God's existence. For philosophers who avoided the mystical dimension of being, God could not be experienced directly, but his existence had to be demonstrated theologically and rationally. Alchemists practiced this knowledge as chemists and doctors who attempted to control forces of nature and bend them to human ends for the purpose of finding cures and remedies (pharmacopoeia) but also for the purpose of purifying substances to their highest possible degree as a means of unraveling human and cosmic secrets. In their search for ways of transmutating one substance into another, alchemists applied the concept that all existence is built of the same elemental substances and principles, whether material or spiritual. All universal processes were seen to repeat themselves in matter; thus, the one who attained recipes of chemical procedures, often developed by craftsmen through their work with metals, could access these secrets directly. The distinction between those who used the knowledge of chemical and physical processes symbolically, allegorically, or practically to mimic creation or to create independently of God were blurred. Some, like Pasikhani, used this knowledge to claim that God was the same as the four elements and that he (Pasikhani) was the purest compound *(murakkab-i mubīn)* and hence was God and the truth. But when Hafez says, "I am the magic poet who by the incantation of my word strews sugar and candy from my pen," he is emulating creation metaphorically through magic. Some of his audience may have viewed his poetry as mental alchemy, and others as satanic.[105] Hafez distinguished his religiosity from that of the philosophers, moving closer to the way of the mystic, in that he partook in the experience of inspiration and revelation expressed through his poetry.

The coalescing and sundering of alchemical, mystical, and philosophical spheres is an old impulse that reemerges in the early modern period to be severed from each other in seventeenth-century Safavi Iran. They have precursors in attacks on Hallaj (d. 922), Yahya Suhravardi (d. 1191), and Ibn-i 'Arabi (d. 1240). By the early modern period when Ibn-i 'Arabi's monism was hegemonic in the central and eastern lands of Islamdom, some—like Mahmud Pasikhani, Muhammad Nurbakhsh (d. 1464), Isma'il Safavi (d. 1524), and Ustad Yusufi Tarkishduz (d. 1593)—practiced it and claimed divinity. Other sufis—like 'Ala Al-Dawla Simnani—vehemently rejected monism. Simnani's ontology construed divine self-manifestation as occurring only through intermediaries who acted as mirrors of the divine, active witnesses of his essence. Simnani dismisses the possibility of an ontological union between God and the human being as he attempts doctrinally to remove any possibility of divine incarnation *(hulūl)*. He challenges the concept of the perfect human being *(insān-i kāmil)* as microcosm of the universe, which had through Ibn-i 'Arabi's philosophy crystallized its cosmic position. In limiting the universality of cosmic potentialities to particular revelatory spokesmen who must be called saints after the prophet Muhammad, Simnani was defining the Muslim monotheistic position. This is the ontology Shah Tahmasb embraced in his *Memoir* as a Muslim king and friend of God *(valī)*. But in the fourteenth century, Simnani's correspondence with Kashani placed him among Ibn-i 'Arabi's critics, in an environment in which the concept of *wahdat al-wujūd* (monism) was both fashionable and hegemonic. The two, however, continued to communicate with one another and deliberated; for the next few generations, Simnani's rationalized sufism would remain in the margins. It was out of tempo with the mood of Iran, Iraq, and Anatolia. It is the blend of Alid, sufi, and *ghulāt* ideas that found articulation in revolutionary movements (Sarbidars, Nurbakhshiyya, Musha'sha') like the Safavis, which attracted believers to their teachings. These movements evoked a late antique way of imagining the cosmos and being, one that Simnani in his monotheism was attempting to supplant with his emphasis on the centrality of one transcendent God and the finality of prophecy after Muhammad. Despite his distancing of heaven from earth, Simnani envisioned the existence of a spiritual guide in every age who reflected the divine for the human. Saints, those special men who could transcend the seven subtle substances *(latā'if)* to attain the ultimate level of I-ness *(al-latīfa al-anā'iyya)*, could actively witness the divine essence. Hence the necessity of a living master and the continuous role of mystical guides who inherited from prophets the station of cosmic axis without which the world would cease to exist. Shah Tahmasb in his *Memoir* imagined himself as one such saint. His visits to the shrine of Simnani signaled his reverence for a new sufi master in the genealogy of the Safavis. Unlike his father, who claimed divinity itself, Shah Tahmasb claimed only to act as divinity's mirror. With the suppression of the Nuqtavis by Tahmasb's grandson's (Abbas I), the Safavis' break with their *ghulāt* past was institutionalized.

The popularity of the Nuqtavis had spread among the Qazvinis *(Turk u Tajik)* during the decade of the second civil war (1576–1590), between the death of Shah Tahmasb and the accession of Shah Abbas I (1587). After Shah Tahmasb's death, Dervish Khusraw built a lodge *(nishīman)* located by his house. There, Turks and Iranians from near and far are reported to have flocked to his cloister *(takkiya)*.[106] Two hundred devotees were said to have congregated daily in his lodge. He engaged with people from every walk of life, spiritual proclivity rather than social rank being the determining factor.[107] We are told that before Shah Abbas I's accession (1587), Dervish Khusraw together with his disciples had spent some years in the lodge, preparing enough food for their subsistence and free from trouble and disturbance.[108] According to the chronicler Natanzi, at this stage in the growth of Dervish Khusraw's movement, it did not appear as though he had acted contrary to the *shari'a*. It was not until the number of his disciples had grown to such an extent that he enjoyed real influence among the people that he was officially perceived as diverging from the prescribed rituals *(adab)* of the *shari'a*. It is only then that the Safavi household developed a real interest in Dervish Khusraw. His fame is said to have grown so that his lodge could no longer contain his followers, and so denizens of his district *(mahalah)* helped Dervish Khusraw build a bigger cloister *(takkiya)*.[109]

From the small sampling of biographical information we possess on approximately twenty Nuqtavi devotees, a sense of their diverse social and ethnic variety emerges. The chroniclers note the mixed ethnic composition of Nuqtavi followers, stating that some Turkmen Qizilbash (Ustajlu and Shamlu) joined the

Nuqtavi ranks as well as Iranians. During the revolutionary phase (1447–1501) of the Safavi movement, the Qizilbash, composed mainly of Turkmen converts to the Safavi cause, had organized themselves militarily into *oymaqs*, a Mongol term loosely translated as "tribe." In the imperial era (1501–1722), however, the Safavis attempted to contain the revolutionary fervor that had won them temporal power. The erosion of Qizilbash Islam was gradual; a long and bloody struggle involving two civil wars (1524–1536 and 1576–1590) had to be fought before the Safavis became true Shahs, for they were politically dependent on the Qizilbash. Loyalty to the Safavi house and to their visionary cause initially had won the Qizilbash a monopoly over positions at court, in the provinces, and in the military. Now Caucasian slaves *(ghulām)* were introduced to supplant the Qizilbash. For the Qizilbash to embrace a Nuqtavi master who aspired to take on temporal power was a religious expression of political rebellion. As some Qizilbash were being denied access to their traditional channels of livelihood, locally as well as at court, they were led or perhaps chose to doubt their devotion toward their Safavi master. The Nuqtavis seem to be the first recorded *ghulāt* movement since the Safavi revolution to have enjoyed a wide following among the Qizilbash, in particular, among prominent dignitaries at court.[110] As the Safavis betrayed the Qizilbash, some Qizilbash revolted against them, using a language that preserved elements forged by the spiritual landscape of Qizilbash Islam, a language that portrays the intimate interplay between the spiritual and the temporal in Safavi Iran. Those Qizilbash who embraced Nuqtavi beliefs aimed at reinstituting sufi and steppe paradigms of authority that had originally given meaning to the relationship between the Qizilbash disciples and their Safavi masters.

Most of the available biographical information concerns individual Iranian Nuqtavis. This may be due to their being artists, like Abul Qasim Amiri, or poets, painters, and calligraphers. Their names are recorded in the well-established genre of biographical dictionaries, the "who's who" of the literati, cherished for their art of poetry. Unlike the medieval genre of biographies of religious men *(rijāl)* that grew out of a need to verify the reliability of transmitters of hadith, biographies of poets were compiled as a sign of respect toward a cultural elite who engaged in poetry, one of the most valued forms of art. That many followers of the Nuqtavis were poets or calligraphers who recited poetry worth noting for posterity in these *tazkire(s)* (biographies) is revealing. The arts and crafts dominate the professional occupations of most of the known non-Qizilbash Nuqtavi devotees. Craftsmen were linked to chivalric circles, which, as we shall see, were arenas of resistance where Muslim, Mazdeans, Armenians, and Jews created communal bonds of solidarity. Nuqtavi devotees were either poets, calligraphers, craftsmen such as quiver makers, musicians, or storytellers. Abul Qasim Amiri's artistic training, for instance, entailed a knowledge of sciences—mathematics, alchemy, philosophy *(hikmat)*, and mysticism *(tasawwuf)*. Some Nuqtavis were also trained in astrology *(nujūm)* and magic *(ramal)*.[111] Others are identified with the life of the wandering mystic *(qalandar* and *rind)*. In this early modern period, the mystical path was an option, a way of life that some embarked on as a profession. Dervish Khusraw, for example, decided to break with his forefathers' occupation of digging wells and chose to wander in search of spiritual nourishment. Ultimately, this became his way of earning a living. For numerous young men of the time, the mystical path offered a way of breaking free from social positions inherited at birth. Another devotee, Mir Ali Akbar (whose pen name was *tashbīhī*, or metaphor), was a *sayyid* from Kashan whose father was a laundryman *(gāzurī)*. For others born into riches, the arts together with the dervish path allowed them to bequeath their wealth to charity or leave it behind to lead the life of an ascetic virtuoso. The example of Abul Qasim Amiri is a case in point.

Both social and ethnic hierarchies seem to be blurred in the dervish cult. With the universalism that permeates Nuqtavi writings, there is an emphasis on the sameness of the human being whether Arab or Iranian. A dualist perception is manifest in the way in which Nuqtavis differentiated Arabs and Persians—more specifically, descendants of the prophet *(sayyid)* and those not possessing a Qurayshi pedigree *(sādah)*: "Whoever are Persians [Ajam] are from the family of Arabs. Whoever is unadorned with this genealogy [*sādah*] is of the family of the prophet [*sayyid*]."[112] Although some devotees of the Nuqtavis are of *sayyid* lineage, there seems to be an underlying social egalitarianism pervading Nuqtavi thought. We shall enter into the importance of Alid lineage among spiritual fraternities *(futuvvat)* in the next chapter; for now it is important to highlight that the geographical regions from which the Nuqtavis emerged were either in the central lands of the Iranian world (Isfahan, Kashan, Yazd) or in the northern Caspian Sea region, the birthplace of the founder of the Nuqtavi movement (Gilan, Amul). These are old centers of Iranian civilization. The nexus of social, professional, scientific, and geographic backgrounds of Nuqtavi devotees confirms the hypothesis that poetry and astrology were two main arteries through which Persianate ideas flowed into and found continuity of expression in early modern Safavi Iran. The egalitarian principles of the Nuqtavis were, of course, attractive to an impoverished sayyid, Persian well digger, or betrayed Qizilbash Turkmen.

News of Dervish Khusraw's popularity must have reached Shah Abbas I, who paid him a visit.[113] In time, they developed a close companionship *(suhbat)*.[114] The chroniclers would like the reader to believe that the Shah subsequently frequented the Nuqtavi cloister in Qazvin and inquired about the disciples *(arbāb-i sulūk)*, only to become acquainted with Dervish Khusraw's ways. The shah is said to have pretended to be an adept and engaged in the rituals of the *takkiya*, offering Dervish Khusraw cash and goods. It is said that following Abbas I's example, many generals (Qizilbash) and high functionaries *(arkān-i dawlat)* also visited him. The dervish, "due to his eloquence," charmed the courtiers. They too became his disciples and offered him inlaid daggers and other precious gifts in devotion and respect.[115]

Dervish Khusraw continued to practice prudence, however, and remained firm in his determination not to utter any words against the *shari'a* so that he would not lose his cloister.[116] His discussions with the shah exposed the way of attaining knowledge of God in accordance to dervish practice.[117] But the truth was soon disclosed. A dervish who enjoyed high standing in his companionship *(suhbat)* divulged the secret nature of Nuqtavi doctrines. The master quiver maker Yusufi had been awarded the special spiritual rank of vice regent *(nā'ib)* and trustee *(amīn)* by his master.[118] Yusufi of Khurasan was also a craftsman, a quiver maker, and because of the Shah's regard for that art, he commissioned Yusufi to make him some quivers. Every time Yusufi came to deliver his handiwork at court, the two would engage in conversations. We are told that the shah spoke with him to obtain privileged information. Yusufi, thinking that the shah had actually been converted to Nuqtavism, trusted his friendly gestures and revealed their secret faith to Shah Abbas I in confidence.[119] A special relationship must have developed between the two for Ustad Yusufi to have divulged the secret mysteries of the Nuqtavis. Yusufi must have felt that Abbas I would embrace their claims and that their veiled secrets, shared by a spiritually select circle of disciples, would be safe with the shah. Although the chronicles claim that Shah Abbas I played the role of a disciple to discover the Nuqtavis' true beliefs, Mobed Shah, writing in the mid-seventeenth century in India, states that an exiled Nuqtavi "trustee" *(amīn)* had told him that, in fact, the Nuqtavis regarded the shah as a "perfect trustee" *(amīn-i kāmil)*.[120] As we have seen in the opening episode of this book, the way in which Shah Abbas I came to deal the Nuqtavi cabalistic predictions points to his enchantment with their doctrines.

The development of an intimate camaraderie between Shah Abbas I and Ustad Yusufi sheds light on two arenas in which bonds of loyalty could be nurtured between "high" and "low," spiritual and temporal, courtly and local, elements in Safavi culture. The sufi hermitage was a space in which, say, a shoemaker could engage in and share a language of secrecy with a sufi master as well as a high-ranking court dignitary. The crafts and the cultivated relationship between an artist and his royal patron represent a second medium through which Yusufi communicated in private with the shah. A whole fellowship of trust and confidence must have developed. Ustad Yusufi's art of quiver making had afforded him special access to the shah, and the example of Yusufi shows how ties could be forged between artists and their royal patrons at the Safavi court. To cite an earlier example, two painters, Ali Asghar and 'Abd al-Aziz, had abducted Shah Tahmasb's favorite page, and to facilitate their escape they had forged the shah's seal.[121] For these two painters to have had access to an adored page at court and to the shah's seal symbolizes proximity to and participation in the most private aspects of Shah Tahmasb's life at court. The association between Ustad Yusufi and Abbas I was perhaps similar to that which existed between Isma'il and his charmed circle of sufi guides who helped organize the Safavi revolution: Lalé Bek, Dede Bek, and Khalifa Bek. In generating a language of secrecy among a spiritually privileged circle of devotees, an alternate reality, a particular way of being and sensing time, was shaped and passed down from master to disciple. Along with their individual commentaries on literary texts (treatise and poetry), they were components of an oral and yet secret knowledge with which masters enlightened their disciples. This alternate sense of reality was their utopia. And when a master like Yusufi, a beholder of such secrets, willed to unveil them, he desired to move beyond the Nuqtavi cosmos as a space to visit in cloisters. He ventured instead to create such an abode in every moment of his existence.

We have discussed some features of Nuqtavi gnosis. Let us now focus on praxis and explore the ways in which Pasikhani's writings were understood and experienced by Nuqtavi believers a century after his death. Yusufi Tarkishduz disclosed to Abbas I the forecast that on the advent of the Muslim New Year (Muharram 1002/1593), a Nuqtavi dervish who had attained unity with God would convert his rank of spiritual monarchy *(saltanat-i ma'navī)* into that of formal sovereignty *(pādishāhi-yi sūrī).*[122] Yusufi believed in divinity on earth, sharing with philosopher poets like Abul Qasim Amiri the notion of the unity of existence, both material and spiritual. Yusufi probably embraced Pasikhani's alchemical view that all existence pervades the four elements, that God is not of a different substance, and that all beings can therefore attain the divine, that purest form, within themselves. Here lies one way of understanding *hulūl,* or divine incarnation, a prominent feature of *ghuluww.*

Three years after the suppression of the Nuqtavis, during a symbolic pilgrimage on foot, Shah Abbas I visited the holy shrine of the eighth Imam Reza in Mashad—a pious journey during which he encountered two Nuqtavis. Dervish Kamal is reported to have questioned Shah Abbas I about the act of holy pilgrimage to a dead man's grave. "Seek the live Imam," the dervish is thought to have said. And when Shah Abbas asked him who this Imam might be, Dervish Kamal responded, "Me." The shah challenged the claim of Dervish Kamal, questioning his divinity: "Let me see if you survive a bullet," to which Dervish Kamal responded sarcastically, "Your Imam Reza died with a [poisonous] grape; you expect me to survive a bullet?"[123] Here Dervish Kamal exposes the inconsistency of Abbas I's belief: the parodox of Nuqtavi and Safavi doctrines of divine incarnation *(hulūl)* is disclosed in this episode. Shah Abbas was engaging in a public act of devotion to a descendant of Muhammad (Imam) who had been sanctified as divine centuries earlier by some Alids and who continued to be clothed in a holy shroud by some Imami Shi'is *(mufawwida).* Shah Abbas's pilgrimage was in veneration of a dead yet holy Imam. Although Dervish Kamal was not of Alid lineage, he claimed sanctity. But the Safavis patronized a "cult of Imams," as they came to limit contact between the holy and the human to the sacred space of a tomb, the site of "the joining of heaven and earth."[124] Notions of holiness that had come to sanctify some holy men in the past no longer applied in the new age of Shah Abbas I as he consolidated one particular Alid lineage, and one genealogy of beliefs. Like the *shari'a*-minded ulama, his survival was linked to a move away from past beliefs.

Another precept *tanāsukh,* or reincarnation, espoused by the Nuqtavis was also expressed by Dervish Kuchak Qalandar, a prominent member of this group. He was a Nuqtavi disciple who chose to take his own life by drinking poison. The Safavi chronicler Iskandar Bek Munshi Turkman states that Dervish Kuchak told his guards, probably immediately before he drank the poison, "We have gone only to be back in the next cycle. Went and went and went the one who went."[125] There is no fear of dying, for Darvish Kuchak is certain that he will return to this world. Iskandar Bek states that essays on the doctrine of the Nuqtavis (*'ulūm-i nuqtah*) were found among the books of a disciple, Mir Ahmad Kashi. According to the chronicler, the Nuqtavis "did not believe in resurrection (*hashr*) and the resurrecting bodies (*ajsād-i qiyāmat*)."[126] They saw the retribution for good and evil acts in the prosperity and destitution of this world. They considered heaven and hell as one. Their gnostic beliefs were also manifest in their espousal of the idea that recompense for enjoining the good and forbidding the evil would occur in this world. The revelations made by prominent Nuqtavi disciples during their trials further reveal their particular beliefs in reincarnation (*tanāsukh*). During his trip to Isfahan (winter 1593–1594), the shah camped out in Kashan, where Mir Ahmad Kashi had been imprisoned. The shah threatened to kill him, and Mir Ahmad responded, "We are not afraid of dying, for once we die, we shall return shortly thereafter in a better form. And every time I come and go, I attain a different perfection. For instance, 320 years ago [1273], I appeared as a beautiful youth and wrote calligraphy so well that everyone praised me. By chance, I recently came across a piece of my calligraphy."[127] Remembrance of past existences resonates with Pasikhani's notion that old souls maintain their unity of spirit and experience, despite their material transformations. A Nuqtavi, Zamani Yazdi (d. 1608–1609 or 1612–1613), believed that he was the famous medieval poet Nizami Ganjavi. He is said to have taken his poetry to Shah Abbas I, presenting it as a reply to Nizami; the shah is then reported to have asked of him: "And how are you going to respond to God?"[128] Clearly, the shah and Yazdi where expressing two very different religious sensibilities, one monotheist and the other reincarnationist. Yazdi's sense of being is encapsulated in his pen name, *rāhguzar-i zamānī*, or "the traveler in time." He wrote:

> In Ganja [Nizami's birthplace] I died in search of seeing [truth].
> In Yazd I arose like the sun.[129]

Imagine how different we would be as individuals if we thought and experienced life cyclically like Zamani Yazdi, "the traveler in time." Here is where we have to take an imaginative leap beyond Safavi attempts to cast such ideas as "satanic" or "irrational" prejudices that are closer to our modern sensibilities than we might like to think. And it is in the name of religion, of one monotheistic God and his divine legislation, that Shah Abbas I and his official historians justified the Nuqtavi suppression. The impact of such a suppression on the individual denizens of Safavi Iran who lingered in a late antique rhythm of time and being was not absolute, for religious movements continued to voice *ghuluww* at the cultural margins, in the form of new incarnations like the Babis. Before we enter the social and cultural dynamics of the absolutist Isfahani era of Safavi rule (in part 3), let us first explore the *ghuluww* of Safavi devotees (Alid) by comparing it to the worldview of the Nuqtavis. And let us not forget the ease with which some Qizilbash could transfer their allegiance to the Nuqtavis and enter their cosmos.

NOTES

1. Sādiq Kiyā, "Nuqtaviyān yā Pasikhāniyān," *Iran Kudeh* 13 (1941): 94.
2. Ibid., 93.
3. Ibid., 20.
4. Ibid., 95.

5. The Qur'an is considered by Muslims to be God's word, a copy of God's scripture contained in a preexistent heavenly tablet *(lawh-i mahfūz)*. See Qur'an 85:22.

6. Kiyā, "Nuqtaviyān yā Paskhāniyān," 32, citing the *Tazkīrat al-a'imma,* by Muhammad Baqir Lahiji.

7. Rabbi Yehudah Ben El'Azar, *Duties of Judah,* ed. and trans. Amnon Netzer (Jerusalem: Ben Zvi Institute, 1995), 250. I would like to thank Vera Moreen Bosch for providing me with this reference as well as for transliterating the passage from Judeo-Persian to the Persian alphabet. For a seminal study of the Kabbalists, see Gershom Sholem, *Kabbalah* (New York: Meridian, 1978).

8. Ibid.

9. Gregory Shaw, *Theurgy and the Soul: The Neoplatonism of Iamblichus* (University Park: Pennsylvania State University Press, 1995), 16. Shaw demonstrates how Iamblichus uses Pythagorean mathematics to overcome the duality of spirit and matter on a cosmic level. Here lies an example from the Roman world of late antiquity of the preoccupation of some thinkers with rejoining the human and the divine at a moment when the two were being forced apart. I would like to thank Peter Brown for having recommended this insightful work to me.

10. Ibid., 1–2.

11. Ibid., 3.

12. Ibid., 3–4.

13. Kiyā, "Nuqtavihān yā Pasikhāniyān," 19, quoting from the *Dabistān al-mazāhib.*

14. Mobed Shah, *Dabistān al-mazāhib,* ed. Rahīm Rezāzādah-yi Malik (Tehran: Kitābkhānah-ī Tahūrī, 1983–1984), 274.

15. Ibid., 273.

16. *"Az Muhammad gurīz dar Mahmud kandar ān kāst va andarīn afzūd."*

17. Kiyā, "Nuqtaviyān," 24, citing Muhammad b. Mahmūd Dīhdār Shirazi, *Nafā'is al-arqām,* MS Majlis Library, Majmu'a #2078, 545, 1391.

18. Kiyā, "Nuqtaviyān," 25, citing Muhammad b. Muhammad Dihdār-i Shirāzī, *Durr-i yatīm,* MS Majlis Majmu'a #1381, 2087.

19. Muhammad Ali Amir-Moezzi, *The Divine Guide in Early Shi'ism: The Sources of Esotericism in Islam* (Albany: State University of New York Press, 1994), 51, makes this connection be-

tween sufi renderings of the colored lights to articulate their notions of the subtle centers of the heart, with early esoteric Imami thought.

20. Mobed *Dabistān al-mazāhib*, 275.
21. Ibid., 275.
22. Kiyā, "Nuqtaviyān" 98–100.
23. James Russell, "Mysticism and Esotericism among Zoroastrians," *Iranian Studies* 26 (1993): 85. The exaltation of an epic hero to a lofty position of spiritual importance is emblematic of the Persianate ethos. Russell cites Shaul Shaked, trans. and ed., *The Wisdom of the Sasanian Sages: Denkard VI* (Colorado: Westview Press, 1979), xxxix, who "observes that it is common for Persian wisdom literature to endow traditional themes with an allegorical religious sense. But Abū Salik Gorgani [900 c.e.] would have none of it. He wrote, "Idolatry is better than the worship of men" [*But parastīdan beh az mardum parastīst*], with the Persian hero-cult in mind."
24. Shaw, *Theurgy and the Soul*, 201.
25. Mulla Sadra defined idol worshipers in his *Kasr al-asnām al-jāhiliyya* as the *ghulāt*, and he tried to distinguish the sufi from the *ghālī*. Rationalist attacks would paint them all with one brush.
26. Mobed, *Dabistan al-mazāhib*, 275.
27. Richard Walzer, "al-Biruni and Idolatry," in *Commémoration Cyrus: Actes du Congrés de Shiraz 1971 et Autres Etudes Redigés a l'Occasion du 2500e Anniversaire de la Fondation de L'Empire Perse* (Leiden: Brill, 1974).
28. Ibid.
29. Mobed, *Dabistān al-mazāhib*, 276.
30. Roy Mottahedeh, "Some Islamic Views of the Pre-Islamic Past," *Harvard Middle Eastern and Islamic Review* 1 (1994): 25.
31. Ibid., 24–25.
32. Sādiq Kiyā *Vazhahāmah-yi Gurgānī* (Tehran: Dānishgāh-i Tehran, 1951), on the Hurufis and Nuqtavis.
33. Mobed, *Dabistān al-mazāhib*, 274: "*Anā wa Ali min nūrin vāhidin wa lahmuka lahmī wa jismuka jismī.*"
34. Shah Tahmasb Safavi, *Tazkire-yi Shah Tahmasb*, ed. D. C. Phillott (Calcutta: Asiatic Society, 1912), 49–51.

35. Mobed, *Dabistān al-mazāhib*, 274.
36. Ibid., 276.
37. Kiyā, "Nuqtaviyān," 101.
38. H. P. L'Orange, *Studies on the Iconography of Cosmic Kingship in the Ancient World* (Cambridge: Harvard University Press, 1953), 10, 20–21.
39. Ibid., 37.
40. Guity Azarpay, "Crowns and Some Royal Insignia in Early Iran," *Iranica Antiqua* 9 (1972): 111–112.
41. Eric Hanne, "The Caliphate Revisited: The Abbasids of Eleventh and Twelfth-Century Baghdad," Ph.D. diss., University of Michigan, 1998, 17–18.
42. Orange, *Studies on the Iconography of Cosmic Kingship*, 87, citing Biruni.
43. See, for example, the Safavi zodiacal plate (date 971/1563) at the Berlin State Museum.
44. Geo Widengren, "The Sacral Kingship of Iran: *La Realita Sacra*," *Contributions to the Central Theme of the Eighth International Congress for the History of Religions* (Rome, April 1955) (Leiden: Brill, 1959), 245.
45. Iskandar Bek Munshi Turkman, *Tārīkh-i Alam Arā-yi 'Abbāsī*, 2 vols. (Tehran: Amīr Kabīr 1971), vol. 1, 347.
46. Kiyā "Nuqtaviyān," 77, citing an untitled Nuqtavi text.
47. Ibid., 81.
48. Ibid., 84.
49. Ibid.
50. Ibid., 77.
51. Mary Boyce, *Textual Sources for the Study of Zoroastrianism* (Chicago: University of Chicago Press, 1984), 20.
52. Kiyā, "Nuqtaviyān," 77, citing untitled Nuqtavi text.
53. Ibid.
54. Ibid., 81.
55. Ibid., 83.
56. Ibid.
57. Ibid., 86. Venus, for example is associated with the first caliph, Abu Bakr (d. 634), as well as with the jurist Shafi'i (d. 820). Mars is associated with the second caliph, 'Umar (d. 644), as well as with the jurist Abu Hanifa (d. 767).

58. Ibid., 84.
59. Ibid., 85.
60. Beyond Nuqtavi circles, there seems to have been a more general construction of such temperamental differences between Arabs and Persians. The Arab polymath al-Suyuti (d. 1505), writing in Mamluk Egypt, compares the Persian language with Arabic and says that revelation is articuated with softness in Persian and with harshness in Arabic. Cited in Shaul Shaked, "Some Iranian Themes in Islamic Literature," *From Zoroastrian Iran to Islam: Studies in Religious History and Intercultural Contacts* (Aldershot: Variorum, 1995), 149.
61. Azhang Ya'qūb, *Hurūfiyah dar Tārīkh* (Tehran: Nashr-i Nay, 1990–1991), 57.
62. Kiyā, "Nuqtaviyān," 85.
63. On the Sarbidars, see John M. Smith, *The History of the Sarbadār Dynasty, 1336–81, and Its Sources* (The Hague: Morton, 1970); T. Petrushevski, "Nahzat-i Sarbidārān," trans. Karīm Kishāvarz, *Farhang-i Irān Zamīn* 10 (1962); Jean Aubin, "La fin de l'etat Sarbidar du Khorassan," *Journal Asiatique* 262 (1974). On the Nurbakhshiya, see Bashir, "Between Mysticism and Messianism." On the Mush'asha', see Ahmad Kasravī, *Musha'sha'īyān* (3rd ed.) (Tehran: Intishārāt-i Sahar, 1977). On the Mar'ashis, see J. Calmard, *EI2*. For a preliminary comparison of these movements, see Bashir, "Between Mysticism and Messianism," ch. 1, "The Religious Guide in Late Medieval Shi'ism (ca. 1335–1500)."
64. Roy Mottahedeh, "The Shu'ūbīyah Controversy and the Social History of Early Islamic Iran," *International Journal of Middle Eastern Studies* 7 (1976): 161–182.
65. Ibid., 161.
66. Ibid., 164.
67. William Tucker, "Rebels and Gnostics: al-Mughīra Ibn Sa'īd and the Mughīriyya, *Arabica* 22 (1975): 33–47; Steve Wasserstrom, "The Moving Finger Writes: Mughīra b. Sa'īd's Islamic Gnosis and the Myths of Its Rejection," *History of Religions* 25 (1985), 1–29; Wassertrom, *Between Muslim and Jew: The Problem of Symbiosis under Early Islam* (Princeton: Princton University Press, 1995).

68. From Muhammad, Ali, and Muhammad b. Hanafiyya, to the Abbasid Ibrahim b. Muhammad, and then back to the Iranians with Abu Muslim.

69. Wilferd Madelung, *Religious Trends in Early Islamic Iran* (Albany, NY: Persian Heritage Foundation, 1988), 9–12. The term *mahdi* is used here in the lower case to refer to the concept of a generic messiah.

70. Mobed, *Dabistān al-mazāhib*, 273–274, 276.

71. The symbol of the western sun has apocalyptic resonance in Muslim eschatological thought and may be associated with Alexander (Dhul Qarnayn), who in some circles was depicted as the sun that rose in the west and set in the east. Ali Akbar Dihkhuda, *Lughatnāme*, 18 vols. (Tehran: Dānishgāh-i Tehran, 1960).

72. For initial efforts in this area, see Marijan Molé, "Les Kubrawiya entre Sunnisme et Shi'isme aux Huitième Siècle de l'Hégire," *Revue des Etudes Islamiques* 29 (1961, 61–142); Louis Massignon, *La Passion de Husayn b. Mansūr Hallāj: Martyr Mystique de l'Islam* (Paris: Gallimard, 1975); Kamil al-Shaibi, *Sufism and Shi'ism*, (Surbiton: LAAM, 1991).

73. Turkman, *Tārīkh-i 'Ālam Ārā-yi 'Abbāsī*, vol. 1, 473.

74. Marshall G. S. Hodgson, *The Venture of Islam: Conscience and History in a World Civilization* (Chicago: University of Chicago Press, 1974), vol. 2; Ahmet T. Karamustafa, *God's Unruly Friends Dervish Groups in Islamic Later Period, 1200–1550* (Salt Lake City: University of Utah Press, 1994).

75. Michael Bonner, *Aristocratic Violence and Holy War: Studies in the Jihad and the Arab-Byzantine Frontier* (New Haven, CT: American Oriental Society, 1996), 125–130.

76. Hodgson, *The Venture of Islam*, vol. 2.

77. For more on this process of the taming of Islamic egalitarianism, see Louise Marlow, *Hierarchy and Egalitarianism in Islamic Thought* (Cambridge: Cambridge University Press, 1997), pt. 2.

78. Kiyā, "Nuqtaviyān," 85, 93.

79. Ibid., 93.

80. Ibid.

81. Sa'di, *Gulistān-i Sa'dī*, ed. Ghulām Husayn Yūsufī (Tehran: Khwārazmī, 1989), 86.

82. Karamustafa, *God's Unruly Friends*, 52–56.

83. Abdul al-Husayn Zarrīnkūb, *Justujū dar Tasavvuf-i Irān* (Tehran: Amīr Kabīr, 1978), 372.
84. Karamustafa, *God's Unruly Friends*, 153.
85. Mobed Shah, *Dabistān al-mazāhib*, on Nuqtavi immigrants in India claiming that Hafez was a Nuqtavi devotee, 277.
86. Hāfiz, *Dīvān-i* Hāfiz, ed. Muhammad Qazvīnī, Qāsim Ghani, Abd al-Karīm Jurbuzahdār (Tehran: Asātīr, 1988), 463.
87. Turkman, *Tārīkh-i 'Ālam Ārā-yi 'Abbāsī*, vol. 1, 473.
88. Ibid.
89. Ibid.
90. Note that Tahmasb did, however, blind the poet Abul Qasim Amiri, a high-ranking Nuqtavi in 973/1565. He also carried out a large-scale purge in Kashan a decade later (981/1573–1574). B. S. Amoretti, "Religion in the Timurid and Safavid Periods," *Cambridge History of Iran*, ed. Peter Jackson and Larence Lockhart (Cambridge: Cambridge University Press, 1986), vol. 6, 645.
91. Although Said Arjomand argues that the Safavi attack on sufis and Sunnis began with the inception of Shah Ismai'l's rule and that the Naqshbandis were the first order to be "ferociously suppressed." *The Shadow of God and the Hidden Imam: Religion, Political Order, and Societal Change in Shi-ite Iran from the Beginning to 1890* (Chicago: University of Chicago Press, 1984), 109–121, Dina Le Gall's dissertation on the Naqshbandis demonstrates that some Naqshbandi shaykhs like Sun'ullah Kuzakunani, the founder of the Naqshbandi *takkiya* in Tabriz, lived there unharmed up to the turn of the seventeenth century. Dina Le Gall, "The Ottoman Naqshbandiyya in the Pre-Mujaddidī Phase: A Study in Islamic Religious Culture and Its Transmission," Ph.D. diss., Princeton University, 1989, 22–31. Studies on particular sufis in their local Safavi contexts need to be conducted before any further generalizations are made.
92. See Sayyid Husayn Modarresi Tabātabā'ī, *An Introduction to Shi'i Law: A Bibliographical Study* (London: Ithaca Press 1984), 50.
93. Turkman, *Tārīkh-i 'Ālam Ārā-yi 'Abbāsi*, vol. 1, 474.
94. Kiyā, "Nuqtaviyān," 59, quoting from a biography of poets *'Urafāt al-'ashiqīn*, written by Taqī al-din Awhadī Baliyānī in the first half of seventeenth century. I would like to thank Setrag

Manoukian for providing me with the relevant folios from the Bankipore Manuscript.

95. Ibid., 63.
96. Ibid., 59.
97. Ibid., 65.
98. Ibid., 66–67. Shah Tahmasb must have been touched by this poem, for he is said to have forgiven Amiri, returned to him the confiscated lands, and placed him on a yearly payroll of thirty tumans. Amiri's name reemerges with the Nuqtavi rebellion under Abbas I. This time he is killed along with his devotees.
99. Nizami, *Leilī u Majnūn,* cited in Johann Christoph Bürgel, *The Feather of Simurgh: The "Licit Magic" of the Arts in Medieval Islam* (New York: New York University Press, 1988), 49.
100. Annemarie Schimmel, *The Triumphal Sun: A Study of the Works of Jalāliddin Rumi* (London: East-West Publications, 1980), 73.
101. Ibid., 74, citing Rumi's *Divan,* ed. Furuzānfar, 2163/2904.
102. Isma'il, *Divan,* 204: 1 and 2.
103. For a general discussion on the categorization and evaluation of these Islamic sciences, see Ibn-i Khaldun, *The Muqaddimah: An Introduction to History,* trans. Franz Rosenthal 1967), 371–411.
104. See Bürgel, *The Feather of Simurgh,* on Nizami, Gulrü Necipoglu, *The Topkapl Scroll: Geometry and Ornament in Islamic Architecture. Topkapl Palace Museum Library MS H. 1956, Sketchbooks and Albums* (Santa Monica, CA: Getty Center for the History of Art and the Humanities, 1995).
105. Bürgel, *The Feather of Simurgh,* 6.
106. Afushtah-yi Natanzī, *Naqāvat al-āsār fī zikr al-akhyār* (Tehran: Intishārāt-i Ilmī va Farhangī, 1971), 515.
107. Ibid., 515–516.
108. Turkman, *Tārīkh-i 'Ālam Ārā-yi 'Abbāsī,* vol. 1, 474.
109. According to Natanzi, *Naqāvat al-āsār,* 517, around two hundred disciples would congregate daily in his cloister. Turkman, *Tārīkh-i 'Ālam Ārā-yi 'Abbāsī,* vol. 1, 474.
110. Afushtah-yi Natanzī, *Naqāvat al-āsār,* 516; Kiyā, "Niqtaviyān yā Pisīkhāniyān," 23, quoting from a contemporary source, Mobed, *Dabistān al-mazāhib,* vol. 1, 273–178. Turkman, *Tārīkh-i 'Ālam Ārā-yi 'Abbāsī,* vol. 1, 476, mentions the name of another Qizilbash who was killed—Budaq Bek Din Oghlu Ustajlu. The

Dabistān al-mazāhib, vol. 1, 277, mentions that Husayn Khan Shamlu was found crying at the *Rawzat al-shuhada* (muharram 1002), and Shah Abbas I asked him why a man from Sham was crying for Husayn. Husayn Khan Shamlu responded: "I am not crying for Husayn; some of our good and young men have also been killed."

111. Mawlana Ayāz Munajjim, for example, was a *ghulām* of Khan Ahmad Shah presented as a gift to Shah Abbas I, who offered the slave to his aunt Zaynab Begum. He was a poet, magician *(ramāl)*, and astrologer and was killed by Abbas in 1020 A.H.1611–1612 C.E. Kiyā, "Nuqtaviyān" 71, citing *'Urafat al'ashiqīn.*

112. Kiyā, "Nuqtaviyān," 91: *har cheh sādāh ast az 'itrāt-i sayyid ast.*

113. Turkman, *Tārīkh-i 'Ālam Ārā-yi 'Abbāsī*, vol. 1, 474, states that Abbas I, while casually strolling through the streets of Qazvin, which he would often do to get acquainted with different groups of people, came across Dervish Khusraw's *takkiya*. But Natanzī, *Naqāvat al-āsār*, 516, states that the news of Dervish Khusraw's fame reached the ears of the shah. One day by chance the shah was walking in the street, and Dervish Khusraw found out about this. He ran out and lured the shah into his *takkiya* with his "smooth talk" *(charb zabānī)*.

114. Turkman, *Tārīkh-i Ālam Ārā-yi 'Abbāsī*, vol. 1, 474.

115. Afushtah-yi Natanzī, *Naqāvat al-āsār*, 516.

116. Turkman, *Tārīkh-i 'Ālam Ārā-yi 'Abbāsī*, vol. 1, 474.

117. Ibid.

118. Natanzī, *Naqāvat al-āsār*, 517; Turkman, *Tārīkh-i 'Ālam Ārā-yi 'Abbāsī*, vol. 1, 474.

119. Natanzī, *Naqāvat al-āsār*, 517.

120. Mobed Shah, *Dabistān al-mazāhib*, vol. 1, 277: "*Va ham az amīnī shanidah keh Shah Abbas amīn-i kāmil būd.*"

121. Qāzī Ahmad Qummī, *Gulistān-i Hunar*, ed. Ahmad Suhayli Khwānsārī (Tehran: Kitab Khanah-yi, Manuchehrī 1973), 140–141; Sadiqi Bek, *Majma' al-khawāss*, ed. 'Abd al-Rasūl Khayyāmpūr (Tabriz: Akhtar-i Shumāl, 1948), 154–155. Royal patronage in the Safavi era remains to be studied. Martin B. Dickson and Stuart Cary Welch's magnum opus *The Houghton Shāhnāme*, 2 vols. (Cambridge: Harvard University Press, 1981) represents a singular attempt to capture the styles and personali-

ties of fifteen painters who collaborated together with their royal patron, Shah Tahmasb, in the creation of the *Houghton Shâhnâme*. As a student of Dickson, Nomi Heger, "The Status and the Image of the Persianate Artist," Ph.D. diss., Princton University, 1997 has pursued a study of the identity of court painters as a group, and their associations with Safavi royal patrons of the sixteenth century.

122. Natanzī, *Naqāvat al-āsār*, 521.
123. Turkman, *Tarikh-i 'Ālam Ārā-yī Abbasi,* vol. 1, 476.
124. See Peter Brown, *The Cult of Saints* (Chicago: Chicago University Press, 1981), ch. 1.
125. Turkman, *Tārīkh-i 'Ālam Ārā-yi 'Abbāsī,* vol. 1, 476.
126. Ibid.
127. Natanzī, *Naqāvat al-āsār,* 525–526.
128. Kiyā, "Nuqtaviyān," 1, citing the *Tazkire-yi Sham'i Anjuman.*
129. Ibid.: "Dar ganjah furū shudam pay-i dīd az Yazd bar āmadam chū khurshīd."

Part II

ALID MEMORY AND RITUAL DRAMA: RELIGIOUS PARADIGMS OF POLITICAL ACTION

FIVE

Abu Muslim:
Victim of the Waning of the Qizilbash

Yes, not only is it lawful [*jāyiz*] to curse him [Abu Muslim], but it is legitimate to curse anyone who is attracted to him, and it is necessary to distance
oneself from him; for he was the leader of the opposition to the Imams,
those whom God has made it incumbent on mankind to be enemies with
their enemies and to love those who loved them. So do not listen to the fast
stories about Abu Muslim, for these have been concocted by storytellers
[*qissahkhwān*].[1]
—Fatwā issued by Shaykh Ali Karaki (d. 1534)

It was through the oral tradition of storytelling that memories of
the heroic feats of the religious warrior Abu Muslim (d. 755)
continued to capture the imaginations of denizens of Safavi Iran
nearly a millennium after his death. At the center of Safavi controversy lay the contours of one such memory, the way in which
Abu Muslim was represented in epics as a "lover" of the family
of Muhammad, who rose to avenge the blood of the betrayed
descendants of the prophet, holy martyrs of early Islam, like Ali
(d. 661) and his son Husayn (d. 680). The epic romance *Abū
Muslimnāme* situated Abu Muslim within an ever-evolving
drama of Alid history, nurturing and partaking in an active charisma that located Abu Muslim within a genealogy of Alid martyrs. When Abu Muslim was assassinated, some of his followers
denied his death, believing that he had gone into occultation
(ghayba) and would soon return *(raj'a)* to establish justice on

earth. Some even claimed to be his reincarnation *(tanāsukh)*; others to have been the site of the incarnation *(hulūl)* of his divine spirit. Throughout the Iranian plateau, *ghulāt* evoking the name of Abu Muslim, entered the battlefield to rebel against the Abbasid Caliph Abu Mansur (r. 754–775), who had killed him. Although these revolts were eventually suppressed, Abu Muslim's heroic role in the Abbasid revolution was memorialized in oral narratives. Not until the rule of Sultan Mahmud Ghaznavi (d. 1030), however, were these narratives recorded by the *qissahkhwān*, the blind storyteller, Abu Tahir Tusi in the eastern Iranian world.[2]

The *Abū Muslimnāme* is an alternative historical narrative of the Abbasid revolution. What remains consistent in all its versions is the basic structure of events leading to the overthrow of the "tyrannical" rule of the Umayyads (661–750), who had usurped the right of the family of the Prophet to rule over the Muslim community. It is this outline that was probably canonized by the panegyrist Abu Tahir, who made use of vernacular traditions, accounts that derived from diverse experiences in the Abbasid revolution. Variations do occur at key points, which manifest the reconstructed memories of particular lineages and meanings associated with Abu Muslim's mission *(da'wa)*, for a variety of groups that lent him support during the revolution produced their own rendering of it. That the genealogies preserved in the *Abū Muslimnāme* correspond to those recorded by medieval heresiographers justifies using them as a historical source rather than relegating them to the realm of myth and fantasy.[3] These epics belong to a similar genre of history as Ferdowsi's *Shāhnāme*, which emplotted the Iranian past, making use of both recorded and oral sources. The Abu Muslim represented in the Abbasid chronicles is but one portrayal and, no less than the others, the product of cultural and political recasting.[4] Moreover, the Abbasid version that has been passed down to us as a master narrative presents a series of historiographical puzzles surrounding the figure of Abu Muslim. The epic histories shed light on some of these puzzles and nuance our reconstruction of the revolution.[5]

The story woven around Abu Muslim's life in the epics also reveals an experience of history that was cyclical, continually connecting the present with past aeons. What seems to the reader as anachronisms are in fact bridges that attempt to heal the aporia of time, emblematic of the ways in which the drama of Alid history was remembered and acted out in "lived time."[6] Historical time and "being in timeness" are embedded cyclically in these narratives.

A different memory drawing on sacred texts *(hadith)* was evoked by religious scholars like Shaykh Ali Karaki, the author of the above *fatwā*. This other historical reconstruction, far from seeing Abu Muslim as a friend of the martyred Alids, cast him as an enemy of Ali and of his progeny (Imams). With the Safavi clash of historical recollections we are entering into a moment of contending Islamic identities. Of course, the confrontation over defining the past had immediate implications for the Safavi present. The diverse ways in which the same past was remembered and narrated highlighted distinct genealogies of heroes and antiheroes, each narrative invoking a particular sense of loyalty, whether embedded in a choice of holy Imams or in alternate readings of the very same events and sacred texts. Safavi polemics against Abu Muslim reveal the relevance of the past to cultural attitudes and practices active in early modern Iran. Storytellers were the target—their tongues were threatened to be cut off, their notebooks ordered to be washed off—for they were the agents through whom a particularly sensitive past was reconfigured and voiced to an audience captivated by Abu Muslim, the protagonist of their stories. With Shaykh Ali Karaki's *fatwā*, a whole history identifying a group of Muslims and their perceived heritage was being erased. In fact, it succeeded in doing so, for today Abu Muslim is absent from the religious imagination of Iranian Shi'is. As we shall see, this history is intertwined with a cultural system *(ghuluww)* presented as irrational and heretical. In the process, certain sacred texts and narratives were canonized as the truth, while epics were relegated to the realm of myth.

Storytellers recounting the chivalric struggles of Abu Muslim and his companions against the perceived injustice of the Umayyads had been used by the early Safavis as missionaries traveled to Anatolia to propagate their visions. The epics of Abu Muslim were recited to recruit new Safavi devotees in Anatolia (Qizilbash), while giving them a sense of the nature of the Safavi mission as lovers of Ali and avengers of the betrayed family of Muhammad. They were to provide the content of an earlier cycle of Alid struggles in which devotees could ground themselves within the present turn of history. These epics had been part of the cultural repertoire of urban devotees of the Safavis in Ardabil as well. The local membership of the Safavi order enjoyed a following among artisans and craftsmen of the bazaar of Ardabil and its surroundings. Members of the Safavi order founded by Shaykh Safi al-din (d. 1334), who appear in his hagiography, *Safvat al-safā*, as well as in the registers of endowments bestowed by patrons on the Safavi shrine *Sarīh al-milk*, represent a variety of professions, from clothiers *(bazzāz)* to painters *(naqqāsh)* and blacksmiths *(āhangar)*. Craftsmen participated in the culture of chivalric circles *(futuvvat)* linked to local spiritual orders *(tarīqat)* like that of the Safavis. The companions of Abu Muslim emerge as well from these professional circles, and as we shall see, the code of ethics that generated bonds of loyalty and camaraderie between them correspond to the prescribed etiquette *(adab)* and conduct delineated in manuals of chivalric corporations.[7] Their gallantry resembles the values of noble kings and warriors from the *Shāhnāme*. Before entering into the social and ethical circles of these chivalric orders, let me take you into the world of the *Abū Muslimnāme*, so that like the devotees of the Safavis, you may gain a sense of the symbolic system through which it speaks and the conceptual network it evokes.

A symbolic inversion is conjured in the *Abū Muslimnāme*. Those in power, the Marwanids, are cast as infidels, the ones who have exited *(khārijī)* from "true" Islam.[8] The epic is narrated from the perspective of the so-called *ghulāt* who see themselves as "true" Muslims *(mu'minīn)*. In fact, those who label groups as *ghulāt* are seen as apostates. These designations focus on love for the family of the prophet. One group is perceived as exaggerating the centrality of the family to Islam. And the other—comprised of the hegemonic Umayyads—is seen as lacking in this veneration to the extent that they have even killed the grandchildren of the Prophet Muhammad over issues of power. Corruption and oppression permeate the sociopolitical landscapes of the narrative. The archetypal tyrant is the caliph himself. The propagators of injustice include everyone from his court functionaries to provincial governors and preachers *(khatīb)*. They are the corrupt squanderers of the public treasury, drunken and depraved. It is within this unjust world order that Alids are living, conscious of a lost utopia that would have existed had Ali and his kin been granted their due authority to rule. A Muslim society ruled by members of Muhammad's family is conceived of as diametrically opposed to the contemporaneous state of affairs in which the Umayyads are in authority.

Such symbols of inversion are culturally recognizable signs of the apocalypse. We should not forget that Muhammad arose within and was embraced as a visionary prophet within a milieu where apocalyptic expectations were pervasive among Jews, Mazdeans, and Christians. With the conquest of the Arabs of the Iranians, some Mazdeans converted to Islam, interpreting this victory as a sign of divine will. They embraced Muhammad as the apocalyptic messiah. Some Mazdeans, however, placed the Arabs within their eschatological scenarios, seeing them as human representations of evil (Ahriman) in the form of "disheveled demons": "On the day of Ctesiphon's capture, Iranians who saw Muslims crossing the [Tigris] river cried out, "The devils have come. By God, we are not waging war against mortals. Rather, we are fighting none other than [evil] spirits."[9] Zoroastrian apocalyptic literature in the post-Islamic era came to represent these "basest of times" as a catalyst for future religious rebirth.[10] Such a binary cognizance of the events that followed the death of Muhammad, during which Ali and his progeny were deprived of rule and killed by members of a rival clan (Umayyad), reveals a Mazdean rendering of circumstances. Some Mazdeans, who continued to experience social discontent as subjects of the eastern realms of Islam, associated their condition with that of the Alid partisans, who had experienced similar injustices and persecution. These shared experiences of failed apocalyptic hopes created an avenue of cooperation and inclusion for Mazdeans and Jews within Alid circles. They were shared spaces of resistance.[11] As we shall see in the pages to come, the narratives of revolt leading to the Abbasid revolution as well as the evidence of rebellion in the post-Abbasid period confirm such syncretic cultural dynamics.

The death of the prophet's grandson Husayn at Karbala is the drama that sets the tone for the *Abū Muslimnāme*. The martyred family of Muhammad is portrayed as the victim of the aggression of the *qawm* (Umayyads), who had usurped the right of leadership of the Muslim community of Ali and his children. Most of the epics written in Turkish that would have been heard by the Qizilbash begin with Husayn holding his half-brother Muhammad b. Hanafiyya (d. 700) in his arms.[12] Foreshadowing the massacre, Husayn gives Muhammad b. Hanfiyya to the famous warrior *(ayyār)* Umar b. Umaya for safekeeping.[13] After Husayn is martyred the following day, Umar searches for Muhammad b. Hanafiyya, who is nowhere in sight. He has disappeared.[14] These exaggerated Turkish versions see Husayn designating his half-brother Muhammad b. Hanafiyya as heir to his authority (Imamate) and envision a line of Imams temporarily stopping *(waqfa)* at Muhammad b. Hanafiyya. The genealogy can be activated in the future, however, with his expected return in another human form—say, like that of Abu Muslim.[15] A movement called the Kaysaniyya enters the historical annals as devotees of this third son of Ali, rebelling in his name (Mukhtar, d. 678) and calling him the Mahdi, a term that would be used by both Sunni and Shi'i alike to designate their eschatological messiah. Some of the followers of Muhammad b. Hanafiyya rejected news of his death and claimed that he had gone into occultation *(ghayba)* and would soon return *(raj'a).* The twin precepts of occultation and return of the dead would become two of the core characteristics of Shi'i cosmology.

That the Turkish versions of the *Abū Muslimnāme* name Muhammad b. Hanafiyya and that the Persian versions that name him survive not in the Iranian lands but in Southeast Asia suggest that the Kaysaniyya lineage was active among Turkish speakers in Anatolia in the early modern period (fifteenth to sixteenth centuries). The Safavis succeeded in erasing Muhammad b. Hanafiyya from their chronicles of Shi'i history and instead canonize Zayn al-Abidin as the legitimate successor of Husayn. Most of the Persian versions written in the Iranian spheres of eastern Islamdom emphasize the succession of Zayn al-Abidin rather than Muhammad b. Hanafiyya.[16]

"Exaggerated" symbols and motifs permeate the *Abū Muslimnāme*(s). The idea of occultation *(ghayba)*—that the divine ones never die but are in hiding and will return in an anthropomorphic form—appears in another scene in which Ali returns in search of his body. After Ali has been stabbed, his two sons Hasan and Husayn are washing their father's body in preparation for burial, when a veiled figure appears to them on a camel. The figure takes the body along with Zul Faqar, Ali's famous sword, and begins to walk away. Hasan, struck by curiosity runs after the figure, who unveils himself as Ali.[17] When Abu Muslim goes on his pilgrimage to Ali's shrine in Najaf, Ali appears in his dream, telling him to go toward Isfahan.[18] In the Turkish version, Muhammad as well as Ali and the Imams appear to Abu Muslim in Najaf and invite him to take revenge for the family. In Karbala, it is Husayn who appears to Abu Muslim in a dream *(vāq'ia),* telling him to acquire a mandate *(manshūr)* from the sixth Imam (Muhammad Baqir). Abu Muslim then visits the Imam (Muhammad Baqir), who is in occultation in the mountains of Lebanon. After spending forty days learning four hadith daily, Abu Muslim prepares for his initiation into the circle of holy Imams. The Imam Muhammad Baqir gives him the standard of Husayn and the turban, mantle, and armband of the Prophet. Muhammad Baqir then issues an order and names him the "father of Muslims" (Abu Muslim). Up to that day, Abu Muslim had been a slave, the servant of God *('abd al-Rahmān)*, but through this holy meeting with Imam Baqir, he is transformed into the savior of Muhammad's community, according to some Alids. The *Abū Muslimnāme* continues in this vein to introduce Abu Muslim, the protagonist of the epic. From the time of his birth, which is juxtaposed in cyclical time with the martyrdom of Husayn in Karbala, the stars reveal his future fame and repute in the name of a Shi'i cause. The massacre at Karbala (680) and the disappearance of Muhammad b. Hanafiyya (d. 700) are juxtaposed with the conception of Abu Muslim in Marv (Khurasan). For the Turkish-speaking audience, forty years of historical time is encapsulated in a description of Abu Muslim's family background. This juxtaposition is imbued with the idea of metempsychosis *(tanāsukh)*, one of the distinctive precepts of *ghuluww* foreshadowing the messianic role of the protagonist. Abu Muslim's father (Asad) dreams *(khwāb)* one night that the whole world has become dark, except for a light shining from under his wife's skirt, which begins to lighten the darkness like day. An interpreter *(mu'abir)* provides the meaning of this dream: "God will give you a son who will lead the world to the right path and will rid it from the Umayyads [Kharijis] and from evil."[19] Although the audience of the narrative is aware of this divination, Abu Muslim's father is told to keep this concealed. Secrecy is key to the power of the Alid missions both in their success in fighting against an "oppressive" status quo and in their potential to attract a whole spectrum of the disenchanted. The audience then becomes privy to this secret, engaging their entry into the successive cycles of Alid struggles in the Islamic era.

Alid sympathies for Abu Muslim are further cemented when the reader is introduced to his father, Asad. Asad's genealogy links him to Abd al-Manaf, a founding father of Muhammad's clan. Asad works in the service of Ibn-i Kathir, the governor *(ra'īs)* of Marv, a partisan of Ali. Asad himself is forced to leave Marv due to his involvement with the pro-Alid opposition in that city.[20] The family sets off for Iraq (Basra), their ancestral hometown. They are forced, however, to settle in the Iranian town of Isfahan, as Halima, Asad's wife is due to give birth to the future Mahdi. On his birth (November–December 721), Abu Muslim's auspicious horoscope is read by the astrologer of the pro-Alid vizier of Hajjaj, Qays b. Amir. The stars reveal that Abu Muslim is marked by Ali and that he will conquer Khurasan with his sword and punish the heretics (Umayyads).[21]

The expectation of divination and of divinely inspired prophecy that was alive in early Islamdom and that was heightened after the tragedy of Karbala and the defeats of Mukhtar (687) and Ibn-i Zubayr (692) translates itself into the atmosphere of the *Abū Muslimnāme* and the character of Abu Muslim. Once Abu Muslim has proved his martial vigor as a chivalrous athlete *(pahlivān)*, fighting a wild tiger and famous wrestlers *(kushtīgīr)*, he receives a revelation from the Prophet Muhammad in a dream. The night of the revelation, he witnesses a man on the execution stand crying aloud that his crime was to have loved Ali and the family of the Prophet. The old man urges listeners not to despair, for the Prophet has informed him of the emergence of a savior from Khurasan, who will destroy the Umayyads. The "exaggerated" notion of God and the Prophet speaking through people seems quite normal in this context. The apocalyptic horizon of truth is also sensed to be imminent through the circulation of horoscopes by astrologers announcing the emergence of a savior.[22] Having heard the news, Abu Muslim returns home, recounts the incident to his mother, Halima, and laments the fact that he possess no weapons to join the partisans of Ali. When Halima tells Abu Muslim of his father's love for Ali and his being martyred for the same cause, Abu Muslim's pious mission takes on a personal dimension.[23]

That night, the Prophet comes to Abu Muslim in a dream, places a crown on his head, and adorns him with a robe and belt

to initiate him into the circle of Alids. Muhammad announces to
Abu Muslim, "You are the one who will take revenge for my
family. What I give you no human being has yet received. Take
revenge from the house of Banu Umayya and kill the
Marwanids."[24] When Abu Muslim responds that he has no
army to avenge the blood of the Prophet's family, Gabriel appears with his famous hatchet. The visions are gone when Abu
Muslim awakens, but in the palm of his hand he finds a sketch
of the hatchet Gabriel had brought him—proof of the reality of
his dream and of his mission.[25] In the Turkish versions, a miracle
is performed at this point further to confirm Abu Muslim's revelation: Halima regains her eyesight, which she had lost after the
martyrdom of her husband Asad. Abu Muslim converts to the
Alid cause, taking up the sword against the villainous
Umayyads, convinced of the purity of his struggle. God is clearly
on his side, for he has witnessed him and his miracles.

When the divine calling of Abu Muslim as the redresser of
Alid truth is unveiled, all his future companions have already
been forewarned of his mission through dreams. His close com-
rades are blacksmiths, bakers, cooks, saddlers, burnishers, and
glass makers. Their professional backgrounds link them to the
bazaar as well as to the chivalrous brotherhoods. It is in a cloister *(takkiya)* of a master *(ustād)* blacksmith *(āhangar)* that Abu
Muslim is first initiated into a community of Alid devotees who
will accompany him loyally throughout his sorties. Familial connections are represented as both biological and devotional. The
cloister is owned by the son of a blacksmith whose father had
been a friend of Abu Muslim's father. The son has now inherited
the father's position as master craftsman and owns a princely
house with many slaves and servants. Attached to his house he
has built a cloister where blacksmith apprentices *(shāgird)* from
his shop congregate with Alid brothers, who, like Abu Muslim,
are given shelter and hospitality. Abu Muslim's mother had told
her son to look up his father's friend in Marv, the blacksmith
who was called Muhammad Khubkar, or the "do-gooder." He
would certainly help Abu Muslim obtain an axe, for not only

was he a master blacksmith but together with Abu Muslim's father had been an Alid sympathizer. Bonds of friendship and loyalty now develop between this second generation of Alid brothers. The blacksmith's son Khurdak-i Ahangar says: "Just as our fathers were brothers, so you are my brother."[26] Devotion for the family of the Prophet was transferred from one generation to another.

Abu Muslim is represented in this narrative as poor. In fact, most of the audience of the epic consists of the downtrodden and the disenchanted. As Abu Muslim is in search of a livelihood and enough money to purchase a weapon, his mother suggests that he look up the blacksmith of Marv. The backing that the blacksmith's son provides for Abu Muslim lends him social, economic, and emotional support. Right away Abu Muslim is incorporated into the social circle of friends of Ali, who craft him his famous heavy axe built with special metal from Zul Faqar, Ali's sword, and provide him shelter and food. In fact, the *takkiya* is one arena from which Abu Muslim is able to gain supporters in every village and town. Secrets are the key to the binding of these communities, and it is only once they are certain of the identity of a lover of the family that they reveal their sentiments and cooperation is forthcoming. Together, they shall "strive to die with a noble name" in retaliation for the blood of the martyrs.[27] As they enter the battlefield, they are conscious that they are reliving the tragedy of Karbala.[28]

Cooperation emerges as well in this narrative between members of other confessional groups, whether Jews, Christians, or Zoroastrians. Conversion is a key theme, and assimilation a basic mechanism for joint action. One of the most significant conversion narratives occurs as Abu Muslim seeks refuge at the house of the Zoroastrian Mahyar-i Gabr, as he is being pursued by the troops of the Umayyad governor.[29] Abu Muslim has just killed a cleric who used abusive language toward Ali during his sermons. Along with his companions, Abu Muslim has taken over a mosque and killed many Umayyad supporters *(khārijī)*, consistently referred to as heretics. The obvious question is posed by the Zoroastrian: "Why take sanctuary [*zinhār*] with a Zoroastrian?" Abu Muslim refers to the Zoroastrian as a broad-minded man *(āzādah mard)*. It is not only due to Mahyar's im-partial character that Abu Muslim has trusted him; the two have much more in common, as shall be revealed.

A general sense of sharing an injustice is evoked between the men. Abu Muslim says that he is fleeing Nasr-i Sayyar, the gov-ernor of Marv, who is his enemy, because of what the Umayyads had done, which pleases neither Muslim, Christian, nor Jew, for the Umayyads claim that they are part of the community of Mu-hammad and yet have martyred their children and continue to insult them. Abu Muslim explains that he has come to a Zoroas-trian seeking refuge because Zoroastrian loyalty is generally greater than that of those who claim to be Muslims (Umayyads).[30] Abu Muslim goes on to divulge a truth that will bind these two men's lineages and histories tightly together: he claims that Zoroastrians and Alids share the same genealogies, for the daughter of the last Sasani king, Shahrbanu, is said to have married Ali's son Husayn: "So it is justifiable for you to feel our pain, since you gave a girl to the family of the prophet [*khāndān-i rasūl*] and this group [Umayyad] has martyred the children of the family. Naturally loving the family would be closer to your heart," he tells, thereby claiming that the two groups shared not only a lineage but also a historical tragedy. Nevertheless, the Islamic conquest marked a different kind of tragedy for Zoroastrians than the Karbala tragedy did for the Shi'is. Karbala, after all, became the life-sustaining narrative for the Shi'a cause. The story of the Zoroastrian princess who was given to Muhammad's grandson then infuses the narrative with an Iranian vigor that constitutes the Shi'ism of the community.[31] But for a Mazdean audience, this shared tragedy creates a space of hope as well, enshrined in a lineage that continues to sustain the divine glory of Iranian kingship *(farr)*—once the Mazdean cosmic struggle against evil has been transferred in the Muslim era onto the Umayyads who had martyred the grandson of the prophet Muhammad and the monarch Yazdgird. The Zoroastrian asks Abu Muslim just how the Iranian princess fell into the hands of Muslims. The fascinating story that follows is corroborated by some of the earliest recorded Shi'i (Kulayni, d. 941) sources, in which vernacular and written traditions converge. The second caliph, Umar (r. 634–644), is reported to have captured the princess Shahrbanu when her father, Yazdgird, fled eastward (Khurasan) and was killed. Umar intended to send the Iranian princess to the bazaar to be sold, but Ali intervened with an important injunction stating that "never shall there be a price placed on the descendants of [Iranian] kings." Ali thus saves the honor of the Persian nobility *(nizhād)*. Umar paid heed to the counsel of Ali and sent the princess to Salman-i Farsi, the Persian symbol of conversion to Islam, for he, a Zoroastrian who had dabbled in Christianity and Manichaeism, was one of the first converts to Muhammad's teachings, and he had served Muhammad, Ali, and his sons Hasan and Husayn loyally. Whenever the name Salman-i Farsi appears in Alid literature, it signifies a channel for the transmission of Persianate ideas. Shahrbanu's independent role in choosing a husband is emphasized, and with her free choice, a marriage of equals is suggested. She tells Salman that she will convert to Islam only if she is seated on a litter *(kiosk)* and has all the companions of the prophet walk in front of her. In true regal manner, this princess demands recognition of her position. Her first choice is Ali, but she says that she is ashamed to take the place of Fatima, the daughter of Muhammad. Her honor does not allow her to do so. Respect is demonstrated here on both sides—Muslim (Ali) for Iranian royalty and Zoroastrians (Shahrbanu) for Muhammad's family. The princess next chooses a handsome man, and when she finds out that she has chosen Husayn, she begins to cry. The night before she had dreamt that the prophet told her that her marriage vow *(khutba)* would be read in the name of Imam Husayn. Shahrbanu is thus portrayed in communication with Muhammad through dreams, and this union of Sasani and Alid blood is shown to be divinely ordained and revealed by the prophet himself.

There is more to the story of this Iranian princess and her Alid husband. Every morning, Shahrbanu is thought to have turned into a virgin again. Her chastity as well as the purity of her progeny through Husayn are thereby highlighted. There seems to be a need in Islamicate literature to inscribe women implicated in any kind of transfer of authority as pure and chaste. Perhaps because women were sûspect, any Muslim male who narrated a tale in which a woman was not impure had to mark her explicitly as pure. Fatima's fate would be similar to that of Shahrbanu. Here, although Shahrbanu refuses to assume Fatima's position, she assumes one of her principal attributes.[32] But Husayn's primacy over his older brother Hasan is confirmed here as well, for it is the authority *(akhbār)* of Muhammad's announcement that God would grant to one of his children a girl who would awaken every morning a virgin that has led Hasan to marry girls and divorce them the following morning in pursuit of that "immaculate" virgin. Once Husayn tells his brother about Shahrbanu, Hasan congratulates him. There are no hard feelings, but it is clear which brother is marked with divine favor and whose descendants shall inherit that favor. The narrator, in fact, interjects that "all *sayyids* [Muhammad's bloodline] according to Arabs and Iranians [Ajam] are born of Imam Husayn."[33]

The cyclical virginity of Shahrbanu links her to a tradition of the Zoroastrian goddess Anahita, the water goddess of fertility whose cult was patronized by the Achaemenid and Sasani kings. *Anahita* means "the immaculate one," and she is represented as a virgin. The mountain shrine in Rayy (central Iran) that became the site of pilgrimage to Bibi Shahrbanu had once been a shrine dedicated to her. The way in which this Zoroastrian legend is used in the *Abū Muslimnāme* to assimilate Zoroastrians with Alids speaks of a cultural symbiosis. Cemal Kafadar has observed a similar atmosphere of cooperation and inclusion between Christian and Muslim symbolic landscapes in Anatolian warrior epics and hagiographies *(Abū Muslimnāme, Battalnāme, Dānishmendnāme, Saltūknāme).* He uses Green-

blatt's work on the ways in which Europeans entered into hegemonic cultural systems of the New World and turned them into
"manipulable fictions" to demonstrate that this phenomenon of
"improvisation" went beyond colonial contexts: "Empathy,
conciliation and improvisation can be seen in some measure as a
proselytizer's tool of trade" in the Muslim frontier literature of
Anatolia as well.[34] In the case of the Shahrbanu-Husayn myth, it
also speaks of the creative ways in which cultural production is
negotiated in a context of resistance, unifying opposition against
more dominant interpretations of the Muslim conquerors. The
myth is applied in a new manner to explain the present as well. I
am referring to the way some Shi'is used this tale not only to create a syncretic context amenable to conversion but as a strategy
to legitimize Husayn's primacy—a point of contention among
different Alid devotees in medieval Islam. Both Kafadar and
Greenblatt's analyses place emphasis on the conscious intentions
of the conquerors, who produce these narratives as manipula-
tions of power. At least in the case of the *Abû Muslimnâme*, this
myth may also represent the ways in which local populations experienced conquest and gave meaning to their conversions.

The confluence of traditions in the *Abū Muslimnāme* is not an
unusual phenomenon in the process of conversion, a process
during which older sites of pilgrimage are transformed into new
sites of religious veneration. Christianity and pagan Mediterranean cultures or Ottoman and Byzantine encounters provide the
most immediate examples of such dynamics of conversion.
What is interesting about the case of Bibi Shahrbanu is that
Zoroastrians continued to keep her cult of shrines alive alongside Shi'i traditions of pilgrimage. Mary Boyce has written
about the shrine outside Yazd, where the "The Lady of Pars"
was visited in three rock-hewn cells by Zoroastrians even in the
1960s, when she conducted her field research.[35] The story
remembered by her Zoroastrian informant is parallel to the
popular Shi'i legend recorded in manuals of pilgrimage
(ziyāratnāme). Neither recall the link to the goddess Anahita,
while both associated it with the female descendants of the last

Sasani king, Yazdgird. The amnesia surrounding Anahita and the memorializing of Shahrbanu reveals what had to be forgotten by new Alid converts as well as by Zoroastrians living in Muslim contexts. For every remembering is as well an act of forgetting. Anahita continued to live as an unconscious memory through the shared virginity of the two figures.[36]

These holy sites were remembered by Zoroastrians as shrines of the daughters of Yazdgird who were fleeing from the Arabs, thirsty and tired. Ahuramazda saves them in the form of a rock that opens and envelops them live. Only their veils stick out of the rock as a public symbol. Zoroastrians recounting this legend to Boyce claimed that their grandparents had seen the veil. The daughter of the Sasani king, Shahrbanu in Shi'i tradition, is running away from Arabs as well, fleeing Karbala and the Umayyads. As she is pursued, she beseeches God for help but being a recent convert from Zoroastrianism, she slips, saying *"yā kūh"* (O mountain) instead of *"yāllāh"* (O God)—a slight mispronunciation that reveals her Mazdean beliefs in mountains as divine refuges. A process of acculturation is illustrated here that allows for shared spaces of overlapping beliefs and common historical tragedies. For the Zoroastrians, this was the advent of Islam, and for the Shi'a, the martyrdom of Imam Husayn. And for Mazdean converts to Islam, both were now blurred in simulacra.

I would like to emphasize that although I am prioritizing the Mazdean elements of syncretism here, Jewish and Christian elements are also part of this shared semiosphere. The story of Mahyar-i Gabr, for instance, is at times transformed into that of Mahyar the Jew. The Jew metamorphizing into the Zoroastrian is symbolic of the mixed cultural spheres emplotted in the narrative of the *Abū Muslimnāme(s)* and portrayed to an audience that was probably just as mixed. That I place emphasis on the Persianate elements is not misrepresenting the landscapes of Iran, in which a majority of the population were originally part of a Mazdean world order. In the same genre of historical narratives that Kafadar analyzes for Anatolian frontier contexts,

Christians who constitute the majority of the local population are the most prominent partners of Muslim warriors of the faith.

On hearing the story of Shahrbanu and Husayn, Mahyar-i Gabr is overjoyed and vows his loyalty to Abu Muslim: "I will hide you and sacrifice myself for you, and I shall not let bad come upon you." And as a further gesture of brotherhood, he offers Abu Muslim a meal in hospitality. Abu Muslim agrees to accept the food on one condition—that Mahyar utter his vow again, this time in the name of his religion *(kīsh)*. Mahyar then vows in the name of his faith that he will keep Abu Muslim's secrets hidden. And thus begins the epic friendship between these two brothers, one Muslim and one Zoroastrian. There is no need for conversion, given that both Alids and Mazdeans are implicated in a combined genealogy that justifies each of them to keep his own faith. Mahyar the Zoroastrian instead vows his loyalty but not his faith, providing grounds for future resistance to conversion.

Abu Muslim's companions fight for him bravely and remain loyal to the end. The epic narrates their many struggles and eventual successes in defeating the Umayyad tyrants and establishing a new Muhammadan political order *(dawlat-i āl-i Muhammad)*. But in the end, Abu Muslim is betrayed and martyred by his patrons (Abbasid). Vengeance hovers over the companions of Abu Muslim at the conclusion of the epic. His brothers are poised to respond to this act of injustice. And Ahmad-i Zemchi, Abu Muslim's appointed vice regent *(nā'ib)*, plays the leading role in the revenge.[37]

The *Abū Muslimnāme* depicts Ahmad-i Zemchi as a hashish-eating dervish who introduces himself as "the messenger of the soul." He instigates the deposition of the Abbasid Caliph al-Mansur (r. 754–775), the assassin of Abu Muslim. The audience listening to this final chapter is left with the impression that the story is not yet over, that retaliation is imminent. History has recorded a series of uprisings in the name of Abu Muslim (Khurramiyya) that plagued the newly established Abbasid ca-

liphate. Some, like Sunbadh and Ishaq the Turk, claimed that
Abu Muslim did not die but went into hiding in a nearby mountain range. They declared Abu Muslim their messiah (Mahdi/
Imam), their prophet, and the incarnation of the divine one and
expected his return to establish the religion of truth, which was
once again betrayed by the Abbasids. Some other groups like the
Mubayyads and the Babakiyya also projected their messianic
expectations onto a living incarnation of Abu Muslim—
Muqanna and Babak. For all these devotees, the different versions of the *Abū Muslimnāme* may have functioned as a historical narrative recounting the life and struggles of an exemplary
warrior messiah, a symbol of justice. But the audience was free
to imagine the lineage of this justice; Abu Muslim could be
viewed as an Alid or as an Iranian savior. The ethnic and
religious mixtures portrayed as brothers of Abu Muslim in this
epic parallel the variety of Alid and Mazdean revolts in the postrevolutionary Abbasid era. For later *ghulāt* groups like the
Khurramiyya, who revolted in central Asia and Iran, these types
of stories may have served as models for their own leaders, such
as Babak. Babak revolted in Azarbaijan (816–838), evoking
Abu Muslim as a heroic symbol who rose against Islam and
called for a return to an Iranian past. Babak's followers in fact
believed that he was the grandson of Abu Muslim, a descendant
of Fatima, the daughter of Abu Muslim.[38] In time, cycles of religious heroic epics began to emerge, like the *Zemchīnāme*, the
Bābaknāme, and the *Junaydnāme*—all of which saw their lineage linked to Abu Muslim.

During the Safavi revolutionary phase, the *Abū Muslimnāme*
was one medium by which the Safavis placed themselves within
the drama surrounding the story of the Alid victims of Umayyad
and Abbasid oppression. The Qizilbash took on the roles of
avengers on those who had usurped the rights of Muhammad's
progeny. Like Husayn and Abu Muslim, Isma'il and his
Qizilbash devotees entered the battlefield and sacrificed their
lives for the beloved family. Isma'il writes in his poetry: "We are
slaves of the Imams, in all sincerity. Our token is to be martyrs

and holy warriors [*ghāzī*]."³⁹ Storytellers *(qissahkhwān)* who recited the epic of Abu Muslim functioned as agents through which such past auras were kept alive in oral culture.

Isma'il's grandfather, Shaykh Junayd (d. 1459), whose name is identical to that of a hero of another Alid epic *(Junaydnāme)*, altered the nature of the Safavi movement from that of a conventional brotherhood to a *ghulāt* movement.⁴⁰ This reorientation of the Safavi order coincided with Junayd's banishment from Ardabil to Anatolia and Syria (1448). There, Junayd spent years (1448–1459) engaging in missionary activities and accumulating Turkmen adepts, Qizilbash, who would enable his grandson Isma'il to establish an empire.⁴¹ The new character of the order was reflected in Junayd's preaching and organizing efforts as he traveled through the regions of Karaman, the Taurus mountains, and Kastamonu. These areas were heavily populated with Turkmen tribes. Other areas that were primarily Turkmen and/or particular targets of Safavi propaganda were Teke (where Shah Quli's messianic uprising originated in 1514); the area near Kirshehir, where Haci Bektash founded his heterodox order in the thirteenth century, including Amasya, Çorum, and Tokat; and the Dobruja in Rumelia, which since Saljuk times had been an area dense with Turkmen and their dervish leaders and a frequent site of popular messianic uprisings.⁴²

Ghuluww had been the motivating force behind many uprisings in Transoxiana and Anatolia. From Ishaq the Turk and Muqanna's rebellions in Khurasan (eighth century) to the Anatolian-based rebellion of Baba Ishak (1240) and Shaykh Bedreddin (1416), the social conditions and beliefs of the Turkish and Persian-speaking population had prompted their participation in messianic uprisings.⁴³

For his Safavi adepts, Junayd, like Abu Muslim for the Khurramiyya, was the reincarnation of the divine one. Fazl Allah b. Ruzbihan Khunji (d. 1521), a Sunni writing at the court of the Turkmen ruler Sultan Ya'qub Aqquyunlu (d. 1490), captures the reverence that Junayd's followers had for him: "[His adepts] openly called Shaykh Junayd God [*ilah*] and his son, son of God

[*ibn allāh*]. In his praise they said: 'He is the Living One, there is
no God but he.' Their folly and ignorance were such that, if
someone spoke of Shaykh Junayd as dead, he was no more to
enjoy the sweet beverage of life; and if someone said that a part
of his body became missing, they would give up the threshing
ground of his existence to the wind of nonexistence."⁴⁴

It is in the context of this geographical relocation—in which
Junayd's brotherhood training became fused with the culture of
Anatolia—that the new direction of the Safavi movement must
be understood. Upon this transformation, Shaykh Junayd took
on the title of sultan—emphasizing the dimension of temporal
sovereignty in addition to his spiritual dominion. Junayd was
the first Safavi mystic to claim the role of ruler as well. In
Anatolia, Junayd actively engaged in *ghaza* against the
Byzantines in Trabezond (1456).⁴⁵ The elements of his claims of
legitimacy were similar to those that had been ascribed to the
Ottoman ruler Osman Ghazi (1301) as he was consolidating
power in Western Anatolia. Legends attribute Osman's devotion
to the *ghaza* to the inspiration of a dervish shaykh, and other
semilegendary sources celebrate the feats of diverses in carrying
on the war against infidels in the company of the early Ottoman
forces.⁴⁶ Kafadar reads these epics as "historical narratives that
represented the frontier society's perception of its own ideals
and achievements."⁴⁷ They allowed the devotee to place himself
within a cycle of history; in each age, new heroes would uphold
similar chivalric ideals and reenact them in the hope of reliving
the drama and tragedy of an Alid past.

In the legendary realm of the *Junaydnāme,* Junayd was a descendant of Ali and a contemporary of Abu Muslim. At the end
of this epic, the reader is sent to the *Abū Muslimnāme* to follow
the story of Junayd.⁴⁸ The *Junaydnāme,* then, equates both
Junayd and Abu Muslim with the Alid cause. The similarities
between the legendary genealogy of Abu Muslim and the real
genealogy of Isma'il are striking.⁴⁹ In the *Abū Muslimnāme,* Abu
Muslim's grandfather is referred to as Junayd, and his father is
Asad. Isma'il's father was Sultan Haydar. Haydar and Asad,

both of which mean "lion," are names attributed to Ali.[50] The Safavis capitalized on kinship ties between Abu Muslim and Isma'il, whether by coincidence or fabrication.[51] Perhaps among Isma'il's devotees, in true *ghulāt* fashion, he was regarded as the reincarnation *(tanāsukh)* of Abu Muslim. Isma'il and his entourage utilized *Abū Muslimnāme*(s) as a means to incite the populace to revolt in the name of Ali and the family of the prophet. Like Abu Muslim's father, who in the epic was martyred while fighting for the Alid cause, Junayd and Haydar were martyred fighting against the infidel Circassians.[52] Both Isma'il and Abu Muslim combined pious and personal motivations in their sorties *(khurūj)*. Beyond the aspect of blood revenge *(tha'r)*, Isma'il and Abu Muslim were fighting for the oppressed "lovers of the family of the Prophet" against the villainous usurpers—the Umayyads and the Ottomans.

Why, then, were these storytellers such a threat to the newly emerging Shi'ism of the Safavi realms, so as to induce Shaykh Ali Karaki (d. 1534) to issue a *fatwā* condemning Abu Muslim and the transmitters of these epics? Was the example of Ali not the impulse behind the expression of Shi'ism? They were literally the "party" of Ali, a term used in the Qur'an for the followers of prophets like Moses and Jesus. Would not any lover of Ali, such as Abu Muslim, be considered a friend? According to Karaki's *fatwā*, that should have been the case:

> God has made it incumbent upon mankind to be enemies with their [Imams'] enemies and to love those who loved them.

Although Shah Isma'il had publicly embraced Shi'ism as the religion of his newly conquered empire, in the first half of the sixteenth century Arab Shi'i (Imami) scholars had rejected his version of Islam, even refusing to emigrate to Iran from Ottoman Sunni territory.[53] Some like Shaykh Ali Karaki, however, accepted Shah Isma'il's patronage, perhaps in the hope of converting the Safavis to a more rationalist interpretation of Shi'ism.[54] Karaki's version of Shi'ism was in conflict with many aspects of Isma'il's religiosity, although Isma'il too was a devotee of Ali. This *fatwā* is one way in which Karaki dealt with the religiosity of his patron. Karaki tells us that the *fatwā* was his response to those "masses" who had been lured by the concoctions of *Abū Muslimnāme* raconteurs. The storytellers' construction of a genealogy of the friends of Ali *(awliyā')* was at variance with Karaki's list. A different memory of the past was preserved in oral history recorded in epics like the *Abū Muslimnāme*. But as Karaki was attempting to consolidate a particular version of Shi'ism, he privileged another recollection of medieval Islam that relied on a distinct corpus of hadith. Such contested memories mark the dynamics of Safavi cultural history.

These *Abū Muslimnāme(s)*, products of the culture of Anatolia, Syria, and Iran, where Safavi devotees had been recruited from the Turkmen and Iranian populations, capture the aura of what being an Alid meant for some Safavi disciples.[55] Embedded in Abu Muslim's narrative, in the characters introduced and in the symbols that relate each actor to a particular episode, lies a genealogy that links three groups of Shi'is who collaborated at a specific moment in history in an Alid revolution against the Umayyads (Kaysaniyya, Khurramiyya, proto-Imamiyya). Subsequent history witnessed one branch of the Alids consolidating temporal authority (Abbasids), eventually breaking away from any association with Ali, in fact, denying his and his sons' claims to succession. They created a new spiritual genealogy—one that saw the prophet's uncle Abbas as heir to Muhammad due to his seniority[56] (see figure 3). Yet some *Abū Muslimnāme(s)* depict Muhammad b. Hanafiyya (d. 700), the third son of Ali born of a concubine, as the heir to the Imamate after the martyrdom of Husayn (d. 680). In practice, then, up to the sixteenth century, these (Kaysaniyya) lineages were still conceived by some as an integral part of the Shi'a. Moreover, for those Qizilbash and Iranian (Tajik) disciples of the Safavis (Junayd, Haydar, and Isma'il) who had been exposed to such versions of the *Abū Muslimnāme,* Imams such as Muhammad Baqir and Ja'far al-Sadiq were seen as partners to a single spiritual lineage that linked Muhammad and Ali to Muhammad b. Hanafiyya, the Abbasid Ibrahim b. Muhammad (d. 749), and the Imamiya Muhammad Baqir (d. 737).[57] I do not intend to imply that the Safavis were a Kaysāniyya offshoot, but the fact that they utilized Kaysāniyya legitimacy confirms that a variety of Alid genealogies were in circulation in vernacular culture. These *Abū Muslimnāme* reflect a conception of the Imamate that saw the transference of authority among the Banu Hashim, crisscrossing between matrilineal and patrilineal lines of both Alid and Abbasid branches. The schematic divisions of the various Shi'i sects inscribed in medieval Shi'i heresiographies are in contradiction to the fluid and overlapping loyalties that the epics draw of early Shi'ism. This is where Shaykh Ali Karaki's recollection of the past clashed with those lovers of Ali who recorded and listened to the epics and recognized them as part of their history.

In 1501, when Shah Isma'il is reported to have proclaimed publicly his allegiance to the Shi'i (Imami) faith, the precise Alid (Husayni/Musavi) lineage of the Safavis had not yet been officially engraved on their family genealogy. It is true that during their revolutionary phase (1447–1501), Safavi guides had played on their descent from the family of the Prophet. The hagiography of the founder of the Safavi order, Shaykh Safi al-din—*Safvat al-safā* written by Ibn Bazzaz in 1350–was tampered with during this very phase.[58] An initial stage of revisions saw the transformation of Safavi identity as Sunni Kurds into Arab blood descendants of Muhammad. Precisely which bloodline was involved remained explicitly vague, for Shaykh Sadr al-din (d. 1392) is recorded as having been clueless as to whether the Safavis were "'Alavis or Sharifs."[59] Although Alid associations had been evoked in Safavi propaganda, the exact form of the genealogy, whether Hasani, Husayni, or, for that matter, Kaysani (Muhammad b. Hanafiyya), remained ambiguous.

It was Husayni descent that Isma'il came to emphasize as he began to take hold of temporal reins: "I am a Husayni, my curse upon Yazid," he writes in his poetry *(Divan)* and personally signs his name "Isma'il b. Haydar al-Husayni" in a sample of his calligraphy preserved in the Istanbul University Library.[60] Now, a second attempt (1508) to further clarify Shaykh Safi's pedigree, this time linking him to the seventh Imam Musa Kazim, was inserted into the *Safvat al-safā*, probably in conjunction with the first political betrayal of a group of Qizilbash.[61] In 1508, Shah Isma'il I massacred a group of loyal sufis from Lahijan—special disciples who had cared for him and given him refuge from the ruling Aqquyunlu Sultan Rustam 9d. 902/1497).[62] These apostles had placed Shah Isma'il on the throne and had for seven years maintained their eminence. Jean Aubin provides us with the nuances of this betrayal.[63] It was a Iranian goldsmith and a *sayyid*—an urban member of the Safavi order from Rasht (Mir Najm al-din Zargar)—who masterminded this takeover. Beyond the ethnic dimension, Aubin sees the massacre of these Lahijani sufis as representative of the tensions between the old landed elite and the new victorious tribal force, between "men of pen" and "men of sword." It represented as well tensions that emerged among a variety of Safavi devotees in a postrevolutionary era where a legally guided rationale *(shari'a)* was judged essential to the maintenance of power and stability.[64] The assault on Abu Muslim and his epics was part of an attempt to (re)describe Shi'i practices and concepts with the aid of tradition-based reasoning. Safavi monarchs attempted to implement these cultural redefinitions, but their Safavi audience continued to resist.

It was not until Isma'il's son Shah Tahmasb had successfully quashed the first civil war (1524–1536) and controlled the Qizilbash that the Husayni/Musavi identity of the Safavis was bolstered, and a rationalist version of Imamism, one that was closer to the textual ideals of Islam, was officially adopted. Hence, Shah Tahmasb's rejection of his father's role as messiah, his public Edict of Sincere Repentance (1534), and his commissioning of the official recension of the Safavi genealogy were recorded in the hagiography of their founding father Shaykh Safi—*Safvat al-safā*, revised by Abu al-Fath al-Husayni in

1533.[65] The newly concocted genealogy of the Safavis revealed no sign of Abu Muslim or of Muhammad b. Hanafiyya. Instead, their bloodline was traced back to the seventh Imam (Musa al-Kazim). Since some Qizilbash and Iranians revered Shi'i Imams such as Muhammad Baqir and Ja'far al-Sadiq and saw them as partners to the spiritual lineage of the Kaysaniyya and the Khurramiyya, perhaps initially this contrived Musavi identity may not have come as a shock. But once Shaykh Ali Karaki banned the recitation of *Abū Muslimnāmes* and issued an injunction sanctioning the cursing of Abu Muslim, it became clear that the *shari'a*-minded version of Imamism was at variance with Qizilbash Islam and that tensions between the *ghuluww* of the Safavi devotees and the rationalism of the *shari'a*-minded were bound to explode.[66]

Hamavi, a student of Shaykh Ali Karaki, preserves this *fatwā* in one of the earliest extant Safavi polemics against Abu Muslim, *Anīs al-mu'minīn*, written in 1531, and draws a picture of the dynamics between the hegemonic culture of the newly established Shi'ism (Imami). Islamdom, says Hamavi, had been in the grip of enemies. Innovation *(bid'a)* and indecencies had spread throughout its domains. Once Shah Isma'il came to power, he attempted to institute the divine law and propagate Imamism. Although he spent most of his hours suppressing "enemies of religion and of the twelve Imams," at the time of his death some of those "upholders of innovation" were still in existence. Isma'il's successor, the Shi'a-propagating Shah Tahmasb, took on the task of ridding the realm of the evil trace of innovation and those rituals that were contrary to Islam. One policy he embarked on was to prohibit storytellers from recounting stories about Abu Muslim: "Prior to the days of Shah Isma'il, the Sunni-tempered fairy tale tellers had woven together myths about Abu Muslim. and some other storytellers, to lure the masses into liking that 'Magian,' had altered these tales [*afsānah*] and had included some sayings of the Imams in them." Although Shah Isma'il had called for the destruction of Abu Muslim's tomb and had ordered the notebooks of these storytellers to be washed out, not long after his death some of the storytellers again began reciting the stories. Shah Tahmasb once again banned the reading of the *Abû Muslimnâme* and ordered that the tongues of those who declaimed the story be cut off.[67] It is no surprise that once Tahmasb moved away from the revolutionary beliefs of his father's generation that had brought the Safavis to power, he forbade the recitation of these stories. The *Abû Muslimnâme* in this imperial context was too much of a venue for *ghulât* temperaments, reminding the populace of Shah Isma'il's former associations with Abu Muslim.

Hamavi goes on to state why he wrote the *Anîs al-mu'minîn*: "From the end of the year 1526, when once again the prohibition of these stories occurred and the cursing of Abu Muslim began, up to this date—that is the beginning of the year 1531—although the masses have been told by the men of religion about the evil state of this man, some remain captivated by the lurings [*ikhtilâb*] of these satanic people. Hence, I decided to write a summary about Abu Muslim's evils, so that some believers, having read this piece, will doubt this man."[68] Here we gain a glimpse of the types of tensions that existed from the inception of the dynasty between the beliefs that brought the Safavis to power and the adopted Shi'ism of the Safavi realm. Both Shaykh Ali Karaki and Hamavi, two representatives of Shi'i (Imami) orthodoxy, saw the religiosity of the populace, in particular the Qizilbash, as heretical—especially because the stories of the Imams had merged with the story of the Mazdean Abu Muslim. Hamavi draws linkages between the instigators of innovation and the *Abû Muslimnâme* raconteurs. He depicts Shah Isma'il and Shah Tahmasb as the destroyers of innovation *(bida')* and the propagators of Shi'ism. Hamavi sees Isma'il and Tahmasb's policy of banning the recitation of epics about Abu Muslim as central to the campaign against innovation. What is even more illuminating is that Hamavi states that Shah Isma'il destroyed Abu Muslim's tomb in Nishapur. This information does not appear in the official chronicles. If this is indeed the case, then Isma'il, on his enthronement and espousal of Shi'ism, openly rejected the messianic claims that had allowed the revolution to succeed. By banning the *Abū Muslimnāme(s)*—the very propaganda tool used by the Safavi movement—and desecrating the tomb of Abu Muslim, Shah Isma'il openly renounced his former identification with the godlike warrior and denounced the hero of his devotees (Qizilbash and Iranians).[69] I am dubious, however, of such historiographical depictions of Isma'il. It is in fact Shah Isma'il's son, Tahmasb, who breaks publicly with the Safavi revolutionary past, and later historical rewritings of Isma'il's reign tend to be back-projections, merging father and son in simulacra.

The Qizilbash, however, refused to heed the call of their spiritual guides and the new religious authorities *(ulama)*. The climate was not ripe for such a ban, given that the Qizilbash still wielded much power and the *Abū Muslimnāme(s)* were too much a part of their cultural heritage for them to forsake their hero overnight. In fact, if one maps the ebbs and flows in the Safavi policy of banning the recounting of *Abū Muslimnāme(s)* onto the political history of the period, one sees that these bans were decreed when Tahmasb was attempting to control the political arena and tame the Qizilbash. The date of Hamavi's *Anīs al-mu'minīn*, in which he complains about Shah Tahmasb's inability to enforce this ban on the storytellers, coincides with the period of the first civil war (1524–1536), which began during the regency of Shah Tahmasb. This marked the first turbulent phase of Tahmasb's rule, when the young king "was buffeted by rival blocs of Qizilbash clans."[70] In the midst of this first civil war, naturally, there was an inability to enforce edicts. The chaos, however, had allowed for a rise in the expression of Qizilbashism for the Safavi Shahs could not enforce their newly adopted version of Shi'ism. It was during the first civil war, when the Qizilbash had open reign, that the tomb of Abu Muslim was rebuilt and his stories recited once again. Moreover, one can argue that since Hamavi was a student of Shaykh Ali Karaki, whose power at court reached its peak in 1531 with the victory of one coalition of the Qizilbash—Shamlu-Ustajlu, 1531 to 1536—Hamavi was propagating the official Safavi line.[71] Once the Shamlu-Ustajlu coalition had attained power, they too publicly embraced the official religion of the Safavi imperium, for the ruling Qizilbash officials engaged in the patronage of Islamicate art, literature, and architecture.[72]

We know from the story of the Nuqtavi Dervish Khusraw that during the second civil war (1576–1590), when the Safavi realms were in chaos, *ghulāt* impulses resurfaced once again. By this time, some Turkmen who had joined the ranks of Dervish Khusraw expressed their piety not as Safavi devotees but in terms of a new Nuqtavi cosmology: the *ghulāt* of some tribesmen *(oymaq)* in reverence toward the Safavi family *(silsila)* had faltered. Shah Abbas I killed the Nuqtavis and many Turkmen supporters of Dervish Khusraw. Now, with the suppression of the *ghuluww* of Safavi devotees and the usurpation of the political role of the Qizilbash by a corps of Caucasian slaves *(ghulām)*, the scene was ripe for a reemergence of anti-Abu Muslim propaganda.

The majority of these polemics coincide with a period during which the power of the Qizilbash—the military and ideological backbone of the Safavi revolution—was waning at court.[73] Shah Abbas I's successor, Safi (r. 1629–1642) inaugurated a reign that saw "slaves of the Safavi household" *(ghulām-i khāssah-yi sharīfah)* in full control of the political arena. Power now lay in the hands of the corps of Caucasian slaves that Abbas I (r. 1587–1629) had introduced for the purpose of supplanting the political influence of the Qizilbash. It had taken a century for the Safavis to consolidate their domains and dilute the power of the Qizilbash. The fact that these disputations began to flourish toward the end of Abbas I's reign—rather than on the inception of the Safavi dynasty, when Shaykh Isma'il took on the title of shah and publicly embraced Shi'ism—is testimony to the concomitant waning of Qizilbash religiosity and political might.[74]

After a lull of nearly a century, toward the end of the reign of Shah Abbas I (r. 1587–1629) we witness a reemergence of polemics against Abu Muslim and the storytellers who recited his epic. These were authored by a group of religious scholars from Isfahan, the new Safavi capital. In an attempt to redefine Abu Muslim's role in the Abbasid revolution and in Sh'i history from a more rationalist perspective, they ignited one of the main debates in seventeenth-century Safavi Iran. This controversy found articulation in a body of literature specified as *radd*, or "refutation," which owes its life to the cleric Mir Lawhi's critique of the prominent sufi-minded religious scholar Majlisi I (d. 1660), who is said to have customarily praised Abu Muslim and the sufi Hallaj from the pulpit *(minbar)* of the old Friday mosque of Isfahan—Masjid-i Jami'-yi 'Atiq.[75] Having tagged Abu Muslim as an enemy of the Imams, Mir Lawhi (alive in 1081/1670–1671) came under popular attack, especially by the sufis.[76] In Mir Lawhi's words, "Since the masses would hear Majlisi I continually voice words of praise about Abu Muslim and that infidel magician Hallaj, when they heard the contrary from this feeble one, they drew swords of vengeance from sheaths of aberration and intended to kill this defenseless soul."[77] The debates gained momentum when some scholars came to Mir Lawhi's defense, thus providing us with a body of twenty disputations in support of Mir Lawhi's assault on Abu Muslim.[78] Clearly, not all men of religion even in the seventeenth century agreed on the position of Abu Muslim in Shi'i history.

At the heart of these polemics against Abu Muslim lies nearly a millennium of friction between the *ghuluww* of Alid devotees and the rationalism of the group of Shi'i scholars.[79] Although an undercurrent of tension between Sunnis and Shi'is and between Iranians and Arabs permeates these refutations, their main thrust revolves around the anti-Shi'a activities of Abu Muslim and the heretical nature of his beliefs. The genealogies of Imams as well as the perceived nature of their authority are at the center of the controversy. Abu Muslim's representation as a holy Imam who shares a common spiritual lineage with the twelve Imams frames the problematics. Abu Muslim's claims to divinity *(hulul)* opened the contentious issue of the authority of the Imams themselves. Were they divine? Did they possess a secondary power from God *(tafwīd)*, or was it due to their knowledge that they were deemed special interpreters of God's message to humanity? These two angles of attack are revealing, for they occur in a transitional context in which the tension between the Alid loyalty of Safavi devotees and the Shi'sim (Imami) of *shari'a*-minded *ulama* was being resolved in favor of the latter. Twelver Shi'i history was being canonized, and homogeneity, the hegemony of one version of history, was being instituted. This Imami version has been passed down until today in the Persianate Shi'i world.

Moreover, the polemics shed light on why Abu Muslim was killed by the Abbasid caliph Mansur (r. 754–775), for whose brother he had fought valiantly and had succeeded in placing as the founder of the Abbasid empire (750–1258). Some of Abu Muslim's supporters claimed he was an Imam, vesting in Abu Muslim the divine authority to role. This topic remains ambiguous in Abbasid historiography, which became the official narrative of early Islam. Abbasid historiography is ridden with revisions written over a century after the revolution, when the Abbasids had already broken from their *ghulāt* past. The Safavi polemics against Abu Muslim add to our modern historical constructions of this past, preserving another contending narrative from the oral culture of popular epics first recorded in the tenth century—the same time that Abbasid history was being revised. Something can be learned here about the nature of Alid and Mazdean support of Abu Muslim and about the mission *(da'wa)* of the Abbasid revolution, requiring us to reconsider the master narrative of early Islamic history.

NOTES

1. Muhammad b. Ishāq Hamavī, *Anīs al-mu'minīn*, ed. Mir Hashim Muhaddis (Tehran: Bunyād-i Ba'sat, 1984), 189.
2. Most of the extant manuscripts name Abū Tāhir Tūsī/Tarsūsī as the compiler of this epic. See Iréne Mélikoff in her introduction to *Abu Muslim: Le "Porte-Hace" du Khorassan dans la tradition epique Turco-Iranienne* (Paris: Adrien Maisonneuve, 1962). The

original Persian version is a product of the renaissance of Persian literature that took place under the Samanids and gave birth to works like the contemporaneous *Shāhnāme*. The Turkish version was recorded later in early modern Anatolia.

3. Here I am totally indebted to Madelung's meticulous research on the Kaysaniyya, *EI2*, which has allowed me to recognize and reconstruct genealogies evoked in each version of the *Abū Muslimnāme*. Although Madelung acknowledges that there is some coalescence between the Muslimiyya and the Khurramiyya, he sees the Kaysaniyya, the Muslimiyya, and the Khurramiyya as separate groups.

4. I would like to thank Michael Bonner for this comment. Bonner emphasized that the idea of an Abbasid "historical core" narrative on Abu Muslim can be opposed altogether.

5. Here I am not pretending to have accomplished a thorough (re)reading of the Abbasid revolution through the *Abu Muslimnāme*. This task remains to be done.

6. Paul Ricoeur, *Time and Narrative*, trans. Kathleen McLaughlin, 3 vols. (Chicago: University of Chicago Press, 1984). I have benefited from Ricoeur's ideas on emplotment, the ways in which events and actions are turned into a story, the processes and mechanisms of the humanization of time through a narrative mode.

7. I will be talking about these manuals in the next section, making use of the *Futuvvatnāme-yi Sultānī* by Vā'iz-i Kāshifī (d. 1504).

8. My interpretations of the *Abū Muslimnāme* have benefited from a lecture delivered at the University of Michigan by Parvaneh Pourshariati as well as our discussions on the subject. She is currently working on the *Abū Muslimnāmes* as a source representative of the Irano-Islamic culture of medieval Khurasan.

9. Jamsheed K. Choksy, *Conflict and Cooperation: Zoroastrian Subalterns and Muslim Elites in Medieval Iranian Society* (New York: Columbia University Press, 1997), 57. Choksy is quoting from Baladhūrī, *Futūh al-buldān* (Leiden, 1866), 263; and Tabarī, *Tā'rīkh*, series 1 (Leiden, 1879–1901), 2440–2441.

10. Ibid., 56.

11. For mixed Jewish and Shi'i contexts, see Steven Wasserstrom, *Between Muslim and Jew: The Problem of Symbiosis under Early Islam* (Princeton: Princeton University Press, 1995).

12. The opening scene of the *Abū Muslimnāme* summarized by Melikoff, *Abū Muslim,* is set in Karbala, the night before the martyrdom of Husayn (680 C.E.). According to Melikoff, this scene appears in all the Turkish manuscripts she consulted. Hasan Isma'ili is currently preparing a critical edition of *Abū Muslimnāme* written in Persian. He has confirmed that none of the extant Persian epics include the martyrdom of Husayn in Karbala as their opening scene. See, for example, the most complete manuscript of the *Abū Muslimnāme* in Persian in the Biblioteque Nationale, MS 860.

13. Muhammad b. Hanafiyya, born in 637 C.E., was forty-three years old in 680 C.E. The point of the episode, however, is to depict the lines of designation *(nass).* Umar b. 'Umaya is a legendary warrior *(ayyār)* who also makes an appearance in the *Mukhtārnāme.*

14. Mélikoff, *Abū Muslim,* 91–92.

15. One group of Kaysaniyya identified by Hamavī and some earlier heresiographers believed that Muhammad b. Hanafiyya was the Mahdi, that he had gone into occultation *(ghayba)* and would return to establish a utopia. Hamavī, *Anīs al-mu'minīn,* 145. See Madelung, "Kaysaniyya," *EI2.*

16. I would like to thank Hasan Isma'ili for confirming this point.

17. Melikoff, *Abu Muslim,* 91. According to Melikoff, this scene appears in different sections of the *Abū Muslimnāmes* she has consulted. Usually it is situated in the beginning of the first chapter before the martyrdom of Husayn, yet it also appears when Abu Muslim goes to Mashad-i 'Ali (as in the case of Belediye, B. 14, for 210–211).

18. Yaghmā'ī, ed., *Abū Muslimnāme,* Supplement Persan 843, f 106 a. I would like to thank Hasan Isma'ili for pointing me to this reference, as well as Ancien Fond Turc 59, f 232 b, and Supplement Turc 1011, f 49 a–b.

19. Yaghmā'ī, *Abū Muslimnāme,* 25.

20. The conflucence of Alid sympathies held by the *ghulāt* and the Shi'a is projected onto the figure of the legendary Abu Muslim. Abu Muslim's Abu Talibid descent rings a Tayyarid bell, for Abu Muslim's father, Asad, is said to be the grandson of Abdul Vahāb, the brother of Ali. This may have been aimed at winning over those disenchanted Tayyarid/Haysāniyya who believed that the Imamate had been passed down to the Tayyarid Abdulluh b.

Mu'awiya (d. 747) after Abu Hashim (d. 716), instead of the Abbasid Muhammad b. 'Ali (d. 743). Islamicate historians and later Imami scholars claim that Abu Muslim was responsible for the killing of 'Abdullah b. Mu'awiya once he had made his sortie *(khurūj)* in 744. This is one criticism that the anti-Abu Muslim polemics highlight in order to portray Abu Muslim as an enemy of the Shi'i. See Ahmad b. Muhammad Pseudo-Ardabīlī, *Hadīqat al-shī'a* (Tehran: n.p., 1964), 556, and Hamavī, *Anīs al-mu'minīn*, 138.

21. Mélikoff, *Abū Muslim*, 94.

22. See Yaghmā'ī, *Abū Muslimnāme*, 37.

23. Ibid., 37: *"Mārā īn madār-i tawfīq bidah keh khūn-i pidar bikunam va nāsizāy-i shāh-i mardān rā barandāzam."*

24. Ibid., 97.

25. Ibid., 97–98.

26. Ibid., 39.

27. Ibid., *"bi nām-i nīk bimīrīm,"* 61.

28. Ibid., 245.

29. I would like to thank Parvaneh Pourshariati for bringing this story to my attention.

30. Ibid., 65.

31. I would like to thank Afsaneh Najmabadi for this comment.

32. Again, I would like to thank Afsaneh Najmabadi for this point.

33. Yaghmā'ī, *Abū Muslimnāme*, 67.

34. Cemal Kafadar, *Between Two Worlds: The Construction of the Ottoman State* (Berkeley: University of California Press, 1995) 72.

35. Mary Boyce, "Bībī Shahrbānū and the Lady of Pars," *Bulletin of the School of Orientale and African Studies* 30 (1967): 30–44.

36. Again, much appreciation goes to Afsaneh Najmabadi for bringing this point to my attention.

37. According to the *Khulāsat al-favā'id*, storytellers had woven new stories about Ahmad-i Zemchi *(Zemchīnāme)*, claiming that Zemchi arose to take revenge for Abu Muslim's martyrdom (f 135a). Ahmad Zemchi's *ghulāt* following is also related in the *Khulāsat al-favā'id*. Tāliqanī states that once Qutayba sent Ahmad-i Zemchi to conquer Yazd, the denizens installed a big stone in a wall in a village near Yazd and called it Ahmad-i Zemchi. They worshipped it as an idol and would circumbulate it (f 125b). The author is quoting from *Tārīkh-i Yazd* "and some

other reliable sources." I have consulted the printed version of Ja'far b. Ja'far b. Muhammad b. Hasan Ja'far's (fifteenth century) *Tārīkh-i Yazd* but could not find this reference.

38. On the genealogy of Babak, through Abu Muslim's daughter Fatima, see Wilferd Madelung, "Khurramiyya," *EI2*.

39. Khatā'ī, *Il Canzoniere di Shah Isma'il*, ed. Ganjei, 101/3: "*Biz Imām qullariz sādiqāneh shahidiq ghāziliq shānumuz dur.*"

40. Michel M. Mazzaoui, *The Origins of the Safavids: Shi'ism, Sufism, and the Ghulāt*, vol. 3, *Freiburger Islamstudien* (Wiesbaden: Steiner, 1972), 71–75.

41. They received the title *Qizilbash* under Junayd's son, Sultan Haydar (1460–1488).

42. For more on Junayd, see *Habīb al-siyar*, vol. 4, 425, *Silsilat al-nasab al-safaviyya, Ahsan al-tavārīkh, Tārīkh-i 'Ālam Ārā-i Amīnī, Tārīkh-i 'Ālam Ārā-i 'Abbāsī*.

43. On Ishaq the Turk and Muqanna sharing Turkic and Soghdian followers, see Gholam Husayn Sadighi, *Les Mouvements Religieux Iraniens au IIe et au IIIe siécle de l'hegire* (Paris: Les Presses Modernes, 1938), 153–154, 169–170. Sadighi is citing Ibn al-Athīr and Ibn al-Nadīm. On Shaykh Badr al-Dīn, see Kissling, "Badr al-Din," *EI2*, and M. Serefeddin, "Simavne Kadisi Oglü Sheykh Bedreddin'e Dair Bir Kitāp," *Turkiyat Mecmuasi (Istanbul Universitesi Enstitusu)*, 3 (1926–1933), 233–256. Mazzaoui, quoting from Kissling, states that Shaykh Bedreddin visited Tabriz in 1402–1403, "possibly attracted by the fame of the Safavis in Ardabil." Mazzaoui, *The Origins of the Safavids*, 62. Melikoff, *Abū Muslim*, 89, also states that the *Abū Muslimnāmes* were used by the followers of Shaykh Beddredin.

44. Khunjī, *Tārīkh-i 'Ālam Āra-yi 'Amīnī* (Minorsky trans.), 66, as cited in Mazzaoui, *The Origins of the Safavids*, 73.

45. Mazzaoui, *The Origins of the Safavids*, 74; John Woods, *The Aqquyunlu: Clan, Confedration, and Empire*, 2nd ed. (Salt Lake City: University of Utah Press, 1999), 139–184.

46. Halil Inalcik, *Cambridge History of Islam*, vol. 1 (Cambridge: Cambridge University Press, 1970) "The Emergence of the Ottomans," 270–271.

47. Kafadar, *Between Two Worlds*, 62.

48. Mélikoff, *Abū Muslim*, 79. See the *Kissah-yi Sayyid Junayd ve*

Reshid-i Arab, Bibliothèque Nationale de Paris, Supplement Turc, MS 636.

49. Melikoff points this out. Ibid.

50. Ibid. The author of the *Khulāsat al-fāvā'id* seems puzzled and refutes the *Abū Mulimnāme's* claim that Abū Muslim's father was Asad b. Junayd. "His father's name was Ahmad and that they say that is father was Asad b. Junayd is an example of the *qissahkhwān's* concoctions; it is not clear among the *ulama* who this Asad b. Junayd is, what kind of a person was he and what were his religious beliefs" (f 122b).

51. The earliest *Abū Muslimnāme* consulted by this author dates from the late Timurid period (late fourteenth century) and contains the same Junaydi genealogy for Abu Muslim. Earlier *Abū Muslimnāme(s)* need to be consulted, if indeed they exist, before this puzzle can be solved. The printed version of the Tehran University manuscript, edited by Iqbāl Yaghmā'ī, and the Majlis Library manuscript, summarized by Muhammad Ja'far Mahjūb in his article "Dāstānhā-yi 'Amiyānah-i Fārsī," *Majallah-yi Sukhan* 10 nos. 1–3 (1959): 167–174, 283–291, 380–386, have been consulted. Both date from the late Timurid period. According to Hasan Isma'ili, who is working on a critical edition of the *Abū Muslimnāme* and the *Junaydnāme,* the Timurid manuscripts are the earliest extant manuscripts written in Persian.

52. Woods, *The Aqquyunlu,* 139–184.

53. Andrew Newman, "The Myth of the Clerical Migration to Safavid Iran," *Die Welt des Islams* 33 (1993): 66–112.

54. See ibid., 78–91, for Karaki's role at the court of Shah Isma'il.

55. Irene Mélikoff, *Abū Muslim 72,* has consulted these two *Abū Muslimnāmes* in Persian (Bibliotheque Nationale, Supplement Persan MS 842, 842 bis, 843–844, sixteenth century). Melikoff notes that one difference between the Persian and the Turkish versions consulted is that in the Persian version Abu Muslim first goes to Imam Muhammad Baqir, who lives in a palace in the mountains of Lebanon, and it is with Muhammad Baqir's approval that Abu Muslim goes to seek out the Abbasid Ibrahim b. Muhammd. See Cemal Kafadar's questioning of the "extreme" Shi'ism of the Anatolians. Love and devotion for the family of Muhammad does not necessarily translate itself into Shi'ism, but in the *Abū*

Muslimnāme(s) a genealogy of Alids as well as precepts such as *ghayba, raj'a,* and *tanāsukh* are manifest, which does represent Alid *ghuluww.*

56. The Abbasids break away from their Kaysāni heritage, making Abbas the successor of Muhammad.

57. The Abū Muslim legends continued to be recited and utilized by *ghulāt* figures like Shaykh Beddredin and Haci Bektash. In addition, one of Haci Bektash's spiritual genealogies links him to the Imamiyya Imams Reza, Musa Kazim, Ja'far al-Sadiq, Muhammad Baqir, and then through Abū Muslim to the 'Abbasid Ibrahim b. Muhammad, Muhammad b. Ali, switching to the Kaysaniyya, Abu Hashim, and Muhammad b. Hanafiyya, and, finally, back to the Imamiyya Husayn, Hasan and Ali. Mélikoff, *Abū Muslim,* 65–66; Abðul Baki Gôlpinarli, "Menākib-i Hācī Bektāsh-i Velī," *Vilāyet-Nāme* (Istanbul: Inkilap Kitabevi, 1958).

58. Ahmad Kasravī, *Shaykh Safi va Tabārash* (Tehran: Nasr va Pakhsh-i Kitāb, 1976), delineates three phases of transformations—Sunni, Sayyid, and Husayni/Musavi—that the genealogy of Shaykh Safi undergoes.

59. Zeki Velidi Togan, "Sur l'origine des Safavides," *Melanges Massignon III* (1959): 346–348, uses a copy of the *Safvat al-Safā* (Ayasofya MS 3099) dated 896/1491, where Shaykh Sadr al-din states, *"dar nasab-i mā siyādat hast likan sūal nakardam keh 'Alavī yā sharīf va mushtabah mānd."* Togan notes that in this Ayasofia manuscript there exists a passage where Shaykh Sadr al-din speaks of his Alid descent without qualifying descent from Fatima or from his Hanafiyya concubine. Also see Yaqub Khan Aqquyunlu's letter addressed to Bayazid II regarding the death of Haydar (d. 1488) in which Yaqub Khan links Haydar to the family of Muhammad *(khāndān-i awliyā' va dūdmān asfiyā').* Nasrullah Falsafī, *Zindigāni-yi Shah 'Abbas-i Avvāl* (Tehran: Chap-i Kayvan, 1960), vol. 1, 3. The letter appears in Feridun Bey's *Münṣeāt al-Selātin* (Istanbul: n.p., 1857–1859), vol. 1, 300–301.

60. Wheeler Thackston, "The Divan of Khatā'ī: Pictures for the Poetry of Shah Isma'il," *Asian Art* (Fall 1988): 57. Isma'il's signature is preserved in the Istanbul University Library; Falsafi provides a photo in *Zindigāni-yi Shah 'Abbās-i Avvāl,* vol. 1, 151.

61. In "Sur l'origine des Safavide," Togan makes use of three manuscripts, two pre-Safavi (i.e., pre-1501) (Leiden MS 2639 dated

890/1485, Ayasofya MS 3099 dated 896/1491) and one Safavi (Ayasofya MS 2123 dated 914/1508) to demonstrate that a tampering with Safavi genealogy takes place: the Safavis are transformed from descendants of the Prophet, without further elaborations, into Husayni/Musavis. Moreover, he demonstrates that the Husayni/Musavi incoporation into the *Safvat al-safā* occurred before Mir Abūl Fath al-Husayni's recension commissioned by Shah Tahmasb in 940/1533. The *Futuhāt-i Shāhī* (927/1520–1521) by Sadr al-din Sultan Ibrāhīm Amīnī Haravī (Kitābkhānah-i Vazīrī-i Yazd MS 5774) is the first chronicle from the Safavi period to include a Husayni/Musavi genealogy for Shah Isma'il.

62. For an analysis of the relationship between the Aqquyunlu and the Safavis, see Woods, *The Aqquyunlu*, esp. 139–184.

63. Jean Aubin, "Revolution Chiite et conservatisme: Les Soufis de Lahejan, 1500–14 (Etudes Safavides II)," *Moyen Orient & Ocean Indien* 1 (1984): 1–40. Aubin, however, assumes that the *Ross Anonymous* is an early source, yet evidence—both art historical and literary—indicates that it was most probably committed to writing in the middle of the seventeenth century. I would like to thank Massumah Farhad for having provided me with the pictorial evidence. For more on the painter Mu'īn Musavvir, whose signed miniatures appear in the earliest manuscripts of the *Ross Anonymous/The History of Shah Isma'il*, see Massumah Farhad, "The Art of Mu'īn Musavvir: A Mirror of His Times," in Sheila Canby, ed., *Persian Masters: Five Centeries of Painting* (Bombay: Marg, 1990). For a study on the dating of the *Ross Anonymous*, see A. H. Morton, "The Date and Attribution of the *Ross Anonymous*: Notes on a Persian History of Shah Ismā'il I," in Charles P. Melville, ed., *Persian and Islamic Studies in Honor of P. W. Avery* (Cambridge: Cambridge University Centre for Middle Eastern Studies, 1990). Morton makes use of the author's annotations to the British Library manuscript of the Ross and proposes the 1680s for its composition.

64. Isma'il II's (1576–1577) flirtation with Sunnism demonstrates the degree to which a *shari'a*-imposed stability, weather Shi'i or Sunni, was an option available to the Safavis.

65. For the 1534 repentance, see Hasan Bek Rūmlū, *Ahsān al-tavārīkh*, ed. 'Abd al-Husayn Navā'ī (Tehran: Bungāh-i Tarjumahra Nashr-i Kitāb, 1978), 249, and Martin B. Dickson,

"Shah Tahmasb and the Uzbeks: The Duel for Khurasan with Ubayd Khan, 930–46/1524–40," Ph.D. diss., Princeton University, 1958, 277–278.

66. Both the official fabrication of Safavi Musavi lineage (1533) and the issuance of this *fatwā* coincide with a period when Karakī attained the peak of his power at Tahmasb's court (1531), symbolized by his ability to secure the position of Sadr for his candidate Mu'izz al-din al-Isfahānī (d. 1545–1546). See Caroline Beeson, "The Origins of Conflict in the Safavi Religious Institution," Ph.D. diss., Princeton University, 1982, 58–65, and Andrew Newman, "The Myth of the Clerical Migration to Safavid Iran," *Die Welt des Islams* 33 (1993): 100.

67. Hamavī, *Anīs al-mu'minīn*, 140–141.

68. Ibid., 145.

69. Isma'il's banning of the *qissahkhwān* does not appear in the main chronicles. It may have been part of his policy to curb the power of the Qizilbash by naming the Tajik, Najm-i Rashtī (1508–1509), and his Tajik successor, Najm-i Thānī (1509–1514), as Vakīl. See Aubin, "Revolution Chiite et Conservatism," 11–13.

70. Martin B. Dickson and Stuart Cary Welch, eds., *The Houghton Shāhnāme*, 2 vols. (Cambridge: Cambridge University Press, 1981), 240 n. 15.

71. See Dickson's "Shah Tahmasb and the Uzbeks" on the civil wars and Caroline Beeson on Karakī's power at court, "The Origins of Conflict in the Safavī Religious Institution," 39.

72. On Qizilbash patrons of the arts, see the Dickson Papers, #84 (University of Chicago, Regenstein Library). To cite some examples: Durmish Khan Shamlu, governor of Herat under Shah Tahmasb; Husayn Khan Shamlu, governor of Qum and later Herat under Shah Abbas I; and Qasim Ali Bek Afshar.

73. When does this wave of debates begin? The earliest in this series of disputations is the *Sahīfat al-irshād* by Sayyid Mīrzā Muhammad Zamān (d. 1041/1630–1631). The author, who knew Mīr Lawhī and his father from Mashad, mentions that on his long-awaited journey to Karbala, he hears of the attack on Mir Lawhi (f 113b; also cited in Ja'fariān, "Rūyrūyi-i Faqīhān va Sūfiyān Dar 'Asr-i Safaviyya," 109). The author could have traveled to Karbala after Shah Abbas I liberated Baghdad (1624) from nearly a century of Ottoman rule. Passage to this holy site *('atabāt)*, however, was safe

only once the Ottomans pulled their forces out of Iraq-i Arab, between Shawwāl 1035/July 1626 and Zul Qadah 1038/June–July 1629, when they once again began their campaigns into Iraq (see Ismail Hami Danishmend, *izahli Osmanli Tarihi Kronolojisi* (Istanbul: Sermet Matbasi, 1960), vol. 3, 343; *Tārīkh-i 'Ālam Ārā-yi 'Abbāsī,* vol. 2, 1053; and the *Zayl-i Tārīkh-i 'Ālam Ārā-yi 'Abbāsī,* 39). In fact, Majlisi, Sr. visited the *'atabāt* the summer (Zul Qadah-Zul Hijja 1037/July–August 1628) before the death of Shah Abbas I (Muhammad Bāqir Khwānsārī, *Rawzat al-jannāt fī ahwāl al-'ulamā wa al-sādāt,* Persian translation by Hajj Shaykh Muhammad Baqir Sā'idī Khurāsānī, 2 vols. (Tehran: Maktabat Ismā'iliya, 1970), vol. 2, 132). According to Mir Sayyid Muhammad, while in Karbala he met a trusted brother from Isfahan at a friend's house, and he asked this Isfahani about the whereabouts of Mir Lawhi. The brother from Isfahan responded that "while Mīr Lawhī had been teaching the people about the Prophet and the Imams. He forbade the masses from venerating Abu Muslim and started cursing that *Khārijī.* It has been a while now that because of these statements he has been bothered" (*Sahīfat al-irshād,* f 113b).

74. Three extant polemics from Shah Tahmasb's (1524–1576) reign were written against Abu Muslim and sufis. There appears to have been a lull until the above-mentioned wave of polemics began to flow toward the end of Shah Abbas I's reign.

75. Sabzavārī (Mīr Lawhī), *Kifāya al-muhtadī fī ma'rīfa al-mahdī,* also referred to as *Arba'īn,* ff 8b and 190a, Tehran University MS 1154.

76. The *Khulāsat al-favā'id* by 'Abd al-Mutālib b. Yahyā Tāliqānī, probably written during the third decade of the seventeenth century, mentions that the sufis took Mir Lawhi's criticism of Abu Muslim to heart. "Those irreligious ones who every day chose a new master [*pīr*] from among themselves took Mir Lawhi's statements personally and told him: you have insulted our masters and their spiritual ancestors" (f 118b).

77. Ibid., f 8b. The *Sahīfat al-irshād* by Mīr Muhammad Zamān b. Ja'far and the *Izhār al-haqq* by Sayyid Ahmad b. Zayn al-'Abidīn, both anti–Abū Muslim polemics, mention this episode.

78. The *Izhār al-haqq* was written in 1043/1634 by Sayyid Ahmad 'Alavī in defense of Mīr Lawhī's critique of Abū Muslim, elabo-

rated in his *Tarjumah-yi Abū Muslim*. Sayyid 'Abd al-Hasīb, the son of Sayyid Ahmad, in 1063/1653 notes on the back of an extant manuscript of the *Izhār al-haqq* that some *ulama* came to Mīr Lawhī's aid and wrote treatises on Abū Muslim in support of Mīr Lawhī's refutation to quell the anger of the masses. A list of seventeen treatises against Abū Muslim is penned in the hand of another contemporary scholar. By 1063/1653, then, seventeen polemics against Abū Muslim had been compiled. (For a list of these disputations, see Āqā Buzurg's *al-dharī'a*, vol. 4, 150–151.) The *Khulāsat al-favā'id* (ff 120a–121a) names three other polemics not mentioned in the *al-dharī'a*: *Hādī al-sabiyān ilā Tarīq al-Imān*, *Zīnat-i majālis al-mu'minīn*, and the *Mīzān al-mahāsin wa al-mashāyin*, also cited in Rasūl Ja'fariān, "Rūyārūyi-i Faqīhān va Sūfīyān dar 'Asr-i Safaviyya," *Kayhān-i Andīshah* 33 (1990): 110. Only three of these treatise seem to be extant—the *Khulāsat al-favā'id*, the *Sahīfat al-irshād* and the *Izhār al-haqq*.

79. Madelung notes with surprise that the popular character of the Kaysaniyya, "reflected in the Persian romance of Abū Muslim, its martyred hero . . . could still in the eleventh/seventeenth century provoke an angry reaction among the Iranian Imami Shi'ite ulama who had no sympathy for this ideological deviation." Wilferd Madelung, *Religious Trends in Early Islamic Iran* (Albany, NY: Persian Heritage Foundation, 1988), 77.

SIX

Fraternal Circles of Alid Piety and Loyalty: Eulogists, Storytellers, and Craftsmen

From within the social milieu of craftsmen, "singers of tales" emerged as professional members of the storytellers' *(qissahkhwān)* guild.[1] Craftsmen and artisans would hear stories like the *Abū Muslimnāme* as they sold their products in bazaars and alleys where they routinely set up their daily shops or in coffeehouses where they socialized after work. It is not only in such public arenas that these stories would be heard, for they also shaped the social and cultural lives of artisans who entered communities *(futuvvat)* of devout lovers of Ali. Bonds were forged between guild members through their participation in chivalric clubs that combined social and work ethics with spirituality. Stories enshrining the lives of the family of the prophet created an Alid identity that gave members of these brotherhoods a sense of belonging to a community and participating in a collective historical struggle. Storytelling was considered a noble way of making a living, as long as the content of the tales centered on the virtuous lives of Ali and his descendants. In *futuvvat* milieus, spirituality was closely tied to a profession, and as long as integrity was maintained, one could engage with honor in material life.

161

With these brotherhoods, we enter into a "world-embracing" form of sufism, which may be why it prevailed in the realm of the crafts.² *Futuvvat* was a mystical sensibility also espoused by the founder of the Safavi order (Shaykh Safi al-din), who is said to have chastised those dervishes who engaged in beggary and mendicancy, enjoining them to return to their families and their occupations to fulfill their productive roles in society.³ Trade and commerce were vital to the economy of Ardabil, in which the Safavi shrine developed and beyond which it extended its spiritual and economic might throughout northern Iran and eastern Anatolia. The spiritual and material livelihoods of the Safavi brotherhood were grounded in the economy of the city.

Futuvvat culture emphasized both physical and metaphysical strength and growth. Knowledge *('ilm)* and power *(quvvat)* were conceived as two sides of the same mystical expression. Whatever one's craft might be, that is what was elevated as an art *(hunar)*, but the disciple had to practice his vocation with sincerity and earn *(kasb)* his livelihood honestly. Certain professional categories, however, were more prestigious. Those "people of words" *(ahl-i sukhan)* who possessed the ability and temperament *(tab')* to write were encouraged to apply their talent to compose eulogies *(maddāhan)* and versify the just struggles of the Alids, turning "the jewels of their (Alid) stories" *(rivāyat va hikāyat)* into poetry.⁴ Amid a hierarchy of artists, the early modern mystic-preacher Va'iz-i Kashifi (d. 1504) regarded eulogists *(maddāhān)* as the most honorable group. Kashifi writes in his manual of chivalry, *Futuvvatnāme-yi Sultānī:* "It is evident that love [*muhabbat*] toward the family of the Prophet [*ahl-i bayt*] is part of Islam, and the one who loves another invariably recites their accomplishments [*manāqib*] and spends time thinking and talking about them. These are the most cherished individuals for the family and the more they display their affection, the more intimate they are with the family. It is clear that the closest people on the path [*ahl-i tarīq*] of the Prophet are his children and his eulogists."⁵ Those who have a beautiful voice or possess oratory skills are to recite these lyric verses as professional "singers of poetry" *(nazm khwānān)* in the bazaars, coffeehouses, or open arenas *(ma'rika)* of towns and cities where such forms of entertainment were current. There were those who displayed their physical talent and dexterity in the martial arts *(ahl-i zūr)* or acrobatics *(rasan bāzī)* or wrestling *(kushtī gīrī)* as emblems of divine favor, and there were some who played games *(ahl-i bāzī)* like jugglery *(huqqah bāzī)*. Here we get a sense of the different artistic forms utilized in the daily battlefield *(ma'rika)* of life, conceived of as part of a larger historical and cosmic struggle against injustice and evil. Verbal and physical strength are but modes of this endeavor.

The Arabic noun *ma'rika,* which literally means "battlefield," is used to designate public spaces for the performing arts: "Know that *'ma'rika'* etymologically *[dar asl-i lughat]* means a battlefield *[harbgāh]* and in idiomatic usage *[istilāh]* it is a locality *[mawzī']* where someone goes and stands and people congregate there *[jam']* and he performs the art *[hunar]* that he possess and they call this locality a *'ma'rika'*."[6] The battle is fought with one's skill, reflecting all those attributes associated with good—justice, knowledge, beauty, compassion, and modesty. Evil is translated onto the oppressors of the family (evil), and the cast of characters involved in the army of Alids (good) fight through their arts to propagate their just cause. Art—whether poetry or acrobatics, storytelling or wrestling—represented everything noble about human beings that allowed them to fight against evil. And thus provides us with a wholly other picture of the power and meaning of the arts, at least in the realm of *futuvvat* culture.

By the seventeenth century, however, many of the guilds associated with the *futuvvat* had lost their status in the realm of Safavi official culture.[7] Storytellers, wrestlers, and acrobats, along with the *Shāhnāme* recitors, were placed among the beggars, grave diggers, and itinerant dervishes *(qalandar)*.[8] Most of our information about Safavi guilds dates from the era of absolutism (1590–1722), when craft organizations had already been transformed from the early days of the order in Ardabil. The Safavis in their imperial mode came to discipline and monopo-

lize these professions, banning storytellers of the *Abū
Muslimnāme* and appropriating some of the popular rituals
such as the mourning processions commemorating the martyrdom of Husayn. In his important study on artisans and guild life
in the Safavi capital city of Isfahan (1590–1722), Mehdi
Keyvani uses Safavi administrative manuals that classify storytellers, jugglers, and wrestlers as third-class professionals within
a hierarchy of guilds. The Safavis used individual craft structures as a mechanism for collecting taxes from craftsmen and
tradesmen.[9] Normally, each guild chose their own chief *(bāshī)*
from among their most skilled members.[10] A government-
appointed religious official *(naqīb)* then certified the position.[11]
One of the functions of this craft master *(bāshī)* was to collect
the pay the group's taxes *(bunīchah)* to the court. Taxes were to
be paid in kind, whatever the craft—sword making, weaving, or
carpentry, for example. These taxes helped supply the needs of
the court, providing stock for the royal workshops *(buyūtāt-i
saltanatī)*. To feed, clothe, and furnish the enormous Safavi
household and its dependents, the palace housed workshops
that were responsible for activities ranging from cooking to tai-
loring to saddle making. Professional organizations of storytellers and wrestlers were not subject to the normal taxes *(barīdah)*
in the seventeenth century, and unlike other guilds they could
not elect their own master but rather were under the direct supervision of senior Safavi government officials.[12] Keyvani provides a few reasons for their low status and strict supervision by
the state. Due to their religious sensibilities, they were seen as
posing a threat to the morality and discipline of the community.
The ban on storytellers who recited the *Abū Muslimnāme* provides strong backing for this assertion. Keyvani goes on to speculate that perhaps these professions were considered inferior as
well because they were not "strictly legal in Islamic law" and
therefore the receipt of revenue from them was forbidden. How,
then, did the Safavi court find ways to tax other religiously ta-
booed activities such as prostitution, gambling, and alcohol?
The survival of pre-Islamic professions like storytelling and

wrestling in the Iranian lands reveals a social channel of continuity of lay religiosity. The transmission of these arts and techniques of the craft came along with an introduction to a whole Persianate worldview that was considered in the seventeenth century as subversive.

In the imperial era of Safavi rule, craftsmen linked to *futuvvat* circles were marginalized by the court. Indeed, the *fatwā* (Karaki) prohibiting the recitation of Abu Muslim's epic history defines them as heretics. Crafts like storytelling were a medium through which aspects of a gnostic past survived, albeit transformed in an Alid idiom. Storytellers broadcast and created memories of a past that fused Mazdean and Alid idioms alive among the religiosity of a lay piety. They were conduits of transmission, both institutional and oral, from master to disciple, generation after generation. They functioned as organic and spontaneous sites of memory—what Pierre Nora has called a *milieu de mémoire*. We shall see, however, that although storytelling was a pre-Islamic mode of orally transmitting history in Iran, in the *futuvvat* circles described by Va'iz-i Kashifi (d. 1504), the content of memory had changed, and history was mediated through Islamic experience. But in the emplotment of this new memory narrative, a symbolic field that evokes patterns of behavior and ethics is communicated from within a Persianate conceptual frame.

I will be coming back to the Persianate ethos permeating *futuvvat* culture and to the question of consciousness of an Iranian identity. But first, I would like to take you into these fraternal bonds and their hierarchical structures as described in the manual of chivalry *Futuvvatnāme-yi Sultānī*, recorded by Vaiz-i Kashifi, who is speaking in a mystical language of Alid Islam. A gem of a source that has not previously been tapped for the purpose of exploring the lives of members of the chivalric circles, the *Futuvatnāme-yi Sultānī* was written at the beginning of the sixteenth century in Timuri Herat by the famous mystic preacher *(vā'iz)* and eulogist Kashifi. He describes in detail the practices and rituals of initiation that shaped Alid fraternities.

Kashifi is most famous for his prose narrative on the life and struggles of the Imams—*Rawzat al-shuhada,* or the *Garden of Martyrs.* This account of the lives of Alid martyrs becomes the main text for the mourning rituals *(rawzakhwānī)* and passion plays *(ta'ziyah)* marking the death of Husayn. Shah Isma'il's court chronicler Khwandamir, writing two decades after Kashifi's death, speaks of his fame among the populace.[13] In fact, Shah Isma'il even commissions a versified version of the *Garden of Martyrs.* Although Kashifi was writing a contemporaneous manual of chivalry from Khurasan in eastern Iran and the Safavi brotherhood evolved in Azarbaijan in the West, the basic structures and ties of loyalties could not be very different, particularly since Kashifi was describing Alid chivalric circles.

Kashifi says he is combining older books on chivalry and quotes them throughout his work.[14] He also states that he is incorporating *futuvvat* practices as he has observed them. Similar to sufi orders that followed the path of Muhammad *(tarīqat-i Muhammadī),* these local orders, as described by Kashifi, consisted of sufi communities of artists and craftsmen with hierarchical organizations and fixed rules and rituals. Kashifi, however, is describing a sufi culture of Alid fraternities *(tarīqat-i Alavī)* that permeates the Irano-Turkic world in early modern Islamdom. That among his popular religious works were both the *Futuvvatnāme-yi Sultānī* as well as the *Garden of Martyrs* suggests that the two texts do emanate from a common cultural arena. After all, the Herati historian Khwandamir states that Kashifi himself had a good voice *(avāz-i khush)* and that he used to preach in the bazaar *(chahār sūq)* of Herat on Fridays and at the shrine of a mystic, Pir Muhammad Khwajah Abu Valid Ahmad, on Wednesdays.[15] The *chahār sūq* was the headquarters of the guilds who occupied particular lanes in the bazaar where their public business was conducted.[16] Sufis and craftsmen were privy to Kashifi's eulogies, which were attended as well by the Timurid ruler Sultan Husayn and his courtiers.

Bound together through vows *('ahd)* of loyalty and codes of etiquette *(adab),* artists and craftsmen entered the spiritual circles of the lovers of Ali. As mystics, they understood their path of transcendence to be indistinguishable from the path taken by Ali, and so they strove to follow step by step the example of Ali and his children, the Imams. It is not only the centrality of Ali as the axis (Qutb) of saintliness that distinguishes this type of ascetic circle. There is a particle emphasis on the mingling of physical and spiritual prowess that takes us into the world of crafts, where an alchemical transformation of spirit and matter fuses apprentice and master through the secrets of the cosmos. Versed in the codes of the many arts and sciences, the master gradually reveals to the initiate particular sets of the truth and of cosmology. Secrets that are part of the oral traditions of the brotherhoods are thus passed on and (re)created anew.

Mysticism and devotion to the family of the prophet expressed themselves in a paternal language of valor that centered around the figure of Ali. Bonds of fraternity tied Muhammad to Ali as the two formed one body cloaked by the same divine light. Muhammad was the seal of prophecy *(nubuvvat)* and Ali the font of sainthood *(vilāyat)*. The Imams, holy descendants of the prophet through Ali and Fatima, represented virtuous and courageous models to be emulated and recalled in the daily lives of participants in the path of *futuvvat*. The oath-taking ceremony was a public act performed in front of a community of brothers as a vow of commitment that bound master to disciple and brother to brother. As the disciple was initiated into this covenant with God, he was made conscious through the recitation of stories that this ritual was a reenactment of the original covenant between Abraham and Ali as father to son, as well as between Muhammad and Ali, as brother to brother. Every relationship that tied members of the order together in the path of learning the arts and initiation into the secrets of the craft was defined through the language of paternity and fraternity and placed within three cycles of time—cosmic time, prophetic time, and the Islamic present.

How these associations between chivalry *(futuvvat)*, mysticism *(tasawwuf)*, and devotion *(muhabbat)* for Alids crystallized around organized circles of craftsmen is beyond the scope of this study. But by the time of the Mongol invasions (1218–1219), sufism had already merged with aspects of this chivalric ethos within craft organizations that venerated Ali as their saint. Historians have tended to see this aspect of sufism as a lesser form of mystic expression, partly because famous sufi masters like Abu Najib Suhrawardi (d. 1168) describe it so, as though mystics from social arenas that engaged in manual labor were unable to realize the complete path and so engaged only in its preliminary stages of transcendence.[17] There has been a tendency in scholarship to view these two mystical forms as separate, perhaps because for us, as well, materiality and spirituality seem to be mutually exclusive. And so their fusion in medieval Islam has been associated with the communal practices of chivalric groups that represented a model for nascent sufi communities of believers. Chivalric groups had, after all, come together around similar notions of equality, camaraderie, celibacy, and justice. And so our modern interpretation of the interplay between sufism and *futuvvat* remains captive to the two seemingly antithetical pictures painted by medieval Islamic sources. Accounts of medieval mystics draw a picture of early communities of men *(fatā'/ javānmard)* living together in harmony and mutual devotion. Men from varied social and ethnic backgrounds were described by these sufis as having broken away from their familial and tribal affiliations to form solidarities based on the utopian ideals of fraternity, hospitality, loyalty, celibacy, and the martial arts. These were ideals that sufis in later periods saw themselves as sharing.

Such cultural forms of Persianate "humanness" that held truth, justice, and wisdom as key values were ideals held by reclusive hermits as well as Irano-Muslim notables. The Persian (Ziyarid) prince Kay Kavus (eleventh century) in his book of advice to his son, *Qābusnāme*, speaks of chivalry *(javānmardī)* as a way of life a prince should follow. But he also places it at the first stages of mystical growth: "Know, O son, that the philosophers [*hukamā*] have imagined humanity and wisdom as a metaphoric [*bi-alfāz*] figure, not a literal body [*bi jasad*]. That figure possess a body, a spirit [*jān*], an intellect [*havas*], and a meaning [*ma'ānī*], just like humans do. And they have said that the body of that image [*surat*] is chivalry [*javānmardī*], and its spirit is truth, and its intellect is knowledge, and its meanings are its characteristics [*sifāt*]."¹⁸ As these different aspects were dispersed among humans, some ended up with the body and nothing else; others with a body and a spirit. And some were possessed of all three. Each individual according to his particular state possess a certain manliness *(muruvvatī)*. Those who have a body are chivalric *(javānmard)*. Those who have a body and spirit are ascetics *(sufis and faqirs)*. And those who have wisdom in addition to body and spirit are philosophers, prophets, and saints. And finally, those who possess inner knowledge *(ma'ānī)* as well as body, spirit, and wisdom are holy ones *(ruhāniyān)* and messengers: "So try, dear son, and endeavor to the extent that you can and according to your aptitude [*miqdār*] to improve [*taraqī*].¹⁹ Here, Prince Kay Kavus is creating a spiritual hierarchy—a gradual progression toward knowledge in which the novice had to begin by attaining a youthfulness of spirit *(javānmardī)*.

Javānmardī was an ideal way of life for Iranian notables to emulate; Kay Kavus places it also among warriors *(ayyār va sipāhiyān)*.²⁰ Warriors like Rustam in the *Shāhnāme* acted as models of chivalry and were represented in the *Shāhnāme* as "youthful, impetuous, trusting to the point of gullibility, eager for friendship and adventure."²¹ The impetus that often spurred them into battle was the murder of an innocent victim, and unjustifiable murder and judicious revenge dominate the first half of the *Shāhnāme*.²² Dick Davis distinguishes two heroic types in the *Shāhnāme*—one self-willed like Rustam and the other more inward like Siyavush. Siyavush is marked by his thoughts and hesitations. In contrast to Rustam, his martial prowess is not given descriptive detail by Ferdowsi.²³ Kashifi includes "people of the sword" as a category of professions separate from "people of words" *(sukhan)* and "play" *(bāzī)* on the battlefield *(ma'rika)* of chivalrous life.[24] Kashifi includes soldiers *(sipāhiyān)* and people of the sword *(ahl-i shamshīr)* in a second group of craftsmen who use handles *(ahl-i qabza)*, like blacksmiths, shoemakers, tailors, butchers, and kabab grillers.[25] Singing poetry and tales, taking up arms, crafting a saddle, or playing games were all part of the combat against injustice.

Alongside such medieval depictions of *futuvvat* piety, we have the court chroniclers who focus on the militant aspect of this culture, a dimension that was part of it and yet one that we tend to see in opposition to asceticism. But some forms of Zoroastrian gnosticism, like that of the Mazdakis, perceived creation and all things material as part of the good because the world had been created by the forces of light. Unlike the Manichaeans, who viewed all materiality as evil, enjoying life and working to earn a living did not prevent the Mazdakis from seeking the truth. For them, it was not materiality per se but rather an inequality in the distribution of material bounties of creation that was deemed unjust. The Mazdakis advocated the sharing of land and women, for they saw them as the main reasons men became greedy, envious, and deceitful. They were causes for social disorder. The mystic mode of the *futuvvat* in early modern Islam embraces similar notions of piety and community. It is in the way that they experienced such metaphysical dimension in the material world, where differences occur with world-rejecting sensibilities among sufis. Members of chivalric circles used both their verbal and physical powers to combat their opponents in daily life. *Futuvvat* clubs prevailed the cities and towns of eastern Islamdom. Initially, they were associated with those lands that had been under Iranian rule, for in the early medieval period (eleventh century), we have no trace of the designation *futuvvat* in Egypt or Syria. Instead, we have *ahdath*.[26]

In medieval chronicles, gallant warriors are represented as rebels, insurrectionists, and plunderers of the ill-gained wealth of the rich, for they were local elements that voiced resistance to regional hegemonies. Naturally, in the eyes of medieval historians, they were bandits, vagrants, and outlaws. But this should not prevent us from seeing some of them as mystics who did possess a communal identity and structure that had the potential to turn into a mass political threat. As a form of resistance, local warriors rose independently in gangs of solidarity against a variety of perceived opponents. Different occupations were grouped into corporations whose patron saints were Ali, Salman-i Farsi, or Abu Muslim. Such affiliations with brotherhoods could offer armed protection in fights for common local interest. As in the case of the Safavis, they had the sociocultural and economic power to mobilize resources and prestige.

Certainly not all medieval *futuvvat* circles were mystically inclined. The Persian local dynasty of the Saffarids (867–911), whose leader was the coppersmith (Ya'qub b. Layth), rose out of one such chivalric fraternity on the eastern frontiers of the Islamic world in Sistan.[27] And when this local dynasty attempted to extend its reach beyond Sistan, other *futuvvat* from Iranian cities extended their support.[28] A regional solidarity bound these craftsmen.

History attests that with the help of such local forms of organization, city notables fought for independence during times of Abbasid decentralization (950–1150), and the Abbasids themselves came to capitalize on local craft associations. Although the situation in Baghdad is particular in terms of the city's role as the seat of the Abbasid household, the power of these communities was evident to the court. The ritualized competitions of games and sports patronized in Buyid Baghdad that pitted Sunni against Shi'i and law schools *(mazhab)* against one another speak of the vitality of this culture manifested in local factionalism.[29] The Buyid, Mu'izz Al-Dawla (r. 936–949), attempted to encourage aspects of *futuvvat* martial arts, like long-distance running *(shātir),* using it to his advantage as he kept close contact with his brother Rukn Al-Dawla (r. 947–977), who ruled in central Iran (Rayy). The martial arts had practical and overreaching functions necessary for centralized political rule. In an attempt to revitalize the authority of the caliphate, the Abbasid Nasir (d. 1225) endeavored to control the local power of chivalric communities by centralizing and patronizing them. Nasir's initiation into the Baghdadi *futuvvat* of Shaykh Abd al-Jabbar made it fashionable in court culture. The caliph, or perhaps his religious advisor, Shihab al-din Umar Suhravardi, must have realized the power of such local associations. After a period of twenty-five years of membership in the Baghdadi *futuvvat*, Nasir attempted to unify the organization beyond Baghdad. Although his ambitions were cut short by Mongol invaders, who put an end to Abbasid rule, his policies did present a stage of further institutionalization and legitimization of the power of the *futuvvat*. Nasir's policies allowed for a flourishing of a genre of chivalric literature, in which sufi spiritual genealogies became canonized within *futuvvat* circles. Such a convergence can be seen from the very early articulation of sufism as a textual phenomenon. The Khurasani Abu Abd al-Rahman Sulami (d. 1021), the first collector of sufi biographies, also wrote the first extant treatise on *futuvvat*, in which both mystical and chivalric currents share a language of piety and loyalty.[30]

Though *futuvvat* seem to have had an earlier organizational existence, emerging in urban circles of towns and cities from Central Asia through the Iranian plateau and Mesopotamia, by the time of the Mongol conquest, *futuvvat* and sufism had merged in the arena of the crafts in these Turco-Iranian territories. Thus, when the spiritual founder of the Safavi order, Shaykh Safi al-din, died in 1334, his craftsmen devotees used their professional skills to build him a mausoleum and decorate it, utilizing their artistic talents. In these circles, Ali had gained the status of an ideal *javānmard*, and Abu Muslim that of the model warrior saint whose acts of revenge in the name of the family of Muhammad were to be emulated. The Mongol invasion concluded the long chapter of Sunni hegemony in the lands of the eastern caliphate, allowing for a public articulation of love for the family of the prophet. A medieval Alid eulogist, Hasan Kashi, acknowledges the Mongol ruler who had converted to Islam—Muhammad Khudabandah Uljaytu (r. 1304–

1317) and his vizier, Rashid al-din—for their patronage of Shi'is that allowed for his poetry finally to be appreciated. Hasan Kashi writes in his *Epic of Imams (A'immahnāme)*, which he dedicates to the Mongol Uljaytu: "It is approximately 650 years since the name of Ali [d. 661] is on people's mouths. Up to the reign of this king [Uljaytu] no one remembered this book, but during his reign he set the foundations for this book to become manifest. Indeed, during his dominion did it finally become history."[31]

With the dwindling of Mongol power in the Islamic east, we witness how an Alid historical consciousness finds new political articulation among mystical and artisanal circles. The Safavis drew their followers from such spheres and were a successful example amid a series of movements (Sarbidars, Hurufi) that made use of the zeal and organization of Alid confraternities to fill a post-Mongol power vacuum. In the same region from which the Safavis arose to establish their first imperial capital, a group of craftsmen (Akhijuk) had attained power in Tabriz (Azarbaijan), albeit for a brief period of three years (1357–1359), until the Mongol successor state of the Jalayirids conquered them.[32] In the fourteenth century, the Ottomans similarly drew support from such fraternities *(akhī)* in consolidating their authority in Anatolia.[33] By this time, the cult of Abu Muslim was widespread among Anatolian fraternities, and the *Abū Muslimnāmes* had been translated into Turkish.[34] Such common narrative memories that instilled a particular love for the family of Ali linked these craft associations regionally. Although the Shi'i tendencies of Anatolian craftsmen warriors *(akhī)* have been disputed, it is difficult to disregard an Alid sense of communal history that saw the blossoming of the prestige of *sayyids* in *akhī* circles, many of which seem to have claimed descent from the eleventh Imam.[35] Despite the problematics of terminology, the saga of Husayn's martyrdom and the veneration of an Alid genealogy shaped a common culture among mystical circles *(futuvvat* and *tarīqat)* like the Bektashis. That a century later the Safavis would recruit

Qizilbash devotees from these Anatolian circles points to the solidarity that could be forged through a sharing of narrative memories and chivalric traditions. In the entourage of Shaykh Safi and his descendants, many names of fraternal brothers *(akhī)* like Akhi Jibra'il and Akhi Farj Zingani are mentioned.[36] The shrine of Shaykh Safi actively participated in the local and regional economy of Ardabil. Among Shaykh Safi's disciples were craftsmen—goldsmiths *(zargar)*, painters *(naqqāsh)*, bakers *(khubbāz)*, barbers *(dallāk)*, and soapsellers *(sābun-furūsh)*.[37] Following the Shaykh's death, craftsmen built a tomb tower and a Dar al-Huffaz, or a chamber for the recitation of the Qur'an, to honor him.[38] The hagiographer of Shaykh Safi himself was the son of a clothier *(bazzāz)*. Isma'il, too, evokes *akhīs* in his poetry *(divan)*: "The *akhīs* who recognize the guide *(pīr)* as true pearls; those whose words is but one are true men."[39] Isma'il, like the founding fathers of the Ottomans, called on such groups of "true men'" *(akhīs* and *ghāzīs)* known for their valor and bravery to join his cause. And it is in the two overlapping genres of the hagiography and the warrior epic that the experiences and actions of such men are represented.[40] Religious and gender diversity are delineated in these narratives not only because they are products of frontier cultures but because craft circles were open to non-Muslims, whether Mazdean, Armenian, Greek, or Jew.[41] Craft circles welcomed a variety of ethnic groups, and both sexes seem to have been allowed to join. Women warriors *(ayyār)* are active in epics such as the Persianate *Samak-i Ayyār* and their Anatolian counterpart—for example, the story of Efromiya, the female warrior of the *Dānishmendnāme*.[42] These chivalric women are not mere characters in epic traditions, for during the rise of the Ottomans a group of Anatolian sisters, Bajiyan-i Rum, played an important role alongside their brothers *(akhī)*.[43] In the lay religiosity of artisanal milieu, gender and ethnic identities mingled in ways that did not conform to Muslim textual ideals. In the final part of this book, we shall see how gendered boundaries would harden with the emergence of a legal culture patronized by the Safavi court and religious seminaries.

Through stories about the Abrahamic family (Adam, Abraham, Muhammad, and Ali) that are narrated using the Qur'an, hadith, and mystical poetry of Attar, Sa'idi, and Rumi as proof texts, the *Futuvvatnāme-yi Sultānī* encapsulates scenarios from the past that each participant must reenact. The stories emanate from three realms of time—creation of the cosmos (God, Adam, and Gabriel), the era of Biblical prophets (Abraham, Moses, and Jesus), and the age of Muhammad's community *(umma)*. This final and contemporary epoch dominates the narrative, although there is a consistent linkage between the present Islamic era and the universal figures who played an important role in the creation and subsequent history of the cosmos. Stories from the Muslim era recorded in the Qur'an and hadith not only relate the moral contours of the righteous characters of the Imams, but their gestures are to be memorized and acted out in ritual and in everyday practice. Each participant is to learn about the history of the holy Imams to place himself within that struggle and better understand personal suffering. Memory of an Alid past is to serve as an elucidation of the present: "Let it be known that narrating and hearing tales has many advantages. First is that one becomes aware of the conditions of the ancients. Second is that when one hears of strange and wondrous [things,] his eyes are opened unto the divine power. Third is that when one hears about the trials and tribulations of the ancients, he finds comfort in understanding that no one has been free of the chains of sorrow."[44] A history of suffering is related orally through "singers of tales" *(qissahkhwānan)*, epics *(afsānahkhwānān)*, and poetry *(nazmkhwānān)*, which the novice is to learn by heart.[45] Here is where the drama of the betrayal of the family of Muhammad forms a shared memory, both of these mystic craftsmen and for Shi'is in general. Both groups venerate the twelve Imams and are summoned to take revenge for their deaths and to redress the injustices they experienced. Through the didactic style of this manual, which uses the question-and-answer format, each initiate into the fraternity is imparted with an awareness of Ali, a knowledge and consciousness of the ways in which Ali tangibly lived with them, through hearing and repeating his words and through the performance of his deeds *(Imitatio Alavi)*. Every item of ritual clothing is associated with an Alid lineage, from the belt girded around the novice at initiation to the cloaks and headgear that symbolize membership in the brotherhood.

Particular to these brotherhoods is that they mix languages of Alid loyalty with sufism in such a way that it is impossible to place them under the rubric of either Shi'ism or Sunnism. Although Muhammad is revered as the seal of the prophets and Ali and his eleven descendants (Imams) as spiritual guides *(pīr)*, the blend of other holy characters from the Islamic past is drawn from both Sunni and Shi'i historiography. Salman-i Farsi appears with the caliph Umar and Uthman as well as Abu Muslim. Remarkably, this Alid piety merges mystic ideals with codes of honor and conduct associated with the milieu of chivalry (artists, craftsmen, and warriors). These codes of honor echo the values of Persianate epic heroes like *Samak-i Ayyār* or Rustam of the *Shāhnāme*. They are the values of chivalry and gallantry *(javānmardī va ayyārī)* that can be traced to an ancient Iranian tradition of "manliness." The Achaemenid inscriptions of Naqsh-i Rustam refer to men *(marik)* associated with a feudal household or a king. These young men *(mariy, ma'riyeh* in Middle Persian, *mirak)* are symbolic wolves *(Mairyo* in the Avesta)—independent fighters who, like wolves, fight in packs.[46] They are girded with a belt of obedience when they take their oaths of loyalty to a princely household or an Iranian king.[47] They are the brothers *(ayyār/yār)* who enter the battlefield in the name of truth and justice in Persian epics like *Samak-i Ayyār* and *Vīs u Ramīn*. And in the Islamic era they are assimilated amid mystic circles of Alid loyalists like those of the Safavis, where such forms of allegiance overlapped linguistically, in that they shared cultural symbols with the Shi'a.

Yet Kashifi specifies that *tarīqat* means following the model of

Ali and his descendants. He places this form of spiritual chivalry within an Islamic framework of mysticism: "Know that the knowledge ['*ilm*] of *futuvvat* is a noble science. It is a branch of mysticism [*tasawwuf*] and of unicity [*tawhīd*]."⁴⁸ He enumerates a number of earlier Muslim mystics who have written about chivalry as his sources and proceeds to locate this knowledge in Ali and his children, the Imams. But the genealogy Kashifi evokes goes back to the creation of the cosmos, all the way to the first man and prophet Adam. Although the nomenclature he makes use of is Abrahamic, he fuses it with a Persianate ethos of chivalry *(javānmardī)*. Kashifi emphasizes that everyone is capable of performing this task. Blood descendants *(sayyid)* are privy to this path; however, *futuvvat* can be attained by anyone.⁴⁹ He thus sanctifies the genealogy of Alids, awarding them direct access to the divine.

Kashifi's manual on chivalry reveals an aspect of sufism that encouraged a variety of mystic expressions, whether with the propagation of piety through "singing stories or poetry" about the Imams or through the cultivation of martial arts, like wrestling and acrobatics. Beyond revealing a whole way of being, this manual situates such virtues within the social and economic milieu of guilds. Now we understand why so many Alid rebellions in the early modern period found followers among craftsmen. As we have seen, the founder of the Nuqtavi movement, Mahmud Pasikhani, was originally a member of the Alid Hurufis. Although the Nuqtavis shared Alid symbols with the Hurufis, they interpreted Ali through Persianate lenses. This asymmetry should be understood in the context of a growing emphasis on the sanctity of the family of Muhammad. Pasikhani had sought to redirect the eminence of Alid sacred lineage *(sayyid)* with his comparison of the moon (Muhammad) and the sun (Mahmud) and his blurring of social distinctions based on pedigree. Instead of Alid kinship, it was a particular Persianate (Ajami) knowledge that would allow transcendence through the paths of *tarīqat* and *futuvvat* indiscriminately.

Whether the *Shāhnāme* was recited along with the *Abū*

Muslimnāme(s) in Alid *futuvvat* circles is unclear. We have isolated instances of guilds, for example, in a southeastern city in Iran—Rashalak in Sistan—where the *Shāhnāme* was recited in the first half of the seventeenth century along with other stories and epics during assemblies.[50] We know that singers of the *Shāhnāme* had their own guilds separate from those of other storytellers. The process of memorizing six thousand lines of poetry was itself a specialization with specific rules and pedagogical techniques.[51] Apart from the *Abū Muslimnāme* and the feats of Muhammad b. Hanafiyya, other Alid narratives portraying the life of Ali, the martyrdom of Husayn, and the struggles of the Imams would have been heard in these circles. I have mentioned that the author of the *Futuvvatnāme-yi Sultānī*, Vai'z-i Kashifi, penned one of the earliest accounts of the Karbala drama. He must have used oral accounts in his *Garden of Martyrs (Rawzat al-shuhada)*, as he says he did for his manual on chivalry.[52] By the seventeenth century, Kashifi's version of the martyrdom of Husayn had become the standard script used during assemblies, recalling the tragedy *(rawzah khwānī)* as well as passion plays *(ta'ziya)* performed as theater in modern Iran (Qajar).

Kashifi emplots religious stories in circulation among a lay piety of artisans and craftsmen into one master narrative. Yet as with the *Abū Muslimnāme(s)*, their contents diverge from what theologians consider legitimate accounts and behaviors. Although the *Abū Muslimnāme* was banned, the fate of this popular ritual of lamentation turned out to be different. Despite Imami *ulamas'* discomfort with the outward expression of weeping, the shedding of blood, the unveiled representation of Husayn's female kin, and the nudity that was displayed during these ritual reenactments of the drama of Karbala, the Safavis came to coopt these mourning processions, manipulating them according to their will.[53] The ritual commemoration of Husayn's martyrdom was a productive mechanism for conversion given that it occupied an emotional space in the imaginations of Sunnis as well.[54] Safavi kings (Abbas II and Sulayman), who literally became the directors of these yearly plays, capitalized on local rivalries that were acted out by craftsmen who usually lived and worked in the same quarters of a city or town.[55] Local rivalries would often play themselves out in the process of casting the characters, who would either be on the side of the victim Husayn or the villainous Umayyads. The Safavis not only used such ritualized violence to centralize their power but were also attempting to achieve social integration through support of such popular religious cults to engage their audience, flaunting their piety through the patronage of the cult of Husayn.[56]

There seems to have been a fear of Iranian stories of warriors and kings entering sufi circles. Shaykh Safi's hagiographer, Ibn Bazzaz, a son of a clothier, recounts a story *(hikāyat)* in which Safi was informed that a disciple, Khwaja Nizam al-din Khwajlu Ardabili, recited the *Shāhnāme* in private *(khalvat)*, while in public *(zikr)* he read from the Qur'an. Safi takes a couple of days before he responds to this accusation of Mazdean tendencies in his order. He first corrects the name of the book and says it must have been the "king of books" (i.e., the Qur'an) rather than the "book of kings" *(Shāhnāme)*. Those who reported this information were simply mistaken. The poem that follows this episode is telling: "We read the book of the Shah [*nāme-yi shāh*] from the notebook [*daftar*] of our hearts [*dil*]. How can you compare the *Shāhnāme* with our book [*daftar*]?"[57] The story creates an opposition between those who recited and listened to the *Shāhnāme* and those who listened to stories from the Qur'an. It is Abrahamic history versus Iranian history. The story also reveals that in Ardabil of the fourteenth century, the center of the Safavi brotherhood, what would be recited during the remembrance of God in private could have been the *Shāhnāme*. Moreover, although Shaykh Safi distinguishes the *Shāhnāme* from the Qur'an, he does not condemn it. Rather, he simply deflects any criticism from his disciple.

We know that Iranian heroic epics continued to be recited by storytellers in the medieval Islamic era. And for some Muslims, they seem to have provided a model for the emplotment of the heroic personae of Ali and the Imams. A medieval Saljuk source—*Kitāb al-Naqz* by Abdul Jalil Qazvini written in 1160 C.E.—reveals the use of these stories in the context of Sunni-Shi'i polemics. The author of the *Kitāb al-Naqz* is responding to Sunni accusations that Shi'is concoct miraculous stories about the feats of Ali and recited them *(manāqib khwānī)* in mosques and bazaars. These stories ascribe to Ali supernatural powers that Iranian heroes like Rustam had possessed. Ali, for example, in the medieval romance of the *Khāvarnāme* is confronted with fighting demons. He is said to have lifted the gates of Khaybar, something one hundred men could not achieve. Or he is reported to have been catapulted by a canon *(manjanīq)* into a fortress protected by five thousand men, which he conquered on his own.⁵⁸ Responding to Sunni critiques of Alid devotees, Qazvini points out that "the believers of Banu Umayya and Marwan after the killing of Husayn could not stand the praise of Ali. So a group of heretics [*khārijī*] and some other irreligious people collected stories of the heroic feats of Rustam and Suhrab, Isfandiyar and Kavus and Zal and recited them to counter the bravery and wisdom of Ali. This innovation [*bid'a*] still remains today [1160 C.E.], and in the community [*umma*] of Muhammad the praising of Zoroastrians [*gabrs*] is an innovation."⁵⁹ Although the intention of the Umayyads had been to counter Shi'i glorification of Ali's heroism, in the process it ensured the livelihood of Persian heroic narratives. That the *Shāhnāme* was associated with Zoroastrians is voiced explicitly; the epic is categorized as other—Zoroastrian and not Muslim. But it is interesting to see the dynamics between these heroic stories, the ways in which the old comes to shape the new. Here we have a Shi'i claiming that Sunnis are using the stories of Iranian heroes to belittle Ali's struggles. The medieval eulogist Shaykh Hasan Kashi in his *Tārīkh-i Muhammadī*, written in 1308 and 1309, mentioned as a model for emulation by the author of our manual on chivalry, Va'iz-i Kashifi, divulges what a contemporary of Shaykh Safi living in the nearby province of Mazandaran (Amul) felt about the *Shāhnāme*.⁶⁰ The fourteenth-century mystic

Hasan-i Kashi was one of the first to versify in Persian his devotion to the family of the prophet:

Dear son [*pisar*], do not read allegorical stories [*qissah-yi mujāz*].
Beware of reading them!
How long will you go on reading the *Shāhnāme*?
Remember promptly, this is a book of sin [*gānah-nāme*].
How much of this reminiscence [*zikr*] of Vamig and 'Uzra?
Remember instead your creator [*khāliq*].
How long will you go on reading about Vis and Ramin?
The story of those corrupt irreligious ones [*fāsiqān-i bī dīn*]—
For how long will you speak about the tales [*hadith*] of Rustam
and Zal?
Playful [*la'b*] and useless imaginary lies [*durūgh-i muhāl*],
The saying of the Zoroastrians [*gabr*] and the people of myths
[*ustūrān*]—
How long will you recite them for the Muslims?
If you wish to read in Persian
So that your spirit [*jān*] may sense comfort [*rāhat*] and familiarity
[*uns*],
There exist stories of Muhammad, the trusted one.
Just as glorious and exemplary as Ali
There exists as well the praise [*madh*] of Ali and his kin
Enough to recite night and day.

Kashi divulges a tension between an active memory of pre-Islamic Persian heroic epics and the unsung stories of Muslim heroes like Muhammad and Ali. In the Iranian lands, Alid histories and identities were in competition on the oral level not with "Sunni" culture but with Persianate culture. Persian speakers seemed to have been more attracted to Iranian epic histories, even if their legal lives were regulated according to Sunni law. Kashi thinks that the medium of the Persian language makes these myths so popular, so comforting. And so he takes it on himself to write eulogies and epics about Ali and his kin in Persian to fill the imaginations of the populace with "true" stories rather than with myths. In this process of conversion, Kashi maintains the symbolic system of the Persianate epic tradition, in which a language of nobility, loyalty, honor, and piety merges with Alid history. In the following passage, he addresses the question of why he uses the medium of Persian poetry to narrate the lives of Ali and the Imams:

> So that they may know and prefer reading them [Alid eulogies]
> For from courtier to peasant their souls yearn, constantly craving Persian poetry.
> Since this is the order of things,
> Perhaps they will read them now and again.⁶¹

With the translation of Alid narratives into the Persian vernacular, the Iranian past was mythologized—thus, our construction of the *Shāhnāme* as myth rather than history.⁶² Here I am assuming that history is not all fact and no fiction. Telling history through myths and in verse was the Mazdean mode of recounting the past. And for Mazdeans, people fought their demons on a daily basis, an aspect that continued to be represented visually in miniatures that illuminated episodes of the *Shāhnāme*. Instead, a new set of legends with claims of being "true" history were attempting to impose themselves. Persianate symbols, however, were translated onto the Alid memories with which they merged (see figure 4). Stories and poetry recited in craft circles where warriors and artisans joined together in chivalric vows of obedience and loyalty acted as a medium for both sharing and (re)shaping the past. Va'iz-i Kashifi's *Garden of Martyrs (Rawzat al-shuhada)* should be seen as an endeavor to propagate that past with a thick Alid coating, and the author did success in memorializing Husayn in the imaginations of inhabitants of the Persianate world on a broader level. Both the Timurid court of Husayn Bayqara (r. 1470–1506) and the Safavis would come to embrace this form of Alid devotion and patronize Kashifi and his works. The Safavi Shah Tahmasb, who quotes from Hasan Kashi in his *Memoir,* built him a shrine in Sultaniya (northwest Iran) and himself engaged in the pilgrimage to this shrine, placing Kashi among the founding fathers of Imami Shi'ism.⁶³ But despite the efforts of the Safavi court and the popularity of this genre of Alid literature, it did not replace the telling and recording of Persian epic histories. What we see instead in the Safavi world is a merging of these two genres, not only within the structure of Alid narratives but, as they continued to be recited side by side, as an integral part of the cultural repertoire of Muslims living in the Persianate zones.[64]

Patterns of behavior and ethics that fashioned notions of loyalty and obedience among these Persian epic warriors fighting the cosmic battle of truth were now translated onto Ali and the Imams fighting for a Muslim truth *(dīn-i haqq)* revealed to Muhammad and fathomed by Ali and his progeny. This code of conduct is embedded in the culture of holy Muslim warriors *(ghāzī)* like Abu Muslim, fighting the infidels and expanding the frontiers of Islam. It is the object of loyalty that has been transformed—from Mazda (wisdom) to a monotheistic Abrahamic God. The rituals of loyalty and types of behavior required find continuity of expression in Alid *futuvvat* contexts. They seem to be self-generating social patterns of piety and of leadership that enjoyed deeper structural roots in cities and towns from Mesopotamia to the Oxus. Whether there existed a consciousness of such continuities—in other words, whether these patterns were identified by some who experienced them as Iranian—is uncertain. But through the singing and memorizing of epic histories in these fraternal communities, traces of a Persianate ethos and worldview seem to have survived alongside a burgeoning Alid memory. Thus it is that some Persianate devotees of the Safavis (Alid) and the Nuqtavis (Mazdean) may have participated in the same craft circles. We know that in seventeenth-century Iran, guilds were open to different confessional groups of Jews, Armenians, and Zoroastrians.[65] Craft professions continued to be an open and active avenue for interconfessional sharing and collaboration. Craftsmen with different religious identities could have joined arms at particular historical judges, during the apocalyptic sorties *(khurūj)* of Isma'il or that of the Nuqtavi—Dervish Khusraw, for example. Whatever their common reasons may have been—whether material concerns prompted by a rise in taxation of their guilds or parallel astronomical readings of celestial phenomena like the conjunction of Saturn and Jupiter—they rebelled together. Kashifi locates the knowledge of *futuvvat* in the human soul *(nafs)*.⁶⁶ Knowledge is portrayed as "a light [*nūr*] from the divine world that with its generous rays [*partaw-yi fayz*], angelic and divine characteristics [*sifāt-i malikī va malakūtī*] will appear in the interior [*bātin*] of the possessor."⁶⁷ This brilliant light is purifying *(tazkiyah)* and cleansing *(asfiyah)*; it allows the human being to defend himself against satanic dispositions *(akhlāq)* and animalistic behavior *(atvār)*. The one who is illuminated by this light is able to act as the agent *(mubashir)* and perpetrator *(murtakib)* of good. The importance of exercising such wisdom through the performance of good deeds is central to the whole ritual and ethical structure of these fraternities. The Zoroastrian mantra of "good thoughts, good words, and good deeds" embedded in Ferdowsi's *Shāhnāme* or in Alid heroic stories about Abu Muslim colors codes of valor and morality that tie members of the *futuvvat* together as a group. In the struggle between good and evil, Iran embodies the good—the central theme running through the cycle of stories of Iranian kings and warriors in the *Shāhnāme*. In the *Shāhnāme*, a family (Nariman) of warriors plays the role of archetypical heroes in the cosmic battle narrated as Iranian history. With the apocalyptic advent of Islam, the *Shāhnāme* leaves the history of the Iranian peoples under Muslim rule open to a future acting and recording. Ferdowsi does, however, end with a telling turn in the history of Iran. The Iranian king Yazdgird flees for his life from the invading Muslim armies and his turned over to the Arab governor of Khurasan by a Persian peasant. The subject betrays the king who merits no better, for he has lost his dignity in flight. It is the warrior Rustam who maintains his honor—fighting to the last drop of blood, becoming the heroic martyr at the hands of the invading Arabs. Is Ferdowsi placing hope for future change in warriors rather than kings?

The medieval Persian epic about the gallant Samak, *Samak-i*

Ayyār, speaks of a milieu of heroic warriors as well. Moral obligations tie two characters and camps together through mutual admiration for a way of being that combines bravery with generosity, humility, and loyalty.[68] The reputation of such men (*ayyār* and *javānmard*) precedes them. Wherever the protagonist Samak goes, he has nameless admirers who spring out of the bazaars. The ways of chivalry are socially recognizable, and they are honored among the populace. Thousands of men and women of the bazaar shriek and cry when they hear that two brothers, the surgeon Zarand, and the butcher Razmaq, have been killed in the narrative, for they embody such dignity.[69] In *Samak-i Ayyār* the brave (*ayyār*) are common people—artisans, traders, spies, and messengers—who join arms together in a moral camaraderie as they embark on the path of professional warriors (*ayyār pīshah*). Their leader, Samak, epitomizes the perfect warrior. He fights in the name of the lineage of the sun king, Khurshidshah, who is depicted as an ideal prince. A Nuqtavi could read this solar genealogy as Persian (Ajami). The narrator informs us that this prince is called the sun king because his birth coincided with the rise of the sun. He is beautiful, erudite, strong, and sound of judgment—a young, moon-faced boy who has the stature of a cypress tree and whose cheeks reveal a green line, traces of a pubescent mustache as though painted by the most deft hand of grand artists.[70] Samak fights on behalf of an exemplary prince who possesses the divine glory (*farr*) symbolized by the sun as well as its noble character. Not only does he represent justice, but he is depicted in sufi poetry (Jami, d. 1492) as the prophet Joseph, portrayed as the symbol of divine beauty. Although *Samak-i Ayyār* was recorded in the thirteenth century, as in the *Shāhnāme,* there is little trace of Islam in it. It is undoubtedly pre-Islamic. It preserves the memory of chivalry for its audience, reinforcing Persianate values and inspiring the ways in which the audience might act them out.

In the Muslim era, Abu Muslim is portrayed through such a Persianate heroic framework. He is fighting, however, not for the sun king, Khurshidshah, but rather for the family of Muhammad, Ali, and his descendants, who are presented as victims of evil and the embodiment of good. Ali at times resembles the Mazdean Lord Wisdom (Ahuramazda). Among Ali Ilahi circles of devotees, for example, he is thought to have preexisted in an original time, perhaps in eternity when there was nothing but purity. Ali is portrayed in many popular stories (Ali Ilahi, *Khāvarnāme*) and miniatures as battling with demons and dragons. Just as Houshang—the son of the first man-prophet—was slain by the black demon and his son Siamak rose to avenge his father, Husayn fights courageously in revenge for the rule usurped from his father Ali. Cycles of revenge stories that provoke the valiant displays of heroes in the *Shāhnāme* mark a new rhythm amid a succession of Alid avengers. Hence, there arose the Alid epic cycles of the *Abū Muslimnāme, Zemchīnāme,* and the *Junaydnāme,* fusing mythological images of Persian warriors with the Muslim nomenclature. In the *Abū Muslimnāme,* it is as an act of revenge against the injustice done to the family of the prophet (Ali and Husayn) that Abu Muslim and his fellow warriors collaborate to overthrow the evil Umayyads. The particular contents of each story are different, and this is where the present is inscribed into the narrative. But the framework that allows for the interpretation of the actions of Muslim historical figures like Ali, Husayn, and Abu Muslim emplotted in prose are identical: they are all fighting for justice in a cosmic battle that links their actions to a universal struggle for good. Ideal values, chivalric virtues, and definitions of loyalty and friendship are shared. Even the particular characteristics of chivalry—generosity, virility, humility, and bravery—are parallel. What is cyclical about such a conception of history is not only that change is understood as a succession of aeons but that in each era warriors play a particular chivalric role and are confronted with the same universal problems, albeit in different historical contexts.

As Kashifi expounds on the etymology of the word *futuvvat,* derived from the Arabi *fatā'* (youth), he associates it with *juwān* the Middle Persian word for "youth" and the practice of *javānmardī* (chivalry):[71] "Know that *futuvvat* linguistically [*az ruy-i lughat*]," he writes, "is a youth [*javānī*] and a *fatā'* is a young man. Some of the grandees of etymology believe that *futuvvat* is [the same as] *javānmardī*."[72] In other words, these etymologists are suggesting a Persian equivalent of the term, with a history prior to Islam. The term *futuvvat* does not appear in Arabic before the advent of Islam.[73] In Persian, *javān* means "youth," and *mardī* is "manliness" or "humanness," so a literal translation would be "young manliness." But the designation *juwān-mardī* existed in Middle Persian (Sasani) to denote a chivalrous individual.[74] Kashifi goes on to present the meaning of the term in the popular usage *('urf-i 'āmm)* of his age—the late fifteenth century. *Futuvvat,* he says, "refers to those who possess praiseworthy characteristics and pleasant temperaments." And in the rendition *(ta'rif)* of famous mystics *(khwāss)*, it is the manifestation of the light of divine creation.

This light is like the Mazdean concept of *fravarti,* those celestial archetypes of the creates of light that act as the tutelary angels of earthly creatures:[75] "In the prologue of the millennia belonging to the period of mixture, which constitutes human history, Ahura Mazda [Lord Wisdom] confronted the *Fravartis* of human beings with a free choice, which is at the origin of their destiny, that is to say, their time, their aeon: either they might dwell in heaven, safe from the ravages of Ahriman, or they might descend and be incarnated in material bodies in order to combat Ahriman in the earthly world.[76] The *fravarti* elect to join the battle on earth, and, as Henry Corbin notes, an entire chivalric ethic is based on this conception. Ahura Mazda is not an all-powerful God imposing the law, imposing trials and sufferings to which the human submits without understanding. Rather, he is one whose companions share his combat, whose suffering they assume, and whom they do not betray. They are the knights of Lord Wisdom, and in Zurvanism they become the suffering members, those who endure affliction because Ahuramazda assumes the features of the active and suffering God, foreshadowing the primordial man of Manichaeism.[77] In Kashifi's work, the *fravartis* have been transformed from an im-

age of celestial archetypes or angels of light to pure light emanating from the divine heavens. And in the chivalric culture described by Kashifi, they are no longer the knights of Ahuramazda but the brave and sacrificial warriors of Ali, fighting
because of his and his family's suffering in the Islamic era.
Some who felt betrayed by the promise of Islam—whether
Alids or Mazdeans—came to explain their predicament through
such frameworks. Cultural forms of chivalry that were linked to
the artisanal class and craft structures were conduits through
which heteroglossia inhabited secrets passed down from master
to apprentice. The collective sense of solidarity in suffering that
was so linked to their cosmic reality gave members of society the
choice of joining arms with the army of good, whomever that
army fought for. The particularities of circumstance found them
at times fighting in the army of Abu Muslim; while at other
times, they were devotees of Isma'il, entering the battlefield
ready to sacrifice their lives.

Kashifi goes on to expound on the spiritual content of this
type of brotherhood: "The meaning of the word *fatā'* is youth,
and it is used for a young man. Although it can only be used for
a youth in reality [*haqīqat*], as a metaphor it can be used for a
person who has attained complete human wisdom [*kamāl-i
fazā'il-i insānī*]: just like a child who is immature, once he develops through the stages of the soul [*nafs*] and attains the state of
the heart [*dil*], he arrives at the stage of youth [*javān*]." Kashifi
explains that youth is just a metaphor for the one who has attained this wisdom, the illuminated one. The wisdom of the *fatā'*
is analogous to the bountiful strength and physical splendor, the
kamālāt, that the body attains at the prime of its youth. Youth is
a metaphor for the fullness and expansiveness of spirit.[78]

Even though Kashifi grounds the chivalric brotherhoods
within the Muslim era and the Alid cause, he presents an interesting interpretation of the Persian traces of this knowledge
(*'ilm*) through the metaphor of clothing. Quoting from a story
preserved by the medieval mystic Attar in his *Qavā'id al-
futuvvat*, Kashifi states that in pagan times during the reign of

Shath Nabi there was no differentiation between chivalry
(futuvvat) and mysticism *(tarīqat)*. Kashifi represents spiritual
chivalry as a pre-Islamic phenomenon, and the essential unity of
sufism and *futuvvat* is expressed in their shared garment—the
cloak *(khirqa)*. In the era of Abraham, one group came to Abraham to complain about the weight of the cloak, which they said
was too much for them to bear. Abraham sends this group in a
boat of mysticism *(tarīqat)* into the sea of truth *(haqīqat)* to an
island of chivalry *(futuvvat)*, where they will be safe from Satan.
This group then asks Abraham to designate a special garment
for them, just as the people of the path *(ahl-i tarīqat)* wore a
cloak. Abraham designates for them the *sharvāl*, which is a Persian word, Kashifi says, for trousers, and the people of Iraq call
these pants *futuvvat*: "It is a part of the cloak [*khirqa*] just as
futuvvat is a part of *tarīqat*."[79] According to Kashifi, the knowledge of *futuvvat* became widespread because most people were
attracted to these trousers.

In the Irano-Muslim tradition, the conflation of Abraham
with Zoroaster was not uncommon.[80] Although Kashifi does not
refer to the beliefs of the group who practiced *futuvvat* as Persian, he does create a link through an item of clothing, using its
Persian designation *(sharvāl)*, typical of members of guilds. The
people of Iraq, a center of gnostic syncretism (Mazdean, Jewish,
and Christian), referred to these trousers as *futuvvat*. Kashifi accounts for the spread of *futuvvat* as well, given that the movement became popular due to its adherents' appealing clothing.
He uses allegory to explain the Persianate lineage of the chivalric
brotherhoods, stating that many different practices have been
associated with the *futuvvat*; he is writing this book to rectify
false attributions. Kashifi's ambiguous representations of the
Persianate idiom in *futuvvat* circles are attempts at forgetting
these traces and instead remembering their Muslim contexts. Although the Alid identity of the *futuvvat* is canonized in Kashifi's
manual, the associations the Mazdean "root paradigms" are introduced metaphorically with the Persian cultural ethos encapsulated in dress. What people wore and the language they spoke

identified and distinguished one group from another. Even though Kashifi internalized memory, rendering it unconscious through metaphor and allegory, with the singing of epics in Persian and the wearing of trousers associated with Iranians, traces of a Persianate ethos and worldview lived on in Alid circles.

NOTES

1. Kāshifī distinguishes between storytellers *(hikāyat gū)* and singers of poetry *(nazm khwān)*. Kashifi, *Futuvvatnāme-yi Sultānī*, ed. Muhammad Ja'far Mahjub (Tehran: Bunyad-i Farhang-i Iran, 1971).

2. See Alexander D. Knysh, *Islamic Mysticism: A Short History* (Leiden: Brill, 2000), 88–99, where he delineates two early styles of ascetism in Eastern Iran (Karrāmiya and Malāmatiya), the former practicing mendicanacy and severe austerity, and the latter rejecting this reclusive style and instead engaging in public life. Both of these movements shared spiritual traits, although their approaches to transcendence were different. Both were incorporated into sufism. The Karrāmiya dissipated as a movement, while the Malāmatiya maintained some cohesiveness. On the Karrāmiya, see J. Chabbi, "Remarques sur le développment historique des mouvements ascétiques et mystiques au Khurasan," *Studia Islamcia* 46 (1977): 5–71.

3. Kishwar Rizvi, "Transformations in Early Safavid Architecture: The Shrine of Shaykh Safi al-din Ardabili in Iran, 1501–1629," Ph.D. diss., Massachusetts Institute of Technology, 2000), 35.

4. Husayn Vā'iz Kāshifī, *Futuvvatnāme-yi Sultānī*, ed. Muhammad Ja'far Mahjub (Tehran: Bunyad-i Farheng-i Iran, 1971), 281.

5. Ibid., 280.

6. Ibid., 275.

7. Mehdi Keyvānī, *Artisans and Guild Life in the Later Safavid Period: Contributions to the Social-Economic History of Persia*, vol. 65, *Islamkundliche Untersuchungen* (Berlin: Klaus Schwarz, 1982), 141–147.

8. Ibid., 54.

9. Ibid., 101–111.

10. Ibid., 47–52. Keyvānī recorded thirty-three main guilds.

11. Ibid., 67–68.

12. Ibid., 53.
13. Rasūl Ja'fariān, *Maqāllāt-i Tārīkhī*, vol. 1 (Qum, 1375), 173; *Rowzat al-safā*, 7, 237; 'Abdullāh Afandī Isfahānī, *Riyāz al-ulamā wa hīyāz al-fuzalā'*, ed. Ahmad al-Husaynī (Qum, 1980), vol. 2, 188–192.
14. Kāshifī, *Futuvvatnāme-yi Sultānī*, 6, mentions the following works: *Tabsirat al-asfiyā*, as well as Khwājū Kamal al-din Abdul Razzāq Kāshī's *Futuvvatnāme*, Attar's *Qavā'id al-futuvvat*, *risālah-yi adab al-futuvvat*, *Futuvvatnāme* of Shaykh-i Kabīr, *'Avarif al-ma'ārif*, *Mursād al-'ibād*, *Hadīqat al-haqīqat*, and Zariyah Isfahani's *Tazkirat al-awliyā'*.
15. Khwandamīr, *Habīb al-siyar*, vol. 4, 170 (Tehran: Kitābkhānah-yi Khayyām, 1954).
16. Keyvānī, *Artisans and Guild Life*, 142.
17. There are some exceptions. Richard Bulliet, *Islam: The View from the Edge* (New York: Columbia University Press, 1994), 162, does talk about the coexistence of these two forms of sufism. Marshall Hodgson, *The Venture of Islam: Conscience and History in a World Civilization*, vol. 2 (Chicago: University of Chicago Press, 1974), 131, speaks of the close association between sufism and *futuvvat* guilds.
18. Kay Kāvūs b. Iskandar b. Qābūs b. Vashmgīr, *Qābūsnāme*, E. j. W. Gibb Memorial Series, 18 (London: Luzac, 1951), 139–152.
19. Ibid., 141–142.
20. Ibid., 143.
21. Dick Davis, *Epic and Sedition: The Case of Ferdowsi's Shāhnāme* (Fayetteville: University of Arkansas Press, 1992), 110.
22. Ibid.
23. Ibid., 118.
24. The *Futuvvatnāme* of Suhrawardi adds a rank between simple adepts of the spoken word *(qawlī)* and those girded by the sword *(sayfī)*. See Claude Cahen, "Futuwwa," *EI2*.
25. Kāshifī classifies artisans and craftsmen into two groups, performers and handle tool users. The first category of performers *(ahl-i ma'rika)* consist of eulogists *(maddāhān)*, water carriers *(saqqāyān)*, orators *(khavāss guyān)*, itinerant showmen *(bisāt andāzān)*, wrestlers *(kushtī gīrān)*, porters *(hammālān)*, rope-acrobats *(rasan bāzān)*, and sheep knuckle players *(tās bāzān)*. The

second category of handle tool users *(ahl-i qabza)* include soldiers *(sipāhiyān)*, trowel users *(ahl-i qabza-yi māla)*, and hammer users, which would involve blacksmiths, coppersmiths, braziers, goldsmiths, and silversmiths *(ahl-i khāsak)*, carding bow users and felt makers *(ahl-i qabzah-yi kamā)*, awl users (who are the shoemakers and saddle makers) *(ahl-i qabzah-yi kūda)*, ironers, tailors *(ahl-i qabzah-yi utū va tāqiya)*, ladle users *(ahl-i qabzah-yi kāfaha)*, pick wielders *(ahl-i qabzah-yi kulang)*, knife wielders (who are slaughterers, butchers, and cooks) *(ahl-i qabzah-yi kārd va sātūr)*, and skewer makers *(ahl-i qabzah-yi sīkh)*. Kāshifī, *Futuvvatnāme*, 276–393. I have used translations here from Keyvāni, *Artisans and Guild Life*, 207.

26. Bulliet, *Islam: The View from the Edge*, 164–165; Claude Cahen, "Futuwwa," *EI2*.

27. On the Saffarids, see Clifford Edmond Bosworth, *The History of the Saffarids of Sistan and the Maliks of Nimruz: 247/861 to 949/1542-3*. (Costa Mesa: Mazda, 1994).

28. Hodgson, *The Venture of Islam*, vol. 2, 128–129.

29. Roy Mottahedeh, *Loyalty and Leadership in an Early Islamic Society* (Princeton: Princton University Press, 1980), 160–162.

30. See Alexander Knysh, *Islamic Mysticism*, 92–94, on the Malamatis of Khurasan and their links to artisanal milieus. Among the names, of their leaders, he lists Hamdun al-Qassār (fuller), Abu Hafs al-Haddad (blacksmith). According to Knysh, Sulami links the Malāmatis to the *futuvvat*. Also see Bulliet, *Islam: The View from the Edge*, 165.

31. Mawlana Shaykh Hasan Kāshī, *Tārīkh-i Muhammadī*, ed. Rasūl Ja'fariān" (Qum: Kitābkhānah-yi Takhassusī-yi Tārīkh-i Islam va Irān, 1998), 28. I would like to thank Rasūl Ja'fariān for providing me with this source.

32. Claude Cahen, "Futuwwa," *EI2*.

33. Mehmet Fuad Köprülü, *Islam in Anatolia after the Turkish Invasion: Prolegomena*, trans. and ed. Gary Leiser (Salt Lake City: University of Utah Press, 1993), 28–30; Köprülü, *The Origins of the Ottoman Empire*, trans. Gary Leiser (Albany: State University of New York Press, 1992); Abdülbāki Gölpīnarlī, "Islam ve Türk Illerinde Fütüvvet Teşkilātī," *Istanbul Universitesi Iktisāt Fakultesi Mecmuasī* 11 (1953): 3–354.

34. Iréne Mélikoff, *Abū Muslim: Le "Porte-Hache" de Khorasan dans la tradition epique Turco-Iranienne* (Paris: Adrien Maisonnere, 1962), 71–83; on Hāji Shādi's version, see particularly 75–76.

35. See Cemal Kafadar's doubts on the Shi'ism of the Anatolian *akhīs*, *Between Two Worlds: The Construction of the Ottoman State* (Berkeley: University of California Press, 1995), 75–76, 171–172. Also see Cahen on the prominence of *akhīs* in thirteenth and four-teenth century Anatolia understood as a channel for 'Shi'itising Anatolian Islam.' Claude Cahen, "Le Problème du Shi'sme dans l'Asie Mineure Turque pre-Ottomane," *Le Shi'ism Imamite* (Paris Presses Universitaires de France, 1970), 120. Cahen, 121–122, points out that a family of *akhīs* in Ankara at the end of the thir-teenth century claimed Alid descent from the eleventh Imam. See Modaressi on Ja'far b. Ali (d. 884–885) who was considered by some Shi'is as the eleventh Imam and the Mahdi (Fathiyya). Some of Ja'far's descendants migrated to Egypt and India. In *Crisis and Consolidation in the Formative Period of Shi'ite Islam* (Prince-ton: Darwin Press, 1993), 85–86, Modarressi speaks of a sufi order in contemporary Turkey that traces its spiritual lineage to Ja'far and call him Ja'far al-Mahdi. He cites the late ninth-century heresiographer Nawbakhti on this group of devotees of Ja'far.

36. Ibn Bazzāz Tavakkul b. Ismā'īl, *Safvat al-safā*, ed. Ghulām Reza Tabātabā'ī Majd (Ardabil: G. Tabātabā'ī Majd, 1994), 182.

37. Ibid., 1094, 1111, 1116, 1121, 1149. Also see Keyvānī, *Artisans and Guild Life;* 154.

38. Rizvi, "Transformations in Early Safavid Architecture," 205.

39. Khatā'ī, *Il Canzonieri di Shah Isma'il*, ed. Tourkhan Gandjei (Na-ples: Institute Universitario Oriente, 1959), (7/11).

40. See Kafadar's illuminating work on the role of such epics as sources for Anatolian frontier culture, *Between Two Worlds.*

41. Hodgson, *The Venture of Islam*, vol. 2, 122. Also see Keyvānī, *Ar-tisans and Guild Life,* 82, 129, 157, 170, 176–184, for the mixed ethnicities represented in guilds of Isfahan in the seventeenth cen-tury. For a list of forty-three crafts and professions held by Arme-nians in seventeenth century Isfahan, see Lutfallāh Hunarfar, "Mashāghil-i Arāmanah-yi Julfa," *Majallah-yi Vahīd* 8 (1964): 68–73.

42. Maria Galland, *Samak-i Ayyār* (Paris, 1987), 142, 154; Kafadar, *Between Two Worlds*, 67–68.

43. Mikāil Bayram, *Bācīyān-ī Rūm: Selçuklular Zamāninda Genç Kīzlar Teşkilātī* (Konya: M Bayram, 1987); Bayram, *Fatma Bācī ve Bāciyān-i Rūm: Anadolu Bacīlar Teşkilātī* (Konya: Damla Ofset Matbaacolokve Ticaret, 1994).

44. Kāshifī, *Futuvvatnāme-yi Sultānī*, translated by Mahmoud Omidsalar in "Storytellers in Classical Persian Texts," *Journal of American Folklore* 97, no. 384 (April–June 1984): 207.

45. See Omidsalar, "Storytellers in Classical Persian Texts," 208–209, for a discussion of three groups of performers—storytellers *(hikāyat gūyān)*, narrative verse singers *(afsānah/qissahkhwānān)* and the lyric verse reciters *(nazm khwānān)* enumerated by Kāshifī. Omidsalar talks about the ambiguity between the *qissah* and *afsanah* raconteurs and concludes that both exist side by side in Persian literature. However, the disputations from the Safavi period are clearly attempting to delegate Persian epics like the *Shāhnāme* and the *Abū Muslimnāme* as myths *(afsānah)*, both of which seem to have been considered as *qissah*, but now *qissah* was to be the canonized versions of the *ulama*.

46. See Mansøur Shaki, "Class System," *E. Iranica*; M. A. Dandamayev, "Barda," *E. Iranica*.

47. Ibid. The *Kārnāmak* refers to them as (h) *adiyār* > (h) *ayyār* > *ayyar* > *ayār* > *yār*.

48. Vā'iz-i Kāshifī, *Futuvvatnāme-yi Sultānī*, ed. Ja'far Mahjub: Bunyād-i Iran, 1971) 5.

49. Ibid., 29.

50. Malik Shah Husayn, *Ihyā al-mulūk*, 252–254, as cited in Keyvānī, *Artisans and Guild Life*, 145. The source dates from the first half of the seventeenth century.

51. Mary Ellen Page, "Professional Storytelling in Iran: Transmission and Practice," *Iranian Studies* 7, nos. 3–4 (1979): 195–215.

52. Scholars of Shi'ism, like Rasūl Ja'fariān, have noted that the *Rawzat al-shuhada* includes information not found in standard Imami texts. *Maqālāt-i Tārīkhī:* Nashr al-Hadi, 1996), vol. 1, 188.

53. Yitzhak Nakkash, "An Attempt to Trace the Origins of the Rituals of 'Ashura," *Die Welt des Islams* 33 (1993): 161–181.

54. For the ways in which Muharram commemorations were used in early modern Nabatiyya to convert Sunnis to Shi'ism, see Werner

Ende, "The Flagellation of Muharram and the Shi'ites Ulama," *Der Islam* 55 (1978): 19–36.

55. Keyvānī, *Artisans and Guild Life*, 202, quotes from Hasan Rumlū's *Ahsan al-tavārīkh* to show that in Tabriz, for instance, individual guilds resided in one quarter, so you had a quarter of the paper makers *(kāghaz-kunān)*, hatters *(kulāh-dūzān)*, and potters *(kūzagarān)*.

56. Medina Zainullina Goldberg makes this observation in her insightful seminar paper entitled "Spiritual and Social Elements of Husayn's Martyrdom: Reading Foreign Accounts of Muharram Commemoration in Seventeenth-Century Iran." She draws a parallel with early modern Muscovy in terms of the significance of local ritual and state building. See Nancy Shields Kollman, *By Honor Bound: State and Society in Early Modern Russia* (Ithaca: Cornell University Press), 1999.

57. Ibn Bazzāz, *Safvat al-safā*, 795.

58. Qazvīnī, *Kitāb al-Naqz*, cited in Rasūl Ja'fariān, *Qissahkhwānān dar Tārīkh-i Irān va Islam* (Qum: Intisharat-i Dalil, 1997), 118–119.

59. Ibid., 120.

60. Kāshī, *Tārīkh-i Muhammadī*, 159–160.

61. Mawlanā Shaykh Hasan Kāshī, cited in Rasūl Ja'fariān, *Tārīkh-i Muhammadī*, ed. Rasūl Ja'fariān (Qum: Kitāb Khānah-yi Takhassusī-yi Tārīkh-i Islam va Irān, 1998), 29.

62. See medieval discussions on history, where Bayhaqi refutes works like the *Shāhnāme* on acount of their mythology and lack of rational discourse. Julie Scott-Meisami, "The Past in the Service of the Present: Two Views of History in Medieval Persia,'" *Poetics Today* 14, no. 2 (1993): 247–275.

63. See the late seventeenth-century biographer of Imami scholars, Āfandī, in his *Riyāz al-ulama*, which states that Kāshī and Muttahar Hillī were the earliest propagators of Imami Shi'ism, cited in Ja'fariān, *Qissahkhwānān*.

64. See Roy Mottahedeh, *The Mantle of the Prophet: Religion and Politics in Iran* (New York: Simon and Schuster, 1985), for his discussion of these two strands (Iranian and Shi'i) that shape the cultural specificity of Iranian religious scholars, like his protagonist Ali Hashemi.

65. Keyvānī, *Artisans and Guild Life*, 176–177.

66. Kāshifī, *Futuvvatnāme*, 8.
67. Ibid., 10.
68. Marina Gaillard, *Le Livre de Samak-i Ayyār* (Paris: L'Institut D'Etudes Iraniennes, 23, 25, 50.
69. Ibid., 50.
70. Ibid., 125.
71. Kāshifī, *Futuvvatnāme*, 9.
72. Ibid.
73. Claude Cahen, "Futuwwa," *EI2*.
74. Mansøur Shaki, "Class System" *E. Iranica,* citing *Denkard,* 723.
75. Maneckji Nusservanji Dhalla, *History of Zoroastrianism* (London: Oxford University Press, 1938), 232–243, 375–378.
76. Henry Corbin, *Cyclical Time and Isma'ili Gnosis: Islamic Texts and Context* (London: Kegan Paul, 1983), 18, citing the *Bundahishn.*
77. Ibid.
78. Kāshifī, *Futuvvatnāme*, 17. The long process of attaining manhood is also emphasized in the epic of *Samak-i Ayyār.* Samak is told that to become a real man *(mardī)* takes at least fifty years of effort; manhood is not about sacrificing your life in an instant. Gaillard, *Le Livre de Samak-i Ayyr,* 25.
79. Kāshifī, *Futuvvatnāme*, 7.
80. The French merchant traveler Jean-Baptiste Tavernier, *Voyages en Perse et Description de ce Royaume* (Chartres: L'Imprimerie Durand, 1930), 79, basing his information on Zoroastrian informants, says that they called their prophet "Ebrahim-ser-Ateucht." The names of Zoroaster and Abraham have been conflated.

SEVEN

Situating the Master-Disciple Schema: Cosmos, History, and Community

Muhammad sanctified Ali as the foremost gallant (*javān-mardtarīn*) with his frequently quoted maxim: "There is no youth [*fatā'*] except for Ali, and no sword other than his [Zul Fiqar]."[1] When Ali in humility asks, "Why me?" Muhammad responds that it is an honor (*sharaf*) with which the brave and the generous are endowed (*mushrif*). Bravery (*shujā'at*) and generosity (*sikhāvatī*) are twin virtues invariably associated with the noble image of Ali, and to be cloaked with such dignity, a disciple must imitate Ali through his words, his thoughts, and his actions. As Kashifi introduces a genealogy of past gallants, patriarchy and sacrifice emerge as central to the constructs of honor and authority. Abraham is placed at the origin of *futuvvat* and is given the appellation *Abu Fityān*, or "Father of the Youth." Since *futuvvat* is imagined as a circle of equality, father Abraham is situated at the "first point [*nuqta*] of the circle."[2] Abraham is cast as the first ascetic who separated himself from luxury and possessed the temperament of a traveler. What set Abraham apart was his willingness to sacrifice his most cherished possession, his son—an act of true submission and devotion to God. This sacrifice places patriarchy at the cultural matrix of the chivalric circles. Knowledge is passed down from Abraham to his sons Isma'il and Isaac. Along with the male

197

seed, it is transmitted until it reaches Muhammad. The axis of
prophecy is Abraham, and its seal is Muhammad. In the same
way that the origin and manifestation of *futuvvat* was located in
Abraham, its pivot was Ali, and its seal was to manifest itself in
the near future with the emergence of the Mahdi born of his
progeny. "Just as Abraham was the axis of prophecy and all
prophets who succeeded him embraced him," writes Kashifi,
"so every master [*sāhib*] of *futuvvat* who follows Ali must be
true to him in every manner. A knowledge whose font is Abraham, whose axis is Ali, and whose seal is the awaited messiah—
what [more] can be said of its nobility?"[3] Abraham, Ali, and the
Mahdi form a triad of exemplary master fathers fusing past,
present, and future.

The relationship between Abraham, Muhammad, and Ali is
depicted as that of a patriarchal family. Abraham is the father,
and Muhammad and Ali are his two sons. Paternal and fraternal
languages of loyalty define Kashifi's representation of master-
disciple associations. Through Muhammad and his example, the
outward dimension of the path to God has been revealed. But
disciples must follow the ways of Ali and his children if they
wish to travel on the spiritual path to the divine. Muhammad is
literally associated with divine law (*shari'a*), and Ali with mysticism (*tarīqat*). Moreover, Muhammad and Ali are brothers, possessors of a single cloak that symbolizes divine knowledge
passed down from father to son and respected between brothers.
Kashifi cites a hadith, a consistent mechanism employed to legitimize his renderings of *futuvvat* loyalties, in which Muhammad
is said to have "tied three knots of brotherhood," binding the
initial core of three hundred Muslims from among those who
emigrated (*muhājirūn*) with him from Mecca to Medina as well
as those Medinese (*ansār*) who had joined the nascent Muslim
community, representing the core circle of Muslim brothers. Ali
is said to have voiced his concern to Fatima, thinking that Muhammad had excluded him in this process. At that moment,
Muhammad walked into the conversation and announced that
he had reserved Ali for himself: "You are my brother in this

world [*dunya*] and in the other [*ākhirat*]."⁴ This symbolic fraternity of early converts to Islam, the quintessential nucleus of true
believers, is meant to reproduce itself with each new initiation of
a brother into its ranks. Each new member is admitted into the
order as a disciple (*murīd*) of a spiritual guide (*pīr*) as well as the
apprentice (*shāgird*) of a master craftsman (*ustād*). But he is also
joined by fellow brothers. He becomes a new son (*farzand*) in
addition to a new brother (*barādar*) once he takes the oath to
join the circle of the lovers of Ali.⁵

As the initiate is cloaked and girded, he recognizes that these
same items of clothing were used when Gabriel and Muhammad
were initiated into the circle of the divinely illuminated and
when Muhammad subsequently admitted Ali into the luminous
circle of God's friends (*awliyā'*). Through this ritual act, the novice is reincarnated as a new member of the family and enters into
a whole new space of time as a completely new person. We have
seen how part of the training of the disciple entailed knowledge
of a shared history of cosmic and historic ancestors. This
mythohistory grounds the disciple within his cycle, which is
shaped by the particularities of his local fraternal contexts. But
it also makes him conscious of the singular cosmic drama in
which the same antagonists meet each other repeatedly in every
epoch.⁶ Stories like that of Abu Muslim that the disciple would
hear in public arenas (*ma'rika*), bazaars, and coffeehouses
would reinforce such a consciousness on a daily basis.

Particular characteristics or signs of chivalry (*javānmardī*) are
enumerated by Kashifi, using biblical figures and Muslim holy
men as exemplars. This Islamic nomenclature is emploted in
Kashifi's narrative inscribing the Muslim era in which they will
be experienced. Joshua is considered a *fatā'* because he pursued
knowledge; the Seven Sleepers because they turned to God. Ali,
like Abraham, is singled out for his brave sacrifice, having slept
in Muhammad's bed the night Muhammad fled for his life to the
nearby cave in Mecca.⁷ Kashifi is presenting the interpretations
of those who believed that being a Muslim meant venerating Ali
at least as much as Muhammad, for Ali held the key to unveiling

the esoteric meaning of Muhammad's prophecy. And in the mystic quest of the *futuvvat* circles, imitating Ali was the path to Islam. Ali is represented as the victim. His opponents, the Umayyads, are the unjust who broke away from the utopian visions of Muhammad. Ali represents the truth; he is the one who possesses knowledge of Islam. He embodies those chivalric characteristics that paragons of truth like Rustam, Siyavush, and Kay Khusraw exude with the rays of their divine glory (*farr*). Ali is wise; he is compassionate and honest, but he is also a brave warrior who with his magical sword (Zul Faqar) performs martial marvels on the battlefield.

The meanings ascribed to Ali's historical actions, seeing him as the heir to the authority of the Muslim community, are interpreted through a dualist mindset. A gnostic binary flows through Kashifi's narrative as he writes about the nature of this knowledge. The novice is conceived as both a social and a universal being. Detailed attention is given to his microcosmic existence in society as he works, eats, and socializes. The small routines of daily life are seen as directly related to a larger cosmic drama. Together, body and spirit, material (*sūrī*) and ideal (*ma'navī*), mediate human behavior. A sense emerges that worldly integrity and harmony correspond directly to a universal order.

Communal responsibility was central to the ethics (*adab*) of the brotherhood and to their conception of a harmonious coexistence. Brothers were expected to treat one another with humanity; arrogance, greed, and envy were to be curtailed to establish genuine bonds of friendship. True (*haqīqī*) friendship was conceived as free of any ulterior motives (*gharaz*). It was a constructive relationship based on mutual respect and sincerity. If a brother detected a weakness in a friend, his duty was to protect him and conceal it from those antagonists who might capitalize on it. A true friend had to try to talk about these weaknesses in private with his brother so that he might correct them. Humanity meant recognizing weaknesses and working together to improve them. Social behaviors likely to provoke discord were to be avoided. Brothers were not to speak behind each others' backs, for instance, to contradict their companions in public, or to search for errors in their utterances. Thus, ties of loyalty were understood to be reinforced through the exercise of humane modes of interaction. To ensure social harmony beyond the fraternal circle, one was to conduct oneself in the same way when among family, neighbors, acquaintances, and even strangers.

Ties with the biological family were to be maintained and cherished. Both mothers and fathers were to be treated with utmost respect (*hurmat*). Their authority was to be honored: children were to listen to the advice of their parents. Parents were to have at least a consenting role when their sons embarked on their obligatory journeys. Brothers were to observe the boundaries of parental respect, never raising their voices when they spoke with mother and father. To ensure an honorable relationship with kin, members of the brotherhood were to avoid dealing with their parents in material matters. Monetary disputes within families were recognized as a source of social discord. Should parents need money, sons were to help them, but they were to avoid any designs over their parents' wealth. It was essential to the maintenance of respect that children express and exercise care and love for their parents without feeling that they were doing them a favor (*minnat*). All motivations with intimate ones were to be pure. What is interesting is that in this biological setting, a distinct hierarchy between father and son is not specified, and reverence toward the mother is highlighed. Kashifi sanctifies the role of mothers. He quotes the prophetic saying that "paradise lies under the footsteps of mothers (*al-jannatu tahta al-ummahat*)."[8]

Does the biological father lose his paternal authority to his son's masters? Hammoudi speaks of these ambiguities as part of the obligatory passage through a feminine role that every disciple must undergo in the path to masterhood under a guide's authority, grounded and sanctified by the concepts and procedures involved in mystical initiation. Hammoudi extends this passage

to every man in a situation of submission who must not only
have the illusion that he is accepting the role but must abandon
for a whle the identity he wants to attain—saint, king, spiritual
guide, father, or virile and dominating man. Hammoudi, of
course, assumes that submission and femininity are synony-
mous. Whatever the gendered associations may be, this transitional inversion that every aspirant to spiritual masterhood must
undergo becomes embedded in the dominant structures of self
and society, according to Hammoudi. It would not be uncommon for a novice's father to be a participant in *futuvvat* culture
as well. Perhaps in such contexts, he temporarily lost his role as
family patriarch.

Despite the programmatic nature of *futuvvat* clubs, there is a
sense of individuality that emerges within these communal
spheres. Traveling, for instance, was essential in the lives of
brothers. Kashifi writes, "Know that man has no choice but to
travel, for from the time that he was a sperm [*nutfah*] he was
traveling and shall travel to the end. His first house was the loins
[*sulb*] of his father, and then he traveled to the womb of his
mother, until he arrived at the third stage, which is this world,
and here he shall travel forty stages (*manzīl*) until he travels toward eternity."[9] Travel possesses ethical, spiritual, and physical
purpose. A brother is to travel as a pilgrim to visit the tombs of
prophets *(anbiyā')*, saints *(awliyā')*, and the Imams, and such
pilgrimages entailed exercising one's spirit *(riyāzat al-nafs)*,
seeking the teachings of spiritual elders *(akābir)*, and tending to
those in the path of God.[10] Travel is seen as beneficial for physical health as well *(sihhat-i badan)*, for to exercise one's body creates transformations in the humors of virtue. The visitation of
saintly graves is seen not merely as a public display of respect
but as an act that curtails laziness and boredom. Travel also has
psychological benefits, for it dissipates the pain of fear *(vahm)*
and anguish *(malālat)* of the unknown.

Travel is also seen as a learning process *(tahsil-i 'ulūm)* because it is through travel that the novice becomes aware of different practices by a variety of groups. Through travel, the disci-

ple is able to observe for himself the wonders of divine creation, to which he has already been introduced through the telling of stories. But seeing something for oneself is a different experience than imagining something that you are told. Travel provides this personal experience of comparison and self-awareness. Separation is seen as a necessary state for consciousness and growth. Longing for friends (*yarān*), brothers (*barādaran*), and relatives (*khwīshān*) is recognized as causing distress. And so there develops a sense of value for one's community, while at the same time one forges new bonds with strangers.[11] In the process of travel, one is able to find new friends who are good (*rafīq-i nīkū*) and with whom one can practice the three virtues (*muruvvat*) of the order—humanity, generosity, and manliness. There is a constant sense of the particularity and universality of the ways of chivalry. And I think that it is within these dynamics of community and cosmos that the novice experiences a sense of self.[12]

In spite of the hierarchical structure of the master-disciple dyad, the *futuvvat* was a fraternal association, bound together as a community of loyal friends of God (*awliyā'*), who were all identified as devotees of Ali. Kashifi quotes from the eighth Imam, Reza (d. 818), whom he refers to as the "honorable sultan of Khurasan," relating the tripartite duty of each brother—to help friends (*rafīqān*), to be open-minded and well intentioned, and finally to be playful and pleasant so long as one does not commit a sin. Solidarity was structured on mutual care and respect in daily spheres of work, friendship, family, and devotion. Feasting was deemed essential to the livelihood of the community. Kashifi delineates an etiquette (*adab*) as to how a novice was to act in festive gatherings—how he was to comport himself in the host's house, his body language, and his table manners. Hospitality was an integral part of communicating the virtues of generosity and compassion on which Alid camaraderie was based. This worldly esotericism is apparent in movements like those of the Mazdaki and Qarmatis, in which social equality is seen as a prerequisite for a harmonious community. The disciples are imagined as individuals living in society and dealing with basic material concerns, engaging in society rather than breaking away from it and living in seclusion. Loyalty to the group was central to their mode of existence. They all identified with the family of Muhammad, and they witnessed the piety of their brothers in devotion—both of which created a trust that nurtured economic solidarity. Artisanal communities of fathers, sons, and brothers of Ali together performed good acts, deeds, and words in society. These seem to have been traditional patterns of relationships that found continuity through the organization of the crafts. Let us see how this schema is enshrined in ritual, marking reincarnation through reenactment.

PERFORMING THE PAST IN THE PRESENT: INITIATION RITUALS AND THE DRAMA OF KARBALA

Four masters initiate the disciple into the charismatic community through an elaborate ritual performed in public. Each is a virtuoso in an art with which he begins to illuminate the novice. Through ritual gestures, these maestros enact their role as patrons and pronounce their expectations of service and loyalty in return. As master craftsman (*ustād*), spiritual guide (*pīr*), Alid "verifier" (*naqīb*), and "father of the covenant" (*pidar-i ahdullah*), each of the four represents a segment of society. Each exemplify many individuals, relationships, collective interests, and institutional aims. Each stands as well for a symbol that distinguishes his particular cosmic character and functions. Through their vows of dedication for the family of the prophet, they consolidate their social, spiritual, and economic capital to work together for the welfare of the community as well as for the pursuit of the struggle for truth.

A key actor whose approval had to be obtained for the investiture was the "Verifier" (*Naqīb*), a title originally used by the medieval Shi'i community to designate their spokesman who would attend to the local interests of the descendants of the prophet (*sayyid*). Most towns where *sayyids* lived had a verifier (*naqīb*) whose responsibility was to determine who was part of the Alid family and to allocate them pensions from the government and pious donors.[13] The post was usually held by an honorable descendant of Muhammad (*sayyid*), representing what comes closest in the Islamic world to an aristocracy of blood. Later in the Safavi era, the Naqib of the capital city of Isfahan was incorporated into the central administration. We have already encountered the Alid verifier in his official capacity as regulator of taxes (*bunācha*) on guilds and guarantor of the appointments of master craftsmen.[14] In the imperial Safavi era, he becomes the intermediary between the guilds and the court as he collects their taxes and oversees their direction.

The Naqib's earlier connections with craft associations came through his central function in the *futuvvat* as the "authenticator" (*shināsandah*) of both the pedigrees of the descendants of the prophet (*sayyid*) and of true chivalry (*ayyārī*).[15] That the Naqib is one of the four masters officiating at the initiation ceremony of the novice links the *futuvvat* directly to a group of professionalized *sayyids*. His function in the ritual is to grant privileges (*imtiyāz*) to those who possess noble (*sharīf*) Alid blood (*nasab*) by providing them with employment (*mansab*) worthy of their rank and status. But first, he must make sure that their pedigrees are indeed genuine and not a fabrication, which he is able to do through his knowledge (*'ilm u dānish*) of genealogy.[16] The Naqib is vested with the power of determining access to nobility.

The Naqib makes sure that those who are not blessed with this holy lineage but who believe in the family are learned in the words and deeds of the Imams, testing them to see whether in reality they are true gallants (*ayyār*). Honor was embedded in lineage (*nijād*), but it was also dependent on a nobility of character (*javānmardī*) assumed to be vested more bountifully with those of "pure" descent. Chivalry (*ayyārī*) is here related to a special knowledge and zeal for the family of Ali. The Naqib authenticates the loftiness of such a disposition, whether through kinship (*nasab*) or through imitative acts of devotion (*ayyārī*) toward the family (Alid). Privilege is distinctly awarded to the bloodline of the Prophet. Sayyids have favored access to apprenticeship in a craft, which secures them a means of livelihood and an honorable status as living symbols of the holy family. As a possessor of Alid charisma, the verifier is himself a manifestation of the family who sanctifies the right to honor this lineage as he delivers each new member into a larger sacred community of Alid fellows.

We have seen how Kashifi distinguishes between *tarīqat* (mysticism) and *futuvvat* (spiritual chivalry). Although he states that these two paths are conjoined, the reason a distinction is made by name is that not everyone can embark on the path of *tarīqat*, "since *tarīqat* is following step-by-step in the footsteps of Muhammad and Ali, and who other than his kin has the power to do that?"[17] But everyone according to his ability can benefit from *futuvvat*. And the *Futuvvatnāme-yi Sultānī* delineates the ways in which these abilities can be channeled through love and service to the family and thereby enhance perfection and intimacy with them. This is one aspect that distinguishes the mystic guild orders from other forms of sufism in which, theoretically, each individual has the potential to attain transcendence through spiritual guidance. In the *futuvvat* circles described by Kashifi, prosperity and honor are first reserved for descendants of Ali and then for their lovers. The initiation ceremony sanctifies the right to honor the family of the Prophet, a right bestowed by the verifier.

The verifier announces the date and place of the ceremony to all the dear ones (*azīzān*), calling the initiated brothers of the community to attend. Initiation is symbolized by the communal drinking of saltwater from a cup and the tying of a belt (*miyān bastan*) with a variety of types of knots, depending on the profession of the novice.[18] At least two girded brothers (*kamarbastah*) have to witness the ceremony, while the four senior members of the *futuvvat* hierarchy perform the rites. The master craftsman (*ustād-i shadd*) together with the spiritual guide (*pīr/shaykh*) of the order stands at the head of the initiation. Both are seated on a prayer rug facing Mecca (*qibla*), around which the ceremony takes place.[19] As an alternative sacred space, the master craftsman and the spiritual guide embody the prayer niche (*mihrāb*) toward which every Muslim faces as they worship in the mosque. They symbolize the two transcendent paths to God—one through prophecy (*nubuvvat*) and the other through sainthood (*vilāyat*). These channels invoke the presence of Muhammad and Ali, respectively.

The verifier begins the ritual as he raises a cup and mixes water and salt, reading a verse from the Qur'an (25: 53):

> And he it is who hath given independence to the two seas (though they meet); one palatable, sweet, and the other saltish, bitter, and hath set a bar and a forbidding ban between them.

Kashifi provides his interpretation of these ritual elements, as though to render them unambiguous for an audience who might read them differently. Clear water represents the purity and genuineness of the novice's heart, and the salt is a metaphor used in the idiomatic expression of respect for the hand that feeds you. The novice entering the *tarīqat* has to be grateful for the patronage he receives from his fathers (*haqq-i namak-i yekdīgar rā ri'āyat kunand*). Purity and loyalty are mixed into this ritual of drinking saltwater, to be passed around at the end of the ceremony for all other members to partake as a community. But the Quranic verse reveals a dualism that infuses the beliefs and practices of the *futuvvat*. A clear boundary is drawn between the binary of sweetness and bitterness, symbolic of the cosmic battle between good and evil into which each disciple is entering. The oath taken by the disciple at initiation entails a manifest knowledge of the opposition between these two forces and the side on which he is fighting.

This ritual of mixing salt with water appears in a variety of manuals on chivalry (*Futuvvatnāme*). Muhammad is said to have performed this "ritual of the cup" as he declared Ali the foremost knight of the community. Henry Corbin in his comparative study of seven manuals of chivalry talks about Muhammad mixing three pinches of salt into the water, symbolizing the tripartite path toward God—*shari'a* (divine law), *tarīqat* (mystical path to gnosis), and *haqīqat* (personal self-realization of gnosis).[20] In a similar ritual that appears in Nusayri (Alid *ghulāt*) liturgy, salt water is replaced by a symbolic "wine of the Angelic world" (*malakūt*). The Nusayris trace their lineage to Abu'l Khattab (d. 762), a disciple of the sixth Imam, Jafar al-Sadiq, who was proclaimed divine. What is of interest to us here is that Imam Jafar is said to have initiated Abu'l Khattab in the same way as Kashifi describes Ali being initiated by Muhammad. Every new novice is acting out identical roles in different cycles of time. But in these Nusayri contexts, there is direct reference to the Persianate lineage of the ritual of the cup. To begin with, the cup is said to belong to the mythical Iranian (referred to as Bahmanian) king Tahmurath.[21] An entire cycle of Iranian history (Bahmanian) is introduced alongside the cycles of Adam, Noah, Abraham, and Moses. Together, all heroes Mazdean and Abrahamic living in different cycles of history are each imagined in the shape of a dome. Time, as Corbin notes, is imagined spatially. All inhabitants of these seven domes have already taken part in the ritual:

> And when the drink has passed to all, then by this cup you hold in your hand, your bodies shall be filled for all the periods and cycles to come. For you belong to the holy of holies, and you were of the Bahmanians [Iranians].[22]

In Nusayri circles as the disciple drinks from the cup, he is aware of his Iranian past, remembering that in every cycle of history brothers not only partook in this same act but were made up of the same substance. Through this imitative process, the novice experiences reincarnation through the seven cycles of history. Moreover, Imam Ja'far manifests himself before Abu'l Khattab, his bright vision proof of the concept of divine manifestation (*tajallī*) on earth. An emptied cup then descends into the assembly as a visible sign that those who have already been initiated, yet are invisible at that moment, are in fact present and indeed drink from the cup. Abu'l Khattab then says:

> Behold this cup has circulated through the temple of all the non-Arabs, throughout all the seven periods of the world. All of them are our brothers in faith and in gnosis. . . . Through this drink you have tasted the knowledge of the *Malakūt* [angelic world], the knowledge of that which was in the first of the centuries and is throughout all the ages and cycles of the world.[23]

We hear echoes of Nuqtavi beliefs here, where the knowledge of the first and the last is recognized as the same. There is a sense of alchemical correspondence between homologous individuals who lived in different cycles of time. Such beliefs enabled Shah Isma'il to claim to be the reincarnation of Feraydun, Kay Khusraw, Alexander, Jesus, Muhammad, and Ali. This entire Iranian cycle of history and Persianate ethos of Nusayri liturgy is erased from Kashifi's manual. Instead, what is remembered is an Abrahamic genealogy in which Persianate traces appear as metaphor, allegory, and allusion. Two different memories are alive here among Alid circles—one (Kashifi) that has forgotten its Iranian past and another (Nusayri) that remembers it as part of its Muslim present. Alid arenas in which both an Iranian past and an Islamic present are preserved side by side facilitated peaceful conversion (Irano-Muslim) but also continued to offer a space in which conversion could be resisted. Both are implicated in a combined genealogy, and this fact justifies each keeping its own identity.[24] A combined Mazdean-Alid genealogy not only opens the possibility for peaceful conversion but allows for durability through a consciousness of this other past. Thus, in Alid circles Irano-Islamic identities (Qizilbash) and the distinct memory of an Iranian past (Nuqtavi) coexisted.

After mixing the water with salt, the verifier lights a lamp (*chirāq*) with five flames. Kashifi explains that the lamp symbolizes the light of the heart, illuminated with the fire of the five core members (*panj tan*) of the holy family—Muhammad, Ali, Fatima, Hasan, and Husayn.[25] The family is visualized as a hand (*panjah*) with the five fingers representing the kinsmen of divine light. The verifier then recites the famous verse from the Sura of Light (24: 35), often quoted by mystics:

> Allah is the light of the heavens and the earth. The similitude of his light is a niche wherein is a lamp. The lamp is a glass. The glass is as it were a shining star. [This lamp is] kindled from a blessed tree, an olive neither of the east nor of the west, whose oil would almost glow forth (of itself) though no fire touched it. Light upon light, Allah guideth unto His light whom he will. And Allah speaketh to mankind in allegories, for Allah is the knower of all things.

The ritual oath of the *futuvvat* has transformed Mazdean myths, recreating them anew within an Alid context. Despite this transformation, a Mazdean "root paradigm," as Victor Turner would call it, is recognizable: "These root paradigms are not systems of univocal concepts, logically arrayed; they are not, so to speak, precision tools of thought. Nor are they stereotyped guidelines or ethical, esthetic, or conventional action. Indeed, they go beyond the cognitive and even the moral to the existential domain, and in so doing become clothed with allusiveness, implications, and metaphor."[26]

In the Persian heroic epic of *Samak-i Ayyār*, the gallant Samak initiates a brother, Ateshak (whose name means "little fire") through an oath of allegiance uttered in the name of God, light, fire, the sun, the bread and salt of virtuous men (*mardān*), and the wise counsels of *javānmards*.[27] All these elements except for the sun are represented in the *futuvvat* initiation rituals. The sun in Mazdean symbology is a manifestation of the creation of fire; it is an icon of truth and justice (*asha*). The manifestation of truth is located in the hearth fire, in the ritual fire, or in the sun. Light is a positive good (*spendta*), and by praying before it the worshipper was helped to fix his thoughts on Mazda himself— on his goodness and on justice and truth.[28] Both fire and the sun continue to be symbols associated with Persian traditions. Although the Qur'anic sura of Light emphasizes that the glow has not been touched by the fire, it is present in the form of a light. The five burners represent the family of truth, hallowed by divine glory (*farr*) passed on through blood (*nizhād*), a luminosity that was bestowed on the household of kings and warriors in Mazdean traditions and that now in the Muslim era enshrines the Alids. Artisans, a fourth functional category that appears in the Avesta, are also enjoined to fight this battle for justice. The rituals and ethics of pre-Islamic chivalrous knights entering the cause of Ahuramazda (good) have been translated here onto the Alid cause.

The fourth actor, whom we have not yet encountered, now enters the ritual. He is designated as the "father of the covenant of God" (*pidar-i ahdullāh*), representing Abraham, the father of all chivalric youths (*Abū Fityān*).[29] He seems to emerge from within the twin structures of spiritual and craft circles. It is he who reads aloud the Quranic verse of the Covenant (36:60–61) that binds the initiate to the order of brave and generous knights of Ali (*futuvvat*). During this public ceremony, he reiterates the centrality of this dualist struggle:

> Did I not charge you, O ye sons of Adam, that ye worship not the devil—Lo! He is your open foe! But that ye worship me? That was the right path.

The covenant instructs brothers to fight in God's army rather than for Satan, as evil (Ahriman) has been translated onto the devil. This cosmic father (Abraham) makes sure that the novice knows the code of ethics of the brotherhood, which he relates to him through twelve phrases (*kalimat*).[30] Obedience and humility are central in the rules and principles he enumerates. In an initiatory act of submission and modesty, the novice is first to ask for God's forgiveness (*astaghfirullāh*). We have seen how brothers are enjoined to be compassionate and generous with one another. Such principles are reconfirmed here as jealousy, envy (*bukhl*), and pride (*kabr*) are shunned. These humane virtues were to create horizontal ties of friendship between brothers, binding them in spiritual marriages. But nobility of character also entailed a sense of deference to superiors and a duty toward them. The novice is forewarned of the expectations of his position as disciple (*murīd*). Generosity and service were kindred tasks of disciples. Brothers were to be devoted to several fathers who were initiating them into a long journey of apprenticeship in spiritual growth and artistic mastery. The ceremonial "father of the covenant" represents the senior patriarch of the cosmic community past and present. The master-disciple paradigm was sanctified by the patriarchal concepts and procedures involved in this process of initiation. The master imposed rules and a hierarchical superiority that had to be respected by the initiate if he desired to become part of the community. In turn, the initiate would achieve a degree of honor that could eventually take him into positions of authority. Such power relations are enshrined in the ceremony.

The "father of the covenant" then reminded the novice that to consider the group (*tā'ifah*) as sacred was among the twelve principles of the brotherhood. Fathers, sons, and brothers surrounded the disciple physically, as spiritual forefathers were evoked as "dear spirits'"(*nafshā*) to be remembered aloud. The recalled genealogy began with Gabriel and Adam, moved into the cycle of prophets inaugurated by Abraham, and finally entered the Muslim era. Here, Kashifi introduces his own Muslim lineage that begins with Ali and extends through the first seven Imams, not mentioning Hasan, to famous medieval mystics like Junayd-i Baghdadi and the two Suhrawardis, Najm-i al-din Kubra and Ala Al-Dawla Simnani. Kashifi mixes a spiritual lineage of Alid Imams together with sufi masters (Kubraviyya and Bektashiyya). Depending on the particular spiritual order and the craft that the disciple is being initiated into, his living masters (*ustād va pīr*) each would then publicly recite their own pedigrees, beginning with those who had initiated them into their dual paths of religiosity. The novice is then installed by spiritual representatives of the masters of the religious arts and sciences, past and present. "Rather than creating a sense of chronological succession by recalling these masters," writes Corbin, "a simultaneous order of spiritual space-time can be visualized, where all are assembled in 'co-presence' with each other."[31]

In the era in which the novice was historically situated the day of his initiation, the presence of Ali, the Imams, and sufi saints were most immediate. Such a consciousness was not only shaped by a knowledge of the initiate's *futuvvat* lineage through an enumeration of exemplars and their actions, but it was experienced through the repetitive performance of acts and words his ancestors were to have rendered historically. The procedure tied each disciple directly to a cast of past holy figures living in different cycles of time, reliving the meaning of their actions and sayings—reinforcing in the process the master-disciple formula.

It is through the initiation into a craft that the disciple joins the circle of Alid lovers; acquiring a master craftsman was a first step to membership. Only once a master took on the responsibility to tutor his apprentice could the disciple join the *futuvvat*. The master would adopt the novice as a son, accepting to initiate him into the secrets of his craft that are intertwined with an entire Persianate ethics and metaphysics. A variety of crafts in which the novice can enter appear in the *Futuvvatnāme-yi Sultānī*. Artisans are divided into two categories: "people on the battlefield "(*ma'rika*) engaged in the crafts of speech (*sukhan*), strength (*zūr*), and play (*bāzī*); and "handle-tool users" (*ahl-i ghabzah*) like soldiers, blacksmiths, tailors, and shoemakers. The novice must spend a period of forty days of initial training before the craft master will take him on as a new student. The language Kashifi uses is paternal, the master (*ustād*) is said to introduce his son (*farzand*) to the community, making sure that all the ritual accoutrements for the initiation ceremony are ready and that the arena (*makān-i vasī'*) in which the assembly (*majlis*) will gather is clean. Although the ceremony is performed in a cloister (*takkiya*) at times established by one of the loyal and wealthier members of the group, according to Kashifi the place is not confined to any institutional building of the *futuvvat*.[32]

After the master craftsman (*ustād-i shadd*) rises from the carpet on which he has been sitting and places his son at his side, he first utters the names of the twelve Imams, along with basic Muslim dicta asking for God's forgiveness (*astaqfirullāh*), martyrdom (*shahādat*), and repentance (*tawba*). As he places his left hand on the forehead of the novice, he reads the first verse of the Qur'an (*fātiha*), confirms the greatness of God (*takbīr*), and once again recites the names of all the spiritual guides (*pīr*) and devotees (*murīd*) of the family (*ahl-i bayt*). He adds a genealogy of craftsmen (*ustād-i shadd*), mentioning his own teachers (*pīr va ustād*). As a eulogist, Kashifi traces his artistic genealogy (*ustād-i shadd*) among the masters of prose elegy (*qurra khwān*). Then the master craftsman takes his left hand and places it on the right shoulder of the disciple and sends blessings (*salavāt*) to Muhammad and his family. Such physical contact is a form of transmission of charisma (*barakat*) from master to disciple.

The whole ritual, according to Kashifi, is a reenactment of Ghadir Khumm where Muhammad is to have confirmed Ali as his successor in a similar manner during the last pilgrimage the prophet made to Mecca. Muhammad is to have sent Ali to the Yemeni tribe of Hamdan to convert them. He places his hand on Ali's shoulder, asking God to render Ali's tongue with truth (*sidq*) and righteousness (*savāb*) and to brighten his heart with the light of guidance and the beam (*partaw*) of knowledge ('*ilm*) and wisdom (*hikmat*). Ali's mission is a success; he converts the Yemenis all in one day. Ali writes to Muhammad about his victory and acknowledges his loyalty and then heads for the hajj that he, Muhammad, and Fatima will perform together for the last time (*hajj al-vida'*). Having completed the rites of pilgrimage with the consciousness that it is his last, the prophet embarks on his return journey to Medina along with a large caravan of believers that includes his most loyal disciples. Stopping in a place called Ghadir Khumm, Muhammad orders a pulpit to be made from camel saddles and from it delivers a speech. After performing the obligatory prayers, Muhammad takes Ali by the hand, saying: "Do you not acknowledge that I have a greater claim on each of the believers than they have on themselves?"[33] And the believers are to have replied, "Yes!" Then Muhammad turns to

Ali and says, "Arise [*yā Ali barkhīz*]!" And Ali rises. Muhammad once again takes Ali by the hand and takes him up to the pulpit, saying, "Of whomsoever I am Lord [*mawla*], then Ali is also his Lord. O God! Be thou the supporter of whoever supports Ali and the enemy of whoever opposes him."[34] Kashifi includes this hadith in his *Futuvvatnāme-yi Sultānī*, translated into Persian and recorded in both Sunni (Ibn Hanbal) and Shi'i canons.[35] The Shi'is are distinct in the way that they interpret this tradition as a confirmation of Ali's succession to Muhammad. The brothers of Kashifi's *futuvvat* seem to believe that Ali was Muhammad's brother, inaugurating the twin path of sainthood (*vilāyat*) embedded in spiritual chivalry (*javānmardī*).[36]

Then the master craftsman leads the novice in prayer, utilizing the ritual girdle made out of a piece of cloth (*shadd*) instead of a prayer stone. This form of *futuvvat* religiosity is distinct from the culture of the mosque. It is a separate religious sphere that has its own particular liturgy and ritual objects. As we have mentioned, there are two figures behind which all the brothers pray. These are the spiritual and professional masters of the order, one representing Muhammad and the other, Ali. The novice is introduced for the first time into the congregational prayer as he prays behind these masters of the crafts and of gnosis. The author of our chivalric manual, Va'iz-i Kashifi, distinguishes between the religious sphere of the mosque and *futuvvat* circles. Among the obligations of the disciple is to be courteous with the *ulama* but to avoid mosques when embarking on the stage of travel away from home: "Do not stop at the mosque (*masjid*) unless necessary (*zarūrat*), and if you can, avoid sleeping there."[37] Here, the religious competition between the mosque and the mystical cloister is clearly stated, yet both spaces coexisted, and the believer was free to choose his path.

After both master and shaykh have prayed for the first time in public with the novice and the whole congregation behind them, the master of the order reads the sermon (*khutba*), which is a mixture of Qur'anic suras. The sermon encapsulates in God's words the basic virtues of the brotherhood already articulated, emphasizing obedience, self-sacrifice, camaraderie, and compassion.[38] Then comes the girding ritual conducted by the master craftsman. Muhammad is to have tied three knots with his handkerchief (*mandīl*) around Ali, each knot representing a divine figure in a lineage beginning with God, extending to Gabriel the *akhī,* and Muhammad the prophet.[39] As the master craftsman comes to tie three knots around the novice, he kisses the girdle (*shadd*) that he had used as a prayer stone. He reads a prayer from Imam Jafar and whispers secrets into the ears of the novice. These secrets uttered in a whisper summarize the role of devotee of the family. The adept is to praise the Imams (*tavallā*) and curse the Alid enemies (*tabbarā'*). He is to enjoin what is forbidden and reject what is prohibited (*amr-i bi al-marūf wa nahy an al-munkar*). Justice (*'adl*) is his mode of behavior as he avoids jealousy and greed and is gallant (*javānmardī*). He is to serve his masters (*bā pīr murīd budan*) following the laws (*shari'a*) of the *futuvvat*. Then the master craftsman distributes the salty water that had initially been mixed by the Alid verifier (*naqīb*), bringing the circle of initiation to a close. To sweeten the conclusion of the ceremony, a sweet (*halvā*) is passed around to all the witnesses of the new covenant. It is the same sweet that Ali and Muhammad are to have eaten after Ali's initiation (Ghadir Khumm) when they returned home and Fatima mixed together the little food that she had in her house—some dates, some bread and oil. Every initiate was aware of this story as he ate the same sweet during his initiation into the brotherhood of devotees of Ali.

During the initiation ceremony, an entire list of girded brothers from the Muhammadan era are evoked. All three sons of Ali including Muhammad b. Hanafiyya are named. Ali was told by Muhammad to tie the belt around loyal companions like the Persian icons of conversion, Salman-i Farsi and Abu Muslim. Famous mystical poets such as the Alid eulogist Hasan-i Kashi, Sa'di, and Khajuy-i Kirmani are honored as members of the brotherhood. [40]

After three days, the son (*farzand*) is brought in front of his master craftsman (*ustād*), who opens his knot, saying: "I gird this son in perpetuity and release him in mortality."[41] Then he puts the sash around the son and ties a knot reciting the Quranic verse 2:286, showing the humanity of this path that recognizes man's weakness and asks God's for forgiveness, just as brothers themselves are to be forgiving (see figure 5). The salt water and sweets are passed on to those witnesses who are present. The son is asked questions concerning the family (*qawm*); answers to these queries are not recorded, according to Kashifi but are rather passed down from mouth to mouth. If the novice responds correctly, he is awarded an elite status (*halvā-yi khwāss*); if not, he is granted general entry (*halvā-yi 'āmm*) to the brotherhood. This act of covenant between the disciple and his masters continues to be renewed yearly through the performance of the drama of Karbala.

An emotional affinity ties disciples as they worked, socialized, and engaged in religious devotion together. We have highlighted the ways in which an Alid memory created a common culture of veneration and lamentation for the family of Muhammad through the recording and recitation of epics like the *Abū Muslimnāme* and eulogies like the *Garden of Martyrs*. The heroes of the *Abū Muslimnāme*, like the brothers of the *futuvvat*, fought with words as well as weapons to vindicate Alid martyrs, ready to sacrifice themselves for the love of this family. Shared notions of chivalry, honor, generosity, bravery, compassion, humility, loyalty, and self-sacrifice distinguished warriors of the family. Chivalrous heroes modeled their behavior in accordance with the image of Ali and the Imams. They imagined the holy family as the embodiment of truth and their opponents as evil murderers. The role of every disciple was distributed along binary lines each representing characters from stories and eulogies constructed around historical events like the martyrdom of Husayn. As devotees of Ali, they shared in a common emotional site of suffering an injustice that gave meaning

to the tragic drama of Karbala. Each gallant directly participated in this life-sustaining narrative both as an audience listening to the stories and as actors performing them in the cosmic
theater of life. Works like the *Abū Muslimnāme* and the *Garden
of Martyrs* memorialized the family along with those who raised
the banner of rebellion in their name. And every year for the duration of ten days, 1 to 10 of Muharram, they reenacted dramas
of Karbala, reconfiguring them with every performance according to the concerns of the day. They were active participants in
the site of communal knowledge, thus partaking in the creation
of a collective memory that was spontaneously lived as ever-
present. As they cursed, wept, and cut their bodies with razors,
every year on the date of Husayn's martyrdom, they (re)experi-
enced in a cyclical rhythm similar feelings of pain and suffering
that bound them together emotionally as a sacred community.

Eulogists and storytellers transmitted the memory of Ali and
his family broadly beyond *futuvvat* circles. Distinguished by
symbols such as a spear (*nayzah*), a standard (*tūq*), or an ax
(*tabarzīn*) they would stand in public arenas (*ma'rika*) and call
people to congregate around their standards as they recited stories in praise of Alids.[42] Those who had a pleasant voice retold
these stories "making sure never to bore the audience."[43] At
times, reciters (*nazm khwānān*) sang these stories with a melody.
As Kashifi has commented, "If such people did not exist, then in
reality the speeches of grandees [Imams and eulogists] would
not be known to everyone."[44] Water carriers (*saqqāyān*) would
transmit these stories daily as they distributed water to the denizens of town and cities. They themselves were seen as reenacting
the role of Abbas, one of Husayn's step-brothers, who is said to
have carried water to quench the thirst of his dying kinsmen at
Karbala. Like Kashifi in his manual on chivalry, each eulogist
who was linked to a craft fraternity provided mythohistoric scenarios for his sons to enact daily. And these became the scripts
from which a yearly public procession of Muharram patronized
by *futuvvat* circles was improvised. Such imitations of past gestures and episodes was a mechanism used during initiation cere-

monies described by Kashifi, in which the disciple was aware of anterior gestures and words of Ali, Salman-i Farsi, and Abu Muslim. For those with *ghulât* temperaments who actually believed that they could remember who they were in their past lives, recalling their professions, recognizing their traces from a past life in calligraphy, or in poetry, this reenactment was not just an artificial suturing of the past and present but a conscious reliving of their previous incarnations.

With the yearly processions of lamentation, disciples relived their previous lives for a period of ten days leading to Husayn's martyrdom. Members of *futuvvat* circles who performed in these processions imitated incarnations of the initial victims of Karbala. And the general public who participated by viewing saw themselves as their supporters—indeed, as the reincarnations of early devotees of the Imams. Kashifi who was a eulogist himself recounted in simple Persian prose the events of Husayn's martyrdom, which lay at the navel of his narrative (*Garden of Martyrs*). The *Garden of Martyrs* became one of the most commonly recited eulogies at private lamentation sessions (*rawzahkhwānī*), initially shaping their reenactment (*shabīh*, "imitation") during Muharram processions, which by the nineteenth century had evolved into staged passion plays (*ta'ziyah*) with professional actors.[45]

European travelers to Safavi Iran are our main source for these yearly carnavalesque plays. They frequently note the simultaneous recitation of elegies as performers acted out in words. Olearius witnessed an elaborate ceremony with recitations of elegies, which took place at the palace of the governor of Ardabil on the last day of Muharram in 1637, and he commented how there is "a very great number of Poets in Persia to write them (guilds) some Verses in commendation of Aly and Hussain." He observed that each guild or "profession" of Ardabil (he counted five) presented its own poet to the governor, and the best one was "bestow[ed] with a Present of water sweetened with sugar."[46] By the mid-seventeenth century, Safavi provincial governors had appropriated the patronage and direction of the Muharram processions, something that had previously been the local prerogative of *futuvvat* circles. Here in Ardabil at the heart of the Safavi order, it was now a government representative who initiated the master of the craft of eulogy taking on the role of the Safavi spiritual guide.[47]

During these processions, elaborate paraphernalia are reported to have been used to enhance realistic representation; paintings illustrating the contents of the stories were also utilized.[48] The Venetian envoy to the court of Shah Tahmasb (r. 1524–1576) notes that "the Sophians [Safavis] paint figures, such as the figure of Ali, riding on a horse, with a sword; and when they see the said figure of Ali, they take hold of their ear and bow their head, which is a kind of reverence. In their squares there are many Persian mountebanks sitting on carpets on the ground; and they have certain long cards with figures; and the said mountebanks holds a little stick and points to one figure after another, and preach and tell stories over each figure."[49] So that the devotee might experience the immediacy of the lives of the Imams, paintings were complemented by graphic representations of the wounded or killed. Husayn's slain children ride naked on horses with their bodies smeared with blood.[50] Naked men mounted on horseback wrapped in sheepskin pierced through with an arrow. The representation of Husayn's dead body and his wounded children provoked emotions of sorrow and grief in the community that aided their yearly transit into the realm of Karbala. The daily reinforcement of these visual and literary elements must have made the annual experiences of Karbala seem much more "real."

Words and images were used to move both performers and onlookers to tears. As Kashifi notes in his manual, eulogists and storytellers had to have direct access to the hearts of their audience. The art of prose and verse eulogy lay in its ability to mesmerize through words. Paintings colored that aura, visually helping both actors and spectators to experience Husayn's passage viscerally. As far as the temporal aspect of experiencing

Karbala, the time of the ritual was deemed to correspond to the time of the sacred events, and the ten days of Muharram were encountered as an organized historical narrative. The narrative was also recorded as sacred memory (at least in *maqātil* literature) as a *lieu de mémoire* that allowed room for interpretation. Similarly, Muharram processions, which represented dramatic personae of Husayn's story intertwined with recitations, could have been organized according to the same "time correspondence" with the "real" events of Karbala. The climax of Ashura came on the tenth day, when Husayn was slain. Olearius notes that the morning after Ashura, "before the Sun was to be seen over the Horizon, the Persians made a Procession, which was to represent the interment of Husayn," commemorating his burial outside of the strict temporal and spacial boundaries of Ashura, as if upholding in "real time" the conventional time order of the story.[51]

Spiritual and emotional elements envelop the participants of the Muharram procession in a sacred space in which the suffering of Husayn and his family are not only remembered but relived through lamentation and recitation of eulogies as well as through realistic representation of martyred bodies, of blood and feuds. A somber frame of mind is created as participants enter the mood of this past cycle: "They all live in sadness; they dress in a positively melancholy fashion and many wear black, which they hardly ever use at other times, nobody shaves their head or their beard, nobody bathes, they do not only abstain from everything they consider sinful but also from every form of delight."[52]

Self-flagellation and body and face cutting were other ways in which disciples induced the experience of common pain. Evliya Chelebi who attended Ashura in Tabriz in 1640 relates that when "some hundred men mingle in the crowd with razors, with which they cut the arms and the breasts of all loving believers . . . the ground appears as if it were blooming with [red] tulips."[53] The blood shed by believers during the Muharram procession in imitation of the shedding of Husayn's blood at Karbala was a powerful reminder of the Imam's martyrdom and a form of direct physical participation in it. The blood of the victim was linked to the act of vengeance in which each disciple vows to engage during initiation. Vengeance took a personal dimension in these Muharram commemorations. The Russian traveler Kotov witnessed in Isfahan (1623) a "dummy made out of hay stuffed into a fur skin, endowed with a bow and arrows made out of splinter and a cup with a tassel. Everyone curses him and spits on him. . . . Later on they take him to the field outside of the city and burn him. This dummy represents the assassin of Husayn and his family."[54] The effigy was that of the hated Shimr, the actual murderer of Husayn, one of the most despised characters in the drama of Karbala. Statues of Umar, the second caliph who is believed by the Shi'a to have usurped Ali's authority, along with a number of the leaders of the Umayyads, the opposing faction involved in the killing of Husayn, are publicly cursed and denounced.[55]

The custom of cursing (*tabarrā'*) the first three caliphs and the enemies of the holy family possessed a long history. The early Safavis integrated cursing as an official ritual in their imperial practice.[56] *Tabarrā'* means "disavowal"' or "disassociation," and it refers to the formula of renunciation uttered by Shi'is living under Sunni hegemony in medieval Islamdom. Sometimes a curse was voiced quietly in the heart (*la'n al-khafī*) to protect the Shi'is from the dominant sect. But at times the cursing was vocalized aloud as a parallel expression uttered alongside praise for the Imams. Such symbolic acts proclaimed the identity of each group, as Shi'i verse reciters (*manāqib-khwān*) praised Ali and vilified the Sunnis publicly in streets and bazaars.[57] Their Sunni counterparts sang the praises (*fazā'il khwān*) of the caliphs and, in turn, cursed Ali. Under the Umayyads (661–750), Ali was publicly cursed from the pulpit. You may recall that one of the first acts of rebellion by Abu Muslim was to have killed the preacher who engaged in such public insults during his sermon against Ali. Shah Tahmasb initially used this practice as a mechanism of public conversion to Shi'ism. Membré notes that wherever the Shah went, he was preceded by a group of *tabarrā'iyān,* or "disavowers," crying out to the beat of a drum "a hundred thousand curses on Umar, Uthman and Abu Bakr."[58] The royal family as well as Qizilbash notables each had their own troop of public cursers. And the recitation of the curse permeated public arenas of the capital city (Qazvin). People were enjoined to denounce the enemies of Ali, and if they refused, they were harassed and intimidated, for they were stigmatized as Alid haters (*nāsibī*).[59] Such transgressions could result in death. As we have seen in Kashifi's manual on chivalry, one of the secrets whispered by the master craftsman into the ear of the adept is a disavowal (*tabarrā'*) of adversaries of the family in affirmation (*tavallā*) of the Alids. Once Shi'ism was proclaimed the hegemonic religion of the empire in Safavi Iran, such curses did not have to be whispered but could be shouted (*la'n-i jalī*).

Public catharsis is achieved through cursing and burning the representations of a number of negative personae involved in the event of Karbala. Medieval enemies were often conflated with current ones; ritual cursing became part of Safavi anti-Ottoman and Uzbek propaganda, for instance. In a letter to the Ottoman Sultan Sulayman, Shah Tahmasb writes, "Witness, that from now on, we will put into effect thus that the *tabarrā'iyan,* who are the fighters of Ali, will freely (*'ala'l itlāq*) curse you in silent recitation and aloud, in the wards and markets of the realms of Azarbaijan, Khurasan, and Iraq. So that the Armenians and Jews will inscribe your name and that of the enemy (Ottomans) on the sole of the foot of an animal."[60] Shah Tahmasb identifies the "disavowers" as fighters for Ali, like the members of the *futuvvat.* Such associations between past and present enemies are embedded in diplomatic discourse and are expressed during the processions as well. The late seventeenth-century traveler Bedros Bedik notes that the Umayyad Caliph Yazid, who actually orders the battle against Husayn, and the Ottomans were cursed together in a procession he witnessed in which the Caliph Yazid's effigy was burnt along with a list of his misdeeds.[61] Is this an enactment of the day of judgment?

Violent fights that broke out during the Muharram procession involved regional rivalries. Tavernier points out that during the elaborate ceremony that he witnessed on the last day of Muharram in 1667, seven men entered the square where the procession was taking place and "carry'd every one a Pike upright in their hands, with every one a Man's Head at the top. Those were the heads of certain Uzbek-Tartars, the neighboring and mortal Enemies of the Persians, which those men had cut off from the shoulders of their conque'd Foes."[62] The theme of vengeance here takes on a presentist dimension in which the severed heads of the Uzbeks, the contemporary Sunni enemies of the Safavis, replaced the heads of Husayn's assassins (Umayyads) from centuries earlier.

The personal dimension of this act of vengeance is rendered even more immediate and absorbing, as blood is shed and martyrdom is achieved through physical engagement in violent fights. Participants in the procession make use of the drama of Karbala to act out their own local rivalries—a symbolic imitation of retaliation against the enemies of the martyred Husayn. The Venetian Vincentio d'Allessandri, who visited Tabriz and Qazvin during Shah Tahmasb's reign, says that the city of Qazvin was divided into two factions; five wards were "Nausitai" (Nimatullahi) and four were "Himicaivartu" (Haydari). According to d'Allessandri, these feuds had a thirty-year history to them; "the king nor any other (could) put a stop to it."[63] Brothers entered contests against outside opponents as part of a public display of their martial arts (*ahl-i zūr*), like wrestling in *futuvvat* practice. Each father and brother's talents (*hunar*) took on a performative aspect as they demonstrated publicly the excellence of their art. In the symbolic battlefield (*ma'rika*), brothers displayed their skill and knowledge, according to Kashifi, just as Adam was taught by God all the names of the angels and the creatures. It is this knowledge that renderes

Adam noble in the eyes of the chivalrous youth. Once God challenges the angels to name the creatures and they fail, Adam is called to the task and having learned the names from God, he rises brilliantly to the occasion: "God (then) made it a point to emphasize each person's nobility based on their knowledge. So Adam rose in this battlefield [*ma'rika*] and showed his art, and God ordered all the angels to bow down to Adam."[64] According to Kashifi, this knowledge is to be used in the battlefield: "Whoever enters [*ma'rika*] without knowledge has no idea of its secret."[65] The quest to discover that cosmic secret is related to the goal of the *ma'rika*, which is to open one's heart and accept the grace of the family. As we have seen, knowledge of the battlefield is performed through the three arts of speech (*sukhan*), strength (*zūr*), and play (*ćazī*). "Strength without knowledge," writes Kashifi, "is like a king without justice, and knowledge without strength is like a just king without an army, and so when knowledge and strength are companions they work together in unison."[66]

Wrestling holds a special place in *futuvvat* culture described by Kashifi. Considered a noble sport patronized by the monarchs (*mulūk*) and sultans, it is traced back to Jacob, who was learned in this art and passed it on to his sons (*farzandān*) to help them to defend themselves.[67] Wrestling, says Kashifi, represents all the beautiful and ugly aspects of people's personalities that are in constant opposition—monotheism (*tawhīd*) and polytheism (*shirk*), piety (*taqvā*) and immorality (*fisq*), certainty (*yaqīn*) and doubt (*shakk*), humility (*tavāzaw*) and vanity (*takbīr*).[68] Although displays of art (*hunar*) such as wrestling matches were enacted at any time during the year between two competing local groups, fractional strife seems to have reached a turning point during Muharram ceremonies. By the age of Shah Abbas I (r. 1587–1629), these spontaneous performances were transformed into ritualized fights between two *futuvvat* factions (Nimatullahi and Haydari), in which the monarch himself participated. Della Valle describes a mourning ritual for the martyrdom of Ali (21 Ramazan 1026/1617) in which Shah Abbas I personally favored one side by joining the procession of one of the congregations. The shah often took pleasure in siding with one of the parties: "After having brought them to blows, he would go and sit at a window to watch the dismal issue of the battle."[69]

The breadth of Safavi control can be seen in the shah's direct involvement in local feuds. Seeking to impose maximum discipline and order, Safavi monarchs came to manage this important arena of social control within their orbit of authority. As Shah Abbas I appropriated the socioreligious function of the Muharram rituals, he severed the connections between the crafts and local sufi orders. The late scholar on sufism, Zarrinkub, notes that Abbas I destroyed the stronghold of the *futuvvat* and replaced them with factions of a deformed kind.[70] Ashura ceremonies shorn of their vitality generated from within local systems of patronage and loyalty had become the tools of Safavi kings—frozen gestures devoid of spirituality. The seventeenth-century poet Khaki Khurasani laments this change:

> Discussion of outer observances and declarations of inward belief are impossible without spiritual guides and master craftsmen.[71]

Safavi historiography has cast Abbas I as the architect of Safavi absolutism. This book aims at refining such a perspective, understanding Abbas I's attempts at centralization as adaptive (re)applications of his grandfather Tahmasb's (1524–1576) royal visions. Furthermore, Abbas I's institutional reforms must be observed within the *longue durée,* mindful of the directions taken by his immediate successors, Safi and Abbas II (r. 1629–1666), which gave shape and permanence to his new orderings.[72] In the seventeenth century as the Safavi Shahs came to centralize their authority, they began to institutionalize a systematic functioning of the Ashura rituals. In a royal attempt to homogenize and control this sacred space, Shah Abbas I's successor (Shah Safi r. 1629–1642), "had ordered the inhabitants of several Persian towns to join their ceremonies with theirs [for] they are made differently everywhere."[73] The royal square of the capital city of Isfahan took center stage for these commemorations. De Montheron, a lay companion of a Carmelite bishop, describes the concluding act of the Karbala narrative, which culminates with Husayn's martyrdom on the tenth day (April 26, 1641):

> On the great square of that town [Isfahan], the most beautiful which exists in Asia and in Europe . . . provided all around with buildings similar in architecture . . . adorned at one end with the great mosque and at one of its sides, with the main portal of the king's palace [Ali Qapu]. At its top, all enriched with gildings and paintings, [and] covered against the inconvenience of the sun with a great veil of gold brocade, [was] the King dressed with a black vest, wearing a black turban (which one does wear only on this occasion) accompanied only by his Great Chamberlain. On the side, under an arcade on the right hand, was the Sadr (who is like their pope) together with the main ministers of the state.[74] In the left hand [arcade were] the king's eunuchs, white and black, about one hundred in number. Down, in the place, was his principal Mulla (who is the first of his doctors), on a scaffold raised 5 or 6 feet high, seated in a chair, narrating in a loud voice the circumstances of the death of this Husayn (whom they hold in an extreme veneration), mixing it sometimes with the praises and prayes for the present King, to which the people answers amin. This sort of predication, which lasts over an hour, is made in that way before the King. A similar one is made, at another end of the square for the common people, by another Mulla, in front of whom [were] five or six hundred crouching women, covered and hidden with a great white cotton shroud, which shown nothing but the eyes . . . to allow them to guide themselves . . . screaming and weeping as if one were wanting to skin them.[75]

A quarter of a century later in 1667, the French traveler Jean Baptiste Tavernier also notes that a "mullah" who recited the lamentation on Hasan and Husayn's deaths "made a prayer for the health of the King [Sulayman] and the propriety of his Kingdom," placing the figure of the shah at the very center of Muharram observances. Tavernier proceeds to describe a fight that erupted among the inhabitants of Isfahan in the presence of

Shah Sulayman (r. 1666–1692): "[T]here were several that went to Sharps, accounting it a great honour to fight smartly in the king's presence; and farther believing that if one be kill'd upon that occasion, he shall be sainted, as indeed everyone gives something toward his interment."[76] The redemptive aspect of suffering and martyrdom were embedded in the public acts of the Muharram ritual; now it was the Safavi monarch representing the Imams who acted as God's intermediary at the day of judgment absolving the sins of the performers.[77]

De Montheron continues to describe the procession (1641) in the central square of Isfahan (Naqsh-i Jahan) performed while the monarch (Safi) and his court were watching from the porch (*tālār*) of the palace (Ali Qapu):

These two predications being over, the first ones of this show (*tamāsha*) enters the square to begin the spectacle. [First] there are the Arabs in great number, representing the Arabs of Medina screaming . . . "where is my Husayn, where is my gallant [*javān*] Husayn?" Then they let go a score of horses, saddled, bridled and armed with arrows, covered with leopard skins, confusedly running here and there, representing Husayn's horses, which fled when he was massacred. Then [they let go] as many camels, some painted in black, loaded with coffers, and naked persons who struggled and screamed as if [they were] in despair, saying his baggage [had been] plundered. After there appeared several machines or biers surrounded with trophies, bows, quivers full of arrows, shields, scimitars, feathers and other similar ornaments. [There were] surrounded by a great number of men, all naked (excepting their privy parts) wounded at their foreheads and at several places of their bodies, where from blood was gushing abundantly. The others, still more frightful, [were] naked, covered with ashes, all surrounded by an apparently infinite number of persons armed with big sticks, screaming and running in a fury as if they wanted to kill each other. . . . All these fancies representing the death of Husayn and all his family with him, which made weep and scream so many men and women, and which lasted 3 or 4 hours passing before the King, may be called with reason a true spectacle of grief. It was finished in the night of this tenth day by a fight of these people in which five of them remained dead on the square and 70 [were] seriously wounded.[78]

By the age of Abbas II (r. 1642–1666), imitators (*shabīhkhwānī*) of the Karbala drama were called to stage their performances at court. Safavi monarchs gradually extended their participation in these rituals as they became directors of the Karbala play partaking, in the creation of a collective Alid memory. Every evening during the first ten days of Muharram, the Shah summoned each town quarter associated with particular guilds to display their rituals and processions at the *Salon de l'ecurie* (*Tālār-i Tavīlah*). As soon as the shah ordered it, the processions entered.[79] And Shah Abbas II acting like a true gallant extended his hospitality feeding the performers throughout the ten days. A space had been constructed that could accommodate the performance of this new court ceremonial. A distinct feature of the building, which was completed by the end of Shah Safi's reign (1635–1636), lay in its openness (*tālār*), which made it particularly suitable for large gatherings, like the addition overlooking the magnificent square of Isfahan that Abbas II added onto the palace during the years 1644 to 1647. The Tālār-i Tavīlah, a long rectangular building comprised of a series of rooms with a *tālār* open on three sides was protected by a roof that rested on wooden pillars.[80] "There was at the entrance into it a partition, like an alcove, with curtains drawn before it, of red cotton, which were taken up and let down with silk strings," recalls Olearius.[81] The theatrical porches with raised platform could have served as a stage around which the king and his extended household engaged in a private Muharram commemoration. Although Shah Safi used this space for New Year celebrations, for Abbas II, the Tālār-i Tavīlah seemed to have served the function of a new center stage for Ashura performances in Isfahan, linking the Safavis spatially and genealogically to this ritual memorializing the family (*ahl-i bayt*). The open battlefield arena (*ma'rika*) where these rituals would be performed in towns and cities was transformed here into a formalized space, enshrining the participation of an Alid king—a potential messiah. Located within the palace precincts, the shah shared this sacred space with his new devotees, his ministers, bureaucrats, craftsmen, slaves, and eunuchs.

The square around which Abbas I had (re)created Isfahan was conceived of as the pivot of the universe from where the expected Mahdi would emerge (see figure 6). To ensure the centrality of the square, he had placed the two lungs through which Muslim cities breath—a mosque and a bazaar—on either side of it. The palace complex was an integral part of the square where amid commerce and devotion, entertainment and displays of power, the apocalyptic theme was performed night and day. The entire complex of buildings surrounding the square can be read as symbols in the Safavi theater of authority. The new addition to the palace complex (*Tālār-i Tavīlah*) came to be utilized as a ceremonial arena for the staging of elaborate rituals and feasting during religious commemorations of Ali's investiture (Ghadir Khumm) or the processional mourning of Husayn. Their performance within the sanctuary of the Safavi abode rather than in the public space of the Maydan signals the binding of Karbala with the holy persona of Shah Abbas II, born of Ali's seed.

Just as the early Safavis constructed their shrine complex in Ardabil around the house of Shaykh Safi al-din, as kings in their new residence of Isfahan they joined their spiritual roles to their royal prerogatives ceremonially. In Isfahan as in Ardabil, palatial and shrine architecture merged; what distinguishes the two is their initial point of conception.[82] Ardabil began as a local sufi shrine and evolved into an imperial memorial. Isfahan, in contrast, was conceived of as the seat of a universal empire, one that inaugurated the new Muslim millennium. The transformed city of Isfahan under Abbas I's successors was thought to mirror paradise. And the Safavis held the key, for as descendants of the family, they were privy to open the gates.

A similar open-space roofed pavilion (*tālār*) had been added by Abbas II onto the Ali Qapu facing the square where polo matches, fireworks, mock battles, and executions were staged. The shah's elevated position in this imperial building where the business of administration transpired allowed him to publicly display his art of governing to his subjects. He does not seem to have mingled as much as his great grandfather Abbas I, who reportedly would personally enter one side of the feuds in the Muharram processions, as discussed, and would also stroll freely through his city, eating food from street vendors, socializing with guests, and playing the host in Isfahan. Abbas II's transfer of the Muharram rituals to the private sanctuary of his abode effectively occluded the denizens of Isfahan; henceforth, the rituals could be observed only by a special audience of courtiers and official visitors.

Sussan Babaie reads the palatial transformations of Isfahan as serving the new needs of Safavi kings, who were for the first time breaking away from the tribal habits of their forefathers, establishing Isfahan as their capital city (*maqārr*) in its essential meaning as the permanent residence of the ruler.[83] As Safavi monarchs became urbanized, they erected structures in which to perform their multidimensional roles as mystic monarchs, representatives of the Imams on earth. Although imperial sites of pilgrimage such as Ardabil, Mashad, and Qum continued to be patronized, the sufi (Ardabil) and Shi'i (Qum and Mashad) idioms of Safavi authority were inscribed in Isfahan, creating formalized urban spaces. As they expanded their city, each king built himself a structure to objectify his reign. Each building served a particular function as a symbol in the Safavi language of power. The vast religious ceremonial space of the Tālār-i Tavīla where Muharram processions were held in Isfahan signals the changing nature of Safavi ritual and politics. Such sufi functions must have been performed at Ardabil during the early life of the Safavi order, for we know about their craft membership. And we know that, locally, Muharram celebrations had been organized by guilds. It is possible that in Ardabil they were first performed in an open space (*ma'rika*) with no architectural embodiment, as Kashifi describes them in his manual on chivalry.

But by the middle of the seventeenth century, the ambassador of the Duke of Holstein to Iran, Adam Olearius (1637), notes that these ceremonies were now performed at the palace of the governor of Ardabil, who even took on the role of initiating the master eulogist.[84] Throughout the Safavi dominion, Muharram celebrations seem to have been integrated into imperial ceremonies of power.

Although there does not seem to be a prototype of the Tālār-i Tavīlah in Ardabil, there is another twin building shared by Ardabil and Isfahan that housed a sufi institution and was first commissioned by Tahmasb. This octagonal domed structure referred to as the *Tawhīdkhānah* (House of Union) in Isfahan stood adjacent to the Tālār-i Tavīlah. That these two holy structures were conceptually coupled between the more public space of the court (*dīvānkhānah*) and the private quarters of the harem (*andarūn*) links them to the charismatic aura of the Shah. In the House of Union *Tawhīdkhānah*, people would take sanctuary, repenting their sins and asking the shah for forgiveness and protection. Weekly, a master (*khalīfat al-khulafā'*) of the Safavi order representing the the mystic-monarch would "follow the rule [*dastūr*] established in the time of Shaykh Safi al-din Ishaq—namely, to gather in the *Tawhīdkhānah* every Thursday evening, dervishes and sufis and to keep them repeating, by way of loud zikr [*zikr-i jalī*], the pious formula: *la ilaha illa'llāh* [there is no god but God]; on Thursday evenings, he distributes to the dervishes bread, sweetmeats [*halva*] and food, and on other occasions, bread and the customary food."[85]

Kishwar Rizwi sees the transformation of the shrine complex in Ardabil during the sixteenth century as a template for future imperial building projects and draws a parallel between the House of Union in Isfahan with the Heavenly Hall (*Jannatsarā*) in Ardabil, which are architecturally identical. The space in Ardabil is one where memory is created; the verse inscribed on its exterior invokes the recalling (*zikr*) of its interior: "Remember Allah with much remembrance" (33:41–43).[86] Rizwi situates the Qizilbash initiation ceremony (*chūb-i tarīq*) in the

Jannatsarā, where poems in praise of Ali written by Isma'il and Tahmasb were recited by devotees.[87] In imperial Isfahan the Safavis continued to initiate members into their transformed brotherhood of Alid lovers, guiding them in devotion (*zikr*) and providing the standard script for Alid memory to be remembered and performed in the present.

To further illuminate the meaning of the new royal setting in which the Muharram rituals were relived, let me end with the messianic tenor they yearly evoked. Chardin in 1666 observes twelve splendid horses harnessed with bridles, saddles, and stirrups made of gold and precious stones standing in two rows of six on each side of the great portal of the palace (Ali Qapu).[88] The horses are symbolic of the twelve Imams, those invisible presences at the Muharram processions located at the threshold of the lofty Gate, Ali Qapu, from which the hidden messiah, the Mahdi, was to manifest himself, exiting the sacred Safavi abode in Isfahan. The gate itself objectified a syncretic Irano-Shi'i icon. Two columns from the Achaemenid palace in Persepolis framed the apocalyptic gateway, while in its threshold was embedded a stone that was to have been removed from Ali's shrine in Iraq (Najaf). The expectation of the return (*ra'ja*) of the twelfth Imam was a reality in early modern Persianate culture. It was this anticipation that Isma'il had played on in his poetry (*divan*), prompting his devotees to enter the battlefield unarmed, ready to sacrifice their lives for their godhead. But as the Safavis began to institutionalize their imperium, Isma'il's son Tahmasb moved away from the messianic image of his father, relegating the manifestation of the hidden Imam to the immediate future. In stables of Safavi cities, saddled horses stood dressed in jewels and gold ready for the advent of the Mahdi.

From beyond the Safavi gates, Isfahanis continued to live this expectation daily as they listened to eulogies and stories in praise of the Imams or as they wrestled and juggled in the battlefield. The central square where such performances were attended by Safavi monarchs and their subjects was surrounded with paintings depicting paradise: "The Painters of Bihzad-like pen and portraitists of Mani-like line painted pictures on those [walls] of all the wondrous creatures and marvelous creations. Thus, every one of the surfaces became like a copy of the wonders of creation [*ajā'ib al-makhlūqāt*]."⁸⁹ Artists and craftsmen (*arbāb-i hirfa*) had through their magical art unveiled the splendors of heaven in this central square of Isfahan.⁹⁰ Divine reflections, whether through images, sounds, or gestures, fused emotions that culminated in the reenactment of the ten days of Karbala, creating a potential turning point. Every year, a space was opened for the possible entry into a new cycle of time. After all, the narrative of the *Abū Muslimnāme* described such apocalyptic chaos in the Muharram processions: The world had gone topsy-turvy. Women mingled with men, and nudity and impurity (blood) were on display. The uprising of Abu Muslim (d. 755) was construed as one of the seventy-two revolts predicted by Muhammad in the name of his betrayed children, the seventy-two victims of Karbala. Abu Muslim's messianic call (*da'wa*) provided a paradigm of what could be actualized after the tragic martyrdom of Husayn, a narrative memory that was imitated by the revolutionary Safavis. But now its future was arrested in Safavi time and space.

By the seventeenth century, the Safavis desired to push the apocalypse into the future while reserving the role of messiah for their progeny alone. Nuha Khoury in her study on the Royal Mosque Abbas I built in the maydan illuminates its meaning through the epigraphic program written in a Shi'i language of authority. Her work brings to life stories and symbols related through the Qur'an, hadith, and accounts of Ali and the Imams that were inscribed on the walls and domes of the mosque as a book on Twelver Shi'i history and ethics. Khoury uses the work of the famous scholar Shaykh-i Baha'i dedicated to Shah Abbas I, *Jāmi' al-Abbasī*, as a mirror of the epigraphic content, revealing an association between these two religious projects of royal patronage. Shaykh-i Baha'i was an eminent representative of the Shi'i clergy (Shaykh al-Islam) and an engineer who helped with the urban development of the city of paradise. Religion, the arts, and politics were working in concert to develop a new city that reflected the image of Shah Abbas I as a pious Imami Shah, the shadow of God on earth, and the inaugurator of a new era of justice, geared for the eschatological arrival of the Mahdi. The stage was set for Abbas I and his sons to act as messiahs in Isfahan, the site of the celestial kingdom. From portal to dome, the mosque's epigraphy memorializes Ali as the ideal gallant and the guide to the city of knowledge.[91] The image of Ali resonates with his construction in chivalric brotherhoods, as well. Episodes we have encountered in our manual on chivalry where Muhammad initiated Ali as his brother, or the famous dictum that Ali is the peerless youth (*fatā'*) are etched on the walls of the mosque, referred to as the second Ka'ba (Mecca).[92] The concepts of brotherhood and the virtues of Ali that are narrated in calligraphy would have been understood by members of Alid craft associations. Although these devotees could not read the Arabic on the walls, they had heard and memorized their content in Persian. A master craftsman's remark would suffice to create an association between these divine letters and their sounds and images. A familiar atmosphere loomed in the royal mosque with the entire south section devoted to Ali. The dome inscription provides the proof of his investiture and righteous cause. And the theme of pilgrimage is engraved above the prayer niche (*mihřab*), transforming the mosque into a holy Alid sanctuary. The path to divine law lay in Mecca (*Ka'ba*), while the mystical quest lay in Isfahan (Ali). On the prayer niche, the drama of Karbala is marked with a hadith that narrates the passion for the martyrdom of Husayn. Words in epigraphy taken from stories that were heard orally are impressed on the prayer niche and performed at court. The image of the shah as sanctuary was engraved in Isfahan, where their blessed abode offered refuge to those who could cross the second most sacred threshold of Ali. In Isfahan, there were twin gates to the truth (Ali)—the mosque (*shari'a*) and palace (*tarīqat*). The mosque, the square, and the palace complex became the stages for Alid history, past and present. "Isfahan" writes Khoury, "was transformed into a holy ground, whether as the battlefield of Karbala, the oasis of Ghadir Khumm, or the city of Mecca where the truth began to be revealed."[93] With the theatrical coronation of the Nuqtavis, Abbas I had orchestrated the "end of the age of metemphsychosis.'" Isfahan was rebuilt as the site of a new era of Safavi universal rule. You may recall that Shi'i hadith had marked Isfahan as a location of future messianic unveilings. The mosque and the palace complex—Tawhīdkhāne, Tālār-i Tavīla—provided a space where the faithful could renew their allegiance to the Mahdi at the end of time. Through the performance of acts of devotion in these arenas (prayer, Muharram, Ghadir Khumm), the past continually recurred in the present. A new cycle of revenge, however, was delayed. With the severing of ties between local guilds and sufi masters throughout the empire, charisma was reserved for the Safavis. Perhaps that explains why in the seventeenth century with the banning of the *Abū Muslināmne(s)* recollections of a past that provided a scenario for rebellion were being erased. A new memory was being created instead, freezing the Alid narrative in space (Isfahan) until a messiah born of Safavi blood would emerge from the palace gate.

NOTES

1. Husayn Vā'iz Kāshifī, *Futuvvatnāme-yi Sultānī*, ed. Muhammad Ja'far Mahjūb (Tehran: Bunyād-i Farhang-i Iran, 1971), also 6.n.4. 20.
2. Ibid., 17.
3. Ibid., 6.
4. Ibid., 146.
5. An analogous relationship is constructed in the Persian epic *Samak-i 'Ayyār*, in which the gallant Samak is adopted by Shuqāl-i Pīlzūr, the master of all *javānmards* in the city of Chin, as his son.
6. I am making use of Henry Corbin's observations on the Nusayri initiation in his "A Shi'ite Liturgy of the Grail," *The Voyage and the Messenger: Iran and Philosophy,* trans. Joseph H. Rowe (Berkeley, CA: North Atlantic Books: 1998), 185.

7. Kāshifī, *Futuvvatnāme-yi Sultānī*, 22.

8. Ibid., 215: *"jannat keh rizā-yi mā dar ān ast andar tah-i pāy-i mādarānast khwāhī keh rizā-yi haqq biyābī ān kun keh rizā-yi mādarānast."*

9. Ibid., 241.

10. Ibid., 242.

11. Ibid., 242–243.

12. Ibid., 244–245: "Take a book [*mushaf, kitābī*] that has verses of the Qu'ran and hadith with you. Carry a pen and inkpot if you are literate. Take a comb, a stove, a cane, and a bowl. The meaning of traveling is *'sayr ilā allah, sayr fī allāhī, sayr bi-allāhī, sayr bi-allāhī fī allāhī.'"*

13. See C. E. Bosworth, "Nakīb," *EI2*; A. Havemann, "Nakīb al-Ashrāf," *EI2*; also see Heinz Halm, *Shi'ism* (Edinburgh: University of Edinburgh, 1991), 49–50.

14. Vladimir Minorsky, *Tazkirat al-mulūk* (London: E. J. Gibb Memorial Series, 1989), 83.

15. Kāshifī, *Futuvvatnāme-yi Sultānī*, 90.

16. Ibid., 89.

17. Ibid., 29.

18. The different knots for belts described by Kāshifī serves as a manual for reading professions into girded individuals depicted in miniatures.

19. Ritual positioning: two carpets *(shaykh* and *ustād-i shadd)* beside which stands the father of the covenant *(pidar-i ahdullāh)* and the novice *(shāgird)*. They are facing Mecca *(qibla)*. Two brothers and the rest of the community pray behind them.

20. Corbin, "A Shi'ite Liturgy of the Grail," 174.

21. Ibid., 192.

22. Ibid., 197.

23. Ibid., 199–200.

24. I would like to thank Afsaneh Najmabadi for bringing this reading of a combined Irano-Shi'i genealogy to my attention.

25. Kāshifī, *Futuvvatnāme-yi Sultānī*, 131–138.

26. Victor Turner, *Dramas, Fields, and Metaphors: Symbolic Action in Human Society* (Ithaca, Cornell University Press, 1974), 64

27. Marina Gaillard, *Le Livre de Samak-e 'Ayyār* (Paris: L'Institut d'Etudes Iraniennes, 1987), 154

28. Mary Boyce, *Zoroastrianism: Its Antiquity and Constant Vigour* (Costa Mesa: 1992), 84.

29. The spiritual chain that Kāshifī enumerates for his path (*tarīqat*) includes Alid eulogists like Dervish Ali Dihqān and Mawlana Hasan-i Kāshī, as well as mystic poets like Sa'dī and Khājūy-i Kirmānī. So the "father of ahdullāh" must represent the revered hierarchy of eulogists and poets related to Kāshifī's profession.

30. Kāshifī, *Futuvvatnāme-yi Sulṭan*, 132.

31. Corbin, "A Shi'ite Liturgy of the Grail," 192.

32. Abu Muslim in his epic is initiated at the *takkiya* of his father's friend, the blacksmith who crafts for him the famous axe.

33. Kāshifī, *Futuvvatnāme-yi Sultani*, 120: "*Alastu awalā bikum mīn anfusukum?*"

34. Ibid.: "*Man kuntu mawlāhu fahaza 'Aliun mawlahu.*"

35. Ibn-i Hanbal, *Musnad*, vol. 4, 281. Similar traditions can be found in many other works such as Ibn Mūjam, *Sunan*, vol. 1, Bab II, 43, no. 116, as cited in Moojen Momen, *An Introduction to Shi'ism: The History and Doctrines of Twelver Shi'ism* (New Haven: Yale University Press, 1985), 15.

36. Kāshifī quotes from Rumi's *Masnavi*: "*zān sabab payghambar bā ijtihād nām-i khud vān Ali mawla nihād kist mawla ān ke āzādat kunad band-i righvat rā az-pāyat barkanad.*"

37. Ibid., 244.

38. The main themes revolve around obedience to Allah, surrender, and self-sacrifice: "O ye who believe! Observe your duty to Allah with right observance, and die not save as those who surrender onto him." (3:102). The concept of camaraderie is emphasized: "And hold fast all of you together to the cable of Allah, and do not separate." (3:103). "The believers are naught else than brothers. Therefore, make peace between your bretheren and observe your duty to Allah that haply ye may obtain mercy" (49:10). Compassion is central: "And in adversity those who control their wrath and are forgiving toward mankind Allah loveth the Good" (3:134). He also reads from the pillars (*arkan*) of the order.

39. Kāshifī, *Futuvvatnāme*, 120. Kāshifī states that the first knot is tied in the name of God, the second in the name of Akhi Jibrail, and the third in Muhammad's name. This points to the three lettered symbols ('*alif, lām,* and *mīm*): '*alif* representing the name of Allah, *lām*

of Jibra'il, and *mīm* of Muhammad. Then it is Muhammad who ties all the knots (*shadd*) around Ali.

40. Kāshifī in a response to a question he himself poses concerning the children of Ali who had been girded says: "Say three: Hasan the chosen [*mujtabā*] who looked like Muhammad, Husayn the martyr [*shahīd*] who was the father of the Imams, and Muhammad b. Hanfiyya who was the manifestation of bravery and generosity (in other words closest to Ali's qualities),"122. In the lineage (*sanad*) of Solomon (Sulaymāniyān), he places Salman-i Farsi, Ali Ansari, and Abū Muslim (123). And in the lineage (*silsila*) of sufis (*faqī*) he enumerates Ala Al-Dawla Simnani, Najm al-din Kubra, Abu Najib Suhravardi, Muhammad Aswad, Mimshad Dinawari, Shaykh Junayd Baghdadi, Shaykh Karkhi, Sultan-i Khurasan Ali Reza, Musa Kazim, Husayn, Ali, and Muhammad (124).

41. Kāshifī, *Futuvvatnāme*, 137: "*Bastam miyān-i īn farzand bi-baqā va gushādam bi-fanā.*"

42. Ibid., 292.

43. Kāshifī insists on the need to entertain and not be boring.

44. Ibid., 281.

45. Most travelers to seventeenth-century Iran (Della Valle, Olearius, Evliya Chelebi, and Tavernier) mention that poetry was recited in the lament of Husayn's martyrdom. See Peter J. Chelkowski on theatrical *ta'ziyah* plays in his edited volume *Ta'ziyah Ritual; and Drama in Iran* (New York: New York University Press, 1979), 4. Also see Yitzhak Nakkash, "An Attempt to Trace the Origins of the Rituals of 'Ashura," *Die Welt des Islams* 33 (1993): 171.

46. Adam Olerarius, *The Voyages and Travels of the Ambassadors Sent by Frederick, Duke of Holstein, to the Great Duke of Muscovy and the King of Persia*, 3 vols. (London: Printed for John Starkey and Thomas Basset, 1669), 236.

47. Craftsmen associated with Alid *futuvvat* circles organized and paid for the expenses of the Muharram commemoration according to Jean Calmard, "Shi'i Rituals and Power. II, The Consolidation of Safavid Shi'ism: Folklore and Popular Religion," in *Safavid Persia: The History and Politics of an Islamic Society*, ed. Charles Melville (London: Tauris), 170.

48. Pietro della Valle, *The Pilgrim: The Travels of Pietro Della Valle*, trans. George Bull (London: Hutchinson, 1990), 144.

49. Michele Membré, *Mission to the Lord Sophy of Persia (1539–1542)*, trans. A. H. Morton (London: School of Oriental and African Studies, 1993), 52.

50. Fedot Afanas'evich Kotov, *Khozhenie kuptsa Fedota Kotova v Persiiu* (Moscow: Izd-vo Vostochnoi lit-ry 1958), 88.

51. Olearius, *The Voyages*, 237.

52. Pietro della Valle's letter dated July 25, 1618, describes Muharram in Isfahan in *The Pilgrim*, 143. Women are noted as active participants in this mourning ritual. In particular, they are said to have been prone to weeping and wailing. Kotov, *Khozhenie kuptsa Fedota Kotova v Persiiu*, 53.

53. Evliya Chelebi, cited in Nakkash, "An Attempt to Trace the Origin of the Rituals of 'Ashura," 175.

54. Kotov, *Khozhenie kuptsa Fedota Kotova v Persiiu*, 88–89.

55. Della Valle, *The Pilgrim*, 127.

56. I would like to thank Rosemary Stansfield-Johnson for sending me a draft of her forthcoming article, "The Tabarrā' and the Early Safavids."

57. On *manāqib khwānī* (reciters of merit), see Ja'far Mahjūb, "The Evolution of Popular Eulogy of the Imams among the Shi'a," in Said Amir Arjomand, ed., *Authority and Political Culture in Shi'ism*, trans. and adapted by John Perry (Albany: State University Press of New York, 1988). Also see P. N. Boratov, "Maddah," *EI2;* Jean Calmard, "Le Chi'isme Imamite en Iran à l'epoque Seldjoukide d'apres le *Kitab al-Naqz*," *Le Monde Iranien et l'Islam*, 1 (1971): 43–67; Rosemary Stansfield-Johnson, "The Tabarrā' and the Early Safavids" (forthcoming), 4.

58. Cited in Stansfield-Johnson, "The Tabarrā' and the Early Safavids," 13.

59. Ibid., Stansfield-Johnson quotes from Isma'il's Sadr Makhdum Sharifi, who was personally harassed by the *tabarā'iyān*. She states that "declaring one's love for Ali was the answer to the charge of heresy against Twelver Shi'ism in this period," 16. See her article "Sunni Survival in Safavid Iran: Anti-Sunni Activities during the Reign of Tahmasb I," for a story of a man who was brought to court with the charge of being a Sunni, *Iranian Studies*, 27, nos. 1–4 (1994): 131.

60. Ibid., cited in Stansfield-Johnson, 14, quoting from 'Abd al-Husayn Navā'ī, *Shah Tahmasb Safavī: Majmū'ah-yi Asnād vā*

Mukātibāt-i Tārīkhī (Tehran: Instishārāt-i Arghavān, 1989), 215. I have altered some of her translations.

61. Calmard, "Shi'i Rituals and Power," 162.

62. Jean-Baptiste Tavernier, John Phillips, and Edmund Everard, *Collections of Travels through Turkey into Persia and the East-Indies* (London: George Monke and William Ewney 1688), 162.

63. Calmard, "Shi'i Rituals and Power," 145.

64. Kāshifī, *Futuvvatnāme*, 276.

65. Ibid.

66. Ibid., 308. Eight different groups are enumerated here: *kushtigīrān, sang gīrān, nāvah kishān, silah kishān, hamālān, mughayir gīrān, rasan bāzān, zūr gīrān.*

67. Ibid., 307.

68. Ibid.

69. Cited in Calmard, "Shi'i Rituals and Power," 145.

70. Cited in Mehdi Keyvānī, *Artisans and Guild Life in the Later Safavid Period: Contributions to the Social-Economic History of Persia* (Berlin: Klaus Schwarz, 1982), 209. Also see Abd al-Husayn Zarrīnkūb, *Arzish-i Mirās-i Sūfiyyah* (Tehran: Amīr Kabīr, 1965).

71. Ibid., cited in Keyvānī, Artisans and Guild Life, 12 [quoting from Khāki-yi Khurāsānī, *Dīvān-i Khaki*, ed. Ivanow (Bombay, 1933)]: "Hadis az zāhir u unvān-i bātin/na-shud bī-pīr u bī ustād-i asnāf."

72. Both Sussan Babaie's dissertation on Safavi palaces in Isfahan (1590–1666) and my own dissertation on the evolution of religious and political culture of Safavi imperial rule in Isfahan (1629–1666) aimed at understanding the reigns of Abbas I's successors (Safi and Abbas II) as active agents in the shaping of new architectural, political, and religious paradigms of authority.

73. Calmard, "Shi'i Rituals and Power," 175 (citing De Montheron, 1641).

74. The Sadr was the minister of religion, justice, and education. He was appointed from among the sayyids and up to this date the office was usually held by a Persian notable. But in 1641 the post is granted to Mirza Habibullah Karaki, a descendant of the Arab jurisconsult Shaykh Ali Karaki (d. 1533), who issued the *fatwā* against *Abū Muslimnāme* reciters. The post of Sadr was now dominated by the Imami clergy.

75. Calmard, "Shi'i Rituals and Power," 174.

76. Tavernier, *Collections of Travels*, 72–77.

77. On the redemptive aspect of suffering during Muharram, see Mahmoud Ayoub, *Redemptive Suffering in Islam: A Study of the Devotional Aspects of 'Āshūrā in Twelver Shī'ism* (The Hague: Mouton, 1978); Nakkash, "An Attempt to Trace the Origin of the Rituals of 'Ashura." The French traveler Tavernier in 1667 Isfahan remarks that "Upon this occasion you shall see a great number of Curtisans that come to the Ceremony fall a weeping, who thereby believe their sins are forgiv'n." Tavernierg Phillips, and Everard, *Collections of Travels*, 162.

78. Calmard, "Shi'i Rituals and Power," 174–175 (translating De Montheron).

79. Ibid., 164. Calmard is quoting Chardin, who refers to Shah Sulayman, vol. 9, 57.

80. Sussan Babaie, "Safavid Palaces at Isfahan: Continuity and Change (1590–1666)," Ph.D. diss., New York University, 1994, 246.

81. Ibid., 247, citing Olearius, *Relation du Voyages* (Paris: Chez Nicolas & Jean de la Coste, 1666), 202

82. See Kishwar Rizvi's "Transformation in Early Safavid Architecture: The Shrine of Shaykh Safi al-din Ardabili in Iran," Ph.D. diss., Massachusetts Institute of Technology, 2000, for a parallel merging of the dual roles in the evolution of the Shrine of Arbabil under Tahmasb and Abbas I.

83. Babaie, "Safavid Palaces at Isfahan." I would like to thank Sussan Babaie for providing me with a copy of her excellent chapter on "The Pivot of the Universe: The Palace and the Rhetorics of Sovereignty in Early Modern Iran," to appear in her forthcoming book, *Feasting in the City of Paradise*. See Robert McChesney, "The Four Sources on Shah Abbas's Building of Isfahan," *Muqarnas 5*, (1988): 103–104, for the designation *maqarr* (seat or abode) from the Arabic root *qarra* (to settle down, become settled, dwell, live, reside).

84. Olearius, *The Voyages and Travels*, 236.

85. Minorsky, *Tazkirāt al-mulūk*, 55.

86. Rizvi, "Transformation in Early Safavid Architecture," 262.

87. Membré, *Mission to the Lord Sophy of Persia*, 2; Rizvi, "Transformation in Early Safavid Architecture," 173–175.

88. Calmard, "Shi'i Rituals and Power," 165 [citing John Chardin, *Les Voyages du Chevalier Chardin en Perse*, ed. L. Langlès, (Paris, 1811), vol. 3, 172 ff.].

89. Babaie, "Safavid Palaces," 167 (quoting Natanzi's *Naqāvat, al-āsār*, 577, translated by McChesney, "The Four Sources on Shah Abbas's Building of Isfahan," 107). I have altered some of the translations. The murals representing paradise were part of the design for the first phase (1590–1501) of the maydan. With the renovations during phase two (post-1602–1603) similar celestial themes are repainted.

90. McChesney, "The Four Sources on Shah Abbas's Building of Isfahan," 107 (citing Natanzi, *Naqāvat al-āsār*, 577).

91. Nuha Khoury, *Ideologies and Inscriptions: The Epigraphy of the Masjid- Shah and the Ahmediye in the Context of Safavid-Ottoman Relations, Muqarnas* (Leiden: Brill, forthcoming).

92. Ibid., 147, 163, 167.

93. Ibid., 192.

EIGHT

Epics and Heresy: Writing Heterogeneity out of Shi'i History

The Safavi polemics against Abu Muslim were part of an effort to rewrite early Islamic history. This Shi'i (Imami) revision of the past had as its impetus the will to create homogeneity amid a diverse Alid culture. If, indeed, polemics in support of Abu Muslim were compiled to counter the assault on this epic hero, their trace has disappeared. We do know, however, that a second wave of refutations against Abu Muslim, dating from the last years of Shah Abbas I's rule (1587–1629), were voiced in opposition to sufi-minded scholars like Majlisi Sr. (d. 1660), who praised the popular Alid hero during his sermons, depicting him as a Muslim crusader and no foe of the Imams.[1] Such men of religion who combined the paths of divine law (shari'a) with mysticism (tariqat), then, would take no offense with the Abū Muslimnāme's portrayal of its protagonist as the lover of the family of Muhammad (ahl-i bayt) who rose to avenge their blood. It becomes clear from the tone of the polemics and the content of some versions of the Abū Muslimnāme(s) that the points raised by the refutations directly bore on the interpretation of the Abbasid revolution articulated in these epics. Moreover, given that the polemics explicitly attack the storytellers who propagated "myths" revolving around Abu Muslim, they will be used as texts that represent the views of those who saw Abu Muslim as a hero of the Shi'a. These polemics attempt to divorce Imami Shi'ism from its own exaggerated past, a past that was still remembered and experienced among the devotees of the Imams in early modern Iran and Asia Minor. They succeeded in canonizing a version of Twelver Imami genealogy and history that remains hegemonic today.

These epics and the polemics they generated preserve a flavor of Safavi vernacular culture at a moment of conflict with a courtly culture that was itself in the process of transformation from an Alid messianic movement to a Shi'i (Imami) theocracy. We know that Safavi missionaries had used the *Abū Muslimnāme* to spread their *ghulāt* beliefs during their revolutionary phase (1450–1501).[2] Just as self-proclaimed messiahs continued to manifest themselves in Alid circles, a cycle of epics recounting the lives of holy warriors took shape around them as well (*Zemchīnāme, Bābaknāme, Junaydnāme*). Revolts and epics together sustained the spirit of heresy through imagined cycles of time. These epics circulated both in the realms of written and oral culture, capturing the points at which words and images animated the past through sound. They were communicative channels through which oppositional practices and cosmologies were voiced, providing a space for emerging forms of resistance to shape their collective actions around an Alid narrative.

Medieval historians like Tabari and Masudi capture an image of men in black congregating around two poles with black banners held by a representative of the family (Sulayman b. Kathir). The rebellion of Abu Muslim in Khurasan was emplotted as an episode that followed the drama of Karbala, and there began in the heartland of Persianate memory the unveiling of the secret mission to take revenge for the family of truth. In medieval chronicles, Abu Muslim chants a verse from the Qu'ran (22:39) as he embraces the cause: "Leave is given to those who fight because they were wronged; surely God is able to help them."[3] Gradually, these men in black espousing a variety of sentiments of betrayal spread throughout the eastern frontiers of Islamdom in defiance of the Umayyads.

In the epic version of history, Abu Muslim spends the first ten days of Muharram—the period of mourning for the martyrdom of Husayn—with the Imam Muhammad Baqir, during which time he receives lessons on divine law (*shari'a*) from him. Before Imam Muhammd Baqir sends Abu Muslim off to make his exit (*khurūj*), he enters a cave and brings forth a secret book composed by Ali, containing Ali's predictions concerning Abu Muslim's role within the unfolding drama of revenge against the Umayyads.[4] Muhammad Baqir reads the divinations aloud to Abu Muslim. He issues him a mandate (*manshūr*) in which the Imam states, "I, Muhammad Baqir, son of Ali Murtaza and deputy [*vakīl*] and executor [*wasī*] of the messenger of God, after seven Imams have sat in the place of my ancestor [Muhammad]."[5] Muhammad Baqir is considered to be the fifth Imam of the Twelver Shi'a (Imami); here, in the *Abū Muslimnāme*, he is the seventh successor of Muhammad through Ali and Husayn, who is succeeded by his half-brother (Muhammad b. Hanafiyya). Such genealogical disputes lay at the center of these debates.

In some versions of the epic, the Alid Imam Muhammad Baqir then sends Abu Muslim to the Abbasid Imam Ibrahim (d. 749), linking these two cousin clans in a single chain of charisma emanating from Muhammad and Ali. When Abu Muslim visits the Abbasid Imam (Ibrahim) with a mandate from his cousin Muhammad Baqir, he is told, "Those who despise Muhammad and Ali will be put to death. Those who refuse to accept the authority of the house of the Prophet will be killed. I have given this mandate to Abu Muslim—*his order is my order.*" The cause of the Abbasids is analogous to the cause of the Alids: together they were reclaiming the usurped authority of the family. In epic history, the Abbasid Ibrahim designated Abu Muslim as his successor. Ibrahim writes a letter to various Shi'i leaders such as Sulayman b. Kathir specifying this point: "Disobeying him [Abu

Muslim] is like disobeying me." Imam Ibrahim then takes Abu Muslim through the rituals of investiture, cloaking him with the mantle and the black turban that Ali wore at Friday prayer.[6] And when Abu Muslim publicly announces his mission, he proclaims, "My aim is to stop the prayer in the name of Marwan [Umayyad], to stop the calumnies against the Caliph Ali, to reinstate the religion of the Prophet, and to destroy the Marwanids [Umayyads] and engage in holy war in the name of Muhammad and Ali."[7]

The Safavi polemicists are sensitive to memories of the past that preserve collaboration between the Alids and the Abbasids against the Umayyads because once the revolution had succeeded, the Abbasids had taken hold of power and killed many Shi'is as well as some Imams.[8] Moreover, since the Abbasids had come in time to embrace the majoritarian tendency among Muslims (Sunni) to maintain a separate identity, it was important for the Shi'a to distinguish their history from the Abbasids, disengaging themselves from an active revolutionary image now that they were forging a "pacifist" theology around the occultation of their last living Imam (874). Instead, the polemicists set out to emphasize Abu Muslim's loyalty to the Abbasids and his enmity toward the children of Ali: "O lover of the family [*muhibb-i khāndān*], know that Abu Muslim was not from the Imamis nor the Twelvers (*Ithna 'Ashari*). In fact, he opposed them."[9] According to one polemicist (Hamavi), the storytellers would claim that "Imam Muhammad Baqir, peace be upon him, issued Abu Muslim a mandate to rule and authorized his mission [*da'wa*] and his revolt [*khurūj*]."[10] That the Imami polemicists deny that Abu Muslim gave his oath of allegiance (*bay'a*) to Imam Muhammad Baqir shows that they were conscious of these types of assertions preserved in some versions of the *Abū Muslim-nāme(s)*—versions utilized by the Safavi propagandists.[11] They dispute the historical validity of any potential linkages between any one of the twelve Imams with Abu Muslim—in particular, Muhammad Baqir (d. 737) and Ja'far al- Sadiq (d. 765). One rebuttal (*Izhār al-haqq*) went to the extent of clarifying the symbolism of the color black, emblematic of the revolution against the Umayyads that conjured its Alid message of martyrdom. A tradition is introduced where Muhammad asks the angel Gabriel the meaning of his black frock (*qiba*).[12] Gabriel confirms that it symbolizes the clothing worn by the children of Muhammad's uncle, Abbas. Black is cast as a symbol identifying the Abbasid household. Rather than a sign of mourning for Husayn, it signifies the harm that they came to inflict on the family (*ahl-i bayt*), killing generations of Imams during their imperial rule.[13]

In the course of such denials and justifications, it becomes clear that epics were not the only source that tied the proto-Imamis to Abu Muslim but that works on the lives and sayings of the Imams related Abu Muslim's episode in the same light.[14] Mowlana Hasan-i Kashi, the Alid eulogist who wrote an early history of the Imams—*Tārīkh-i Muhammadī*—during the Mongol period, extols Abu Muslim as a gallant who raised his sword in the name of the Alid cause: "A hundred booklets [*pārah-kitāb*] in that age were written about this story [*fisānah*]."[15] Hasan-i Kashi's verse narrative on Abu Muslim is an adaptation from these epics. These may have been utilized by popular men of religion, like Majlisi Sr., to confirm Abu Muslim as a friend of the Imams, justifying his praising of him from the pulpit of the mosque in Isfahan during his sermons. Moreover, Imam Muhammad Baqir was clearly not the only Twelver Imam implicated in the revolt of Abu Muslim, for denials surround Imam Ja'far al-Sadiq, a contemporary of Abu Muslim.[16]

Inasmuch as this aspect of epic accounts corresponds to the ones preserved in a variety of "legitimate" sources such as canonized dictums (*hadith*), they are read here as one interpretation of what transpired among the family of the Prophet (*ahl-i bayt*) during the Abbasid revolution. This interpretation emanated from a time in which the Imamis had not yet established themselves as a separate group, wheras the refutations were written at a time when the Imamis had not only gone sectarian but had established themselves as the official religion of the Safavi empire. They had the institutional backing to enforce a single version of Shi'i (Imami) memory. Any source depicting a heterogeneous context of the early Imamis would be refuted. Such attempts to create a linear and homogenous image of the past were not a new phenomenon. Once the Imamis began to consolidate themselves as a distinct group with their specific legal and theological teachings, religious scholars such as Kulayni (d. 941) and Ibn-i Babuya (d. 991) began reinterpreting the early history of the Imams.[17] Those artisans who were members of chivalric brotherhoods and who considered themselves lovers of Ali and his children did not embrace such renderings of history. Due to the nature of the Safavi movement, which saw its history linked to Alid groups such as the Kaysaniyya, some of whom had come to incorporate Imam Muhammad Baqir into their genealogy (*silsila*), new fire was added to the explosive history of relations between a group of rationalist Shi'i scholars and the excess of their devotees.

Some Shi'i hadith, one of the principal sources used in Islamic law, contain traces of ties between the proto-Shi'i Imams and Abu Muslim. Hamavi acknowledges that traditions ascribed to Ali, Muhammad Baqir, and Ja'far al-Sadiq have these two Imams forecast the rebellion of Abu Muslim and the Mongols, for example.[18] He reinterprets these texts as examples of the miraculous foresight possessed by these Imams. They need not be interpreted, he suggests, as praise and support for Abu Muslim or the Mongols.[19] The Mongols are generally viewed favorably by the Imamis, because they ended Sunni hegemony (1258) and patronized Shi'i scholars. Some Mongol rulers like Uljaytu (r. 1304–1317) are even considered to have been Shi'i. For the Mongols who were either pagan or Nestorian, Muslim sectarianism had political implications; therefore it was pragmatic to support minority religious traditions.

The juxtaposition of Abu Muslim and the Mongols in these Shi'i traditions points to a tendency to construe them both as Shi'a sympathizers. Hamavi instead argues that the rise of the Mongols can be read as a retaliatory move against Abu Muslim's revolt: "For history shows that Abu Muslim Marvazi was sent with a mission [*da'wa*] to Khurasan by the Abbasids to conquer the people of that province. After approximately 520 years of Abbasid rule, Hulegu and his troops descended from Khurasan upon Mu'tasim, the last of the Abbasid caliphs—and annihilated that group."[20] Yet the fact remains that the Abbasids began as an Alid *ghulāt* movement and in their imperial mode distanced themselves from this past. This initial point of cooperation, however, left its mark in the epics and histories.

Hamavi continues to refute the alleged connections between Abu Muslim and the Imamis. He argues against the medieval Shi'i scholar, Shaykh Abu Ali al-Fazl al-Tusi (d. 1153–1154), who states that Abu Muslim had given his oath of allegiance (*bay'a*) to the family before Saffah (r. 750–754), succeeded the caliphate. Hamavi insists that "according to works of prominent Imami *ulama*, Abu Muslim Marvazi was against the family of Muhammad [*ahl-i bayt*] from the very beginning to the very end of his life."[21] He proceeds to legitimize his argument by quoting his prominent teacher, Shaykh Ali Karaki, the author of the injunction against *Abū Muslimnāme* raconteurs. According to Karaki, before Abu Muslim gave his oath of allegiance to the Banu Abbas, he did indeed meet with the children of Ali and pretended to be their friend. Then he turned his back on them and embraced the Banu Abbas.[22] Karaki reads this as a conspiracy. He sees Abu Muslim's flirtation with the children of Ali as a ploy to convince the Umayyads that Abu Muslim was voicing his revolt (*da'wa*) in the name of the Alids (Banu Ali), so that the Abbasids (Banu Abbas) would be free of suspicion.[23] Karaki's conspiratorial interpretation of Abu Muslim's actions could support Hamavi's claim that Abu Muslim was always an enemy of the family, yet it does not dispel the allegations that the descendants of Ali met with Abu Muslim and that promises of support may have been given.

Another polemicist—Taliqani in his *Khulāsat al-favā'id*—tries to blame the Sunnis for concocting stories about Abu Muslim's relations with the Alids: "They [Sunnis] say that Ali at the battle of Siffin [in 657 against the Umayyad contender Mu'awiyah] asked, 'Where is Abu Muslim?' And Muhammad b. Hanafiyya responds that he is at the end of the battlefield. Then Ali responds: 'I do not mean Abu Muslim Khulani. I mean the one who will lead our armies and will rise from the east with black banners fighting such a battle that through him truth will be placed back in its central position,' and the reason that the Sunnis ascribe this to Ali is so to say that Ali testifies that the Abbasids would bring the truth back."[24] The Abbasids are to have fabricated this tradition so that they could gain legitimacy from Ali in the name of the true cause.

A second encounter after the victory over the Umayyads makes its way into recorded history. Muhammad b. al-Husayn Kaydari (seventh/thirteenth century) writes that Abu Muslim made one last contact with Ja'far al-Sadiq toward the end of his career.[25] Once Abu Muslim had linked his lineage to that of the Abbasids and had claimed divine incarnation (*hulul*) and the Imamate, he is said to have turned to Ja'far al-Sadiq in desperation when al-Saffah died (754). To challenge the Abbasid Imam, Abu Ja'far (r. 754–775), who had just succeeded his brother, al-Saffah, Abu Muslim offers the position to Ja'far al-Sadiq. Abu Muslim's messenger arrives in Medina and hands Ja'far al-Sadiq the invitation. Imam Ja'far takes the letter and in an angry tone tells the messenger to leave the gathering. The response is ambiguous. Both Hamavi and Taliqani quote the Imami scholar Kulayni (d. 941), who clarifies this response with a tradition in which the relater, Fazl-i Katib, was to have been present at Ja'far's gathering when Abu Muslim's messenger arrived in Medina. Ja'far is said to have responded, "There is no answer to your letter. Leave our gathering."[26]

In the later Safavi polemics, a greater emphasis is placed on Ja'far's rejection of Abu Muslim's offer. The pseudo-Ardabili categorically dismisses any connections between Ja'far al-Sadiq and Abu Muslim.[27] He stresses that Abu Muslim was a missionary (*dā'ī*) of the Abbasid Ibrahim, who sent him to Khurasan. Once Ibrahim was killed, his two sons, Saffah and Abu Ja'far, were sent to Kufa and took refuge in the house of Abu Salama.

Although Abu Salama knew that Ibrahim had designated Saffah as his successor, he was not convinced of Saffah's abilities as a ruler. The pseudo-Ardabili, using the medieval historian Mas'udi as one of his sources, recounts the same story related by Hamavi about the first letter addressed to Ja'far, yet his evidence is more damning. He states that two (some argue three) letters were written to the Alids inviting them to succeed the Abbasid Ibrahim.[28] One letter was sent to Ja'far al-Sadiq, who burned it and said, "What do I and Abu Salama have to do with one another? Abu Salama is not of our Shi'a. He is of the Shi'a of the family of Abbas [*Banu Abbas*]."[29]

Whose Shi'a (partisan) was Abu Muslim after all? Certainly, according to these refutations, he was no Shi'a of the Alid Imams. With the Safavi polemics against Abu Muslim, we witness the Alids clash among themselves over "legitimate" genealogies, attempting to erase the heteroglossia that had colored Alid expression of loyalty. Those particular characters and their relationships to one another that are at the center of debate encode a time when Alid devotion was diverse. Responding to this fluid image, the authors of these disputations were presenting a different picture. Instead, they insisted on one true genealogy of twelve Imams that had become dominant (Imami) only in time. The Imamis came to rewrite early Shi'i history, attempting to place themselves at the very inception of the struggle against those who betrayed the family of the Prophet, the Umayyads. They drew a picture of a fixed and continuous growth of support surrounding a single Alid patrilineage of Muhammad's descendants through his grandson Husayn, the son of Ali and Fatima. This genealogy is constructed as divinely predetermined. According to Shi'i (Imami) traditions, this list had been presented to Muhammad by the angel Gabriel in the form of a heavenly scroll where the names of twelve descendants of Muhammad, through patrilineal descent from Husayn, had been enumerated—a genealogy legitimized by the Imamis.[30]

The *Abū Muslimnāme(s),* heresiographies, and local and universal histories, however, trouble the homogeneous picture drawn by official Imami sources, which reveal many other active genealogies involved in the Alid struggle against the Umayyads. To begin with, Ali had three sons—Hasan, Husayn, and Muhammad b. Hanafiyya. In addition, he had a brother, Ja'far al-Tayyar, and a paternal cousin, Abdullah b. Abbas (see figure 3). Either their children led rebellions themselves, or calls for revolt were evoked in their names. The disputations concern a particular moment in the past, when resistance against the Umayyads was most visible among members of Muhammad's household (Hashimi). Cooperation as well as rivalry between branches of this extended family occurred over half a century after the death of Husayn (d. 680). It is out of this nucleus of Alids that one branch, the Abbasids, succeeded to capitalize on the revolutionary movement and secure temporal power for themselves. Within a generation, they broke away from the apocalyptic spirit that had brought them to power. They also broke away from their Alid loyalties and genealogy, creating a new direct line to Muhammad not through Ali but through Abbas, Muhammad's brother. The family of Muhammad (*ahl-i bayt*) was thus redefined.

Another lineage of Alids (Imami) from among this nucleus succeeded in cementing a position for themselves in the realm of religious knowledge and spiritual authority. It is thanks to Imams like Ja'far (d. 765), Husayn's great grandson, who gained recognition and respect through knowledge rather than armed rebellion, that Imam Ja'far was able to survive Abbasid suspicion, at least initially. What happened before Ja'far, or a century after his death, was another matter, for the *ghulāt* continued to create movements around the Imams, and splinter groups mushroomed up to the disappearance of the twelfth Imam (874 c.e.).[31] These groups continued to divinize the Imams, forming new branches around each subsequent Imam (there were six) until the Imamis decided that the twelfth in line would be the last (874), delaying the appearance of the living Imam on earth to the imminent future.

The polemics focus on historical inconsistencies narrated around the lifetimes of the first six Imams. They carry along with them particular memories of a past that color the way people experienced the Safavi present. These debates bring to the surface older contentions that had fused similar centrifugal impulses in the past, rewriting early Islamic history from the view of one tendency among many currents and shades of Shi'ism. What makes it difficult for a historian is that the "standard narratives" that survive on this early history of Islam derive from two voices that established themselves as hegemonic—one Abbasid and the other Imami. These two therefore rewrite the past teleologically, describing a linear process toward their ascendancy through two distinct Sunni and Shi'i narratives on early Islam. Both the Abbasid version that becomes the standard text for Muslim history and the Imami version that becomes the sanctioned text of Shi'i oppositional history continue to dominate our modern constructions of this past.[32] The Safavi debates over Abu Muslim's role in the Abbasid revolution provide a space for retrieving such lost narratives.

Succession following Ali's son, Husayn, was a sensitive point of contention for the Imamis in early Shi'i history. Many lovers of the family of Muhammad came to express their devotion toward a third son of Ali, Husayn's half-brother, Muhammad b. Hanafiyya. The earliest extant Imami heresiographer, Nawbakhti, utters a first revisitation of early Islam focusing on the role of Shi'is (Imamis) in this history. The timing of this rewriting is revealing of its intent, for it was recorded when the twelfth Imam was believed to have just gone into occultation (*ghayba*), and an expectancy of his return (*raj'a*) was rife among followers (Imamis).[33] Nawbakhti writes that some followers of Hasan and Husayn had been perplexed by the dissonance between the life experiences of the two sons of Ali. The oldest son, Hasan, had given an oath of allegiance to Mu'awiyyah, the man who had usurped his father's dominion. In contrast, the second son, Husayn, had taken up arms to fight for his right and had been killed in the battlefield. These confused lovers of Alids either turned to join the majority of Muslims (Sunnis) or came to follow a third son of Ali, Muhammad b. Hanafiyya, born not of Fatima but of a slave concubine, and regarded him as an equally legitimate heir to Ali.[34]

To rewrite early Imami history was not an easy task, for to erase these relationships and yet maintain other crucial ties that were necessary to legitimate their movement would be tricky. The historical linkages between Husayn, Muhammad b. Hanafiyya, and Mukhtar (d. 687) preserved in a variety of texts presented one such problem for the Imamis. The first armed Alid movement after the death of Husayn (d. 680) was led by a man named Mukhtar, who murdered many of those responsible for Husayn's death. Even though these sources speak of the political pragmatism of Mukhtar's ambitions, he did create a momentum among proto-Shi'is by capitalizing on the killing of Husayn that came to be the life-sustaining drama of Alid identity. Mukhtar's revolt politicized the death of Husayn. Any Shi'i lineage that would weave Husayn into its genealogy and focus on his role as martyr would have to deal with Mukhtar, who had killed many opponents of Husayn but had done so in the name of Muhammad b. Hanafiyya, the third son of Ali. Playing with the prevalent messianic mood that cast this third son as the expected Mahdi, Mukhtar's revolt lay the foundation in Shi'ism for the central paradigm of future Imams as messiahs, expected saviors who took up arms to redress the corruption and establish truth and a just order.

One of the first recorded instances of the usage of the messianic term *Mahdi* occurs when the third son of Ali is his deathbed (Kaysaniyya merging with Mukhtariyya).[35] Mukhtar had played on the discontent of the new non-Arab converts to Islam (*mawali*) who expected to be treated equally according to the ideals of this new divine vision of the Qur'an. By incorporating new converts, he introduced many Mazdeans and Jews into Shi'i circles, infusing Shi'i messianism with diverse cultural systems. According to Dinawari (d. 894), "Most of those who responded to al-Mukhtar were [Arabs] from the tribe of Hamdan and Persians [who were] in Kufa [and] whom Mu'awiyah had enrolled in the military. They were called al-Hamra [the Reds]."[36] These Iranian converts were soldiers who had surrendered in battle; they were members of the Sasani military class whose emblem was red. By the time of Mukhtar's revolt, there were said to have been twenty thousand (Hamra) in Kufa.[37] Yemeni Jews and their particular cosmologies and myths were present among the early followers of the Alids, but so were Persian cultural forms. And although historians have called Mukhtar's movement a *mawali* (clients) movement, acknowledging Mukhtar's heavy use of Persian converts, they have tended to gloss over this channel of entry of Mazdean ideas into Shi'ism, either focusing on the Jewish influences or rejecting the nationalist claims of Iranian scholars, who, granted, have exaggerated such influences.[38]

What this Imami early revisionist Nawbakhti does is to distance the figure of Muhammad b. Hanafiyya from Mukhtar, claiming that the third son did not accept the role as Imam or messiah, which Mukhtar had propagated for him.[39] Mukhtar was portrayed as acting independently in revenge for the assassination of Husayn. And so those Shi'is who did follow Muhammad b. Hanafiyya were separated as a group, the Kaysaniyya, from the core that would come to represent the Imamis.[40] They were called the "pure" Kaysanis, those who located their messianic aspirations around the third son of Ali. Through such a disentaglement of Muhammad b. Hanafiyya from Mukhtar, Muktar's actions against the assassins of Husayn could be incorporated into a narrative of Imami history.

Time, however, would further complicate Imami revisions, for messianic aspirations continued to be voiced around the Kaysaniyya nucleus: a series of Alid offshoots incorporated these first three sons of Ali within their genealogies. The Abbasids emerged from among such a Kaysani collective of Alid movements, some of whom "exaggerated" their veneration for members of this family in that they considered them divine. Abu Muslim, identified by the polemicists as a Kaysani, enters the scene of Alid history at this point with his pivotal role in Khurasan that led to the success of the Abbasid revolution. In the fifty years following the death of Mukhtar (d. 692), it is in the name of the Alids that most rebellions are voiced.[41] But by the time of the successes of this anti-Umayyad revolution, only two members of Ali's bloodline had survived the struggle, the grandsons of Hasan and Husayn, for Muhammad b. Hanafiya's son (Abu Hashim) had died without an heir.[42] And some Shi'is continued to expect both their imminent returns (pure Kaysaniyya or Hashimiyya). Others claimed that Abu Hashim had transferred his authority through a written will to his Abbasid cousin, Muhammad b. Ali. And some others claimed that he had transferred it to another cousin, Abdullah b. Muawiyya, the grandson of Ali's brother (Ja'far al-Tayyar). Abdullah b. Muawiyya had led a rebellion into the heartland of Iran (Ahwaz, Jibal, Isfahan, Fars, and Kirman) and controlled the region for a few years (744–748). When he fled from the Umayyad forces to find a safe haven in Khurasan, the eastern territories where his Abbasid cousins had been active recruiting supporters, he was instead imprisoned and killed by Abu Muslim. The polemicists use this killing as a justification for the claim that Abu Muslim was against the Alids. The stage was thus set for the children of Abbas, Muhammad's nephews, who had not yet shed blood in the name of their uncle, to take on the challenge. The Abbasids would be the ones who would maintain themselves as the rulers of the Islamic world for the next half millennium. The united family (Hashemi) movement that put an end to Umayyad rule saw the emergence of one Abbasid cousin who came to quash the *ghulāt* around his (Tayyari) cousins and around the Abbasids themselves. Ironically, even though the second Abbasid ruler, al-Mansur, who executed Abu Muslim named his son the Mahdi, this so-called messiah broke from the Kaysaniyya lineage, thanks to which he could make such divine claims. Instead, a new patriarchal chain of transmission was constructed through their eponymous father "Abbas," the brother of Muhammad. They argued that Abbas had been next in line to succession due to his seniority. The central figure of Ali is erased with this Abbasid fabrication. The Abbasid al-Mahdi also killed a group who came to his palace thinking they were coming to prostrate in front of God. It is after the assassination of Abu Muslim and the public break with a *ghulāt* Alid (Kaysani) past that a new series of rebellions in the name of Abu Muslim and the Alids burst forward into central and eastern Persianate landscapes—Soghdia, Nishapur, Qumis, Tabaristan, Rayy.

In this revolutionary phase when the identity of the messiah was veiled to protect him from the Umayyads, different branches of Muhammad's family—his children as well as those of his two brothers, Abbas and Abu Talib (Ali's father)—each concentrated on particular territories. Loosely organized factions that were not divided along rigid genealogical or ideological lines formed the opposition movement. Groups tended to shift allegiances between the several candidates from among Muhammad's family (Banu Hashim).[43] In the process of the consolidation of Abbasid power, the family of Muhammad had been (re)configured, and these Imami polemics speak of a time when the family no longer included all the Hashemite cousin clans but had come to limit kinship to another patrilineage from Ali and Husayn. They were crystallizing a Twelver genealogy that would distinguish them from the Abbasids as well as from the variety of rival Alid lineages—Kaysani and Isma'ili.

It becomes clear in the process of the arguments employed by the polemicists who portray Abu Muslim as an enemy of the Shi'i that the Safavi Imami definition of the Shi'a had evolved from that which shaped Shi'i identity in the first two centuries of Islam. When Abu Muslim was fomenting his rebellion against the Marwanids (740s), the distinct Fatimid lines of the proto-Seveners (Isma'ili) or the proto-Imami Imams had not yet taken shape. At the time, this definition of the *ahl al-bayt* had not yet crystallized, nor was it the only one in circulation.[44] Mukhtar (685–687), as we have seen claimed that the Imamate had passed from Ali to his three sons—Hasan, Husayn, and Mu-

hammad b. Hanafiyya. This indicates that descent from Muhammad through his daughter Fatima was not unanimously
considered a superior pedigree, as it came to be in later Shi'i history. It was not until the era of Ja'far al-Sadiq (d. 765), most
probably after the Abbasid revolution (750), that the proto-
Imamis began to develop their own doctrine of *nass*, the designation of a successor by the Imam—an idea they borrowed from
the *ghulāt*. Only then did the Fatimid/Imami lines begin to take
shape—those very lines now engraved on Imami genealogical
trees. The notion of inheritance of the Imamate by designation
from father to son was in the process of formation, and even after the deaths of Ja'far, Musa Kazim, and the subsequent generations of Imams (there were four), their Shi'a followers were split
on the issue of a successor.[45]

The conception that the Imamate could be passed down to, or
transferred among, members of the Banu Hashim is reflected in
the various genealogies of the Kaysaniyya *ghulāt* and is indicative of a broader meaning of the *ahl al-bayt*—the *bayt* being that
of the Banu Hashim and not the Banu Muhammad. The various
groupings of the Kaysaniyya (Tayyarids, Abbasids, Harbiyya,
etc.) who like Mukhtar held the belief that the Imamate had
been passed down to all three sons of Ali were most visible in
this period.[46] This crisscrossing between the lines of the Abu
Talibids and those of the Abbasids was the norm. Perhaps it
reflects local tribal notions of honor and legitimacy that allowed
collateral members of a clan to attain positions as "elders" of
that clan authority to extend beyond patrilineal succession.

The Safavi polemicists construct Abu Muslim as a Kaysani,
separating themselves from him genealogically: "It has been
proven that Abu Muslim was a Kaysani and believed in the
Imamate of Muhammad b. Hanafiyya after Ali, and after him
his son Abu Hashim, and then the Abbasids."[47] To explain why
the Abbasids (Abu Ja'far) eventually kill Abu Muslim, they
point to the *ghulāt* nature of Abu Muslim's beliefs: "Abu Muslim claimed divine incarnation [*hulūl*] and would say that God
had been reincarnated in Adam and that after that he had been

incarnated in all Prophets until the prophet Muhammad and after Muhammad, God was incarnated in me." In these polemics, Abu Muslim is represented as an exaggerator who marks his lineage within an Abrahamic language.[48]

Abbasid historiography did have to address the issue of assassinating the man who won them their revolution; they accuse Abu Muslim of being arrogant and of transgressing his boundaries of authority—placing his name above the caliph's in formal correspondences or wanting to marry into the Abbasid family. But the official Abbasid sources shy away from specifying the nature of Abu Muslim's arrogance. The *Abū Muslimnāme* features what could have been construed as arrogant behavior, revealing that Abu Muslim was either considered by some as their Imam or claimed the title himself. According to this epic, Abu Muslim should have taken over the reigns of temporal power. Nawbakhti, the first revisionist Shi'i historian, identifies a group among the proto-Abbasids (Rawandiyya) who had kept secret their belief in the authority (*vilāyat*) of Abu Muslim, claiming that the Imamate had passed from the Kaysani (Abu Hashim) to Abu Muslim (Rizamiyya).[49] This claim to the Imamate, although erased from Abbasid rewriting of their revolutionary past, is preserved in these epics and in Imami heresiography (Nawbakhti) and is also highlighted in the disputations over Abu Muslim that occur in the Safavi period. Such a memory of Abu Muslim's mission had been kept alive in Imami circles, and they came to capitalize on it to discredit Abu Muslim along with traces of his entanglement with their Imams (Muhammad Baqir and Ja'far al-Sadiq)—traces that survived both in vernacular traditions like the *Abū Muslimnāme(s)* and in sayings of the Imams. So in (re)writing early Islamic history, albeit from two different perspectives, the Imamis retained a layer of this lost past erased from Abbasid official memory.

Ambiguity surrounds Abu Muslim's background: he may have been a freeborn descendant of Persian nobility (Buzurgmihr), a Persian slave, a Kurd, or a member of the Abbasid or Alid (Asad b. Junayd) family.[50] The diversity of competing claims sheds light on the different meanings Abu Muslim's mission held among his diverse followers, with each constructed origin manifesting a particular role played by Abu Muslim within a variety of imagined histories. The abjectness of Abu Muslim as a Kurd, or Persian, issued from an Abbasid perspective. Persianate movements simply imagined that Abu Muslim was an Iranian who rose to restore Persian rule. The polemics instead cast Abu Muslim as a slave, opening the possibility of his Persian descent; however, they dispute the Alid descent of Abu Muslim, which is preserved in the *Junayðname* and *Abū Muslimnāme* but does not appear in medieval sources, whether Imami or Abbasid. In a reconstruction of the processes through which events surrounding the Abbasid revolution were transformed into an idealized view of the past, Jacob Lassner concludes that Abu Muslim could not have been of Abbasid blood either.[51] Why else would he be denied an Abbasid bride? The Abbasids were noble Arab descendants from the Prophet, and Abu Muslim then must have been just a client, probably of Persian origin; the two could never merge in marriage.[52] Moreover, Lassner argues that once Abu Muslim was executed by al-Mansur (r. 754–775), members of his bloodline would have risen to avenge him.[53] Those who rose evoking Abu Muslim's name in revenge, were, however, not blood relatives but his chivalric brothers.

In the middle of the eighth century, upon Abu Muslim's assassination, a series of messianic movements spread from Transoxiana through the Iranian heartland into eastern Anatolia. Despite their diversity, two languages can be discerned within these movements—one Persianate and the other Alid. Persianate *ghulāt* (Khurramiyya) preserved a substratum of Mazdean beliefs that centered on the figure of Abu Muslim, the savior (Saoshyant) who would restore truth and justice. They placed him within a Mazdean apocalyptic cosmology. Abu Muslim came to represent the chivalric warrior who along with his army had fought against the Arabs (Umayyads) and was betrayed by them (Abbasids). In this narrative, Abu Muslim's mission was thus understood as a restorer of a Persian dispensation.

Another language of *ghuluww* expressed itself within an Alid idiom (Khattabiyya), focusing its reverence and loyalty on the family of Ali.[54] In these circles, Abu Muslim was also seen as a messiah, but he was imagined to be restoring justice in the name of the descendants of the Prophet (Imam). Their exaggeration lay in the way in which they divinized the Imams and located hope in their ability to recreate Muhammad's Medina. Both Alid and Persianate devotees shared in the hope for change that was imagined as an apocalyptic break with the past and an unveiling of hidden secrets. By the tenth century, one group among the Alids (Jafari/Imami), which would become hegemonic in early modern Iran, came to distance itself from this past. But *ghuluww* continued to mingle with even this Twelver group of Imams. Messianic expectations were expressed toward every Imam after Ja'far, denying their deaths, deifying them, and awaiting their return. Even though Ja'far al-Sadiq seems to have refused to take on the role of Messiah during his lifetime, that did not stop some of his followers, like Abu'l Khattab (d. 755), from claiming that Ja'far was God and Abu Khattab himself his prophet. And it is from within this Alid messianic milieu that another Shi'a group creating their legitimacy through Ja'far's son would succeed by the tenth century to establish a separate empire (Faitimid-Isma'ilis) in North Africa as rivals to the Abbasid Caliphate.

These Alid and Persianate cultural systems shared in their belief in reincarnation (*tanāsukh*), in the potential for the divine to exist in a human being (*hulūl*), and in the eventual return (*raj'a*) of past messiahs—three key precepts of *ghuluww*. They differed when it came to the particular lineages of their divines and the myths associated with them. I would like to emphasize that despite the schema I am presenting here to emphasize salient features among these groups, the elasticity and overlap of Persianate and Alid circles should not be underestimated. For within this "semiosphere," a variety of cultural forms shared symbols and codes as well. These signs could be read differently, however, creating a variety of versions of the same code. In Bakhtian terms, these "texts"—revolt, heresiographies, chronicles, and epics—are dialogical, inscribing different meanings. A common code may have been used to communicate to various groups both a sense of unity and conflict, but at particular moments of rebellion these methods of encoding the past clash.[55] The examples I will be delving into are selected precisely because they reveal the intimacy between Alid and Persianate languages that come to be severed at apocalyptic moments when the truth is finally unveiled.

Persianate genealogies of Mazdean kings and prophets were at times interspersed with those of Alid Imams. They maintained a recollection of belonging to an Iranian past. And although they included Alid figures, thereby emplotting Muslim-times in their historical consciousness, they always had an option to return to a Persian past while experiencing the Islamic present. This past was embodied in Mazdean symbols like the sun of the Nuqtavis or the four letters particular to the Persian alphabet. The Persianate ethos was active in Muslim imaginations through texts like the *Shāhnāme*, one of the most accessible and immediate *lieux de memoire* for conveying this past through stories about Iranian kings, warriors, mystics, and rebels. Distinct from these Persianate circles, Alids placed themselves within a Judeo-Christian pedigree of prophets that saw Ali and his progeny as successors of Muhammad. Yet in this moment of history, a variety of belief systems did share in a lived Muslim time. It was the past and the contours of the future that divided Alid and Persianate *ghulāt*.

The Abbasids had sent their missionaries to Iraq and to the eastern frontiers of Islam, lands populated mainly by Iranians but also by Turks. At this point natives of Khurasan were just beginning to feel the physical presence of the Arab conquerors, while Iranians and Turks of course did not all share in their religious beliefs.[56] The official Zoroastrian priesthood through the

patronage of Sasani kings had enforced one version—
Zurvanism of Mazdaeans—but their hegemony faltered under
Islam. Mazdean reformists like the Manichees and Mazdakis
had some space to breathe. Manichees who had fled Iran due to
Sasani persecution began to return from exile. In Khurasan,
where Buddhism was also prominent, Abu Muslim, among others, successfully converted many Mazdeans to the Alid cause
and thus created a culturally diverse Khurasanian army that
would be crucial to the Abbasid victory. As we have seen, this diversity is preserved in the *Abū Muslimnāme(s)* in which Zoroastrians, Jews, and Christians joined the mission of Abu Muslim. The revolts that ensued in the name of Abu Muslim attest to
the diversity of his followers.

The Safavi polemicists Hamavi and Taliqani note that once
the news of Abu Muslim's assassination had reached his Zoroastrian devotees, his deputy Sunbadh the Gabr revolted to reclaim
the blood of Abu Muslim.[57] "And a large number of them considered Abu Muslim as God [*khudā*] and a group who considered him as Imam joined Sunbadh and in a short time the number of Sunbadh's troops reached 100,000."[58] These Mazdeans
believed in the divinity of Abu Muslim, and some of his followers are to have considered him their Imam, a term used by the
Shi'a for the hereditary representatives of the Prophet. The
mixed Alid and Mazdean followers of Abu Muslim who congregated around Sunbadh are attested in medieval sources.[59] Nizam
al-Mulk (d. 1092) the Saljuk vizier captures the way in which
Sunbadh was remembered in the eleventh century by opponents
of *ghuluww*. In the post-Islamic period, Sundbad is referred to as
a Magian (Majūsī) and a follower of the Mazdaki religion. He is
said to have claimed "that Abu Muslim had not been killed but
that when the Abbasid caliph al-Mansur (r. 754–775) tried to
kill him, he recited the greatest name of God, and turned into a
white dove, and escaped from his hands; he was now in a brazen
fortress where he dwelt with the Mahdi and Mazdak; soon all
three would appear and their chief would be Abu Muslim with
Mazdak as his vizier."[60] This messiah was probably Muhammad

b. Hanafiyya, Ali's third son, around whom the anti-Umayyad opposition coalesced.

Alids (Kaysaniyya) and neo-Mazdakis (Khurramiyya) seem to have coalesced toward the end of Umayyad rule. A dual language of appeal and following is recorded in Nizam al-Mulk (d. 1092), who writes that "when the Rafidis [Shi'a] heard mention of the Mahdi, and the Mazdakis the name of Mazdak, a great multitude gathered at Rayy. . . . Whenever he [Sunbadh] was alone with Zoroastrians, he would say, 'According to one of the books of the Sasanis which I have found, the Arab empire is finished.' . . . And to the Khurramdins he would say, 'Mazdak is a Shi'ite and his command is that you make common cause with the Shi'a.'" Sunbadh's syncretic language was an early articulation among religious movements in the Iranian world that voiced this ever-tempting return to a time before Islam when the Persians ruled—a refrain we have heard with the Nuqtavis. It is not only a restoration of Mazdean cosmology that Sunbadh was advocating, for he also claimed that the days of the Muslims were over and that the time of the Sasanids had arrived.[61] Political and religious hegemony were imagined as twins never to be sundered. But already here at its initial utterance Mazdean aspirations merged with Alid messianic expectations.

Sunbadh was one of the first agents (*dā'i*) of Abu Muslim to rebel in the name of Abu Muslim in Khurasan—Nishapur and Qumis. Whatever the relationship between Abu Muslim and Sunbadh may have been, Sunbadh acted in retaliation for Abu Muslim's death, taking over his treasury as though he were of Abu Muslim's family. The family ties here were not of blood but of religious confraternity. The layers of Persianate ideas alive in these early expressions of Islam are palpable through the symbols evoked in these rebellions. As we have seen with the Nuqtavis, the sun was a central icon of identity. Revenge was expressed in terms of destroying the dominion (*mulk*) of the Arabs, substituting the sun instead of the Ka'ba as the holy direction of worship.[62] This binary opposition between the Ka'ba and the sun is a recurring construction among Persianate religious movements—a metaphor for the "old" and the "new," Persian and Arab. Although the Nuqtavis equate the two in their alchemical views on creation, both in essence being the same yet still differentiating between them, Sunbadh set out to destroy the Ka'ba. And in the process he attracted much support in the Iranian heartland (Rayy, Jibal, Tabaristan), probably in opposition both to the Iranian landed nobility and religious elite who had become partners with Arab conquerors.[63] The image of Abu Muslim as the destroyer of elites both among Arabs and Iranians is preserved in medieval historiography.[64] The way in which history is understood by these Persianate movements reinforces a Mazdean binary, where change is viewed as a radical break with the present and a return to the past. With a belief in shifting cycles of authority, rhythms of change in the Islamic era were imagined in these circles in terms of overthrowing the Arabs and inaugurating a new cycle of the Persian past. The idea of the successive incarnation of the divine in humans opened this space for renewal.

Abu Muslim had tried to maintain a "half-way position between Arabs and Iranians. Many non-Arabs who had hoped for great things from the revolution regarded him as their spokesman and were outraged when he was killed."[65] The versatility of Abu Muslim, which may have had political intent behind it, drew many Mazdaki adherents to his cause during his lifetime. He was adopted by Persianate *ghulāt* as an anti-Arab and anti-Muslim hero.[66] Islamic sources refer to these diverse neo-Mazdaki groups under the umbrella of the "joyous religion" (*Khurramiyya*), perhaps alluding to their beliefs that sacred ownership of land and women should be shared by the community as a method of achieving a just and harmonious society free of inequalities.[67] "Mazdak preached the elimination of desire through fulfillment."[68] But this language of material and sexual equality had a particular resonance for some Mazdeans who were closely encountering their new Arab/Muslim conquerors for the first time. Zoroastrian practices of endogamy and Mazdaki communal sharing of women and wealth were prohib-

ited under Islam. Revolts in Khurasan and western Iran did coincide with an increased physical presence of Arabs. What provoked the Khurramiyya revolt in Azarbaijan (758–759), for
example, was that the Abbasid caliph al-Mansur had for the first
time settled Yemeni tribal groups from Basra in various parts of
the province. Many Arab shaykhs migrated to the area, building
themselves castles as they dominated the inhabitants. The
Khurramiyya of Jibal and Azarbaijan rose up in defiance of
Arab colonization and the heavy-handed Abbasid rule.[69]
The ideals of social justice expressed in these neo-Mazdaki revolts came to appeal not only to those Persian converts to Islam
who remained on the social and cultural fringes of Abbasid
society but to the Turks of Transoxiana as well, who were
now being touched by the expansive swords of Islamic dominion. By the eleventh century, Persianate *ghuluww* had spread
throughout Arab, Judeo-Christian, Persian, and Turkish landscapes.

Although apocalyptic ideals of equality permeated Muhammad's visions, political realities impinged on such objectives in
the imperial phase of Muslim expansion, and in time Islamic
egalitarianism was shorn of its social implications.[70] As an or-
phan, Muhammad was responding in part to the circumstance
of having been born into a patriarchical and tribal society in
which social status and prestige were awarded to the sons of distinguished fathers (*hasab* and *nasab*). To the east, Sasani kings
were centralizing their authority, solidifying a hierarchical society that saw power invested in the hereditary households of
priests and kings. Such shifts had excited a populist temper,
which responded to the concentration of power, both political
and religious, in the hands of a privileged and hereditary priestly
and military elite. This mood was expressed in rebellions like
that of the Zoroastrian reformer, Mazdak (fifth century). Muhammad's vision, too, was egalitarian, and his program of social
justice was voiced in the language of messianism, a familiar
mode through which such aspirations were articulated in the

premodern world. Not only did Muhammad pose a moral challenge for the Arabs; he also sought to eliminate social hierarchies, for all Muslims were to be equal in the eyes of one God,
Allah. Tensions between these ideals and realities of social difference gave voice to a wide range of resistance, whether
through the literary movement of the Shu'ubiyya or the
Persianate and Alid rebellions that emerged throughout the eastern landscapes of medieval Islamdom.

The polemicists mention a series of revolts by a group that
they identified as the Khurramiyya, who believed in the Imamate
of Abu Muslim and who denied his death, claiming that "he will
never die until he makes his manifestation and fills this world
with justice." Some accepted Abu Muslim's death and believed
that the Imamate was passed down to his daughter Fatima
(Babakiyya)—a new genealogy of Persianate divines carried
through a female vessel who shared her name with Muhammad's immaculate daughter.[71] The Khurramiya revolts spread
from Khurasan throughout the central Iranaian landscapes of
the Jibal, Caspian, and Azarbaijan. In the ninth century (816–
838), a self-proclaimed descendant of Abu Muslim through
Fatima named Babak—Mutahhar son of Fatima bint Abu Muslim—led the Khurramiyya (neo-Mazdaki) movement in Ardabil,
the very same region from which the Safavids would emerge five
centuries later. Maqdisi visits this region in the middle of the
tenth century, and he states that although the Khurramiyya were
divided into many groups, they all were unified in their belief of
the return of Abu Muslim's children. They believed in reincarnation and that prophets despite their different laws are of one single spirit, so that revelation was a never-ending process. They
were also dualists, in that they believed in the binary forces of
light and dark.[72] The Babakiyya *ghūlat* who were awaiting the
messiah from Abu Muslim's line continued to be cited in the late
medieval period.[73] They were referred to in Azarbaijan as the
"wearers of red" (*surkh jāmigān*), just like the Qizilbash, who
wore red turbans. Isma'il's father, Haydar, who instituted the

red crown of the Qizilbash, is said to have embraced the beliefs of these Khurramiyya (Babakiyya).[74]

A particularity of the Khurramiyya was their play with nature, drawing on their knowledge of astrology, the occult, and the physical sciences (geometry and mathematics). These were channels through which Persianate ideas lived on as former components of a Mazdean cosmology. Mazdak, for example, is remembered by Nizam al-Mulk as "well versed in astrology, and from the motions of the stars he foretold that in that age a man was to appear who would introduce a religion to cancel the Zoroastrian, Jewish, Christian, and idolatrous faiths."[75] Mazdak's prediction turned out to be a Muslim reality. Mazdak is represented as having deceived the Sasani king Qubad with his construction of a hole under the fire temple, sending his minions into this tunnel to answer his questions as though God were speaking to him. Another Khurrami divinity, Muqanna, who revolted after Abu Muslim's assassination, is to have been famous for his ability to bring the moon out of a pit (*māh-i nakhshab*). Adding to these theatrical representations of holiness, Muqanna would wear a green veil covering his luminous face. When his believers insisted on Muqanna demonstrating his divinity, one account has it that he gave them mirrors and had them reflect the rays of the sun on one another. Then they were told to look at him, and with the reflection of the sun that had struck their eyes, instead of Muqanna they saw but blinding brightness. This ingenious mechanism is noted in some histories without contempt but with bewilderment. Nevertheless, we have seen in Safavi attacks on the Nuqtavis an emphasis on casting these kinds of acts as "magic" and "trickery." Already in the medieval age, some heresiographers (Abu Ma'ali's *Bayān al-adyān*) reveal their rational tenor, critiquing such practices as magic; they list the claims of "fake" prophets and then proceed to unveil their tricks. In this age of monotheistic logic, only God and his spokesmen (prophets, Imams, and *ulama*) can bewilder the believer. We are at the brink of momentous change when agents of old mentalities are alienated, relegated to the realm of magic.

A variety of genealogical mixtures differentiate this cluster (Khurramiyya) of Persianate religious movements. They are those like the Nuqtavis who combine Alid and Mazdean holy figures. Sunbadh is to have claimed that Abu Muslim did not die, that he would return together with Mazdak and the Mahdi who was possibly Muhammad b. Hanafiyya.[76] And Muqanna placed Abu Muslim in a long line of Judeo-Christian prophets from Adam to Noah, Abraham, Moses, Jesus, and Muhammad, Ali, and Muhammad b. Hanafiyya. Then Muqanna was to have been incarnated with Abu Muslim's divine spirit. These mixed Alid (Abrahamic) and Persianate genealogies show a coalescence of the Khurramiyya with some factions of the Kaysaniyya.[77] One difference we see between the early Kaysaniyya offshoots and the Muslimiyya ones is that lieux of occultation have moved into Persian topographies. No longer do self-proclaimed messiahs take refuge in the Razavi mountains between Mecca and Medina; now they hide in the Alburz mountain range on the Caspian sea. This geographical shift to the heartland of Iran also mirrors a new phase of Alid history experienced through Persianate senses of time and being. In some distant landscapes like Transoxiana, where Muqanna led his revolt and ruled for fourteen years (Kasj and Nasaf) he converted many Turks to his beliefs. Biruni, the polymath historian, claims that when he is writing his book on the history of ancient chronologies, devotees of Muqana still existed in Transoxania, professing their beliefs in secret while embracing Islam in public.[78]

The medieval Imami heresiographer Nawbakhti expounds on Khurramiyya (neo-Mazdaki) cosmology. Although in his schema of heresy he separates the Khurramiyya from the Alids (Kaysaniyya), in his narrative he states that the Khurramiyya nevertheless emanated from such earlier Alid movements:[79]

The Khurramdiniyya started exaggeration [*ghuluww*] claiming that the Imams at the same time as being God were prophets, and messengers of God and angels. They talked about shadows [*suvvar zillī*] and the reincarnation [*tanāsukh*] of the spirit and believed in cycles and reincarnation and denied resurrection and the day of judgment. They believed that there is no other place of existence other than this world and the meaning of the last day [qiyâma] and resurrection is the separation of the spirit from the body and its return into another body. If they have been good, then they will encounter good, and if they have been evil, then they will encounter pain and sorrow, and in the body that they enter they will exist happily or will be tortured. They believe that the body is their paradise or hell, and so long as they are, so they move from one body to another. When they are in the body of good people, they are happy and have a good future, but if they enter ugly bodies such as that of the dog, or monkeys, or pigs, or snakes, or scorpions, or reptiles, or those who mull around dung, they will be in pain and suffering and will have a sour future so they will move from one body to another and be in perpetual hardship.[80]

Nawbakhti encapsulates the dualist cosmology of the Khurramiyya *ghulāt*, who did not believe in a heaven or a hell. They imagined time cyclically: death invariably led to rebirth in better or worse forms, depending on the quality of goodness attained during each lifespan. Nawbakhti provides details on the mechanics of reincarnation that parallel Nuqtavi beliefs. He also asserts that in arenas of medieval resistance, Alid and Persianate cosmologies had been laced together. Alid movements reveal a Persianate sense of time and being—an ethos from which different strands come to unravel themselves genealogically in postapocalyptic moments. "Whenever the Khurramiyya [neo-Mazdakis] have arisen," noted Nizam al-Mulk, "the Batinis [Alid/Isma'ilis] have made common cause with them and strengthened them; and whenever the Batinis appear, the Khurramiyya combine with them and assist them with men and resources; for the origin of these two religions is the same, and they have but one object—to corrupt the faith."[81] One could argue that this syncretic picture is drawn by an opponent of the Alids (Isma'ilis)—Nizam al-Mulk—to debase this Persianate version of Islam (Alidism), casting its origins in a "pagan" past of Mazdean religious systems. But the history of Alid expression (rebellion and epics) divulges a shared Mazdean cosmology with a following that maintained a sense of "Iranianness" through a collective memory of a past to which some invariably desired to return.

Take, for example, a group of Alids–Qarmatis–who had congregated around a son of Imam Ja'far, Isma'il, and established a utopian enclave in Bahrayn on the Persian Gulf in 899. The Qarmatis believed that the line of Imams, descendants of Ali and Fatima, had stopped with their seventh descendant, Muhammad b. Isma'il. Two groups of proto-Shi'is split over who would succeed the sixth Imam Ja'far (d. 765). The Qarmatis placed their messianic expectation with the line of Isma'il, who had been designated by his father Ja'far as heir but who had died prematurely. This group of proto-Seveners claimed that Isma'il's son had then inherited from his father the divine authority to rule. Still another group of proto-Twelvers argued that because Isma'il had died before his father, his succession was void and instead another son, Musa Kazim, was the designated successor. These two groups of Seveners (Isma'ili) and Twelvers (Imamis) would become the most prominent factions among the Shi'is.

The Qarmatis claimed that when Isma'il's son had died, he had actually gone into hiding (*ghayba*) and would soon emerge as the Mahdi of the seventh and final dispensation ending the *shari'a*, for the truth would finally be revealed in full. The history of the human race was divided into seven cycles, each of which was inaugurated by an Abrahamic prophet who revealed a new truth (*shari'a*). This divine spokesman (*nātiq*) was succeeded by a silent one (*sāmit*), whose duty it was to unveil the deeper meaning (*bātin*) of the new book. So each dispensation also brought forth seven Imams who were to be consulted in esoteric and exoteric matters and who were to make sure that the divine law was followed. The seventh Imam of every era became the new Prophet (*nātiq*) of the following era. The Islamic era was situated within the period of the sixth dispensation of Abrahamic prophets (Adam, Noah, Abraham, Moses, Jesus):

Muhammad was the speaker; Ali, the silent one; and Muhammad b. Isma'il, the seventh Imam.[82] Prophets and Imams, rather than kings, were the pioneers of universal change in Ismai'li (Alid) history. But the conception of history as a succession of dispensations that would inevitably lead to a final era of unveiled truths and utopian lawlessness on earth was central to Mazdean cosmology.[83] Not only does this cyclical conception of history speak from within a Mazdean framework; the doctrine of the divine heptad is also central to Zoroastrianism: "Zaratusthra taught that God had made this sevenfold world with the help of six lesser divinities whom he brings into being to aid him."[84]

Based on astrological speculations over a century after the Abbasid revolution, the Qarmatis first emerged in Kufa (874) during the very same year that the twelfth Imam of the Twelver Shi'is went into occultation *(ghayba)*. Their timing does not seem to be mere coincidence. Once the political activism of the Twelvers ceased with their adoption of the doctrine of occultation, those Seveners who had been practicing it broke their silence and began to take arms in the name of their hidden Imam (Muhammad b. Isma'il). As Shi'is, the Qarmatis too rose in opposition to the Abbasid caliphs to take revenge in the name of the Alid cause but through the intermediary of one particular lineage of the descendants of Ali. They were able to establish their rule in Bahrayn in 899, at which time they abrogated the *shari'a* and set up a utopia in preparation for the return of Muhammad b. Isma'il.

Another branch of Seveners (Isma'ili/Alid) established the Fatimid empire (909–1171) in North Africa as a rival Shi'i caliphate to the Abbasids (750–1258). The founder, 'Ubaydullah (d. 934), claimed to be the awaited messiah–Muhammad b. Isma'il–and in an attempt to win over Qarmati dissenters, incorporated many of their doctrines. Yet the Fatimids found themselves continually amending those doctrines to suit their own political ends. The main doctrinal problems centered on the difficulty of accommodating the various Fatimid rulers who declared that the series of Imams ending with Muhammad b. Isma'il had been reactivated with 'Ubaydullah (al-Mahdi, r. 909–934), the reincarnated Imam. 'Ubaydullah modified the Qarmati doctrines by stating that Muhammad b. Isma'il was indeed the seventh Imam of the sixth era and that he would return as the messiah of the seventh era. Yet a new heptad of Imams was added to this sixth era. Now the eschatological scenario would be fulfilled by the messiah only after this new series of seven Imams had appeared. So 'Ubaydullah made room for seven more Fatimid rulers to appear, before the *shari'a* would be abrogated and justice established.

Once the seventh Fatimid ruler, Zahir (r. 1121–1135), emerged, however, this new scheme had to be abandoned, and the eschatological scenario of the Mahdi was postponed to some time in the future. The significance of these doctrinal amendments—the necessity of adding a new series of Imams—meant that the abrogation of the *shari'a* and the establishment of a utopia, which was key to *ghulāt* aspirations, was continually postponed. Once in power, the Fatimids had problems implementing one of the fundamental ideals of their supporters. Eventually, they abandoned these ideals and went orthodox. They suppressed gnostic tendencies in their doctrines and relegated the advent of the final messiah to the distant future. The doctrinal evolution that the Fatimids underwent, from their initial revolutionary stage to their establishment as an empire (909) in North Africa, is telling of a type of taming characteristic of *ghulāt* movements that succeeded in establishing themselves politically.[85] Their story is similar to that of the Abbasids, and, as we shall see, the Safavis.

Qarmati opposition to Fatimid orthodoxy was manifest from the very beginning of the reign of the first ruler, Imam 'Ubaydullah. The Qarmatis broke away from the Fatimid Isma'ili's (909–1171), reaffirming their belief in the imminent return of their anticipated messiah from the family of the prophet (Muhammad b. Isma'il).[86] They continued to imagine themselves within the last Muhammadan cycle and in the tenth century were still awaiting the return of their seventh Imam–Muhammad b. Ismai'il–to inaugurate the final era of history as seventh speaker. Islam was then to be abrogated, for a complete revelation of past hidden esoteric truths was to take place. What exactly this truth would contain seems to have been understood in different ways by various Qarmati devotees.

We have seen how the son of the founder of the Qarmatis in Bahrayn, Abu Tahir Jannabi, sacked Mecca during the pilgrimage season (930), slaughtering the pilgrims and throwing their corpses into the holy well of Zamzam. His most sacrilegious act was the carrying off of the black stone from the Ka'ba, the locus of circumbulation at the holiest shrine of Islam.[87] Muslims believed that the Ka'ba had been built by Abraham and that the black stone embedded in the eastern corner of the structure was to have been brought down by the angel Gabriel. Before the advent of Islam, the Ka'ba had housed 360 idols of those Arab tribes who were protected by Muhammad's ancestors, the Quraysh. Although reconfigured, the Ka'ba was preserved by Muhammad as a sacred sanctuary, emptied of all its idols save for the black stone. One account claims that Abu Tahir smashed the black stone and hung its pieces in a mosque in Kufa, the Alid center in Iraq.[88] Whatever the details of this episode may have been, violating the sanctity of the month of yearly Muslim pilgrimage and entering the holy city with arms already marked a breach with Islam, just as Muhammad's transgression of the Qurayshi truce month had signaled his rupture with pagan Arabia (Jahiliyya). Removing the black stone from the Ka'ba, as Madelung states, was a "palpable demonstration of the end of the era of Islam."[89] But for some Qarmatis (Alid), it could have meant the relocation of the black stone to the center of true Islam located in the city of Kufa (Iraq), the dominion of Ali and his devotees.

In the tenth century, some Qarmatis associated the conjunction of Saturn and Jupiter (27 October 928 c.e). with the end of Arab hegemony. Like the Nuqtavis, who had broken away from Alid circles (Hurufi), the Qarmatis (Isma'ili) came to interpret this astrological conjunction in a language of Persianate messianism. Where this tenth-century (928) planetary conjunction of Saturn and Jupiter was placed within the history of the Qarmatis and of Islam differs from that of the Nuqtavis. Nevertheless, they both share a sense of cyclical time that fashioned their parallel conceptions of change in terms of a return to a time before Islam when the Persians ruled. And as we have seen, some Qarmatis of Bahrayn anticipated a Persian messiah who would restore the rule of justice and truth. Yet not all Qarmatis embraced Abu Tahir's massacre at Mecca, especially when two years later (September and October 931), he relegated his rule to a Persian from Isfahan who claimed that he was the Mahdi. The Isfahani Messiah abolished the *shari'a* and sanctioned the worship of fire and the cursing of Muhammad and his family. For the Qarmati leader, Abu Tahir, the truth meant a return to a Persian past. Some Qarmatis (Ismai'lis), as Madelung points out, expected an Alid revealer of deeper truths to be grounded in Jewish, Christian, and Muslim scriptures; nevertheless, for some devotees the cycle of Muslim prophets (Muhammad) and silent ones (Ali) represented but an intermediary epoch in the history of the world.

Let me end with a last example of an Alid setting from which a Persianate messiah arose. The Parsis (or Parsiyan) from Azarbaijan were remnants of the Khurramiyya followers of Babak (d. 837).[90] There are regional and cultural parallels between this group and the Safavis, separated by four hundred years. Initially, the Parsis had accepted Isma'ilism, concealing their true beliefs. They joined a group of Isma'ilis (Nizari) who, like the Qarmatis of Bahrayn, had broken with imperial (Fatimid) Shi'ism and established a utopian enclave in an impenetrable mountain fortress, Alamut, awaiting the day of resurrection. Once the founder Hasan-i Sabbah (1090–1124) died, however, a weaver named Budayl rose from among them and said, "The truth is with the Parsis: the Isma'ilis are people clinging on to the exterior of religion [*mardum-i zāhirand*]."[91] He claimed that the two sons of "Dihkhuda Kay Khusraw, the chief of this group [Nizaris], were the reincarnation of Muhammad and Ali, and that Budayl himself was Salman-i Farsi: all three were God."[92]

Budayl traced the Imamate back to the ancient kings of Iran, beginning with Jamshid, whom he recognized as the first rightful Imam. He argued that the prophetic chain had been passed from the Kayanis to the Arabs—Muhammad, Ali, and Muhammad b. Hanafiyya—and then back to the Persians with Abu Muslim. Although "Abu Muslim's heroic effort to break the Arab domination and restore justice" had failed, his grandson Gawhar "would complete his work and restore the Persian religion and the dominance of the Mahdi."[93] Budayl's message portrays the kind of syncretic process in effect between Alid and Persianate belief systems in the twelfth century. Budayl expressed his claims from within Islamic traditions. He made use of Islamic vocabulary and characters such as Muhammad, Ali, and the Imams. Initially, he joined the Isma'ilis (Nizari). The Alid cause, once again, provided a space for different lineages of *ghuluww* to be experienced and articulated by a variety of resistance movements. But when Budayl claimed to be the reincarnation of Salman-i Farsi, the symbol of Persian conversion to Islam, and applied the principle of divine incarnation to himself, claiming to be God, he abrogated the *shari'a* and openly broke with Islam. For some Persianate messiahs, "Islam was just a brief interval in the religious tradition of Iran."[94] The Safavis emerged four centuries later from within this milieu, performing an Alid version of the apocalyptic scenario.

By the twelfth century, when Budayl made his sortie (*khurūj*), *ghulāt* ideas of occultation (*ghayba*) and return (*raj'a*) had already become an integral part of Imami doctrine.[95] The anticipated emergence of the Mahdi was an accepted cultural paradigm, recorded in canonized traditions (*hadith*) relating to the day of resurrection (*qiyāma*). This model, however, was open to a variety of interpretations by a host of *ghulāt* groups throughout Islamdom. Budayl's message demonstrates how one group utilized this paradigm of return to express its particular aspiration to establish a Persian order in opposition to the existing Arabo-Islamic regime. Perhaps due to their oppositional stance toward Islam, they continued to embrace these doctrines, which allowed them to maintain a distinct identity as other. Chivalric rituals, epics, and rebellion were media through which they practiced and created this memory. Budayl was a weaver who must have been exposed to such recollections in craft circles (*futuvvat*). Moreover, because of the Alid oppositional stance toward mainstream Islam, Alid and Persianate cultures intermingled in battlefields of resistance. Given the belief that revelation never ceased, that Muhammad was not the seal of the prophets, and that Mazdak or Abu Muslim's spirit could migrate (*naskh*) into different human beings at any given time, their movements constantly found rejuvenation and continuity.

Shah Isma'il too played on the *ghulāt* spirit of the Qizilbash and his craftsmen devotees to establish the Safavi empire. Remember that in his poetry Isma'il names his prior incarnations—Jamshid, Rustam, Alexander, Jesus, and Ali—from a list of Mazdean kings and Abrahamic prophets of Islamdom's cultural past. This savior who had come "to suffer death in his soul on behalf of all souls" also played on associations with Abu Muslim. Raising the banner in the name of the family of Muhammad, both Abu Muslim and Isma'il entered the battlefield as avengers of Alid blood. They were crusaders of the true religion (*dīn-i haqq*), which had been lost and abandoned.

As we have seen, the *Abū Muslimnāme(s)* portray Abu Muslim and Shah Isma'il as sharing similar divine lineages, which were used as tools, with Shah Isma'il's poetry, to signal to their audience the codes and symbols present in their syncretic visions. In true *ghuluww*, Shah Isma'il may have been regarded as the incarnation of Abu Muslim. For an audience that would have been attracted to Safavi revolutionary discourse, Abu Muslim constituted a multiplex symbol. His image resonated with a range of referents amid chivalric circles, which could be assumed, accentuated, or practiced at particular junctions of history. Each decoding drew from the particular craft and sufi milieus in which the interpreter had been socialized. We have seen how chivalric communities created and performed Alid memory, fusing emotional bonds through ritual. But Abu Muslim conjured a dual image. For Persianate imaginations, he was a symbol of anti-Arab resistance who would inaugurate a cycle of return to Persian glory. For Alid imaginations, Abu Muslim was a martyr who took up arms against the oppressors of the *ahl-i bayt*. The ambiguity surrounding Abu Muslim may have inspired the Nuqtavis, who had already mingled in Alid circles (Hurufis) to join the Safavi movement. Nuqtavi devotees could associate with Isma'il's poetry in which his Persian cultural heritage as the reincarnation of Iranian kings like Feraydun and Kay Khusraw was intertwined with his Alid identification with Ali, Husayn, and Abu Muslim.

With the establishment of the Safavi imperium, an Alid messianic language was accentuated. But in time even this expectation was delayed. Once in power, Shah Isma'il's successors embarked on a different course of action than that taken by the Fatimids to suppress the *ghulāt* nature of their revolutionary movement. Had doctrinal alterations been necessary, they would not have sufficed, for the Qizilbash were not only a religious force; they were the military backbone of the Safavi imperium as well. The transition was to be gradual, involving two civil wars, institutional reforms, and the transformation of an entire way of being and experiencing time. In the process of conversion, however, Imamism and *ghuluww* once again intermingled, touching the religiosity of even the staunchest cleric. On the doctrinal level, Safavi Imami scholars did not have to come up with major alterations, something that Fatimid-Isma'ili doctrine could not avoid. Given that the concept of the awaited messiah was already a calcified cultural paradigm, traditions were initially introduced that implicitly drew parallels between Isma'il and the awaited Shi'i Mahdi.[96] A century later, however, once the Qizilbash had waned, these messianic dicta were replaced by ones that depicted the rise of Isma'il as a sign leading to the advent of the hidden messiah. Here, too, the appearance of the Mahdi was postponed. Yet once it became clear to the Qizilbash that their revolution had been betrayed, the Safavis–like the Fatimids–had to contend with movements like that of the Nuqtavis.

Let us move into such Safavi transformations, exploring the shifting modes by which the absoluteness of power was expressed and the ways in which this discourse impinged on arenas of socialization.

NOTES

1. The first wave of polemics against Abu Muslim began in the early sixteenth century, as you may recall, with the injunction of Shaykh Ali Karaki (d. 1534).
2. According to Abd al-Husayn Zarrinkub, storytellers referred to as "Sufiyān-i Ardabil" would recite stories about Muhammad b. Hanafiyya and Abu Muslim to draw parallels between the nature of Abu Muslim's *da'wa* and the aims of the Safavi revolutionaries. Zarrinkub unfortunately does not quote his source. See *Dunbālah-yi Justijū dar Tasavvuf-i Iran* (Tehran: Amīr Kabīr, 1987), 228–229; also quoted by Rasūl Ja'fariān, "Rūyārūyi-i Faqīhān va Sūfīyān dār 'Asr-i Safaviyya," *Kāyhān-i Andīshah* 33 (1990): 110; and Ja'fariān, *Dīn va Siyāsat dar Dawrah-yi Safavī* (Qum: Intishārāt-i Ansāriyān, 1991), 235.
3. Elton L. Daniel, *The Political and Social History of Khurasan under Abbasid Rule, 747–820* (Minneapolis: Bibliotheca Islamica, 1979), 25 [citing, Tabarī, *Tārīkh*, vol. 2 (1954)].
4. There exist hadith related from Ali where he foretells the revolt (*khurūj*) of Abu Muslim and the Mongols.
5. Here reference is made to that hadith ascribed to Ali about the sortie of Abu Muslim and the Mongols. The polemists pick up this point and reinterpret this hadith. The variation occurring in this Bāqiriyya/Muslimiyya version of the *Abū Muslimnāme* distinguishes itself from the two previous *ghulāt* genealogies, for it views Imam Muhammad Bāqir as the successor of the Abbasid Imam Ibrāhīm.

6. Iréne Mélikoff, *Abū Muslim: Le "Porte-Hache" de Khorasan dans la tradition epique Turco-Iranienne* (Paris: Adrien Maisonneuve, 1962), 116–117.

7. Ibid., 119.

8. Although three versions of the *Abū Muslimnāmes* draw connections between some of the proto-Imami Imams and Abū Muslim, the Hāshimiyya/Bāqiriyya version sees Abū Muslim as inheriting his divine spark from Ibrahim through Muhammad b. Hanafiyya and passing it on to Muhammad Bāqir. In the Bāqiriyya/ Muslimiyya version, Abū Muslim, by way of Muhammad b. Hanafiyya, inherits his *nass* from Imam Muhammad Bāqir, who is in *ghayba*. Finally, in the Bāqiriyya/Imami recension, Abū Muslim makes his *da'wa* in the name of Imam Muhammad Bāqir and in his capacity as *nā'ib* (vice regent) to that Imam.

9. Muhammad b. Ishāq Hamavī, *Anīs al-mu'minīn*, ed. Mīr Hāshim Muhaddis (Tehran: Bunyād-i Ba'sat, 1984), 145.

10. Ibid., 159; and the *Sahīfat al-irshād*, Mar'ashī Library, MS 4014, f 114a.

11. For a discussion of the *bay'a*, see Emile Tyan, "Bay'a," *EI 2*.

12. Ibn Babuya's *Man lā yahduruhu al-faqīh* introduces this hadith. The hadith is mentioned in the *Izhār al-haqq* and the *Khulāsat al-favā'id*, Mar'ashi Library, MS 4014.

13. Ibn Babuya, quoted in the *Izhar al-haqq* by Sayyid Ahmad b. Zayn al-Abidīn Alavī Mar'ashi Library, MS 4014, f 107a.

14. See, for example, 'Abd al-Jalīl Qazvīnī's *al-naqz* (sixth/twelfth century), where he states that Abū Muslim made Saffah caliph in Baghdad, stopped the cursing of Ali, defeated the Banu Umayya and the Marwanids, and was both a Shi'i and a believer. As cited in Askar Huqūqī, *Tahqīq dar Tafsrī Abū al-Futūh* (Tehran: Tehran University, 1967), 12. Also see Nūr Allah b. Abd Allah Shūshtarī's (d. 1019/1610) *Majālis al-mu'minīn*, 2 vols. (Tehran: Kitābfurūshī-i Islāmīyah, 1986), for another description of Abū Muslim as a good Imami Shi'i.

15. Mawlanā Shaykh Hasan Kāshī, *Tārīkh-i Muhammadī*, ed. Rasūl Ja'farīan (Qum: Kitābkhānch-yi Takhassusī-yi Tārīkh-i Islam va Irān, 1998), 133–135.

16. See Muhammad ibn Abd al-Karīm Shahristānī's *al-Milal wa-al-nihal*, ed. M. R. Jalālī Nā'īnī (Tehran: n.p., 1971), 178–179; Ali b. al-Husayn Mas'ūdī, *Murūj al-zahab (Les Prairies d'or)*, trans. c.

Barbier de Meynard, 9 vols. (Paris: L'imprimerie Impériale, 1861–1877; Hamavī, *Anīs al-mú minīn,* and 'Abd al-Muttalib b. Yahyā Tāliqānī, *Khulāsat al-favā'id* (Mar'ashī Library, MS 4014) (both quoting Muhammad b. al-Husayn Kaydarī's *Kifāyat al-barāya fi Ma'rifat al-anbiya wa al-awsiya*); Mélikoff, *Abū Muslim,* 72 (citing S. Muscati, "Studi su Abū Muslim); Marshall Hodgson, "Ghulāt," *EI2.*

17. See, for example, Muhammad b. Ya'qūb Kulaynī, *al-Kāfī, ilm al-dīn,* ed. 'Ali Akbar Ghaffārī (Tehran: Maktabah al-Islāmiyah, 1957–1960), in which he introduces a hadith that clarifies Ja'far al-Sādiq's response to Abū Muslim's invitation, as recorded in the *Anīs al-mu'minīn* and the *Khulāsat al-favā'id.* Ibn Babuya's *Man lā yahduruhu al-faqīh* introduces a hadith in which Gabriel comes to the Prophet wearing a black gown, and the Prophet asks him the meaning of the black garment. The hadith portrays the Banū 'Abbās as having been harmful to the *ahl-i bayt.* This is mentioned in the *Izhār al-haqq* and the *Khulāsat al-favā'id.*

18. In his *al-Kāfī,* Kulaynī includes one such hadith from Muhammad Bāqir. Hamavī, *Anīs al-mu'minīn,* 137.

19. According to Hamavī, these predictions do not indicate that the Imams considered these people as good from the very beginning. This statement is intended for the Mongols, who eventually under Khudābandah (d. 1317) converted to the Imami faith. Hamavī, *Anīs al-mu'minīn,* 138.

20. Ibid.

21. Hamavī continues to refute the alleged connections between Abū Muslim and the Imamis. He argues against the medieval Shi'i author of the *I'lām al-warā,* who states that Abū Muslim had made a *bay'a* with the *ahl-i bayt* before Saffah succeeded the caliphate. Shaykh Amīn al-Islam Abū Ali al-Fazl b. al-Hasan al-Hasan b. al-Fazl al-Tūsi (d. 1153–1154), the author of the *I'lām al-warā,* is quoting from the *Nawādir al-hikma* by Muhammad b. Ahmad b. Yahya al-Qummī, who relates it from Bakr b. Abi Bakr Wasitī. Hamavī, *Anīs al-mu'minīn,* 136.

22. Ibid. This is the version preserved in the *Milal wa al-nihal* by Muhammad Shahristani, as quoted in Hamavī, *Anīs al-mu'minīn,* 178–179.

23. Ibid.

24. Tāliqānī, *Khulāsat al-favā'id,* f 135b.

25. Hamavī, *Anīs al-mu' minīn*, 178, quoting Muhammad b. al-Husayn al-Kaydarī (thirteenth century). Also recorded in the *Khulāsat al-favā'id*, f 132a.

26. Ibid.

27. *Hadīqat al-shī'a* was not written by Muqaddas Ardabīlī (d. 1585). The work must have been written after 1055/1645, given that the pseudo-Ardabīlī states that in his day people visited the tomb of Shaykh Abū al-Futūh 'Ijli Shafi'i in Isfahan, thinking that it was the tomb of Shaykh Abū al-Futūh Rāzī. Chardin states that in 1055/1645, a marble inscription with the name of Shaykh Abū al-Futūh was found in Isfahan (Cemetary of Chamalan), and some *ulama* thought that it belonged to the Rāzī, who had compiled the famous commentary on the Qur'an (Abū al-Futūh). Two mosques and a tomb were built there. Later, a mulla called Mīr Lawhī, using a historical passage, proved that Shaykh Abū al-Futūh was buried in Rayy and that this Rāzī was a Sunni Turk and heretic. According to Chardin, two thousand people demolished the mosque and the tomb. John Chardin, *Les Voyages du Chevalier Chardin en Perse*, ed. L. Langlès (Paris: Le Normant, 1811), vol. 8, 20. Chardin's last departure from Isfahan was in 1086–1087/1677. The *Hadīqat al-shī'a*, then, must have been written between 1055/1645 and 1086–1087/1677, for the *Hadīqat al-shī'a* quotes from the *Hādī ilā al-nijāt* by ibn-i Hamzah, a contemporary of Abūl-Futūh Rāzī, to prove that Rāzī was buried in Rayy. But the pseudo-Ardabili mentions that people still visit that tomb, thinking that it is the tomb of Shaykh Abū al-Futūh. This raises the possibility that Mīr Lawhī may have himself written this polemic ascribed to Ardabīlī. For further discussions on the dating of the *Hadīqat al-shī'a*, see Mehdi Tadayyun, "Hadīqat al-shī'a yā kāshif al-haqq?," *Ma'ārif* 2 no. 3 (1985): 453–469. Tadayyun argues that the *Hadīqat* was not written by Ardabīlī and was composed some time between 1070/1659 and 1100/1688.

28. One letter was written to Abdullah b. Hasan b. Hasan b. Ali, who accepted the leadership of the Abbasid movement. A second letter was written to Umar b. Ali b. Husayn, the brother of Muhammad Baqir, who refused it. The third was sent to Ja'far al-Sādiq.

29. In other words, he is of the Hashimiyya/Kaysaniyya. Ahmad b. Muhammad Pseudo-Ardabīlī, *Hadīqat al-shī'a* (Tehran: n.p., 1964), 554.

30. Sayyid Husayn Modarresi-Tabātabā'ī, *Crisis and Consolidation in the Fromative Period of Shi'ite Islam* (Princeton, Darwin Press, 1993), 99–105.

31. Ibid., 54–99; also see al-Hasan b. Musā Nawbakhtī, *Firaq al-shī'a*, ed. Muhammad Sādiq Bahr al-Ulūm (al-Najaf: al-Matba'ah al-Haydarīyah; 1936).

32. Isma'ili narratives also need to be included here to rewrite early Islamic history.

33. Note that this Nawbakhti is from the same family as the Zoroastrian astrologers working at the court of the Abbasids discussed in part 1.

34. The medieval historian Tabarī cites a hadith to demonstrate how clear Ali was, according to one tradition, about the equality and love he felt for all three of his sons. Although a hierarchy is delineated among his three sons, it closely mirrors the succession story of this third son of Ali as heir to Husayn's Imamate. Ali is on his deathbed, and after having addressed his two sons born of Fatima about certain things they should remember, he turns to Muhammad b. Hanafiyya and asks him to commit to heart what he has commended to his two brothers. Ali says, "And I commend the same to you and also reverence for your two brothers to whom you owe a great duty. Follow their commands and do not decide any matter without them." To Hasan and Husayn, he says, "I commend him to you too for he is your brother and your father's son, and you know that your father loved him." Tabarī, *The History of al-Tabari: The First Civil War*, trans. and ann. G. R. Hawting (Albany: State University of New York Press, 1987), vol. 17, 219, based on a report by Jundab b. 'Abdullah.

35. It had apparently been used for Husayn. Tabarī refers to Husayn as "Mahdi son of the Mahdi [Ali]." *The History of al-Tabarī: The Victory of the Marzanids*, trans. and ann. Michael Fishbein (Albany: State University of New York Press, 1990), vol. 21, 546.

36. Cited in Tabari, *History,* vol. 21, 8.

37. Michael G. Morony, *Iraq after the Muslim Conquest* (Princeton: Princeton University Press, 1984), 10–11 (citing Tabarī). This group of Persian converts (Hamra) to Islam joined Muslim armies as allies of the Arab tribe Tamim. These Arabs of Tamim had been Mazdean converts.

38. For a Jewish emphasis in Shi'ism, see Steven Wasserstrom, *Between Muslim and Jew: The Problem of Symbiosis Under Early Islam* (Princeton: Princeton University Press, 1995). For a nationalist reading of Persian influences, see Abd al-Husayn Zarrinkub, *Bāmdād-i Islam* (Tehran: n.d., 1967).

39. Medieval Imami scholars like al-Sharīf al-Murtada acknowledge that Muhammad b. Hanafiyya did originally regard himself as Imam but realized his error and then recognized Zayn al-Abidin. On the creation of a separate category of heresy, the "Kaysaniyya," see Wadad al-Qadi, "The Development of the Term *Ghulāt* in Muslim Literature with Special References to the Kayasāniyya," in *Akten des VII. Kongresses für Arabistik und Islamwissenschaft Göttingen,* ed. Albert Dietrich (Göttingen: Vandenhoeck & Ruprecht, 1976).

40. Despite some problems in the way in which Wadad al-Qadi generalizes these early revisions of Imami heresiographers, she does outline a process that is important. Wadad al-Qadi does not use later heresiographers like Abū Ma'āli, who trouble her schema. Instead, she tends to make assumptions, basing her arguments on formal categories that are embedded in these early heresiographers. But even in the narrative of Nawbakhti, for example, the author creates linkages between the Kaysaniyya and the proto-Imamis as well as the *ghulāt* that need to be addressed in the study of *ghuluww.*

41. Other than the Khariji rebellions against the Umayyads, the Kaysani and Alavi revolts were most prominent. Followers of Mukhtar (685–687) set up a state in Nisibin (690). After Abū Hashim's (Kaysani) death in 716, Hamza b. 'Umarah Barbari revolted in Medina and Kufa and claimed that Muhammad b. Hanafiyya was God and Hamza was his Prophet. Bayan, a supporter of Hamza, continued this rebellion in Kufa, claiming that Muhammad Bāqir (Husayni) had named him his successor. Mughīra joined Bayan's rebellion, and both were killed in 736 by the Umayyads. Khidash, the missionary of Muhammad b. Ali Abbasi, is killed by him in Khurasan (Nishapur) in 736 due to his extremist Alid ideas. Muhammad Bāqir's brother, Zayd b. Ali, takes on an active role and revolts in Medina; he is killed in 740, and his son Yahya b. Zayd continues his rebellion in Khurasan where Kufan Shi'is had been exiled earlier by the governor of Iraq,

and is killed in 744. These two grandsons of Husayn are linked by marriage and blood to the Kaysanis, Zayd b. Ali marries the daughter of Abū Hāshim, so Yahya is a descendant of both Husayn and well as Abū Hāshim. And finally, the Tayyarid/ Kaysani (Abdullhah b. Mu'awiyāh), who had inherited his rule from the Kaysani Abū Hāshim, revolts after the death of his Husayni cousins Zayd and Yahya. His revolt spreads through Iraq and into Isfahan and Fars (744–747); he is joined by Zaydis, Abbasids, and Kharijis. When he flees to Khurasan, Abū Muslim kills him on behalf of the Abbasids. Abdullah b. Mu'awiyah's sortie should be understood in the context of the 126/744 Hashimi gathering at al-Abwa' near Medina where supposedly the Hasanid (Nafs al-Zakiyya) is considered as the Imam of the Shi'is (al-Tabarī, *History*, vol. 3, 143ff). The Abbasids are to have agreed, but the Husayni Ja'far is to have withdrawn his approval. Clearly, so did Abdullah b. Mu'awiyah, for he made his sortie right after this meeting in 744.

42. The Husayni, Ja'far al-Sādiq (d. 765) and the Hasani, Muhammad b. Abdullah (Nafs al-Zakiyya, d. 762). The latter would revolt after the Abbasid takeover.

43. Jacob Lassner, *Islamic Revolution and Historical Memory: An Inquiry into the Art of 'Abbāsid Apologetics* (New Haven: American Oriental Society, 1986), 91.

44. Marshall G. S. Hodgson argues that "it need no longer be regarded as strange, as it used to be, that so many Shi'ites could accept as Imam non-Fātimids, like Muhammad b. Hanafiyya; for it is now recognized that for the early Shi'ites as for the other Arabs, it was descent in the male line which counted—that is, from Ali and not primarily from Muhammad's daughter. Indeed, the whole family of Ali was given precedence: any descendants of Abū Tālib could become Shi'ite leaders—and, so far as relationship to the Prophet entered the case, even the other uncles were not ruled out." "How the Early Shi'a Became Sectarian," *Journal of the American Oriental Society* 75 (1955): 1.

45. Tāliqānī, *Khulāsat al-favā'id*, f 129b, using Mas'udi and Kaydari as sources, indicates that the theory of primogeniture was part of the political culture of Arabia and was in fact later used by the Abbasids to legitimize their claims. The *Khulāsat* argues that Abū Muslim denied the Imamate of Ali on the basis of tribal notions of

inheritance. Abū Muslim claimed that "the Imamate is hereditary and that after the Prophet the Imamate was the right of 'Abbās, for so long as there is an uncle, the inheritance is not passed on to the nephew."

46. It is perhaps in relation to these type of claims that Zayd attempted to distinguish his candidacy as a Fatimid and denied the doctrine of designation (*nass*), claiming that it was necessary only to be pious and rebellious to seek the Imamate.

47. Hamavī, *Anīs al-mu'minīn*, 147.

48. Tāliqānī, *Khulāsat al-favā'id*, f. 131a, also mentioned in Pseudo-Ardabīli, *Hadīqat al-shī'a* (Tehran: n.p., 1964), 556.

49. Nawbakhtī, *Firaq al-Shī'a*, 75.

50. Lassner, *Islamic Revolution and Historical Memory*, 103–120.

51. On Abū Muslim represented as a descendant of Salit b. Abdullah b. Abbas, the brother of Ali and uncle of Ibrahim, Abū al-'Abbās (al-Saffah) and Abū Ja'far (Mansur), see Lassner, *Islamic Revolution and Historical Memory*, 113.

52. Ibid., 106. Another Abbasid, Isa, who is to have claimed authority over Mansur, was not killed. If Abū Muslim had been of Abbasid blood, he too would not have been killed.

53. Lassner remarks that the only recorded case of a client marrying a Muslim was the mock marriage between Ja'far Barmaki and Harun al-Rashid's sister, Abbasah. On this matter, Ibn Khaldun, *The Muqaddimah: An Introduction to History*, trans. Franz Rosenthal (Princeton: Princeton University Press, 1967), vol. 1, 28–29, notes: "How could she link her pedigree with that of Jaf'ar b. Yahya and stain her Arab nobility with a Persian client? His ancestors had been acquired as a slave, or taken as a client, by one of her ancestors, an uncle of the Prophet and noble Qurayshite [that is, al-'Abbās]. How could it be that al-Rashid would permit himself to be related to Persian clients?" Ibid., 120.

54. A third tendency can also be discerned emerging as well from an Abrahamic milieu, which embedded a core of Jewish beliefs (Isawiyya, Mansuriyya). See Wasserstrom, *Between Muslim and Jew*.

55. See Yuri M. Lotman, *The Universe of the Mind: A Semiotic Thoery of Culture* (Bloomington: Indiana University Press, 1998), 131–142, on the notion of boundary.

56. See Richard W. Bulliet, *Conversion to Islam in the Medieval Period: An Essay in Quantitative History* (Cambridge: Harvard University Press, 1979), and Bulliet, *Islam: The View from the Edge*, (New York: Columbia University Press, 1994), as well as Parvaneh Pourshariati, "Iranian Tradition in Tus and the Arab Presence in Khurasan," Ph.D. diss., Columbia University, 1995.

57. Hamavī, *Anīs al-mu' minīn*, 190; Tāliqānī, *Khulāsat al-favā'id*, 135b.

58. Tāliqānī, *Khulāsat al-favā'īd*, f. 135b, is quoting from Kaydari, the author of *Kifayat al-baraya* and a student of Nasir al-din Tusi. Hamavī also mentions this account of Sunbadh.

59. Shahristānī, *al-Milal wa-al-nihal* (521 A.H.), 132, states that the *ghulāt* Shi'ites in Rayy are called Mazdakis and Sunbadhis (also cited in Gholam Hossein Sadighi, *Les Mouvements Religieux Iraniens au IIIe siècle de l'heqire* (Paris: Les Presses Modernes, 1938), 148. The author of the *Tabsirat al-avam* confirms that they are called in the same manner in Qazvin and Ray.

60. Tūsī, Nizam al-Mulk, *Siyāsatnāme*, ed. Murtazā Mudarris, Chahārdahī (Tehran: Tehran University, 1955), 212.

61. Ibid., 190.

62. Hugh Kennedy, *The Early Abbasid Caliphate: A Political History* (London: Croom Helm, 1981), 64.

63. Ibid., 184.

64. Muhammad Mirkhwand, *Rawzat al-safā*, ed. 'Abbās Zaryāb (Tehran: Intishārāt-i ilmī, 1994), zvol. 3, 404–405), citing Pourshariati, op. cit. n. 56, 215.

65. Ibid., 212 (citing Kennedy, *The Early Abbasid Caliphate*, 65).

66. Ibid., 65.

67. The Islamicate sources tend to equate the Muslimiyya and the Khurramiyya. But there does seem to be territorial specificity when referring to the Neo-Mazdaki movements in western Iran (Azarbaijan, Rayy, Hamadan, Isfahan) as the Khurramiyya is used. See part 1 for a discussion of these neo-Mazdaki beliefs and their resonance in Nuqtavi spheres.

68. Patricia Crone, "Kavad's Heresy and Mazdak's Revolt," *Iran: Journal of the British Institute of Persian Studies* 24 (1991): 27.

69. Those revolts in "Inner Khurasan" like Bihafarid (Khwaf) and Sunbadh (Nishapur) occurred in regions that had remained out-

side the domain of Arab infiltration, where Zoroastrian fire temples abounded and mosques were rare. See Pourshariati, "Iranian Tradition," 210.

70. See Louise Marlow, *Hierarchy and Egalitarianism in Islamic Thought* (Cambridge: Cambridge University Press, 1997). Marlow traces the taming of Islamic egalitarianism through didactic literature of courtly and religious culture in which hierarchy is rationalized. She does not, however, emphasize the apocalyptic context from which Muhammad rose and was embraced, nor does she read these Persianate revolts as reactions to such shifts in discourse.

71. Tāliqānī, *Khulāsat al-favā'id*, f 134, quoting from Mas'udi's *Murūj al-zahab* and Kaydari's *Kifaya al-abraya*.

72. Sadighi, *Les Mouvements*, 201–202.

73. Abū Dulaf visits Bazz in the mid-tenth century.

74. Bidlisi, *Sherefname*, f. 127b, cited in Hassan Pirouzdjou, *Mithraïsme et Emancipation: Anthropolgie Sociale et Culturelle des Mouvements Populaires en Iran au VIIIe, IXe et du XIVe au Début du XVIe siècle: Le Cas du Mouvement Safavide* (Paris: Harmattan, 1999), 138.

75. Tūsī, Nizam al-Mulk, *Siyāsatname*, 195.

76. Although this information comes from a later and hostile source (Nizam al-Mulk), the Khurramiyya mixing with Harithiyya, and the Janahiyya mixing with Mazdakis are mentioned in medieval heresiographies as well.

77. The Harithiyya were *ghulāt* suporters of Abd b. Mu'awiyya (d. 748). Khidash was killed in 736 by the Abbasids for having extremist ideas, such as the belief that the Imamate moved from the Abbasids to Khidash, like some claimed for Abū Muslim. Also the Rizamiyya, radical anti-Abbasid followers of Abū Muslim who reject al-Mahdi's break with the Kaysaniyya lineage is an example.

78. Mubayyids are still identified in twelfth century; see Wilferd Madelung, "Mubayyida," *EI2*.

79. Nawbakhtī, *Firaq al-shī'a*, 60.

80. Ibid., 61.

81. Nazim al-Mulk, *Siyāsatnāme*, Drake (trans.), 238.

82. The preceding six Imams being Ali, Hasan, Husayn, Zayn al-'Abidin, Muhammad Bāqir, and Ja'far.

83. The history of the human race was divided into seven dispensations, each of which began with a *nātiq* (speaker) who revealed a new *shari'a*. This *nātiq* was succeeded by an *asās/sāmit* (silent one), whose duty it was to reveal the deeper meaning *(bātin)* of the new book. Each dispensation also brought forth seven Imams, who were to be consulted in legal matters and who were to make sure that the *shari'a* was followed. The seventh Imam of every era became the new *nātiq* of the following era—revealing a new book for this new dispensation.

84. Mary Boyce, *Textual Sources for the Study of Zoroastrianism* (Chicago: University of Chicago Press, 1984), 12. For Mazdean influences in Isma'ili cosmology, see Henry Corbin, *Cyclical Time and Isma'ili Gnosis: Islamic Texts and Contexts* (London: Kegal Paul, 1983).

85. The year 953 was chosen by Wilferd Madelung "Karmatī," *EI2* because it marks the accession of al-Mu'izz (r. 953–74), who revised the Fatimid-Isma'īlī doctrine to win over Qarmatī dissent among the Eastern Isma'īlī communities. He reaffirms the central Qarmatī belief that Muhammad b. Isma'īl is the hidden Imam but adds that his acts are to be executed by his descendants, the Fatimid caliphs. He also gives entree to Qarmatī/neo-Platonic cosmology, accepting into Fatimid doctrine the earlier neo-Platonists like Nasafi and Abū Hātim Rāzī. However, with these doctrinal revisions he fails to win over the Qarmatīs of Bahrayn. The Ikhwān al-Safā writing in 960 c.e. from Basra repudiate the Fatimid claims to the Imamate as well. This date marks the permanent split between the religious doctrines of the Qarmatīs and the Fatimids. After 953 Qarmatī communities outside of Bahrayn were rapidly absorbed into the Fatimid-Isma'īlīs.

86. The Fatimid caliph 'Ubaydullah al-Mahdi (d. 934) had claimed the Imamate of the anticipated Isma'īlī Mahdi (Muhammad b. Isma'il) for himself. For a detailed history of the Isma'īlīs, see Farhad Daftary, *The Isma'īlīs: Their History and Doctrines* (Cambridge: Cambridge University Press, 1990); Heinz Halm, *The Empire of the Mahdi: The Rise of the Fatimids,* trans. M. Bonner (Leiden: Brill, 1996).

87. Wilferd Madelung, *Religious Trends in Early Islamic Iran* (Albany, NY: Persian Heritage Foundation, 1988), 96–97.

88. Muhammad b. Ahmad al-Bīrūnī, *The Chronology of Ancient Nations* (*al-āthār al-bāqiyah*), trans. and ed. Edward Sachau (London: Allen, 1993), 196–197.
89. Madelung, *Religious Trends in Early Islamic Iran*, 96.
90. Wilferd Madelung, "Khurramiyya," *EI2*. In Islamic sources, the name *Khurramiyya* is applied to religious movements founded by Mazdak (in the late sixth century) and to various Abū Muslimiya groups that claimed he was still alive—Hanafiyya, Muslimiyya, Rizāmiyya, Fātimiyya, Sinbadiyya, Ishāqiyya, Muqanna, Mubādiyya, Muhammiraiyya, Rāwandiyya. Khurramiyya revolts continued with Babak (revolts in Azarbaijan, 816–838) and beyond his death until 1125 C.E., when they were last mentioned to have been active in Hamadan. Wilferd Madelung, "Khurramiyya," *EI2* [quoting al-Bundarī, *Mukhtasar Zubdat al-Nusrā*, ed. M. T. Houtsma (Leiden, 1889) 124].
91. Madelung, *Religious Trends in Early Islamic Iran*, 10.
92. Ibid.
93. Ibid., 11.
94. Ibid.
95. Sayyid Husayn Modarresi-Tabātabā'ī, *An Introduction to Shi'i Law: A Bibliographical Study* (London: Ithaca Press, 1984), 40. The theologian and jurist al-Shaykh al-Mufīd (d. 1022) of the *usūliyya*/rationalist school was successful in discrediting the *akhbāriya*/traditionalists of Qum, who regarded the attribution of any supernatural element to the Imams as a sign of *ghuluww* and a religious deviation.
96. See the *Khulāsat al-tavārīkh*, vol. 1, 79. Also see Sayyid Husayn Modarresi-Tabātabā'ī, *Zamīn dar Fiqh-i Islāmī* (Tehran: Daftar-i Nashr-i Farhang-i Islāmī 1984), vol. 2, 222 n. 84), for a discussion on the extent to which the early Safavi *ulama* ascribed legitimacy to these shahs using hadith that had until then been evoked only when speaking of the advent of the Mahdī. Modarresi does not explicitly state that mahdist legitimacy was implied by the use of these hadith; I have taken the liberty of making such a conjecture.

Part III

CRAFTING AN IMPERIAL
SAFAVI IDIOM

· NINE ·

Mirroring the Safavi Past: Shah Tahmasb's Break with His Messiah Father

It struck my feeble [*shikastah*] mind that I should pen a Memoir [*tazkīre*] relating my circumstances [*ahvālāt*] and encounters [*sarguzasht*] from the beginning of my reign (1524) up to this day (1562). How has my state [*ahvālam*] transpired? So that it may remain in the path of memory [*sabīl-i yādigār*] throughout the ages [*rūzigār*]. Let it serve as a "mirror" [*dastūr al-amal*] for my noble descendants [*awlād-i amjad*] and loyal friends [*ahbāb*], with the hope that whenever it may come to the attention of Alids [*muhibbān*], it be remembered with blessings [*du'ā-yi khayr*]. Since it has been written without much effort [*bī takalluf*], let it not be exposed to nit-picking [*khurdah gīrī*], and let it be considered free of the taint of doubt [*rayb*], lies [*kizb*], and dissimulation [*riya'*][1]

—Tahmasb b. Isma'il b. Haydar al-Safavi al-Musavi al-Husayni

SITUATING SHAH TAHMASB (r. 1524–1576) AND THE EARLY SAFAVIS

As we have seen, the author of the *Memoir* was born into a genealogy that awarded him spiritual authority by virtue of descent from the famous mystic Shaykh Safi al-din (d. 1334). Denizens of early modern Islamdom who were immersed in the ubiquitous culture of mysticism imagined charisma (*barakat*) to flow biologically from one generation to another. Shah Tahmasb's dominion was not only endowed with spiritual au-

295

thority, for he had inherited his father's kingly throne within a cultural milieu that joined the holy intimately with the human, in particular with, paragons of truth and justice—mystics, monarchs, and messiahs. Shah Tahmasb's *Tazkire* is symbolic of his endeavor to set a new tempo for Safavi sovereignty in a post-apocalyptic age.[2]

Shah Tahmasb's father, Shah Isma'il (r. 1501–1524), had conquered Iran and Iraq with his Turkmen armed disciples, the Qizilbash, who venerated him as the incarnation of God on earth. Thus, as the first spiritual guide of the Safavi brotherhood to assume temporal dominion, Shah Isma'il fused the dual meaning of the title *shah* current in the political and religious cultures of the central and eastern lands of Islamdom. That the Persian designation for monarch—*shah*—had become a current appellation for spiritual guides and even for holy men like Ali speaks of a history of convergence and similitude. Shah Isma'il claimed to be the reincarnation of a host of prophets and kingly heroes from Iran's cultural past. "Prostrate thyself! Pander not to Satan! Adam has put on new clothes, God has come," writes Isma'il in his poetry composed as he, together with the Qizilbash, conquered Safavi Iran. In an attempt to add temporal power to the already existent Safavi spiritual dominion, these Qizilbash allegedly entered the battlefield unarmed, thinking that Isma'il's miraculous powers would shield them.[3] Shah Isma'il identified himself as well with the awaited Mahdi in early modern Islamdom, in an era that marked the end of the first millennium of Muslim rule, a time when millenarian expectations were widespread. To further validate his messianic claim, Isma'il placed himself within a special Alid lineage of the family of the Prophet Muhammad, from whose bloodline the messiah was to emerge at the end of time. Isma'il depicts this apocalyptic moment in his poetry:

The heroic crusaders [*ghāzī*] have come forth with
   "crowns of happiness" on their heads

The Mahdi's period has begun.
The light of eternal life has dawned [upon] the world.[4]

The appropriated idiom of the Muslim chiliastic Messiah carried with it the promise of a paradise on earth, and so Isma'il merged divine justice with this worldly kingship. Moreover, it was not a title that Isma'il merely played with; in practice, he performed the functions expected of a messiah king. Shah Isma'il is to have shared his booty with his Turkmen disciples and divided the conquered territories into appanages, which they administered as governors and tutors of Safavi princes. Although descendants of Muhammad (*sayyid*) were singled out as a privileged group and awarded stipends and tax immunities, a form of communism was instituted whereby craftsmen and merchants were exempted from supra-Islamic commercial taxes, and soup kitchens were set up for the poor.[5] It is no surprise, then, that throughout Isma'il's reign his treasury was often empty. Yet as the eyewitness Venetian diplomat Sanuto relates, such generous bestowal affirmed Isma'il's role as "God on earth" for the sensibilities of those whom he came to rule.[6]

Whether his followers perceived Isma'il as God or messiah, these were tough acts for any son to follow. This particularity renders Tahmasb's portrayal of his reign and of his character an even more fascinating narrative of the life of a king who had to deal with the image of a godlike father. Through his *Memoir*, Tahmasb rejected his father's role as messiah-God as he cast his own role as saintly king (*shah vilāyat*). That Tahmasb decided to personally record such a recasting of his father and a casting of himself is telling. He must have wanted to make sure that future generations would judge him and his father in accordance with his own rendering of the two, rather than trusting contemporaneous or future court historians to translate their reigns. Tahmasb was securing himself a role in the recording of the history of the rise and consolidation of Safavi rule. His *Memoir* encapsulates a moment of disruption in early Safavi discourse, an opening of a space for subtle transformations in the cultural meanings of authority, loyalty, and masculinity. Tahmasb does succeed in consolidating the way for a (re)interpretation of Isma'il's revolutionary discourse in later Safavi historiography, but he fails to imprint himself as saint.

We still need to determine how much of this (re)interpretation of Isma'il can be attributed to Tahmasb's innovation or rather to a prevailing mood that was searching for a more acceptable rendering of Isma'il in the postrevolutionary Safavi era. Although the two principal court historians of Isma'il's reign continue to play with the categories of temporal and spiritual authority, each chose to emphasize one of the numerous icons with which Isma'il had identified in his poetry.[7] Two distinct rubrics of legitimacy were evoked by these first-generation Safavi historians as a means of distinguishing the spirit of Shah Isma'il's authority.

The first court historian, Khwandamir, who completed his work *Habīb al-siyar* on the death of Isma'il (1524), makes use of an apocalyptic language that merged worldly conquest with divine kingship to characterize Isma'il's rise to power. Khwandamir implies the messianic role of Isma'il using mixed symbols of Persianate kingship (*shāhanshāh*). To encapsulate Isma'il's authority, he draws on three key emblems of sovereignty—sword, sun, and crown—to recount a telling dream that Shaykh Safi had in his youth. The dream is framed as a prophecy
· forecasting the future emergence of Shaykh Safi's progeny to universal supremacy. And history, the unfolding of events that led to the success of Shah Isma'il, is introduced as proof of Shaykh Safi's divination. Khwandamir adds his own interpretation of the dream, as though to make it clear to an audience for whom these symbols might enjoy a multitude of meanings: "The author of these words asserts that anyone who is enlightened and who will reflect upon the interpretation of this dream will know for certain that the sword represents the manifestation [*zuhūr*] of the blade of the victorious-bannered, world-conquering king [*pādishah*]. And the crown along with the sun refer to the blazing crown on the august head of that holy one."[8] The term *zuhūr* (manifestation) enjoys a particular meaning in Shi'i

apocalyptic rhetoric and designates the unveiling of the messiah, who, since his occultation (874 C.E.), had remained invisible to the world at large. And the Persian title of kingship (*pādishah*) is evoked here in the context of the world-conquering mission of the messiah. Isma'il's mandate of sovereignty is located within the Irano-Islamic idiom of the messiah-king. The adjectives of the "resplendent" sun and the "blazing crown" (*tāj-i vahhāj*) invoke pre-Islamic Persian attributes of sacral kingship. Although the term *Mahdi* or its analogue, the *Lord of the Age* (*sāhib-i zamān*), is not used explicitly by Khwandamir, his eliciting of mixed metaphors of Persianate regal and sacred vocabulary within the language of Alid apocalyptic implies a messianic role for Shah Isma'il.

Amini was another court historian commissioned by Isma'il to write his history, which he completed only at the beginning of the reign of Shah Tahmasb (1531). In his casting, Isma'il was a crusader (*ghāzī*) who had succeeded in establishing Shi'ism, the true Muslim faith.[9] Interpreting the same dream of Shaykh Safi, Amini's emphasis is different: he asserts that the marriage of temporal authority (*hukm-i vilāyat*) and spiritual authority (*nūr-i vilāyat*), or the marriage of the sword and the sunlike crown, will materialize only once the "sword of holy war [*ghaza*] take[s] on the expanse of the whole universe."[10] Here, at the beginning of Shah Tahmasb's reign, we already witness a move away from the messianic claims of Shah Isma'il. Rather, Isma'il is remembered as having "uprooted, as much as he could, the forms of oppression and innovation" that had plagued the eastern lands of Islam.[11] As holy warrior, Isma'il's aura continued to thrive on his inherited spiritual charisma (*nūr-i vilāyat*), but such an attribution also specified the nature of his worldly conquest (*hukm-i vilāyat*). Isma'il was a fighter for the faith. In the name of Islam, his motivations and success were placed within the rhetoric of "holy war."[12] It is neither as God nor as divinely guided messiah but as a saintly warrior (*ghāzī*) that Isma'il became *shah* of Safavi Iran in this version of history. Isma'il's initial campaigns (1500–1501) into Christian-dominated Georgia and his establishment of Shi'ism as the religion of the Safavi domains comprises the central revolutionary events around which his image is shaped. Isma'il is eulogized with the epithet *dīn panāh*, or "refuge of religion."[13] Both of these languages of sovereignty were part of the repertoire that he had used to describe his eclectic mission in his poetry as well as in coins minted in his name and inscriptions engraved on mosques commemorating him. Numismatic and epigraphic vestiges attest to Isma'il's continued associations with the hidden Imam (messiah) and his appropriation of a medley of roles not only as the "just and perfect Imam" (*imām al-ādīl al-kāmil*) but also as holy warrior (*al-ghāzī*) and "friend of God" (*al-valī*).[14] By isolating one of these roles, each historian came to reflect on a particular audience's sensibilities, whether sedentary or nomadic, that had now become entrenched within the Safavi imperial system. These two options of imagining Isma'il—holy warrior or messiah king— were open for a second generation of Safavis to reconsider.

The written sources that we have from Shah Tahmasb's reign divulge a multiplicity of ways in which Isma'il's messianic claims were understood by the second generation. Tahmasb's brother, Sam Mirza (d. 1567), for example, writing a classic biography (*tazkire*) of poets probably a decade before Tahmasb wrote his memoir (1550), emphasizes Isma'il's role as holy warrior (*ghāzī*) as well.[15] But he also refers to their father using the new title of "master of an auspicious conjunction" (*sāhib qirān*).[16] The title of *sāhib qirān* denotes a world conqueror who establishes a universal dominion by force of arms. In the memory of Muslim historians, Alexander, Chengiz Khan, and Timur represented such universal sovereigns, revealing a mentality that understands continual suceess in the battlefield to signify divine favor. Tahmasb's brother preferred to frame their father with majestic titles that deemphasized his holy claims. There is no trace of Isma'il's role as messiah. Yet the messianic coloring of Shah Isma'il I's claims continued to shape the way in which the Safavi mission was described in other sources. Amir Mahmud, the son of Khwandamir, writing at the same time as Sam Mirza, refers to Shaykh Safi as the Imam of the age (*Imām-i zamān*).[17] The messianic role of Isma'il is projected back to his ancestor Safi, and Isma'il's rise to power is related as being divinely inspired (*ilhām-i ghaybī*).[18] Isma'il is guided by the Imams rather than embodying the awaited twelfth Imam himself.[19] But Amir Mahmud refers to Isma'il as subsuming all titles of Muslim sovereignty—imam, caliph, sultan, *sāhib qirān*. Again, like his father a generation later, Amir Mahmud implies Isma'il's role as Mahdi.

Religious (Imami) scholars from Tahmasb's period initially legitimized Safavi rule on messianic grounds as well. It had been common among Islamic scholars and aspiring reformers to relate eschatological traditions to political uprisings and vice versa.[20] Less common, however, had been the attempt to ascribe Shi'i (Imami) legitimacy to a government on grounds that it was indeed that just order (*dawlat-i haqq*) that the messiah was to establish at the end of time.[21] With the rise to power of Shah Isma'il, some prominent Safavi clergymen from Tahmasb's age related prophetic traditions paralleling the advent of the messiah.[22] These prophetic dictums had customarily been employed only when discussing eschatological events relating to the advent of the Mahdi.[23] Initially, then, Imami clerics implied that Safavi rule was legitimate on the basis of messianic rather than religiolegal (*shar'i*) legitimacy.[24] The expectation of an imminent rise of the messiah seems to have lingered in the imagination of Safavi denizens beyond the death of Isma'il. Some continued to understand Isma'il's role as the eschatological messiah who establishes justice on earth. But there were certain realities that had to be accounted for. Isma'il had been defeated in 1514 by the Ottoman Sultan Selim after thirteen years of steady conquest. How could a messiah be defeated on the battlefield? After this defeat, Isma'il went into retreat for the rest of his life, engaging in hunting and drinking wine (*bazm u razm*). Aubin sees this as symbolic of Isma'il's asceticism, but how did his disciples interpret it? With the death of Isma'il, the expectation of a Safavi messiah seems to have been transferred onto his son Tahmasb.

Early in Tahmasb's reign, while his power was still tenuous, he seemed to have played on the possibility of his messiahship, at least publicly. The Venetian envoy to Tahmasb's court in 1534 speaks of Tahmasb as practicing the by then common ritual of keeping a white horse in his stable harnessed for the immediate occasion of the arrival of the messiah and reports that Tahmasb was saving his favorite sister, Sultanim ("my sultan" in Turkish), for the Mahdi.[25] We know that Tahmasb's relationship with his uterine sister was an intimate one. She is one of his closest confidants, to whom he trusted diplomatic relations with the Ottomans. Sultanim was economically independent, as we can tell from her many charitable endowments of public works for the religious establishment, and was never married.[26] In Tahmasb's *Memoir*, she appears to him in a dream as she prepares his bed for him, placing four beautiful Georgian concubines at each corner of the room. Conquest, whether sexual or territorial, is implied in this dream. Had Tahmasb reserved Sultanim for himself as a prerogative of the hidden Imam? Whatever the nature of the relationship between Tahmasb and his sister Sultanim, Tahmasb's reign continued to echo expectations of sounds of apocalyptic trumpets signaling the manifestation of the messiah. Such hints were engraved in an inscription in a shrine in Isfahan that characterized the era of Tahmasb's ascendancy as the vanguard (*muqaddima*) of the army of the "Lord of the Age" (*al-jaysh li-sahib al-zamān*).[27]

The official court historian Ghaffari, writing at about the same time (1563–1564) as Tahmasb, presents two chronograms for the accession of Tahmasb—the "end of time" (*ākhir al-zamān*) and the "shadow (*zill*) of God on earth."[28] In his *Memoir*, Tahmasb applies the title "shadow" of God on earth to himself. Embedded in pre-Islamic Iranian (Sasani) notions of sacral kingship within a Muslim monotheistic framework, the title epitomized the essence of kingly patrimonialism, according to which the political ethos of divine kingship was reserved for the monarch, whose role as God's representative on earth entailed the promulgation of Muslim sacred law. With the theory of the shadow of God on earth, political power was dispossessed of sanctity, making way for the emergence of a body of religious scholars who were privileged due to their knowledge of the sacred law to mediate between God and the world.[29] The domains of religion and politics were beginning to be split into two distinct loci of authority. With his *Memoir*, Tahmasb confirmed the Safavi break with a messianic and godlike father image; it is not as God but as his shadow that Tahmasb saw himself. Yet Tahmasb did not present an alternative representation for Isma'il. Perhaps in constructing his own saintly monarchy, Tahmasb was suggesting one such role for his father as well.[30]

The diversity of titles ascribed to Isma'il reveals the multitude of ways in which the Safavi revolution was understood by those who participated in it as well as those who came to play a role in the consolidation of Safavi imperial power. Prior to the revolution, the Safavi order had included a variety of followers— Turkmen tribesmen, urban craftsmen, shopkeepers, merchants, and landowners. I am assuming that their beliefs were not homogeneous and that the variety of symbols evoked by Isma'il represents a confluence of the many ways in which Safavi disciples fathomed the visions of their spiritual guide. Moreover, once Isma'il conquered the Safavi domains with his Qizilbash, new regional groups were incorporated into the system such as bureaucrats and local notables.[31] And by the time Shah Tahmasb was writing his *Memoir* (1562), a group of Arab immigrant clerics as well as Caucasian slaves were beginning to be incorporated into the Safavi court.[32] The fluidity of the renderings of Isma'il reflects the diffuse and contending centers of power in this period. Tahmasb had just emerged from a thirteen-year civil war. These struggles for power would eventually determine which version of Isma'il's story would be adopted as the "official" history of the Safavis. Isma'il would not take on the role of messiah in this version of the Safavi story; rather, he was portrayed as the precursor of the messiah who by establishing the "right order"—namely, Shi'ism (Imami)—would carve the way for his advent of the hidden Imam.[33]

Tahmasb's construction of himself in the *Memoirs* is shaped in contrast to a reflection of Isma'il's original holy aura. Isma'il's divine luster acts as the mirror on which Tahmasb's personality is refracted. Ironically, although Tahmasb commits his *Memoir* to writing so that his own image would remain in the "path of memory" (*sabīl-i yādigār*), later Safavi historiography chose to focus on one feature of Tahmasb's pious self-imaging—his religious (Shi'i) devotion and will to enforce Islamic law throughout his "god-protected" domains. The image of Tahmasb as saint (*valī*) did not find permanence in the minds of future generations of Safavis who rewrote their own past. In official Safavi historiography, the epitaph *dīn panāh*, or "refuge of religion," is inscribed alongside the name and reign of Shah Tahmasb.[34] Later Safavi historians project Tahmasb's policies back onto his father Isma'il, merging the two figures in simulacrum.

The cultural and political climate of the time stimulated such shifts in legitimizing symbols and paradigms of authority. In the two centuries prior to the rise of Isma'il, the lands of Iran, Mesopotamia, and Asia Minor had experienced a period of decentralization with the collapse of Mongol hegemony (Ilkhanid, 1258–1335). Turkmen factionalism (*mulūk al-tawā'if*) had created a mosaic of diffuse and ever-shifting centers of power. A series of Alid millenarian movements issuing from sufi circles attempted to gain regional control in all four corners of the Iranian plateau as well.[35] In this era of decentralization, the local power of sufi orders was enhanced. They provided a sheltered space for the continuity of economic and cultural life in localities consistently threatened by invading armies. In the case of the Safavi order, we can now ascertain that they enjoyed extensive economic and commercial power in northwestern Iran (Ardabil Tabriz, Gilan, and Mazandaran). Merchants and craftsmen found it beneficial to enter into business transactions with the Safavi order, perhaps to ensure a solid, nontaxable income for those who sold property and goods to the shrine.[36] Due to the respect awarded locally to sufi orders as well as the economic power of sufi institutions, regional rulers patronized and protected them. This was not only an act of devotion but a means of consolidating their own local authority. And so the orders could use this leverage to protect those residents who had become partners with the shrine from the extraction of extra taxes and tributes customary of invading armies. Such circumstances charged the political authority of sufi brotherhoods. Their choice of an apocalyptic language of revolt, however, clearly indicates that there was an Alid revival in this period. The impulses behind such a rekindling remain ambiguous, but it is probable that with the Mongol conquests of the central and eastern lands of Islamdom, when the core regions of Islam came under the control of non-Muslim rulers for the first time, there was a rapprochement between Sunni and Shi'i Islam. Moreover, many Muslims came to place their hopes with the betrayed family of the Prophet (Alids), who from the beginning of the expansion of Islam had contested the worldly ways of the Sunni Muslim caliphs who took over the leadership of Islamdom as the successors of Muhammad (Umayyads and Abbasids, 650–1258).

There seems to have been another element active in this era, when Muslims experienced their first encounter with non-Muslim colonizers. It expressed itself in the will to reinstate the ways of the ideal community of Muhammad and to cut down the "filthy trees of unbelief" (*shajarah-yi khabīsah-yi kufr*) that had rooted themselves in Muslim landscapes with the rise of Mongol imperialism (1257–1350s).[37] Modern Safavi historians have located a desire for security and stability based on a more legal control of society in this post-Mongol chaos (1356–1501).[38] A confluence of circumstances—political decentralization, demographic shifts due to the influx of large numbers of Turkic nomadic peoples, and Alid messianic movements—forged a dynamics of interests. Certain social groups in these regions gravitated toward a desire for stability and continuity in their political and economic lives. Impulses to control and rationalize power can be detected in the Timurids and Aqquyunlu empires, which the Safavis came to absorb. The powerful Aqquyunlu minister of religion and finances (Sadr and

Mostawfi) Qadi Isa Saveji, for example, had attempted to re-
form administrative practices.³⁹ The establishment of sacred law
was the medium through which he articulated his centralizing
reforms.⁴⁰ His patron, Sultan Yaqub (d. 1490), symbolically denounced wine drinking and issued a general prohibition against
the consumption of alcoholic beverages by all Muslims of his
capital city of Tabriz in 1488.⁴¹ Qadi Isa's reforms aimed at ac-
cruing the stable revenues so necessary for centralization, and
these policies probably led to his being hung a year after his
Aqquyunlu patron, Yaqub Bek, was killed in 1490.⁴² Shah
Tahmasb attempted to do the same, although he succeeded in in-
stituting and maintaining order. Whereas Isma'il made use of the
Turkmen Qizilbash to conquer and administer his domains, it
was Tahmasb who began to abate their *ghulat* temperament in
conjunction with his administrative experiment of breaking
Qizilbash-Safavi corporate sovereignty and enforcing the sacred
law.⁴³

Key to this breaking away from the radical past of the Safavis,
is Tahmasb's delegation of his religious authority, doctrinal and
legal, to the Shi'i jurisconsult (*mujtahid*) Shaykh Ali Karaki
through a noteworthy decree in 1533. Although Shah Isma'il
had patronized Karaki from the onset of his conquests of the
Safavi territories, the *firman* (decree) symbolized the new directions of Safavi rule. Karaki had ascribed to Isma'il the title of
just Imam (*imām al-adil*), playing on the double entendre embedded in this designation that denoted both the hidden Imam
as well as the just temporal ruler. For a Shi'i cleric to evoke such
a title in the context of Isma'il's revolutionary rhetoric highlights
the messianic layer of the appellation.⁴⁴ It also confirms Isma'il's
role as religious arbiter. After all, the Imam articulates sacred
law himself. Not needing the intermediary of religious scholars
to interpret the law for him, the Imam embodies divine law. But
with this *firman,* Karaki is ranked alongside the Imams and is
given eleven titles that are far from being normative effusions of
epistolary prosody (*saj*). The most significant of these epithets is
"deputy of the Imam" (*nā'ib al-imām*). Shah Tahmasb is here

actualizing a title that only recently had entered the realm of Shi'i discourse. And it is Karaki himself who had introduced the argument that the clergy are the general representatives, the *nā'ib al-'amm* of the Imams, distinguishing them from the four "gates" (*bāb*) who were the Imam's special delegates, the *nā'ib al-khāss*. This amounted to a theoretical revolution in Imami doctrine. The authority of the *ulama* became a direct reflection of the authority of the Imam himself. Tahmasb was denying his own Imamate and instead was designating Karaki as the ultimate arbiter of the faith. Tahmasb was bolstering Safavi authority on the basis of his patronage of a learned religious elite who possessed the knowledge to interpret sacred law. Karaki's title of the "seal of the jurisconsults" placed him at the head of this learned group. His endeavors would carve the way for the clergy to act as the Imams on earth, appropriating all their prerogatives, whether in collecting taxes or in leading the Friday congregational prayers. Karaki was now the ultimate arbiter of Shi'i doctrines and practices, even if he did not have the support of the Shi'i clerical community at large.[45] As you may recall, it is Karaki who wrote the first *fatwā* against singers of Abū Muslim's epic.

Shah Tahmasb confirms his commitment to the contents of the decree in an important episode he narrates in his *Memoir* where he reaffirms the authority (*ijtihād*) of Karaki.[46] With this *firman*, Tahmasb separates the mosque from the sufi cloister and paves the way for the eventual sundering of the religious and political spheres in the next century of Safavi dominion.[47] Jean Aubin remarks that Tahmasb is the real founder of the Safavi dynasty and was "hoisted to power through his father's charisma."[48] His *Memoir* and the rejection of his father's messianic heritage must be understood in this context.

The eponym *Safavi* (born of the pure Shaykh Safi), which was used to designate Tahmasb's dynastic household, which ruled in Iran for two centuries (1501–1722), encoded the complex interface of contemporaneous meanings and shapes of spiritual and temporal rule. The two-hundred-year dominion of the Safavi household offers a picture of the ways in which paradigms of authority shifted, reflecting in the process broader mystical, philosophical, and religiolegal tensions that had activated impulses toward change in Safavi society.[49] Culturally, we must imagine the Safavi age as an era of impassioned debate over an ontology of spirit and matter, as attempts were made to define boundaries between heaven and earth and to limit chaos through reason and divine law. We are witnessing the clashes, adoptions, compromises, and synthesis between two worldviews or ways of being and sensing time, one emanating from a monotheistic world religion and the other from a substratum of Mazdean cosmologies that predate it.[50] To the historian, the variety of symbols the Safavis came to draw on in time communicates cultural processes of transformation in early modern Islamdom (Ottoman and Mughal) in general, and Iran in particular.[51]

TAHMASB'S RENDERINGS OF THE SELF: PIETY, AUTHORITY, AND MASCULINITY

Throughout the last part of the book, we will be focusing on the shifting meanings and loci of authority (*vilāyat*) in the Safavi age. I read the *Memoir* as Tahmasb's personal narrative weaving together his twin journeys to kingship (*shah*) and sainthood (*valī*). It is Tahmasb's construction, or sincere perception, of what saved him all through his tumultuous reign as he struggled to maintain his temporal dominion, which was consistently threatened by his rival brothers, Sam and Alqas Mirza. Tahmasb's survival narrative attributes his political success to his being divinely protected, thanks to his devotion and commitment to a particular Alid lineage and set of Muslim precepts. Perhaps Tahmasb really came to believe in time that he was divinely protected, as he survived a turbulent thirteen-year regency (first civil war, 1524–1536) and a series of poison plots that threatened his life. Tahmasb is writing his life story forty years into a reign that spanned over half a century (1524–1576).

And in his *Memoir,* Tahmasb links his piety and his faith in God to his military and political success, which enabled him to overcome adversaries and maintain security both internally as well as along his western (Ottoman) and eastern (Uzbek) frontiers. From the very beginning of his reign, Tahmasb represents himself as being in communication, through the world of dreams, with Ali, the paternal cousin and son-in-law of Muhammad. Ali smiles at him in confirmation of Tahmasb's first victory in the battlefield at age fourteen against the Uzbeks—the Battle of Jam in 1528. Ali even reveals to him the location of the offensive, which seems to have been crucial to a strategic Safavi victory. Even though Ali cautions Tahmasb that his affairs shall not be determined by political victories, making it clear to his audience that temporal rule does not embody the totality of his authority, Tahmasb still had to take possession of his military power. And by including this military episode as the first in the series of seven dream accounts that span the narrative of his reign, Tahmasb links his assumption of military power to his personal relationship with Ali. This was a friendship that he developed on his own—a special companionship that would allow him access to sainthood and kingship on earth.

Dreams are the most visceral medium through which Tahmasb communicates with Ali. Tahmasb divulges his understanding of these metaphysical encounters: "It is this feeble-minded one's opinion that whoever sees Ali [*hazrat-i amīr al-muminīn*] in his sleep [*khwāb*], whatever he may say will come true."[52] Ali is objectified as the truth (*haqq*), and Tahmasb depicts himself as being privy of divine access to Ali through dreams. Tahmasb describes the intensity of this form of communication. Every time Tahmasb dreams of Ali, he awakes with a tangible sense of this contact and with a certainty of the meaning of the encounter. The night he records his first dream (1528) in the battlefield, Tahmasb writes, "When morning came, I knew that the Uzbeks had been defeated and had fled."[53] Tahmasb venerated Ali in his autobiography as a father and "perfect guide," whereas Isma'il, his biological father, is absent as a presence to be honored and respected. Tahmasb chose not to designate his father as his spiritual guide or model, something that would have been common in mystical circles. Rather, it is a paternal language of authority that Tahmasb reveals as he comes to narrate his life story and his relationships whether with his ever-present guide Ali, his rebellious brothers Sam and Alqas Mirza, or the Ottoman Sultan Sulayman and his sons Selim and Bayazid.[54]

Tahmasb continuously referred to Ali as "My Lord" (*āqā-yi man*).[55] *Āqā* is a Mongol term denoting seniority and a variety of patrilineal kinship ties—fathers, paternal uncles, older brothers. The term is also applied with reverence to other forms of "superior" beings—such as God or members of Muhammad's holy family (*sayyid*)—that surpass biological ties. In Tahmasb's conception of loyalty and devotion, paternity and fraternity are not bound by consanguinity.[56] Such constructs are most likely shaped by paradigms of authority prevalent in mystic orders that bind disciples in obedience and submission to their spiritual masters. Here I have been inspired by the anthropologist Abdella Hammoudi's study on the cultural foundations of Moroccan authoritarianism. Hammoudi illustrates how sets of emotional relations between master and disciple evolved in mystic initiations and extended beyond sufi circles to attain a new credibility as the main operative power relations in the social and political life of sixteenth-century Morocco. I see Tahmasb as attempting to delineate one such cultural schema of domination and submission, in which mystical, familial, and imperial ethics appear as replicas of one another, each reinforcing the other.

With the *Memoir*, Shah Tahmasb defines his authority (*vilāyat*), choosing one definition of holiness amid a medley of available forms that his father, Isma'il, had embraced collectively. Through Tahmasb's narrative, we gain a glimpse of the nature of the piety that allowed him to claim the special status of friend of god (*valī*) and are introduced to the cast of holy friends in his newly constructed (Musavi) genealogy. As we have seen one character, Ali, emerged as Tahmasb's ever-present companion. From the very rise of Islam, when leadership of the *umma,* the Muslim community, fell out of the hands of the Prophet's nuclear family, a group of lovers (*muhibbān*) of Ali had congregated around him and his descendants. The betrayal of the family of the Prophet was subsumed in the pivotal event of the martyrdom of Muhammad's grandson Husayn, Ali and Fatima's son, by the Umayyad clan, who would come to rule Islamdom for the next century (682–740). The martyrdom of Husayn in Karbala is located at the "navel of the narrative" of Shi'i history.[57] Partisans of Ali continued to imagine and hope for a time when leadership in the Islamic community would return to the family of truth and justice, who were privy to the inner (*bātin*) meanings of Islam due to their bloodline. Alid genealogy was the site in which some Muslims located their hope (*dār al-imān*) for an ideal polity within Islamdom. And there was a group among these supporters of Ali who we are told "exaggerated" their love for him to the extent that they considered Ali as divine and omnipresent, accessible to those who were endowed with a virtual and visceral awareness of him. For those devotees of Ali who supported the Safavi revolutionary call (*da'wa*), Isma'il had represented such a hope because Tahmsab's father had placed himself within one such lineage and Alid drama of history. Although in public Tahmasb rejects his father's role as messiah, he maintains Isma'il's genealogical associations as well as his particular coloring of Alid veneration. Tahmasb could have very well included these lines written by his father in his *Memoir* to capture his hue of Alid devotion:

> Know for certain, Ali is the Sea of Truth [*haqīqat*], he is the eternal
> life of honor.
> Those who do not recognize Ali as truth [or God] are absolute unbelievers.[58]

Tahmasb, however, alters the nature of Isma'il's Alid loyalty. Unlike his father, he does not claim to be the incarnation or manifestation of Ali on earth but rather is Ali's friend (*valī*) and

intimate companion; therefore, he would reject the following
lines ascribed to Isma'il:

> In me is prophethood [and] the mystery of Holiness.
> I am God's eye [or God himself]; come now, O blind man gone
>   astray, to behold the truth I am the Absolute doer of whom they
>   speak.
> Sun and Moon are in my power. [59]

In fact, in the later Safavi period, many *ghulāt* lines like these
are edited out of Isma'il's poetry.[60] As Tahmasb begins to consolidate his power, he prefers to toy with the idea that his reign is
but a prelude to the unveiling of the hidden Imam and clubs to
death a group of Qizilbash who venerated him as the messiah
(1551). His Edict of Sincere Repentance (1556) and his decree
designating the jurist Karaki as the vice regent of the Imams
(1533) are public confirmations of his rebellion against his father's image. In conjunction with such public acts, Tahmasb provides in his *Memoir* a more personal face to the recorded acts
that survive from the Safavi official past. A particular Alid lineage (Musavi) and narrative continue to be appropriated in
Tahmasb's story of his reign. But Alid *ghulāt* loyalty is reserved
for Ali alone. In Tahmasb's newly adopted cosmology, there is
no room for new revelations and prophetic experiences.

Why would Shah Tahmasb choose the genre of autobiography, specified as *tazkire,* to render a personal—in his view, more
honest—version of history for his Safavi heirs, for future Shi'i
lovers of Ali as well as for his western (Ottoman) and eastern
(Adil/Qutb Shahis) neighbors?[61] The choice is intriguing because
the genre was unusual for a ruler in premodern Islamdom.
Babur (r. 1526–1530), the founder of the Indo-Timurid
(Mughal) dynasty in India, is another exception; at least this is
what historiography claims.[62] But, obviously, Babur's authoring
of a first-person narrative was not "the only real autobiography
in the Islamic lands." These two near contemporaneous memoirs of Muslim rulers need to be studied together, particularly
given the fact that both rulers were educated in the same cultural

milieu of the Timurid court that nurtured the "high" arts and sciences. [63] Both texts are early examples of an effervescence of royal memoirs that would emerge from the eastern world of Islamdom. Moreover, these personal narratives demonstrate a self-consciousness despite the absence of a hyperconscious Western modern self and in spite of their issuing from non-Western arenas. Babur and Tahmasb's memoirs expose the cultural chauvinism of Western scholarly assertions that "autobiography is not to be found outside of our [Western] cultural area; one would say that it expresses a concern peculiar to Western man."[64] It also opens the question of why the West defines its identity so strongly in terms of autobiography.[65]

For Shah Tahmasb to write a prose narrative in the first person was particularly distinctive. His father and predecessor, the holy messiah king Isma'il, had expressed his divine visions in the more conventional form of sufi poetry—conventional, that is, for mystics like Attar and Hafez as well as for aspiring messiahs like Fazlullah Astarabadi (d. 1394) or Shah Nimatullah Vali (d. 1430). Shah Tahmasb was attempting to relate a different message and portray his singularity through the medium of a first-person narrative in prose. This *tazkire*, I shall argue, was a vehicle for Tahmasb to chisel a new image of himself as pious Shi'i mystic king, deviating from that of his godlike father, Isma'il.

Although Tahmasb found a way to express himself that gave him some autonomy from his father, writing about himself involved defining his relationships with Ali, his father, brothers, sons, the Muslim community at large, and, ultimately, God. My work on the *Memoir* corroborates Natalie Davis's study on boundaries and the sense of self in the completely different context of sixteenth-century France—a study in which she questions Jacob Burkhard's dictum that the discovery of self in the Renaissance was predicated on an ability to distinguish oneself from a group.[66] Davis contends that within this embeddedness in a group identity people worked out strategies for self-expression and autonomy. In fact, she maintains that poverty and powerlessness impeded such self-descriptions rather than immersion in a group. In his attempt to engrave one such novel image in the imaginations of his contemporaries as a model of sovereignty for his Safavi descendants to emulate, Tahmasb drew inspiration from a variety of available genres, including versified mystical diaries (Ruzbihan Baqli's *Kashf al-asrâr*), hagiographies of mystics (*manâqib*), and biographical dictionaries of religious scholars or poets, mixed in with Irano-Islamic "mirrors of princes."

It is through the medium of dreams, seen as a communicative and experiential channel with the divine, that Tahmasb narrates his mystical journeys so directly linked to his day-to-day experiences. Dreams punctuate focal events in Tahmasb's personal narrative as he carefully dates them. One wonders whether Tahmasb may have kept an earlier diary that he used for the writing of this *Memoir.* He must have been familiar with Babur's *Memoir,* for Babur had solicited Isma'il's aid to fight for his dominion. Tahmasb was certainly conscious of the annals style of chronicling the events and lives of individuals, prevalent among Safavi historians. When Babur's son Humayun takes refuge at the Safavi court in 1544, Tahmasb orders that a calligrapher be assigned the task of recording Humayun's day-to-day activities while a guest in Iran.[67] Biography as a literary form occupied a unique and familiar space in medieval Islamicate written culture. Because Islamic scholars relied on second-person reported deeds and sayings uttered by the Prophet as a sacred source of divine law, knowledge of the whereabouts and character of the "transmitters" was crucial to determining the trustworthiness of the report. In the process of this inquiry into the lives of the transmitters of the Prophet's axioms, a genre of biographical dictionaries crystallized that in time extended beyond religiolegal spheres into mysticism, the arts, and the administrative sciences. Biographical writing came to encompass every social and occupational category.[68] Diaries as a form of modern-day note taking—jotting down dates of birth, deaths, important events, and even recording first-person accounts that are incorporated into the entries of biographical dictionaries—were research tools that provided a medium for the shaping of the personal diary.[69] Historically, diaries "were the source from which the materials were derived for two types of historiography: the biographical and the annalistic."[70] By the early modern period, there were several mediums through which Muslims could express themselves in the first person, whether through mystical poetry, captivity memoirs, or dream books (*khwābnāma*).[71] Although accounts of dreams do appear in many kinds of Islamicate literary forms, their conjoined use in the midst of a first-person narration serves a distinct purpose, revealing the nature and persona of the seer/autobiographer.

The permeation of dreams in a variety of Islamicate genres—whether biography, poetry, hagiography, or history—speaks of a culture that thought of dreaming as an integral part of the experience of being. It alludes to a culture that was mindful of human experience in both the realm of sleep and the realm of wakefulness. All pious Muslims dreamed, it was thought, for dreams were understood as palpable experiences that distinguished the individual as the recipient of God's favor.[72] A typology of dreams that evinces a hierarchy of potential dreamers can be discerned from the preliminary work that has been conducted on the significance of dreams in Islamicate cultures.[73] All dreams assume a relationship between the dreamer and the divine. A third party enters at times into this equation as the dream interpreter, a sort of official storyteller who canonizes the "real" meaning of the dream.[74] Prophets like Joseph in the Qur'an are blessed with knowledge of the symbols divulged in dreams, and thanks to their preferred status, they can publicize the future.[75]

All sorts of authority figures from sultans to mystics and theologians come to cite dreams as a means of legitimizing their power. Each dream narrative reveals the particularity of the dreamer's relationship with God as well as their related roles on earth. Roy Mottahedeh characterizes the relationship between the Muslim ruler and God as compactual.[76] Through the act of making a dream public, the ruler pledges his faith in God and promises to serve God and his creation with justice and compassion. In return, God protects the dominion of the sovereign. With the seven dreams recorded in his *Memoir*, Tahmasb defines the nature of the compact he was negotiating with God through Ali. The example that Mottahedeh provides—a "dream of sovereignty" that the Buyid ruler Rukn al-Dawla is said to have had, foretelling his unexpected victory in Isfahan against the Samanids—is significant because of the way in which it is culturally understood. According to Rukn al-Dawla's vizier, Ibn al-'Amid, who narrates and interprets this dream, God saved his patron's dominion because he had "formed an 'intention' that was 'correct' for a king, and because the king had made the appropriate vows."[77] There exists an interactive role between sovereign and God in this compact. The ruler has to commit himself to God and to the Muslim community. He has to promise to engage in public works and show kindness toward his subjects.

Tahmasb's portrayal of himself throughout this *Memoir* encompasses all of these general characteristics. Like Rukn al-Dawla's representation by his vizier, Tahmasb personally confirms his rule through dreams in the image of a king who has entered a compact with God, confirming his status as shadow of God on earth. Tahmasb acts as the interpreter of his dreams, and as a first-person narrator of his dreams, he reveals how he responds to these dreams. As Mottahedeh points out with his customary acumen, such dream vows also serve the purpose of articulating one's commitment to a particular group. In the case of Tahmasb, he vows his personal and formal promise of service to the partisans of Ali (Shi'is). But as an aspiring Alid saint (*vali*), Tahmasb records dreams that represent an esoteric layer of this compactual relationship, for the dream grants the seer access to divine inspiration and inner prophecy. The active role of the dreamer lies in fulfilling his obligation of ruling with justice and in allowing him to enter into the kingdom of heaven and hence claim the status of living saint. Dreams in Shi'ism represented a continuing source of inspiration for the Imams. As we shall see with Tahmasb, such visionary dreams lend themselves to a more allegorical or symbolic interpretation. They are closer in content and imagery to the visionary dreams of mystics like those related by Ibn al-Arabi, Sohrawardi, and Najm al-din Kubra. Dreams served the narrative purpose of legitimizing new ideas as well, whether theological, legal, or metaphysical. The people who were in the world of dreams identified the seer with a particular genealogy and interpretation of Islam. They also sanctified the seer. For Tahmasb to have dreamt of Ali is an obvious sign of his Shi'i faith; however, he also hopes that the dream will win him the status of *valī*, or saint, which ultimately is a socially sanctioned station. The ways in which one experienced the world of dreams—whether asleep (*khwāb*), awake, or semiawake (*vāqī'a*) or whether one heard or saw a holy figure in one of these states—was an indication of how close the dreamer was to the divine. Dreams served as a measuring stick in the ontological relationship between spirit and matter, a mediating channel between the realms of heaven and earth. As we shall see through the progression of Tahmasb's dreams, from his first dream in which he sees Ali smile at him to his final dream in which he experiences the brilliant presence of God, Tahmasb maps out his eventual ascent to heaven.

Tahmasb's writing reflects a refined education, which began in Herat (1516–1522), the former capital of the Timurid court of Husayn Bayqara (r. 1469–1506). Husayn Bayqara was the last and perhaps the greatest Timurid patron of the arts. Tahmasb entered a vibrant courtly milieu of painters, calligraphers, poets, and musicians, who now created in the name of their new patrons, the conquering Safavis (1510–1513). The six years of Tahmasb's childhood that he spent in Herat between the ages of two and eight sparked his early passion for painting. Tahmasb was not only an avid patron of the visual arts in his youth but also a good painter and calligrapher in his own right. According to the court historian Qazi Ahmad, Tahmasb was "drawn toward this wonder-working art, in which he was a master."[78] We even have one of his signed miniatures, which reveals a sense of humor and the playfulness of this king who paints a caricature of a royal butler by shaping his belly appropriately in accordance with his name Karpuz "Melon" Sultan. His academic education would have included the religious sciences—Qur'an and hadith—as well as poetry and history. So there is no doubt about Tahmasb's ability to have written this piece, particularly given that it is written in simple Persian and at times in a laconic style. Tahmasb displays his knowledge of religious and secular literature, quoting his preferred poets throughout—Nizami, Hafez, and Sa'di. His choice of Persian over Turkish is indicative of his cultural identification. The Timuri-Mongol ruler Babur, on the other hand, chooses to write his memoir in Chagatay Turkish. These royal choices of a particular language of personal expression reveal a historical moment, when mixed Turco-Iranian cultural spheres (Ottomans, Safavis, Uzbeks, Mughals) that used Persian as their main literary language began to assert their cultural singularity.

So I am reading Tahmasb's *Memoir* both discursively and structurally as a new Safavi icon that represents the subtle features of a royal face that has matured through the long and arduous process of consolidating his father's newly conquered domains. Having survived a turbulent regency and having secured his Ottoman and Uzbek borders, Tahmasb speaks from a position of security, at times with a tinge of bitterness, as he looks back on the early years of tumult and betrayal. Through this reconstruction of history, Tahmasb voices a imperial language of power, presenting a new rationale for control that reflects a novel balance that the Safavi house had finally effected with the Qizilbash, the landed Iranian elite (Tajik), and the Shi'i ulama. We should not forget that although Tahmasb had established himself as king and protector of the *shari'a*, he still aspired to be recognized as saint. And as a would-be saint, he expressed feelings and beliefs that cannot be separated from his political conduct.

What Tahmasb believed or wanted us to believe was that order (*nizām*), security (*amniyat*)—and justice (*'idālat*)—and by

extension the Safavi realms—had been bestowed on him thanks
to his devotion to Ali. Due to his status as a pious Muslim, forgiving and merciful toward his rebelling brothers and individual
Qizilbash generals, compassionate to the plight of the poor and
the aging, he was indeed a true ritual- and law-abiding king.
Tahmasb associates himself with the station (*tabaqa*) of kings
who distinguished themselves from all of humanity (*kull-i afrād-
i insān*) due to their special (*khāss*) status.[79] Selected by God,
their duty was to act as the axis around which stability on earth
flowed. In his preface, Tahmasb refers to God as king (*pādishah*)
and takes on the role of a monarch on earth enforcing the divine
prohibitions against wine, adultery, prostitution, gambling, and
the visual arts. In Tahmasb's *Tazkire*, there is no trace of his former appreciation of painting. He is writing no longer as a patron
of the visual arts, for with his Edict of Sincere Repentance in
1556 (*tawba*) he had banned painting, a fine aspect that
conflicted with the culture of Muslim anti-iconoclasm.
Tahmasb's Edict of Sincere Repentance, which is a pivotal event
narrated in his *Memoir*, is once again framed through a dream
that he has in the holy Shi'i city of Mashad. This is the dream
that prompts Tahmasb to break publicly with his father's culture
of drinking, yet another symbol of Isma'il's *ghulāt* ways. Wine
was central to the religious rituals of Qizilbash Islam.[80] The prohibition of wine meant breaking with an antinomian way of being closely linked to mystical dancing, music, singing, and gaz-
ing at beautiful male youth (*amrad*), all of which were ritual
mediums of union with the divine. Tahmasb bans all these transcendental rituals in his decrees and edicts of sincere repentance,
categorizing them along with wine, sodomy, and the wonder-
making art of painting as undisciplined passions.
   The culture of drinking was part of the cosmology of those
sufis who believed in worldly union with God, and wine was a
metaphor for transcendence in sufi poetry. Tahmasb literally rejects wine as a way of attaining divine union, further clarifying
his position within the ongoing cultural clash between
ontologies of spirit and matter.[81] Throughout his *Memoir*,

Tahmasb reserves divinity for God alone (*hazrat-i pādishah*) and prophecy to Muhammad, the seal of the prophets (*khātam al-nabiyin*). Although he characterizes Muhammad as human, quoting the hadith, "I was a prophet, while Adam was still between water and clay," he moves away from *ghuluww* toward Muhammad, though still maintaining a monist (*wahdat-i wujūdī*) sensibility when he speaks of Ali. Tahmasb asserts his Shi'ism, confirming Ali as the direct successor of Muhammad by designation and right (*bar vasī va bar haqq*). He depicts Ali not only as the victorious "lion of God" (*asadullāh al-ghālib*) but as the site of supernatural and occult manifestation (*mazhar al-'ajā'ib va al-qarā'ib*), thereby revealing the particular exaggerated hues (*mufawwida*) of his Alid devotion. Ali and Muhammad are of the same light (*nūr*), flesh (*lahm*), blood (*dam*), body (*jism*), and spirit (*rūh*). In the hierarchy of divinity, they hold equal status. Tahmasb preserves a *ghulāt* flavor of Qizilbash devotion to Ali, in that he represents Ali as divine, but Isma'il's claim to messiahship is rejected in his cosmology that sees no room for prophecy after Muhammad and Ali. All those who follow them can only be their friends and close associates or their delegates on earth. Alid charisma is transferred to Tahmasb as a member of Ali's family. In Tahmasb's cosmology, humans can see and communicate with the divine through dreams, particularly those special ones who are blessed with an Alid pedigree.

In the process of breaking from his father's claims to divinity, Tahmasb broke from the warrior (*ghāzī*) temper of his father's persona and thus found himself needing to redefine current notions of masculinity (*mardānagī*). True, there is no braver than Ali in the battlefield, but Tahmasb often recalls Ali's dictum "that battle is but a ruse" and so chooses to fight wisely and justly rather than respond militarily to every provocation of the Ottomans.[82] The historical memory of Ali opting for arbitration to secure unity among Muslims shaped Tahmasb's imaging of his holy hero. Ali's representation as a valiant warrior (*asad allah*) is dulled, while his wisdom and concern for the well-being of the Muslim community are highlighted. Tahmasb is here redefining the notion of manliness (*mardānagī*) linked to the image of Isma'il as a warrior who immersed himself in the culture of hunting, feasting, and banqueting (*bazm u razm*) after his defeat by the Ottomans (1514), all aspects of world-embracing asceticism. Instead, it is wisdom, peace, devotion, and humility that delineates the manliness or "humanness" (*āqā'ī*) of Ali, and, by reflection, Tahmasb. Tahmasb's preference for fishing over hunting wild boars is symbolic of this new, perhaps more urbanized style of masculinity that seems to be closely tied to the world-rejecting sufism.[83] Tahmasb's fear of impurity toward the end of his life verges on paranoia. His court chronicler states that he considered most objects ritually impure (*najis*): he would throw half of his food into the water and fire; he would not eat at formal banquets; he would spend one whole day in the *hammām* and the next clipping his nails: "He abstained from all the pleasure [*lizzat*] of life and for nearly twenty years he did not mount a horse."[84] Tahmasb, thus, altered the font of Isma'il's sufism.

With Tahmasb's abdication of virility, his display of modesty in the presence of his master (Ali and God), his habits of abstention and bodily control, we are dealing with a process of submission, which Hammoudi characterizes as part of the obligatory passage through a feminine role every disciple must follow. In the path to masterhood, the adept submits to the guide's authority, grounded and sanctified by the concepts and procedures involved in mystical initiation. Hammoudi associates this feminine passage with every man in a situation of submission who must give himself the illusion that he is accepting the condition of obedience. But I think in the case of early modern Iran, it is not necessarily a gendered stage, for it involves a personal choice that Tahmasb makes to follow a particular mystic path. As an ascetic virtuoso, Tahmasb rejects attributes of violence, pleasure, and virility associated with a culture of chivalry (*javānmardī*) that tied members of guilds to mystical orders through the veneration of Ali as their patron saint. With Tahmasb's renunciation of his father's world-embracing sufism, he alters the font of his authority and masculinity. He also emphasizes an altered image of Ali as generous and wise rather than a valiant lion in the battlefield.

Through a dream that he has in his grandfather's (Shaykh Haydar) house in Ardabil, Tahmasb presents his most explicit statement rejecting Isma'il's mission (*da'wa*). In the dream, Tahmasb cannot distinguish between two words—*zuhūr* (manifestation) and *khurūj* (sortie)—that Shaykh Safi utters to him. When he awakes, he wonders what Shaykh Safi could have uttered to him and concludes that it must have been *khurūj*, for *zuhūr* is a special word reserved for the Mahdi. He wonders what exactly *khurūj* means, and in the course of his narrative, it becomes clear that he is defining it as victory over the Ottomans. Emphasizing a future manifestation of the Mahdi, Tahmasb thereby rejects his father's claims as Mahdi and divine, claims preserved in Isma'il's poetry, in coins, and in epigraphy. Later editions of Isma'il's poetry censor those lines where he refers to himself as Mahdi. He dismisses the messianic layer of the meaning of *zuhūr* applied to Isma'il in the early chronicles like that of Khwandamir. I have addressed Tahmasb's curious silence surrounding the figure of Isma'il throughout his narrative, which is finally broken when Tahmasb addresses his father's defeat at Chaldiran (1514); the chroniclers and Sam Mirza, in contrast, just gloss over it as if it were just any old defeat. Tahmasb deals with Chaldiran directly, once again in the context of a discourse on chivalry (*marδanigī*).

Tahmasb records a taunting remark that the Ottoman Sultan Sulayman, Hazrat-i Khwandigar, addresses to him: "Your father Shah Isma'il fought with my father [Selim I], you claim to be brave, come and fight, and if you will not fight, then desist from your claims of bravery."[85] Tahmasb's response to Sulayman, which he records in the *Tazkire,* encapsulates some of the predominant features of his new language of power. He first quotes from the Qur'an (2:191) that God is the greatest of all beings: "And in his words he has said do not throw yourself into perdition while making holy war [*jihad* and *ghaza*]. So how can I issue a *fatwā* of war between two Muslim armies, when in number the one is ten times the size of my army, and thus expose these Muslims to such danger? My father on that day he fought with your father, Durmish Khan [Shamlu Lalé and paternal cousin] and the other Qizilbash generals [Amirs], and most of the army was inebriated. They had drunk wine all night and began the song of war, and this was so irrational [*nāma'qūl*] and improper.[86] From that time on, whenever the story of Chaldiran comes about, I wish bad prayers upon Durmish Khan, who deceived my father in battle."[87]

Not only does Tahmasb justify Isma'il's defeat, but he provides pious reasoning for his own nonengagement in war with Sulayman, characterizes Qizilbash drinking habits as irrational (*nāma'qūl*) and incorrect behavior, and proceeds to introduce his first Edict of Sincere Repentance (*tawba*). Tahmasb introduces a dream (*khwāb*) that he has in the holy city of Mashad, in which he hears the prayer leader of Medina, Mir Sayyid Muhammad, telling him to establish the *shari'i* prohibitions (*man'āhī*) so that he will be assured victories over the Ottomans and the Uzbeks. Tahmasb insists on the prohibitions despite the response of the Qizilbash generals, who resist the ban on wine, arguing that it is a necessary accouterment of sovereignty (*zarūri-yi saltanat*). It must have been a difficult decision that required Tahmasb to furnish cogent proof for his actions. He promises the Qizilbash that he will sleep that night with an intention (*niyat*) to seek a sign of divine guidance. That night, in a half-conscious dream (*vāqi'a*), he sees the market-inspector (*muhtasib*) of Mashad, Mir Hadi, holding his hand by the tomb of Imam Reza. The message is clear; he awakes, recounts the dream to his generals, reenacts it, and enforces the edict. Once the realms of sleep and wakefulness converge, he says, "Thank God that my realm and my troops have repented from wine, all my domains [*mamlikat*] have now became pure." Tahmasb claims that he was twenty years old then (1534) and composed the following quatrain:

With the waters of repentance did we wash away the stains
of pulverized emerald [hashish] and liquefied ruby [wine].

Unlike his father, Tahmasb did not claim to be that messiah
who could abrogate the *shari'a;* instead, he portrayed himself as
a mystic king who ruled his realms with justice and reason. His
special status as "sufi guide" allowed him to maintain communication with the divine through dreams. And as an Irano-Islamic
monarch, Tahmasb claimed as well a special stature (*makhsūs,
mumtāz*) designed and protected by the grace of God to maintain temporal and moral order as the shadow of God on earth.
Tahmasb encoded this role in his choice of the chronogram for
his accession as "shadow" *zill* (900 + 30), thus rejecting his
chronicler Amir Mahmud's chronogram of eschatological messiah (*akhir al-zamān*).

At times, Tahmasb voices his image as a just Muslim monarch, upholding the Shi'i cause, building mosques, maintaining
order and the humility of a dervish to account for his early impotence. He also attempts to mitigate his passivity toward Ottoman assaults but in the process legitimizes his politics. Through
the intermediary of seven dreams, Tahmasb communicates with
the holy (Ali, Shaykh Safi al-din, and Shaykh Shihab al-din
Ahari), consulting with them over imperial matters, whether
military or religious. Unlike his father, whom early chroniclers
(like Khwandamir, 1524) portray as the locus of divine authority and inspiration (*bar zabān-i ilhām bayān kard*), Tahmasb positions himself within that comfortable distance of dreams that
had become a recognized mystical medium of communicating
with the divine—an accepted distance between the holy and the
human.[88] In limiting the universality of cosmic potentialities to
particular revelatory mediums of dreams and loci like Imams
and sufis after the prophet Muhammad, Tahmasb was also
affirming the Muslim monotheistic position of one transcendent
divinity as well as the centrality and finality of monotheistic
prophethood. Alas, Tahmasb was breaking away from the
ghulāt heritage of his father, grandfather, and great-grandfather.

Tahmasb lays out this new cosmology and ontology in his preface and weaves it into the seven dreams and twelve royal episodes in the body of the *Memoir.*

LOYALTY, GENEROSITY, AND COMPASSION:
TAHMASB'S CHIVALRIC LANGUAGE
OF PATERNITY

Let me provide you with a few more layers of Tahmasb's political context as a way of delving deeper into the *Memoir* and pondering the element of representation in it. In his address to the
Ottoman ambassadors who had arrived in the Safavi capital,
Qazvin (16 July 1562), Tahmasb surrendered Bayazid, the renegade son of Sulayman, and thus composed for the occasion a
history of Ottoman-Safavi relations seven years after the signing
of their peace treaty of Amasya.[89] Tahmasb pays special attention to his relationship with the Ottoman sultan Sulayman and
his grand viziers Ibrahim and Rustam Pasha throughout the
three Safavi-Ottoman wars.[90] The *Memoir* ends somewhat awkwardly with the Bayazid affair (1559–1562), which involved the
rebellious son of Sulayman, who took refuge in Safavi territory.
Tahmasb uses the episode to delineate his understanding of the
nature of reciprocity and mutual esteem this new alliance with
the Ottomans entailed. Tahmasb positions himself as paternal
king, chiding Bayazid for disobeying his father Sulayman (*valī
nimat*) and for not having honored his filial duties (*huqūq-i
vālidayn*): "He [Bayazid] has been ungrateful to his father and
has rebelled and not respected those filial duties which are required to be observed according to Qur'anic verses and divine
axioms. What right [*haqq*] have they [Bayazid and Selim] to
fight when Sulayman [*hazrat-i khwandigār*] is seated robust and
healthy on the throne?" This background sheds light on the
meaning of the magnificent gift of the illuminated "Book of
Kings," known as the Houghton *Shāhnāme,* that Tahmasb
sends four years later to Selim (r. 1566–1582), the successor and
son of Sulayman. Tahmasb acts like a protective father toward

Selim, whose succession he feels he had safeguarded thanks to Tahmasb's suppression of Selim's brother's (Bayazid) earlier ambition to rule. As the senior patriarch of the Muslim community, Shah Tahmasb bestowed the *Shāhnāme,* representing the most creative endeavors of Safavi painters and calligraphers, to his Ottoman son Sultan Selim on his accession. Beyond the artistic splendor of this generous gift, the choice of the text, the "Epic of Kings," is symbolic of the self-image Shah Tahmasb wished to transmit.[91] We have seen how in the *Shāhnāme* Iranian kings, princes, and warriors—descendants from the noble bloodlines of charismatic rulers and fearless heroes—are constantly challenged to balance the temporal with the spiritual, to succumb to the temptations of power and the arrogance it can foster. Kings are to rule their sons and subjects with justice, and they are to obey the king with reverence. Such is the advice Tahmasb offers through his gift to his new son Selim, who will now have to deal with the vicissitudes of kingship. Along with the generous offering of the *Shāhnāme,* Tahmasb sends the new Ottoman sultan a Qur'an. These two treasures—the *Shāhnāme* and the Qur'an—exhibit the features of Tahmasb's twin language of Irano-Islamic authority.

The rhetoric of paternity Tahmasb develops in his narrative conveys the way in which fathers should treat their sons, as well as the nature of reciprocity such filial bonds anticipate. Tahmasb applies this account to reflect on loyalty and obligation within the Safavi household, as well. What he intersperses in the Safavi-Ottoman narrative are the other, more internal yet equally pivotal events of his life. His relationship with the Qizilbash and with his own family, particularly his rebelling brothers, Sam and Alqas Mirza, structures the rest of his narrative.[92] Tahmasb seems to have had to account for the killing of old loyal Qizilbash disciples of his father from important Turkmen tribes, like the Ustajlu and Takkalu, during his troubled regency, although he continues to refer to his realm (*mamlikat*) as the domains (*vilayat*) of the Qizilbash. After all, the Qizilbash had conquered the Safavi territory and shared in its rule and administration. Yet what the chroniclers allude to through their annal-style recording of events, Shah Tahmasb states openly.[93] He divulge the machinations of independent-minded Qizilbash generals like Ulamah Takkalu and speaks of these disclosures and punishments as fortunate turns of events, acts of God that secured him his kingship through his troubled regency. And this is where Tahmasb's closing statement in his preface (*dîbâchah*)—excusing himself for his simple style but speaking the truth free of stains of dissimulation and lies—rings true. Tahmasb is presenting his personal story, which perhaps the official chroniclers with their ornate literary (*munshiyânah*) style are unable to divulge completely.[94] Tahmasb is critical of the recalcitrant Qizilbash generals and couches his criticism in the language of justice: kings are responsible for the security and well-being of their subjects. "What use is war between the generals [*amîr*]?" he says. "Let us tend to the populace [*reaya*]."

Although the master dominates with all his authority, he often needs to display tenderness and care toward a disciple who is being tested. Here lies an ambiguity inherent in the figure of master-saint-king, who is to be generous and modest as well as dominating. Throughout his narrative, Tahmasb constantly mediates between these roles. The way Tahmasb relates to his disciples is not so different from the way he relates to his brothers, but the role of disciple brother seems just as ambiguous. Their submission does not exclude either feelings of ambivalence or awareness of the transitional nature of their submissive role, and they often act on this awareness.[95] Tahmasb relates quarrels that arise between himself and his brothers and disciples, in which dissent and violence is not precluded. Tahmasb uses episodes relating his brothers' betrayals to reflect on loyalty and obligation within the larger Safavi patrimonial household, as well as within the Muslim community. His relationship with his army composed of disciples and his relationship with his own kin are reflective of one another. In response to his renegade brother's assertion to Sulayman that he enjoys Qizilbash backing, Tahmasb tries to resolve the ambiguity: "The Qizilbash," he says, "would have their heads chopped off before they remove their crowns [*taj*] in the path of sufiness [*sufīgarī*] there is but one spiritual guide [*murshīd*] and even if there may be one hundred thousand princelings [*pādishāhzādah*], they [Qizilbash] would not even look at them." Although we know that this was not the case, here, I think, is an example of the license the *I* voice granted Tahmasb as a means of expressing his expectations of devotee loyalty.

Notions of respect and allegiance—whether in familial, military, or religious contexts—are expressed through the filial language of paternity and fraternity used in mystic circles, in which the disciple is referred to as a "son" and the master as "father." In response to his renegade brother's claims that the Ottoman Sultan Sulayman has called him his son (*pisar-i man*) and has given him troops and money, Tahmasb says: "Kingship [*mulk*] is not mine, nor yours, nor Sulayman's. There exists a God, and sovereignty is his, he will give to whom he pleases. [W]hat are all these worldly things good for when you have sold your faith? I am not as stupid [*ablah*] as you to prattle about this worldly power." His critique of his rebellious brother holds true for the Ottoman sultan as well. To Sulayman, Tahmasb questions why two Muslim rulers should go to war with one another: "we [Tahmasb] shall not sell religion [*dīn*] for worldly concerns [*dunya*]." In other words, two Muslim brothers should not fight one another because religious solidarity should be placed above territorial gains. Tahmasb goes on to frame his brother's rebellion against him as a rebellion against God. Faith and kinship ties are sanctified, as a holy hierarchy of paternal authority is delineated progressively from God to Ali to Tahmasb, to his brothers, sons, his generals, disciples, and subjects. Tahmasb articulates a discourse of social arrangements that sheds light on the cultural foundations of this style of domination, in which the master-disciple schema is the most potent metaphor of community.

Tahmasb's sensitivity at not being considered a Muslim and an equal to Sulayman is expressed in Ottoman imperial rhetoric.

Tahmasb records a *fatwā* issued unanimously by Ottoman men of religion (*ulama, mashāyikh*), in which the Safavis are called infidels (*kāfir*). The *fatwā* confirms that it is religiously lawful (*halāl*) to loot the property or kill the people and wives of all those (from *sipāhī* to *reaya*) living under the Safavi shadow, whether Muslim, Armenian, or Jew. Tahmasb responds, "I said this is a fine *fatwā*. We who pray, fast, go on the pilgrimage, pay alms, and follow all the requirements of religion [*dīn*], they call me an infidel! The Lord above will judge between us." Even as he attempted to embrace a more acceptable version of Shi'ism, Tahmasb's particular Alid heritage exposed him to traditional attacks by Sunnis against the outcast "heretics" (*rāfizī*). His Edicts of Sincere Repentance, his officiating Safavi Alid (Musavi) genealogy with the new recension of the *Safvat al-safā* (1533), his naming of jurisconsult Shaykh Ali Karaki as the vice regent of the Imam (*nā'ib al-imām*), and his whole language of piety expressed in this memoir should be understood in this self-conscious light.

As a Muslim, Tahmasb continuously speaks of Sulayman with respect but blames Sulayman's viziers, Ibrahim and Rustam Pasha, for their machinations and evil intentions with Safavi renegades like Ulamah Takkalu and Alqas Mirza. He calls Sulayman's grand vizier Ibrahim Pasha an opium addict (*taryākī*) who gets bold when he is high and says, "Whatever I command, Sulayman will follow," and when sober, claims that he is but a slave of Sulayman and has no choice but to follow his orders. Tahmasb respects Sulayman's role as holy warrior (*ghāzī*), fighting against the Christians (*farangī*) so much so that when Sulayman is on *jihad* against Austria in 1532, he says that this is why he refuses to attack the Ottomans. The cynical interpreter would want to see this claim as an excuse for Tahmasb's inability to attack the Ottomans that year. In either case, Tahmasb's language of Muslim fraternity is telling of his choice of identity. As much as Sulayman is glorified, 'Ubaydullah Khan the Uzbek ruler is demonized as an uncouth beast with no education or respect for Islam. Tahmasb does criticize Sulayman,

however, for not contacting him directly to inquire about his rebelling brother Alqas Mirza. Tahmasb utilizes his own behavior
toward Bayazid to point a finger of insolence (*bī adabī*) at
Sulayman. Using knowledge in his rhetoric of power, Tahmasb
is surprised that the Ottomans have not read works on biography (*sirat*), history (*tārīkh*), and the *Bustan* of Sa'di to understand the basic principles of sovereignty and ethics.[96]
By way of the Alqas Mirza episode, Tahmasb illuminates his
sense of family loyalty, whether ties of the womb "breaking
uterus-bonds" (*silah-i rahim*) or Muslim fellowship. His most
emotional and heartfelt words are found in his discussion of the
betrayal of his favorite brother, Alqas Mirza. Quoting from the
poet Hatifi's *Timūrnāme*, he writes, "I would say Alqas and myself are like Timur and Shahrukh, 'like two swords in one scab-
bard.' Out of all my brothers and children I loved him most."[97]
As an example of affection for Alqas, Tahmasb states that he
had made sure that 250 tomans be given yearly to the *sayyids* of
Mashad to pray at the shrine of Imam Reza for the longevity of
his brother's life. Although Tahmasb gives Alqas Mirza a chance
to repent, out of his "ignorance" Alqas sells his religion (*dīn*) for
temporal power (*dawlat*). Tahmasb exposes his emotions; he
speaks of his melancholy, as he cries and curses his brother: "I
had such a heartache and became very depressed and started to
cry."[98] Even though Alqas was not a uterine brother, Tahmasb
loved him more than his womb brothers (*karāndāsh*) and his
own children.
Notions of respect and loyalty—whether genealogical, political, or religious—are expressed through the filial language of paternity and fraternity. Tahmasb uses the language of paternal
kinship to articulate the nature of the alliance formed between
Alqas and Sulayman, with Alqas boasting to Tahmasb that
Sulayman has called him "my son" (*pisar-i man*). And Tahmasb
is dubious of the Ottoman prince Bayazid when he calls him
simply "Shah Tahmasb," whereas Selim, he says, calls him "my
father" (*pidaram*). What led Alqas astray, according to
Tahmasb, was his embracing of evil ways that were contrary to

the precepts of Islam. Once Alqas Mirza began drinking and engaging in sexual improprieties (*fasq u fujūr*), he abandoned the straight path of devotion and loyalty to God, the Imams, and his older brother. Within the context of the patrimonial language of kingship of the shadow of God on earth, drinking and sexual vices are framed as uncontrolled passions that usher in irrational and chaotic behavior.[99]

Although on the surface we could target Tahmasb as a fabricator fictionalizing his narrative, the way in which he uses fiction is revealing of his message. Tahmasb projects onto the past, and at times masks things he may have felt uneasy about. He attempts, for example, to show that he was in control three years after his accession, when in reality the year 1527 marked the ascendance of a faction of the Qizilbash (Takkalu oymaq) that secured his reign. True, his kingship was then temporarily secure, but he was only thirteen years old and would have to wait another seven years before his reign would be free of different Qizilbash coalitions attempting to place his brother Sam Mirza on the throne. Although Tahmasb has himself appointing governors and bestowing titles (*laqab*) on the leading Qizilbash generals, viziers, and ministers of religion/education (*sadr*) early in his regency, he does draw a progressively more active picture in time. His revisions are rendered with humility; he reports of his first battlefield experience, for instance, by saying simply, "I took a few more steps."[100] With the control of one tribe— Takkalu Hegemony—Tahmasb says, "in Qazvin, now in reality I became *pādishah* [monarch]. I eliminated enemies. In an auspicious hour, I entered the palace [*divānkhānah*] of my father in Qazvin."[101]

That Tahmasb felt it necessity to expose Qizilbash politics and disloyalty toward him is revealing of the shifting nature of Safavid-Qizilbash power and loyalty. In so doing, he was defining the relationship between the Safavi house (*dūdmān*) and the Qizilbash (*oymaq*) in this imperial phase, an ambivalent alliance that seems to have held together thanks to the charisma of Isma'il but one that is shattered with Isma'il's death. Its disintegration finds articulation, as Martin Dickson sees it, with the first civil war that marked the initial twelve years of Tahmasb's reign (1524–1536).

Tahmasb chooses seven dreams that characterize the first two phases of his reign as he maps out his progressive wielding of temporal power along the stations of his spiritual growth.[102] His dreams center around two pivotal events that mark the closure of each stage (1534 and 1555) of his life rule, and their themes set the tone for the future. Tahmasb is writing his *Memoir* during the third phase of his life (1555–1576), which we have characterized as an age of extreme piety during which he became obsessed with ritual purity and physical renunciation. This last stage of Tahmasb's life is his phase of sainthood, and the two final visionary dreams he presents toward the end of his narrative confirm for the audience Tahmasb's initiation into the circle of the "friends of God." The dream event that marks the end of Tahmasb's turbulent regency is the repentance dream (1534), in which he vows his commitment to God and to the Imams at the holy site of the tomb of the eighth Imam in Mashad. This is the event (Edict of Sincere Repentance) that is constructed by Tahmasb as the reason for his ability to campaign successfully against dissidents within his realms and to contain the continual invasions of the Ottomans and the Uzbeks during his second phase of consolidating Safavi dominion (1536–1555).

As Shi'i saint, Tahmasb introduces two last dreams in which God manifests himself to him. The first of these twin dreams (1550) links Tahmasb's attainment of peace with his Ottoman and Uzbek neighbors to God's protection of his throne. This is five years before the peace of Amasya is signed with the Ottomans and is narrated right after the irksome *fatwā* by the Ottomans in which the Safavis were called infidels. With this dream, Tahmasb demonstrates God's judgment on the issue of who is a good Muslim. He sees three moons in the sky—one in the middle and the other two flanking it on the west and east. The western moon is very high, while the eastern moon is small. An illuminated person (*shakhs-i nūrānī*) informs Tahmasb that the western moon represents Sulayman, the eastern moon is 'Ubaydullah the Uzbek, and the one in the middle is himself. Gradually, the eastern moon moves to the middle of the sky, is torn out of the sky, falls onto the earth, and disappears. Afterward, the western moon likewise falls to the earth and vanishes: "And the middle moon like a fluttering piece of paper in the sky slowly descends until it arrived on top of the raised floor [*suffah*] of the throne [*shāhnishīn*] that is in Qazvin where they had laid out my place, on top of the pillows on which I sit."[103]

Four years later (1554), God appears to Tahmasb in the form of a brilliant Qur'anic verse written on the page of the sky:

> I saw in the sky toward Mecca [*qibla*] where the sun set in the evening [west] a dusty line in the sky as though drawn on the page of the heavens. And indeed the one on the ceiling of the sky was more brilliant than the calligraphy of a royal edict [*tamgha*] written on foreign [*farangī*] paper. I read that line that was this verse (Qur'an 2:137):

> But God will suffice thee as against them.
> And he is the all-hearing, the all-knowing.

> I began to shiver when seeing that line, and anxiety filled me. I saw that the verse was like an oscillating wave and the portion of the sky surrounding it was shaking as though the sky was about to be shattered. And I witnessed that the line and the prayer niche [*mihrāb*] were trembling as if a door of the sky had opened up. From agitation I awoke.

This verse represents the refrain that frames Tahmasb's narrative, the particular circumstances of his life story; his longevity of rule and survival are portrayed as divinely devised and planned. To explain his trembling and bewilderment once he awakens from these dreams, Tahmasb draws a revealing analogy. He says that his frenzy must be due to having been in God's imposing presence (*partaw-yi nūr-i hazrat-i illahi tajallī va zuhūr kardah bud*), something like Moses must have experienced in the Sinai (as recorded in *Qisas* and *Akhbār*) and Muhammad during his ascension (*mi'raj*). Tahmasb's dramatic closure presents these divine encounters as proofs of his sainthood, which encapsulates the successive distancing in time between the holy and the human, within Muslim monotheistic historiography— from Moses's vision of God to Muhammad's veiled encounters (*pas-i pardah-yi hijâb*), through which he becomes the spokesman (*mutikallim*) of God. And finally, as a "friend of God," Tahmasb the Alid saintly king comes to communicate with the divine in the realm of dreams.

Unlike his father, who claimed to be the messiah/God, Tahmasb positions himself within the millieu of dreams, which had become recognized means of communicating with the divine from an accepted distance. In limiting the universality of cosmic potentialities after the prophet Muhammad to particular revelatory mediums like dreams and loci like the Imams and sufi masters, Tahmasb was also affirming the monotheistic position of one transcendent divinity as well as the centrality and finality of prophethood. As he was breaking away from the *ghulat* heritage of his father, Tahmasb was taking yet a few more steps in the long process of the Islamization of the Iranian world.

NOTES

1. Shah Tahmasb, *Tazkire-yi Shah Tahmasb,* ed. D. C. Phillott (Calcutta: Asiatic Society, 1912), 12. Contemporary historians have neglected this gem of a source. Except for Martin B. Dickson, who uses it extensively in "Shah Tahmasb and the Uzbeks: The Duel for Khurasan with Ubayd Khan, 930–46/152–40," Ph.D. diss., Princeton University, 1958, and in Martin B. Dickson and Stuart Cary Welch, eds., *The Houghton Shāhnāme,* 2 vols. (Cambridge: Harvard University Press, 1981), and Cornell Fleischer, who used it for "Alqas Mirza," *E. Iranica,* the source remains untapped. Martin Dickson introduced me to the *Tazkire.*

2. The Arabic term *tazkira* is the verbal noun derived from the root *z.k.r. Zakara* in the first form signifies the act of remembering, recalling, recollecting, talking, citing, reporting or relating. Its verbal noun or gerund *tazkira* denotes a message, note, a reminder, or momento. In early modern Irano-Turkic cultural spheres, the

term pronounced as *tazkire* is used to designate one category amid the variety of forms of Islamic biographical literature (*tabaqāt*). Generally, in the Persianate world the *tazkire* records the lives of the members of a particular profession, such as poets, painters, calligraphers, or mystics. In this period, the most common form of *tazkire* was that of poets, which combine anecdotes relating the personality or experiences of the poet with selections from the poet's work. But *tazkire* is also a medium for narrating the lives of mystics and masters of popular religious brotherhoods. The genre of spiritual biography or hagiography (*maqāmāt* or *manāqib*) concentrates on a singular saint or founder of an order so as to memorialize the particular teachings and practices of that order. See John E. Woods, *The Aqquyunlu: Clan, Confederation, Empire,* 2nd ed. (Salt Lake City: University of Utah Press, 1999), 228–229. Also see Ahmad Gulchīn-Ma'ānī, *Tārīkh-i tazkirah'hā-yi Fārsī,* 2 vols. (Tehran: Kitābkhānah-yi Sanā'ī, 1970–1972).

3. In his introduction to *Tazkirāt al-mulūk* (London: Gibb Memorial Series, 1989), 13, Vladimir Minorsky quotes a Venetian merchant (now identified by Aubin as Domenico Romano) who was in Tabriz in 1518: "This Sophy is loved and reverenced by his people as a God and especially by his soldiers, many of whom enter into battle without armor, expecting their master Ishmael to watch over them in fight." Hans Roemer quotes a Qizilbash battle cry without citing the source: "My spiritual leader and master, for whom I sacrifice myself (Qurban oldigim pirüm murşidim)." *Cambridge History of Iran,* ed. Peter Jackson and Lawrence Lockhart (Cambridge: Cambridge University Press, 1986), vol. 6, 214.

4. Khatā'ī, *Il Canzoniere di Shah Isma'il,* ed. Tourkhan Ganjei (Naples: Institudio Orientale) 249:12.

5. Jean Aubin, "L'Avenement des Safavides Reconsideré (Etudes Safavides III)," *Moyen Orient & Ocean Indien* 5 (1988): 42, refers to Isma'il's policies as "le communism des Qizilbsh." In Aubin, "Shah Ismā'īl et les Notables de l'Iraq Persan (Etudes Safavides I), "*Journal of Economic and Social History of the Orient* 2 (1959): 50 he says, "il fet toutes biens communs." On the Safavi connection with Babaki, see Fazl Allah b. Rūzbihān Khunjī-Isfahānī, *Tārīkh-i' 'Ālam Ārā-yi Amīnī,* ed. John E.

Woods (London: Royal Asiastic Society, 1993), f. 140b. See Patricia Crone, "Zoroastrian Communism," *Comparative Studies in Society and History* 36 (1994), on the Khurramiyya. Isma'il is to have shared booty in Georgia in 1500 and in Baku in 1501. Quotes from foreigners confirm this, like Marino Sanuto, *I diarii*, ed. Federico Stefani, Guglielmo Berchet, et al. (Venice: Visentini, 1879–1903), vol. 7, 529–531 (cited in Aubin, "Shah Ismā'il," 40): "Hommes de grand justice et sans aucune avidité, beaucoup plus liberal qu'Alexandre, aussi prodigue de tout, car comme l'argent lui vient il distribue aussitôt. De sorte qu'il parait un Dieu sur terre." In 1515, the Venetian Alfonso de Alberqurque speaks of the largesse of Isma'il with money. Aubin, "Shah Ismā'īl," 52)

6. Ibid., Aubin, "Shah Ismā'īl," 40, quoting Sanuto.

7. Both historians of Isma'il's generation—Amini and Khwandamir—used the symbols of the sun, the crown, and the sword to describe Isma'il's authority. These symbols that were cast as an inheritance from the founder of the Safavi spiritual order, Shaykh Safi al-din (d. 1334). They are related to Isma'il through the medium of two dreams singled out from the multitude of dreams associated with the mystic Shaykh Safi in his hagiography the *Safvat al-safā,* first recorded by Ibn Bazzaz a generation after the death of Safi and commissioned by his son Shaykh Sadr al-din. In one dream, Shaykh Safi is seated on top of a mountain, Qaf, with a sable hat on his head and a sword around his waist. He is confused as to what he a mystic is doing with a sword. He tries to draw his sword but is unable to. He next attempts to lift his hat and consecutively for three times as he raises his hat the sun shines from his head like a brilliant halo (*Safvat,* 87). Shaykh Safi's spiritual guide, Shaykh Zahid (d. 1301), from whom he inherits his order interprets this dream for him. He states that the sword represents the "mandate of sovereignty" (*hukm-i vilāyat*) and the sun represents the "light of sainthood" (*nūr-i vilāyat*). It is no wonder that later Safavis choose this dream that embeds both temporal and spiritual authority to delineate Isma'il's power. This core narrative derived from a dream recorded in Safi's hagiography becomes the text through which the Safavis redefine themselves as they cast Isma'il in relation to Safi to translate the Safavi mystical past into their

imperial present. See Sholeh Alysia Quinn, *Historical Writing during the Reign of Shah 'Abbās: Ideology, Imitation, and Legitimacy in Safavid Chronicles* (Salt Lake City: University of Utah Press, 2000), ch. 4, on the historiography of Safavi origins.

8. Ghiyās al-dīn Khwāndamīr, *Tārīkh-i Habīb al-siyar,* ed. Jalāl al-din Humā'i (Tehran: Kitābkhānah-yi Khayyām, 1954), vol. 4, 414; also cited in Quinn, *Historical Writing.*

9. Quinn, *Historical Writing,* 105 (citing Sadr al-dīn Sulṭan Ibrāhīm Amīnā-Haravī, *Futūhāt-i Shāhī* Kitābkhānah-yi Vazīrī-yi Yazd MS 5774, f 246a).

10. Ibid.

11. Ibid.

12. See Cemal Kafadar, *Between Two Worlds: The Construction of the Ottoman State* (Berkeley: University of California Press, 1995), for a similar *ghaza*-colored reinterpretation of the rise of the Ottomans in later Ottoman historiography, particularly Introduction, ch. 1, and ch. 2.

13. Quinn, *Historical Writing* (citing Amīnī-Haravī, *Futūhāt,* f. 246a).

14. In a firman dated 911/1501 inscribed in the Friday congregational mosque of Isfahan, Isma'il is referred to as the "successor of the age" (*khilāfat al-zamān*), the just and perfect Imam (*imām al-ādīl al-kāmīl*), the guide (*al-hādi*), the crusader (*al-ghāzī*), and the friend of God (*al-valī*). Cited in Andrew Newman, "The Myth of the Clerical Migration to Safawid Iran," *Die Welt des Islams* 33 (1993): 70–71.

15. Sam Mirza, *Tuhfah-yi Sāmī* (Tehran: Ilmī, 1973–1974), 7. See Cornell Fleischer, *Bureaucrat and Intellectual in the Ottoman Empire: The Historian Mustafa Ali (1541–1600)* (Princeton: Princeton University Press, 1986), 279–283, on the sixteenth-century Ottoman historian Mustafa Ali Efendi's (1541–1600) description of Islamicate titles of sovereignty.

16. Mirza, *Tuhfah-yi Sāmī,* 7.

17. Amir Mahmud, *Zayl-i Tārīkh-i Habīb al-siyar* (Tehran: Nashr-i Gustarah, 1991–1992), 21.

18. Ibid., 43.

19. Ibid., 56.

20. For the Bab's use of hadith in his sortie, see Abbas Amanat, *Resurrection and Renewal: The Making of the Bābī Movement in*

Iran, 1844–1850 (Ithaca: Cornell University Press, 1989), 193–197.

On Islamicate scholars who linked the apocalyptic circumstances of the manifestation (*zuhūr*), recorded in hadith literature, to political upheavals, also see ibid., 89–93.

21. See Sayyid Ahmad Husayni's *Fihrist-i Nuskhahā-yi Khattī-yi Kitābkhānah-yi 'Umūmī-yi Hazrat-i Ayatullāh al-uzmā Najafī Mar'ashī*, vol. 4, 154–155, MS 1381. This anonymous work, dedicated to Shah Tahmasb in 974/1566–1567, is a commentary on the hadith relating the just order that shall be established at the end of time. It attempts to draw parallels between the just order evoked in this hadith and that of the Safavi order. It has also been noted by Sayyid Husayn Modarresi that some Safavi scholars considered Safavi rule the *dawlat-i haqq*—the utopia-like order that the Mahdi is to establish in Imāmī eschatology. Sayyid Husayn Modarresi-Tabātabā'ī, *Zamīn dar Fiqh-i Islāmī* (Tehran: Daftar-i Nashr-ī Farhang-i Islāmī, 1984), vol. 2, 222 n. 84.

22. Qāzī Ahmad Qummī, *Khulāsat al-tavārīkh*, ed. Ihsān Ishrāqī (Tehran, 1984), 79.

23. See, for example, the various monographs on the *ghayba* in Aqa Buzurg, *al-Dharī'a ila tasānīf al-shi'a* (Tehran: 1936–1978), vol. 16, 74–85.

24. Ibid. For example, *Arba'īn 'Uqāb*, written for Shah Tahmasb. See Muhammad Taqī Dānishpazhū, *Fihrist-i Nuskhahā-yi Kitābkhānah-iy Dānishgāh-i Tehran*, (Tehran: Tehran University Press), vol. 3, 1069, MS 1116. Also see Āqā Buzurg, *al-Dharī'a*, vol. 1, 419.

25. Michel Membré, *Mission to the Lord Sophy of Persia (1539–1542)*, trans. A. H. Morton (London: School of Oriental and African Studies, 1993), 25–26.

26. Maria Szuppe, "La Participation des femmes de la famille royale à l'exercise du pouvoir en Iran Safavide au XVIe siècle," pt. 1, *Studia Iranica* 23 (1994): 249, 251.

27. The inscription (*katība*) appears in the shrine of Khwajah Shah Hasan in Isfahan (dated 962/1554). Lutfullāh Hunarfar, *Ganjīnah-yi Āsār Tārīkh-i Isfahān* (Isfahan: (Kitābfurùshi-yi Saqafi,) 1965), 388. Also cited in Newman who omits the phrase "vanguard of the armies" and focuses rather on the title of "Lord of the Age." The distinction here is important for Tahmasb is referred to not as the hidden Imam but as a precursor of that

awaited messiah. Newman, "The Myth of the Clerical Migration," 94.

28. Ahmad b. Muhammad Ghaffārī, *Tārīkh-i Jahān Arā*, ed. Hasan Narāqī (Tehran: Kitābfurūshī-yi Hāfiz, 1963), 281. Also late in 1570, Tahmasb's historian 'Abdī Bek Khwajah Zayn al-'Abidīn 'Alī Shīrāzī, in *Takmīlat al-akhbār*, ed. 'Abd al-Husayn Navā'ī (Tehran: Nashr-i Nay, 1990), 60 refers to his chronogram (*bi hisāb-i jummāl*) as the equivalent of the "end of time" (*ākhar-i zamān*).

29. See Said Arjomand, *The Shadow of God and the Hidden Imam: Religion, Political Order, and Societal Change in Shi'ite Iran from the Beginning to 1890* (Chicago: University of Chicago Press, 1984) for an excellent analysis of patrimonial kingship in the Irano-Islamic world. For a discussion on the theory of the "shadow of God on earth," see particularly 7, 95, 98, 181, 229.

30. You may recall that the historian Amir Mahmud already refers to Isma'il as *shāh vilāyat* in 957/1550.

31. See Aubin, "Shah Ismā'īl," and "L'Avènement des Safavides"; Arjomand, *The Shadow of God*.

32. Andrew Newman challenges the standard scholarly accounts that place the large migration of Arab Twelver clerics to Safavi Iran at the inception of Safavi rule (1501) with their proclamation of Imami Shi'ism as the religion of their domains. Newman adduces a number of cogent reasons for the refusal of many Arab Imami clerics residing in Sunni Ottoman lands, one of which is the nature of Isma'il's messianic claims to power. He argues that it is not until the latter half of Tahmasb's reign (probably after 1555 with the Treaty of Amasya) when the Safavi domains have become more stable and have gradually moved away from the original "exaggerated" rhetoric of Shah Isma'il. See Newman, "The Myth of the Clerical Migration."

33. A series of alternative roles are played within later Safavi historiography. According to Arjomand, *The Shadow of God*, 80, Abdi Bek writing his *Takmilat al-akbār* in 1571, says in 1499/905: "Leaflets announcing to those expecting the appearance of that majesty [Isma'il] who is the prelude to [the appearance of] the Lord of the Age were disseminated in every direction." Hassan Bek, Rumlu, *Ahsan al-tavārīkh*, ed. 'Abd al-Navā'ī (Tehran: Bungāh-i Tarjumah va Nashr-i Kitāb, 1978), writing in 1577, re-

fers to Isma'il as Khāqan Sikandar Sha'n—that is, *Sāhib Qirān* (10). Memory of Isma'il's messianic discourse lived on into the third generation of Safavi court historians. Qāzī Ahmad Qummī, Shah Abbas I's court historian, who had been born into a family of religious scholars, records a hadith he had heard from Shaykh-i Bahā'ī, concerning the *zuhūr* of Shah Isma'il. Shaykh-i Baha'i had heard this hadith from his father, the sound scholar, Shaykh Husayn 'Abd al-Samad al-'Amilī, who highlights characteristics of the Mahdī that seem to be tailored to Shah Isma'il: "[I]ndeed when a man from Ardabil . . . a man of my family, will enter Tabriz on a white horse with twelve hundred cavalrymen and a red cloth on his head." Qāzī Ahmad goes on to link yet another prominent Shi'i cleric with this hadith. He states that "Hasan b. Sayyid Ja'far al-Amīn al-Karakī, my father's teacher, told me: In the beginning of the reign of Shah Isma'il, when I was going on a pilgrimage to Mashad, I arrived in Tabriz. . . . the Shah was out hunting. The day he returned from his hunt, along with the residents of Tabriz we went to greet him. In fact, the Shah was riding on a white horse that day and due to some trouble with his eye he was wearing a red scarf on his head and he had 12,000 cavalrymen with him. At that time, this hadith that I had come across a couple of years ago sprang to my mind." Qāzī Ahmad, Qummī, *Khulāsat al-tavārīkh*, vol. 1, 79.

34. You may recall that Isma'il's historian Amini refered to his patron as the refuge of religion in 1532. Rumlu, in his preface to *Ahsān al-tavārīkh*, refers to Tahmasb with the same title, *dīn panāh*.

35. From the northern Caspian Sea region of Mazandaran (Mar'ashī, Mīr-i Buzurg, d. 1379), to eastern Iran (Sarbidar, 1336–1381, and Nūrbakhshis, Muhammad Nūrbakhsh, d. 1464) and into the southwest (Musha'sha', Muhammad b. Falāh d.1462), Alid claimants emerged from within sufi circles as apocalyptic messiahs. On the Sarbidārs, see John M. Smith, *The History of the Sarbadār Dynasty, 1336–81, and Its Sources* (The Hague: Mouton 1970); I. Petrushevski, "Nahzat-i Sarbidārān," trans. Karīm Kishāvarz, *Farhang-i Irān Zamīn* 10 (1962): 124–224; Jean Aubin, "La fin de l'etat Sarbidar du Khorasan, " *Journal Asiatique* 262 (1974): 95–118. On the Nūrbakhshiya, see Shahzad Bashir, 1997. On the Musha'sha', see Ahmad Kasravī. *Musha'sha'īyān*, 3rd ed. (Tehran: Intishārāt-i Sahar, 1977). On

the Mar'ashīs, see J. Calmard, EI2. For a preliminary comparison of these movements, see ch. 1 of Bashir, ""Between Mysticism and Messianism: The Life and Thought of Muhammad Nurbakhsh (d. 1464)," Ph.D. diss., Yale University, 1968, ch. 1, "The Religious Guide in Late Medieval Shi'ism (ca. 1335–1500)."

36. I am relying here on the illuminating work of Kishwar Rizvi, "Transformations in Early Safavid Architecture: The Shrine of Shaykh Safi al-din Ardabili in Iran," Ph. D. diss., Massachusetts Institute of Technology, 2000.

37. Woods, *The Aquyyunlu*, 8 [quoting Mu'izz al-Din Pir Husayn Muhammad Kart (d. 1370/771)]. In 1345/750, he announced the reestablishment of Islamic sacred law in place of the "filthy trees of unbelief" and customs of unbelievers (*rusūm-i kufẹar*). *Farā'id*, Tehran MS 618–620. Also quoted in Aubin, "L'Avènement des Safavides," 31.

38. Aubin, "Shah Ismā'īl," 47. B. S. Amoretti, "Religion in the Timurid and Safavid Period," in *Cambridge History of Iran*, ed. Peter Jackson and Lawrence Lockhart (Cambridge: Cambridge University Press, 1986), vol. 6, 611. Each historian characterizes the age of Mongol hegemony differently, either as the rise of "paganism," or as Barthold refers to the permeation of the irrational, and Meier as an environment that nurtures spiritualism. See Allesandro Bausani "Religion under the Mongols," in *Cambridge History of Iran*, vol. 5, ch. 7.

39. Woods, *The Aqquyunlu*, 140–145.

40. Aubin, "Shah Ismā'īl," 47.

41. Woods, *The Aqquyunlu*, 141.

42. Ibid. The urban population of Tabriz and the religious leaders become alienated from Sultan Ya'qub due to the canceling of immunities and stipends—an animosity that may have helped support Isma'il's quest for power.

43. Scholars have focused on a couple of indications to argue that Isma'il does himself attempt to clamp down on *ghuluww*. Arjomand, for instance, includes the testimony of an Italian merchant who claims that Isma'il was not happy to be called God or Prophet. Sanuto, however, states the opposite. Arjomand also interprets Isma'il's killing of *ghulāt* followers of Baba Shah Quli in this light. Fear of political destabilization with the influx of new

tribal elements from Anatolia may be the cause for this action, rather than Isma'il's rejection of his *ghulāt* beliefs. See Arjomand, *The Shadow of God,* 110. As mentioned above Isma'il continues to be referred to as the hidden Imam on coins minted as late as 924/1518 in the holy Shi'i city of Mashad, where he is referred to as *al-imām al-adil* and *al-sulṭan al-adil.* Cited in Newman, "The Myth of the Clerical," 71.

44. Newman, "The Myth of the Clerical," 85, points out the ambiguities surrounding the title *imām al-adil* in Imami discourse. He also points out that in Karakī's essay on Kharāj, although he is addressing clerical criticism of Karakī's association with Isma'il, Karakī here refers to Isma'il not as the just Imam but as the unjust *(jā'ir)* Imam. This is an indication that Karakī had no choice but to conform to Isma'il's holy claims, yet in his doctrinal essays written in Arabic he was addressing a different audience and hence could openly characterize Isma'il as other Shi'i clerics had done as a false claimant to the Imamate.

45. Moreover, with this decree, Karakī is given the right to mint coins in Hilla and becomes the ruler of the autonomous enclave in Iraq.

46. Tahmasb, *Tazkire,* 14. Tahmasb writes about the intellectual debates *(mubāhisāt-i 'ilmī)* between the Mujtahid al-zamān (Karakī) and the Sadr (Ghiyās al-dīn). Tahmasb confirms Karakī's knowledge *(ijtihād)* over Mīr Ghiyās al-dīn Mansūr.

47. Arjomand, *The Shadow of God,* posits a separation between religion and politics by the age of Tahmasb. The situation is a bit more complicated, for in the *Memoir,* Tahmasb continues to draw on his spiritual authority.

48. Aubin, "L'Avènement des Safavides Reconsideré," 126.

49. Tensions are manifest in a body of disputations and edicts as well as in messianic revolts and court cabals. See Arjomand, *The Shadow of God,* introduction, on the theoretical implications presented by the Safavi case for the study of the role of religion and politics in premodern societies.

50. Ibid., 2.

51. Ibid. For a Weberian and metahistorical analysis of this phenomenon, see Arjomand, *The Shadow of God.*

52. Tahmasb, *Tazkire,* 21–22: *"Itiqād-i bandah-yi za'īf Tahmasb al-Safavi al-Musavi al-Husayni īn ast keh har kas keh hazrat-i amīr*

al-muminīn salvāt allah alayhī rā dar khwāb bīnad ānchāh īshān farmāyand hamān mīshavad."

53. Ibid., 12: "*Chūn subh shud dānistam keh Uzbek shikast khurdah.*"
54. See Arjomand, *The Shadow of God*, for a discussion of patrimonial Safavi kingship.
55. Dehkhoda, *Lughatnāme*, "āghā."
56. This is a common aspect of Turco-Iranian cultures. Babur, for example, speaks of Umar Shaykh Mirza's (grandson of Timur) relationship with his sufi master Khwaja Ahrār (1403–1488) in paternal terms. To emphasize their intimacy, Babur says Khwaja Ahrār called Umar Shaykh Mirza "my son." Babur, *Bāburnāme: Chaghatay Turkish Text with Abdul-Rahim Khankhanan's Persian Translation*, ed. W. M. Thackston and Khan Abdul-Rahim (Cambridge: Department of Near Eastern Languages and Civilizations, Harvard University , 1993), vol. 1, 13.
57. Mieke Bal, *Reading "Rembrandt": Beyond the Word-Image Opposition* (Cambridge: Cambridge University Press, 1991), 18–24.
58. Khatā'ī, *Il Canzonieri*, 7/8 and 194/43.
59. Ibid., 15/6 and 204/1–2.
60. We still need to study exactly which lines are censored from Isma'il's poetry.
61. We also need to study the manuscript tradition of Tahmasb's *Tazkire*. A segment of his *Tazkire* is preserved in the *Bayāz-i Mukālimah-yi Shah Tahmasb bā Ilchiyān* (MS. Dorn 302, St. Petersburg, 1601–1602). We have a copy in Berlin that was edited by Keyvani. This copy had been recorded for Humayun Qutbshah The *Tārīkh-i Ilchi-yi Nizāmshāhī* (971/1563) written by Khurshah uses it and says that Tahmasb sent his *Memoir* to Ali Adil Shah of Bijapur.
62. Babur, *The Bāburnāme: Memoirs of Babur, Prince and Emperor* trans., ed., and ann. Wheeler M. Thackston (Washington, DC: Freer Gallery of Art and Arthur M. Sackler Gallery, Smithsonian Institution, 1996), 10–11. Thackston does speak of a flourishing of the "royal memoir in the Timurid and Mughal contexts." Babur's memoir, however, is one of the earliest examples. He names Sultan Husayn Mirza's in Chagatay, Babur's daughter Gulbadan Begum, who kept her diary and recorded her brother's

life in the *Humāyūnāme*. Jahangir (r. 1605–1627) writes a memoir as well as Akbar's (r. 1556–1605) Persian translation of the *Bāburnāme* in 1589.

63. Both Babur and Tahmasb were sent at a young age to provincial seats as governors under the supervision of *atabeks* (surrogate fathers). Their education entailed not only the martial arts but also the visual arts and religious sciences. Tahmasb was sent to Herat at age two (1516). Herat was the former Timurid capital (since the reign of Shahrukh r. 1405–1447) and represented the cultural center of the Timurid cultural synthesis (Turco-Iranian). Babur was appointed governor of Andizhand at ten or eleven farther east of Herat in the Feragana valley (Transoxiana).

64. Georges Gusdorf, "Conditions and Limits of Autobiography," in *Autobiography: Essays Theoretical and Critical,* ed., James Olney (Princeton: Princeton University Press, 1980), 29. Also see Stephen Dale's comment that despite the patronizing attitude of Roy Pascal in *Design and Truth in Autobiography* (Cambridge: Harvard University Press, 1960), Pascal acknowledges that the *Bāburnāme* does manifest characteristics attributed to "classical" European autobiographies like that of Rousseau and Goethe: "[The *Bāburnāme*] would occupy a significant place in the history of autobiography had it belonged to Europe," 22, cited in Stephen Dale, "Steppe Humanism: The Autobiographical Writings of Zahir al-Din Muhammd Babur, 1483–1530," *International Journal of Middle East Studies* 22 (1990): 2 n. 8.

65. I would like to thank Helmut Puff for bringing this point to my attention.

66. Natalie Zemon-Davis, "Boundaries and the Sense of Self in Sixteenth-Century France," in *Reconstructing Individualism,* ed. Thomas C. Heller, Morton Sosna, and David Wellbery (Palo Alto: Stanford University Press, 1986).

67. Muhammad Taqī Muqtadirī, "Pazīrā'ī-yi Shāhānah," *Nashriyah-yi Vizārat-i Umūr-i Khārija* 2 (1956–1957): 48–56. The contents of this decree are described in this article; unfortunately, there is no reference to the location of the decree.

68. Michael Cooperson, "The Heirs of the Prophets in Classical Arabic Biography," Ph. D. Diss., Harvard University, 1994, ch. 1 on *tabaqa* and *tā'ifa*.

69. Ibid., as well as George Makdisi, "The Diary in Islamic Historiography: Some Notes," *History and Theory* 25 (1986): 173–185. Makdisi argues that "historiography owes its existence in Islam to the existence of this hadith criticism" (174). He is drawing on Sir Hamilton Gibb's statement that the "composition of biographical dictionaries in Arabic developed simultaneously with historical composition." Makdisi, "The Diary," 175 [citing Bernard Lewis and P. M. Holt, eds., *Historians of the Middle East,* Vol. 4, *Historical Writing on the Peoples of Asia* (London: Oxford University Press, 1962), 54–58].

70. Ibid., 175.

71. For a list of Ottoman personal literature, see Cemal Kafadar, "Self and Others: The Diary of a Dervish in Seventeenth-Century Istanbul and First-Person Narratives in Ottoman Literature," *Studia Islamicus* 69 (1989): 121–1500. Also see Jonathan Glustrom Katz's work on the dream diary of a Moroccan sufi from the fifteenth century, *Dreams, Sufism, and Sainthood: The Visionary Career of Muhammad al-Zawāwī* (Leiden: Brill, 1996).

72. Ibid., 208, citing Malik ibn Anas, *al-muwatta',* vol. 2, 957 (1951).

73. Gustave E. von Grunebaum and Roger Caillois, *The Dream and Human Societies* (Berkeley: University of California Press, 1966), 6–10.

74. Kafadar, *Between Two Worlds,* 133, characterizes the role of the dream interpreter as the "notary of its contractual character."

75. Qu'ran 12.

76. Roy Mottahedeh, *Loyalty and Leadership in an Early Islamic Society* (Princeton: Princeton University Press, 1980), 66–67.

77. Ibid., 67.

78. Dickson, "Shah Tahmasb," 45.

79. Tahmasb, *Tazkire,* 1: "*va īn tabaqah rā az kull-i afrād-i insān biqāyat-i khāss makhsūs va mumtāz namūd.*"

80. Particularly after Isma'il's defeat in Chaldiran where the chroniclers and even Sam Mirza, Isma'il's son and Tahmasb's brother, speak of Isma'il partying (*'aysh*), drinking wine, and hunting, to the exclusions of virtually everything else, while still maintaining complete Qizilbash loyalty. Aubin understands Isma'il's hunting and wining as symbolic of his delegation of temporal authority to

his viziers or vakils, maintaining his spiritual role (*irshād*) through his withdrawal from worldly affairs and his continued messianic role of justice, bestowing all booty to his followers (empty treasury).

81. Hasan Bek Rūmlū, *Ahsān al-tavārīkh*, ed. 'Abd al-Husayn Navā'ī (Tehran: Burgāh-i Tarjumah va Nashr-i Kitāb, 1978), 635, states that Tahmasb exaggerated his abstention from drinking: "*va dar nakhūrdan-i sharāb ghuluww-i 'azīm dāsht.*"

82. Tahmasb, *Tazkire*, 49–51, quotes from Ali like "*hukm bāzī dārad*" (governing entails games). It is interesting to note that Ferdowsi in his *Shāhnāme* has Afrasiab voicing this dictum—yet another example of processes of Persianate conversion.

83. Ibid., 38. It is such a saintly image that Tahmasb constructs for himself through examples of his fishing in the nude (*birahnah*) or in his last dream when a herd of wild boars are roaming by the royal encampment and Tahmasb kills a token wild boar to show that he can indeed hunt but prefers not to. He leaves this play for "the kiddies" and the Qizilbash (68). Abolala Soudavar reads this "passivity" during Tahmasb's later years and ascribes it to a possible ophthalmic disease that he may have inherited from his father, Muhammad Khudabandah. What is important is that Soudavar senses this shift in Tahmasb's temperament from his readings of the chronicles and art historical evidence, yet the *Tazkire* is helpful here as a source that illuminates the reasons behind such a shift in Tahmasb's self-representation. Abolala Soudavar, "Between the Safavids and the Mughals: Art and Artists in Transition," *Iran: Journal of the British Institute of Persian Studies* 36 (1999): 52. I would like to thank the author for providing me with a copy of this article before its publication.

84. Hasan Bek Rūmlū, *Ahsān al-tavārīkh*, ed. 'Abd al-Husayn Navā'ī (Tehran: Bungāh-i Tarjumah va Nashr-i Kitāb, 1978), 635.

85. Tahmasb, *Tazkire*, 28.

86. Note that the historian Amir Mahmud (in 1550) attributes Durmish Khan's defeat not to drinking but rather to his faulty military strategy. Durmish Khan is dead at the time that Amir Mahmud is writing.

87. Tahmasb, *Tazkire*, 28–29. I wonder whether plate 145 in the *Houghton Shāhnāme* that Tahmasb gives as a present to the Ottoman Selim II, depicting the inebriated Iranian camp attacked by

Turanian (Turkish) troops at night, is not a representation of Chaldiran. The narrative of the *Shāhnāme* story resembles Tahmasb's description of Chaldiran. Spies of Piran, the commander-in-chief of the Turanian army of Afrasiab, reports to the king that the Iranians were "carousing about drunkedly in their cups night and day" in their encampment at Girowgird. Dickson and Welch, *The Houghton Shāhnāme*, vol. 2, plate 145.

88. Khwāndamīr, *Tārīkh-i Habīb al-siyar*, vol. 4, 453.

89. The St. Petersburg manuscript (MS. Dorn 302), *Bayāz-i Mukālimah-yi Shah Tahmasb bā Ilchiyān*, needs to be studied in relation to the *Tazkire*.

90. The first war occurred between 1528 and 1535. The second Ottoman War erupted during the Alqas episode between 1545 and 1549. The third invasion of Sulayman (Nakhjavan in 1554), which leads to the peace of Amasya (1555), ends with the Bayazid episode from 1559 to 1562.

91. Dickson and Welch, *The Houghton Shāhnāme*, state that this illuminated album was probably initiated by Shah Isma'il in his Tabriz atelier as a gift for his son Tahmasb's accession.

92. He does not discuss his problems with his son Isma'il Mirza, who has been in prison (Qahqahah) since 1557, five years before the *Memoir* was penned. However, his brothers Alqas and Bahram Mirza are dead, and Sam and Isma'il are in prison. Also there is a silence concerning women like Sultanim and Pari Khan Khanum, except for a dream reference to Sultanim.

93. For example, when he narrates "The Takkalu Disaster" (*āfat-i Takkalū*) (1531), he says that the Afshars, Ziadoghlu, and Ustajlu are upset at the four-year Takkalu hegemony of power.

94. Dickson, "Shah Tahmasb," corroborates information from the chronicles to piece together such implications. Also see Babur, *The Bāburnāme: Memoirs*, for Thackston's remarks on the *Baburnāme*, where Babur also claims to speak the simple truth; his version corroborates with contemporaneous histories of Babur's reign.

95. I am using Abdellah Hammoudi's characterization of master-disciple roles here. See his *Master and Disciple: The Cultural Foundations of Moroccan Authoritarianism* (Chicago: University of Chicago Press, 1997).

96. Tahmasb, *Tazkire*, 46.

97. Ibid., 43.
98. Ibid., 61.
99. Muhammad Taqī Dānishpazhū, "Yik Parda az Zindigāni-yi Shah Tahmasb-i Safavī," *Majallah-yi Dānishkadah-yi Adabiyyāt va 'Ulūm-i Insāni-yi Mashad 7*, no. 4 1972): 966–988 provides a copy of the *A'īn-i Shah Tahmasb*, (Tahmasb's manual on ethics), where he prohibits drinking, dancing, music, sodomy (*amrad*), and women riding on saddled horses and holding onto their reins.
100. Tahmasb, *Tazkire*, 11.
101. From the beginning of his reign, Tahmasb is trying to show that he was in control. He states that "I made him [Kopek Sultan Ustajlu] partner with Div Sultan," or "I replaced him [Qazi Jahan Qazvini] instead of Mirza Shah Husayn," 3. Only once the Takkalu gain power, however, in 1527/993 does he say that in reality he became *pādishah*. See Dickson, "Shah Tahmasb," on this matter.
102. The first four dreams Tahmasb narrates fall into the first phase of his turbulent regency (1524–1536), when he was jockeyed between different coalitions of the Qizilbash (*oymaq*). His historian Rumlu states that in this youthful phase, Tahmasb was inordinately fond of painting, calligraphy, riding Egyptian asses, and disporting with people of his own age (Rumlu, cited in Dickson, "Shah Tahmasb,"). These four dreams are about his military conquests of the Uzbeks. The first dream occurs at the Battle of Jām, when Ali smiles at him, signaling his victory. Ali and Husayn are present in the second dream he has in Herat (16 June 1535/14 Zul Hijja 941). In this dream, Ali asks Tahmasb to build him a dome like Imam Reza's in Mashad. Ali could be referring to the conquest of Balkh and the Mazar-i Sharif, where one myth has it that Ali's body lies. This hypothesis makes even more sense because the Ottomans are in possession of Najaf, the other site of Ali's grave. The third dream occurs in Mashad, where Tahmasb institutes his Edict of Sincere Repentance (1534). And the fourth dream takes place at Ardabil. Ali and Shaykh Safi are the holy communicators. Here victory over the Ottomans is confirmed as well as the nature of Isma'il's mission, rejecting his manifestation (*zuhūr*) as the Mahdi (1 September 1535/941).
103. Ibid., 67.

TEN

The Isfahani Era of Absolutism:
1590 to 1666

With the suppression of the Nuqtavis, Shah Abbas I attempted
to circumscribe a way of being and sensing time that saw no
bounds to prophetic revelation, perpetually bringing forth new
messiahs, uncovering deeper layers of the truth. He relied on the
shari'a-minded in this process, for they provided him with a sacred forum through which to attack the *ghulāt* and legitimize
the absoluteness of his rule. The public image that Abbas I was
cultivating resonates with his efforts to control the free mingling
of the temporal with the spiritual, an atmosphere that was characteristic of the age during which his mystic ancestor Isma'il
proclaimed himself shah of Iran. Abbas I's presence as a disciple
at the Nuqtavi cloister shows how far this Safavi monarch had
moved away from the godlike image of Isma'il. Publicly, Abbas I
was not playing the role of spiritual master. Although the chroniclers continue to refer to the shah as the perfect guide (*murshid-
i kāmil*) and to the Qizilbash as sufis, they did so sentimentally
and piously. In the Isfahani phase of Safavi rule (post-1590),
these titles were largely ceremonial, retaining the element of
obedience that was required of a disciple toward his master.
Nevertheless, Abbas I was still captivated by things esoteric;
otherwise, he would not have been so drawn to the Nuqtavis or
have been so accepted in their world.

What had convinced Shah Abbas I that the ways of the Nuqtavis were heretical was their disrespect for the precepts of the divine law and their intention to overthrow him. In his role as propagator of Shi'ism, the monarch was certainly concerned with the Nuqtavis' rejection of Muhammad as the "seal of the Prophets." Nevertheless, what induced their suppression was the Nuqtavis' desire to extend their spiritual puissance over Safavi dominion. The chronicles insist that it was foremost out of religious concerns that the Nuqtavis were eliminated. The "imaginary religion and politics" of the exaggerators were paired and could only be attained on earth. *Shari'a*-minded Imamism, however, allowed for their separation into two distinct realms on earth, relegating their reunion to the end of time and the advent of the Mahdi. Isfahan was visualized and constructed by Shah Abbas I and his descendants as the stage for one such apocalyptic event. With the execution of the Nuqtavi masters, the role of messiah was reserved for an Alid descendent from the Safavi branch of this holy household.

Shah Abbas I's decision to eliminate the Nuqtavi movement was also influenced by his court astrologer's renderings of the stars. According to Nuqtavi readings, the sixteenth-century "greatest" conjunction of Saturn and Jupiter signaled the fall of the Safavis and the (re)establishment of Iranian dominion. The court astrologer, Jalal al-din Muhammad Yazdi, on the other hand, announced that "the reading of the stars and the verses of the Qur'an pointed to the execution of an important individual from those related [*mansūbān*] to the sun, who were the temporal rulers in particular."[1] Adducing Qur'anic confirmation of his planetary readings, the astrologer concurred that upheaval might take place in Iran. The Persianate sun had been incorporated in Muslim astrology as a symbol of royalty—the abode (Leo) of the monarch in the heavens. Using Mazdean interpretive frameworks, Yazdi translates the Nuqtavi forecast for the shah, erasing the anti-Islamic layers of these predictions. He personalizes their meaning, stating that the conjunction of the two unlucky planets fell into the first house (*tarb'i*) of the shah's horoscope and that the rising star was in the perigree (*hazīz*) of decline and calamity. Jalal al-din Yazdi, then, suggests that the shah abdicate for a period of three days, during which time the effect of the ill-fated conjunction was most threatening. Now the power of reading the future was reserved for courtiers.

Once the authorized reading of the stars and the Qur'an too spelled Shah Abbas I's abdication, he decided to annihilate the Nuqtavis. The shah's personal and public role in this affair is fascinating. The manner in which the Nuqtavis' forecast was dealt with—the fact that the shah abdicated the throne in favor of a Nuqtavi trustee (*amīn*)—illustrates the seriousness of that threat and Shah Abbas I's enchantment with their geomatrical calculations. The transfer of the throne to a rival Nuqtavi for a three-day period during which he was in the highest risk of losing his authority is indicative of the real nature of the Nuqtavi menace. In addition, the abdication scenario presented an opportunity for the shah to expose the impotence of the Nuqtavis and the paradoxical nature of their forecast. Beyond his possible belief in the cabalistic doctrines of the Nuqtavis, the shah had to contend with many high-ranking Qizilbash functionaries who had become Dervish Khusraw's disciples. Of course, Shah Abbas I's abdication and Ustad Yusufi's coronation was a farce. Ustad Yusufi was placed on the throne once all the influential Nuqtavi disciples had been imprisoned, leaving them absolutely no room to maneuver. Yet Shah Abbas I took great care to authenticate this coronation, as though it were a prediction that was now going to be fulfilled through his role as restorer of a just Alid kingdom, emphasizing an alternative finale preserved in shared Persianate and Alid apocalyptic discourse.

A new millennium of rule was established in Isfahan, the city of paradise, thus creating and controlling the script of the past and the present in the hope that this would secure them permanence in the future. Following the suppression of the Nuqtavis (1593), Shah Abbas I proceeded to amass control in the hands of a newly reconfigured Safavi household, relying heavily on an elite corps of slaves (*ghulams*), individual Turkmen lovers of the

Shah (*shāhīsivān*), Shi'i scholars (*ulama*), and Armenian mer-
chant-bankers in this process.[2] And he embarked (in 1601) on
yet another symbolic act, a pilgrimage on foot from Isfahan to
Mashad—a public performance of pious devotion to Imam
Reza, the son of the eponymous Imam, Musa Kazim, of the
Safavi house. Abbas I rendered this act of piety with reverence
for Imam Reza as part of a vow (*nazr*) he had made in which he
asserted his public commitment to the Imami faith.[3] His subsequent endowment of all his personal estates as a benefaction to
the "fourteen imaculate ones" may have been linked to this very
vow, which he had promised to fulfill in the name of the family
of the Prophet. The first lands Abbas I endowed (1602–1603)
were those surrounding the sacred threshold of Imam Reza's
tomb and the courtyard of the mosque.[4] This sacred topography
was to provide space for those members of Shah Abbas I's
household who would rest in eternal proximity to the eighth
Imam. Mashad was replacing Ardabil, site of the tomb of the
founder of the Safavi brotherhood, Shaykh Safi al-din, as the
Safavi holy locus. The transfer of the capital from Qazvin to
Isfahan, in the heartland, reflects this centrifugal mood. The
move away from Anatolia toward Fars signaled both the
Iranization and Imamification of the empire. The Maydan-i
Naqsh-i Jahan and the Masjid-i Jadid-i Shah came to represent
the era of Safavi absolutism as universal monarch and awaited
messiah. Those who played a role in the process of making
Isfahan into a capital city represented the new pillars on which
Safavi despotism was founded. As the protector of Shi'ism,
Abbas I engraved the Persianate symbol of the sun on Safavi
coins. Just as the Nuqtavis imagined Ali, in Isfahan he was in-
deed speaking a "Persian version of Arabic."[5]

Shah Abbas I's inherited role as perfect guide, his sufi lineage,
and his devoted Qizilbash were the essential elements of the
"classical age" of Safavi rule. In the Isfahani era, these components took on a ritualistic function. Unlike Isma'il I, who was
still bound to the just role of Messiah and to the revolutionary

power structure of the Safavi movement, Shah Abbas I maintained these, ceremonially donning the red crown of the Qizilbash in public. This transformation is reflected in the chronicles in which the red (*qizil*) headgear, introduced by Shaykh Haydar (d. 1488) to symbolize the "exaggeration" of the Qizilbash, was translated into the twelvefold crown (*tāj-i Ithna 'asharī*).[6] Shi'ism and kingship gained emphasis over the halo of mystic headgear.

Such transformations in the discourse of sovereignty had been accompanied by practical changes in the social and political structure of authority. A major obstacle that lay in the path of Safavi absolutism was the Qizilbash, who had championed the ideology of the Safavi revolution. With their help, the Safavis had conquered Iran and Iraq, setting up their imperium. The Qizilbash, composed mainly of Turkmen tribesmen, were privileged members both of the Safavi brotherhood and the politico-military administration of the empire. They were a military elite introduced into the sociopolitical mix of the Iranian domains. Their allegiance to the Safavi shahs found a variety of manifestations, one of which was taking up arms to actualize the ecstatic visions of their perfect guide. During the revolutionary phase (1447–1501), the Qizilbash had organized themselves militarily into groups (*oymaq*), a Mongol term loosely translated as "tribe." Members of a particular tribe or locality in Anatolia and Syria had converted to Qizilbash Islam; the tribe, however, had not converted en masse. Qizilbash religiosity created the structure around which individuals coalesced into a single group, like the Shamlu, Ustajlu, or Takkalu. A belief system then entered into the dynamics of a set of Turco-Mongol kinship ties in the process of reformulation. In the imperial era (1501–1722), the Safavis attempted to contain the revolutionary fervor that had won them temporal power. An individual could no longer convert to Qizilbash Islam; to become a Qizilbash, one had to be born into the *oymaqs* that had originally associated themselves with the Safavi house.[7] Now blood ties were solidifying the spiritual bonds that had formerly brought the tribes together, and Qizilbash Islam was to be channeled to Ottoman Anatolia for export only.

Although the internal organization of these tribes remains to be studied, some general points can be made concerning their nature. The modern historian need not conjure an image of dissonance to understand the spiritual and political dualism embedded in the Qizilbash system. Alid, Sufi, and Turco-Mongol steppe concepts of authority, for example, were harmonious in the context of tribal stratification. Spiritually, all members of the Safavi order were equal as disciples (*murīd*). We have seen the ways in which bonds of loyalty and obedience were created and experienced among brothers and fathers of Alid chivalric circles, forging vertical and horizontal solidarity. Masters and their deputies (*khalīfa*), selected from each clan, were their superiors in esoteric matters. Similarly, according to steppe political theory, all members of a clan were considered equals among equals. One member, the khan, theoretically the eldest collateral member, represented the entire clan. In the classical age of Safavi rule (1501–1590), the main tribes had at least two courtly appointed delegates—a *khān, sulṭan,* or *bek* and a *khalīfa*—who represented them in the imperial arena politically as well as spiritually. Both concepts of equality and hierarchy lay at the core of steppe and sufi systems. Ultimate power to appoint, demote, or execute resided in Isma'il, for he was the perfect guide, the god shah for whom the Qizilbash continued to devour enemies alive in ritual submission. Subsequent Safavi shahs, however, would have to procure the total obedience of the Qizilbash, which Isma'il, the conquering messiah, enjoyed.

It still remains for Safavi historiography to explore the levels of interplay between spiritual rank and political status, as well as the interaction between horizontal and hierarchical, local and imperial, concepts of authority in the classical age. It is clear, however, that spiritual authority did translate itself into political power for more individuals than just the shah. Loyalty to the Safavi house and to their visionary cause won the Qizilbash a monopoly over positions at the court, in the provinces, and in the military. During the classical age, these arenas became the near exclusive preserves of the Qizilbash. The charmed circle of sufis who had surrounded the infant Isma'il during his days of refuge in Gilan (1494–1499) received special rewards. Those handful of devoted Qizilbash who had served Isma'il's father, Sultan Haydar (d. 1480), and had protected and trained Isma'il and his brothers—those who Jean Aubin terms the "sufis of Lahijan"—initially received the most esteemed and politically influential posts at court and in the battlefield.[8]

Proximity, trust, and the type of loyalty developed between a spiritual master and his disciple were basic components on which these choice imperial posts were shaped. These elements came to define the role that functionaries would enjoy at the Safavi court. The creation of these posts institutionalized the intimacy that had developed through a language of Alid secrecy that Isma'il shared with his revolutionary apostles. The titles of three Lahijani sufi loyalists—that of Dede, Lalé, and Khalifa—reflect the mixture of Turco-Mongol and sufi forms of authority absorbed in the Safavi revolutionary power structure.[9] Isma'il's childhood preceptors in matters profane and perhaps spiritual—Lalé Bek (Husayn Bek Shamlu) and Dede Bek (Abdal Bek)—both received the most important imperial military functions, Amir al-Umara and Qurchi Bashi.[10] Isma'il's spiritual mentor, Khulafa Bek (Khadim Bek Talishi), was to administer justice at court and in the battlefield as the Divan Begi.[11] After all, Isma'il was establishing a just utopia, and despite his public allegiance to Imami Shi'ism, initially it was the Qizilbash who would enforce law and order. Moreover, on the conquest of Baghdad and the Shi'i holy shrines in 1508, this same Khalifa Bek was awarded a new imperial title, that of chief spiritual deputy of the realms, Khalifat al-Khulafa, along with the governorship of Baghdad. For the Qizilbash, political and spiritual authority were intimately intertwined.[12] By 1508, even though Isma'il had linked himself with the "orthodox" lineage of the twelve Imams and had toured the Shi'i shrine cities with the prominent Imami cleric Shaykh Ali Karaki (d. 1534), it was the Qizilbash who captured Baghdad and the Khalifat al-Khulafa who would govern and protect it. So long as the Qizilbash maintained their political sway, the religious dyarchy that the Safavis had created with their profession of Imami Shi'ism would exist in conflict. Isma'il's successor, Tahmasb (1524–1576), attempted to subdue the religiosity of the Qizilbash, but it would be his grandson Abbas I who would possess the real power to enforce it systematically.[13] Qizilbash Islam would maintain its hegemony for nearly a century, and the Safavis would have to cater to their revolutionary personae.

For seven years, these "sufis of Lahijan" enjoyed political eminence, but the Qizilbash aspired to administer the Safavi domains collectively; and another pressure group composed of local Iranian notables and craftsmen shared in that aspiration. Turco-Mongol concepts of corporate sovereignty defined the political relationship between the Qizilbash and their Safavi mystic kings. It is true that the Qizilbash were disciples of their Safavi godhead, but they did expect to share in the governing of the newly conquered domains. The dynamics between these two interrelated hierarchies, one spiritual and one political, distinctively shaped the structure of power and loyalty in Safavi Iran. Shortly after the conquest of Baghdad, a coalition of Qizilbash led by the Ustajlu clan, in collaboration with newly conquered Iranian notables, and the Alid master goldsmith, Amir Najm-i Lahiji, disciple of the shah, asserted their political role and checked the hegemony of the "sufis of Lahijan."[14] A more equitable balance of power was struck among the devotees of the Safavis. Yet throughout these power struggles, Qizilbash loyalty toward Isma'il remained unwavering. In fact, up to his death, although Isma'il had retreated from the public life of chivalric hunting and wine, the Qizilbash continued to "dutifully obey the writ of his commands: no one of any eminence entertained the slightest thought of opposition."[15]

In accordance with steppe tradition, Isma'il parceled out his domains among the Turkmen tribes and sent his sons as governors to their appanages. These Safavi princes were assigned a Qizilbash tutor (*lalélatabek*), directly linking the fate of a princeling with a single tribe. Through such a practice of land distribution, the Qizilbash became partners in the Safavi corporation, each receiving an appanage referred to as *tuyul* for their tribe, as well as a dynastic member, female or male, with which to participate politically in the system. Although Tahmasb continued to appoint Safavi princes as titular governors, sending out first his royal brothers, Sam (d. 1567), Bahram (d. 1549), and Alqas Mirza (d. 1550), he was forced to rethink the notion of corporate sovereignty; for the Qizilbash were in open revolt the first twelve years of his reign (1524–1536) using him and his brother, Sam Mirza, as rallying points around which to achieve a more advantageous position.[16] The belief that charisma was transmitted to all collateral members of the Safavi house allowed the Qizilbash to unite around different members of the Safavi family to express their political aspirations. Their loyalty lay with the Safavi household (*dūdmān*), and at times, as in the case of Pari Khan Khanum (b. 1548), Shah Tahmasb's daughter, it was through a female member of the Safavi family that they aspired to rule collectively. The Safavi candidate would have to fight for sole representation of the household, all members of which were qualified to rule. Here, Turco-Mongol concepts of corporate sovereignty colored succession politics within the Safavi house. It would be the Safavi shah's military prowess and political sagacity that would earn him total obedience. Indeed, Shah Tahmasb had to quash the first civil war, before, in his own words, he "became padishah in fact [*bi haqîqat*]."[17] Only then could he begin to solidify Imami religious institutions and elaborate on the new language of sovereignty that he had developed in his *Memoir* and that would in time secure him supreme authority as the shadow of God on earth.[18]

It was Tahmasb's grandson, Abbas I (r. 1587–1629), who (re)applied his centralizing reforms and succeeded to assume the image of a just Shi'i monarch, engraving his grandfather's self-portrayal as the "shadow of God" permanently in Safavi historiography. Abbas I dismantled the appanage system and abated the power of the Qizilbash. He had grown up during a decade of civil war (1576–1590) that followed Shah Tahmasb's death (1576). Similar to the first civil war (1524–1536), this anarchy was typical of the nature of classical Safavi-Qizilbash succession politics. Each individual tribe or bloc of tribes fought for the regency of their particular Safavi princeling. These princes, who had been sent out to the provinces, were placed under the guardianship of the Qizilbash provincial governors. The governor's role as tutor to the Safavi prince provided him and his tribe with the political clout necessary to enter the game of imperial politics. These Qizilbash governors were the makers or breakers of kings. Initially, however, the princeling who ensured the political survival of that Qizilbash general and his tribe was at the mercy of the Qizilbash, who brought him to power. Isma'il I, Tahmasb, and Isma'il II all fought for their independence, and Shah Tahmasb (1524–1576) eventually achieved it. Although Shah Tahmasb began introducing slaves into court service, the struggle with the Qizilbash nevertheless began anew upon the ascendance of his successors.[19]

Abbas I must have been aware of how the Qizilbash had used his ancestors as pawns. They had placed his nearly blind father, Muhammad Khudabandah (r. 1577–1587), on the throne once they had become disenchanted with his uncle Isma'il II (r. 1576–1577) because of his massacre of prominent Qizilbash (including the Khalifat al-Khulafa) and his flirtation with Sunnism. Abbas I had also witnessed the execution of his mother, Mahd-i Ulya (d. 1581), for her involvement against the hegemony of the Qizilbash (Ustajlu). He himself had grown up with the Qizilbash (Ustajlu) in Khurasan, observing them closely. His personal experience, strong character, and political sagacity allowed him to pick up once again on the efforts of his grandfather Tahmasb to consolidate authority within the hands of the Safavi household. Like his grandfather, he used a new elite of royal slaves (*ghulam*) and the *ulama* as a solution to this problematic relationship with the Qizilbash.[20]

Within the first year of his reign, Abbas I displayed his political sensibility. He capitalized on the triumph of his Qizilbash regent, Murshid Quli Khan Ustajlu, to help put an end to the civil war that had plagued the empire for over a decade. He waited wisely until his regent first eliminated Qizilbash opposition to his rule. Once the Ustajlu Khan had massacred Qizilbash dissenters who had supported the candidacy of a rival Safavi princeling, Abū Talib, Abbas I unveiled his personal plot. As soon as all potentially threatening male members of the royal family had been incarcerated and influential Qizilbash opponents of Murshid Quli Khan's cabal executed, Abbas I felt that the time was ripe for him to assert his independence from his regent. At age seventeen, Abbas I assassinated the very man who had utilized him as a pawn in pursuit of personal power within the context of Safavi-Qizilbash tribal politics. His aunt, Zaynab Begum, acted as his advisor. As the daughter of Shah Tahmasb who saw her sister, Pari Khan Khanum, and brother, Isma'il II, eliminated by the Qizilbash, Zaynab Begum certainly retained an institutional memory of Qizilbash-Safavi relations. She remained loyal throughout Abbas I's reign as his confidant in her capacity as head of the Safavi harem. From the outset of his reign, Abbas I relied on the *ghulāms* and the *shāhīsivāns* to carry out the purge against those loyal to his Qizilbash tutor, the Ustajlu Khan. They were the agents through whom Abbas I could consolidate his authority within the Safavi household.

Abbas I ended the second civil war (1576–1590) that had erupted on Tahmasb's death, removing the Qizilbash rebellious governors, Afshar and Zul Qadr, from their appanages in Fars and Kirman.[21] These two Qizilbash tribes had governed the southern provinces from the time of Isma'il's conquest in 1503. They had asserted their independence and refused to pay allegiance to the new shah. Abbas I sent his newly appointed commander of his army, a royal slave, to conquer his dominion from these Qizilbash rebels. And he named this newly converted Caucasian *ghulām*, Allah Verdi Khan, governor of Fars (1595), appointing under him an administration of three hundred slaves.

In consolidating power, Abbas I made use of the royal slaves that Tahmasb had begun to train as palace pages. He increased their number and thoroughly introduced them into the central and provincial administration.[22] At the turn of the seventeenth century, the granting of gubernatorial positions, formerly reserved domains of the Qizilbash, to slaves was rare, in contrast to the reign of Shah Safi (1629–1642), during which it had been the norm.[23] Two years after Allah Verdi Khan was named governor of Fars, Isfahan was proclaimed the new Safavi capital. The southern flank that this new slave governor came to conquer formed a secure cradle above which Shah Abbas could build his capital city in commemoration of the Safavi household's triumph over the Qizilbash. The Qizilbash lost their privilege to receive appanages, along with their laleships, a key element in their bid for equal participation in Safavi politics.

At this stage of centralization, to which I refer as the Isfahani phase of Safavi rule (1590–1722), the Safavis had begun to alter the political and religious landscape of Iran. Shah Abbas I's reforms had far-reaching social implications, particularly for the Qizilbash, who were used to being regarded with special honor and respect. For many Qizilbash, this meant that they no longer enjoyed political and economic privilege, and also that many of the Qizilbash tribes were now governed by the slaves who had been named governors of the provinces in which they lived.[24] Positions for the Qizilbash in the army and in the provincial and court administrations had become much harder to secure now that slaves were being trained in large numbers. The *ghulāms* were groomed at court and owed allegiance to the shah as ruler of the Iranian lands, rather than to a spiritual master whose rule extended over the domains that lay between heaven and earth.

According to Shah Abbas I's (1587–1629) official court chronicler, Iskandar Bek Munshi Turkman, around 330,000 slaves were captured by Abbas I on his Georgian campaign (1614–1615).[25] This date, then, marked the first significant influx of *ghulāms* into the Safavi system. The chronicler explains that "since some of the tribes [*oymaq*] did not possess qualified

candidates to take on high posts once their Qizilbash generals
[*amīr*] and governors had died, a *ghulām* was appointed, due to
his justice, skill, bravery, and self-sacrifice, to the rank of amir of
that clan [*īl*], army [*qushūn va lashkar*], and to the governorship
[*hukūmat*] of that region [*ulkā*]." The whole tribal structure of
the Qizilbash had been affected by Abbas I's centralizing reforms. The Qizilbash Khan/Bek who guaranteed the political
and economic interests of the tribe was rendered impotent once
he was officially replaced by a slave to whose authority he had
to be subservient. The local power of the Qizilbash general was
thus undermined, creating fissures in the intricate web of tribal
and sufi allegiances and loyalties that had enhanced Qizilbash
solidarity. Even the Tajiks (artisans and notables) must have felt
awkward being governed by slaves who were recent converts to
Islam and culturally alien to the Iranian lands. As you may recall, Safavi control of guild activities, whether commercial or ritual, had also severed local ties of patronage that bound craftsmen to sufi circles. Such social transformations would allow for
the exercise of absolute power by the newly reconfigured Safavi
household.

Centralization in the Safavi context was tantamount to the
shattering of the religious and political power of Safavi devotees—Qizilbash and artisans. In the case of the Qizilbash, who
constituted the military backbone of the Safavis, centralization
fractured the tribal structure of the Turkmen tribes that had facilitated powerful Qizilbash resistance to the Safavis. Within the
religious domain, it also served to tame the Qizilbash in an attempt to convert them to Imami Shi'ism, for originally it had
been Alid loyalty that had acted as the cement that bound each
tribe together. Qizilbash reactions to the beginning of Abbas I's
absolutism made their mark throughout the domains in the
form of messianic rebellions and armed confrontations. The in-
creasingly bureaucratized and Imamized empire of Shah Abbas I
and his successors—Shah Safi (1629–1642) and Abbas II (1642–
1666)—must have been an important factor in fomenting
Qizilbash dissatisfaction and hostility toward the Safavis.

Barely three years had passed since Shah Abbas I had put an end to the civil war (1576–1590) and asserted Safavi control over the tribes when some Qizilbash joined the Nuqtavis. The Nuqtavi order provided the Qizilbash with a channel through which opposition could be voiced. Dispossessed of a royal princeling, they abandoned this saintly family and became disciples of a new master.

The conquest of Isfahan encapsulates Abbas I's novel practice of power and his use of religious scholars in the process. Upon Abbas I's accession, his regent, Murshid Quli Khan Ustajlu, had himself named governor of Isfahan and named a slave as his deputy.[26] To effect their hegemony, the Qizilbash employed slaves as well. Once Abbas I had executed his Qizilbash regent, the slave vice governor, Yuli Bek, fortified the citadel and acted as the independent ruler of Isfahan. Even Shah Abbas I's arrival in Isfahan (1589) did not dissuade the rebel governor from his folly. To avoid armed conflict, the shah appointed a delegation to negotiate with the slave. The choice of Shaykh-i Baha'i, the famous chief jurist (Shaykh al-Islam) of Isfahan, as the head of this negotiating team reveals the extent of respect and authority he enjoyed.[27] Shaykh-i Baha'i's father, Shaykh Husayn b. 'Abd al-Samad, had served Shah Tahmasb in his capital city of Qazvin as chief jurist (1556–1563).[28] He was one of the emigrant scholars from southern Lebanon who had been patronized by Tahmasb in an attempt to spread Shi'ism throughout his domains. But he had been demoted and sent to Herat (1569–1573), where Abbas I's father was governor.[29] The grandson of Shaykh Ali Karaki, the author of our *fatwā* against Abū Muslim, was favored instead. Families of Arab scholars were competing among themselves for Safavi patronage, and Baha'i's father eventually left Iran, choosing to live in the Shi'i enclave of Bahrayn. From Bahrayn he wrote to his son Shaykh-i Baha'i: "If you seek this world alone, then go to India. If you desire the next world, then you must come to Bahrayn. But if you desire neither this world nor the afterlife, then stay in Iran."[30] Shaykh-i Baha'i decided to remain in Safavi Iran and managed to secure himself an important position as Shaykh al-Islam in Isfahan. And now with Shah Abbas I, he would play a pivotal role in the consolidation of imperial Safavi Shi'ism. The choice of Baha al-din also reveals Shah Abbas I's reliance on the local authority of the *ulama* in this new phase of his reign. The trust between the Safavi monarch and the Shi'i scholar was mutual. The crowds of mourners that are said to have filled the Maydan-i Naqsh-i Jahan, the central square in Isfahan, for Shaykh-i Baha'i's funeral (1621) attests to his popularity and his success in creating a tolerant religious community in Isfahan where Shi'is, Sunnis (Shafi'i), and sufis could all express their piety toward the family of Muhammad.

Baha'i's presence as chief negotiator achieved its intended aim: the slave was persuaded to surrender the citadel. Shah Abbas I had chosen him because of the status he enjoyed within the Isfahani community as a pious and learned scholar, and the *ghulām's* capitulation illustrated his esteem for this dignitary in particular and perhaps for Islam in general. The Islamization of these new Caucasian converts in the palace schools does not seem to have been superficial. The rebellious slave's allegiance to Shi'ism, or regard for the persuasive arguments that Baha'i may have employed, eventually overcame his personal motivations. Having avoided armed conflict, Shah Abbas I was able to recover the city of Isfahan and proceed to reconquer his empire, which had been shattered by over a decade of civil war from the center outward. Shaykh-i Baha'i was to play yet another role in the construction of Isfahan as a capital city as a consultant-architect and engineer in the drafting of the map for this new capital.[31]

The Friday prayer mosque that Abbas I built as a symbol of the Shi'i community, which his Safavi ancestors had finally secured after a thousand years of Alid struggle, required the legal and theological expertise of Shaykh-i Baha'i to be actualized. Abbas I's reinstatement of Friday prayers as official practice, neglected since the days of Shah Tahmasb placed him in the position to build the first Safavi Friday prayer mosque, which still stands today as a central religious icon to his name in Isfahan. Even though Tahmasb had patronized the practice of Friday prayer under the guidance of a learned jurist (*mujtahid*), he had used the communal mosque already standing in Qazvin. Imami theologians in the sixteenth century continued to debate the legality of performing the Friday prayer during the occultation of the Imam. Shah Abbas I's commissioning of this mosque (1612) once he reconquered Safavi frontier territories—Ottoman, Georgian, and Uzbek—provided him with a religious motive to build a mosque from the booty captured in holy war. With the erection of this mosque, Abbas I, like his grandfather, entered religious controversies and authorized one school of thought. Thanks to Baha'is treatise which is written in Persian (*Jâm'i-yi Abbâsî*) and delineates Shi'i ethics and practice for his new patron king to emulate—Shah Abbas I acquired the legal backing for this monumental enterprise.[32] Shaykh-i Baha'i supported the practice of Friday prayer during occultation, his premise being the importance of communal prayer for creating a sense of unity amid a religiously diverse Safavi landscape. The epigraphic program of the Masjid-i shah mirrors the contents of Baha'is treatise, as these two imperial projects come to embody a diversity of Alid symbols that were part of the classical Safavi idiom but were now being reshaped within Shi'i theological contexts. It is important to note the consciousness with which Abbas I reenacted Tahmasb's legacy. In the inscription of the foundation text, dated 1616, of the mosque, Shah Abbas I dedicates "the spiritual reward [*thawâb*]" of his pious act to the "soul of his grandfather, the greatest, the most honorable, the most magnificent Shah Tahmasb."[33]

The institutional changes that were a product of Abbas I's legacy did not occur in a vacuum. The transformations in Qizilbash and *futuvvat* structures and the introduction of slaves into the Safavi imperial system translated themselves onto the religious sphere and entered a dynamic phase for the debate of religious styles. The hegemonic culture of the dervish cult attracted some mystically minded *ulama* like Shaykh-i Baha'i to sufi ways, which the *shari'a*-minded *ulama* considered blasphemous. Coupled with a curbing of Qizilbash authority from above was a patronizing court attitude toward the humble dervish. This attitude propagated by Abbas I's court is captured in an anecdote recounted by a Shi'i biographer, Tunukabuni (d. 1890–1891), who revels in the use of stories to paint personalities and their milieu.[34] Although Tunukabuni is a later source and has been criticized for giving theatrics priority over facts, he preserves traces of Shah Abbas I's religious policy, for which he is remembered two centuries later.

Tunukabuni writes about a prominent scholar, Sultan al-Ulama, who came from a long line of sayyid notables (Mar'ashi) from the Caspian Sea region of Mazandaran. Sultan al-Ulama's ancestor was a famous mystic who in the late medieval period had established his temporal kingdom. The Safavis had awarded this family with important religious and political positions. His father was the minister of justice, religion, and education and Sultan al-Ulama held the post of grand vizier of Shah Abbas I. The biographer notes that on Sultan al-Ulama's return from Mecca, news reached Shah Abbas I's ears that his vizier did not perform the ritual (*harvalah*) religiously recommended (*mustahabb*) during his pilgrimage.[35] For such arrogance in the house of God, Shah Abbas I chided Sultan al-Ulama: he was to wear a dervish cloak, carry a battle-axe (*tabaržin*) on his shoulder, and perform the ritual in the Maydan-i Naqsh-i Jahan, in front of the shah and his courtiers.[36] The associations implicit in this anecdote between the Ka'ba and the central square of Isfahan are evident. The Maydan was the second Ka'ba as is inscribed on the walls of the new Friday prayer mosque. The parallels between respect for the authority of God and that of the shah are also inscribed in this memory of Abbas I. Total obedience implicit in the master-disciple schema was transposed onto the highest functionary at court, who was expected to submit to the authority of the Safavi shah despite his noble lineage.

Beyond reinforcing the hierarchical structures of authority, this episode illustrates the public court attitude toward the mystic. The itinerant dervish having donned his cloak of obedience had to respect Islam above all and by association the shah, whose role it was to enforce the *shari'a*. As the empire was centralizing, the Safavi court was making use of universal rather than regional symbols of sovereignty. His grandson rejected the image of saint that Tahmasb had cultivated toward the end of his reign, for it represented the antithesis of Shah Abbas I's vision of an urbanized empire. Wandering dervishes were too suggestive of the *ghulāt* heritage of the Qizilbash, an aspect that had added to the fluidity of his grandfather's rule and the decentralization of the Safavi domains. Abbas I still played on the sufi cult: he publicly engaged in the rituals of the Nuqtavi order. But this was done in his capacity as disciple rather than master. As vice regent (*nā'ib*) to the Mahdi, he could still gain legitimacy through his public respect for sufism. Because sufiesque *ghulāt* movements with political aspirations kept emerging, however, a real choice had to be made. So long as *ghuluww* was alive in the empire, religious groups with political aspirations would continue to arise and threaten the stability of the Safavi imperium.[37]

THE SAFAVI HOUSE TRANSFIGURED:
GENDER AND PATRIARCHY

Three years after Shah Abbas I's death, on 20 February 1632, a bloody massacre marked the dramatic end to Safavi classical rule at the court in Isfahan.[38] Forty women of the harem were killed. All of Abbas I's grandsons born to his daughters were blinded. Representatives of political networks who had served this family for a generation and had in fact forged blood ties with them were either executed or discharged. A faction of royal slaves introduced by Abbas I to consolidate his dominion expunged prominent Qizilbash (Shaykhavand) and sayyid notables (Mar'ashi) who had married into the Safavi bloodline.[39] The Safavi household was being redefined within a single patrilineage born of Shah Ismai'il (Haydari), who gained ascendancy as a sacred genealogy protected by a new elite of loyal slaves. The massacre finalized the succession of Abbas I's grandson, Shah Safi. In the process, the slave faction had to rid the court of opposition to its rule, as well as quell another messianic rebellion in the provinces led by a disenchanted Qizilbash, Dervish Reza, who now claimed to be the long-awaited Alid Mahdi. The hegemony of a faction of royal slaves would last through the reign of Shah Safi (1632–1642) only to be toppled in the third year of the reign of his successor-son, the second Shah Abbas, in May 1644, and replaced by remnants of the "lost generation" of Safavi devotees (Shaykhavand cabal). These two reigns—Safi and Abbas II—will be read together as a transitional phase during which the new features of an imperial Safavi idiom were debated and given shape.

An analysis of the cabals that formed around the accessions of Shah Safi and Shah Abbas II will reveal the dominant pressure groups at court during this period of transformation in Safavi history.[40] A study of the politics of succession can be fruitful, especially because the era in question was one in which the nature of authority was revised. Successions represent a natural arena for participants of a dynastic system to demonstrate their aspirations through their support of a particular candidate. Moreover, throughout the nearly four decades (1629–1666) of these two monarchs' reigns, the political rivalries described by the chroniclers surfaced at the junction of these two accessions to the Safavi throne.

During the celebrations of Id-i Khizr al-Nabī, on Friday night, 20 February 1632, all the sons born of Shah Abbas I's daughters were blinded in the harem precincts.[41] It is no coincidence that this yearly festival celebrating a cult of the saint of fertility, Khizr, was chosen as the occasion for the massacre of female members of the extended Safavi family. In eastern Persianate cultural spheres, Khizr is still evoked at childbirth, and women appeal to him for offspring. This invisible saint is believed to make his presence felt every year at the end of winter, leaving his imprints on puddings that women have baked in anticipation of him. His visit into the earthly realm is viewed as a blessing for the coming year for biological and agricultural productivity. Khizr is related to the Zoroastrian water goddess Anahita, and some of her former sanctuaries in Iran were rededicated to him (Pīr-i Sabz).[42] The invisibility and anonymity of Khizr is translated into a multitude of identities depending on the cultural landscapes in which he is reshaped in the Islamic era. In Anatolia, the Greek and Armenian Christian populations merge him with St. George. Beyond these indigenous layers of the cult of Khizr, he represents for sufis a spiritual master and guide into the metaphysical world. According to mystical Qur'anic exegesis, he is the mysterious character who is said to have guided Moses when he was searching for the "junction of the two seas" (*majm'a al-bahrayn*). Khizr is also to have assisted Alexander, Dhu'l Qarnayn, in his expedition to the boundaries of the world in search of immortality. Sufis cast him in the role of a spiritual guide along the journey of initiation, he holds the key to esoteric knowledge.[43] His presence at the Safavi court was to be ominous for the women of the family in 1632. Ironically, the Safavi female sex was rendered sterile on a day when fertility was commemorated. The massacre can be read as a metaphor for a syncretic way of being that Khizr symbolized, which was now officially being suppressed.

Zaynab Begum, who had served her nephew Shah Abbas I loyally as his confidant, also fell victim to the great massacre. Although her life was spared, she was evicted from the harem and banished to her house.[44] Among the forty harem women who were executed was Shah Abbas I's daughter Zubaydah Begum, who had fought for the candidacy of her son Sayyid Muhammad Khan Shaykhavand.[45] Clearly, the harem lay at the center of succession politics. Its composition, however, would alter drastically as Safavi royalty were liquidated—male cousins dispossessed of rule and their mothers, who had the potential of bearing more sons, deprived of reproduction. Adam Olearius, the secretary of the Holstein Embassy at the court of Shah Safi (1637), illuminates the intricate thread of alliances binding this cabal (Shaykhavand). Shah Abbas I's daughter, Zubaydah Begum, the mother of a rival Safavi cousin, worked from within the harem to overthrow Shah Safi. A couple of attempts to poison the young monarch had failed, according to Olearius. Although the shah fell sick for two months, the poison had not been strong enough:[46]

> As soon as he had recovered, he caused an exact inquiry to be made, whereby it was discovered, by means of a woman belonging to the Harem, who had been ill treated by her Mistreas, that the poyson had been prepared in the appartment of the women, and that his [Safi] Aunt, Isa Khan's [Qurchi Bashi] wife, had caused it to be given him.[47]

A history of Safi's reign written by Muhammad Husayn Tafrishi, which ends abruptly on the occasion of the bloody massacre, is the only extant Persian source that links the massacre to the shah's illness, as well as to the attempts to murder him.[48] The chronicler writes that "during the period that the Shah fell ill (September 1631), some evildoers and ill-thinkers had farfetched ideas, thinking that if something happened to the monarch, God forbid, they could follow and obey Abbas I's grandsons [nasvab]. And some simple-minded ones obeyed this. After a couple of days [following his recovery], the Shah ordered the killings of the children of a prominent Qizilbash general [Qurchi Bashi] and the other princes."[49]

Harem linkages with the outer court (birūn) are constructed by Olearius as well as the contemporaneous Persian chronicler through a cousin of Shah Abbas I's, Isa Khan Qurchi Bashi, who headed an elite military corp of men culled from among the Qizilbash. Shah Abbas I had entrusted Isa Khan Shaykhavand with this royal corps because of their familial ties and must have felt that he could rely on his cousin's loyalty more than that of other Qizilbash leaders. Isa Khan was a descendant of Shah Isma'il's grandfather, Junayd: he symbolized not only the *ghulāt* persona of this ancestor but a branch of the Safavi family that had been incorporated into the Qizilbash system of tribes in the sixteenth century. The Shaykhavands represented the ancien regime. In addition to blood and spiritual ties, Isa Khan had been betrothed to Abbas I's daughter, Zubaydah Begum—a further measure taken to ensure obedience. The Shaykhavand cabal based its claim on the Turco-Mongol theory of succession, according to which once the descendants of the "eponymous" ruling line had become extinct, the eldest member from a cousin clan could form a "neo-eponymous" state.[50] Iskandar Bek Munshi Turkman explains that the Shaykhavand candidate was considered a potential successor to Abbas I because people thought no one from the Safavi family was left to ascend the throne, for they were not aware of the existence of Prince Safi in Isfahan.[51] As a descendant of Shaykh Junayd, Sayyid Muhammad Khan was a member of the Safavi (eponym) extended household.[52] In addition, his mother, Zubaydah Begum, was the daughter of Abbas I. It could be argued, therefore, that the right to the throne belonged to Sayyid Muhammad Khan—that is, according to Turco-Mongol culture.

In this process of centralization, in the rationalization of power, the Safavis, like the Ottomans (1301–1924), came to rely on a legal and religious basis for their dominion, one closely linked to the promise and ability to enforce the *shar'ia*. Authority was being redefined in Safavi Iran (1501–1722), emphasizing aspects of urbanized Islam, more particularly in its Imami Shi'i ethos, which is essentially patriarchal. Early modern Muslim empires like the Ottomans and the Safavis initially observed Turco-Mongol political practice, in that they shared power that was distributed in the form of appanages among the entire dynastic house, male and female.[53] And so women played a formative role at court and in the imperial life of Safavi dynasties. In practice, land belonged to the paramount ruling family as a whole. Like Safavi men, female kin too engaged in politics to protect their patrimony. Moreover, both male and female Safavi blood was believed to be laced with a divinely bestowed charisma, which is why princesses in the seventeenth century were blinded along with their brothers for fear that they may lay claim to the throne. All females, whether descended from male or female blood, could rule—a phenomenon particular to the Safavis.[54] In seventeenth-century practice, in fact, female members were blinded as well as males, except for three or four males of close kin. This practice, which the perceptive French observer of Safavi Iran Jean Chardin terms *la politique Persane*, was exercised by the later Safavis to limit rule to a direct and fixed patrilineal succession.

The involvement of the ambitious daughter of Shah Tahmasb, Pari Khan Khanum (d. 1578), in the succession politics that followed her father's death reveals the extent to which the Safavis regarded sovereignty as being vested in the ruling family as a whole—that is, both male and female descendants were cloaked with authority. Perhaps this particular definition of the household (*dūdmān*) also invoked ancient Iranian notions of the *farr* (New Persian) or *khvaranah* (Avestan), a divine grace bestowed on the dynastic family.[55] Because both Turco-Mongol and Iranian ideals of sovereignty see power vested in the ruling family, it is difficult to assess whether such ideas were derived from central Asian or Iranian heritage. I tend to understand these practices as an aspect of cultural reinforcement, with shared conceptions enhancing continuity.

Although some chroniclers delineate the extent to which political participation for the preservation of the hearth of Safavi rule was seen as a prerogative of the female bloodline, already at the turn of the seventeenth century reactions were voiced in the chronicles against Pari Khan Khanum's successful rallying of political support and maintenance of order between both interregnums that led to the accessions of her brother, Isma'il II, and her nephew, Muhammad Khudabandah. These reactions aimed at delegitimizing female power. Shah Abbas I's chronicler, Iskandar Bek Munshi Turkman, speaks of the power this princess wielded among the Qizilbash: "not one of them dared to contravene her orders. And most of the generals, convening at the house of the princess Pari Khan Khanum, offered their services as per custom [*bi tarīq-i ma'hūd*]. They understood that such attendance enhanced the lofty rank and honor of kingship. The deputies [*vakīl*] of the above-mentioned princess arranged for more majestic rituals [*ā'īn*] and ceremony [*tuzūk*] and pomp [*tumturāq*] than during the days of Shah Tahmasb, and her attendants and chamberlains maintained order according to kingly customs [*bitarīq-i salātīn nazm u nasq-i dargāh mībudand*]."[56] The chronicler has her rival brother, Isma'il II, voice his discontent with the Qizilbash generals who had been convening at Pari Khan Khanum's residence. Chiding them, he is to have said; "Have friends [*yārān*] not understood that interference by women in matters of the realm [*umūr-i mamlikat*] is not worthy of royal honor [*lāyiq-i nāmūs-i pādishāhī*] and that it is shameful for men to associate with the veiled and chaste of the Safavi royal house?"[57] In an attempt to legitimize his right to rule over his sister, Shah Abbas I's chronicler uses Ismai'il II as his mouthpiece to argue that females are not only unworthy of rule but that their exercise of political power tarnishes male honor. The chronicler (d. 1633) who is projecting this attitude back in time has Isma'il II (d. 1577) invoke another set of traditions in Islamdom to counter the claims of his sister.

As the Safavis began to centralize power in the hands of a single male of the Safavi house, this new political theory that reserved and limited legitimacy to the patrilineal successors of the eponymous founder of the Safavi dynasty Isma'il was enforced. This time, Shah Abbas I's chronicler has a prominent member of the Safavi cousin clan, Isa Khan Shaykhavand, confirm the new discourse of authority: "Sovereignty and kingship is the right of Shah Isma'il and Tahmasb's family, who having sent their dust-and-wind borne opponents to hell with the fire of their well-tempered swords, revealed and manifested Imami Shi'ism and spread it throughout the world."[58] One century after the Safavis came to power, on the succession of the first Safavi shah, Shah

Safi (r. 1629–1642), to be enthroned in the imperial capital of Isfahan (1590–1722), Iskandar Bek Munshi Turkman was expounding on the new type of political theory that was in the process of replacing the classical Safavi synthesis between Turco-Mongol and Iranian political systems. According to this chronicler, what separated Isma'il and his male lineal descendants from other members of the Safavi extended family was that his descendants had reinvigorated Shi'ism in Iran. Hence, as propagators of Shi'ism, Isma'il's descendants were sole heirs to its dominion. At the turn of the seventeenth century, as Shah Isma'il was being cast as the founder of an Imami Shi'i empire, the idea of an eponymous dynastic clan and a sacrosanct family (*dūdmān*) was replaced by the concept of a fixed patrilineage in which succession passed to the next generation through primogeniture.

As the court was becoming urbanized, the nature of male royal power took on feminine characteristics, in that shahs too were secluded in the heart of the palace (*qafes*)—secluded, that is from the battlefield, a means through which they could assert their masculinity and control. It was the concubine mother who now would become more powerful. The newly established "cage" system instituted by Abbas I may have been the impetus for this shift from the active political participation of aunts, sisters, and daughters of Safavi monarchs to the predominance of the role of the queen mother. Abbas I had personally experienced the insecurities of the crown and had abandoned the practice of sending out princes to the provinces.[59] In this fashion, the power of prominent Qizilbash leaders, who were customarily designated as guardians (*lalé*) to the royal princes, was contained. Confining the princes to the harem precincts further tightened the umbilical cord between the prince and his mother and strengthened her role and the role of the eunuchs who guarded the harem.[60] The "cage" system, while restricting the role of the Qizilbash guardians, enhanced the role of Shah Safi's mother—and by extension, that of the harem—in politics. Mothers of princes could legitimize their political agency not only as wives of current kings but as guardians and representatives of future Safavi monarchs. In the process, new members of the household—such as eunuchs of the harem and elite slaves, whose function was to maintain the power of the Safavi family—gained in prominence. Power was further concentrated in the harem, the heart of the Safavi court: political power was transferred from the dynastic family/clan to a slave royal household. The massacre of all competing cousins delayed opposition to a new generation of the descendants of Shah Safi, thus creating a clean slate.

Through a reconfigured household, Shah Abbas I's successors, Safi and Abbas II, ruled his city of paradise—through military slaves, concubines, and eunuchs. Although both genders would have to exert their power through intermediaries, the classical era during which they had shared in the protection of their patrimony had lapsed. Now the construction of royal Safavi power would emphasize patrilineality and patriarchy, principles central to the cultural matrix of Islam.[61] These two organizational principles of kinship found religious sanction through the ritual of coronation. Instead of the Khalifat al-Khulafa, a revered representative of the Safavi order, placing the red crown symbolizing spiritual dominion on the king's head, the monarch was girded by a Shi'i clergyman, and coins were minted in his name. Shah Safi's name was called out during the sermon (khutba) of the Friday prayer at the royal mosque, Masjid-i Shah, built by Abbas I. Urbanization had ushered in an era in which political legitimacy would be derived from temporal rule sanctioned by divine law and through descent from a patrilineage of Fatima and Ali's sons and grandsons. Imami legitimacy may have also served the Safavi will to limit charisma to the person of the shah and religious scholars, rather than to the entire dynastic family. Such legitimacy served the shari'a-minded as well, who were attempting to limit the influence of sufis and even mystically minded philosophers, to reserve the role of intermediary between believer and God for the awaited Mahdi and for themselves.

Like his grandfather Tahmasb, Abbas I enjoyed a long reign that stretched over four decades. Both monarchs felt secure enough, internally as well as externally, to alternate the factor of Qizilbash dependency. In a step designed to alter the existing order, Abbas I (re)introduced the royal corps of slaves into the topography of the central (*andarūn*) and the provincial (*birūn*) administrations.[62] Both came to rely more heavily on regional notables (*sayyid* and *Tajik*) with strong local ties in the process. Abbas I took the major leap and placed a religious notable, Sultan al-Ulama, in the all-powerful seat of grand vizier,[63] (see figure 7). With Shi'i sanction, local support, and royal slaves, the power of the crown could be freed of Qizilbash control. Although Abbas I was cautious to maintain a structural equilibrium between these powerful elements of the empire (*ghulāms*, *ulama*, *sayyids*, Turks, and Tajik), the balance became precarious when the autocrat was gone.

The struggles over succession that surfaced on the death of Shah Abbas I finalized the victory of one faction of slave elites at court. Indeed, the Qizilbash had lost their political hegemony. Shah Abbas I's reforms had set in motion a dynamic that perpetuated the Isfahani phase of Safavi rule beyond his reign, and with the accession of the slave cabal's candidate, Shah Safi (1629–1642), a new imperial language of power was ritualized in his support. Officially, Safi's candidacy was sanctioned over that of his rival cousin, Sayyid Muhammad Khan Shaykhavand, a descendant of Haydar's half-brother, Khwaja Muhammad, for the right to sovereignty and kingship was said to have rested with the patrilineal descendants of Haydar—Isma'il and Tahmasb—who with the sword revealed and manifested Imamism and spread it throughout the world.[64] Shah Safi was the first Safavi monarch to be enthroned by a cleric, Mir-i Damad, who in turn was one of the first native Iranians (Astarabadi) in the history of the Safavi empire to have achieved the rank of grand jurisconsult (*mujtahid*).[65] The grandees who had been with Shah Abbas I in Mazandaran arrived in Isfahan

nineteen days after Shah Safi had been made king.[66] Denizens of
Isfahan had already heard Shah Safi's name being called out by
Mir-i Damad during the sermon (*khutba*) of the Friday prayer
he recited at the magnificent Masjid-i Jami'-i Jadid, the royal
mosque Shah Abbas I had built as a symbol of his affirmation
and adherence to Imamism.[67]

Parallels can be drawn with medieval Alid history. Although
Husayn's half-brother Muhammad b. Hanfiyya and his
Kaysaniyya devotees were politically active, in the rewriting of
Shi'i (Imami) history, it is Husayn's male descendants who were
sanctified as legitimate heirs to Ali's charisma. As propagators of
this new faith in early modern Iran, Isma'il's patrilineal descendants were to be the sole heirs to Safavi dominion. Imami legitimacy separated his direct descendants from collateral members
of the Safavi extended family, particularly from Junayd, who
reeked of *ghuluww*. Legitimacy was thus reserved for the
Haydari line alone, who had revived and would continue to defend Shi'ism in Iran. In the Isfahani phase, Turco-Mongol notions of an eponymous dynastic clan and Indo-Iranian notions
of a sacrosanct family (*dūðman*) were replaced by the concept of
a fixed patrilineage in which succession passed to the next generation through primogeniture.

The Safavi goal of centralization could not be achieved within
the framework of classical Safavi political culture. The particular blend of Turco-Mongol and sufi paradigms of authority was
being overshadowed by a new synthesis in which notions of Iranian kingship merged with Shi'i symbols to shape a new language of temporal authority. It is at this moment that Shah
Abbas I's image as shadow of God on earth is inscribed in Safavi
historical memory, and Tahmasb and his father Isma'il together
are cast as propagators of Imami Shi'ism, who put an end to the
innovation of the *ghulāt*. The gradual shift to a self-consciously
logical conception of political rule parallels the Safavi public rejection of gnosticism and other syncretic forms of cultural practice that were located beyond the pale of textual and normative
Islam in the post-Mongol era.

The successions of Safi and Abbas II and the political factions that formed around these two candidates demonstrate the radical change that the Safavi system had undergone by the third decade of the seventeenth century. To begin with, there were no longer civil wars but rather revolts in the provinces—Gilan and Qazvin—that were quelled by a new provincial administration that relied heavily on slave governors. The Qizilbash as a coalition of varying tribal solidarities had lost their political clout at court. We no longer observe blocs of Qizilbash forming opposition groups. Rather, as in the case of the Shaykhavand cabalists, individual Turkmen formed alliances with traditional political actors, like local notables, Sayyid and Tajik. But this time, they rallied against groups of slave elites (*ghulām*). Tribal participation in the factions at court occurred on an individual basis, with Turkmen family members who collaborated with networks outside the tribal system being represented. The social formations of the cabals encapsulate the changes in the nature of participation stimulated by Abbas I's attempt to break Qizilbash solidarity, which had by then been eliminated as a cohesive political force.

Both the messianic revolt of the Qizilbash Dervish Reza (1631) and the rise of the Shaykhavand cabal act as testimony to the waning of the Qizilbash as a hegemonic political and religious force. Resistance and dissent were voiced through an apocalyptic scenario and court faction. And there very well may have been a connection between the messianic claims of Dervish Reza and the Shaykhavand cabalists. The Shaykhavands included not only a descendant of Junayd but also a famous sayyid—Mar'ashi—whose ancestor was a revered mystic king of Mazandaran. These two families—Shaykhavand and Mar'ashi—shared a history of partnership in the Safavi *ghūlat* venture. During their revolt (1631), the self-proclaimed messiah Dervish Reza and his devotees had headed for the shrine of Imamzadah Shahzadah Husayn on the outskirts of Qazvin, where they took sanctuary. For the denizens of Qazvin, this shrine, marking the burial place of the infant son of Imam Reza, was the most important site of visitation and congregation. When Shah Tahmasb had moved his capital to Qazvin (1555), he had the shrine rebuilt and enlarged, fostering the Safavi tradition of veneration for the family of Muhammad.[68] Accompanied by a couple of his devoted followers, Dervish Reza entered the shrine complex and congregated around the tomb of Mir Faghfur, the grand Mar'ashi sayyid of Qazvin, whose family had held the hereditary post of superintendents *(mutavallī)* of that shrine for generations.[69] The disciples of Dervish Reza declared that their spiritual guide would bring Mir Faghfur back to life.[70] I read this messianic revolt as a provincial act of resistance by the ancien regime attempting to revivify the revolutionary ideals of the Safavi Alid mission.

Traditional forces came into direct conflict at court against a new elite of slaves.[71] Their vested interest in the maintenance of political, economic, and religious autonomy helped forge the Shaykhavand alliance against an emerging faction of slave elites. Members of the cabal had initially allied themselves with the Safavis. In so doing, some prominent landed sayyid families had been successful in maintaining their regional authority. For generations before the rise of the Safavis, their fathers had engaged, like the Mar'ashi's, in the administration of local religious and political affairs. The Safavis had solicited their help early on to consolidate their empire: they had formally been incorporated into Abbas I's court as courtiers and sons-in-law *(dāmād)*.[72]

Sultan al-Ulama represents the way in which Abbas I had utilized a distinguished member of the religious milieu, whose sayyid ancestors enjoyed much regional power and prestige. He was descended from a long line of local rulers *(vālī)* of Mazandaran, the Mar'ashi dynasty of Tabaristan founded by a mystic, Mir-i Buzurg (d. 1379).[73] Mir-i Buzurg was a disciple *(khalīfa)* of the famous Shaykh Hasan-i Juri, from whose order another Alid messianic dynasty of the Sarbidars (1336–1381) in Khurasan emerged. Regional histories of the Caspian Sea speak of Mir-i Buzurg's tomb in Amul as a popular place of pilgrimage in the fifteenth century.[74] His Alid descent gave him eminence not only among sufi orders and confraternities but among the broader population of Mazandaran. Although Arabs were already settled in this region in the tenth century, Mazandaran remained heavily populated by Persians who maintained their particular northern dialects. Shi'ism (Zaydi) had entered Caspian sea landscapes early in medieval times, providing common spheres for Alid and Mazdean languages to cross-fertilize. The Mar'ashi mystic king lived, in fact, in the very city—Amul—from which our Alid eulogist, Hasan-i Kashi, writing in 1308 and 1309, complained a generation earlier that people listened to the *Shāhnāme,* constantly craving to hear warrior epics sung in Persian. And so he decides to compose a *Book on the Imams* in Persian in the hope that perhaps the audience will listen to stories about the valor of Ali and his children. The Mar'ashi may have engaged in this conversion that translated Alid history through Mazdean frameworks and epic structures into the Persian language.

In Isfahan, too, Sultan al-Ulama must have enjoyed the popular support attached to his lineage. His ancestor Nizam al-Din Ali had moved from Mazandaran to Isfahan in the fifteenth century. His own links to the famous Shahristani sayyids of Isfahan, through his mother, further strengthened his local connections. By the time of the rise of the Safavis, the Mar'ashis in Isfahan were revered among the Alid community as the descendants of Mir-i Buzurg (*sādāt-i khalīfa*). Sultan al-Ulama's grandfathers had already received patronage from Shah Isma'il and Shah Tahmasb, but it was not until the reign of Abbas I that Sultan al-Ulama's father, Mir Rafi al-Din Muhammad, received an official post at court, that of minister of religion, justice, and education (Sadr)—a position historically held by sayyids in the sixteenth century.[75] But while his father was Sadr (1617–1624), Sultan al-Ulama was nominated to the post of grand vizier (1623–1624). In his biography of poets, Nasrabadi notes with surprise "that in past times no *sayyid* family [*silsila*] had enjoyed such good fortune and had been elevated to both of these lofty positions simultaneously."[76]

Sultan al-Ulama's family had strong economic interests in Isfahan as well. They were probably linked through the culture of Alid brotherhoods with craftsmen and the bazaar. A relative of Sultan al-Ulama in Isfahan—Mir Qutb al-Din Mahmud— was entrenched in these millieus; it was due to his objections, along with those of Mirza Muhammad Amin, the Naqib al-Nuqaba of Isfahan, that Shah Abbas abandoned his original plan to redevelop the old market district in Isfahan. Instead, the shah decided to build a new commercial district by the Maydan-i Naqsh-i Jahan. Robert McChesney speculates that the Mar'ashis of Isfahan (*sādāt-i khalīfa*) must have been "wealthy, with substantial investments in both land and commercial real estate."[77] McChesney argues that Mir Qutb al-Din's opposition to Abbas I's plans for renovating the old market district, indicated that his family's economic interests had been at stake. Mir Qutb al-Din represented a network of local ties between the religious and the commercial sectors in Isfahan. With the introduction of royal slaves who would supervise and invest in the new urban development of Isfahan, these economic interests were threatened.

One of the members of the slave cabal, Muhibb Ali Bek (Lalé Bek), was the teacher of the royal corps of slaves. His position had allowed him to cultivate paternal ties with some of his students, emotional bonds of dependency that fostered patron-client relations once they were manumitted and entered the world of Safavi politics as free Muslims. Muhibb Ali Bek had probably assembled his former novices like Rustam Bek (Sipahsalar) and Çelebi Bek Evoghlu (Ishik Aqasi Bashi of the harem) to secure the position of this group of slaves at court who attached themselves to the Haydari line of the Safavi monarchs. Lalé Bek had been influential during the reign of Shah Abbas I. His name, Muhibb Ali Bek b. Muhammad Quli Khan, appears on an inscription at the main entrance to the Masjid-i Shah in Isfahan, the royal mosque built by Abbas I, for he had supervised (*mushrif*) the building of the mosque. Once the mosque complex had been completed, he was given the superintendency *(tawliyat)* it. In addition, he must have been wealthy, given that after Abbas I, he was the major donor to the endowment *(waqf)* of the Masjid-i Shah.[78] His alliance with the chief merchant, Malik al-Tujjar Mulayim Bek, points to an important force that bound this faction together—financial interests. Not only was the new elite of slaves infiltrating the administration of the provinces and the inner court, but slaves also became major participants in the economy of Isfahan. Moreover, they established ties with the Armenian community of merchants that Abbas I had settled in the suburb of Isfahan (Julfa) as his personal silk merchants, bankers, and diplomats.[79] Slaves, Armenian merchants, and Shi'i religious scholars would be the new pillars on which Safavi absolutism was consolidated in Isfahan.

Representatives of two Safavi cousin clans, the Shaykhavands and Pirzadahs, who shared in the family charisma, collaborated with Abbas I's aunt, daughter, and son-in-laws.[80] These cabalists represented, at least symbolically, Safavi revolutionary ideals. The Shaykhavands bear it in their name as "vessels of the shaykh," for they were descendants from Shaykh Junayd, who embodied excess.[81] During the reign of Shah Tahmasb (1524–1576), the Shaykhavands had officially been incorporated into the system and were considered as Qizilbash.[82] The Pirzadahs descended from the spiritual master Shaykh Zahid-i Gilani of Shaykh Safi. Shaykh Zahid had married his daughter to Safi and had sent him as a missionary to Ardabil. When he died (1301), Safi took over the order despite the objections of some devotees who followed Shaykh Zahid's son in Gilan.[83] Ardabil, however, grew to become the center of gravity of the Safavi branch of this order. The descendants of the Shaykhavands and the Pirzadahs were thus associated with the charisma of the order. They also owned land in Ardabil, the seat of Safavi mysticism and commerce.[84] The eventual loss of the economic and political privileges of the Pirzadahs and the Shaykhavands in Ardabil was linked to the consolidation of Safavi power within one patrilineage.[85] For these cabalists, Abbas I's introduction of a slave elite coupled with the integration of revenues from provinces (*khassah*) into his private treasury provoked the fracturing of social and spiritual networks bound historically to the Safavi brotherhood.

Unlike the Ottomans who married their sisters and daughters to slaves, this new Safavi elite of slave converts to Islam would be deprived of blood ties with Safavi females. Whereas Safavi women had been married to elites in the sixteenth century, now they would be kept for male relatives of the family. The practice of *musāhirah*, the cementing of alliances through marriage, was a tool employed by the Safavis to consolidate and legitimate power. Until the days of Abbas I, these marriages had occurred mainly between the Safavi royal family and the Qizilbash. With Abbas I's reforms, royal marriage with *sayyid* religious notables became the mode.[86] Sultan al-Ulama, for example was given Abbas I's daughter, Aqa Begum, in marriage. This consolidated the existing kinship ties between the Mar'ashis of Mazandaran and Shah Abbas I (Abbas's mother was herself a Mar'ashi), finally incorporating the Caspian Sea province under direct Safavi dominion. Unlike the Ottoman system, *ghulām*s were not betrothed to Safavi princesses. Abbas I's strategy of marriage alliances with *sayyid* notables was one way of linking the fate of the crown (*tāj*) with that of the turban (*'amāmah*). Partners to these unions were expected to serve the Safavis with loyalty now that their interests had converged. The equation, in fact, worked both ways: Safavi sons-in-law (*damād*) could now use these dynastic ties to resist change from within the system. Such was the strategy of the Shaykhavand cabal. But the new elite of slaves would have different access to the harem, through slave concubines, the dominant mode of procreation for Safavi monarchs in the seventeenth century.

For the duration of the reign of Shah Safi, his slave household—concubines, eunuchs, and military slaves—would dominate the court, vying among themselves for power. The dynamics of change saw a group of slaves consolidate their authority both militarily and within the harem. A key figure active in the centralizing project at Shah Safi's court was his grand vizier nicknamed Saru Taqi, "Blondie" (1634–1645), by Shah Abbas I. Saru Taqi was technically not a slave, in that he was not a Caucasian convert to Islam who had been separated from his roots and groomed at court for imperial service. Although Saru Taqi was a non-Qizilbash from Tabriz, he should be classified as a eunuch because he had been castrated by Abbas I for having engaged in the act of sodomy. Rumor had it that the castration was for sodomy and for the kidnapping of a young boy.[87] That he did not enjoy the typical access and support provided to "men of the pen" and "men of the sword" in sixteenth-century Iran placed him within the social world of slaves. Saru Taqi had risen through the provincial administration, neither from within the Qizilbash tribal system nor through the new corps of slaves. He had been elevated through his own merits, acting as a loyal servant of Shah Abbas I. Saru Taqi had supervised Shah Abbas I's creation of two new towns in Mazandaran, a development project that involved the building of trade routes and the resettlement of fifteen thousand families from northwestern Iran (Qarabagh, Shirvan, and Georgia). On Abbas I's death, he held the position of governor of the shah's motherland, Mazandaran. Saru Taqi maintained Safavi control over this province, quelling rebellions in the neighborhood province of Gilan as well as the Dervish Reza revolt in Qazvin. Indeed, he performed the loyal role *ghulām*s were to play for the Safavi household. Saru Taqi had the added advantage of being a eunuch who could enter the harem, the most private arena of family politics.

With Shah Abbas I's death, Saru Taqi made his way to Isfahan, the center of power. The key to his success at court lay in his close relation with a slave, Ughurlu Bek, who served in the civil administration, *dārūghah* of accounts.[88] This slave's access to Shah Safi was through his daughter, who was an influential concubine in the harem. The Safavi slave system then allowed for slave children, both male and female, to participate in politics as free Muslims. The influence of this slave's daughter in the harem coincides with the year of Abbas II's birth. Within harem politics of the postcage system, it was conventional for the first women who gave birth to a male heir of a monarch to gain polit-ical status.[89] Saru Taqi's connection was with Abbas II's mother. Beyond the fact that the dates of the influence of Ughurlu Bek's concubine daughter align with the birth of Shah Abbas II and the access that Saru Taqi had to the shah through his slave patron, later political alliances confirm this circumstantial evi-dence.

When Safi died (1642), the accession of his son, Abbas II, took place quite smoothly. Saru Taqi maintained his position as grand vizier, eliminating those *ghulāms* like Rustam Bek, whose ally in the harem was probably Safi's Georgian concubine mother, to consolidate power within his faction.[90] Foreign trav-elers like Chardin speak of the close relationship between Saru Taqi and Abbas II's mother, Anna Khanum.[91] Chardin describes their friendship and close collaboration in his discussion of Saru Taqi's assassination by a rival Turkmen—the Qurchi Bashi, Jani Khan Shamlu, three years after Abbas II ascended the Safavi throne (1645):

> The power of mothers of Persian kings loom large when they [shahs] are at a young age. Abbas II's mother had much influence, which was absolute. They [queen-mothers] were in close contact with the prime minster and would help each other mutually. Sary Taqi was the agent and confidante of the queen mother, he would gather immense fortunes for her. She governed Persia at her will through her minister.[92]

The harem connection was key to Saru Taqi's success in at-taining the lofty position of grand vizier. But this time around, it would be mothers who would play a prominent role in politics through their sons. Chardin, writing between 1665 and 1677, observes that the "palace of women," where a form of private council was held, caused most trouble for the Safavi "minis-ters." The council included mothers of shahs, favored concu-bines, and eunuchs. If the ministers did not rule according to the interest of these *personnes cheries*, they risked ruin.[93] Although Saru Taqi had connections in the outer court—Ughurlu Bek and

Mirza Muhammad Majlis Nivis—his faction remained ineffective without support from the inner court (*andarūn*). Since the heart of the pro-Safi slave faction lay in the harem, with the person of Safi's mother, it could be matched only from within. Ironically, Saru Taqi's castration turned to be a political blessing. Along with the altered role of the harem, the position of military slaves and eunuchs had improved. The *ghulām* connection with the harem was strong, whether through female relations living in the harem, or through peers—other eunuchs in the harem—who had studied with them in the palace school.

Chardin goes on to describe the way in which in the Isfahani phase the queen mother engaged in the political arena. Saru Taqi was assassinated by another courtier, the Turkman Jani Khan, probably with the consent of the reigning monarch, Abbas II, who was attempting to gain his independence from his mother and her slave allies. Chardin states that Anna Khanum was furious at the assassin of her ally Saru Taqi. She sent one of the principal eunuchs, probably the elder, *rish sefid* of the harem to the culprit, Jani Khan, asking him to explain his actions. The assassin, Jani Khan, responded rudely, calling Saru Taqi a dog and a thief, and then proceeded to insult the queen mother personally:

> Saru Taqi was a dog and a thief who should have been killed long ago. Tell this to the grand duchess and tell her that he was a true scoundrel of Julfa . . . and I shall prove within five months that this cursed dog has exhorted two hundred thousand pounds. He [Jani Khan] was saying this to irritate the queen mother because the revenue of this suburb is the appanage of the king's mother and not one dime can be levied without her orders.[94]

Chardin represents the queen mother as receiving tax revenues from the Armenian community of Julfa. He calls this income her *taxe de la Chaussure,* stating that this tax was an old Persian custom practiced since Achaemenid times when Egypt fell under Persian domination. The revenue from the most famous among the cities of the realm was set aside for the wife of the sovereign as "footwear expenditure." The Armenians had been introduced by Abbas I as his bankers and financiers, who traded Persian silk for European silver.[95] They were a major source of revenue with which Abbas I, Safi, and his successor Abbas II would construct Isfahan as the city of paradise. Saru Taqi was one of the most important builders for the new Safavi household, as he used his own money to erect a mosque and a bazaar in Isfahan. He even had supervised the building of an important religious site of pilgrimage, the tomb of Ali in Najaf, which Shah Safi's new slave general had recaptured from the Ottomans in Iraq in 1631.[96] The Safavi slave household were agents through which a new imperial idiom was crafted in Isfahan, inscribed visually through buildings and articulated discursively in the Shi'i rhetoric of kingship.

Saru Taqi supervised the addition of the roofed structure Talar onto the Ali Qapu palace, the threshold from which the hidden messiah was to manifest himself. This vast stage was superimposed onto the lofty gate that commanded a panoramic view of the entire square from which Abbas II could display his bravura of power. Saru Taqi was the administrator who built spaces for Safi and Abbas II in which they could direct the yearly Karbala dramas, imposing their control through urbanized ceremonial structures that allowed them to partake in the creation of Alid collective memory. These vast open arenas were intended for the performance of lavish commemorations and feasts that allowed the monarchs to manage social and religious expression within their orbit of authority.

With the assassination of Saru Taqi, Sultan al-Ulama, one of the main participants of the Shaykhavand cabal, was (re)appointed as grand vizier, bringing to a close a decade of slave hegemony. And the young Shah Abbas II was able to break from his powerful mother, now that her ally, the eunuch Saru Taqi was dead. Abbas II's appointment of two religious scholars of *sayyid* descent as grand vizier (Sultan al-Ulama in 1655 and the Sadr Mirza Muhammad Mahdi in 1661) indicates that he had opted for a solution similar to the one his grandfather and namesake, Abbas I, had arrived at by the end of his reign in 1629. A representative from the religious establishment was placed at the pinnacle of temporal power, backed by an administration in which Persian (Tajik) bureaucrats, Turkmen, and slaves shared power.[97] The policy of incorporating the Shi'i clergy within the Safavi court had been part of the Safavi strategy to impinge on the *ghuluww* of their devotees. But there was an entire controversy over the question of authority that had come to polarize the religious community in Isfahan. Such dynamics would affect the texture of imperial Safavi discourse and practice. Let us move from the palace into the mosque, the theological seminaries and public arenas of socialization where culture was lived and debated.

NOTES

1. Iskandar Bek Munshī Turkmān, *Tarīkh-i 'Ālam Ārā-yi 'Abbāsī* (Tehran: Amīr Kabīr, 1971), vol. 1, 474.
2. *Shāhīsīvan* literally means "those who love the shah." They were recruited from among the different Qizilbash tribes. In return for an official post, they were ready to break away from tribal loyalties and fight for the person of the shah.
3. Turkmān, *Tārīkh-i 'Ālam Ārā-yi 'Abbāsī*, vol. 2: 610–612.
4. See Robert McChesney, "Waqf and Public Policy: The Waqf of Shah 'Abbas, 1011–1023/1602–16," *Asian and African Studies* 15 (1981): 169–170.
5. Ahmad Kasravī, in his "Tārīkhchah-yi Shīr u Khurshīd," *Armaghān* 11, 7 (1930): 542–554, argues that Shah Abbas I was the first Safavi monarch to incorporate the symbols of the sun and the lion on his coins. Kasravī argues that the first Muslim ruler to have used the *shir u khurshid* (sun and lion) was Ghiyas al-din Kay Khusraw II (1236–1246) of the Anatolian Saljuqs. He had a sample of this coin in his possession. Kasravī brings textual proof as well. Ibn-i 'Abri in his *Mukhtasar Tavārīkh al-duval* notes this in an interesting story about Ghiyās al-din, who falls in love with a beautiful Georgian woman and wants to have her face engraved on his coins. The religious scholars resist, but Ghiyās al-din insists.

They arrive at the solution of using the motif of the lion with a sun behind it, the sun being the face of the Georgian woman! Abbas I, according to Kasravī, revives this motif (minus the Gorgi women) and uses Ghiyās al-din's coin as a pattern (because of the placement of the sun behind the lion). So Kasravī adduces that although he has never seen the *shīr u khurshīd* on Ilkhani, Qara/Aqquyunlu, or Timuri coins, the motif must have been used since Abbas I had access to it. John Woods has filled in this gap for us. He reports: "The earliest *shīr u khurshīd* coins I know of offhand are the dirhams minted by Ghiyās al-din Kay Khusraw II (I have two in my collection). I also have a dirham of the Ilkhan Arghun (1284–1291) with an eagle and sun and a copper fals of Ghazan Khan with only a sun. Finally, I have a copper coin of Hamza Aqquyunlu (1435–1444) with a *shīr u khurshīd*. These are the only pre-Safavid items I have." I would like to thank John Woods for kindly sharing this information with me.

6. Turkman, *Tārīkh-i 'Ālam Ārā-yi 'Abbāsī*, vol. 2, 882.

7. Martin B. Dickson, "Shah Tahmasb and the Uzbeks: The Duel for Khuransan with Ubayd Khan, 1930–46/1524–40," Ph. D. diss., Princeton University, 1958.

8. See Jean Aubin's excellent study on the Lahijani sufis in his "Revolution Chiite et conservatisme: Les Soufis de Lahejan, 1500–14 (Etudes Safavides II)," *Moyen Orient & Ocean Indien*, I (1984): 2–9. Aubin, however, assumes that the Ross Anonymous is an early source, yet evidence—both art historical and literary—indicates that it was most probably committed to writing in the middle of the seventeenth century. For a study on the dating of the Ross Anonymous, see A. H. Morton, "The Date and Attribution of the *Ross Anonymous*: Notes on a Persian History of Shah Ismā'il I," in *Persian and Islamic Studies in Honor of P. W. Avery*, ed. Charles P. Melville (Cambridge: Cambridge University Centre for Middle Eastern Studies, 1990), 179–212. Morton makes use of the author's annotations to the British Library manuscript of the Ross and proposes the 1680s for its composition.

9. Delineating the cognomen *dede* is more nuanced than that of *lalé* (mentor) and *khalīfa* (spiritual deputy). In the early Ottoman context of Turkmen frontier culture, *dede* was used synonymously with the appellation *baba*, designating the spiritual leader of a

group of dervishes or of a tribe. In the Iranian context of the mid-sixteenth century, the term *dede* seems to have moved away from its spiritual associations, for it is used synonymously with *lalé* to designate preceptors of Safavi princesses. The fact that both Lale Bek and Dede Bek received purely militaristic posts, while Khalīfa Bek was also awarded the post of Khalīfat al-Khulafā is indicative of the nature of evolution the term was undergoing in the context of sedentary Safavi rule. I would like to thank Cemal Kafadar for his insights on the use of the term *dede* in Ottoman frontier culture.

10. Lalé Bek was the Amīr al-Umarā, the chief of all the military forces of the combined *oymāqs*. He also received the honorary title of *vakīl*, the temporal lieutenant of the shah symbolizing the true trust that Isma'il had bestowed on him. Dede Bek was named Qūrchī Bāshī, the chief of the three thousand elite royal guards culled from all oymāqs.

11. The Dīvān Begī, also referred to as the Amīr-i Dīvān, adjudicated matters of *'urf*. According to the *Tazkirat al-mulūk*, he sat four days a week, jointly with the Sadr, in the *kishīk-khānah*: "There, directed by the *sadr*, he interrogated (*bāz-khwāst*) those guilty of the four capital crimes, namely, murder, rape, blinding, and breaking of teeth." Vladimir Minosky, *Tazkirat al-mulūk* (London: Gibb Memorial Series, 1989), 50. He also executed *shar'ī* decisions, maintained order in the city, and had control over provincial tribunals. Twice a week he sat in his house and heard civil cases of common law (*da'vihā-yi hisāb-i 'urf*). Ibid., 51.

12. The Khalīfat al-Khulafā was the deputy of sufi affairs acting on behalf of the shah, appointing his representatives in the provinces—all of which were chosen from among the Qizilbash. See Minorsky, *Tazkirat al-mulūk*, 12. The degeneration of this post at the end of Shah Abbas I's reign is indicative of the changes going on in this period. See the list of civil officials Turkmān, *Tārīkh-i 'Ālam Ārā-yi 'Abbasi*, vol. 2, 1084–1093 at the death of Abbas I; no mention is made of a Khalīfat al-Khulafā. The office does survive to the reign of Shah Sultan Husayn, yet its function seems to have been transformed, for not only is it bestowed on a sayyid—in the classical age, it was awarded to the Qizilbash only—but it entails the enforcement of purely *shar'ī* matters. See Shah Sultan Husayn's

firman for the appointment of a Khalīfat al-Khulafā in Rasūl Ja'fariān, *Dīn va Siyāsat dar Dawrah-yi Safavī*, (Qum: Intishārāt-i Ansāriyān 1991), 426.

13. The religious history of sixteenth-century Safavi Iran remains to be studied. The current dialogue between Arjomand, Newman, and Stewart revolving around the role of the Imami *ulama* in early Safavi history is a positive move in this direction.

14. Aubin, "Revolution Chiite et conservatisme," 1–40.

15. Ghiyās al-dīn Khwāndamīr, *Tārīkh-i Habīb al-siyar*, ed. Jalāl al-din Humā'i (Tehran: Kitāb Khānah-yi Khayyām, 1954), vol. 4, 602, as quoted in Dickson, "Shah Tahmasb and the Uzbeks," 14.

16. For the role of Husayn Khan Shamlu in the grand sedition (1531–1534) that attempted to poison Shah Tahmasb and place the more pliant seventeen-year-old prince Sam Mirza, see Dickson, "Shah Tahmasb and the Uzbek," 265–295.

17. Shah Tahmasb, *Tazkire-yi Shah Tahmasb* (Berlin: Asiatic Society, 1923), 14, as quoted in Dickson, "Shah Tahmasb and the Uzbeks," 96. During the turbulent phase of Tahmasb's regency (1524–1536), he had to overcome a civil war characterized by inter-*oymaq* rivalries over the regency and over key administrative posts. Ibid., 12, 51–53, 265–292.

18. See Said Arjomand, *The Shadow of God and the Hidden Imam: Religion, Political Order, and Societal Change in Shi'ite Iran from the Beginning to 1890* (Chicago: University of Chicago Press, 1984), 105–122.

19. Forty thousand *ghulāms* had been incorporated into Shah Tahmasb's court in 1533 and 1534. Sharaf Khan Bitlisī, a Kurdish prince who was a *ghulām* at Tahmasb's court, writes in 1596: "From the age of nine to twelve, from 1551 to 1554, I was a page at the inner palace. For it was the Shah's policy to educate the sons of illustrious families along with the princes of the realm" Martin B. Dickson and Stuart Cary Welch, eds., *The Houghton Shāhnāme* (Cambridge: Harvard University Press, 1981), 242a n. 30. This statement by Bitlisi indicates that under the reign of Tahmasb (1524–1576) a system of palace schools existed, whereby children from prominent families were trained. This system must have then been thoroughly institutionalized under 'Abbas I to accommodate a larger number of *ghulām*s. For a similar type of development un-

der the Ottomans, see Halil Inalcik, *The Ottoman Empire: The Classical Age, 1300–1600*, trans. N. Itzkowitz and C. Imber (London: Wiedenfeld and Nicholson, 1973), 78–85, and Barnette Miller, *The Palace School of Muhammad the Conqueror* (New York: Arno Press, 1973).

20. See Dickson, "Shah Tahmasb and the Uzbeks," 12, 51–53, 265–292.

21. It would take another two years before Abbas I could put an end to the second civil war that for fourteen years had placed the Safavis at the mercy of the Qizilbash. For example, the Qābūshān movement in the second year of Shah Abbas I's reign was a revolt of the Qizilbash *umarā* against Safavi *dūdmān* control of the *oymaqs*. The second civil war (1576–1590) did not end until the fourth year of Abbas I's reign, when the Zul Qadr and Afshar *oymaqs* where pacified in Fars and Kirman and *shāhīsīvāns* from the same *oymaqs* replaced them.

22. After Shah Abbas I's Georgian campaign in 1025/1616–1617—during which approximately 330,000 slaves were reportedly captured—he began to utilize them thoroughly in the administration of the Bīrūn and the Andarūn. Turkmān, *Tārīkh-i 'Ālam Ārā-yi 'Abbāsī*, vol. 2, 900–901.

23. This author has come across only one example, apart from Allah Verdi Khan, of a *ghulam* holding such a post. In the sixth year of 'Abbas I's reign (1000–1001/1592) Iskandar Bek Munshī Turkmān speaks of Jamshid Bek, a slave (*ghulām-i khāssah-yi sharīfah*) who was the governor of Qazvin. Turkmān, *Tārīkh-i 'Ālam Ārā-yi 'Abbāsī*, vol. 1, 449.

24. Ibid., vol. 2, 1088. Twenty-one *ghulām*s held such positions at the death of Abbas I.

25. Ibid., vol. 2, 875.

26. Iskandar Bek Munshī Turkmān states that Isfahan had been *khāssah* (crown) land since the days of Shah Tahmasb. As governor of Isfahan, Murshīd Qulī Khān would have access to its revenue. Yuli Beg was named acting governor in 995/1587. He rebelled in 997/1589.

27. Afushtah-yi Natanzi, *Naqāvat al-asār fī zikr al-akhyār* (Tehran: Intishārāt-i Ilmi va Farhangī, 1971), 334–335. Shaykh-i Bahā'ī was the son of Shaykh Husayn (1512–1576), a first-generation

Arab *mujtahid* émigré from Jabal 'Amil. He was betrothed to the daughter of Shaykh 'Alī Minshar (d. 1576–1577), the former Shaykh al-Islam of Isfahan who had been appointed by Tahmasb. In 1553, when Bahā'ī and his father arrive in Isfahan from Jabal 'Amil, Shaykh 'Alī held that position. Bahā'ī inherited this post from his father-in-law on his death. For more on Bahā'ī, see Devin Stewart, "A Biographical Notice on Bahā' al-Dīn al-'Amilī," *Journal of the American Oriental Society* 3 (1991): 563–571.

28. Devin Stewart, "The First Shaykh al-Islam of the Safavid Capital Qazvin," *Journal of the American Oriental Society* 3 (1996): 387–405.

29. For the controversy between Shaykh Husayn al-Hārithī and Sayyid Husayn b. al-Hasan al-Karakī that led to this demotion, see ibid.

30. Ibid., 394.

31. Seyyid Hossein Nasr, *Cambridge History of Iran*, vol. 6, 668.

32. See Nuha Khoury's chapter on the dynamic relationship between Baha'i's *Jām'i-yi Abbasi* and the Masjid-i Shah. Nuha Khoury, *Ideologies and Inscriptions: The Epigraphy of the Masjid-i Shah and the Ahmediye in the Context of Safavid-Ottoman Relations, Muqarnas* (Leiden: Brill, forthcoming).

33. Ibid., 43–44.

34. Mīrzā Muhammad Tunukābunī, *Qisas al-'ulamā*, 2nd. ed. (Tehran: Intishārāt-i 'Ilmiyya Islāmiyya, 1985), 268.

35. The *harvalah* is a pace adopted by the pilgrims at Mecca.

36. The *tabarzīn* is an axe (*tabar*) used as an arm and usually placed on the saddle (*zīn*). It also was an implement carried by dervishes. See the Muhammad Husayn b. Khalaf Tabrīzī, *Burhān-i Qāti'* ed. Muhammad Mu'īn (Tehran: Ibn-i Sina, 1963), n. 2.

37. Dervish Reza (d. Zul Hijja 1040/July 1631), a Qizilbash (Afshar) who had served in the Safavi provincial administration, claimed to be the awaited Mahdi, and rose up against the Safavi order two years after Shah Safi's accession.

38. According to the Shi'is, the day the Prophet Muhammad first received his revelation is celebrated on the 27th day of Rajab. The sources refer to this day as the *Id-i Khazr al-Nabī.*

39. The main actors around which this slave cabal was formed were Muhibb Ali Bek, Rustam Khan, and Khusraw Khan. For details on

these factions, see my dissertation and the forthcoming book by Sussan Babaie, Kathryn Babayan, Ina Baghdiantz-McCabe, and Massumeh Farhad, S*laves of the Shah: New Elites of Isfahan (*London: I.B. Tauris, 2003).

40. This study of cabals formed at the courts of Safi and 'Abbas II has been inspired by Le Roy Ladurie's work on the cabals formed at the court of Louis XIV, Emmanuel LeRoy Ladvrie, *Le Territoire de l'historien,* vol. 2, 1978.

41. The three sons of Isā Khān Shaykhāvand were executed, in addition to one of his grandsons born of Sayyid Muhammad Khān. The four sons of Sulṭan al-'Ulamā were blinded, and he was fired and placed under house arrest. The four sons of Mīrzā Rafī al-Dīn Sadr were blinded, and he was also fired and placed under house arrest. Mīrzā Rizā's son was blinded. The sons of Mīrzā Muhsin Razavī, the Mutavallī of the shrine of Mashad, were blinded, and he lost his job. Takhtah Khān Ustājlū was killed. Muhammad Tāhir, the vizier of Isā Khān, was also killed.

42. See Mary Boyce, "Bibi Shahrbanu and the Lady of Pars," *Bulletin of the School of Oriental and African Studies* 30 (1967): 32, and Mīrshokrā'i, *Tahlīl az Rasm-i Sunni-yi Chihilum-i Bahār, Kirmanshenasi,* Kirman (1982), 365–374, cited in Anna Kransnowolska, *Some Key Figures of Iranian Calendar Mythology* (Krakow: Univesitas, 1998).

43. See Kransnowolska, *Some Key Figures of Iranian Calendar Mythology,* ch. 7 on Hazrat-i Khizr.

44. According to the *Zubdat al-tavārīkh,* Zaynab Begūm arrived only on this date with the body of Shah 'Abbas from Mazandaran and was thrown out of the Andarūn (f 85b). It is not certain whether she had switched sides and had joined the Shaykhavand cabalists once her partners to the Safi cabal had broken her trust in them. One can, however, state with certainty that a new powerful figure had arisen within the ranks of the harem women, leaving no room for Zaynab Begūm.

45. 'Abbas II built a mausoleum (1067/1656–1657) for the three sons of Isā Khān and Zubaydah Begūm. Sayyid Muhammad Khān's daughter, Badr-i Jahān Begūm, who died in (1062/1651), is also buried in that mausoleum. Another tombstone, with no writing or ornaments, exists in the mausoleum. Lutfullāh Hunarfar

Ganjīnah-i Asār-i Tārīkhi-i Isfāhān (Isfahan: Kitābfurūshi-yi
Saqafī, 1965), speculates that this is the tombstone of Zubaydah
Beğum. 547.

46. Olearius does not provide us with any dates for Zubaydah Beğum's attempts to poison Shah Safī. According to the chronicles,
Shah Safī fell sick in Qazvin ten months after the Bloody Mab'as
massacre. The *Khuld-i Barīn* states that the Shah went on Qishlāq
to Qazvin, in Takhaqūy 1042–1043, he entered Qazvin on 19
Jamādī al-Avval 1042/1 December 1632. He remained in Qazvin
until after the Nowruz celebration, 20 March 1633/9 Ramazan
1042. If this indeed is the occasion on which he was poisoned, then
Zubaydah Beğum may have been trying to poison Safī in retaliation for the killing of her three sons, who were victims of the
Bloody Mab'as massacre. However, given Olearius states that
forty harem women were killed due to their collusion with
Zubaydah Beğum, to argue that Zubaydah Beğum's action was
strictly personal and vindictive is missing the mark. If, in fact, the
poisoning involved forty women, then it was part of a larger anti-
Safī scheme. Zubaydah Beğum's central role in this poisoning links
the assassination attempt to the Shaykhāvand cabal. This allows
us to assume that the discovery of the poisoning attempt probably
occurred before the massacre and may in fact have prompted the
Bloody Mab'as massacre. This hypothesis has been confirmed by a
source from Safī's reign, written by Muhammad Husayn Tafrishī.
He connects the Shah's illness with the attempts to replace him, as
well as with the Bloody Mab'as massacre. Untitled manuscript,
Flügel I, 281 (1), *A Sketch of Shah Safī's Reign from 1038/1629–
1041/1631-2*. This history also appears in the Chester Beaty Collection, MS 345, Catalogue of Persian Books.

47. Adam Olearius, *The Voyages and Travels of the Ambassadors Sent
by Frederick, Duke of Holstein, to the Great Duke of Muscovy
and the King of Persia*, 3 vols. (London: Printed for John Starkey
and Thomas Basset, 1669), vol. 6, 269.

48. Tafrishī states that two months after the Shah entered Isfahan
(Wednesday, 2 July 1631) he fell sick for a week. His sickness was
linked either to the heatwave in Isfahan or to his overindulgence in
wine. Mīr Muhammad Husayn Tafrishī, *A Sketch of Shah Safī's
Reign from 1038/1629–1041/1631-2* (Flügel I, 281(1), Chester
Beaty Collection, MS 384), f 34a.

49. Ibid., ff 35a–b.

50. Martin B. Dickson, "Uzbek Dynastic Theory in the Sixteenth Century," in *Trudy 25-ogo Mezhdunarodnogo Kongressa Vostokovedov* (Moscow: Tehran: Kitābfurūshi-yi Islāmiya, 1963) vol. 3, 208–217.

51. Turkman and Vāli *Zayl-i Tārīkh-i 'Ālam Ārā-yi 'Abbāsī*, 87. The *Zayl* also mentions that Sayyid Muhammad Khān was eighteen years old.

52. According to the *Khuld-i Barīn*, Sayyid Muhammad Khān was eighteen years old, and due to the fact that he was related on his father's (Isā Khān Shaykhāvand) side to the Safavi *dūdmān* (who were the grandchildren of Sultan Junayd and the sons of the paternal uncle of the Safavis) and that on his mother's side, he was the grandchild of 'Abbas I, he was worthy of this grand position (f 47a). At some point the *Khuld-i Barīn* refers to Sayyid Muhammad Khān as Sayyid Muhammad Khān Tafrishī (f 47b). As for Shah Safi, he was also eighteen years old.

53. Lawrence Krader, *Social Organization of the Mongol-Turkic Pastoral Nomads* (The Hague: Mouton, 1993); Mansur Haider, "The Mongol Traditions and Their Survival in Central Asia (Fourteenth to Fifteenth Centuries)," *Central Asiatic Journal* 28, nos. 1–2 (1984): 57–79; Morris Rossabi, "Khublai Khan and the Women in His Family," In *Studia Sino-Mongolica: Fesctschrift für Herbert Franke*, ed. W. Bauer (Wiesbaden: Steiner, 1979), 153–180.

54. In the case of the Sasanis, two females, Purandokht and Azarmidokht, ruled—once again when no legitimate male candidate was alive. Historians have often interpreted this as diminishing the validity of female legitimacy to rule, for it was permitted only in a context in which no rival men were alive. Nevertheless, women surfaced at such times, and the fact that female sovereignty was actualized—even if only on occasions when the dynasty could become inactive—demonstrates its legitimacy.

55. See Richard Frye, "The Charisma of Kingship in Ancient Iran," *Iranica Antiqua* 4 (1964): 36–54; Frye, "Pre-Islamic and Early Islamic Culture in Central Asia," in *Turco-Persia in Historical Perspective*, ed. R. Canfield (Cambridge: Harvard University Press, 1991), 41–42. On the notion of divine grace (*khvaranah*) in Avestan literature, see Mary Boyce, *A History of Zorastrianism* (Leiden: Brill, 1975), 66–68. On the legitimacy of matrilineal de-

scent, see Mansour Shaki, "The Sassanian Matrimonial Relations," *Archiv Orientālnī* 39 (1971): 322–345; A. Perikhanian,
"Iranian Society and Law," *The Cambridge History of Iran,* ed.
Ihsan Yarshater, vol. 3 (2) (Cambridge: Cambridge University
Press, 1983), 693. On family law and succession and the *stūr*-suc-
cessorship where "the son and successor provided by the *stūr*
might be separated by several generations from the man who was
this son's legal father and whose heir he was, by a whole chain of
epikleros-daughters (in practice these would be the legal father's
daughters, granddaughters, great granddaughters, etc.)." Ibid.,
654. Also note the Feraydun cycle of the *Shāhnāme* in which
Feraydun is separated from Manuchihr his successor by seven
epikleros-daughters.

56. Turkmān, *Tārīkh-i 'Ālam Ārā-yi 'Abbāsī,* vol. 1, 201.
57. Ibid.
58. Iskandar Bek Musnhī, Turkmān and Muhammad Yūsuf Vālih,
Zayl-i Tārīkh-i 'Ālam Ārā-yi 'Abbāsī, ed. Suhaylī Khwānsāri,
(Tehran: Kitābfurūshi-yi Islāmi, 1938–1939), 87.
59. This practice was terminated with the killing of Safī Qulī Mīrzā, in
Bars 1023–1024/1614. Safī Qulī Mīrzā, Shah 'Abbas's talented
son, had been killed on the order of his father on charges that he
was fomenting a revolt, along with some Circassian *ghulāms* who
were related to his mother, against 'Abbas I. Röhrborn states that
the last time that a *shāhzādah* was sent out to the provinces was in
the year 1000/1591–1592. Turkmān, *Tārīkh-i 'Ālam Ārā-yi
'Abbāsī,* vol. 1, 444.
60. For a parallel development in Ottoman politics, see Leslie Pierce,
*The Imperial Harem: Women and Sovereignty in the Ottoman
Empire* (London: Oxford University Press, 1993).
61. For an illuminating discussion by an anthropologist on patriarchy
and patrilineality in Islam, see Elaine Combs-Schilling, *Sacred Performances: Islam, Sexuality, and Sacrifice* (New York: Columbia
University Press, 1989).
62. A parallel solution had already been adopted by the Ottomans two
centuries earlier. The Ottoman *kul* (slave) system had been incorporated to facilitate their conquests and strengthen their central
authority. See Inalcik, *The Ottoman Empire,* and G. Necipoglu,
*Architecture, Ceremonial and Power: The Topkapi Palace in the
Fifteenth and Sixteenth Centuries* (Cambridge: MIT Press, 1991).

63. Iskandar Bek Munshi Turkmān provides us with a chronogram that perhaps best describes the extent of Sultan al-Ulama's power. His chronogram, prepared for the date of Sultan al-Ulama's appointment as grand vizier, reads, "The vizier became the shah—the sultan—the *dāmād* (brother-in-law)"—that is, the vizier who became the shah is the sultan who was the *dāmād Vazīr shāh shud sultan dāmād*. The chronogram, however, can also be read as "The Sultan who was the *dāmād* became the vizier of the shah." (*vazīr-i shāh shud sultan dāmād*). Both readings of the chronograms arrive at the date 1033/1624. *Tārīkh-i 'Ālam Ārā-yi 'Abbāsī*, vol. 2, 1013. His religious function as legal consultant, teacher and at times Friday prayer leader made him a popular public figure with access both to the *Birūn* and the *Andarūn*. He could simultaneously strengthen the religious community while paying lip service to the Safavi *pādishahs*. Muhsin al-Husayni, 'Āmili, *A'yān al-shī'a* (Beirut: Matba'at al-Insāf, 1960) 240. One can detect some indignation on behalf of the *A'yān's* author against the soiling of spiritual hands in the materialism of courtly affairs. This issue divided the Imami *ulama* from the time of Shah Isma'il I to that of Muhammad Reza Pahlavi. Despite Sultan al-'Ulama's soiled hands, he commanded respect within the religious community. All the biographies of *ulama* (*rijāl*) speak well of his intellectual abilities and consider him among the good scholars of his age.

64. Turkmān and Vāli, *Zayl-i Tārīkh-i Ālam Ārā-yi 'Abbāsī*, 87.

65. Mīr Muhammad Bāqir Dāmād, better know as Mīr-i Dāmād. His maternal grandfather was the famous Shaykh 'Alī Karakī. His father, Shams al-Dīn Muhammad, was from Astarabad.

66. He had in fact been girded with a sword.

67. Turkmān, *Tārīkh-i 'Ālam Ārā-yi 'Abbāsī*, vol. 2 632. Shah Safi's first Julus: 4 Jamadi al-Thani 1038/28 January 1629. Mīr-i Damād read the *khutba* in Safi's name four days after his accession, on Friday 8 Jamadi al-Thani 1038/1 February 1629. According to the *Khulāsat al-siyar,* however, the *khutba* was read one day after his accession, Tuesday 5 Jamadi al-Thani 1038/29 January 1629. Sikkes were coined in the name of Safi five days after his accession, on Saturday, 9 Jamadi al-Thani 1038/2 February 1629. The *urdu* arrived in Isfahan nineteen days after Shah Safi's accession, on Saturday, 23 Jamadi al-Thani 1038/17 February 1629, when a second coronation was held.

68. Sayyid Husayn Modarresi-Tabātabā'ī, *Bargī az Tārīkh-i Qazvīn* (Qum: Mar'ashī Library Press, 1982), 33. Shāhzadah Husayn was the infant son of Imam Rizā, the eighth Imam. The tomb of Shāhzadah Husayn was famous and well known by the twelfth century. By the sixteenth century, it became a public shrine visited by Sunnis and Shi'is alike. Once Tahmasb moved his capital to Qazvin (1555), he rebuilt the shrine (Turkmān, *Tārīkh-i 'Ālam 'Ārā-yi 'Abbāsī*, vol. 1, 95–96). It was probably finished in 968/1560–1561, and by the middle of the sixteenth century, it was a popular place for congregation. *Tārīkh-i Shūshtar*, 887 from 'Alā al-Mulk Husaynī Mar'ashī, (d. 990–992), Qāzī 'Askar, and Sadr of Gilan.

69. Muhammad Yusūf Vālih Isfahānī's *Khuld-i Barīn* (f 45a) is the only source that mentions the fact that the rebels congregated around the tomb of Mīr Faghfūr. The *Khulāsat al-siyar* (120) states that they took refuge in a nearby chamber (*hujrah*) without naming the person buried in that tomb: "*panāh bi hujrah'ī ki dar ān havālī būdah.*" In his detailed study on the history of Qazvin, Modarresi Tabātabā'ī identifies Mīr Faghfūr as Sharīf Mu'ayan al-Dīn Faghfūr/Faghfūl, a former Naqīb of Qazvin and the son of Shams al-Dīn Muhammad of the Ma'rashī sayyids of Qazvin. Mīr Faghfūr lived in the first half of the ninth/fourteenth century and held the hereditary post of Mutavallī of the Shāhzadah Husayn shrine in addition to the powerful post of Muhtasib and Naqīb al-Ashraf.

70. *Khuld-i Barīn*, f 45a.

71. Muhammad Yūsuf Valī makes a revealing remark about the nature of the Shaykhavand cabal. When Chirāgh Khān Pīrzādah was assigned the task of assassinating the engineers of this cabal (*arbāb-i fitnah va fasād*), he states that Chirāgh Khān became the abolisher of old families. *Khuld-i Barīn*, f 47a.

72. See Jean Aubin's study on the role of Tajik notable families in the first century of Safavi rule, "Shah Ismā'īl et les Notables de l'Iraq Persian (Etudes Safavides I)," *Journal of Economic and Social History of the Orient* 2 (1959): 37–81.

73. Mīr-i Buzurg was a disciple of Shaykh Hasan-i Jūrī, from whose *tarīqat* the Sarbidārs emerge. For more on Mīr-i Buzurg, see Sayyid Zāhir al-Dīn Mar'ashī, *Tārīkh-i Tabaristān va Ruyān va Māzandarān*, ed. by M. H. Tasbīhī (Tehran: Intisharāt-i Itilā'āt,

1966), and his *Tārīkh-i Gīlān va Daylamistān*, ed. M. Sutūdah (Tehran: Intisharāt-i Itilā'āt, 1968); Mīr Taymūr Mar'ashī, *Tārīkh-i Khāndān-i Mar'ashī-i Māzandarān*, ed. M Sutūdih (Tehran: Intishārāt-i Itilā'āt, 1977); I. Petrushevsky, *Kishāvarzī va Munāsibāt-i Arzī dar Irān-i Ahd-i Mughūl*. trans. Karīm Kishāvarz (Tehran: Bungāh-i Tarjumah va Nashr-i Kitāb, 1976–1977). Abbas's mother, Mahd-i Ulyā, was a Mar'ashi from Mazandaran and was related to Sulṭan al-'Ulamā'.

74. Sayyid Zāhir al-Dīn Mar'ashī, *Tārīkh-i Tabaristān va Ruyān va Māzandarān* (292, 330, and 350, where he mentions the rebuilding of Mīr-i Buzurg's tomb in 840 A.H.) and in his *Tārīkh-i Gīlān va Daylamistān* (16–18, 29, 32, and 39). Turkmān, *Tārīkh-i 'Ālam Ārā-yi 'Abbāsī*, vol. 1, 147–148. Sultan al-'Ulama's great-great-grandfather, Sayyid Hidāyatullāh, was a *nadīm* (companion) at the court of Isma'il I. Sayyid Hidāyatullāh's son, Mīr Sayyid 'Alī, had been patronized by Shah Tahmasb.

75. Mīr Shujā al-Dīn Mahmūd, Sayyid Hidāyatullāh's grandson, was a famous scholar. On the Mar'ashi's in Isfahan, see Robert McChesney, "The Four Sources on Shah Abbas's Building of Isfahan," *Muqarnas 5* (1988): 118.

76. Nasrābadī, *Tazkirah-yi Nasrābadī*, ed. V. Dastgirdī (Tehran: Armaghān, 1973). 15.

77. McChesney, "Four Sources on Shah Abbas's Building of Isfahan," 118.

78. For more on Lalé Bek, see McChesney, "Four Sources on Shah 'Abbas's Building of Isfahan," 179; McChesney, "Waqf and Public Policy," 122–123.

79. Ina Baghdiantz-McCabe, *The Shah's Silk for Europe's Silver: The Eurasian Trade of the Julfa Armenians in Safavid Iran and India (1530–1750)*, ed. Michael Stone (Atlanta: Scholars Press, 1999).

80. The two men of religion at court, the Grand Vizier, Sultan al-Ulama and the Sadr, Mirza Rafi al-Dīn, who joined this cabal, were both members of notable sayyid families—Mar'ashī and Shahristānī. Sultan al-Ulama was a Mar'ashī *sayyid* from Mazandaran; Mirzā Rafi al-Dīn was a Shahristānī *sayyid* from Isfahan.

81. The Shaykhavands were a branch of the Safavis who descended from the non-Haydarī line of Shaykh Junayd's offspring. Shaykh Junayd had two sons, Haydar Sultan (born of Uzun Hasan's sis-

ter), who represented Isma'il's silsilat, and Khwajah Muhammad
(born of a concubine), from whom the Shaykhavands descend. See
the *Silsilat al-nasab al-Safaviyyah*, 67.

82. See Masashi Haneda on Tahmasb's coining of the title
Shaykhavand and their incorporation into the Qizilbash oymāq
system. *Le Chah et les Qizilbash: Le System militaire Safavide,*
(Berlin: Klaus Schwarz Verlag, 1987), 133.

83. The Pīrzādahs and the Safavis were also related by blood. Safi al-
din Ishaq was married to the daughter of his *pīr,* Shaykh Zāhid-i
Gīlānī. The Pīrzādah Chirāgh Khān Zāhidī initially pushed for the
Shaykhavand candidate. Later, however, he turned against the
Shaykhavands and divulged the intentions of these cabalists.
Iskandar Bek Munshi Turkmān provides us with Chirāgh Khān's
possible motivations, which evolved around local Ardabilī politics
and rivalry between the Shaykhavands and the Pīrzādahs. The
Shaykhavands lived in Ardabil, where Shaykh Sharīf Bek, Chirāgh
Khān's father was the *mutavallī* of Shaykh Safi al-din's shrine. The
Zayl-i Tārīkh-i 'Ālam Ārā-yi 'Abbāsī states that Chirāgh Khān did
not get along with Isā Khān Shaykhavand (Qūrchī Bāshī) because
in his time the Shaykhavands did not respect his father, Shaykh
Sharīf Bek. Turkmān and Vālih, *Zayl-i Tārīkh-i 'Ālam Ārā-yi
'Abbāsī* , 87 and 92.

84. Shaykh Husayn, *Silsilat al-nasab al-Safaviyyah* (Berlin:
Chāpkhānah-yi Irānshahr, 1964), 106. That these associations
were alive in the seventeenth century is manifest in the *Silsilat al-
nasab al-Safaviyyah,* written by a Pīrzādah, Shaykh Husayn during
the reign of Shah Sulayman (1666–1694). Shaykh Husayn tells
that his father, Shaykh Abdal, had visited Abbas I at court in 1009/
1600–1601 to pay homage to the shah. Abbas I showered Shaykh
Abdal with gifts and stated, "You are the offspring of our *pīr,* due
to this blessing you should enter our service." The author of the
Silsilat al-nasab al-Safaviyyah adds, "It is because of this that my
father came to be referred to as Pīrzādah [descendant of the *pir*]."

85. See, for example, the *Silsilat al-nasab al-Safaviyyah,* 104, for the
soyūrghāls and *mu'āfīs* granted to the descendants of Shaykh
Zāhid-i Gīlānī during the reigns of Shah Isma'il and Shah
Tahmasb.

86. Of the six known daughters of 'Abbas I, five were married to members of prominent *sayyid* families or *ulama.* Shāhzādah Beğum was

married to Mīrzā Muhsin Razavī; Aqā Begum to Sultan al-Ulamā'; Havā Begum to Mīrzā Rizā Shahristānī (Sadr) and after his death to Mīrzā Rafī al-Dīn Muhammad (Sadr); Shāhr-i Bānū Begum to Mīr 'Abdulazīm (Dārūghah of Isfahan); and Malik Nisā Begum to Mīrzā Jalāl Shahristānī (the *mutavallī* of the shrine of Imam Rizā). Zubaydah Begum, the sixth known daughter of Abbas I, was married to Isā Khān Shaykhavand, the namesake of the Shaykhavand cabal. In addition, Abbas I's grandaughter Gawharshād Begum, the daughter of Sultān Muhammad Mīrzā (blinded in 1030/1620–1621) was married to Mīrzā Qāzī, the Shaykh al-Islam of Isfahan. Nasrullāh Falsafī, *Zindigānī-yi Shah 'Abbas-i Avval* (Tehran: Chāp-i Keyvān, 1955), vol. 2, 198. Also see Jean Chardin, *Les Voyages du Chevalier Chardin en Perse*, ed. L. Langlès, 10 vols. (Paris: Le Normant, 1811), vol. 9, 564.

87. This rumor is preserved in Chardin, so I am assuming that it was in circulation at court and related to Chardin by his eunuch informant.

88. Ibid.

89. For the role of the wife who bears the first son (Haseki Sultan) of the Ottoman sultans, see H. A. R. Gibb and H. Bowen, *Islamic Society and the West*, pt. I, 2 vols. (London: Oxford University Press, 1950, 73; on the *haseki/has odalik* women chosen for the sultan's bed, see Inclcik, *The Ottoman Empire* 86; also see Leslie Pierce's *The Imperial Harem*, for the changing role of the Ottoman harem in the period of Ottoman sedentarization.

90. We know from a *waqfnāme* dated Rajab 1053/September–October 1643 that Shah Safi's mother survived her son and endowed a Qur'an for Safi's mausoleum located in the Sitti Fātima mosque in Qum. Sayyid Husayn Modarresī-Tabātabā'ī, *Turbat-i Pākān: Āsār va Banāhā-yi Qadīm-i Mahdūdah-yi Kunūnī-yi Dār al-mūminīn-i*, 2 vols. (Quinn: Chāpkhānahayi, 1957) vol. 1, 152.

91. Anna Khanum was Circassian according to Nasrallāh Falsafī, "Sarguzasht-i Sāru Taqi," in *Chand Maqalah-yi Tārīkhī va Adabī*, (Tehran: Tehran University, 1964), 301. See Willem Floor, "The Rise and Fall of Mirza Taqi, the Eunuch Grand Vizier (1043–55/1633–45)," *Studia Iranica* 26 (1997): 237–266, who questions my analysis of Saru Taqi and court politics during the reigns of Safi and Abbas II detailed in my dissertation (1993). One of the objections he raises is that Abbas II's mother could not have collabo-

rated with Saru Taqi for she was dead. He cites Falsafi's article to back his point but has misread the Persian, which in fact confirms that she was alive during the early reign of her son Abbas II. Most of my analysis is based on information from the Persian court chroniclers, in this case Kamal ibn Jalal Munajjim, *Zubdat al-tavārīkh* (Royal Asiatic Society, MS Morley 43, 1677), f. 102b, where the author records the death of Anna Khanum (*khānūm-i vālidah va hakīmah*) in 9 Shaban 1957/9 September 1647.

92. Chardin, *Les Voyages du Chevalier Chardin en Perse*, vol. 7, 306–307, 314.
93. Ibid., vol. 5, 237.
94. Ibid., vol. 5, 315.
95. See Baghdiantz-McCabe, *The Shah's Silk for Europe's Silver.*
96. On Saru Taqi and his building projects see Sussan Babaie, "Building for the Shah: The Role of Mirza Muhammad Taqi in Safavid Royal Patronage of Architecture," in *Safavid Art and Architecture*, ed. Sheila Canby (London: British Museum, 2002). These holy Shi'i shrines in Mesopotamia had just been recaptured from the Ottomans, who had held them from 1587 to 1623.
97. See my dissertation, "The Waning of the Qizilbash," Ph.D, diss., Princeton University, 1993, for details on these administrative shifts.

ELEVEN

Shaping a Mainstream:
Mystics, Theologians, and Monarchs

THE SAFAVI COURT AND THE SHI'I
RELIGIOUS ESTABLISHMENT

With the dismissal of Sultan al-Ulama (1632) as grand vizier during the reign of Shah Safi (1629–1642), the only remaining cleric at court was the minister of religion, justice, and education—(Sadr) Mirza Habibullah Karaki. Mirza Habibullah was a descendant of the famous jurisconsult, Shaykh Ali Karaki (d. 1534), whose help Shah Isma'il and Tahmasb had solicited to bolster their Shi'i legitimacy.[1] This minister's great-grandfather had enunciated the first Safavi *fatwā* against the singers of the tale of Abū Muslim in an attempt to break with the *ghulāt* religiosity of the early Safavis. This family of Arab (Imami) immigrant scholars) would continue to be favored by the Safavi court throughout the sixteenth century. But unlike his great-grandfather, Mirza Habibullah was not a scholar of any standing within the clerical community.[2] He himself is quoted as having said that among his contemporaries no Shi'i jurist existed in Iran or in the Arab world.[3] A religious judge from Shiraz Shaykh Ali Naqi Kamira'i preserves this comment in one of his works dedicated to Shah Safi—*Himām al-thawāqib* (1634–1635). There he complains that men of religion had been deprived of divine rule

403

(hukūmat-i shar'ī), for they had lost their positions at court to courtiers *(darbāriyān)*.[4] This work, written three years after the expulsion of the Shaykhavand cabalists, points to the resentment that a number of *ulama* felt toward the removal of Sultan al-Ulama. It is as well a critique of some new converts to Islams—Caucasian slaves—who dominated Shah Safi's court. Kamira'i's comment confirms that in this period a group among the Shi'i clergy argued that political rule was a prerogative reserved for jurists—a revolutionary stance in Shi'i theology that Ayatollah Khomeini would institute with the Islamic revolution in Iran (1979). Chardin locates these debates two centuries earlier. He states in a famous passage:

> The clergy, their devotees, and those who profess the strict observance of religion maintain that in the absence of the Imam the royal throne must be occupied by an impeccable jurisconsult [*mouchtehed massoum*]—a term that signifies a man of pure morals who has mastered the sciences to such a perfect degree that he can respond on the spot and without hesitation to all the questions concerning religion and civil law [*droit civil*].[5]

Chardin identifies a salient view among "the people of the church and their devotees . . . all of whom professed the strict [*étroite*] observation of religion." He situates this attitude within the group of *shar'ia*-minded scholars. But Chardin goes on to report that the majority of the *ulama* argued that the right to temporal power lay with a direct descendent of the Imams and that it was not necessary that he be learned. He adds that this opinion was dominant because it awarded the current shah (Sulayman) legitimacy to rule.[6] And yet Chardin states that some men of religion openly criticized the Safavi monarchs and attacked the dominant opinion. These religious dissenters (Usuli) claimed that the "vicar of the Imams" should not only be a *sayyid* but also be immaculate and learned in theology and law:

> How could it be possible, say the clergy, for these *na mouqayyed* or impious kings, to use their own terms—consumers of wine carried away by their passions, to be the vicars of God, communicate

with heaven, and receive the necessary enlightenment to guide the faithful believers? How could they resolve a case of conscience and the doubts of faith, in the required manner of the lieutenant of God, they who can barely read? The Supreme throne of the universe belongs exclusively to a *mouchtahed,* or to a man who possesses sanctity and the sciences, transcending the community of men.[7]

The community of religious men was not a homogeneous group. The subject of authority polarized them. The particular function and role of the jurist in the dual spheres of the temporal and spiritual divided them. Some openly criticized the Safavi monarch, who drank and indulged in carnal passions. In their eyes, such depravity coupled with illiteracy could hardly merit the gift of God's grace and knowledge. Only pious scholars learned in God's words and teachings could attain the lofty throne of the universe: they were the true representatives of God on earth. One such scholar, in fact, threatened Shah Abbas II's rule. Mulla Qasim, in 1664, openly preached that the monarch should abdicate in favor of the son of Mirza Qazi, the foremost religious notable (Shaykh al-Islam) of Isfahan, for only he was worthy of kingship. Mulla Qasim's choice was predicated on descent from a pure line of the Imams and from Shah Abbas I's granddaughter. Moreover, he was learned in the religious sciences. Mulla Qasim's critique of Shah Abbas II reflected a consciousness that the Safavi's were not true descendents of Ali—that they had in fact fabricated their genealogy a century earlier.

Chardin tells us that Mulla Qasim had been a teacher *(mudarris)* in Isfahan. Cleansing himself of all association with the court, he had retired to a cloister, where he conducted his daily sermons. Both denizens and grandees of Isfahan had been attracted to his teaching. In particular, Chardin relates that even Abbas II's grand vizier Muhammad Bek (1659–1661) was an ardent follower. Chardin provides us with the gist of Mulla Qasim's sermons:

He [Mulla Qasim] would say that the king and his court were despicable transgressors of the law, that God desired the extermination of this cursed branch and the restoration of another pure lineage of the Imams. He declared this loudly and daily, almost straight into the ears of the king and his ministers. And when he was asked where this pure breed could be found, he would answer that the son of the Shaykh al-Islam should be elected, for he is the foremost judge of civil law and of canon. This judge was the brother of the grand vizier, currently in the ministry, and his son, who this seditious one [Mulla Qasim] was speaking about, was born to him by a daughter of Abbas the Great, betrothed in marriage because of his great integrity and his profound knowledge.[8]

The authority of Shah Abbas II was threatened by those men of religion (Usuli), who saw the jurist as the sole heir of political power during the Imam's occultation. As the supremacy of Safavi monarchs was being questioned by elements within the religious community, an intellectual climate that attempted to divorce theology from philosophy and mysticism had already began to gain ground among the *ulama*. The debates *(rudūd)* centered on the locus of spiritual authority on earth. These two controversial angles of dispute intersect over the meaning and practice of authority in general as the *shari'a*-minded were attempting to reserve both spiritual and temporal dominion for the jurist. The intellectual debates in progress among the *ulama* certainly had a life of their own. They coincided, however, with a period in Persianate history during which messianic rebellions against the Safavis—Nuqtavis in 1593 and Dervish Reza in 1631—had been suppressed and Qizilbash Islam was waning at court. The crown, now more than ever, needed to rely on legal *(shar'ī)* rather than popular legitimacy to rule. Court patronage supporting any of these religious currents would allow for one school of thought to assert itself. After all, it was the court-appointed minister of religion, justice, and education who awarded religious posts from that of the Shaykh al-Islam and judges *(qāzī)* of the major cities of the realm to the teachers of seminaries.

The contentious interplay between *ghuluww,* mysticism, philosophy, and theology divided Muslims throughout medieval history over questions of transcendence and immanence. These tensions and the dynamic impulses they generated are rendered more palatable in the Safavi context, thanks to a written exchange *(radd)* between proponents of these styles of thought. Unlike the polemics against Abū Muslim, the subsequent wave of attacks against mystics represents both the views of the *shari'a*-minded and the sufi-minded men of religion. Although the voice of the so-called *ghuluww* remains silent, these polemics highlight the particular tenor of discord—both in the realm of theory and practice—thus providing us with a texture of the spiritual landscape of Safavi devotees.

The *ghuluww* of Safavi disciples, the vitality of sufism as a socioreligious force, and the respect philosophy enjoyed among intellectuals had minimized the early attacks by *shari'a*-minded *ulama,* like Shaykh Ali Karaki, against Abū Muslim and the famous "drunken" mystic Hallaj (d. 922). Despite isolated instances of calumny that continued to surface during the reign of Shah Tahmasb (1524–1576), figures like Dervish Khusraw—although under close scrutiny—maintained their cloisters and their practices.[9] By the age of Shah Abbas I (1587–1629), once religious scholars were recruited for a variety of clerical posts, perhaps due to the marriage that had taken place between intellectual styles from Jabal Amil and Iran, prominent scholars like Shaykh-i Baha'i and Mir-i Damad found the *shari'a*-minded quest for God insufficient.[10] To their studies on religious sciences *(fiqh* and *hadith)* they added philosophy *(hikmat)* and mysticism *('irfān).* Due to their stature in both religious and political elite circles, so long as they were alive, polemics against sufism and philosophy would not be well received and were in fact rare in this period.[11] Mir-i Damad and Baha'i trained a generation of students who, like their mentors, would synthesize philosophy or sufism with the purely rational quest for God.

The variety of charismatic savants teaching in Isfahan provided students of Shi'ism with the option of pursuing all three quests simultaneously. Many indeed were inspired and took advantage of the knowledge of these trend-setting scholars.[12] It was due to such a scholastic environment that Mirza Rafi'a Nai'ni (d. 1669–1670), the famous jurist and mystical philosopher patronized by Abbas II, could study theology and law with Mir-i Damad, as well as mysticism with Mir Findiriski.[13] Thanks to the patronage of some of their teachers with links to the Safavi court, these students formed the pool from which important clerical posts of the realm, posts such as that of Shaykh al-Islam and Friday prayer leader, were to be filled. This is not to say that all students trained by these teachers accepted the eclectic approach of their mentors. Some students of Baha'i and Mir-i Damad (like Mir Lawhi and Sayyid Ahmad b. Zayn al-Din al-Amili) rejected this synthesis. They were in fact the authors of the polemics against Abū Muslim that would lead to a vocal attack against sufis and philosophers under Abbas II.[14] But much of this denunciation of *ghuluww,* couched in an attack against the Alid cultural hero Abū Muslim, came from students who had studied in religious centers outside of Isfahan, like Mashad.[15] Until the reign of Shah Sulayman (1666–1694), Isfahan remained the stronghold of the mystics and philosophically inclined students of Baha'i, Mir-i Damad, and Mir Findiriski.[16]

I have argued that the attacks on Abū Muslim found articulation once the power of the Qizilbash had waned at the Safavi court and the political scene was ripe for such an assault. In addition, by the time the first extant polemic against Abū Muslim was penned in Isfahan, both Mir-i Damad and Baha'i had passed away.[17] Sultan al-Ulama had just been fired from his post as grand vizier (in 1632), and the three leading proponents of an eclectic approach to God—Mir Findiriski (d. 1640), Mulla Sadra (d. 1640), and Majlisi Sr. (d. 1660)—were not to receive Shah Safi's patronage.[18] Some—like Majlisi Sr. and Muhsin-i Fayz (both students of Baha'i or Mir-i Damad) came to defend and condemn the gross generalizations voiced by *shari'a*-minded clerics, generalizations that saw famous mystics like Hallaj,

Bistami, Ibn-i Arabi, and even Rumi as heretics (*mulhid* and *zindiq*).[19] Debates within the religious community centering on Abū Muslim resurfaced toward the end of Abbas I's reign. Apparently due to Majlisi Sr.'s praising of Abū Muslim from the pulpit of the old mosque in Isfahan where he held the post of Friday prayer leader, his opponent Mir Lawhi is said to have written a tract in condemnation of Abū Muslim—*Tarjumah-yi Abū Muslim.* Mir Lawhi, having labeled Abū Muslim an enemy of the Shi'a (Imami), came under popular attack to the degree that his life was threatened. Some came to his defense, penning a series of essays on his behalf.[20] The controversy between Majlisi Sr. and Mir Lawhi over Abū Muslim must have gained momentum at the junction of Dervish Reza's revolt (1631) and the victory of the new elite of slaves at Safi's court (1632). A body of twenty disputations (*rudūd*) in support of Mir Lawhi's assault on Abū Muslim would be compiled during the next two decades.[21] The denunciation of the *ghulāt* was made public in the streets of Isfahan as seminary students and devotees actively participated in the debate.

Deliberations on Abū Muslim, sufism, and the political role of the jurist were in circulation within the Isfahani community, when Sultan al-Ulama was named to his second tenure as grand vizier under Abbas II (in 1645). Once he regained power, the Shaykh al-Islam of Isfahan, Miza Qazi, an appointee of the slave cabalists, was fired.[22] Instead, Shaykh Ali Naqi Kamira'i, the judge from Shiraz who had attacked Shah Safi's policy precluding men of religion from rule, was named the chief religious dignitary of Isfahan. Abbas II must have been aware of the discontent among some *ulama* (Usuli); thus, (re)naming a religious scholar to the post of grand vizier (Sultan al-Ulama), as well as Shaykh Ali Kamira'i as chief religious dignitary, was aimed at appeasing those elements.[23]

By this time, a second wave of disputations directly attacking sufism had surfaced. One such polemic, the *Salvat al-Shī'a*, written in 1650, includes a list of six injunctions against the unlawful deeds of mystics.[24] Both Habibullah Karaki (Sadr) and the Shaykh al-Islam of Isfahan (Kamara'i), appear in the list of religious scholars who condemned sufis. The grand vizier, Sultan al-Ulama, however, remained silent on this issue—an indication that he was not opposed to sufism. The debates were played out, and until the death of Sultan al-Ulama no one option had been embraced by Abbas II's court.

But once Sultan al-Ulama passed away (1655), Shah Abbas II publicly bestowed favors on mystics, whether wild or sober.[25] A contemporaneous Turkman chronicler, Vali Quli Shamlu, claims that in 1659 the monarch formally invited the philosophically minded cleric Muhsin-i Fayz to Isfahan. At the time when he was writing his history—the *Qisas al-khaqani*—Fayz was still said to have been leading prayer *(pīshnamaz)* at the new mosque built by Shah Abbas I (Masjid-i Jam'i).[26] It is clear from the contents of his response to a request by Shah Abbas II asking him to lead the congregational prayer at the royal mosque that he had held that post for only a short time—a tenure that caused much controversy among the Isfahani community.[27] The discord his appointment generated among the Imamis revolved around the legality of Friday prayer during the occultation of the hidden Imam; it touched as well on the mystical temperament of Muhsin-i Fayz.

Five years after Sultan al-Ulama's death in 1660 Shah Abbas II met with two dervishes from the Ottoman empire—Dervish Mustafa and Dervish Majnun. These two mystics had been guests at the homes of the monarch's private doctors, Hakim Muhammad Husayn and Hakim Muhammad Sa'id. The dervishes from Anatolia had requested to meet with their famous Safavi counterparts, Mulla Rajab Ali and Dervish Muhammad Salih, who had just received grants *(in'ām)* from the monarch. A courtly assembly was arranged for the occasion of this meeting, and one of the participants was Muhsin-i Fayz. Shah Abbas II's official chronicler, Muhammad Tahir Vahid, refers to Fayz as the "*mujtahid* of the age" *(mujtahid-i zamān)* and depicts him as a traveler on the twin paths of mysticism and law *(haqīqat va sharī'at)*.[28] Shah Abbas II desired to preserve this marriage. That Shah Abbas II was personally attracted to the ways of the mystic is clear: the court chronicler referred to his patron as the dervish-loving monarch.[29] We have seen how this shah (re)played a saintly aura, just like his ancestor Shah Tahmasb had done. And he was the monarch who took on the role of directing the Karbala commemorations, bringing them within the sacred space of the palace in Isfahan to be performed in the newly constructed Hall of Stables *(Tālār-i Tavīla)*, positioning himself at the center. Political motivations may have played a part in shaping Shah Abbas II's policy of patronage toward mystics. Administratively, his reign represented a break with that of his father, Shah Safi, which witnessed the predominance of a slave elite. Abbas II's religious policy also symbolized a break with his father. The chronicles are filled with instances in which the monarch interacts with and patronizes dervishes. These elements are completely lacking from the histories of the reign of Shah Safi. The religious policy of the slave elite at Shah Safi's court had been predicated on a rupture with the sufi features of the classical Safavi idiom. The slave elite shaped their religiosity as they came to impinge on the power of those social groups linked to mystical circles and endowed with local and regional power during the sixteenth century. Ideologically, the *ghulams* forged their image of sovereignty with elements that were averse to popular symbols of religiosity. They broke with the custom of the Safavi order in which the king was initiated by a master; instead it was a Shi'i religious dignitary who now performed the investiture of the new Safavi monarch.

The polemics against Abū Muslim that flourished in this period serve as testimony to the antipopulist mood that prevailed at Safi's court. Shah Safi patronized scholars like Sayyid Ahmad b. Zayn al-Abidin Alavi and Mulla Muhammad Tahir Qummi, both of whose positions against sufis were well know.[30] Sayyid Ahmad Alavi wrote one of the earliest tracts against Abū Mus-

lim—*Izhār al-haqq*—in 1633 to 1634, during the reign of Shah
Safi. Mulla Muhammad Tahir Qummi penned a couple of treatise against sufis—in particular, it is said, against his teacher
Majlisi Sr.'s defense of sufism.[31] We know as well that none of
these philosophically minded scholars who received patronage
from Abbas II (such as Majlisi Sr., Mulla Sadra, and Sabzavari)
dedicated any of their works to Safi. Although Shah Safi's court
seems to have favored the *shari'a*-minded *ulama*, they did not allow them direct access to political power.

Shah Abbas II may have chosen to deal with these religious
controversies in Isfahan, supporting elements within the community who could rival those clerics (Usuli mujtahid) who laid
claims on temporal rule. The traditionalists (Akhbari) were one
such group. These Shi'i scholars argued that every Muslim who
perfected his knowledge of Arabic could read the teachings of
the Imams. Once the believer had read and studied the traditions
(akhbār), he could attain an accurate understanding of the law.
In so doing, the Akhbaris undermined the special role of the jurists *(faqīh)*, who claimed to be the sole possessors of the knowledge *(ijtihād)* that enabled them to interpret the divine law. In
supporting elements within the religious establishment who did
not believe in the all-encompassing role of the jurisconsult, Shah
Abbas II encouraged opposition to the political claims of jurists
on legal grounds. In addition, Shah Abbas II patronized the
philosophically minded, who negated the concentration of
power within one ideological current. They undermined the
power of the jurists on intellectual grounds. And finally, on the
social level, dervishes could compete with legal scholars for
adepts, given that their religiosity was more palatable to the
denizens of Isfahan.

DEBATING AUTHORITY: MYSTICS, PHILOSOPHERS, AND THEOLOGIANS

Throughout medieval Islamic history, the relationship between
the philosophical, the mystical, and the *shari'a*-minded men of

religion has been tinged with an undercurrent of hostility. At times, these tensions rose to the surface, resulting in stringent waves of polemics and persecutions that polarized these three often interchangeable paths toward divine truth. It was during such times that the *shari'a*-minded *ulama* would term the styles of thought and practices of mystics and philosophers as "heretical," accusing them of deriving their ideas from non-Islamic sources, whether Mazdean belief systems or Greek philosophy.[32] Sufis were branded as *zindiqs*, an appellation used in medieval Islam during the Abbasid inquisition (779–787 C.E.), which sought to undermine the popularity of Manichaeans who had infiltrated the Abbasic household, the court, and the inhabitants of Baghdad.[33] In the Islamic era, the association of Mani with heresy had a long history behind it that continued to shape Muslim consciousness of the abject other. Sufis were also accused as well of being atheist *(mulhid)*. Both these defamatory terms— *zindiq* and *mulhid*—were employed against the so-called *ghulāt* throughout Islamic historiography up to the sixteenth century with the Nuqtavi Dervish Khusraw. In time, just as the term *ghulāt* came to be ascribed to a whole variety of perceived nonconformists, so did the designation *zindiq*. Often the two terms were used synonymously. Although the appellations *zindiq* and *ghulāt* were adopted indiscriminately for all types of religious dissenters, serving as negative icons in attacks by the *shari'a*-minded, parallels constructed between sufi beliefs and those of the *zindiq* are not all fantastic fabrications devised by their detractors. Sufis were accused of embracing specific precepts like divine incarnation *(hulūl)*, unicity of being *(ittihād)*, and reincarnation *(tanāsukh)*—doctrines also ascribed to the *ghulāt*. From self-portrayals of the Nuqtavis preserved in their writings, we know that these doctrines were part of their cosmology. They were not fiction. Philosophers, on the other hand, were accused of providing the theoretical framework that legitimized the claims of the Manichaeans *(zindiq)*. As I have argued throughout this narrative, some of these "heretics" did indeed give meaning to Islam using Persianate interpretive lenses, but they were Muslim. They placed themselves within the Muslim era and incorporated Muslim prophets and saints in their genealogy of holy men. The *ghulāt* used a Muslim vocabulary as well to explain their worldview. It is in the meaning ascribed to these holy beings and to cyclical turns of time where singularity from other readings of Islam emerges. Sufism, Shi'ism, and Illuminationist philosophy were spheres in which various renderings of Islam overlapped. Insofar as the marriage between these religious quests was not always fused with the fire of the more literalist interpreters of Islam, a harmony prevailed. Particular historical contexts, like that of Safavi Iran, shed light on our understanding of these dynamics and help delineate the nature of difference. Whether charges of Manichaeism *(zandaqah)* were trumped up or not, the *ghulāt*, the sufis, and the philosophers shared religious sensibilities—and these threatened the *shari'a*-minded quest for God.

Heresy trials against sufis illustrate the historical circumstances—and outline patterns—that led to the persecution of mystics such as Abū al-Husayn Nuri (d. 907), Hallaj (d. 922), and Ayn al-Quzat (d. 1131).[34] Beyond the religious context of Hallaj's execution, for example, it has been read as one motivated by political concerns.[35] Although the mystic Hallaj may very well have been the victim of political factionalism at the Abbasid court, both the nature of the charges leveled against him and the historical factors that colored the reasons behind his execution are revealing. Hallaj was accused of practicing Manichaeism, believing in divine incarnation, and being an apostle of the Isma'ilis (Qarmati) at a time when the ideology of some Qarmatis had posed a threat to Abbasid rule in Iraq and Bahrayn.[36] Hallaj's links to the Qarmatis were not mere fabrications that conveniently suited the Abbasid political agenda. He is said to have enjoyed good relations with Abū Sa'id Jannabi, the founder of the Qarmati state in Bahrayn, for example.[37] This is not to say that Hallaj was a Qarmati. Hallaj had sanctioned that the individual unable to perform the pilgrimage could reconstruct that ritual in a special room containing a replica of the

Ka'ba. His prosecutors argued that this was inspired by the Qarmatis, who at the time were propagating ideas against the hajj.[38] A year after Hallaj's execution, Abū Tahir, the youngest son of Abū Said Jannabi, led a series of campaigns in southern Iraq, raiding pilgrimage caravans. Finally, in 930 Abū Tahir sacked Mecca and captured the black stone during the hajj season. The Qarmatis may have been inspired by Hallaj and borrowed some of his ideas, interpreting them to fit into their own beliefs and aspirations. A dynamic may very well have existed between the *ghuluww* of some Qarmatis and the beliefs of Hallaj, particularly since Hallaj did make use of Qarmatian vocabulary and motifs.[39]

Hallaj, in an attempt to explain his predicament, drew four concentric circles and proceeded to delineate the variety of ways in which his teachings were received:

> The denier remains in the outermost circle. He denies my state since he cannot see me, he charges me with *zandaqah* and accuses me of evil. The inhabitant of the second circle thinks that I am a divine master [*'alim rabbānī*]. And he who attains to the circle of reality forgets and is hidden from my sight.[40]

The *shari'a*-minded scholars who were furthest from understanding Hallaj accused him of being a Manichaean. Those, perhaps like the Qarmatis, who claimed familiarity with his teachings, misunderstood him, for they saw him as divine. And those who realized the real meaning of his words attained the truth and vanished. It is clear from Hallaj's statement that a relationship existed between the two groups who confounded his quest. The rationalists whose temperament hindered them from recognizing the essence of Hallaj's mission came to define him in accordance with the way in which the second group perceived him. The term *zindiq* and its precise use here, referring to those who espouse the concept of divine incarnation, was colored by the way in which some devotees saw Hallaj as a divine being. In reality, then, the charges against Hallaj were directed against those *ghulāt* who viewed Hallaj as godlike. Had Hallaj expressed his views at a time when *ghuluww* posed no direct challenge to the political establishment, he probably would have still been misconstrued and would have remained a controversial figure. His trial and execution, however, might have been avoided.

The traditional undercurrent of tensions between these three religious styles was kindled in Safavi Iran once a figure like Mulla Sadra, in true Ghazalian fashion, attempted to fuse metaphysics and mysticism with theology.[41] This time around, however, it was within the context of Shi'ism (Imami) that the synthesis was being posited. Sadra's views were certainly controversial for the *shari'a*-minded, who did not believe in transcending beyond rational proofs. The religious judge of Shiraz (Shaykh Ali Naqi Kamara'i) in one of his works *(Himām al-thawāqib)* dedicated to Shah Safi voiced his resentment toward the shah who had commissioned Mulla Sadra to translate the *Ihyā' 'Ulūm al-dīn* of Ghazali into Persian.[42] Mulla Sadra spoke of the interplay between experience and formal knowledge—which incorporated a balanced degree of both variables.[43] He was one who practiced what he preached. Of his experience during his retreat to Kahak, where he had settled for some years due to "the hostility of his [my] contemporaries to extinguish the flames of his [my] soul," he writes: "I came to know divine secrets that I had never before comprehended, mysterious enigmas unveiled themselves—in a manner that rational argumentation had never before been able to unfold. Better said, all metaphysical secrets that I had known through rational proofs, now, finally I had experienced the intuitive perception—the direct vision."[44]

For a reader untrained in metaphysics, these statements, taken out of context, may sound like remarks the *ghulāt* would utter. Mulla Sadra, with his revival of Suhravardi's illuminationist (Ishraqi) philosophy, however, was attempting to reunite the spiritual exercises of the "real" mystic, who was driven by self-purification, with the method of the philosopher, who in his pursuit of wisdom ultimately sought knowledge of the self. It is clear from the defense that Mulla Sadra provides in his *Kasr asnām al-jāhiliyya,* where he attacks those assumed sufis who know nothing of mysticism *(tasawwuf)* and gnosticism *(irfān),* and in his *Sih Asl,* where he criticizes the ignorant *shari'a-*minded *ulama,* that like Hallaj he too was trying to draw distinctions around the two groups who had misunderstood his ideas. Mulla Sadra was responding to the vulgar and superficial categorizations that lumped mystics and philosophers with "exaggerators." He was responding as well to those assumed sufis who claimed to be in direct contact with God. Four decades later, Muhsin-i Fayz, in his *Muhākama bayn al-mutasawwif wa Ghayrihim* (written in 1072/1660–1166), would still attempt to make these distinctions. By that time, however, twenty tracts against sufis and philosophers had been compiled by the *shari'a-*minded: the debates had reached their peak.[45] Muhsin-i Fazyz himself speaks of the futility of his writing, but since the question has been posed and every question deserves an answer, he says, an attempt shall be made to respond to this query in accordance to what has been understood from the Qur'an and the hadith.[46]

Both Fayz and Sadra's voices are critical for understanding the different dimensions of these polemics. In their attack on supposed sufis, whom they call *mutasawwif*—literally, those who are turning into sufis—they distinguish between those assumed sufis with *ghulāt* colorings and sufis like themselves. They speak of the ways in which the popularization of sufism and the dervish cult were perceived as creating social discord. They single out public arenas of the marketplace and sufi cloisters as sites of disorder. In addition, both Fayz and Sadra attribute the *shari'a-*minded *ulama*'s aversion to mysticism and philosophy to their narrow-mindedness, a predicament that had led them to define the sufi in such broad terms as to encompass those so-called sufis along with the piety-minded mystics and philosophers. Here we begin to see how a socioreligious phenomenon such as the popularization of sufism was capitalized on by the *shari'a-*minded to discredit their traditional opponents—mystics and philosophers.

"Today" says Sadra, "the word *sufi* is used to refer to any individual who attracts a following and who has assemblies gorging on stew [*āsh*], mystical concerts [*sama'*], clapping and stamping."[47] Amid Sadra's repertory of words, he uses the term *sufiesque (mutasawwif)* most frequently to refer to those pretenders to sufism. At one point he uses the term *dervish*, perhaps the more untainted designation, one that characterizes the type that these so-called sufis enacted. Of the influences Sadra sees as having affected this group, he singles out their exposure to popular beliefs during their childhood. Youth are deemed most prone to these ways. They embraced these beliefs due to their association with ignorant persons—associations that would prevent them from seeking true knowledge and wisdom *(ma'rifat)*.[48] Their ignorance and rejection of the divine law led them to repeat words of ecstasy *(shathiyat)* that others had voiced. Clueless as to their meaning, they uttered them and identified themselves with sufis like Hallaj. Mimicking his words, they would say, "I am the truth/God" *(ānā'l-haqq)* or those of Bayazid Bistami's, "Glory be to me" *(subhānī)*. Perhaps they would even mimic the words Sadra had uttered during his spiritual retreat in Kahak.

Sadra sees these utterances as "worse for the general public than deadly poison, for they are attracted to these types of sayings, and anyone can weave such words together."[49] Although Sadra defends Hallaj and Bistami, he seems to agree with Ghazali (d. 1111) that these are words that need to remain in private, as social chaos can arise if they are vocalized. It is probably on the same grounds that other mystically inclined scholars like Muhsin-i Fayz, Mulla Rafi'a Na'ini, and Mawlana Muhammad Baqir Sabzavari felt that the sufi ritual of recalling God *(zikr)* need not be recited aloud.[50] As for those "assumed" sufis, Sadra feels that they had no respect for formal knowledge and considered intuition and experience the only true means of attaining God. That is why Sadra in his *Kasr asnām al-jāhiliyya* emphasizes the need to acquire knowledge of the divine law and to follow the pillars of Islam before any self-purification and transcendence could occur.[51] These sufis he sees as unlearned and, therefore, as charlatans and pretenders. Gnostics *('arif)*, says Sadra, are rare individuals.[52] To attain gnosis *(ma'rifat)*, one must begin by "worshipping in accordance to the *shari'a* without which spiritual exercises are confusing and confused."[53] Sadra concludes by saying, "If one sways from studying the *shari'a,* he will not attain the type of devotion a philosopher arrives at nor the spiritual state of a sufi—in that case he is lost."[54]

This telling representation distinguishing the "assumed" mystic from the "real" one—that the sufi pretender had no interest in the pursuit of Muslim knowledge and prescribed rituals—isolates sufism as a site of syncretism where other ways of being and experiencing time shaped cosmology and practice. Mulla Sadra was partaking in a project of conversion where the *shari'a* lay at the core of mystical inspiration and philosophic inquiry. This is not a portrayal uttered solely by Sadra, for it permeates the criticism of the rationalist polemics. Qummi, in his *Tuhfat al-akhyār* (1075/1664–1665), states that the followers of Hallaj and Bistami, inasmuch as they have abandoned their quest for knowledge, prevent their adepts from seeking knowledge *('ilm)* and reason *('aql)*, hindering them from attaining God.[55] The anticlericalism of these sufi pretenders is manifest in their rejection of formal knowledge. According to the pseudo-Ardabili, some "claim that they are the only ones who understand God. But the followers of the path [*shari'a*] of Muhammad recognize that these people have ceased to observe the precepts [*ahkām*] of the divine law and the quest for religious knowledge. Furthermore, this group claims that rational and transmitted [*'aqlī u naqlī*] proofs force one to desist from progressing on the spiritual path for one cannot understand God through these means."[56] They say "reading religious books is forbidden [*haram*]. Whatever the *ulama* arrive at in seventy years or more of study can be attained in an hour of guidance with the spiritual master."[57] This rationalist discourse however, unlike the utterances of Mulla Sadra, stopped short of moving beyond the *shari'a* as a blueprint for religious, political, and social order.

"And I saw a man" says the pseudo-Ardabili, "who not only was unlearned in the religious sciences [*'ulūm-i dīniyah*] but was illiterate, and just because he interpreted the *Gulshan-i rāz*, people considered him to be above the *ulama* of the age."[58] These types of people, according to the pseudo-Ardabili, "are numerous and have fooled the masses and have given themselves the name of sufis, so that perhaps they may gain respect among the masses, or perchance they hope to fool those among the masses who have no inclination [*mayl*] toward the *ulama*."[59]

It is no surprise then that Mulla Sadra was determined to identify the "true" sufi, who in addition to his pursuit of formal religious knowledge and rational proofs engaged in the spiritual quest for God. Qummi and the pseudo-Ardabili instead blurred the distinctions between the type of mystic Sadra talked about and the omnipresent phenomenon of exaggeration. Threatened by this situation, which certainly challenged the role of the *shari'a*-minded, legal scholars *(ulama al-dīn)* came to project this menace from "assumed" sufis onto mystics and philosophers in general. The connections, however, are not far-fetched, for these supposed sufis reflect the image and spoke the language of the "real" sufis. We have seen in the case of Dervish Khusraw how sufism acted as an arena from which his *ghulāt* aspirations came forth. The polemicists too speak of how heretics *(mulhid)* are often mistaken for dervishes. The pseudo-Ardabili names a group of "Sufis" (Shamrākhiyya) and says of them: "This group is from among the groups [*firqah*] who in reality [*bātin*] are heretics [*mulhid*] but use mysticism [*tasawwuf*] as a sanctuary [*panāhgāh*] for their corrupt idea."[60] In another section he says, "Ignorant ones consider these kinds of people as dervishes."[61] "And some Shi'is have been fooled by them, insofar as some of them venerate Ali."[62] These polemics encapsulate heteroglossia where Alid loyalty and gnosticism overlapped in spaces of resistance now cast as excess by rationalist Muslim tendencies.

Although Mulla Sadra does not explicitly use the word *ghulāt*, as the pseudo-Ardabili will when describing these groups, he states, "They say that they are friends [*awliyā*] of

God and claim closeness to him. They hear meaningless sayings and words of ecstasy [*shathiyāt*] thinking that they are intuitions and miracles [*kashf u karāmāt*]. They think that they are hearing divine words. At this time I see a group of these blind ones who claim that their leader has attained gnosis [*ma'rifat*] and that he is in the process of seeing God, and to his stupid disciples he says that they have attained God and are near him. While no inspiration has befallen him, he says, 'I shall send down something like what God has sent down.'"[63] Here Sadra refers to this fake master as a Manichaean *(zindiq)*.[64] The picture Sadra paints of this so-called master is one who in practice claims something very close to prophethood, at times articulated under the rubric of a saint *(valī)*, yet making use of sufi terminology—an example of the synthesis between *ghuluww* and sufism, an inkling of the nature of Shah Isma'il's movement.

Mulla Sadra was observing this phenomenon in 1618, two decades after the second civil war had come to a close and four years after slaves *(ghulām)* were being thoroughly incorporated into the Safavi system. The Qizilbash were just beginning to wane. The issue of *ghuluww* was still a sensitive one to broach explicitly. Hamavi's earlier attack against Abū Muslim (in 1531), for example, makes use of the word *bid'at*, or "innovation," and refers to Abū Muslim as an Alid deviant (Kaysani). The term *ghulāt* is never used.[65] Even with the second wave of attacks against Abū Muslim (1626–1649)—toward the end of Abbas I's reign and into Safi's—the key icon "Kaysaniyya" is used with reference to innovation to mark Abū Muslim and his devotees as other than the Twelver Shi'is. It is only in the *Hadīqat al-Shī'a*, written in 1648 to 1649 and falsely attributed to the dead scholar, Muqaddas Ardabili (d. 1585), that the term *ghulāt* is used candidly. The essential meaning ascribed to the "exaggerators"—that these individuals claimed to be divine, through precepts such as incarnation and reincarnation—is identical to the descriptions of this group found in Mulla Sadra, Hamavi, and other polemists who were alive and writing within the Safavi realm and who refrained from the use of the term

ghulāt. The pseudo-Ardabili, however, uses *ghuluww* synonymously with *bid'a*.[66]
    Here the pseudo-Ardabili provides us with a thread that ties
the *ghālī* Abū Muslim together with the sufis—the common belief in unitive fusion *(ittihād)* and divine incarnation *(hulūl)*. The
connection lies in questions concerning the soul, the individual,
and the divine, and their interrelationship—issues that preoccupied the so-called *ghulāt* and were taken up by sufis and philosophers. The meaning that they ascribed to the relationship between the individual and the divine in this world in terms of
being and time were imbued with Mazdean and Gnostic
cosmologies. These attitudes were controversial in the Safavi
context of centralization, where attempts at homogenizing religious belief systems were underway. These linkages, however,
shed light on the perception of intercultural dynamics that are
translated onto the evolution of Safavi polemics from their initial anti-Abū Muslim (Alid exaggeration) stage to the subsequent wave directed against sufis and philosophers. The
Hadīqat al-Shī'a by the pseudo-Ardabili begins with an attack
on Abū Muslim and leads into an attack against sufis. This particular format allows us to place the *Hadīqat al-Shī'a* in time, for
it is the work that connects both waves of disputations, falling
squarely in the middle of the two. It provides us as well with a
negative representation of the processes and production involved in the interplay between Alid loyalty, sufism, and
ghuluww.
    The pseudo-Ardabili, in an exposé of sufism and its historical
linkages to *ghuluww*, provides a variety of technical terms that
were used to refer to sufis. Although the connections he draws
between terms, individuals, and movements are distorted and
often historically inaccurate, the meanings he ascribes to these
genealogies are illuminating. He begins with the word *sufi*, originally used, he says, to identify the followers of the "first" mystic,
Abū Hashim (d. 776) from Kufa (Iraq).[67] The medieval Shi'i
heresiographer and author of *Usul al-diyānah* is said to have regarded Abū Hashim as an apostate *(mulhid)*, for he was known

for his belief in divine incarnation *(hulūl)*, which he shared with Christians (Nusrani).[68] The polemicist is creating a narrative whereby Shi'is from the very inception of Islam were opposed to mystics due to their embracing of non-Muslim (in this case, Christian) precepts. Abū Hashim's adepts, says the psuedo-Ardabili, were called sufis because they wore woolen clothing *(sūf)*. The famous Sunni religious scholar Sufyan al-Thawri (d. 778) took up this path, and so his disciples were called Sufiyanis. The ecstatic mystics Hallaj and Bayazid Bistami later continued this tradition, and insofar as their followers believed in divine incarnation *(hulūl)* and unitive fusion *(ittihād)*, they were called Incarnationis and Unitarians (Hulūliyya and Ittihādiya). And since a group among their adepts were fanatics in their belief in unitive fusion *(ittihād)*, they came to espouse the concept of unity of being *(wahdat-i wujūd)* and were accordingly called Wahdatiyya:

> Those who had *ghuluww* toward their shaykhs and believed in their divinity, on the basis of *hulūl* and *ittihād* they were called *ghulāt* and *ghāliya* and *ghāwiya*, and since they invented a path [*tarīqa*] and a sect [*mazhab*], they mixed profanities [*kufr*] together with Islam, and our Imams called them innovators [*mubtadi'*], and once they began using some terminology, they called it *tasawwuf*, and the *ulama* called them sufiesque [*mutasawwif*].[69]

"For the Shi'is," says the pseudo-Ardabili, "*ghulāt* means those who believe that some of the twelve Imams were God, and for the Sunnis, *ghulāt* are those sufis who consider their Shaykhs as Allah."[70] Prominent Shi'i scholars, like Shaykh Mufid and Ibn-i Babuya, according to the pseudo-Ardabili, considered sufis as "exaggerators." He adds, "And it is certain [*yaqīn ast*] that they are effects [*āsār*] of the *ghulāt*."[71] Finally, the pseudo-Ardabili provides us with a condensed definition of the so-called sufi: "One who believes in divine incarnation [*hulūl*], unitive fusion [*ittihād*], or unity of being [*wahdat-i wujūd*], which is *ghuluww*, and all of these are considered to be blasphemy [*kufr*] in Shi'ism. Know that there are many who do not believe in God [*hazrat-i haqq*]."[72] The pseudo-Ardabili remarks with certainty that sufis are remnants of the *ghulāt* as he attempts to erase an entire syncretic history of esotericism in Shi'i Islam (Imami).[73] Although the *shari'a*-minded polemicists use the terms *sufi* and *ghulāt* indiscriminately, it is clear that the pseudo-Ardabili is referring to those mystics with transcending coloration who breathed life into arenas of opposition, giving shape to new forms of Muslim religiosity (Shi'ism and Persianate Sufism) that were now at the center of controversy. "Exaggerated" beliefs are ascribed to the followers of "real" sufis like Bistami—rather than to Bistami himself. In addition, the pseudo-Ardabili sees divine incarnation and unitive fusion as the doctrinal mechanisms through which sufi masters and Shi'i Imams come to be revered as divine. In so doing, the pseudo-Ardabili demonstrates how *ghuluww,* Alid loyalty, and sufism merged in the disciple who due to his sense of being and time viewed the mystic and Imam as godlike messiahs. This merging is seen as a new path *(tarīqat)* toward God—a fourth path that combines non-Islamic precepts with the language and practices of sufis. Hence, the pseudo-Ardabili creates a new category that encompasses the beliefs of assumed sufis like Shah Isma'il and Dervish Khusraw, the sufiesque *ghulāt.*

In an attempt to discredit sufism in general, the pseudo-Ardabili links the sufi heritage with that of the Sunnis. Whether through the ties that early mystics were said to have had with Sunnis like Sufiyan al-Thawri or through the similar manner in which they venerated their shaykhs, an attempt is made to cast sufism into a Sunni mold. Sectarian antagonisms were certainly alive at the time and translate themselves onto most of these polemics. Qummi provides evidence for the fact that Shi'is were never sufis: "An important indicator is that in all those cities that are known to be centers of Shi'ism, such as Qum, Astarabad, Sabzavar, Jabal 'Amil, and Hilla, one cannot find a single ancient cloister [*khāniqāh*]. Even famous mystics like Attar and Jami, who have written books about sufi masters and consider Hallaj and Bistami as friends of God [*awliyā'*], have not mentioned a single spiritual master from Qum, Astarabad, Sabzavar, Hilla, or Jabal 'Amil."[74] Sectarianism, however, is not the impetus behind these polemics. Just as the opponents of Hallaj tried to discredit him by branding him a Shi'i, so these Imami polemicists attempted to discredit sufism by defining it as a Sunni practice.

Majlisi Sr. is the other link that ties these two waves of polemics together. We know that the disputations *(rudūd)* against Abū Muslim were first articulated by Mir Lawhi in opposition to Majlisi Sr., who praised Abū Muslim from the pulpit *(minćar)*. We also know that the first set of polemics against mystics transpired between Majlisi Sr. and his *shari'a*-minded student Muhammad Tahir Qummi.[75] Mir Lawhi provides us with the background to these refutations. In the course of Mir Lawhi's attempt to confirm the sufi proclivities of Majlisi Sr., he informs us that "thousands of copies" of the *Tawzīh al-mashrabayn* and the *Usūl al-fusūl al-tawzīh* were in circulation in Isfahan. These books dealt with "the rejection and affirmation, the truths and fallacies, of mysticism [*tasawwuf*] disputed between Majlisi Sr. and Mullah Muhammad Tahir Qummi, the Shaykh al-Islam of Qum."[76] According to Mir Lawhi, it all began "when a certain man in Qum [Mulla Muhammad Tahir Qummi] wrote a treatise with the intention of guiding the masses, and a certain Ali Bek from among the adepts of Hallaj [*murīdān-i Hallaj*] stole it and circulated it in other towns. He showed it to some religious scholars, none of whom paid attention to the disputation. Finally, he brought it to Isfahan and disclosed it to Majlisi Sr., who wrote a warning [*inhā'*] directed against his rebel student: "Whoever from among the people of religion [*ahl-i dīn*] sees this polemic should beware!"[77]

Majlisi Sr.'s defense of figures such as Hallaj links him to the sufis, who in the language of the Safavi polemicists are referred to as the "adepts of Hallaj." Majlisi Sr. belonged to the circle of religious men who, like Shaykh-i Baha'i (d. 1621), had been assimilated into the hegemonic culture of the dervish cult to the extent that he revered the same cultural heroes. Baha'i himself had a large popular following. Yet it is not clear whether he flaunted his godlike aura. The populist dervish cult seems to have influenced some men of religion more than others. According to Mir Lawhi, the populace regarded Majlisi Sr. as a saint. Although Mir Lawhi's voice is embittered by Majlisi Sr.'s popularity, Chardin, who visited his tomb in Isfahan shortly after his death, confirms the fact that people venerated Majlisi Sr. as a prophet.[78] "People in that day and age," says Mir Lawhi, "revered the deeds and acts [ḥālāt va kamālāt] of that scholar [Majlisi Sr.], to such an extent that after his death, they did not think the Mahdi [ṣāhib-i zamān] could hold a candle to him. They ascribed miracles to his mule and broke pieces off his grave and wore them as amulets."[79]

In the eyes of the denizens of Isfahan, Majlisi Sr. possessed a spark of divinity. The ghulāt sensibilities of the populace, which led them to seek constant guidance and communication with a living god or prophet, were directed at dervishes as well as clerics like Majlisi Sr. This holy role, just like the one dervishes played in the religious cosmology of the masses, had repercussions for the shari'a-minded, who were attempting to reserve that status for the awaited Mahdi. The early debates among Shi'i men of religion concerning the divine or human nature of the Imams, which had been articulated during the period of the Imams' presence, an era in which ghuluww and Imamism had once before come into close contact, were revived here.[80] This time they centered on the divine qualities of other intermediaries between God and the believer—mystics, philosophers, and theologians.

Seventeen years after the Hadīqat al-shī'a was written, during the last year of Abbas II's rule, once the attacks against sufis were at their peak and the court was clearly patronizing mystics, Majlisi's rebellious student Qummi writes of the followers of Hallaj and Bayazid Bistami: "It is not like the followers of Hallaj and Bayazid think that with spiritual exercises one can become an Imam and a caliph and can attain such a high stature. This

group considers obedience to their masters as obligatory, and
they call them Imams and caliphs, and this is why their spiritual
guides, when they get the chance, emerge as messiahs
[*khurūj*]."[81] Qummi goes on to cite an example of one such phenomenon. Nurbakhsh (d. 1464), he says, "who was a grand
master of this group [*tayifa*], made claims that he was the Mahdi
and the Imam and made his sortie [*khurūj*] during the reign of
Shahrukh."[82]

Once again, Qummi, although he refrains from using the term
ghulāt, ascribes a meaning to the term *bid'at,* or "innovation,"
that embodies the essence of *ghuluww*—the belief in the potential divinity of human beings.[83] "If one asks what are these miracles [*kashf*] through which some of the followers of Hallaj and
Bistami claim they have attained unitiy with God [*wahdat-i
wujūd*], we know what they mean by miracles," says Qummi.
"In response we say that people with these invalid [*bātil*] spiritual exercises act contrary to the *shari'a,* insofar as they go into
seclusion for forty days and refrain from eating meat and stay in
dark places alone so that their temperament [*mazāj*] becomes
corrupt, and they start seeing visions and have dreams in which
they ascend to heaven and to the throne and see God in the form
of their master, and sometimes they even see themselves as God
and think that they have attained their quest and that in reality
they are God."[84]

The *ghuluww* of the assumed sufis described here by Qummi
and the pseudo-Ardabili may appear to be a fantasy aimed at
discrediting their "real" sufi opponents. Yet it is difficult to dismiss these charges on such grounds, for how are we then to account for the philosopher Sadra's depiction of the contemporaneous group whose master utters words like "I shall send down
something like what God has sent down." In fact, if we then
place these polemics within their historical context, we see that
these kinds of claims were not anomalous. Qummi himself
speaks of Nurbakhsh (d. 1464), who claimed to be a messiah.
Shah Isma'il, too, played on the sensibilities of his devotees,
claiming in his poetry that he was the manifestation of the truth,

that, indeed, he was God himself. We know as well that figures like Dervish Khusraw continued to espouse these beliefs or at least to speak in this millenarian language well into the seventeenth century.

To argue that the *ghuluww* of some Qizilbash and craftsmen devotees of the Safavis did not play an active role in the cultural landscape of early modern Iran is to overlook much. After all, Turkmen (Qizilbash) lived side by side with Iranians (Tajik), both in the provinces and in the cities. Not only did they intermarry at court, on the battlefield, and in the marketplace, but together they also engaged in the rituals of the dervish lodge as disciples of Dervish Khusraw. It was through mystical arenas that conversion of the populace to Shi'ism (Imami) was also taking place in Safavi Iran. The *Qisas al-khāqānī*, written contemporaneously with Qummi's disputation (*Tuhfat al-akhyār* in 1664 to 1665), enumerates a list of twenty dervishes engaged in the process of converting the general public to Islam. The Turkmen author of the chronicle, Vali Quli Shamlu, speaks of a mullah in Mashad, Shaykh Muhammad Ali Muazzin, whose efforts at proselytizing entailed basic ritual teachings of the five daily prayers and of what was prohibited *(harām)* and enjoined *(halāl)* in Islam.[85] On two occasions, this shaykh is reported to have taken groups of new converts from the province of Khurasan to the hajj. And it is from the central treasury *(khazanah-yi 'amirah)* in Isfahan that he received the financial support of Shah Abbas II to undertake these pilgrimages.

It was not only in Safavi frontier lands of the east that conversion was occurring. Another dervish, Mir Muhammad Baqir, is mentioned as one whom "since his adolescence had been in seclusion in the town of Sichan close to Isfahan. Now [1655–1666] he is busy guiding [*hidāyat*] nomads [*sahra nishīnān*], [and] it is known that he converted many opponents to Islam."[86] Islam was just beginning to be embedded in the daily practices of nonliterate denizens of Safavi Iran, and in the process the religiosity of mystical agents of this transformation colored the language and cosmos of these new members of the Muslim community *(millat)*.[87] But the process worked both ways, for the new Muslims carried some of their beliefs into their interpretations of Islam, filtering Shi'ism and Shi'i figures through their own vernacular lenses. New coatings of local beliefs continuously painted Muslim identities. Some familiar layers may have been reinforced at every merging; those who perceived divine qualities in a master continued to pose a problem for rational monotheists like Qummi, who saw the necessity of building a wall between heaven and earth. The "exaggerating" sensibilities of the populace did not stop short of viewing spiritual guides as gods; some polemists like Mir Lawhi saw these attitudes translating themselves onto the work of even the staunchest Shi'i scholars.[88]

Kindled by the competition over religious posts and new converts as well as Mulla Sadra's attempt to unite all three quests—*shari'a, tariqat, haqiqat*—in one, the longstanding hostility between theologian and mystic finally exploded.

NOTES

1. Mirza Habibullah was the son of Mīr Sayyid Husayn, whose mother was Shaykh Ali Karakī's daughter.

2. See, for instance, 'Abdullāh Afandī Isfahānī, *Riyāz al-Ulamā wa hīyāz al-fuzalā*, ed. Ahmad al-Husaynī, 6 vols. (Qum: Matba'at al-Khayyam, 1980), 70. sarcastic comments concerning Mirza Habibullah's scholastic abilities.

3. Sayyid Husayn Modarresi-Tabātabā'ī, *Introduction to Shi'i Law: A Bibliographical Study* (London: Ithaca Press, 1984), 53. The author is quoting from Kamarā'ī's *Risāla dar Ithbāt-i Luzūm-i Wujūd-i Mujtahid dar Zamān-i Ghaybat*, 2–3.

4. Ahmad Munzavī, *Fihrist-i Nuskhaha-yi Khattī-yi Fārsī*, vol. 2, 117, also quoted in Said Arjomand's *The Shadow of God and the Hidden Imam: Religion, Political Order, and Societal Change in Shi'ite Iran from the beginning to 1890* (Chicago: University of Chicago Press, 1984).

5. Jean Chardin, *Les Voyages du Chevalier Chardin en Perse*, ed. L. Langlès, 10 vols. (Paris: Le Normant, 1811), vol. 5, 209.

6. Ibid., 215: "It is, as I have just stated, the dominant opinion because it legitimizes and confirms the rights of the reigning monarch."

7. Ibid.

8. Chardin, *Les Voyages du Chevalier Chardin en Perse*, vol. 5, 216–217. For the Vizier Muhammad Bek, see Rudi Matthee, "The Career of Mohammad Beg, Grand Vizier of Shah Abbas II (r. 1642–1666)," *Iranian Studies* 24 (1991): 17–36.

9. Shaykh Ali Karakī's *Matā'in al-mujrimiyya fi radd al-sufiyya*, probably written in 1526; the *Anīs al-mu'minīn* by Hamavī written in 938/1531; and the *'Umdat al-maqāl fi kufr ahl al-zalāl* by Shaykh Hasan b. Shaykh Ali Karakī, written in 972/1564–1565.

10. Prior to the Safavi age, some scholars like Ibn Fahd (d. 841/1437) and Ibn Abī Jumhūr al-'Ahsāī had also combined these different quests for God, yet they were anomalies rather than the norm.

11. Only one extant refutation has come to my attention. The author of the *Arba'īn hadīthan fi radd al-sūfiyya* is anonymous—an indication that one could not openly attack sufis in this period. This work was composed in 1016/1608. The work consists of forty hadith attacking *tassawuf* and sufis in addition to a section relating prominent theologians' condemnation of sufis. Mạra'shī Library, MS 4578.

12. During Abbas I's reign, for example, one could study in Isfahan with Mīr Damad, Shaykh-i Bahā'ī, 'Abdullah Shūshtarī, Mīr Findiriskī, and Sultan al-Ulama.

13. Afandī, *Riyāz al-'ulamā*, vol. 5, 193.

14. Ibid., vol. 1, 39.

15. Mīr Lawhī first studied in Mashad with his father, Amīr Sayyid Muhammad Sabzavārī, who also taught Mīr Muhammad Zamān b. Ja'far Razavī (d. 1041/1631–1632)—author of the anti-Abū Muslim polemic, the *Sahīfat al-irshād*. Mīr Muhammad Zamān, in turn, was the teacher of Shaykh Zayn al-Dīn b. Muhammad Shahīdī, author of the *Sihām al- māriqa*. *Riyāz al-'ulamā*, vol. 5, 104, and the *Sahīfat al-irshād*, f 112b.

16. We know that within the clerical community, the greatest scholars of Safi's and Abbas II's reigns still adhered to the more eclectic school of thought: Mulla Sadra, Muhammad Taqī Majlisi Sr., 'Abd al-Razzāq Lāhījī, Muhammad Bāqir Sabzavārī, and Muhsin-i Fayz.

17. The *Izhār al-haqq* (1043/1633–1634) was written by Sayyid Ahmad, a student of Bahā'ī and Mīr-i Damad. Sayyid Ahmad was also the son-in-law of Mīr-i Damad. The first in this series of polemics against Abū Muslim, the *Sahīfat al-irshād* by Sayyid Mīrzā Muhammad Zamān, was written between 1626 and 1629 in Mashad. The fiery exchange between Mīr Lawhī and Majlisī Sr. seems to have been oral. I have found no trace of a manuscript of Mīr Lawhī's *Tarjumah-yi Abū Muslim,* in the Tehran University catalogue of manuscripts and in the *Tazkirat al-qubūr.*

18. Majlisi Sr. had tried to court Shah Safī, but Safī paid him no heed. In the following section, I shall discuss Majlisī Sr.'s dream—preserved in the *Rawzāt al-jannāt*—that portrays this courtship. In the same fashion, Nasrābādī informs us that once Mīr Findirskī returned from India, Shah Safī is said to have paid him a visit, but Nasrābādī sarcastically states, "In spite of this honor, his situation did not change." In other words, he was granted neither an official post nor a stipend. Muhammad Tāhir Nasrābādī, *Tazkirah-yi Nasrābādī,* ed. V. Dastgirdī (Tehran: Armaghan, 1973), 153. Both Mulla Sadra and Mīr Findiriski died during the last years of Safi's reign. Neither received grand burial sites.

19. Muhsin-i Fayz studied with Bahā'ī and Mulla Sadra.

20. From the *Izhār al-haqq wa miyār al-sadq* (1043/1633–1634), written by Sayyid Ahmad b. Zayn al-'Abidīn 'Alavī, we learn that this polemic was written in defense of Mīr Lawhī's criticism of Abū Muslim.

21. A list of seventeen *radds* appears in a manuscript of the *Izār al-haqq,* penned in 1063/1653.

22. *Zubdat al-tavārīkh* and the *Qisas al-khāqānī,* f 282a. Mīrzā Qāzī was the son of Tabīb Kāshifā, the Shah's doctor at court (d. 1075/1664–1665). He wrote a commentary on the *Usūl al-kāfī* and the *Jām-i Jam* concerning the good and the evils of wine. The *Zubdat al-tavārīkh* (f 82b), *Khulāsat al-siyar,* and the *Khuld-i barīn* name Mīrzā Qāzī along with the *ghulām* cabalists (Lalé Bek and Khusraw Mīrzā) in Isfahan as being present and arranging for Safi's accession.

23. Sultan al-Ulama, however, seems to have paid lip service to both the philosophically and the *shari'a*-minded tendencies among the religious community, allowing for these debates to continue openly.

24. The author of the *Salvat al-Shi'a* appears as a certain Mutahhar b. Muhammad al-Miqdādī: perhaps it was penned by Mīr Lawhī himself under a pseudonym. The list of those who wrote these polemics includes both the *shari'a*-minded *ulama* and the philosophically inclined ones: Shaykh Ali Naqī (Shaykh al-Islam), Mullā Hasan Ali Shūshtarī, Nūr Allah Ali Muftī, Mīr Sayyid Ahmad, Rafī al-Dīn Muhammad Nāīnī, Mawlana Muhammad Bāqir Sabzavārī. Rasūl Ja'fariān arrives at the conclusion that the *Salvāt al-Shī'a* was written by Mir Lawhi. See his "Rūyārūyi-yi Faqīhān va Sūfiyān dar 'Asr-i Safaviyyah," *Kayhān-i Andīshah* 33 (1990): 116.

25. *Qisas al-khāqānī*, f. 284b. Dervishes who received patronage from Abbas II in the form of land grants, *takkiya* or *'ināms* included the following:

 (1) Shaykh 'Imād-i Māzandarānī is said to have been the *murshid* of the notables (*'ayāns* and *ashrāf*) of Astarabad (*Qisas al-khāqānī*, 285a–285b).

 (2) Aqā Muhammad Sālih-i Lunbānī Isfahānī also had a following among the notables (*ashrāf* and *a'yān*) of Isfahan. Shah 'Abbās II frequently engaged in *suhbat* with him at his cloister *(dervish khānah)* and showed generosity *(ihsān)* toward his disciples *(murīd)* (*Qisas al-khāqānī*, f 286a). The shah offered him a piece of land *(bāgh)* and an *imārāt* (soup kitchen), along with a cloister in the town of Lunbān.

 (3) Sayyid Mu'īzz took up domicile in Bābā Rukh al-Dīn's shrine in Isfahan. On Friday nights, many sufis *(ahl-i tasawwūf)* who wanted to attain the paths of *haqīqat* and *ma'rifat* through the guidance of this shaykh would congregate there. The shah would provide him with a yearly recompense (*Qisas al-khāqānī*, f 286b).

 (4) Mawlana Hakīm Rajab Ali Tabrizī studied *fiqh* and then traveled to Konya to visit the *zāviyah* of Rūmī, where he engaged in the purification of his soul and found many adepts among the disciples of Rūmī. Later he moved to Isfahan, where the shah visited him often (*Qisas al-khāqānī*, f 277b).

26. Ibid., f 277a. Although Shah Abbas II's official court historian, Muhammad Yusuf Vālih, does not specify that Muhsin-i Fayz held

the post of Friday prayer leader, he does mention a couple of occasions during which the shah prayed with Fayz in Isfahan at the Masjid-i Jam'i. The first of these (1065/1654–1655) happened to be right after Sultan al-Ulama's death. Sultan al-Ulama had probably led the prayer while he was grand vizier.

27. See Rasūl Ja'fariān, *Dīn va Siyāsat dar Dawrah-yi Safaviyyah* (Qum: Intisharat-i Ansariyan, 1991), 449, for a facsimile of the *farmān* of Shah 'Abbās II to Fayz as well as his reply (*Fihrist-i Danishgāh*, dated Zul Qa'dah 1066/August–September 1656. Letters 29–31, MS 4602 entitled "Majmū'ah"). In 1065/1654–1655 Fayz refuses to lead the Friday prayer despite Abbas II's request, for it had caused much dissent within the Imami community, negating its purpose of fomenting unity.

28. Muhammad Tāhir Vahīd Qazvīnī, *'Abbāsnāme*, ed. I. Dihqān (Aṙak: Kitābfurūshi-yi Dāvūdī, 1950–1951), 255.

29. Ibid.

30. Sayyid Ahmad b. Zayn al-'Abidīn 'Alavī dedicated his *Lavāmi'-yi Rabbānī dar Radd-i Shubūāt-i Nasrānī*, to Shah Safī. Husaynī, Sayyid Ahmad, *Fihrist-i Kitābkhānah-yi 'Umūmī-yi Hazrat-i Ayatullah al-'Uzma Najafi Mar'ashī*, Qum: Mihr-i Ustuvār, vol. 6, 379–380. Muhammad Tāhir Qummī dedicated his *Jāmi'-yi Safavī* to Shah Safī. Mar'ashī Library Fihrist, vol. 11, 17.

31. Muhammad Tāhir Qummī, *al-Fawā'id al-dīniyya* (Tehran University Library, MS 2479), al-Tihrānī, Āqā Buzurg, *al-dharīa*, vol. 16, 335; Qummī, *Tawzīh al-mashrabayn*, al-Tihrānī, Āqā Buzurg, *al-dharīa*, vol. 4, 495.

32. Heresiographers like al-'Asharī, Nawbakhtī, and al-Baghdādī speak of Christian (Nasrānī), Hindu, and Manichaean influences on the beliefs of these heretics.

33. Georges Vajda, "Les Zindiqs en Pays d'Islam au Debut de la Période Abbaside," *Rivist a degli Studi Orientali* 17 (1938): 173 and 182. Vajda names two members of the Abbasid family, the son of Dawud b. Ali and a certain Ya'qub b. al-Fadl. He also names the son of the Abbasid Vazir Abū 'Ubaydullah, who is implicated through the inquisition against the Manichaeans, 186–187.

34. Carl Ernst's *Words of Ecstasy in Sufism* (Albany: State University of New York Press, 1985) examines the trials of these three sufis.

35. Ibid., 109–110.

36. Wilferd Madelung, *Religious Trends in Early Islamic Iran* (Albany, NY: Persian Heritage Foundation, 1988), 96–100.

37. Louis Massignon, *La Passion de Husayn b. Mansūr Hallāj: Martyr Mystique de l'Islam* (Paris: Gallimard, 1975), vol. 3, 194; Henry Corbin, *Histoire de la Philosophie Islamique* (Paris: Gallimard, 1964), 276.

38. Madelung, *Religious Trends in Early Islamic Iran*, 36.

39. Massignon, *La Passion de Husayn b. Mansūr Hallāj*, vol. 3, 194.

40. Hallaj, *Kitāb al-tawāsir*, vol. 5, 2–5, as cited in Carl Ernst, *Words of Ecstasy in Sufism*, (Albany: State University of New York Press, 1985), 145.

41. Corbin argues that Haydar Amulī (fourteenth century) had tried to cement this marriage earlier.

42. Ahmad Munzavī, *Fihrist-i Nuskhahā-yi Khattī-yi Fārsī*, 6 vols. (Tehran: Chāpkhānah-yi Shirikat-i Sihāmī, 1969), vol. 2, 1716 and 928: *Himām al-thawāqib* and the *Jāmi'-yi Safavī*.

43. See James Winston Morris, *The Wisdom of the Throne: An Introduction to the Philosophy of Mulla Sadrā* (Princeton: Princeton University Press, 1981), 7–12.

44. Henry Corbin, "La Place de Molla Sadrā Shirāzī (d. 1050/1640) dans la Philosophie Iranienne," *Studia Islamica* 18 (1963): 93. Corbin is quoting from the prologue to Sadrā's *Asfār al-arba'a*. Dānīshpazhū in his introduction to Mulla Sadrā's *Kasr asnām al-jāhiliya* speculates that Mulla Sadrā must have left for his exile sojourn in Kahak after 1021/1612–1613. We are sure that he remained in exile up to 1039/1629–1630, given that Muhsin-i Fayz writes that he studied with Sadra in Qum between 1033–1039/1623–1630.

45. The *Sihām al-māriqa*, written between the years 1650 and 1664 by Shaykh Ali Shahīdi, enumerates nineteen disputations against sufis.

46. Kashanī Muhsin-i Fayz, *Muhakama bayn al-mutasawwifa wa ghayrihim*, published in the *Nashriyah-i Danishkadah-i Adabiyāt-i Tabriz*, 2, Year 9 (1957): 118.

47. Sadr al-Dīn Muhammdad Shīrāzī (Mulla Sadra), *Kasr asnām al-jāhiliyya*, ed. M. T. Dānishpazhūh (Tehran: Matba'at Jami'at, 1962), 62.

48. Ibid., 16.

49. Ibid., 58.

50. Both Mulla Rafī'a Nā'īnī and Mawlānā Muhammad Bāqir Sabzavārī issued *fatwās* against singing and dancing, two activities that had become mixed with the *zikr*. These *fatwā(s)* are preserved in the *Salvāt al-shī'a* by Muttahar b. Muhammad al-Miqdādī, ff 103a–b. Fayz speaks out in his *Muhākamma bayn al-mutasawwifa wa ghayrihim*, 125, against *zikr*'s being recited aloud.

51. Mulla Sadra, *Kasr asnām al-jāhiliyya*, 51–52.

52. Ibid., 50.

53. Ibid.

54. Ibid., 52.

55. Muhammad Tāhir Qummī, *Tuhfat al-akhyār* (Qum: Intishārāt-i Nūr, 1973), 13–14. Qummī sees the fact that this group does not emphasize knowledge *('ilm)* and the recitation of the Qur'an—a fundamental pillar of Islam—as *bid'a* (148). The *Tuhfat al-akhyār* was written in 1075/1664–1665.

56. Pseudo-Ardabīlī, Ahmad b. Muhammad, *Hadīqat al-shī'a* (Tehran: n.p.), 1964. 581.

57. Ibid., 582.

58. Ibid., 591.

59. Ibid., 592.

60. Ibid., 580. On the Shamrākhiyya, see the al-'Alavī, Abū Ma'ālī Muhammad b. Husayn *Bayān al-adyān* (Tehran: Intishārāt-ii Ilmi va Farhangī, 1997), 558.

61. Ibid., 582.

62. Ibid., 570.

63. Mulla Sadra, *Kasr asnām al-jāhiliyya*, 24–26.

64. Ibid., 26

65. For an analysis of the variety of meanings ascribed to the term *ghulāt* in Muslim heresiography, see Wadad al-Qadi, "The Development of the Term *Ghulāt* in Muslim Literature with Special Reference to the Kaysaniyya," in *Akten des VII. Kongresses für Arabistik und Islammissenschaft Göttingen*, ed. Albert Dietrich (Göttingen: Vandenhoeck & Ruprecht, Abhandlungen der Akademie der Wissenschaften in Göttingen, 1976).

66. In addition, according to Rasūl Ja'farīān, an anonymous source, the *Kitāb al-arba'īn fī matā'in al-mutasawwifīn*, written during the reign of Shah Sultan Husayn (1694–1722), is said to have used the word *ghulāt* when depicting the *wujūdī* sufis. Ja'farīān speculates that the author is the grandson of Shahīd-i Thānī (d. 966/1559),

the son of Shaykh Ali Shahīdī (author of the *Sihām al-māraqa*—
another disputation) and a student of Majlisi Sr. "Rūyārūyi-i
Faqīhān va Sufiyān dar 'Asr-i Safaviyya."

67. The pseudo-Ardabīlī is probably referring to Abū Hāshim, the first
known sufi in Islam. The author of the *Bayān al-adyān* refers to his
followers as the Hāshimiyya (*Bayān al-adyān*, 47). He is also said
to have ascribed colors, tastes, and smells to God. *Tabsirah al-avāmm*, 75.

68. According to Muhammad Muhsin Āqā Buzurg al-Tihrānī, *al-dharī'a ilā tasānīf al-Shī'a*, 25 vols. (Tehran: n.p., 1936–1978) vol.
1, 181, the *Usūl al-diyāna* by Muhammad b. Nimatullah b.
'Abdullāh concerns the different sects and religions of Islam.

69. Ahmad b. Muhammad Pseudo-Ardabīlī, *Hadīqat al-shī'a* (Tehran:
n.p., 1964), 560. *Ghāwiya* comes from the Arabic root *ghawa*.

70. Ibid., 565.

71. Ibid.

72. Ibid., 599.

73. For this history, see Mohammad Ali Amir-Moezzi, *The Divine
Guide in Early Shi'ism: The Sources of Esotericism in Islam* (Albany: State University of New York Press, 1994).

74. Muhammad Tāhir b. Muhammad Husayn Qummī, *Risālah-yi
Radd bar Sūfiyān*, Mar'ashī Library, MS 4014, ff 76a–b.

75. These two tracts are preserved in the *Tawzīh al-mashrabayn* and
summarized in the *Usūl al-fusūl*.

76. Muhammad b. Muhammad Lawī Sabzavārī (Mīr Lawhi), *Arba'īn*
(Tehran University, M S1154), f 189a.

77. Ibid., f 189b–190a.

78. In a detailed description of the various districts of Isfahan,
Chardin mentions the tomb of Majlisi Sr. that is located beside the
masjid-i jām'i-i 'atīq. Chardin, *Les Voyages du Chevalier Chardin
en Perse*, vol. 8, 6.

79. Ibid., f 8b.

80. On these early tendencies and debates, see Modarresi-Tabātabā'ī,
An Introduction to Shi'i Law, 27.

81. Qummī, *Tuhfat al-akhyār*, 25.

82. Ibid., 25, and Qummī, *Risālah-yi Radd bar Sūfiyān*, f 85b. According to Qummī, Hallaj too claimed to be God (*Radd bar Sūfiyān*,
f 74b). Muhammad b. Muhammad b. 'Abdullāh (795–869/1392–
1464) was the disciple of Ishāq al-Khutlānī, who gave his pupil the

name Nurbakhsh. He received the title Mahdi due to his descent from Imam Musa Kazim, and he was proclaimed caliph by some of his followers. Shahrukh (807–50/1404–1446) arrested him in 826/1423; his life, however, was spared. In the headings of his *ghazal*(s) he is referred to as "Imam and Caliph over all the Muslims." D. S. Margoliouth, "Nurbakhsh," *EI1*.

83. Qummī, *Tuhfat al-akhyār,* 80. Qummī states "followers of Hallaj and Bayazid are into innovation [*bid'a*]." Qummī says "one *bid'a* of this group is their belief in *tanāsukh;* those who believe in *tanāsukh* are *zindiq(s)* and *mulhid(s).*" 112.

84. Ibid., 61–62.

85. Valī Qulī Shāmlū, *Qisas al-khāqānī*, Bibliothèque Nationale, MS Suppl. Pers. 227, f 282 b.

86. Ibid., f 285a.

87. Valī Qulī Shāmlū explicitly refers to the role of these dervishes in bringing opponents of Islam under the umbrella of the community of Islam *(millat-i Islam).* See, for example, his biography of Mīr Muhammad Bāqir Ardastānī, f 285 a.

88. Muhammad b. Muhammad Lawhī Sabzavārī (Mīr Lawhī), *Arba'īn* (Tehran University, MS 1154), f 29b: "This *ghuluww* and fanaticism of the masses in regard to crazy ones is not reserved to them, but superstition extends itself into all aspects even when it has to do with the *ulama* or the so-called *ulama* [*'ulamā nimāyān*]."

TWELVE

Conversion and Popular Culture

As the polemicists were painting a jaundiced picture of the intellectual milieu, tolerance manifested itself in public spaces of Isfahan in the ways in which the sacred and the profane coexisted side by side. Sources beyond courtly and religious circles, like the biographies of poets or European travelogues, depict an age in which the learned and popular mingled at court at the same time as they intersected in mosques, in sufi lodges *(takkiya),* and in coffeehouses *(qahvahkhānah).*[1] The synthesis was most visible—or perhaps most thorough—in sufi circles. There *ghuluww* had made its strongest impact. Such a fluid image does not contradict the one drawn by the authors of this oppressive discourse, for the disputations against sufis and the *ghulāt* are reactions to the very open-mindedness and syncretic processes that were unfolding within the culture of mystics, whether poets, storytellers, craftsmen, or philosophers. But when these two types of sources are viewed together, the tainted image can be peeled away from the less distorted one. Just as the voices of philosophers like Mulla Sadra and Muhsin-i Fayz helped refine the range of *ghuluww* amid mystic circles, these unofficial sources provide some texture to the contexts in which inhabitants of the Safavi realm experienced religion.

The *Stories of Monarchs (Qisas al-khāqānī)*—penned at the same time that Qummi composed his polemic against sufis,

Tuhfat al-akhyār, written in 1664 and 1665—names many dervishes who had followers among the notables and denizens of Astarabad (Shaykh Imad-i Mazandarani), Mashad (Shaykh Mu'min and Shaykh Muhammad Ali), Sabzavar (Dervish Hajji Muhammad), and Isfahan (Aqa Muhammad Salih and Sayyid Mu'iz).[2] The polemicists speak of the prestige that was to be gained by participating in the culture of sufism, which was a means of socializing and like all such arenas provided opportunities for forging connections—particularly given that social distinctions were blurred in these circles. A disciple, whether court functionary or baker, shared with other devotees the same spiritual status and submission toward a common master. Here in the intimacy of the cloister, where worldly distinctions were temporarily blurred, fraternal and paternal bonds would have been nurtured. Sadra believes that "most of those people hang out in cloisters [*sawāmā'*] so as to make their presence known or stay in the lodge [*khāniqāh*] so that piety [*zuhd*] and miracles [*karāmāt*] became associated with their names.[3] Prestige and honor continued to be gained through the dervish cult in the first half of the seventeenth century.

It was in public arenas such as coffeehouses, bazaars, and central squares that the mix of religious currents and eddies flowed through the Safavi imperium. Here in these spaces, mullahs, dervishes, and qalandars spoke of their religious quests—some genuinely believing in their mission, others seeing it as a profession and a means of gaining a livelihood. Whatever the intentions of these religious men, the populace was exposed to different religious tendencies and practices. At least up to the age of Sulayman (1666–1694), the choice to follow or abandon a particular jurisconsult *(mujtahid),* preacher *(vā'iz),* or dervish seems to have been as free as the flow of the currents. The contents of the polemics against sufis were debated in these spaces, as they were articulated in theological seminaries, the courtyard of the mosque, or the sufi cloister. Here the ideas of mystics would have been heard—voices that the rationalist *ulama* attempted to expunge from the legitimate map of Shi'ism toward the end of Shah Sulayman's reign (1689).

The coffeehouse was a place of cultural exchange frequented by a wide variety of denizens—from the shoemaker to the poet and the young dandy.[4] Chardin, who first traveled through Iran at the end of Abbas II's reign (1664–1665), speaks of the coffeehouse as a grand structure with high ceilings—usually the most beautiful space in the city—for here the inhabitants met for pleasure.[5] Coffeehouses in big cities ordinarily had a fountain at their center and platforms along the walls on which people would sit *À la manière orientale*. They were most crowded in the early mornings and in the evenings. People would pass their time drinking coffee, served with a hookah and some tobacco. Chardin depicts the coffeehouse as a place where one could tune into the latest news and where political criticism was voiced in full liberty, free of government scrutiny, for the court was not concerned with what people said.[6] While some were chatting or playing games like chess, poets would rise and recite their poetry; storytellers, their epics; and mullahs, their sermons. Dervishes would speak of human vanity and of worldly materialism. People were free to listen or to ignore them completely:

> The speeches of mollahs or dervishes are moral lessons similar to our sermons, but it is not scandalous to ignore them. No one is obliged to leave his game or his conversation in order to listen. A mollah stands up in the middle or at one end of the coffeehouse and begins to speak out loud, or a dervish suddenly enters and admonishes the gathering about the world's vanity, of its wealth and honor. It happens often that two or three people talk at the same time, one at one end, and one storyteller [*faiseur de contes*] at another. Ultimately, there is here ample liberty. The serious man, of course, would not dare engage in pleasantries, each does his harangue and listens to whom he pleases. The speeches end usually by saying: enough of sermons, in the name of God, go tend to your affairs. Then, those who have made these speeches ask for

something from the bystanders; they do this very modestly and without importunity, because if they act otherwise the master of the coffeehouse would not let them enter again, hence the one who wants pays.[7]

The situation, however, seems to have been more controlled half a century earlier during the reign of the autocrat Shah Abbas I (1587–1629). Tavernier, who made six voyages to Iran between 1636 and 1663, says that Shah Abbas I, realizing that people discussed affairs of the realm in the coffeehouse, feared that cabals against the court would be formed. The shah then ordered a mullah to go to the main cafés in Isfahan and preach about law, history, and poetry.[8] Abbas I was particularly sensitive to political dissent, for he was in the process of curtailing the power of the Qizilbash. Sending court-sponsored mullahs to preach in coffeehouses allowed him to extend his control beyond the court and into these public arenas.[9] Mullahs would expose participants of the culture of the coffeehouse to the official version of Imami Shi'ism—in an attempt to frustrate other religious style, in particular, the sufiesque *ghulāt*. Abbas I himself participated in the culture of the coffeehouse. Nasrabadi, the compiler of biographies of over one thousand poets living in Isfahan, uses the coffeehouse as a main source for his recordings of poetry. The proliferation of poets from all social strata in the seventeenth century, many of whom composed poems as a means of mystical expression, points to the democratization of a genre that prior to the Safavis was the privilege of a courtly elite.[10] Poets assembled in coffeehouses, where they recited their verse, and others responded to them by creating their own. One day, according to Nasrabadi, as Mullah Shukuhi, who was a calligrapher from Hamadan, was sitting in an Arab coffeehouse *(qahvahkānah-yi Arab)* famous for its young boys with locks *(zulf dār)*, Shah Abbas I walked in and inquired about his profession.[11] Mulla Shukuhi responded that he was a poet, and the monarch invited him to recite a verse. The poet sang a verse on love associating the beloved with the petal of a rose *(barg-i gul)*.

Shah Abbas I praised the poet but criticized his metaphor, which he found too austere *(nāmulāyim)*. As the story demonstrates, Shah Abbas I did not hesitate to enter and participate in a public sphere—whether coffeehouses or the Nuqtavi cloister, where controversial practices were in circulation. According to Tavernier, the court of Shah Safi (r. 1629–1642) continued to send religious preachers to coffeehouses. After a couple of hours of entertainment, the mullah would stand up and tell everyone to go to work.[12] By the age of Abbas II (1642–1666), however, the owner of the coffeehouse seemed to be able to set the tempo of the currents that flowed in and out of his shop.[13]

Not all public arenas were controllable—a point that must be kept in mind when analyzing the effectiveness of court policies. The bazaar, for instance, was a conversion ground for proponents of popular religious styles, acting as channels through which craftsmen and shopkeepers as well as female and male shoppers would be converted. Although the market inspector *(muhtasib)* oversaw the affairs of the bazaar, it seems that qalandars and sufis maintained access to them. Tavernier speaks of a cave by the city of Isfahan where qalandars had taken up residence. The cave, he says, was also a site of worship for Zoroastrians, who visited it two or three times a year.[14] Transcultural encounters continued to take place in holy sites shared by both Zoroastrians and Muslim mystics, who every day at three or four o'clock in the afternoon would make their way to the bazaar in Isfahan. Splitting up into teams, an elder dervish along with a young novice each headed for their designated corners. From one craftsman stall to another they would go, teaching their beliefs in the form of a play.[15] The older dervishes would pose questions that the youth would attempt to answer. After such exhortations, it is said that the dervishes would circulate "horrible" seasonal flowers and herbs (see figure 8). In return, they would receive alms.[16] Dervish culture was a channel through which vernacular systems continued to breathe freely within the Muslim semiosphere.

These herbs referred to by European travelers may very well have been psychoactive drugs. Travelers speak of a drug culture that was widespread in Isfahan, one that infiltrated both courtly and popular circles.[17] Although the court, according to Chardin, had attempted to limit the use of opium, this effort had been unsuccessful, for people had a general inclination toward it. It is rare, he says, to come across one in ten individuals who does not engage in this habit.[18] Cabarets, says Chardin, where a concoction of opium drinks *(cocenar/kokenar)* were served—at times not far from a mosque—were as common as coffeehouses. He speaks of a famous street in Isfahan, the Harun-i Vilayat in the district of Sayyid Ahmadiyan, where such opium dens were abundant. From his description of this street we also acquire a flavor of the larger community in which the sacred and the profane coexisted in Isfahan—how Jews, Armenians, Muslims, and "heretical Turks" shared these spaces:

> There is always an abundance of people who drink, converse, take fresh air, or visit the mausoleum of Harun Velaied, which is close by, and is one site of pilgrimage for the Persians where it is alleged that miracles occur, and people, mostly women go in crowds. It is a big mausoleum, well built in accordance to the saint's body, or as others interpret it, the saint of the region [*pays*]. He has no particular name, for they do not know precisely who this alleged saint was. The Turks who are Muslim heretics, the Jews and the Christians of whatever sect they may be, all say that he [the saint] was of their religion.[19]

In *Beliefs of Women ('Aqā'id al-nisā')*, a social satire mocking the popular beliefs of Isfahani women ascribed to the cleric Aqa Jamal Khwansari (d. 1710), the author divulges local rituals that in Isfahan had been synthesized with Islamic norms and practices.[20] The female reproductive role pervades local custom in the *Beliefs of Women*. Female fertility lies at the core of numerous rituals of shrine visitation that are invariably linked to the figure of Ali. The author places one of the fasts of Ali *(ruzah-yi Murtiza Ali)*, particularly recommended for young girls who want a good husband, in the same district of Isfahan where Jews, Armenians, and Turks engaged in devotion.[21] The contemporaneous French traveler, Jean Chardin, speaks of this minaret located in the district of Sayyid Ahmadiyan in Isfahan.[22] According to him, sterile women and newlyweds had great faith in this mosque. Much like the dervish cult served to bring together different social and ethnic groups, female religiosity linked all these individuals with the tempo of local beliefs shared by Zoroastrian, Armenian, and Jewish minorities living in Isfahan. The blurring of confessional lines was not limited to gendered ritual spaces. Even though they traveled primarily through and between female spaces, women were remarkably mobile. The degree to which socializing, whether during religious holidays or in the bathhouse, is given priority over religious duties demonstrates the extent to which women were participants in Isfahani society and active in formulating theology, synchronizing their lives with their devotional obligations. The details of cultural transmission through mothers may be lost to the historian, but we must not forget that these women did indeed pass on rituals and attitudes to their sons and daughters.

Isfahani society was geared toward communal socializing and entertainment. Some denizens of Isfahan spent wakeful hours in a state induced by the drinking, eating, or smoking of a variety of drugs, from hashish to opium. It would not be uncommon, according to Raphael du Mans, to come across individuals hallucinating in the street—speaking with or laughing at angels.[23] People in an altered state of consciousness would have been attuned to the world of miracles and the supernatural—to the magic theater of forms and figures. The sharpening of perceptions that is said to result from the ingestion of psychoactive drugs would have allowed the individual to experience new realities while in a consciousness-expanded state. According to mystics, the transcendental experience is not restricted to drug-induced states. It can be brought on in a variety of ways—sensory deprivation, fasting, or disciplined meditation. Those, however, who engaged in the drug culture would have been open to the religious orientation of the dervishes, for they would already have had visions of the unseen, experienced a different realm of space and time, and perhaps already sensed the presence of something powerful like God. Drugs were also used, along with music and dance, as a means of attaining a higher state of consciousness or a state of ecstasy. Qummi criticizes these ascetics: "[They] eat hashish so as to quicken" the process of attaining God.[24] The dreams and visions some sufis have of sitting on God's throne and seeing their master and themselves as the manifestation of God—something they call miracles, Qummi says— are similar to the hallucinations of qalandars who eat hashish *(bang)*"[25] (see figure 9). It is very possible that these mystics incorporated drugs in their initiation of craftsmen or *bazaaris*.

Mulla Sadra locates the marketplace as a recruiting ground for mystics with exaggerating tendencies. He sees this public space of conversion as a socioeconomic threat: "[T]hese peoples' power is such that some craftsmen [*san'atgarān*] and artisans [*pishāhvarān*] leave their jobs and follow them—what left of the common folk!"[26] The pseudo-Ardabili speaks of merchants as targets of this group. "Some of them go to weak-minded peoples' homes and voice their satanic whispers, and they go to the homes of the *bazaaris*, who know nothing of religious principles and sit with them and talk with them in order to fool them."[27] Craftsmen and artists are among the most visible professions who abandon their work and don the dervish cloak in the near contemporaneous *Biography of Poets* written by Nasrabadi.[28] Names of merchants *(tujjār)*, however, appear more frequently as patrons of cloisters *(takkiya)*, along with court official and the shah.[29] Despite the efforts by Safavi monarchs in the seventeenth century to severe the ties between local guilds and sufi masters through their direct control over guild organizations and their participation in the Karbala commemorations, craftsmen continued to be attracted to the ways of local dervishes.

Beyond these public arenas where the religiosity of sufis, dervishes, and *ghulāt* converged, in the private space of cloisters *(takkiya)* the performance of miracles, and rituals like the recalling of God *(zikr)* and mystical concerts *(sama')* provided for syncretism as well. The *shari'a*-minded polemists ridicule sufi rituals of transcendence as games and attribute the popularity of the mystical way to its entertainment value: "They attend these people's assemblies [*majlis*] because they like to listen to music and sing and play and swirl and tumble. They join this group and brag that they are the disciples of these people, and some go to these places due to the stews that they serve."[30] Qummi sees youth as being particularly attracted to the clioster *(khāniqāh)*, for they are "seduced by worldly amusements [*lahv u la'b*]—love and being in love [*'āshiqī*]."[31]

The popularization of sufism, and the attraction of some members of Safavi society to this style of being, is a price that movements must pay once they become mainstream. Similar to the punk culture of today, where the so-called punk is void of any ideology and merely maintains the appearance of one, Qummi says of assumed sufis, "[W]hen one asks them what sainthood [*vilāyat*] means, they say it means being a bachelor and homeless."[32] Some sufis seem to have donned the dervish cloak and the air of a master to earn a living. Inasmuch as sufism was in vogue, it was manipulated by many who had ulterior motives. For some it was a profession, for others a fad to follow, and for some, like Dervish Khusraw, a stage in a cyclical journey of time. Perhaps for some it was a conscious facade to veil their *ghuluww*, and for others a means of converting the populace to Shi'ism, and yet it remained a genuine quest for God.

The name of Shaykh Ali Mashadi surfaces both in the polemics against sufis and in Vali Quli Shamlu's *Stories of Monarchs (Qisas al-khāqānī)*. Two dimensions of this shaykh emerge from these representations. The rationalist discourse places him in the category of sufi "pretenders," portraying him as a popular charlatan whose sole motivation was money. Of his activities in Isfahan, the author of the *Hidāyat al-avāmm* writes:

Under the guise of a sufi, [he] would claim things, and under the pretext of having many debts, he would acquire money from people. After a while, once people realized the truth about this man, he moved to Khurasan and there he began engaging in the same business. When people started doubting him once again, he said: "All that I do has been approved by Mullah Muhammad Muhsin Kashi [Muhsin-i Fayz], and in his assemblies some of his adepts would engage in these very acts. And he did not prevent them from committing these acts; in fact, he would tell them what to do and delighted in it too."[33]

It is through a letter written by a curious denizen of Mashad addressed to the philosopher Muhsin-i Fayz that the nature of these abject acts becomes apparent. The letter reads as follows: This humble one, Muhammad Muqim Mashadi, would like to inquire about the integrity [*salāhiyat*] of Mawlana Muhammad Ali Mashadi, who having come to Mashad from Isfahan claimed in gatherings and assemblies that during the *zikr* and recitation from the Qur'an, singing love poetry and going into ecstasy [*vajd namudan*] and dancing and not eating meat and taking up the retreat [*chilah*] and other things that sufis perform as rituals of worship have been sanctioned by you. In addition, he claims that in your grand *majlis*, at times these types of rituals would take place. We ask you to verify the validity of these claims for the Shi'is of Mashad.[34]

In response to Muhammad Muqim Mashadi's query as in his *Muhakama bayn al-mutasawwifa wa ghayrihim*, Fayz speaks against the ritual recalling of God *(zikr)* that is recited loudly.[35] The *zikr*, he says, in accordance with the Qur'an, and some hadith, should be recited quietly. In addition, he highlights another "ugly" act of this group *(tāyifa)*: "[A]mong the words of unity [*tawhīd*] they include other things and change words around and include poetry in the middle of their *zikr* and clap their hands and sing and dance, and they call this worship."[36] Sadra, four decades earlier, had also condemned the practice of intertwining poetry with the *zikr*, seeing it as a main attraction of these assumed sufis' assemblies:

Poems describing the beauty of lovers, sweethearts, and the beloved, about pleasure and union and about the pains of separation [are recited]. Most of those present at these assemblies are ignorant folk who have hearts full of bodily desires and interiors that are prone toward the pursuit of pleasure. This is why poems recited in tone are aimed at letting out this hidden inner desire and sickness.[37]

It is through sufi poetry—couched in the ambiguity of metaphors and allegories—that many of the motifs of *ghuluww* preserve their vitality. They would have been evoked in the ritual remembering of God, for the rationalist authors like Qummi openly attack mystics like Rumi, Attar, Jami, and even the more "orthodox" Sana'i:

> It has been recounted that their masters, like the Mulla from Rum, and others used musical instruments in their *zikrs,* and up to this date in their cloister [*mawlavīkhānah*] in Baghdad this is being practiced. According to the religion [*mazhab*] of our Imams, these things are considered illegal [*harām*]. It is true that many Shi'is have great respect for the Mulla from Rum, despite the fact that this man was an Uzbek, and in accordance to what has been related, he was a Sunni judge. Most probably because some Shi'is have seen that he has praised Ali in his divan they have thought that he is a Shi'i and have been fooled. Many Sunnis have written books in praise of Ali; this is no reason to be considered a Shi'i. Know that this man has written things in his *masnavi* that do not mesh with Shi'ism. In addition, this lost soul [Rumi] was a disciple of Shaykh Muhyi al-din. He has composed many lines of poetry portraying his enthusiasm toward that satanic shaykh. He has said that once truth [*haqīqat*] is attained, the *shari'a* shall be void [*bātil*]. There is no doubt that this is outright blasphemy [*kufr*], for the meaning of these words is that once an individual attains the rank of truth [*haqiqat*], he no longer has any obligations and according to him the *shari'a* will expire![38] (See figure 10.)

In an attempt to define a Shi'i devotee, the pseudo-Ardabili distinguishes between love for Ali and the embracing of Shi'ism. Just as Abū Muslim was rejected as a Shi'a, here Rumi's loyalties are made plain. But the excess of Rumi according to the polemists is obvious through the verses of his poetry *(masnavi).* He was not only a monist, but he ignored divine law:

> One of the things that they (devotees of Rumi) say is that prayer, fasting, the hajj, and other precepts [*ahkām*] of the *shari'a* were set up so that one could cleanse [*tahzīb*] his behavior, given that our behavior has already been cleansed and we have already attained the gnosis [*ma'rifat*] of objects and the knowledge of God, and having attained God, we do not need to follow the precepts of the *shari'a* and nothing is incumbent upon us.[39]

That these groups refused to follow the pillars of Islam points to their anticlericalism, yet a deeper layer of *ghuluww* lies in this attitude. The early *ghulāt,* as we have seen in the first parts of this book, believed in establishing a utopia on earth: their utopia, by definition, was one in which everything was licit: there was no longer a need for the *shari'a.* Such a representation speaks of groups that did not make the observance of Muslim rituals such as prayer or fasting, a condition for inclusion in their circles. They allowed room for converts to incorporate their former beliefs and practices as new Muslims. The authors of the disputations against sufis, however, emphasize the centrality of the *shari'a* as a prerequisite for being Muslim, for the *shari'a* was a marker of core rituals and behavior without which conversion could be nebulous. The Qur'an could no longer be interpreted alongside poetic exegeses. Some sufis strove to hasten the encounter with God—an encounter that was promised by the Qur'an in the hereafter and one that poetry allowed the devotee to experience in the now. In this holy rendezvous, they too shared in the desire for immediacy. Yet unlike the *ghulāt,* they did not believe that every individual was capable of this nearness and worthy of this acquaintance. As Sadra remarked, gnostics *('ārif)* are a rare phenomenon. This mystical longing for union with God—or desire to collapse eschatology, as Roy Mottahedeh puts it—translated itself into mystical poetry and fused the metaphors of lover and beloved.[40] Despite the ambiguity of sufi poetry, some did recognize the code.

For Shaykh Ali Mashadi to have used sufi poetry during his *zikr*—a time when God was "remembered" and closeness to him attempted—may have meant that he was trying to strip all allegory and metaphor from Rumi's lines of poetry. His intent may have also been to speak in a popular language and to attract those who were accustomed to listening to and reciting poetry while they worshiped. Once again, as in the case of Hallaj, the polemics are colored by the ways in which some interpreted these lines with a *ghulāt* impulse.

Intoned evocation of God accompanied by clapping and dancing mixed with mystical poetry and epics *(qissas)* are cast as sufi innovations.[41] The two sources—mystical poetry and epics—are symbolic repositories for *ghulāt* ideas. According to Mulla Sadra, "the fake charlatans take the word *zikr* into their taverns [*kharābāt*] and they consider *zikr* to mean making all kinds of noises and utterances and telling stories [*qissas*]. And boy what kinds of stories are being concocted in this day and age by the so-called preachers [*vā'iz*] and storytellers!"[42] The pseudo-Ardabili also sees Persianate epics such as the *Shāhnāme* as a means through which Zoroastrian ideas were kept alive. He refers to these epics as fake stories of the Gabrs (Zoroastrians).[43]

Qummi sees Rumi as having espoused *ghulāt* precepts like reincarnation *(tanāsukh)*. His poetry, Qummi believes, acts as evidence for such an assumption. He cites the example of Qazizadah Lahiji, the commentator of the *Gulshan-i rāz*, who claimed that Muhammad's spirit could be reincarnated."[44] Rumi, he says, not only believed in the reincarnation of Muhammad's spirit, but according to the *Majālis al-'ushshāq*, Rumi is said to have consoled his followers by telling them not to mourn his death, for the spirit of Hallaj became manifest in Attar 150 years later.[45] Once again, Qummi is providing the opinions of those who interpreted Rumi's *Masnavi* and Mahmud Shabistari's *Gulshan-i rāz* (composed in 1317) in a spirit of *ghuluww*. The illiterate man at whom the pseudo-Ardabili was pointing a finger for having attracted a large following while commenting on the *Gulshani-i rāz* may have been interpreting Shabistari's lines in the same vein. The words uttered by the Nuqtavi disciples of Dervish Khusraw before their death are in tune with those that Rumi is said to have voiced. The Nuqtavi Mir Ahmad Kashi, himself a poet, is to have uttered, "[W]e are not afraid of dying, for once we die, we shall return shortly thereafter in a better form."[46] Although Shah Abbas I's official chronicler, Iskandar Bek Mumshi Turkman, asserts that once the Nuqtavis were massacred, the way of metempsychosis was abolished in Iran. It was through the medium of mystical poetry and epics such as the *Shāhnāme* that this ethos lived on for those who spoke the code. What distinguished the philosopher's definition of the "real" sufi from the sufiesque *ghulāt* was that the "real" sufi believed in the Muslim version of eschatology—in the idea of resurrection and the afterlife. The mystic who recognized the futility of this-worldly existence—for all that really mattered was the encounter with God in the hereafter—anticipated divine union impatiently and desired it immediately. Other mystics like the sufiesque *ghulāt*, however, held onto the idea of cyclical history and hence a different cosmology. It was not in the hereafter that such holy encounters would occur, for there was no afterlife. Everything—even the meeting with God, which in reality was an encounter with the self—occurred in this world.

Mir Lawhi enumerates Shaykh Muhammad Ali Mashadi's trespasses, writing, "[S]ome wise men who are aware of the state of that evil one [Shaykh Ali Mashadi] know that he made higher claims than God, the Prophet, and the immaculate Imams. He engaged in singing in the mosque, and some genuine believers attacked him, but none of his followers turned against him; in fact, they drew closer to him. What business do the common folk have with the teachings [*aqwāl*] of the *ulama al-dīn*?"[47] Mir Lawhi's elitism surfaces here: "Their opinions are warranted on matters concerning mules, camels, and stables"![48] Vali Quli Shamlu, however, provides us with another representation of Shaykh Ali Mashadi. This Turkmen chroniclers' perspective, of course, is one that sees the dervish cult as a legitimate path for a Muslim to tread. He is exemplary of the way some Qizilbash who converted to Islam constructed their religiosity. We know that he was at least a second-generation Muslim, for his father, Hajj Davud Quli Shamlu, is said to have died after his pilgrimage to Mecca and Medina.[49] Vali Quli Shamlu, who held the post of financial secretary *(mustawfi)* of Sistan and superintendent *(nâzir-i buyûtât)* of Zul Faqar Khan, the governor of Qandahar's workshops, speaks of a mountain in Sistan where allegedly one of the sons of Daniel was buried. It was a popular site of visitation. One day Vali Quli visits that mountain with the intention of building a water reservoir, but he could not find any building material. Subsequently, he dreams that two redhead dervishes show him a spot in the mountain where there was an abundance of material. The next day he heads there. Lo and behold, there was a quarry![50]

That Vali Quli Shamlu saw the mystic quest for God as part and parcel of a syncretic Muslim tradition is apparent from his amateur history. Although he was writing about the reign of Abbas II—who by nature or practice had an inclination toward dervishes—he wrote this history as a hobby. Perhaps due to his own proclivity, he spends many pages describing the dervish cult—more than Muhammad Tahir Vahid, the official court chronicler of Abbas II. At the end of his history Vali Quli lists the names of dervishes from Dervish Baba Kalb Ali, the nudist who lived in a cave near Kuh Giluyah, to sufi-minded alims like Shaykh Tunukabuni, *shari'a*-minded polemicists like Shaykh Ali Shahidi, and populist preachers like Shaykh Muhammd Ali Mashadi. Out of the forty-four religious men mentioned, nineteen were famous dervishes or shaykhs who had a lodge *(khâniqâh)*.[51]

It is through Vali Quli Shamlu that we learn that Shaykh Muhammad Ali Mashadi had in fact been trained in the religious sciences *('ulūm-i dīnī)* by the famous *shari'a*-minded jurisconsult *(mujtahid)* of Mashad, Mir Muhammad Zaman (d. 1631–

1632), the author of a disputation against sufis *(Sahīfat al-irshād).*[52] Shaykh Muhammad Ali is exemplary of those clerics who found the rational knowledge of God to be insufficient and sought to add the intuitive and experiential aspect to his quest.[53] Vali Quli Shamlu says that he became a disciple of Dervish Hatam, a wise mystic from Khurasan. Once this dervish died, Shaykh Muhammad Ali—whom he refers to as his "Highness" *(hazrat)*—built a cloister by his house and began guiding those "lost in the desert."[54] He is said to have attracted a large following to his lodge. "He would perform the five daily prayers along with the congregation at the Masjid-i Jami' of Imam Reza," writes Vali Quli Shamlu. "And upon the completion of the afternoon prayers, he would preach to the populace so that many of the people of aberration and ignorance would repent from their improper ways and would begin to engage in the worship of God."[55] In the year 1652, the desire to go on the hajj filled his heart. Along with a large group of pilgrims, whom he had encouraged to make the pilgrimage, he began his journey from Mashad to Mecca. He took many poor people along with him and paid their way: "This humble one has heard from a reliable source that after this peerless shaykh returned from that trip, he owed fourteen hundred tumans. In a short while, it was granted to him as a freely bestowed gift from the Central Treasury [*khazānah-i 'amirah*]."[56] In 1655, he once again led a large group of converts to Mecca and met their expenses.[57]

It is not only in the person and style of Shaykh Muhammad Ali that one sees the merging of oral and written cultures; at the court of Abbas II, this synthesis is apparent as well. When the two Ottoman dervishes—Dervish Majnun and Dervish Mustafa—visit Isfahan (1660), an assembly is held at court. According to the official court chronicler of Abbas II, Muhammad Ali Mashadi was present at that occasion along with other famous philosophers, sufis, and jurisconsults like Mulla Rajab Ali, Muhsin-i Fayz, and Hakim Muhammad Sa'id, the personal doctor of the shah.[58] This courtly assembly *(majlis)* epitomizes the synthesis in process during a period when polemics against mystics were at their peak and "exaggerating" sufis and philosphers were being lumped together[59] (see figure 11).

It is probably soon after this courtly assembly in Isfahan that Muhammad Muqim Mashadi wrote to Fayz, inquiring about the permissibility of music, poetry, and dance during the *zikr* of Shaykh Ali Mashadi—aural, sensory, and sensual performances. Such ritual forms may very well have been practiced at court. In Isfahan, too, this Shaykh, whom Vali Quli Shamlu says is known as "the preacher" *(al-muazzin)*, seems to have attracted large crowds of believers. Mir Lawhi equates Shaykh Mashadi with Majlisi, Sr., in that the masses followed both these men blindly. Although "the preacher" was a learned scholar in Isfahan, and the Isfahanis showered him with affection, he was the very man who, according to Mir Lawhi, made higher claims than God, the Prophet and the immaculate Imams as he sang poetry and epics in the mosque.[60] Here we have another category of sufis, who combined the paths of *shari'a* and *tariqa* but who took on a more populist style in their religious expression and teaching. The way in which the populace viewed these figures, attributing godlike qualities to these holy men, caused them to be accused of heresy. The multifaceted approach that they used in their commemoration of the divine allowed them to experience him viscerally. The *ghuluww* of the populace infused the religiosity of men of religion, like Majlisi Sr. and Shaykh Muhammd Ali Mashadi. The ways of the sufis touched all layers of society; such forms of public veneration and charisma were a reality that the *shari'a*-minded *ulama* had to compete with. *Ghuluww*, then, became the emblem through which they came to discredit their traditional opponents, the sufi-minded *ulama*.

As Shi'ism (Imami) was expressed with a mystical flavor, a hierarchy of religious posts were being crystallized throughout the Safavi imperium. Mulla Sadra sees the professionalization of the Imami religious establishment as widening the existing rift between the variety of religious quests. "Currently the designation 'jurist' [*faqih*]," he says, "is being used for a person who with an invalid *fatwā* and an unjust ruling seeks access to governors and sultans."[61] "In the past, the title 'jurist' was ascribed to a person based on his knowledge of the truth and the hereafter. He was considered on the basis of his heart and soul. His preoccupations were with cleansing one's behavior and transforming the bad into good, rather than with the knowledge of the rules of usury or divorce, with the dividing of inheritance and land, or with legal ruses."[62] The institutionalization of clerical posts filled by court appointees and the growing need for judges to adjudicate Shi'i law gave rise to specialized clerics who had been hastily trained in the practical religious sciences—particularly in aspects of contractual *('uqūd)* law. These half-baked jurists competed for positions against scholars who had been trained in philosophy and mysticism in addition to jurisprudence. These specialized clerics harbored a professional grudge against the more eclectic men of religion, thus providing them with an incentive to discredit sufism and philosophy. Sadra reproaches these assumed theologians "whose knowledge does not add up to more than six months of study" but who, nevertheless, have the audacity to attack "those who have spent fifty years of their life studying these subjects and have devoted their lives and energies to this pursuit and have given up grandeur and prestige."[63] These apprentice lawyers had little tolerance for mysticism or philosophy, what was left of the variety of religious orientations that had taken refuse under the umbrella of the dervish cult.

Sadra utters these words from his retreat in Kahak in 1618. Internal debates among the men of religion had only recently materialized into verbal attacks against Sadra and one anonymous tract against mystics and sufism. Both Mir-i Damad and Baha'i, the two bastions of eclecticism, were still teaching in Isfahan.[64] To study under the auspices of prominent scholars favored by the court provided a student with a better chance of advancing in the Safavi system. Traditionally, however, status among the Shi'i clerical community depended not only on the teachers with whom one studied and the scholarship one produced but also on the following one could muster. With the professionalization of religious learning, once posts needed to be

filled in haste, the importance of sound and innovative scholarship seems to have been overshadowed.[65] A scholar could gain
status simply by producing a *fatwā* that sanctioned the secular
policies of the Shah. Because this was an age when both the
court and the clergy were attempting to acquaint the masses
with the main pillars of Shi'ism, a cleric who enjoyed a popular
following would also have been a favorite candidate for patronage. One who could attract the minds and souls of believers to
his teachings would have captured the attention of the court and
enhanced his prospects of being assigned to an important religious office.

From Kahak in the 1620s, Sadra paints yet another picture,
one of popular culture colored by mystical sensibilities. This
need for immediate satisfaction—for a tangible contact with the
divine—rendered the dervish-type figure's religiosity more appealing to a wide variety of professions, from the artisan to the
cleric and bureaucrat. A mystic turned messiah like Dervish
Reza (d. 1631) would continue to attract a large following from
among the elite and the populace a decade later, threatening the
sovereignty of the Safavis. Sadra speaks as well of the way in
which associating with the dervish cult was still seen as a means
of acquiring social prestige.[66] The number of followers one attracted could determine one's rank, status, and wealth in society.
Such competition seems to have given birth to both amateur
sufis and theologians *(faqīh).*[67] The commercialization of religion and the rivalries it nurtured certainly added to existing tensions between the *shari'a*-minded, sufi-minded, and philosophically minded.[68] Tensions between the sufi lodge and the mosque
permeate the polemics of the time.[69] Key official posts such as
that of Shaykh al-Islam, or Friday prayer leader, however,
would have provided a cleric with a forum through which to
broaden and maintain a following.[70] Mir Lawhi likens the hold-
ers of these posts and the jealousy and insecurity that pervaded
them to the pigeon player who is constantly concerned that his
pigeons will fly off onto another person's roof.[71]

Some men of religion like Majlisi Sr., in an endeavor to con-

vert the masses, came to render Shi'ism (Imami) more palatable
to the common people. Majlisi Sr. attempted to join the cloister
with the mosque. Following Shaykh Baha'i's suit, in addition to
scholarship on theology and Shi'i traditions (*fiqh* and hadith), he
wrote treatises in Persian geared toward conversion. He dealt
with rituals such as prayer and the hajj—works intended to fa-
miliarize the general public with the correct way of worship according to the Imamis.[72] Here aspects of vernacular culture
trickled into the written culture of the learned *ulama*. Just as
Shaykh Ali Mashadi had adopted from the dervish cult the practice of utilizing poems and songs in his sermons, so Majlisi Sr.
wrote treatises in which the spiritual converged with the rational
culture of Imami legal discourse. Not only were these treatises
written in the vernacular, but their language was simplified to
attract a broader audience. Moreover, Majlisi Sr. popularized
specific prayers and rituals of pilgrimage and came to legitimize
them through mystical mechanisms, such as revelatory dreams
and divine inspirations.[73]

The French missionary Raphael du Mans situates Majlisi Sr.
in the competition underway over the post of the Friday prayer
leader at the old mosque in Isfahan, Jami'-yi Atiq. According to
du Mans, Majlisi Sr. claimed that the Mahdi appeared to him in
the course of a dream and presented him with a prayer *(al-
Sahifat al-sajjadiyah)* inscribed on a tablet in Kufic script.[74] In
the famous Shi'i encyclopedia of traditions *(Bihar al-anwar)*, his
son, Majlisi Jr., devotes a section to the utility of the report regarding the *al-Sahifat al-sajjadiyah*, attributed to the fourth
Imam, Zayn al-Abidin.[75] Here he includes facsimiles of this
prayerbook's chain of transmission reported by his father,
Majlisi Sr., who solidifies the technically weak ascription
through the means of a revelatory dream:

> In the spring of my youth or perhaps a short while before that, I
> was in search of closeness with God. Then in the world of dreams
> I was blessed with the holy presence of the *sāhib-i zamān*, who ap-
> peared to me in the old mosque [*Jami'-yi 'Atīq*] in Isfahan. I asked

him about some problems I had recently encountered. Then I said, O son of the prophet of Allah, given that I am unable to serve you forever in your presence, hand me down a book that I may obey. That holy one granted me an old *Sahifat*. When I awoke, I found that *Sahifat* among the endowed books of Aqa Qadir. I took it and studied it with Shaykh-i Baha'i, and I copied my *Sahifat* from it and checked it several times with the copy that Shaykh 'Abd al-Samad, the grandfather of Shaykh-i Baha'i had copied, and that copy had been taken from a manuscript penned by the hand of Shahid II. And due to the blessing of the Mahdi [*sāhib-i zamān*] copies of the *Sahifat al-sajjadiyah* are widespread and can be found in every Muslim town, especially in Isfahan. It is rare to find a house in that city that does not contain a copy or several copies of the *Sahifat*. And its popularity is proof of the validity of my dream.[76]

Majlisi Sr. awards a high status to this prayerbook, referring to it as the psalms of the family of Muhammad and the bible *(injīl)* of the Shi'is *(ahl al-bayt)*.[77] A number of religious men have since supplemented this collection with additional prayers from the fourth Imam, Zayn al-Abidin, and the *al-Sahifat* is indeed in use today.[78] Majlisi Sr. was engaging in the canonization of Zayn al-Abidin as the successor or Husayn, rather than Muhammad b. Hanifiyya, who has successfully been erased from Shi'i history. Specific prayers to be recited on particular occasions can be found in this prayerbook—in times of sickness, to resist the evil of the devil, to request rain, while in search of a good augury, during the 'Id-i Fitr (Feast of Ramazan), and on Fridays.[79] These prayers were meant to circumvent the need to consult with a dervish during times of crisis or daily tribulations. Once again, the nature of these prayers reflect Majlisi Sr.'s attempt to integrate popular concerns into mainstream Shi'ism (Imami)—questions, say, that a farmer would have about his crops or a mother would have about a sick child. These were the types of questions previously addressed to dervishes. Now, however, instead of consulting with a dervish about the auspiciousness of a daughter's wedding, the circumcision of a son, or a commercial trans-

action, the believer had the option of reciting a prayer from the
fourth Imam.

Qummi refers to Majlisi Sr.'s pretensions, omitting the use of
his name, for to insult one's teacher while he was still alive
would be ill conceived. He speaks of a certain falconer *(qūshchī)*
from Qum, Jamshid Bek, who was barely literate. Jamshid Bek
goes to Isfahan, and on his return he claims, "When in Isfahan I
was praying behind the prayer-leader [*pishnamāz*]. During the
recitation of the prayer he showed me the preserved tablet
[*lawh-i mahfūz*]."[80] This Qummi ascribes to a vision induced by
the hashish the falconer must have ingested prior to prayer.[81]

Meanwhile, the court too emphasized that the *ulama* should
desist from writing complicated and flowery prose—a tendency
that discouraged the populace from seeking their advice.[82]
Chardin speaks of a mullah who received two hundred thrashes
and was chastised by the grand vizier for having written in a
convoluted and compliment-ridden language. The grand vizier
reproaches him, saying:

> I have other things to do than to read your nasty compliments and
> to sort out the chaos of the requests you write. Use a clearer and
> simpler style, or do not write for the public; otherwise I shall have
> your hands cut off.[83]

For a public accustomed to the earthy language and fantastic
aura of a dervish, the transition to the scholarly and rational discourse of the *ulama* was not easy. Some clerics realized the need
to broaden their audience to encompass the seminary student,
the court official, the soldier, the baker, and the farmer. Religious men like Majlisi Sr. and Shaykh Ali Mashadi styled their
teachings in the vernacular of the common believer. In addition
to simplifying the language of liturgy and ritual, Majlisi Sr. began to take on functions of the spiritual master—roles that had
endowed these holy men with a luminous radiance. The power
of divination *(kashf)*, of being so in tune with God and his will
as to be able to read into man's destiny, was enjoyed by mystics

and saints *(awliyā')*. Majlisi Sr. embodied this spirit, which Shah Tahmasb a century earlier attempted to represent in his autobiography.[84] Both monarch and mystic used the icon of Ali and the communicative channel of dreams to draw a saintly image of themselves. Majlisi Sr. writes of one such encounter with Ali:

One year I was able to visit the holy shrines, and when I entered Najaf, the hot season had begun and I decided to stay there all summer and for that reason I returned the horse I had rented to his owner. That night I dreamt of Ali, who showered me with kindness. He said: do not stay in Najaf beyond this date. I asked him to allow me to remain in his presence for a while longer. But he did not pay heed to my request and instead said: Shah Abbas I will die this year and Shah Safi will replace him. It would not surprise me if there were much upheaval in your cities. God wills it that during such times you be in Isfahan and that people be protected by your guidance. So I returned to my country [*mamlikat*]. Once in Isfahan, I recounted my dream to someone who told it to Shah Safi when he paid a visit to the seminary *(madrasah-yi safaviyya)*. Shah Abbas I was in Mazandaran then. Shortly afterward, he died.[85]

These are the words of a man who had a sense of a religious mission. Ali commands him to guide the Isfahani community and to counsel the Safavi monarch as well. Like Shah Tahmasb (d. 1576) and his ancestor Shaykh Safi al-din (d. 1334), Majlisi Sr. seems to have become aware of his calling at a young age. He is to have seen the Mahdi in his dreams during his youth. At age four, he is said to have encountered God, heaven, and hell. Even at that early age, he reportedly guided children, giving them advice in accordance to hadith he had learned from his father, a poet.[86] Moreover, in the seventeenth century, it was a Shi'i scholar like Majlisi Sr. who expressed his piety in terms of mystical visions.

Shah Safi, however, did not seek Majlisi Sr.'s guidance, for he did not shower this holy man with favors, yet another indication of the religious policy of Safi's court. Majlisi Sr.'s relationship with Rustam Bek, the slave architect of the reigning court faction, seems, in fact, to have been laden with competition. A later source relates a conversation that took place between the slave general and the mystic.[87] Majlisi Sr. is said to have asked Rustam Khan during an assembly, "While you are busy establishing order amid the troops, or when the trumpet and drums are sounded announcing the launching of the battle, do you feel grandeur and authority to such an extent that you may exit from obedience to God?" Rustam Khan is said to have replied cunningly, "It is strange for you to think that these types of grand illusions overcome one at such times and not while one is praying or reciting the call to prayer!!"[88]

During the reign of Abbas II, Majlisi Sr.'s aspirations blossomed. The dervish-loving Shah Abbas II commissioned him to translate into Persian his commentary on a classic Shi'i canonical work in Arabic—al-Saduq's *Man la yahduruhu al-faqīh*. To his post as seminary teacher *(mudarris)* was added that of Friday prayer leader (Imam Jum'a) of the Old Mosque in Isfahan *(masjid-i jāmi'-yi 'atīq)*.[89] He continued to be vocal in his defense of mystics, for he responded to the tract Qummi, his student, Shaykh al-Islam of Qum, wrote against them and spoke from the pulpit in defense of controversial figures such as Abū Muslim and Hallaj.[90] Majlisi Sr. also wrote a treatise in defense of Rumi, who, as we have seen, was not spared accusations of heresy by Qummi.[91] His popularity continued to flourish. Some of his followers endowed him with divine qualities. Mir Lawhi once again provides us with a perhaps exaggerated picture: "A man by the name of Ali Reza Ardastani, because of his fanaticism and ignorance, would say that when Majlisi Sr. returned from his pilgrimage to Mecca, two people were in his service. They refused to part his company. Once Majlisi Sr. realized that they would not leave, he asked them who they were. One said, 'I am Husayn b. 'Ali b. Abi Talib,' and the other said, 'I am the Lord of the Age.'"[92] Here, some so-called fanatics were ascribing the role of Ali or perhaps that of the Prophet to Majlisi Sr., for in some Shi'i (Imami) traditions on eschatology, the advent of the Mahdi was to be accompanied by the appearance of figures such as Muhammad, Ali, and the Imams.

Indeed, the popularization of Majlisi Sr.'s preaching went beyond the production of popular religious manuals in Persian, for he actively engaged in the mystical quest. Mir Lawhi claims that Majlisi Sr. was a disciple of a certain Mir Qasim and that it was in his circle that the love of singing filled Majlisi Sr.'s heart.[93] Although his son, Majlisi Jr.—the *shari'a*-minded Shaykh al-Islam of Shah Sulayman (1666–1694)—attempted to dispel the sufi proclivities of his father, evidence indicates that this denial was prompted by the political and religious vicissitudes of his age. Within a generation, centrifugal impulses had so altered heteroglossia that now Majlisi Jr. was embarrassed by his father's eclecticism. The way in which Majlisi Jr. voices his defense of his father is very telling, however. He claims that his father frequented the sufis to infiltrate their ranks, become familiar with their doctrines, and subsequently convert them from within.[94] That it was necessary for a jurist to destroy the sufis by infiltrating their ranks points to their prominence and to the nature of the competition between mystics and theologians. Without their silencing, the rationalization of religion could not attain dominance. Mir Lawhi, two years after Majlisi Sr.'s death (d. 1660), states that the sufis of Isfahan (Hallajis) believed that Majlisi Sr. associated himself with them, praised Hallaj and Bayazid Bistami daily from the pulpit, and talked about their miracles and inspirations to claim that he himself performed miracles.[95] These devotees of Hallaj, according to Mir Lawhi, believed that Majlisi Sr. was able to lure the general public into following him because of his membership in their brotherhood.[96] Mir Lawhi was certainly jealous of Majlisi Sr.'s popularity, but he was also reacting against Majlisi Sr.'s attempts to legitimize heteroglossia.

That the issue of performing miracles is such a central point of contention in these polemics and a criticism that the *shari'a*-

minded address to the sufi-minded sheds light on the essence of these debates. The rationalists saw the performance of miracles as a function reserved to the prophet Muhammad, Imams like Ali, and the awaited Mahdi—those who had been imbued with divinity. Some sufis, however, ascribed such functions to their masters, whom they also imagined as possessing a divine spark. The sufiesque *ghulāt* extended this function to dervishes and, more generally, to charismatic figures who were particularly perceptive and in tune with the cosmos. Messianic figures like Dervish Reza (d. 1631), for instance, were expected to perform miracles such as raising the Mar'ashi *sayyid* (Mir Faghfur) from the dead. Sufi-minded scholars like Majlisi Sr. also adopted this function, yet the types of miracles he seemed to perform occurred through the medium of inspirational dreams, dreams in which Ali or one of the Imams revealed a truth or foretold an event. *Shari'a*-minded jurists like Mir Lawhi perhaps to stem competition from charismatic mystics, attempted to reserve this divine authority for the "friends of God"—the Imams and the awaited Mahdi.

Whatever Majlisi Sr.'s motivations, he spoke in a language that had wide appeal, engaged in the rituals of the sufi lodge, and did not condemn popular activities such as singing or the recitation of Rumi's poetry, which would have certainly alienated sufis.[97] Mir Lawhi claims that Majlisi Sr. had a regular minstrel *(mutrib)* and a singer in his service. In addition to these, says Mir Lawhi, there were a number of minstrels and singers who were commissioned by Majlisi Sr. to perform at weddings and banquets.[98] Singing, dancing, and clapping were key activities of mystical ritual worship. Refraining from issuing a *fatwā* in condemnation of these rituals signaled one's support for popular sufism. By 1650, we know of six prominent clerics, not all of whom were *shari'a*-minded, who condemned these three activities and branded them illicit *(harām)* and immoral *(fasq)*.[99]

However much Majlisi Jr. would have denied such portrayals of his father, some did venerate Majlisi Sr. as a saint. Chardin uses the words "saint" and "prophet" when observing the way in which visitors paid homage to Majlisi Sr.'s tomb in Isfahan. According to Chardin:

> [U]nder the dome bearing the name of the dervish's shrine [lies] the grave of a certain Mohammad Taqi, who was the priest of this mosque or Pich Namaz, during Abbas II. He was recognized as a saint during his life, which he led in extreme detachment from the world; the populace venerated him as a prophet. He predicted his death, they say, three months before it occurred, while being in perfect health.[100]

Mir Lawhi says that the masses prostrate themselves in front of Majlisi Sr.'s tomb and circumambulate it. He complains that "most of the famous scholars of Isfahan were the teachers of Majlisi Sr.; why did they not build them a tomb and a dome and a mausoleum and make their burial grounds similar to shrines of the Imams?"[101] The popular sensibilities of believers led them to venerate Majlisi Sr. as a godlike figure—just as Hallaj was viewed by some of his followers. Quoting from one of his own works, *I'lam al-muhibbin*, Mir Lawhi says, "[T]his *ghuluww* of the masses in regard to crazy ones is not reserved to them, but superstition and *ghuluww* penetrates all aspects of life, even when it comes to men of religion or pretenders who consider the uneducated sufi or the evil beliefs of the philosophers as mighty.[102] And yet Abbas II built Majlisi Sr. a sumptuous tomb out of respect and veneration.

What worried jurists like Mir Lawhi and Qummi was that the common people were getting carried away in their devotion to these religious men, whether theologians, masters, or dervishes. Such sentiments were further aggravated, given that the dervish-loving Shah Abbas II was encouraging these orientations and styles of thought. The majority of the polemics against sufis were written during the reign of Abbas II. Mir Lawhi, using the pseudonym "Muhttahar b. Muhammad al-Miqdadi," voices concern in his *Salvat al-shi'a:* "Although they [sufi] have been condemned and have been punished by the minister of religion, justice, and education [Mirza Habibullah Sadr], they have not stopped their activities."[103] The date cited by Mir Lawhi after which sufis ignored the injunctions of the rationalist *ulama* coincides with the accession of Abbas II—16 May 1642. "From the end of the year 1642 up until today, that is, the middle of the year 1650," says Mir Lawhi, "these cursed ones do not stop their nonsense and idle talk."[104]

This is why Muhammad Tahir Qummi, the rebellious student of Majlisi Sr., makes a point of defining who saints are according to Shi'i (Imami) legal scholars. Qummi sees Safavi denizens as afflicted with an illness brought on by an epidemic of sufism. In this age of rampant disease, the Mahdi plays the role of doctor. In the introduction to one of his treatises against sufis, *Tuhfat al-akhyār*, written during the last year of Abbas II's reign, he speaks of the Mahdi as the "doctor of the sick of this age. Although he may be absent and hidden and is unable to touch the hands of the patients, the benefits of his existence are many, and the religion of Islam is standing firm due to it."[105] Qummi refers to the *ulama* as the students of the Imams who have taken on the role of doctors and healers, for they are the ones who possess knowledge of the Imam's utterances and deeds and who have recorded them in books:[106]

And know that the children of this age, because they did not know themselves nor their duties, engaged in this-worldly pleasures and forgot about trying to remedy their illness and contracted many other sicknesses that deprived them of closeness with God. Many of those who have become famous have become so due to the fact that they have drunk wine with the ignorant and have contracted their disease. One cannot be cured reading books by Socrates, Galen, and Plato or books written by the followers of Hallaj and Bayazid. . . . The followers of Hallaj and Bayazid have dissuaded their disciples from seeking knowledge and associating with the *ulama*, for they consider knowledge ['*ilm*] and reason ['*aql*] as preventing the believers from attaining God. . . . Above all, they claim that through spiritual exercises [*riyāzat*] one can become an Imam and a caliph.[107]

Know that the term saint [*awliyā'*] generally has two meanings. At times one says the Friends of God [*awliyā'-yi allah*], meaning those who by God's command are caliphs, Imams, amirs, and in authority over the community [*umma*], and are learned in all the pillars [*ahkām*] of the Shari'a and there is no doubt that authority [*vilāyat*] in this particular context means the *amīr al-muminīn* Ali and his eleven illustrious descendents . . . and there are many proofs for the caliphate and imamate of the Twelve Imams in the Books of Forty Traditions [*arba'īn*]. . . . Know that the rank of love [*muhabbat*] and authority [*vilāyat*] is also reserved for the wise, the *ulama* and their followers, and not for the ignorant and crazy who revere ignorant ones and ascribe the rank of master [*qutb*] and saint [*valī*] to them.[108]

Qummi reserves the title of saint *(valī)* for Ali and the eleven Imams, as well as for the learned *ulama* who guide the community during the occultation of the Mahdi. In another of his polemics against sufis, *Radd bar Sufiyān*, Qummi argues that "although the Mahdi is hidden from our sight, and we cannot see the other Imams, their sayings have been preserved: the religious and legal scholars [*ulama al-dīn*] have compiled their sayings [hadith]."[109] Sufi masters like Nurbakhsh and philosophers like Ibn-i 'Arabi cannot be messiahs *(mahdi)*, Imams, or caliphs, according to Qummi. Like Majlisi Sr., Qummi was addressing the need to see the divine or be touched by his healing hand. Qummi is less flexible in accommodating this popular need, however. In his view, the populace will have to make do with the fact that the Mahdi cannot perform a physical examination. The need for visceral contact will be met by the *ulama*, who instead of miracles or revelatory dreams consult books on theology and law—books written by religious scholars on the Imams—to find remedies for believers. Addressing the popular messianic expectation, Qummi says, "God willing, the reign of Shah Abbas II will be linked to the rule of the Lord of the Age."[110]

But the populace continued to crave close contact with the divine. They longed for an intimate relationship with the holy—a relationship as tangible as the ones they experienced among themselves. The idea of a distant and invisible God was too abstract, for understanding God through his words recorded in texts was not quite the same as seeing, hearing, or feeling him. The idea of the awaited Mahdi in Imami Shi'ism provided hope of a future tactile relationship with the divine. And believers had expectations of miracles from the holy. Sufi masters, dervishes, and the *ulama,* each in their own fashion, took on the function of performing miracles. The mystical cleric performed auguries with the Qur'an or experienced communicative dreams with the Imams and the Prophet. The sufiesque *ghālī,* in contrast, performed miracles that impinged on the essence of monotheism, crafting the arts, and hence was labeled a magician. Qummi blames the dervish cult for nurturing this religious style that raised the devotee's expectations, a style that he believes devalues the miracles performed by the Prophet and the Imams and undermines the role of the *ulama* as well.[111]

Some *shari'a*-minded *ulama* like Majlisi Jr. catered to the messianic craving of Safavi denizens. Here Majlisi Sr.'s endeavors served as a model for his son. Majlisi Jr. certainly played on his father's popularity, allowing him to inherit a following.[112] Although he repudiates his father's saintly aura and the sufi culture that had endowed him with divine charisma, Majlisi Jr. maintains some of the popular functions that his father had introduced into mainstream Shi'ism. Two monographs on the occultation and return of the Mahdi reflect Majlisi Sr.'s sanctioning of his father's attempts to render Imami Shi'ism congruent with popular beliefs. Just as Majlisi Sr. would come to canonize the function of divination in Imamism with his revival of the genre of *Ikhtiyārāt al-ayyām,* so did he forecast the date on which the messianic expectation would materialize.[113] According to the numerological *abjad* system of interpretations of the Qur'an, he predicted that the Mahdi would appear in sixty-five years (1730–1731).[114] A generation earlier, bibliomancy had been exercised by mystics like his father Majlisi Sr.[115] Now, his *shari'a*-minded son was enshrining this synthesis in written word. Mir Lawhi finds this appalling.

"Due to the vicissitudes of the age," writes Mir Lawhi, "the act of knowing your Imam-i Zaman was postponed to this time. Some Shi'is, both elite and popular [*khāss u 'āmm*], asked questions about the occultation and return of the Mahdi, and Majlisi Jr. began to talk about this and wrote a book on the subject of his return [*raj'a*]. People debates this issue, and some believers came to me, so I wrote this piece."[116] Mir Lawhi criticizes Majlisi Jr.'s attempt to please the Safavi household by using weak and contradictory tradition, portraying its rule as one of the signs leading to the advent of the Mahdi. In addition, Mir Lawhi sees this as a gimmick to attract the attention of the masses.

In the fifteenth century, a new interest in the Mahdi had given birth to a series of monographs on the subject.[117] Four centuries had gone by since the first wave of extant works on the occultation and advent of the messiah—a wave that had tried to provide an eschatological framework for the disappearance of the twelfth Imam.[118] Once the power of the Saljuks and Mongols had waned and aspirations of regional rulers, some of whom were Shi'is, began to materialize, a series of books on the occultation were penned.[119] These works coincided as well with a wave of messianic revolts. Mystical figures like Nurbakhsh and Ibn-i Falah had pretenses of being Mahdis and proclaimed the advent of his rule.[120] Sayyid Muhammad Ibn-i Falah, the foster son of Ibn-i Fahd, did indeed establish his rule (Musha'sha') in Khuzistan, only to be toppled by Shah Isma'il Safavi, a new claimant to mahdihood. A century later, Majlisi Jr. wrote the next two works on the advent *(zuhūr)* and return *(raj'a)* of the Mahdi.[121]

A study of works on the Mahdi's occultation remains to be conducted before we can determine the degree to which they attempt to legitimize their patron's claims. There is no doubt, however, that these works were addressing the popular messianic expectation that played an important role in the realm of political theology. Imami scholars during the reigns of Tahmasb (r. 1524–1576) and Muhammd Khudabandah (r. 1577–1587) used traditions on the Mahdi's emergence *(khurûj)* recorded in Numani and Tusi's *Kitâb al-ghayba* to draw connections between the rise of Shah Isma'il and the advent of the Mahdi: they represented Safavi rule *(dawlat)* as the just rule that was to be established at the end of time.[122] Shaykh Baha'i, his father Shaykh Husayn b. Abd al-Samad, and Hasan b. Sayyid Ja'far al-Karaki are also said to have related a tradition ascribed to Ali in which they associate a messianic scenario with the rise of Isma'il.[123] A century later, Majlisi Jr. comes to view Ismai'l's revolution as one of the many successive signs of the advent of the lord of the age. Moreover, he predicts that the Mahdi will make his appearance in sixty-five years (1730).[124] Here Majlisi Jr. was accommodating the popular messianic expectation promising the denizens of Safavi Iran a utopia in the near future. He was also responding to those "heretics," such as Dervish Reza's followers, who saw their masters as Imams and Mahdis, for by linking Safavi rule to the just rule of the Mahdi, he was reserving the role of messiah for the Safavi house. This was the reigning Safavi political theology during the last two decades of the seventeenth century.

Some *shari'a*-minded like Mir Lawhi, however, contested Majlisi Jr.'s accommodating views on the Mahdi. Mir Lawhi makes no such concessions and criticizes Majlisi Jr.'s pretensions:

Why did the honorable preacher [the Akhund—Majlisi Jr.] not restrain himself or refrain from designating a time for the emergence [*khurûj*] of the Lord of the Age [*sâhib-i zamân*]. If the preacher considers himself to be partners with God in the knowledge of the imperceptible [*'ilm-i ghayba*] and if he claims that he is aware of divine secrets, he should not determine the time and should not exceed that limit. There exists many things that may enter one's mind that are mere murmurs of the devil. Many hadith point to the fact that only God can determine the time of the Manifestation [*zuhūr*] of the Mahdi.[125]

Mir Lawhi does offer some solace to the Shi'i. He states that the messiah will soon emerge but that until such a time, no one can ascribe that role to a particular figure, nor can one determine the time of his advent. He urges the Shi'i community to be patient and have faith in his coming:

> It should not remain a secret from the Shi'is that the Sunnis believe the Mahdi is a descendant of Imam Husayn and that he shall make his appearance at the end of time, filling this world with justice as it was formerly filled with injustice. O dear one, know that although many do not believe in his existence in this and every age and although the heretics [*malāhidah*] do not believe in the existence of God [*hazrat-i haqq*], this does not affect our religion [*dīn*]. Their lack of belief does not weaken our religion [*mazhab*].[126]

Tensions between vernacular and written cultures of Shi'ism (Imami) would remain kindled among the diversity of believers. Once Shah Sulayman appointed Majlisi Jr. as chief religious dignitary of Isfahan Shaykh al-Islam in 1689, however, this dynamic interplay was temporarily suspended. With the banning of sufi lodges, Greek philosophy, wine, sodomy, singing, dancing, and clapping, the jurists secured their position among the ranks of the men of religion. The legitimate map of Imami Shi'ism was redrawn, pushing *ghuluww* outside the boundaries of the mainstream. In the process, Shi'ism, however, which had from its very inception fused different cultural systems, came to (re)invigorate its gnostic and cyclical framework. In this (re)mapping of the quest for God, the one who trod only the path of the *shari'a* was recognized. Now that spiritual masters and dervishes were stripped of their institutions and rituals and philosophers of their privileged knowledge of God, the function of saint *(vali)* was reserved for a descendant of Muhammad—

perhaps a future Safavi monarch—and the scholars of religion and law. Let me end by going back to the *Memoir* of Shah Tahmasb (written in 1562), expounding on the life of this text and the living image of Tahmasb. In writing a personal narrative, the end of the story of one's life remains to be told by those who survive. It is the future that acts as the mirror that reflects the past. And so in the path of historical memory, Shah Tahmasb's godly father, Isma'il, overshadowed Tahmasb. And his absolutist grandson, Abbas I (r. 1587–1629), captured the limelight in the seventeenth century. Within the century-long process of the consolidation of Safavi rule—Tahmasb's reign spanned half of it—the directions Tahmasb took to centralize his dominion would be followed and thoroughly institutionalized by his grandson. Tahmasb had begun to break with the messianic tendencies of his father and incorporate the Shi'i clergy *(ulama)* and household slaves *(ghulām)* to tame the religious temperament and political independence of the Qizilbash. These were key reforms that his grandson would enforce by the end of the civil war (1576–1590) that followed Tahmasb's death, finally securing Safavi dominion for another century. Abbas I reiterated the master-disciple discourse of dominance, but this time it was shorn of its spiritual content. Safavi sainthood was reserved for their dead ancestor Safi, around whom the brotherhood had originally taken shape. His shrine was patronized as a site of pilgrimage and veneration. But it is the shrine of the eighth Imam in Mashad, Imam Reza, that would become the center of Shi'i piety, an icon of Safavi imperial sovereignty. Isma'il's rise to power was interpreted as a symbol signaling the imminent emergence of the eschatological messiah. And the Safavi monarchs had taken on the role of the shadow of God on earth. This title rooted in pre-Islamic Iranian (Sasani) notions of sacral kingship, and with the Safavis it was voiced with a Muslim vocabulary. It epitomized the essence of kingly patrimonialism, which reserved the political ethos of divine kingship for the monarch, whose role as God's representative on earth entailed the promulgation of the sacred law. In so doing, a body of religious scholars became privy due to their knowledge of how to mediate between God and the world. These men of religion claimed sole access to God through his words. Dreams were the most immediate way in which they could transcend. The domains of religion and politics were severed into two distinct sites of authority. Tahmasb's image as saint could not survive in such a context. The manuscript tradition attests to the fact that as Abbas I enforced his centralizing reforms, the *Memoir* fell into oblivion.[127] It would not be copied for another century, when the Qajar dynasty (1785–1925) would revive it as a memorial to Safavi kingship.[128]

NOTES

1. Muhammad Tāhir Nasrābādī began to write *Tazkirah-yi Nasrābādī*, ed. by V. Dastgirdī (Tehran: Armaghān, 1973), in 1083/1673–1674. Chardin traveled in Iran in 1667 to 1669 and in 1673 to 1676. Valī Qulī Shāmlū began to write his *Qisas al-khāqānī*, Bibliothèque Nationale, MS Suppl. Pers. 227, in 1073/1662–1663. Both the dates 1076/1665–1666 and 1085/1674–1675, however, occur in the text.

2. Valī Qulī Shāmlū, *Qisas al-khāqānī*, ff 282b–288a. Nineteen dervishes are enumerated under the rubric of the *ulama*.

3. Sadr al-Dīn Muhammdad Shīrāzī (Mulla Sadra), *Kasr Asnām al-jāhiliyya*, ed. M. T. Dānishpazhūh (Tehran: Matba'at Jāmi'at, 1962), 142.

4. To gain a sense of the variety of people who frequented the coffeehouses, see Nasrābādī's *Tazkirah*, as well as Jean-Baptiste Tavernier's *Les Six Voyages du Jean Baptiste Tavernier*, 2 vols. (Amsterdam: Chez Johannes van Someren, 1678), vol. 2, 132. Tavernier says that "even those Persians of moderate means do not hesitate to frequent the *qahvahkhānah* daily."

5. For the dates of Chardin's travels, see John Emerson's article on Chardin in the *Encyclopedia Iranica*. Chardin's journey to Iran took place on Zul Hijja 1078/April 1667–January 1668. In 1080/1669, he stayed in Isfahan for six months. His second journey

found him in Isfahan for two and a half years (9 Rabī' al-Awwal 1084–1087/24 June 1673–1676).

6. Jean Chardin, *Les Voyages du Chevalier Chardin en Perse*, ed. L. Langlès, 10 vols. (Paris: Le Normant, 1811), vol. 4, 68: "[T]he government did not care what the world would say."

7. Ibid., 68–69.

8. Tavernier, *Les Six Voyages du Jean Baptise Tavernier*, vol. 2, 132.

9. See Robert McChesney, "The Four Sources on Shah Abbas's Building of Isfahan," *Muquarnas 5* (1988): 109, for Abbās I's inclusion of coffeehouses in his plan of Isfahan [Jalāl al-Dīn Munajjim Yazdī, *Tārīkh-i 'Abbāsī* (1005/1596) (Tehran: Intishārāt-i Vahīd, 1987): 112, for the actual mention of coffeehouses in a *farmān* dated 1012/1603–1604 in which the shah delineates the design of the Naqsh-i Jahān.

10. See Paul Losensky's discussion of this phenomenon in his *Welcoming Fighani: Imitation and Poetic Individuality in the Safavid-Mughal Ghazal* (Costa Mesa: Mazda, 1998), 137–145.

11. Nasrābādī, *Tazkirah-yi Nasrābādī, 239*

12. Tavernier, *Les Six Voyages du Jean Baptise Tavernier*, vol. 2, 132.

13. Those *qahvahkhānah* owners enumerated by Nasrābādī were participants in the dervish cult. For a sampling, see Nasrābādī, *Tazkirah-yi Nasrābādī*, 109, 112, 136.

14. Tavernier calls these people dervishes. He describes that they wore skins of lamb and were half-naked; they may have been Qalandars. Raphael du Mans, who provides a detailed classification of the different ascetics, sees the Qalandars' clothes as one distinction between them and dervishes. Tavernier, *Les Six Voyages du Jean Baptise Tavernier*, vol. 2, 117; Raphaël du Mans, *Estat de la Perse en 1660*, ed. Charles Henri Auguste Schefer (Paris: Leronx, 1890), 216: "Their garments are the most grotesque that they could imagine so as to attract bystanders; they are covered with sheepskin and are half-naked."

15. Tavernier says that they taught them about law—but it is highly unlikely that it was about the *shari'a*.

16. Tavernier, *Les Six Voyages du Jean Baptise Tavernier*, vol. 2, 137.

17. On the drug culture, see Chardin, *Les Voyages du Chevalier Chardin en Perse*, vol. 4, 78; du Mans, *Estat de la Perse en 1660*, 140.

18. Chardin, *Les Voyages du Chevalier Chardin en Perse*, vol. 6, 78.

19. Ibid., vol. 7, 450–451. See Lutfullāh Hunarfar's *Ganjīnah-i Āsār-i Tārīkh-i Isfāhān* (Isfahan: Kitābfurushi-yi Saqāfī, 1965), 360–369, for more on this shrine. According to Hunarfar, the Hārūn-i Vilāyat was built by Shah Ismā'īl in 918/1512.

20. Aqā Jamāl Khwānsarī, *'Aqā'īd al-nisā*, ed. Mahmud Katīrā'ī (Tehran: Tāhirī Press, 1970), 1. This essay provides a colorful view of the female sex through five token Isfahani women: Kulthūm Nanih, Bibi Shah Zaynab, Khālah Jan Aqa, Baji Yasaman, and Dede Bazmārā. In his preface *(dībāchah)*, Aqa Jamal delineates his audience as "any women who is of age *(keh sinī dāshtah bāshad)* and who is inclined to superstition *(khurāfāt)*." What the author meant by "superstition" can be read as vernacular traditions practiced by Isfahani women in the seventeenth century. The *Beliefs of Women* is written in a genre *(risālah)* that religious scholars *(mujtahid)*, emulated by seminary students *(tālib)* as well as the community of believers, used to clarify practice for those who questioned how the *shari'a* affected daily life. This point is made by the editor, Mahmud Katira'i, ibid., 7–8. See my chapter on this satire, "The *'Aqā'īd al-nisā*: A Glimpse at Safavi Women in Local Isfahani Culture," in Gavin Hambly, ed., *Women in the Medieval Islamic World* (London: St. Martin's Press, 1998).

21. Ibid., 7.

22. Chardin, *Les Voyages du Chevalier Chardin en Perse*, vol. 7, 446. I have not been able to locate this minaret in Hunarfar's *Ganjīnah-i Āsār-i Tārīkh-i Isfāhān*. It must have survived into modern times, for the editor of the *'Aqā'īd al- nisā* quotes from Sādiq-i Hidāyat's *Nayrangistān*, where he refers to the minaret of *Sar Birinjī* in Isfahan and the survival of this practice, as well as the recitation of the same verse preserved in the *'Aqā'īd al-nisā* by Isfahani girls who visit this shrine (51–52).

23. du Mans, *Estat de la Perse en 1660*, 140.

24. Muhammad Tāhir b. Muhammad Husayn Qummī, *Tuhfat al-akhyār* (Qum: Intishārāt-i Nūr, 1973), 62.

25. Ibid., 62. Although cannabis and opium are not technically hallucinogens like lysergic acid diethylamide (LSD) and mushrooms, they could be processed so that their ingestion either as an infusion or in solid form would induce hallucinations. See "Opioid Analgesics and Antagonists," in Louis Sanford Goodman and Al-

fred Gilman, *The Pharmacological Basis of Therapeutics: A Textbook of Pharmacology, Toxicology and Therapeutics for Physicians and Medical Students* (New York: Macmillan, 1985).

26. Mulla Sadrā, *Kasr asnām al-jāhiliyya*, 25.

27. Ahmad b. Muhammad Pseudo-Ardabīlī, *Hadīqat al-shī'a* (Tehran: n.p., 1964, 597.

28. Nasrābādī, for example, mentions a perfumist *(attar)*, Ustad Ali Qulī Māhīr, who was in search of a master (141); a bookbinder turned painter, 'Arif-i Kirmānī, who went into retreat (382); a calligrapher, Sāyirā, who also retreated to a *takkiya* (51).

29. Although the name of one merchant *(tājir)* from Tabriz, Hajji Isma'īl Khan, appears as a sufi (31), most merchants appear as endowers and disciples of sufis. To cite an example, Hajj Safi Qulī Bek, a seller of pearls *(murvārīd)*, built a cloister *(takkiya)* for Dervish Muhammd Sali in Isfahan (44).

30. Pseudo-Ardabīlī, *Hadīqat al-shī'a*, 596.

31. Qummī, *Tuhfat al-akhyār*, 49.

32. Muhammad Tāhir b. Muhammad Husaym *Risālah-yi Radd bar Sufiyān*, Mar'ashī Library, MS 4014, f 86b.

33. As quoted in Rasūl Ja'fariān, "Rūyārūyi-yi Faqīhān va Sūfiyān dar 'Asr-i Safaviyyah," *Kayhān-i Andīshah* 33 (1990): 106.

34. Ibid.

35. Ibid., and Muhsin-i Fayz Kāshānī, *Muhākama Bayn al-Mutasawwifa wa Qayrihīm*, 125.

36. Muhsin-i Fayz, *Muhākama*, 125.

37. Mullā Sadrā Shīrāzī, *Kasr asnām al-jahiliyya*, 57.

38. Qummī, *Risālah-yi Radd bar Sufiyān*, f 81b. The pseudo-Ardabīlī also quotes this line from Rumi, *Hadīqat al-shī'a*, 577.

39. Pseudo-Ardabīlī, *Hadāqat al-shī'a*, 577.

40. Roy Mottahedeh, *The Mantle of the Prophet: Religion and Politics in Iran* (New York: Simon and Schuster, 1985), 145.

41. For a discussion on the classical tension between "permitted" chanting and "illicit" forms of singing, see James Winston Morris, "Situating Islamic Mysticism: Between Written Traditions and Popular Spirituality," in *Typologies of Mysticism: The Quest for God in Judaism, Christianity and Islam*, ed. Robert Herrera (Washington, D.C.: Catholic University Press, 1992), sec. 4.

42. Mulla Sadrā, *Kasr asnām al-jāhiliyya*, 56.

43. Pseudo-Ardabili, *Hadīqat al-shī'a*, 585.

44. Qummī, *Tuhfat al-akhyār*, 112–113.
45. Ibid., 114. The *Majālis al-'ushshāq* was written by Kamāl al-Dīn Husayn Tabasī Gazurghā'i (d. before 930/1524).
46. As cited above.
47. Muhammad b. Muhammad Lawlī Sabzavāhī Mir Lawhi, *Arba'īn* (Tehran University, MS 1154), f 10a.
48. Ibid.
49. Nasrābādī, *Tazkirah-yi Nasrābādī*, 93.
50. Ibid.
51. Shāmlū, *Qisas al-khāqānī*, ff 276a–288b are names of the *ulama*, and ff 282b–288b are dervishes and shaykhs.
52. Ibid., f 282b. Mīr Muhammd Zamān's name appears as the teacher of another *shari'a*-minded polemist, Shaykh Ali Shahīdī, author of the *Sihām al-māraqa*. On Mīr Muhammad Zamān as teacher to Shaykh Ali, see Afandī Isfahānī *Riyāz al-'ulamā* (Qum: Matba'at al-Khayyam, 1980), vol. 5, 104.
53. Ibid., f 282b.
54. Ibid.
55. Ibid.
56. Ibid.
57. At some point after his return from Mecca, he decided to go to Isfahan and settled down there. Valī Qulī Shāmlū, writing in 1076/1666–1667, says Shaykh Ali Mashadī is still in Isfahan, busy reading books of hadith.
58. Muhammad Tāhir Vahīd Qazvīnī, *'Abbāsnāme*, ed. I. Dihqān (Arāk: Kitābfurūshī-yi Dāvūdī, 1950–1951): 255.
59. That same year the shah endowed a *takkiya* for Fayz on the banks of the Zayandirūd, and Mīrzā Muhammad Sālih, the shah's doctor, was named superintendent *(mutavallī)* of that shrine. *'Abbāsnāme*, 256.
60. Sabzavārī (Mīr Lawhī), *Arba'īn*, ff 9b–10a.
61. Mulla Sadra, *Kasr asnām al-jāhiliyya*, 62.
62. Ibid., 65.
63. Mulla Sadra, *Sih Asl*, 81–82.
64. In 'Abdullāh Afandī Isfahānī, *Riyāz al-'ulamā wa hīyāz al-fazalā'*, ed. Ahmad al-Husaymi (Qum: Matba'at al-Khayyam, 1980), vol. 2, 324, in the biography of Majlisi Sr., notes that Majlisi Sr. was the first grandee to take on the post of Imam Jum'a of Isfahan

since the death of Mir-i Damad and Baha'i—implying that both Mir-i Damad and Baha'i had held this post earlier.

65. For Mīrzā Habībullah Karakī's statement that no *mujtahids* existed in this period (Safi), see above.

66. Mulla Sadra, *Kasr asnām al-jāhiliyya*, 142.

67. Ibid., 91 and 130. Other polemicists who make this point include Mīr Lawhī, Qummī, and Kāshānī. Fayz and Sadra add *faqīhs* to the list.

68. The competition over religious posts motivated many of the rivalries, adding to the already existing polemics against sufis. Yet these polemics cannot be dismissed as being motivated simply by power and money. Qummī, for instance, already held the post of Shaykh al-Islam of Qum.

69. See, for example, Qummī's *Tuhfat al-akhyār*, 81, in which he says that *khāniqāhs* are built to render the mosque less appealing.

70. Mīr Lawhī, *Arba'in*, f 23a.

71. Ibid., f 23b. Mīr Lawhī speaks of the times when Muhsin-i Fayz would come to perform the prayer at the court mosque, the Masjid-i Jām'i-yi Jadīd, and Mīrzā Muhammad 'Abd al-Hasīb al-'Amilī would then go to the Masjid-i Jām'i-yi Qadīm (where the two Majlisīs were Imam Jum'as) as a guest, yet he was never asked to lead the prayer or be the *vā'īz* for a few Fridays due to jealousy and competition. The *'Abbāsnāme* and the *Qisas al-khāqānī* speak of Fayz performing the prayer in the Masjid-i Jāmi'-yi Jadīd in 1065/1655, 1068/1657–1658, 1071/1661 and 1076/1665–1666. Majlisī I died in 1070/1660. Mīrzā Muhammad 'Abd al-Hasib died after 1058/1647–1648.

72. Mahdavī's version is also preserved in the *Riyāz al-'ulamā*, vol. 2, 318. For a less detailed version, see the *Bihār al-anwār* (Tehran: Maktab al-Islāmiyya, 1972), vol. 110, 43 and 45.

73. Majlisī Sr. popularized two religious manuals—the *al-Sahīfat al-sajjādiya*, a compilation of prayers to be recited on specific occasions, and the *Ziyārat al-jāmi'at al-kabīra*. Mir Damad also has a *al-Sahīfat al-kāmila;* see the *Amal al-āmīl*, vol. 2, 249, and the *al-dharī'a*, vol. 15, 15.

74. du Mans, *Estat de la Perse en 1660*, 58.

75. Muhammad Bāqir b. Muhammad Taqī Majlisī Jr., *Bihār al-anwār* (Tehran: Dūr al-Kutub al-Islāmīyah, 1949–1968), vol. 110, 43–66.

76. Sayyid Muslih al-Dīn Mahdavī, *Zindigināmah-yi 'Allamah Majlisī*, 2 vols. (Isfahān, n.d.), vol. 2, 385, quoting from the first edition of the *Bihār al-Anāwr*, vol. 25, 148. I am using this quote, for it provides more information about the content of Majlisī Sr.'s dream than the Maktab al-Islāmiyya edition of the *Bihār al-anwār* available to me. Mahdavī's version is also preserved in the *Riyāz al-'ulamā*, vol. 2, 318. For a less detailed version, see the *Bihār al-anwār* (Tehran: Maktab al-Islāmiyya, 1392/1972), vol. 110, 43 and 45.

77. Majlisī Jr., *Bihār al-anwār*, vol. 110, 43.

78. See Āqā Buzurg Tihrānī's *al-dharia*, vol. 15, 18–19, for six different compilations.

79. Majlisī Jr., *Bihār al-anwār*, vol. 110, 44–46. The 'Id-i Fitr is the ritual celebration marking the end of Ramazan, the Muslim month of fasting.

80. Qummī, *Tuhfat al-akhyār*, 71.

81. Ibid.

82. Chardin, *Les Voyages du Chevalier Chardin en Perse*, vol. 3, 200.

83. Ibid.

84. His son, Majlisī Jr., later comes to canonize this role with the revival of a genre of literature referred to as *Ikhtiyārāt* (almanacs or a list of propitious moments or days on which to perform a specific act).

85. Muhammad Bāqir, Khwānsārī, *Rawzāt al-jannāt fī ahwāl al-'ulamā wa al-sādāt*, ed. Sayyid Muhammad Taqī al-Kāshifī, 8 vols. (Tehran: n.p., 1970), vol. 2, 322 (Persian translation).

86. Sayyid Muslih al-Dīn, Mahdavi, *Zindigīnāmah-yi 'Allamah Majlisī* (Isfahān, n.p., 1969–1970), vol. 2, 381.

87. 'Abd al-Hayy Razavī Kāshānī (1152/1739–1740), the author of a second *Hadāqat al-shī'a*.

88. Kashānī, *Hadīqat al-shī'a*, f 41, as cited in Rasūl Ja'fariān, "Intiqād az Vazī'at-i Jāmi'i-yi Dīnī-i Asr-i Safavī," *Kahyān-i Andīshah* (1991): 159.

89. According to the author of the *Rawzat al-jannāt*, the post of Imam Jum'a had been vacant since the death of Mir-i Damad (1039/1630), vol. 2, 324.

90. Mīr Lawhī, *Arb'īn*, f 8b.

91. Sayyid Muslih al-Dīn, Mahdavī, *Zindigīnāmah-yi 'Allamah Majlisī*, vol. 2, 399.

92. Mīr Lawhī, *Arba'īn*, f 8b. This story also appears in the *Tazkirat al-qubūr*.

93. Ibid., f 187b.

94. Majlisī Jr., *Sayr va Sulūk* (written in 1086/1675–1676), quoted in Ma'sūm Ali Shah's *Riyāz al-siyāhat*, 616–621, and in his *Tarīqat al-haqā'īq*, vol. 1, 270.

95. Mīr Lawhī, *Arba'īn*, f 190a.

96. Ibid.

97. Mīr Lawhī states that Majlisī Jr. argued that singing is illegal *(harām)*, "whereas his father Muhammad Taqī spent his life in song and just like Shah Mīrak Zarkish, he had an official minstrel and singers." *Arba'īn*, f 187b.

98. Ibid., f 188a.

99. These six *fatwās* are recorded in Ahmad b. Zayn al-'Abidīn 'Alavī's (d. 1043/1633–1634) *Izhār al-haqq wa miyār al-sadq*. The *fatwās* were issued by Mīrzā Habibullāh Karakī, The Sadr of Safi and 'Abbās II (1041–1063/1632 to 1652–1653); Mīrzā Rafi al-Dīn Nāī'nī, a famous *'arif*; Mawlānā Muhammad Bāqir Sabzavārī, the Shaykh al-Islam and Imam Jum'a of Isfahan under 'Abbās II, also an *'arif*; Shaykh Ali Naqī Kamirā'ī, Qāzī of Shiraz under 'Abbās I and Safi and Shaykh al-Islam of Isfahan under 'Abbās II; and Mīrzā Nūr al-Dīn 'Ali Muftī. These *fatwās* have also been preserved in the *Salvāt al-shī'a* by Muttahar Muhammad al-Miqdādī, written in 1060/1650. According to the author, many learned scholars have written these kinds of *fatwās*. Ja'fariān speculates that the author is probably Mīr Lawhī. The *Salvat al-shī'a* is a synopsis of the *Tawzīh al-mashrabayn*.

100. Chardin, *Les Voyages du Chevalier Chardin en Perse*, vol. 7, 6.

101. Mīr Lawhī, *Arba'īn* f 189b; Hunarfar, *Ganjīnah-i Āsār-i Tārīkhī-yi Isfāhān*, 158–161.

102. Ibid., f 30a. This work appear in the *al-dharī'a*, the *'I'lām al-muhibīn*, vol. 11, 95–96.

103. Muttahar Muhammad [Mīr Lawhī] al-Miqdādī, *Salvāt al-shī'a wa Quvrat al-sharī'a*, Mar'ashī Library, MS 4296 and MS 4014, f 96b.

104. Ibid., f 102b.

105. Qummī, *Tuhfat al-akhyār*, 9.

106. Ibid., 10.

107. Ibid., 14, 24–25.

108. Ibid., 30.

109. Qummī, *Risālah-yi Radd bar Sufiyān* ff 77a–b. Here Qummī is referring to the four Imāmī canons of *hadith*: Muhammad b. Ya'qūb Kulaynī's (d. 328/939) *al-Kafī fī 'ilm al-dīn*, ed. 'Alī Akbar Ghaffārī (Tehran: 1957–1960); al-Sadūq's (d. 381/991) *Man lā yahduruhu al-faqīh*; and Tūsī's (d. 460/1017) *Tahzīl al-ahkām* and *Al-istibsār fī-mā ikhtalafa min al-akhbār*, ed. Hasan al-Mūsāwī Kharsān (Najaf: Dār al-Kutub al-Islāmiīyah, 1956).

110. Qummī, *Tuhfat al-akhyār*, 30.

111. Ibid., 100

112. Mīr Lawhī, *Arba'īn*, f 190b

113. The *Ikhtiyārāt* literature had first been popularized as a genre by Razī al-Dīn Ali b. Mūsā Ibn-i Tāwūs (589–666/1193–1266). Ibn-i Tāwūs was himself a sufi-minded *'alim* and is said to have met the Mahdī in Samarra. Moojan Momen, *An Introduction to Shi'i Islam: The History and Doctrines of Twelver Shi'ism* (New Haven: Yale University Press, 1985), 314.

114. Muhammad Bāqir b. Muhammad Taqī, Majlisī, Jr., *Raj'a*, Abū Zarr Bīdār (Tehran: Risālat-i Qalam, 1988). 16–17.

115. Chardin, *Les Voyages du Chevalier Chardin en Perse*, vol. 4, 436.

116. Ibid., f 7b.

117. For a list of the various works on the *ghayba* (*Kitāb al-ghayba* and *Risāla fī al-ghayba*), see Āqā Buzurg-i Tihrānī's *al-dharī'a*, vol. 16, 74–83.

118. Based on the list of extant works on the subject of occultation recorded in *al-dharī'a*, the first was written by Fazl Ibn-i Shāzān (d. 260/873–874). Nearly a century would pass before Abū Ja'far al-Shalmaqānī (d. 323/935) and al-Numānī (d. 342/953–954) would each write the Imāmī versions of the *ghayba*. By this time Islamdom was traveling through its Shi'i century, and powers such as the Hamdānids and the Buyids had placated 'Abbāsid hegemony. This gave rise to three more monographs by al-Sadūq (d. 381/991), Shaykh Mufīd (d. 413/1022), and Shaykh al-Tāī'fa (d. 461/1068–1069), capping what seems to be a first wave of writings on the *ghayba*.

119. Bahā' al-Dīn Ali b. Qiyās al-Dīn 'Abd al-Karīm al-Nīlī al-Najafī, a teacher of Ibn-i Fahd (841/1437), seems to have been the forerunner in this new wave of *Kitāb al-ghayba(s)*. Sayyid Husayn Modarresi has pointed out, however, that since no Shi'i bio-

graphical dictionaries exist from these centuries, some *Kitāb al-ghayba(s)* could have gone unnoticed.

120. Both these figures had studied with Ibn-i Fahd. Momen, *An Introduction to Shi'i Islam*, 102 and 314.

121. Shaykh Ali Karakī seems to have been the first Safavi 'alim to have written a book on the *ghayba*. Āqā Buzurg, however, points out that Karakī's book on the *ghayba* is about the backbiting and gossip *(ghayba/iqhtiyāb)* that his opponents had instigated against him; only one chapter covers the occultation of the Mahdī. The author was unable to check the treatise itself now published in a three-volume work entitled *Rasā'il al-muhaqqiq*. Abd al-Razzāq Lāhījī (d. 1121/1709) would also write his treatise on the *ghayba*; this too would be about slander rather than occultation.

122. Sayyid Husayn Modarresi-Tabātabā'ī, *Zamīn dar Fiqh-i Islāmī*, 2 vols. (Tehran: Daftar-i Nashr-i Farhang-i Islāmī, 1984), vols. 2, 222, fn. 84.

123. Qāzī Ahmad Qummī, *Khulāsat al-tavārīkh*, 2 vols., ed. Ihsān Ishrāqī (Tehran: Tehran University Press, 1980 and 1984), vol. 1, 79.

124. Majlisī, Jr., *Raja*, 16–17.

125. Mīr Lawhī, *Arba'īn*, ff 38a–39a.

126. Ibid., f 190b.

127. A copy of the *Bayāz-i Mukālimah-yi Shah Tahmasb bā Ilchiyān* (Dorn, MS 302, St. Petersburg, dated 1010/1601–1602 with two miniatures) is extant from the early reign of Shah Abbas. This manuscript was probably housed in the library of the shrine of Shaykh Safi in Ardabil, which fell into Russian hands in the nineteenth century.

128. According to Paul Horn, "Die Denkwürdigkeiten des Schah Tahmasp I. von Persien," *Zeitschrift der Deutschen Morgenländischen Gesellschaft* (Leipzig), 44 (1890), he saw a manuscript of the *Tazkire* in the possession of the Qajar king (Nasir al-din Shah), which was an original copy written in the hand of Tahmasb. The Qajar courtier and historian Ittimād al-Saltanah includes the *Memoir (Ruznāmah-yi Shah Tahmasb)* in his *Matl'a al-Shams*.

Epilogue

We began our cyclical journey with the greater Mediterranean world of late antiquity when prophets like Jesus, Mani, and Muhammad entered the debate over authority with a monotheistic response and universal vision. The book focused on a microhistory of Safavi Iran as a way of capturing some early modern alternatives—manifestations of the dialogue between Semitic, Indo-Iranian, and Hellenic cultures that continued to resist the monotheist impulse to delay the meeting of the holy with the human until the end of time. I would like to close with a larger picture of the history of modernity in Iran to trace a trajectory into the future of some of the book's actors, the motifs they invoked, and the desires they revealed. My conclusions will be brief; they are afterthoughts on the significance of the Safavi episode in Islamic history—particularly in those lands where the Persian language came to dominate politically.

Throughout the narrative, I have tried to identify a Persianate ethos recognized and practiced by a variety of ethnic group (Persians, Turks, Kurds) and religious groups (Alid, Imami, Mazdean) living in Anatolia, Syria, Iraq, and Iran—each providing its own particular renderings. Mazdean and Alid features of Persianate culture shared symbols such as the Persian language, the sun, the mystic, the monarch, the messiah, and the ritual commemoration of the drama of Karbala, creating a sense of "group belonging" that I have at times referred to as an *iden-tity*.[1] This cultural system uttered in the Persian dialect was transmitted through epics like the *Shāhnāme* and the *Abū Muslimnāme* and translated into Turkic dialects spoken as far east as Samarqand and westward all the way to Istanbul. Identification with a Persianate ethos was not necessarily bound to a territory, a body that would be grounded in modern Iran with the advent of the West and the entire imperialist project of modernity that mapped the contours of nation-states.[2] Attempts to confine heteroglossia, to fuse a single Persianate language, were visible impulses in the Safavi world. In this centrifugal process, lands that came to be controlled by the Safavis *(mamālik-i mahrūsah)*, referred to in the chronicles as Iranzamin, the "Land of Iran," were marked by binary tensions between Alid and Mazdean idioms. Although a spectrum of meanings ran through these two poles, their dialectic shaped the rhythms of history that permeated Safavi oral and written culture. I have emphasized a number of ways in which common signs were given signification through these two sites of representation and how each came to incorporate shared icons into their particular cognitive styles, memory narratives, and ritual expressions. Explorations into the cosmos of the Qizilbash and Nuqtavis served as examples, providing social and political texture for these symbols as well as glimpses into the ways in which they were experienced. In early modern Safavi Iran, Mazdean and Alid domains of signification overlapped, and as we saw with the Nuqtavis and Qizilbash, boundaries were porous; one could easily slip into the universe of the other.

By the end of seventeenth century, with the writing of an oppressive Safavi discourse and the physical assault on sufi *ghulāt*, cyclical time—the "way of metempsychosis"—was to have officially been silenced. The successful erasure of *ghuluww*-tainted figures—Ali's third son, Muhammad b. Hanafiyya, and his avenger, Abū Muslim—from the pages of Shi'i history was accompanied by an enumeration of excesses that violated the tenets of Islam. A decree in 1694 was to be read in all mosques, in some even inscribed in stone: provincial governors, aldermen, and judges were to enforce the word of God.[3] Functionaries who had neglected the *shari'a* in the past were punished. Wine bottles from court cellars were publicly smashed in the central square of Isfahan. Music and dance were to cease at all weddings and in male and female gatherings. Sodomy, prostitution, and gambling were banned. Coffeehouses were closed down. Opium and "colorful herbs" were declared illegal. Islamic garb was to be enforced. In the name of divine law, these practices were marked as abhorrent. Although these *shari'a*-based denunciation were not new impulses, with the Safavi patronage of Shi'i scholars, judges, and preachers, the foundations of a religious establishment were actualized. Through institutions like the mosque, theological seminaries, and religious endowments *(waqf)*, the Shi'i clergy could now take part in the game of politics. Hence, a new stock character entered the dynamics of Iranian history—the jurisconsult *(mujtahid)* who was privy to knowledge of the word of God. These Shi'i scholars challenged charismatic mystics thanks to a theological school (Usuli), which sanctioned the position of specialists in divine law as the sole intermediaries between the believer and God. In the absence of the hidden Imam, these specialists not only claimed direct access to God; some, like Mulla Qasim in Safavi Isfahan and Khomeini in contemporary Iran, would argue that political rule was reserved for them as well. With the Islamic Republic of Iran in 1979, the *mujtahid* would eclipse the figure of the monarch.

Idealists and visionaries continued to voice their desire for alternative visions of justice. A longing for immediate contact with the holy and a hope to experience a utopia on earth was expressed through a familiar apocalyptic language of change. The break with cyclical time and a gnostic way of being had not been complete in Safavi Iran. Believers continued to anticipate messiahs who emerged from mystical circles, unveiling new cycles of revelation. Groups like the Ahl-i Haqq and the Nusayris in western Asia, the Naqshbandis in the east, and the Alevis in Turkey still practice these beliefs. Political vicissitudes shaped the degree to which so-called "exaggerated" utterances could be voiced publicly or on the margins of secrecy. Today in republican Turkey, with the rise of a *shari'a*-minded consciousness organized into political parties, the secular government has in fact encouraged Alevi expression in the hope of mitigating religious orthodoxy. Heresy and orthodoxy continue to define each other; what distinguishes each meaning has much to do with the one who does the defining. For some Shi'i *ghulāt*, revenge was no longer articulated against the Sunni oppressors of the family of the Prophet. Although they continued to resist the hegemony of rationalist theologians patronized by monarchs like the Qajars (1785–1925), a new enemy had emerged on the scene with the advent of Western imperialism, whether in the form of the British or the Russians. Some dervish groups came to interpret colonialism as a sign of the end of time.[4] In central Asia (Marv), the Englishman Joseph Wolff, traveling in the middle of the nineteenth century, captures some of these readings. As one dervish claimed, "[T]he English people are now Timur, for they are descendants of Ghengis Khan. The Inglees will be the conquerors of the world." Another Turkmen is held to have said that "the Russians shall be the conquerors of the world," while a dervish from Patna framed the British dominance of India in apocalyptic terms.[5] The different ways in which the West was incorporated into the consciousness of Muslims reveals not only a strand that read colonial rule as old prophecies foretold in the corpus of Muslim eschatological traditions, but other Muslims perceived the West as a site of cultural, spiritual, and political resistance.

Apocalyptic thinking continued to resonate with the ways in which history was interpreted and lived by a variety of Muslims in nineteenth-century Qajar Iran. Astrological calculations in synchronicity with Shi'i eschatological traditions set the date 1844 as a fatal year when a variety of millenarian responses were voiced within the Shi'i community—Nimatullahi, Isma'ili, Babi—and, beyond, among a heteroglot Christian, Zoroastrian, and Jewish population living in Persianate landscapes.[6] Some, like the Nurbakhshi Hajji Muhammad Na'ini, chose to emphasize a return to the Persian past, claiming that "ere long will Iran be made the shrine around which will circle the people of the earth."[7] Others, like the Bab, articulated change from within the Shi'i paradigm of the return of the Hidden Imam to initially declare himself as his gate in 1844 and then to go public as the Imam himself (1848)—the manifestation of God. Yet it would be another prophet, Mirza Husayn Ali Nuri, known as *Baha'ullah,* the "Glory of God" (1817–1892), who emerged out of the Babi movement with a universal vision that had evolved through its Mazdean and Abrahamic cycles to express an alternative worldview cognizant of a new global reality. Baha'ullah continued to repudiate the hegemony of a Shi'i rationalist school (Usuli), which sought to seal prophecy after Muhammad as a solution to the debates over authority that the Imami community had to revisit with the occultation of the twelfth Imam (874 c.e.) and a renewed expectation of his appearance. Echoing traditions of *ghuluww,* Baha'ullah saw revelation as a process, each cycle progressively illuminating new layers of the divine message. As Ismael Velasco has aptly put it, "Baha'u'llah appropriated not merely the pre-Islamic past but, crucially, the non-Islamic present, to predicate a post-Islamic future."[8] Persianate religious dissent had throughout Islamic history challenged cultural hegemonies that attempted to rationalize religion, severing direct and intimate contact between the holy and the divine in the name of Islam. Those Persians who embraced Baha'ullah's message—whether Shi'i scholars, Qajar royalty, courtiers, sufis, craftsmen, Zoroastrians, or Jews—were responding to similar pressures. Critical of the Shi'i clerical establishment, Baha'ullah imagined a utopia where religious liberty and human equality fostered heteroglossia. What distinguished Baha'ullah from other like-minded Iranian reformists was that he was speaking as the spokesman of God. Baha'ullah's ideal society was not secular, for he lamented the spiritual and ethical decay in the West, associating it with the erosion of religion and its replacement with reason.[9] Instead, Baha'ullah legitimized the sovereignty of monarchs but independently of clerical authority. These two

bodies were to remain separate but joined, a tradition he recalled back to the "Covenant of Ardashir," locating it within a
Persian genealogy of sovereignty. Baha'ullah was speaking in the
language of Persianate culture for an audience who understood
it. But as Juan Cole has persuasively argued, Baha'ullah was ascribing meanings to the notion of justice that were now indeed
global ideals that had found realization in the American Bill of
Rights, the French Declaration of the Rights of Man and Citizen, and even the religious freedom and equality of minorities
expressed in the Ottoman Tanzimat.[10] Such ideals were being
encountered at a time when Europe was building world empires,
expanding militarily into Islamic territories. An insidious cultural imperialism provoked a crisis of identity, shaping a multitude of "Muslim" constructions of itself and the "West" until
this day. Baha'ullah was critical of European militarism, but he
admired European technological advancements and egalitarian
beliefs. He used examples of Achaemenid glory and tolerance to
bolster pride so as to shake the Iranian out of his sorry state of
subjugation, rejecting the racist orientalist arguments internalized by some Iranians, seeing themselves as inferior to the Europeans.[11] As Velasco has succinctly put it:

> Baha'ullah appropriated the idiom not just of Persianate Islam,
> but also of the West and used it to resist its cultural hegemony. In
> other words, the Baha'i teachings opened an avenue for a new,
> post-Islamic identity that promised to overcome and finally re-
> solve the cultural (and by implication political and social) tensions
> of the day. They also posed an unmistakable challenge to the exist-
> ing order. What was seen by some Persians as the fulfillment of Is-
> lam was regarded by others as its open subversion.[12]

Baha'ullah articulated his universal language of liberty and
justice from within the framework of Shi'i *ghuluww*. Only after
Bahai'sm was established as a new religion, however—defining
itself as the fulfillment of Shi'i messianic expectations, breaking
with the *shari'a,* and unveiling a new universal revelation—did
Babism became tagged as *ghuluww*.[13] As in the case of the

Nuqtavis, the public revelation of a new order that promises paradise on earth marks the boundaries of *ghuluww*. But unlike the universalism of the Nuqtavis, whose alchemical conception of the cosmos imagined all spiritual and material creation as equal, Baha'ullah's universalism transcended the Nuqtavi need to emphasize a Persian Ajami identity. Perhaps this had something to do with the particular historical context of each prophet. After Mongol rule, Pasikhani was confronted with a fragmented Caspian Sea region, in which a plethora of regional messianic movements rose in the name of Ali and emphasized the prestige of Muhammad's family *(sayyid)*. Baha'ullah, on the other hand, lived in an age in which not only Iran but the entire Abode of Islam was colonized by the West. The advent of technicalism and European world hegemony ushered in an era in which localisms no longer remained isolated within regional dynamics but were now intimately connected to a global society. What happened in Tehran came to matter to London and Paris, just as these two European capitals would prevail on Tehran. The late antique language of apocalyptics in its Abrahamic mode shared by Jewish, Christian, and Muslim cultures was indeed a unifying system. It took a consciousness like that of Baha'ullah to recognize this and to creatively reinterpret eschatology as a spiritual revolution that promised the integrity and freedom of all citizens of the world.

Identification with a Persian past and the will to return to it resurfaced in modernity, although it took on a very different incarnation in the form of Iranian nationalism with the chauvinistic flair characteristic of nationalist visions. Binary tensions between what was officially identified as Mazdean and Alid continued to mark the history of Iran. The Safavis as agents of official culture had produced a dominant discourse that crystallized this dual image, shaping a sense of "Iranianness" for the future denizens of modern Iran. The ebb and flow of Iranian history gravitated around imaginations in which both Shi'i and Iranian symbols were used to construct narrative memories. How governments manipulated these two symbolic repositories, which aspects were appropriated, redefined, and branded as excess shaped the trajectory of the history of modern Iran.

I have isolated three memory hooks on which a Persian past fastened itself—the Persian language (alphabet, poetry, and epics), the solar calendar, and the physical ruins of pre-Islamic Iran. These symbolic resources would be mobilized and reanimated during the next three centuries following Safavi rule. Both the successor dynasties of the Qajars (1785–1925) and the Pahlavis (1925–1979) began to rewrite Iranian history with different degrees of emphasis on pre-Islamic Iran, supplanting or writing out Shi'ism in the process. Safavi representations of the Mazdean sun, a symbol of sacral kingship, and the Shi'i lion, evoking Ali's chivalric struggles for truth, were fused together, serving as twin symbols of monarchy. Qajar imagery added a crown that enshrined the lion and sun as though visually asserting the power of kingship over civil and religious domains. A process was set in motion that formalized the lion-and-sun symbol into a national emblem of Iran written into the first Iranian Constitution of 1906. Afsaneh Najmabadi has unraveled this fascinating trajectory, exposing the layers of meaning and the iconic shifts embedded in this single sign that continues to enjoy multiple associations of "Iranianness."[14] Her readings illuminate the gendered and sexual impulses behind the evolution of this icon, relating it to the project of modernity that introduced ideals such as romantic marriage and heterosexual love under the gaze of the West. In the process of standardizing this symbol, she delineates the ground that was laid out for competing and contesting meanings of "Iranianness" to emerge in time. Just as the sun came to shine its feminine face and the masculine lion became her partner, the lion and sun came to be associated with early Qajar kingship. Gradually, as the sun began losing all her feminine features toward the end of Qajar rule, she was transformed into an abstract circle, finally to be desexualized by Reza Shah Pahlavi. In an Irano-Muslim culture in which male homoeroticism was the norm, it would not be embarrassing for a monarch to be associated with a bigendered imperial logo. But as the Western perception of sodomy as "unnatural" became internalized by an elite of Iranians exposed to the West, the female figure had to be veiled in a male-dominated national iconography.[15]

With the Pahlavis, the lion-and-sun symbol became so associated with an oppressive Westernizing monarchy that the Islamic Revolution that toppled it replaced it with Arabic calligraphy inscribing the monotheism of the new regime. With the victory of a rationalist interpretation of the word of God, a single language of Shi'ism was imposed by a Shi'i clergy that had now established a theocracy as agents of God and perhaps at the behest of the Mahdi himself embodied by Imam Khomeini in the popular imagination. It was a Persian past that was now being erased. As Najmabadi points out, although the lion had a definite iconic association with Ali in Safavi and Qajar visual culture, it was eliminated in the era of Islamic rule as a national symbol. Returned to its previous religious domain, it was to be displayed in banners hoisted during Muharram commemorations marking the martyrdom of Husayn. Although in 1979, Ali and his progeny had in reality appropriated the authority of monarchs and messiahs, and religion and politics had merged once again, the lion had been contaminated by Pahlavi kingship with its reintroduction into a Persian symbolic field. The lion that had been a symbol of Rustam's heroism in the *Shāhnāme* and an Irano-Semitic icon of kingship in medieval Iran was marked with the figure of Ali and would be fused during the Safavi episode with Shi'ism. The lion was returned to its old domain of identification with the Qajars and Pahlavis defined by their opponents, the Islamic republic, as a sign of the historically corrupt regimes of Persian shahs. What was deemed as old was in fact a synthesis of the old and the new, for Ali and the Imams were now speaking in Persian.

Ironically, the West, with its interest in archaeology and its reintroduction of Greek histories, preserved an interpretation of the Iranian past beyond what had been commemorated in Ferdowsi's *Shāhnāme*—that the ruins of Persepolis and the

Sasani palace of Ctesiphon would provide the legitimacy for a new form of Persian revival. French archaeologists who had a monopoly over Iranian antiquities under the late Qajars began to provide scientific backing to a mythohistory of Persian glory.[16] In a step to reclaim Iran's integrity as a nascent nation-state, Reza Shah revoked the French concessions of 1895 and 1900 through an act of parliament in 1927 and came to personally protect the material remains of an Iranian past for his program of nation building. With his establishment of the Museum of Iran Bastan (1937) inspired architecturally by the Sasani Palace at Ctesiphon, Reza Shah began to codify a singular meaning for these ruins. No longer were they signs of Persian glory that alerted Arab or Iranian Muslims to the success of Islam and the mutability of Persian kingship, but rather they were to be read and felt as sights of ancient pride to be recalled into the present sense of "Iranianness." Reza Shah officially recast his nation as *Iran*, a term used locally, rather than the Western appellation *Persia*, which had entered European discourse through the Greek designation of their enemy, the Persians who ruled from Fars. He also chose a new name for his family, adopting the term *Pahlavi*, which designated the ancient language of Iranians before the Arab conquest, before Arabic words colonized the Persian alphabet. Although it is related that Reza Shah had forgotten his own Iranian past, prompting him to ask an American orientalist, Donald Wilber, the meaning of the word *Pahlavi*, Reza Shah was not only responding to an Iranian inferiority complex toward the West.[17] A current of Iranian nationalism was active among scholars like Sadiq Kiya and Ibrahim Purdavus, the very first professors who taught in the Department of Archaeology, established in 1937 at the Tehran University by Reza Shah. Sadiq Kiya published his research on the Nuqtavis in a journal he had established with like-minded colleagues entitled *Iran Kudeh*, "The Land of Iran." Such Persian impulses had been voiced earlier in Qajar Iran by intellectuals and politicians like Akhunzadah and Mirza Aqa Khan Kirmani. These men confirmed Ferdowi's project as a *lieu de mémoire*, seeing it as a pivotal text for the community of Persian culture and its resilience against Arab dominance. It was thanks to Ferdowsi that they believed the fate of Iranians did not resemble that of the Egyptians.[18] The Persian language became the privileged site for nationalisms and anti-Arab sentiment to mine. And we must not forget that these voices were uttered at a time when Iran's Muslim neighbors were expressing their own versions of Arab and Turkish nationalism. The rejection of Arabs and, by association, of Islam prompted an Iranian identification with Europe. Already, orientalism had marked Islam as backward, despotic, and carnal. The Persian linguistic kinship with French or English through its Indo-European past served as a bridge to the West that could save Iran's face from its Islamic taint. A movement to purge the Persian language of Arabic words produced a genre of writing in pure Persian *(pārsīgarī)* that had a previous incarnation in Safavi Iran.[19] A genealogy can be traced from the Nuqtavis who fled to India—Azar Kayvanis—to a nascent nationalism voiced in the form of Zoroastrian revivalism and the preservation of the Persian language. Dictionaries were the most fashionable mode of this expression, compiling lexicons of Persian unfettered by Arabic. But such movements underscored Persian superiority, deemphasizing the universalist dimension of Nuqtavi thought—two different directions in which the Bahai faith and Persian nationalism took.

Both Pahlavi monarchs, father and son, manipulated these tendencies and exaggerated the identification of Iran with its pre-Islamic past. Structurally, they derooted the clerical establishment, depriving it of its legal and educational functions. The clergy retreated into their mosques from which a new revolution remembering a Shi'i past would emerge. Along with such institutional changes, which had cultural and political reverberations, Muhammad Reza Shah broke with the Islamic calendar and instead inaugurated a new era that would reckon time through solar calculations beginning with the reign of the Achaemenid monarch Cyrus. His 2,500-year commemoration of Persian monarchy at the site of Persepolis was the most extreme of the many manifestations of Pahlavi revival and was the brainchild of another orientalist, Arthur Pope, who surveyed Iranian art and architecture. The new Western factor would complicate the complex dynamics of Iranian identity formation, whether in the territory of Iran or among an Iranian diaspora living in the West since the Islamic Revolution.

Persian xenophobia under the Pahlavis gave voice to a variety of opposition, both secular and religious. Among the clergy, Khomeini was the most vocal. Breaking the silence of contemporary accommodating clerics, Khomeini blamed the Pahlavis for Iran's enslavement by the West. He argued for the incompatibility of monarchy and Islam, quoting Muhammad as his source. Even intellectuals like Al-i Ahmad and Ali Shariati, who had toyed with Marxism, spoke in the common language of Shi'i Islam represented by Khomeini. Each, of course, placed a different emphasis on the centrality of Shi'ism for the Iranian. For these men voicing a spectrum of Iranian malaise, the Persian revival and its concomitant obsession with the West was deemed foreign to the Iranian populace at large. Iranians not only knew nothing of this Persian past, but a consumerism was infesting Iran that ate at the soul of every citizen; even the villager was struck by it. Al-i Ahamd located this "spiritual enslavement of Iranians to the alien God that Europe had injected into Iranian imagination" at the height of Iran's confusion.[20] He coined a word for this disease—*gharbzadegī* (Euromania)—and likened it to "locusts in fields of wheat who infest the wheat from within, leaving behind only skin."[21] Despite Al-i Ahmad's break with his own clerical heritage and his candid critique of the rigidity, hypocrisy, and superstition of clerics, his ensuing struggles to find a home for himself in Iranian political life left him with an emotional longing that was filled by those Shi'i memories and rituals that made him an Iranian—something that became clear to him during his pilgrimage to Mecca. The Iranian revolution of 1979 spoke in this very language of cultural resistance, and, as Al-i Ahmad had anticipated, it would be a revolution of the "word," for only if the word were uttered from within its religious domain (Shi'i) could it have the power to succeed. But as the Islamic Republic came to eliminate the sun-and-lion symbol, and as it attempted to eradicate Persian New Year celebrations, the discipline of archaeology, and Achaeminid and Sasani history prominent in Pahlavi textbooks, these sites are rooted in Iranian cultural imaginations. Today, they are sites of resistance both inside the boundaries of Iran and among exile Iranians in the West. Whether nostalgia or kitsch, the lion-and-sun emblem on coffee mugs and the revival of Zoroastrian studies in Iran as well as among amateur scholars in exile show that the Persian past is now a living and organic *milieu de memoire*. The Islamic Republic appropriated these sites somewhat reluctantly as the war with Iraq necessitated a revival of nationalism. Shi'ism as a universal ideology has not freed itself of the referent that is Iran, at least in this cycle of history.

During the millennium-and-a-half history of conversion of former Sasani dominions to Islam, Mazdean and Alid idioms have been the most vocal styles of expression. Mystics, monarchs, messiahs, and, more recently, mullahs have been endowed with the authority to privilege particular memories and historical narratives, either merging the two languages, as Shah Isma'il did, or rejecting Shi'ism, as did the Pahlavis. And we have the counterexample of Khomeini, who asserted the hegemony of Shi'ism over a Persian past. Such binary dynamics exhibit diametric responses, influencing the cyclical processes of change—moving to and from an Arab (Islamic) present to a Persian past. What is constantly shifting is what continues to be constructed at every turn of history as "Iranian" and "Shi'i." Despite attempts from the rise of Islam up to the Islamic Revolution in Iran to reject one for the other, the duo has resisted separation. Continuities are not linear: they do not necessarily live on in their distinct domains, for in every (re)invention of "Iranian" or "Shi'i" both elements have already been merged: they have lived previous incarnations in each other's fields of representation. What is seen as Shi'i in one cycle of history is actually imagined as Iranian in another age.

Since the rise of colonialism, a third icon—the West—has joined this duo to create a triangle that marks the tensions that motivate change in Iranian society. Western democratic ideals that were embraced by Baha'ullah are now the platform for reformist clerics like Khatami in Iran, who emphasize the rule of law and civil society in the language of Islam. The prospect for mystics, monarchs, and messiahs seems gloomy today, but we should not forget that Baha'ullah appeared and was embraced just over a century ago. And that in the 2001 presidential elections in Iran, a young sufi from Ardabil presented himself as a candidate. It is difficult for many of us living in this age of reason to believe in messiahs or in reincarnation. The rationalist project of Abrahamic monotheisms has, indeed, succeeded in severing the holy from the human. Although many educated citizens of the world would ridicule *ghulāt* beliefs, relegating them to the realm of superstition and magic, some continue to dream of justice and union with the divine in apocalyptic terms. This book offers itself as a bridge to a past to which we are now blind—a guide not only for exploring another culture, another mentality, but for understanding that world on its own terms.

NOTES

1. See Rogers Brubaker and Fred Cooper, "Beyond Identity," *Theory and Society*, 29, nos. 1–4 (2000): 1–47, for the problematic over use of the term *identity* in academic discourse. The authors emphasize the importance of contextualizing such cultural manifestations and developing a richer vocabulary to conceptualize social and cultural heterogeneity. In this study, I have foregrounded the particularity of Safavi historical contexts.

2. See Firuzeh Kashani-Sabet, *Frontier Fictions: The Shaping of the Iranian Nation, 1904–1946* (Princeton: Princeton University Press, 1999), for the dual blending of an imagined and material (geography, maps, wars) community that forged the modern nation of Iran.

3. Abū Tālib Mīr Findiriskī, *Tuhfat al-'ālam*, Tehran University Microfilm, MS 4955, f 206a. According to Rasūl Ja'fariān, this decree

was circulated throughout Iran, for it appears as an inscription *(katībah)* on mosques in Kashan, Lahijan, Tabriz, and Luristan. *Dīn va Siyāsat dar Dawrah-yi Safavī* (Qum: Intishārāt-i Ansāriyān, 1991), 441–445.

4. See Abbas Amanat, *Resurrection and Renewal: The Making of the Bābī Movement in Iran, 1844–1850* (Ithaca: Cornell University Press, 1989), 82–83, where he mentions the Khāksār and Jalālī messianic interpretations of Western hegemony.

5. Ibid., 83.

6. Ibid., 96, where Amanat is quoting Qatīl al-Karbalā'ī.

7. Ibid., 97. Amanat dates this utterance as approximately 1806 to 1818.

8. Ismael Velasco, "Academic Irrelevance or Disciplinary Blind-Spot: Middle Eastern Studies and the Baha'i Faith Today," *MESA Bulletin* 35 (Winter 2001): 188–198. I would like to thank Ismael Velasco for having shared his perceptive article with me, which has inspired this conclusion.

9. Juan Ricardo Cole, *Modernity and the Millenium: The Genesis of the Baha'i Faith in the Nineteenth-Century Middle East* (New York: Columbia University Press, 1999), 44–46.

10. My readings of Baha'ullah have benefited from Cole's positioning him within a larger context of world history.

11. Juan Cole, *Modernity and the Millenium*, 8.

12. Velasco, "Academic Irrelevance or Disciplinary Blind-Spot?," 192.

13. I would like to thank Afsaneh Najmabadi for this insightful comment.

14. Afsaneh Najmabadi, *Women with Mustaches and Men without Beards: Gender and Sexual Anxieties of Iranian Modernity* (Berkeley: University of California Press, forthcoming). This entire section on the lion-and-sun icon is based on Najmabadi's innovative reading of Iranian modernity.

15. See Afsaneh Najmabadi for this argument and for another layer of the eclipse of the sun, the advent of the modern Iranian women in the public domain. My narrative here draws on her arguments.

16. See Kamyar Abdi, "Nationalism, Politics, and the Development of Archaeology in Iran," *American Journal of Archeology* 105 (2001): 51–76, for an insightful survey of the uses and abuses of archeology in the nationalist project of Iran.

17. Ibid., 63. Abdi cites this quote from Donald Wilber's _Reza Shah Pahlavi: The Resurrection and Reconstruction of Iran_ (New York: Exposition Press, 1975), 163.

18. Muhammad Tavakoli-Targhi, "Refashioning Iran: Language and Culture during the Constitutional Revolution," _Iranian Studies_ 23, nos. 1–4 (1990): 81.

19. Ibid. Tavakoli-Targhi speaks of this Persian purification movement in the context of constitutionalism in Iran. And in his article "Contested Memories: Narrative Structures and Allegorical Meanings of Iran's Pre-Islamic History," _Iranian Studies_ 29, nos. 1–2 (1996): 149–175, he hints at a connection between Azar Kayvan, who emigrated from Safavi Iran to Patna, and what he terms a neo-Mazdean revival through the production of texts like the _Dasātīr_ and the _Dabistān al-mazāhib_. He does not develop this lineage to nationalist discourses of the twentieth century, however.

20. I am quoting from Roy Mottahedeh, _The Mantle of the Prophet: Religion and Politics in Iran_ (New York: Simon and Schuster, 1985), 298, which captures the vicissitudes of Persian political culture through key figures of Iranian history. His perceptive reading of Al-i Ahmad has influenced my understanding of modern Iran. His book is a gift to Iranian historiography not only because of its methodological innovations (the mixing of history, allusion, and fiction) but also because of Mottahedeh's clarity of thought and the ease with which his prose flows makes the reading of Iranian history a joy.

21. Mottahedeh, _Mantle of the Prophet_, 296, has captured this metaphor used by Al-i Ahmad in his _Gharbzadegī_.

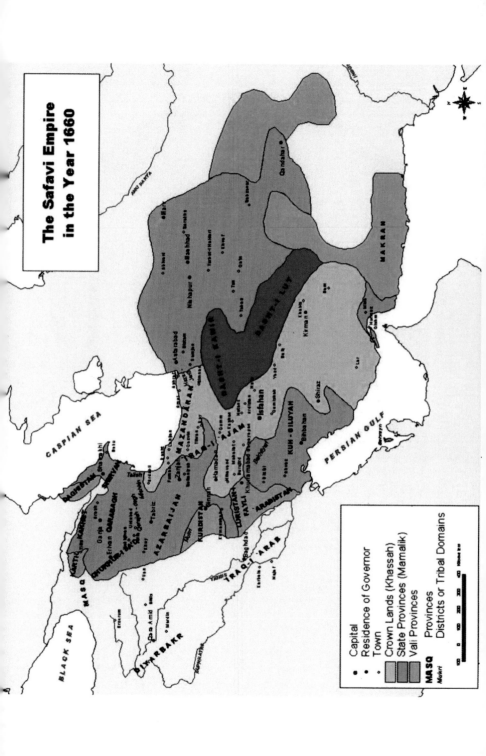

The Safavi Empire in the Year 1660

Figure 1. Silver-Gilt Plate, Iran, Sasanian, 7th century.
Gift of Arthur M. Sackler, S1987.113, Courtesy of Arthur M. Sackler Museum,
Washington, D.C.

The Zoroastrian goddess of fertility and war, Anahita (the immaculate
one), investing the Sasani king with a ring of sovereignty, representing
the *farr* (divine glory). He is crowned with crescent and sun, twin
symbols of kingship.

Figure 2. From a *Fālnāme*, Iran, probably Qazin, mid-16th century.
TKS H1702, Courtesy of the Topkapi Palace Museum and Library.

The signs of the zodiac from a *Book of Divination* attributed to Ja'far
al-Sadiq, where Leo is represented by the sun rising behind the lion's
torso.

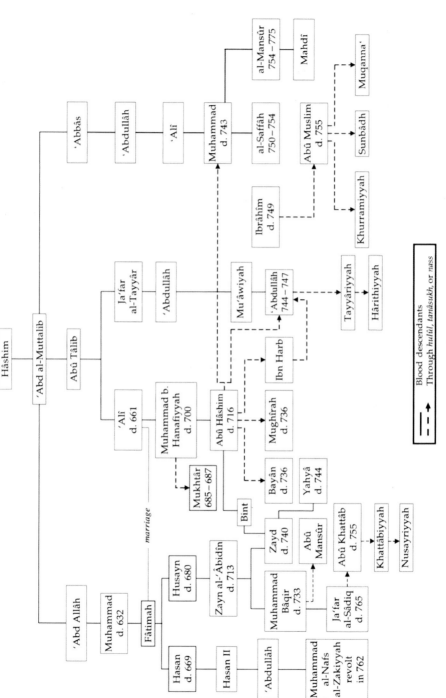

Figure 3. A Genealogical Chart of Alids and Early Ghulāt

Figure 4. Imam Reza Fighting a Demon, from a *Fālnāme,* Iran, probably mid-16th century.
Ancient Collection O. Homberg and Gareth Windson, MAO984, Courtesy of the Louvre.

This book of *Divination* attributed to Ja'far al-Sadiq was prepared for Shah Tahmasb (1524–1576). The illustration represents Imam Reza fighting a demon, reflecting the ways in which Persianate symbols are translated onto Alid figures.

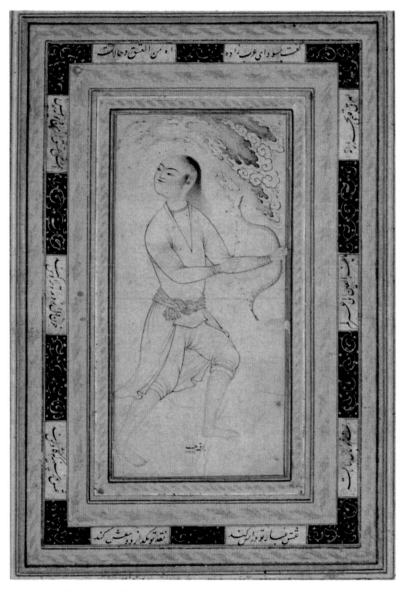

Figure 5. Signed by Habib, *Young Man with a Bow,* Iran, Khurasan, late 16th century.
Lent by the Art and History Trust, LTS1995.2.62, Courtesy of the Arthur M. Sackler Museum, Washington, D.C.

Perhaps a depiction of a newly girded novice initiated into a confraternity. His bow may be a ritual representation marking his entry into the guild of bow-makers.

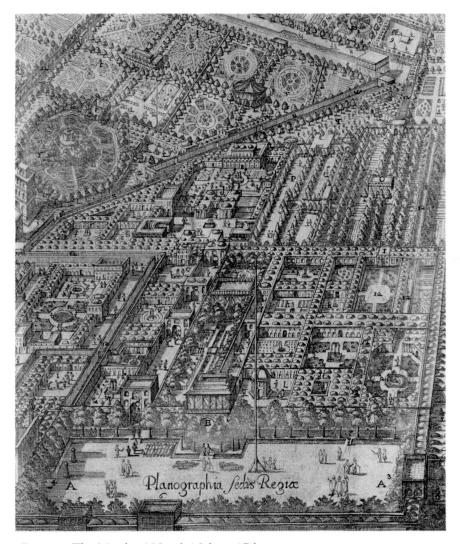

Figure 6. The Maydan-i Naqsh-i Jahan, 17th century.
From Engelbert Kaempfer, *Amoenitatum Exoticarum Politico-physico medicarium: variae relationes, observationes & descriptiones rerum Persicarum & Ulterioris Asiae,* Lemgovnaie, 1712 (#107189) 179, Courtesy of the Library of Congress.

A seventeenth-century rendering of the Maydan-i Naqsh-i Jahan in Isfahan and the palace complex.

Figure 7. Attributed to Mu'in Musavvir, *The Vizier Khalifa-Sultan,* Iran, Isfahan, circa 1650.
Lent by the Art and History Trust, LTS1995.2.88, courtesy of the Arthur M. Sackler Museum, Washington, D.C.

The religious scholar Sultan al-Ulama turned Grand Vizier (1623–1632, 1645–1654). Is he offering his patronage here to Shah Abbas II after a decade of estrangement from the Safavi court?

Figure 8. Signed by Reza Abbasi, *Young Dervish,* Iran,
Isfahan, circa 1590–1595.
Lent by the Art and History Trust, LTS1995.2.76, Courtesy of the
Arthur M. Sackler Museum, Washington, D.C.

A barefoot dervish clad in a sheepskin cloak offering herbs.

Figure 9. Men Drinking a Mixture of Wine and Bang, Probably
Iran, first half of the 17th century.
Read Albums, MS M.386 f. 6v, Courtesy of the Pierpont Morgan
Library, New York.

Dervishes engaging with their devotees as they prepare mixtures
of hashish (*bang*) and wine. This mixture is offered to initiates,
some of who have attained altered states and others who are in
its pursuit.

Figure 10. Mevlana Rumi Participating in Samā', from Dervish Mahmud
Mesnevi Khan, *Tarjumah-yi thawāqib-i manāqib*, Baghdad, 1590s.
MS M466f.21v, Courtesy of the Pierpont Morgan Library, New York.

Figure 11. Sultan Muhammad, *Heavenly and Earthly Drunkenness,*
from the *Divan of Hafez,* Iran, Tabriz 1526–1527.
The Arthur M. Sackler Museum, Harvard University Art Museums 1988.460.3,
promised gift of Mr. and Mrs. Stuart Cary Welch Jr., partially owned by the
Metropolitan Museum of Art and the Arthur M. Sackler Museum, Harvard
University, 1998, in honor of the students of Harvard University and Radcliffe
College. Photo by Allan Macintyre.

A poetic allusion to the practice of *ghuluww* at the court of the early
Safavis, where Qizilbash, qalandars, dervishes, and other courtiers joined
in ecstasy.

APPENDIX

Bibliography of Sources Cited

Abdi, Kamyar. "Nationalism, Politics, and the Development of Archaeology in Iran." *American Journal of Archeology* 105 (2001): 51–76.

Afandī Isfahānī, 'Abdullāh. *Riyāz al-ulamā wa hīyāz al-fuzalā*'. Edited by Ahmad al-Husaynī. 6 vols. Qum: Matba'at al-Khayyām, 1980.

Afushtah-yi Natanzī. *Naqāvat al-āsār fī zikr al-akhyār*. Tehran: Intisharat-i Ilmi va Farhangi, 1971.

Al-'Alavī, Abū Ma'ālī Muhammad b. Husayn. *Bayān al-adyān*. Tehran: Sipihr, 1997.

'Alavī, Ahmad b. Zayn al-'Ābidīn. *Izhār al-haqq wa mi'yār al-sadq*. Mar'ashī Library, MS 4014.

Amanat, Abbas. *Resurrection and Renewal: The Making of the Bābī Movement in Iran, 1844–1850*. Ithaca: Cornell University Press, 1989.

'Āmilī, Muhsin al-Husaynī. *A'yān al-shī'a*. 4. ed. Beirut: Matba'at al-Insāf, 1960.

Amīnī-Haravī, Sadr al-dīn Sultan Ibrāhīm. *Futūhāt-i Shāhī*. Kitābkhānah-yi Vazīrī-yi Yazd MS 5774.

Amīr Mahmūd, ibn Khwāndamīr. *Tārīkh-i Shah Ismā'īl va Shah Tahmasb-i Safavī (Zayl-i tārīkh-i habīb al-siyar)*. Edited by Mahmud Ali Jarāhī. Tehran: Nashr-i Gustarah, 1991–1992.

Amir-Moezzi, Mohammad Ali. *The Divine Guide in Early Shi'ism: The Sources of Esotericism in Islam*. Albany: State University of New York Press, 1994.

Amoretti, B. S. "Religion in the Timurid and Safavid Periods." In *Cambridge History of Iran*. Edited by Peter Jackson and Lawrence Lockhart, Vol. 6. Cambridge: Cambridge University Press, 1986.

Arjomand, Said. *Authority and Political Culture in Shi'ism*. SUNY Series in Near Eastern Studies. Albany: State University of New York Press, 1988.

———. "Religion, Political Action, and Legitimate Domination in Shi'ite Iran: Fourteenth to Eighteenth Centuries A.D." *European Journal of Sociology* 20 (1979): 59–109.

———. *The Shadow of God and the Hidden Imam: Religion, Political Order, and Societal Change in Shi'ite Iran from the Beginning to 1890*. Chicago: University of Chicago Press, 1984.

Aston, Margaret. "The Fiery Trigon Conjunction: An Elizabethan Astrological Prediction." *ISIS* (1970): 159–187.

'Aṭṭar, Farīd al-Dīn. *Tazkirat al-awliyā'*. Tehran: Intishārāt-i Zavvār, 1967.

Aubin, Jean. "Shah Ismā'īl et les Notables de l'Iraq Persan (Etudes Safavides I)." *Journal of Economic and Social History of the Orient* 2 (1959): 37–81.

———. "L'Avènement des Safavides reconsideré (Etudes Safavides III)." *Moyen Orient & Ocean Indien* 5 (1988): 1–130.

———. "La fin de l'etat Sarbidar du Khorasan." *Journal Asiatique* 262 (1974): 95–118.

———. "La Politique religieuse des Safavides." In *Le Shi'isme Imamite*. Paris: Presses Universitaires, Colloque de Strasbourg (6–9 mai 1968), 1970.

———. "Revolution Chiite et conservatisme: Les Soufis de Lahejan, 1500–14 (Etudes Safavides II)." *Moyen Orient & Ocean Indien* 1 (1984): 1–40.

———. "Le Temoignage d'Ebn-i Bazzaz sur la Turquisation de l'Azerbaijan." In *Melanges Gilbert Lazard, Studia Iranica Cahier 7*, Paris 1989.

Ayoub, Mahmoud. *Redemptive Suffering in Islam: A Study of the Devotional Aspects of 'Āshūrā in Twelver Shī'ism*. The Hague: Mouton, 1978.

Azarpay, Guity. "Crowns and Some Royal Insignia in Early Iran." *Iranica Antiqua* 9 (1972): 108–115.

Babaie, Sussan. "Building for the Shah: The Role of Mirza Muhammad Taqi in Safavid Royal Patronage of Architecture." In *Safavid Art and Architecture*. Edited by Sheila Canby. London: British Museum, 2002.

———. *Feasting in the City of Paradise*, forthcoming.

———. "Safavid Palaces at Isfahan: Continuity and Change (1590–1666)." Ph.D. diss., New York University, 1994.

Babaie, Sussan, Kathryn Babayan, Ina Baghdiantz-McCabe, and Massumeh Farhad. *Slaves of the Shah: New Elites of Isfahan*. London: I.B. Tauris, 2003.

Babayan, Kathryn. "The Waning of the Qizilbash." Ph.D. diss., Princeton University, 1993.

———. "The '*Aqā'īd al-nisā*': A Glimpse at Safavi Women in Local Isfahani Culture." In *Women in the Medieval Islamic World*. Edited by Gavin Hambly. London: St. Martin's Press, 1998.

———. "The Safavi Synthesis: From Qizilbash Islam to Imamite Shi'ism," *Iranian Studies*, 27 (1994): 135–161.

———. "Sufis, Darvishes, and Mullas: The Controversy over Spiritual and Temporal Dominion in Seventeenth-Century Safavi Iran." In *Safavid Persia*. Edited by Charles Melville. London: I.B. Tauris, 1996.

Babur. *Bāburnāme: Chaghatay Turkish Text with Abdul-Rahim Khankhanan's Persian Translation*. Edited by W. M. Thackston and Khan Abdul-Rahim. Cambridge, MA: Department of Near Eastern Languages and Civilizations, Harvard University, 1993.

———. *The Bāburnāme: Memoirs of Babur, Prince and Emperor*. Translated by Wheeler M. Thackston. Washington, DC: Freer Gallery of Art and Arthur M. Sackler Gallery, Smithsonian Institution, 1996.

Baghdiantz-McCabe, Ina. *The Shah's Silk for Europe's Silver: The Eurasian Trade of the Julfa Armenians in Safavid Iran and India (1530–1750)*. Edited by Michael Stone. Atlanta: Scholars Press, 1999.

al-Bahrānī, Yūsuf b. Ahmad. *Lu'lu'āt al-Bahrayn fī al-ijāzāt wa tajārim rijāl al-hadīth*. Edited by Muhammad Sādiq Bahr al-'Ulūm. Beirut: Dar al-adwa', 1966.

Bailey, H. W. *Zoroastrian Problems in the Ninth-Century Books.* Oxford: Oxford University Press, 1943. Reprint, 1971.

Bakhtin, M. M.. *The Dialogic Imagination: Four Essays.* Edited by Michael Holquist. Vol. 1, *University of Texas Press Slavic Series.* Austin: University of Texas Press, 1981.

Bal, Mieke. *Reading "Rembrandt": Beyond the Word-Image Opposition.* The Northrop Frye Lectures in Literary Theory, Cambridge New Art History and Criticism. Cambridge: Cambridge University Press, 1991.

Bal, Mieke, Jonathan V. Crewe, and Leo Spitzer, eds. *Acts of Memory: Cultural Recall in the Present.* Hanover, NH: University Press of New England, 1999.

al-Barqī, Ahmad b. Muhammad. *al-mahāsin.* Edited by Jalāl al-Dīn Husaynī Muhaddis Urmavī. Tehran: Dār al-Kutūb al-Islāmīyah, 1950–1951.

Bashir, Shahzad. "Between Mysticism and Messianism: The Life and Thought of Muhammad Nurbakhsh (d. 1464)." Ph.D. diss., Yale University, 1997.

Bausani, Allesandro. "Religion under the Mongols." In *Cambridge History of Iran.* Vol. 5. Edited by J. A. Boyle. Cambridge: Cambridge University Press, 1968.

Bayram, Mikāil. *Bā ciyān-ī Rūm: Selçuklular Zamāninda Genç Kīzlar Teşkilāti.* Konya: M. Bayram, 1987.

———. *Fatma Bācī ve Bā ciyān-i Rūm: Anadolu Bacīlar Teşkilātī.* Konya: Damla Ofset Matbaacolok ve Ticaret, 1994.

Beeson, Caroline. "The Origins of Conflict in the Safavi Religious Institution." Ph.D. diss., Princeton University, 1982.

al-Bīrūnī, Muhammad b. Ahmad. *The Chronology of Ancient Nations (al-Āthār al-bāqiyah).* Translated and edited by Edward Sachau. London: Allen, 1993.

Blanchot, Maurice. *The Writing of the Disaster.* Translated by Ann Smock. Lincoln: University of Nebraska Press, 1986.

Blochet, Edgar. *Catalogue des Manuscrits Persane de la Bibliothèque Nationale.* 4 vols. with *Supplement.* Paris: Imprimerie Nationale, 1905–1934.

Bonner, Michael. *Aristocratic Violence and Holy War: Studies in the Jihad and the Arab-Byzantine Frontier.* Vol. 81, American Oriental Series. New Haven, CT: American Oriental Society, 1996.

Bosworth, Clifford Edmund. *The History of the Saffarids of Sistan and the Maliks of Nimruz: 247/861 to 949/1542-3.* Vol. 8, Columbia Lectures on Iranian Studies. Costa Mesa: Mazda Publishers in association with Bibliotheca Persica, 1994.

Bourdieu, Pierre. *Outline of a Theory of Practice.* Vol. 16, Cambridge Studies in Social Anthropology. Cambridge: Cambridge University Press, 1977.

Boyce, Mary. "Bibi Shahrbanu and the Lady of Pars." *Bulletin of the School of Oriental and African Studies* 30 (1967): 30–44.

———. *A History of Zoroastrianism.* Leiden: Brill, 1975.

———. *Textual Sources for the Study of Zoroastrianism.* Chicago: University of Chicago Press, 1984.

———. *Zoroastrianism: Its Antiquity and Constant Vigor.* Vol. 7, Columbia Lectures on Iranian Studies. Costa Mesa: Mazda Publishers in association with Bibliotheca Persica, 1992.

Brockelmann, Carl. *Geschichte der Arabischen Literatur.* 2 vols. and 3 suppls. Leiden: Brill, 1937.

Brown, Peter. *The Making of Late Antiquity.* Cambridge: Harvard University Press, 1978.

———. *The World of Late Antiquity: From Marcus Aurelius to Muhammad.* London: Thames and Hudson, 1971.

———. *The Cult of Saints.* Chicago: Chicago University Press, 1981.

Brubaker, Rogers, and Frederick Cooper. "Beyond Identity." *Theory and Society* 29, nos. 1–4 (2000): 1–47.

Bulliet, Richard W. *Conversion to Islam in the Medieval Period: An Essay in Quantitative History.* Cambridge: Harvard University Press, 1979.

———. *Islam: The View from the Edge.* New York: Columbia University Press, 1994.

Bürgel, Johann Christoph. *The Feather of Simurgh: The "Licit Magic" of the Arts in Medieval Islam.* New York: New York University Press, 1988.

Cahen, Claude. "Le Problème du Shi'isme dans l'Asie Mineure Turque pre-Ottomane." In *Le Shi'isme Imamite*. Paris: Presses Universitaires de France, 1970.

———. "Le Chi'isme Imamite en Iran á l'epoque Seldjoukide d'apres le *Kitāb al-naqz*." *Le Monde Iranien et l'Islam* 1 (1971): 43–67.

Calmard, Jean. "Shi'i Rituals and Power. II, The Consolidation of Safavid Shi'ism: Folklore and Popular Religion." In *Safavid Persia: The History and Politics of an Islamic Society*. Edited by Charles Melville. I.B. Tauris, 1996.

———. "Mohammad b. al-Hanafiyya dans la Religion Popularie, le Folklore, les Lègendes dans le Monde Turco-Persan et Indo-Persan." *Cahier d'Asie Centrale*, nos. 5–6 (1998): 201–220.

Chabbi, J. "Remarques sur le développment historique des mouvements ascétiques et mystiques au Khurasan." *Studia Islamica* 46 (1977): 5–71.

Chardin, Jean. *Les Voyages du Chevalier Chardin en Perse*. Edited by L. Langlès. 10 vols. Paris: Le Normant, 1811.

Chelkowski, Peter J. *Ta'ziyah, Ritual, and Drama in Iran*. New York: New York University Press, 1979.

Choksy, Jamsheed K. *Conflict and Cooperation: Zoroastrian Subalterns and Muslim Elites in Medieval Iranian Society*. New York: Columbia University Press, 1997.

Cohn, Norman Rufus Colin. *Cosmos, Chaos, and the World to Come: The Ancient Roots of Apocalyptic Faith*. New Haven: Yale University Press, 1993.

Cole, Juan Ricardo. *Modernity and the Millennium: The Genesis of the Baha'i Faith in the Nineteenth-Century Middle East*. New York: Columbia University Press, 1998.

Collingwood, R. G. *Essays in the Philosophy of History*. Austin: University of Texas Press, 1965.

Combs-Shilling, Elaine. *Sacred Performances: Islam, Sexuality, and Sacrifice*. New York: Columbia University Press, 1989.

Cooperson, Michael. "The Heirs of the Prophets in Classical Arabic Biography." Ph.D. diss., Harvard University, 1994.

Corbin, Henry. *Cyclical Time and Isma'ili Gnosis: Islamic Texts and Contexts*. London: Kegan Paul, 1983.

————. *Histoire de la Philosophie Islamique.* Paris: Gallimard, 1964.

————. *En Islam Iranien, Aspects Spirituels et Philosophiques.* Paris: Gallimard, 1971.

————. "La Place de Molla Sadrā Shirāzī (d. 1050/1640) dans la Philosophie Iranienne." *Studia Islamica* 18 (1963): 6–113.

————. *The Voyage and the Messenger: Iran and Philosophy.* Translated by Joseph H. Rowe. Berkeley, CA: North Atlantic Books, 1998.

Crone, Patricia. "Kavad's Heresy and Mazdak's Revolt." *Iran: Journal of the British Institute of Persian Studies* 24 (1991): 21–42.

————. "Zoroastrian Communism." *Comparative Studies in Society and History* 36 (1994): 447–462.

Daftary, Farhad. *The Ismā'īlīs: Their History and Doctrines.* Cambridge: Cambridge University Press, 1990.

Dale, Stephen. "Steppe Humanism: The Autobiographical Writings of Zahir al-Din Muhammad Babur, 1483–1530." *International Journal of Middle East Studies* 22 (1990): 37–58.

Daniel, Elton L. *The Political and Social History of Khurasan under Abbasid Rule, 747–820.* Minneapolis: Bibliotheca Islamica, 1979.

Danishmend, Ismail Hami. *İzahlı Osmanli Tarihî Kronolojīsī.* 4 vols. İstanbul: Sermet Matbasi, 1960.

Dānishpazhū, Muhammad Taqī. *Fihrist-i Kitābkhānah-yi Markazī-yi Dānishgāh-i Tehřan.* Vol. 18. Tehran: Dānishgāh-i Tehran, 1961.

————. *Fihrist-i Mikrufilmhā-yi Kitābkhānah-yi Markazī va Markaz-i Asnād-i Dānishgāh-i Tehran.* 3 vols. Tehran: Dānishgāh-i Tehřan, 1969.

————. "Yik Parda az Zindigāni-yi Shah Tahmasb-i Safavi." *Majallah-yi Dānishkadah-yi Adabiyyāt va 'Ulūm-i Insānī-yi Mashad* 7, no. 4 (1972): 966–988.

Davis, Dick. *Epic and Sedition: The Case of Ferdowsi's Shāhnāme.* Fayetteville: University of Arkansas Press, 1992.

Della Valle, Pietro. *The Pilgrim: The Travels of Pietro Della Valle.* Translated by George Bull. London: Hutchinson, 1990.

Dhalla, Maneckji Nusservanji. *History of Zoroastrianism.* London: Oxford University Press, 1938.

Dickson, Martin B. "Shah Tahmasb and the Uzbeks: The Duel for Khurasan with Ubayd Khan, 930–46/1524–40." Ph.D. diss., Princeton University, 1958.

———. *Unpublished Papers. Middle East Department, Joseph Regenstein Library.* Chicago: University of Chicago.

———. "Uzbek Dynastic Theory in the Sixteenth Century." In *Trudy 25-ogo Mezhdunarodnogo Kongressa Vostokovedov.* Moscow: Izdvo vostochnoi lit-ry, 1963.

Dickson, Martin B., and Stuart Cary Welch, eds. *The Houghton Shāhnāme.* 2 vols. Cambridge: Harvard University Press, 1981.

Dihkhudā, Alī Akbar. *Lughatnāme.* 18 vols. Tehran: Dānishgāh-i Tehrān, 1960.

Dīnawarī, Abū Hanīfah Ahmad b. Dāwūd. *al-Akhbār al-tiwāl.* Edited by Abd al-Mun'im 'Āmir. Cairo: Wizārat al-Thaqāfah wa-al-Irshād al-Qawmī, 1960.

Doerfer, Gerhard. *Türkische und Mongolische Elemente im Neupersischen.* 4 vols. Wiesbaden: Steiner, 1963–1975.

Du Mans, Raphaël. *Estat de la Perse en 1660.* Edited by Charles Henri Auguste Schefer. Paris: Leroux, 1890.

Encyclopaedia Iranica. Edited by Ihsan Yarshater. London and Boston: Routledge & Kegan Paul, 1982–.

Encyclopaedia of Islam (EI2). Edited by H. A. R. Gibb et al. 2nd ed. 4 vols. Leiden: Brill, 1954–.

Encyclopaedia of Islam (EI1). Edited by M. Th Houtsma et al. London: Brill Ltd., Luzac & Co., 1913–1936.

Ende, Werner. "The Flagellation of Muharram and the Shi'ites Ulama." *Der Islam* 55 (1978): 19–36.

Ernst, Carl. *Words of Ecstasy in Sufism.* Albany: State University of New York Press, 1985.

Ergun, Sadeddin Nuzhet. *Hatayi Divāni: Shah Ismā'īl Safevī Edebi Hayati ve Nefesleri.* Istanbul: Maarif Kitāphanesi, 1956.

Falsafī, Nasrallāh. "Sarguzasht-i Sāru Taqi." In *Chand Maqālah-yi Tārīkhī va Adabī.* Tehran: Tehran University 1964.

———. *Zindagānī-yi Shah 'Abbās-i Avval.* Tehran: Chāp-i Kayvān, 1955.

Farhad, Massumeh. "The Art of Mu'īn Musavvir: A Mirror of his Times." In *Persian Masters: Five Centuries of Painting*. Edited by Sheila R. Canby. Bombay: Marg, 1990.

Ferdowsi. *Shāhnāme*. Edited by Jules Mohl. 4 vols. Tehran: Intishārāt-i Ilmī va Farhangī, 1995.

———. *Shāhnāme*. Edited by Jalāl Khāliqī Mutlaq. 6 vols. New York: State University of New York Press, 1978.

———. *Shākh-name; Kriticheskiĭ Tekst, Pamīātniki Literatur Narodov Vostoka; Teksty. Bolshaīā Seriīā*. Edited by A. Y. Bertel et al. Moscow, 1960–1971.

Feridun, Bey. *Mecmu'a-yi Münşeat-i Feridun Bey*. īstanbul: Takvimhāne-yi Āmire, 1848–1850.

Findiriskī, Abū Tālib Mīr. *Tuhfat al-'ālam*. Tehran University Microfilm, MS 4955.

Fleischer, Cornell. "The Lawgiver as Messiah: The Making of the Imperial Image in the Reign of Süleymān." In *Soliman le Magnifique et son Temps: Actes du Colloque de Paris Galeries Nationales du Grand Palais*. Edited by Gilles Veinstein. Paris: Ecole du Louvre, 1990.

———. *Bureaucrat and Intellectual in the Ottoman Empire: The Historian Mustafa Ali (1541–1600)*. Princeton Studies on the Near East. Princeton: Princeton University Press, 1986.

———. *Mediterranean Apocalypse*. Princeton: Princeton University Press, forthcoming.

Floor, Willem. "The Rise and Fall of Mirza Taqi, the Eunuch Grand Vizier (1043–55/1633–45)." *Studia Iranica* 26 (1997): 237–266.

Fragner, Bert. *Repertorium Persischer Herrscherurkunden*. Freiburg: Klaus Schwarz Verlag, 1980.

Frye, Richard. "The Charisma of Kingship in Ancient Iran." *Iranica Antiqua* 4 (1964): 36–54.

———. "Pre-Islamic and Early Islamic Culture in Central Asia." In *Turco-Persia in Historical Perspective*. Edited by R. Canfield. Cambridge: Harvard University Press, 1991.

Gaillard, Marina. *Le Livre de Samak-i Ayyār*. Paris: L'Institut D'Etudes Iraniennes, 1987.

Gazārghā'ī, Kamāl al-dīn Husayn Tabasī. *Majālis al-'ushshāq.* Bānkipore, MS 663.

Geertz, Clifford. *The Interpretation of Cultures: Selected Essays.* New York: Basic Books, 1973.

Ghaffārī, Ahmad b. Muhammad. *Tārīkh-i Jahān Ārā.* Edited by Hasan Narāqī. Tehran: Kitābfurūshī-yi Hāfez, 1963.

Gibb, H. A. R., and H. Bowen. *Islamic Society and the West.* Part I, 2 vols. London: Oxford University Press, 1950

Gölpīnarlī, Abdülbāki. "Islam ve Türk Illerinde Fütüvvet Teşkilātī." *Istanbul Universitesi Iktisāt Fakultesi Mecmuasī* 11 (1953): 3–354.

——. "Menākib-i Hācī Bektāsh-i Velī." *Vilāyet-Nāme.* Istanbul: Inkilāb Kitābevi, 1958.

Golsokhri, Shohreh. "Isma'il II and Mirza Makhdum Sharifi: An Interlude in Safavid History." *International Journal of Middle East Studies* 26 (1994): 477–488.

Goodman, Louis Sanford, and Alfred Gilman. *The Pharmacological Basis of Therapeutics: A Textbook of Pharmacology, Toxicology and Therapeutics for Physicians and Medical Students.* New York: Macmillan, 1985.

Gulchīn-Ma'ānī, Ahmad. *Tārīkh-i Tazkirah'hā-yi Fārsī.* 2 vols. Tehran: Kitābkhānah-yi Sanā'ī, 1970–1972.

Gurevich, Aron. *Time as a Problem of Cultural History: Cultures and Time.* Paris: n.p., 1976.

Gusdorf, George S. "Conditions and Limits of Autobiography." In *Autobiography: Essays Theoretical and Critical.* Edited by James Olney. Princeton: Princeton University Press, 1980.

Hāfez, *Dīvān-i Hāfez.* Edited by Muhammad Qazvīnī, Qāsim Ghanī and Abd al-Karīm Jurbuzahdār, eds. Tehran: Asātīr, 1988.

Haider, Mansur. "The Mongol Traditions and Their Survival in Central Asia (Fourteenth to Fifteenth Centuries)." *Central Asiatic Journal* 28, no. 1–2 (1984): 57–79.

Hāirī, 'Abd al-Husayn, et al. *Fihrist-i Kitābkhānah-yi Majlisi-i Shu'rā-yi Millī.* 21 vols. Tehran: Majlisi-i Shu'rā-yi Millī, 1965.

Hakīm Ruknā-yi Kāshī. *Dişan.* Tehran: n.p., 1973.

Halm, Heinz. *The Empire of the Mahdi: The Rise of the Fatimids.* Translated by M. Bonner. Leiden: Brill, 1996.

————. *Shi'ism.* edinburgh: Edinburgh University Press, 1991.

Hamavī, Muhammad b. Ishāq. *Anīs al-mu'minīn.* Edited by Mir Hāshim Muhaddis. Tehran: Bunyād-i Ba'sat, 1984.

Hammoudi, Abdellah. *Master and Disciple: The Cultural Foundations of Moroccan Authoritarianism.* Chicago: University of Chicago Press, 1997.

Hanbal b., Ishāq. *al-fitn: Jam' fīhi adadan min al-ahādīth wa-al-āthār al-muta'allaqah bi-al-masīh al-dajjāl.* Edited by Amir Hasan Sabrī. Vol. 8–9. Beirut: Dār al-Bashā'ir al-Islāmīyah, 1998.

Haneda, Masashi. *Le Chah et les Qizilbash: Le System militaire Safavide.* Berlin: Klaus Schwarz Verlag, 1987.

Hanne, Eric. "The Caliphate Revisited: The Abbasids of Eleventh- and Twelfth-Century Baghdad." Ph.D. diss., University of Michigan, 1998.

Haravī, Sadr al-Dīn Sulṭan Ibrāhīm Amīnī. *Futūhāt-i Shāhī.* Kitābkhānah-i Vazīrī-yi Yazd, MS 5774.

Heger, Nomi. "The Status and the Image of the Persianate Artist." Ph.D. diss., Princeton University, 1997.

Heller, Thomas C., and Christine Brooke-Rose. *Reconstructing Individualism: Autonomy, Individuality, and the Self in Western Thought.* Stanford: Stanford University Press, 1986.

Herzig, Edmund. "The Armenian Merchants of New Julfa: A Study in Premodern Asian Trade." Ph.D. diss., Oxford University, 1991.

Hidāyat, Sādiq. *Nayrangistān.* In *Farhang-i 'Āmīyānah-yi Mardum-i Irān.* Tehran: Nashr-i Chishmah, 1999.

Hodgson, Marshall G. S. "How the Early Shi'a Became Sectarian." *Journal of the American Oriental Society* 75 (1955): 1–13.

————. *The Venture of Islam: Conscience and History in a World Civilization.* 3 vols. Chicago: University of Chicago Press, 1974.

Holt, P. M., Ann K. S. Lambton, and Bernard Lewis, eds. *The Cambridge History of Islam.* Cambridge: Cambridge University Press, 1970.

Horn, Paul. "Die Denkwürdigkeiten des Schah Tahmasp I. von Persien." *Zeitschrift der Deutschen Morgenländischen Gesellschaft* 44 (1890).

Hunarfar, Lutfallāh. "Mashāghil-i Arāmana-yi Julfa." *Majallah-yi Vahīd* 8 (1964): 68–73.

———. *Ganjīnah-yi Āsār Tārīkh-i Isfahān.* Isfahan: Kitabfurūshi-yi Saqafī, 1965.

Hunt, Lynn, ed. *The New Cultural History.* Berkeley: California University Press, 1989.

Huqūqī, Askar. *Tahqīq dar Tafsīr-i Abū al-Futūh.* Tehran: Tehran University, 1967.

al-Hurr al-'Āmilī, Muhammad b. al-Hasan. *Amal al-'āmil.* Edited by Ahmad al-Husaynī. 2 vols. Baghdad: Maktab al-Andalūs, 1965–1966.

al-Hurr al-'Āmilī, Muhammad b. al-Hasan. *Wasā'l al-shī'āh ilā tahsīl masā'il al-sharī'a.* Edited by Abd al-Rahīm Rabbānī, Muhammad b. Alī Sharīf al-Rāzī, and Abū al-Hasan Sha'rānī. Tehran: Maktabat al-Islāmīyah, 1961.

Husaynī, Sayyid Ahmad. *Fihrist-i Kitābkhānah-yi 'Umūmī-yi Hazrat-i Āyatullāh al-'Uzma Najafī Mar'ashī.* 20 vols. Qum: Mihr-i Ustuvār, n.d.

Ibn Bābūyā [al-Sadūq]. *Man lā yahduruhu al-faqīh.* Edited by Ali Akbar al-Ghaffarī. Qum: Jamā'at al-Mudarrisīn, 1972–1975.

Ibn Bazzāz Tavakkul b. Isma'īl. *Safvat al-safā.* Edited by Ghulām Reza Tabātabā'ī Majd. Ardabil: G. Tabātabā'ī Majd, 1994.

Ibn-i Khaldun. *The Muqaddimah: An Introduction to History.* Translated by Franz Rosenthal. Princeton: Princeton University Press, 1967.

Inalcik, Halil. *The Ottoman Empire: The Classical Age, 1300–1600.* Translated by N. Itzkowitz and C. Imber. London: Wiedenfeld and Nicholson, 1973.

———. "The Emergence of the Ottomans." In *Cambridge History of Islam.* Vol. 1. Cambridge: Cambridge University Press, 1970.

Isfahānī, Muhammad Ma'sum b. Khwajagī. *Khulāsat al-siyar.* Tehran: Intishārāt-i 'Ilmī, 1989.

Isfāhānī Muhammad Yūsuf Vālih. *Khuld-i Barīn.* British Library, MS 4132.

Iqbāl, Abbās. *Khānadān-i Nawbakhtī.* Tehran: Tahurī, 1966.

Islam Ansiklopedisi. 12 vols. Istanbul: Milli Egitim Basimevi, 1940–1978.

Ja'farī, Ja'far b. Muhammad. *Tārīkh-i Yazd.* Edited by Iraj Afshār. Tehran: Bungāh-i Tarjumah va Nashr-i Kitāb, 1960.

Ja'fariān, Rasūl. *Dīn va Siyāsat dar Dawrah-yi Safavī.* Qum: Intisharat-i Ansariyan, 1991.

———. "Intiqād az Vazī'at-i Jāmi'ī-yi Dīnī-yi Asr-i Safavī." *Kayhān-i Andīshah* 37 (1991): 155–165.

———. *Qissahkhwānān dar Tārīkh-i Irān va Islam.* Qum: Intishārāt-i Dalīl, 1997.

———. *Maqālāt-i Tārikh-ī.* 3 vols. Qum: Nashr al-Hādī.

———. "Rūyārūyi-i Faqīhān va Sūfīyān dar 'Asr-i Safaviyya." *Kayhān-i Andīshah* 33 (1990): 101–128.

Jamasp Namak or "The Book of Jamaspi." Translated by Jivanji Jamshedji Modi. Avesta, 1903 [2001]. Available from http://www.avesta.org/pahlavi/jamaspi.htm.

Kafadar, Cemal. *Between Two Worlds: The Construction of the Ottoman State.* Berkeley: University of California Press, 1995.

———. "Self and Others: The Diary of a Dervish in Seventeenth-Century Istanbul and First-Person Narratives in Ottoman Literature." *Studia Islamica* 69 (1989): 121–150.

Karamustafa, Ahmet T. *God's Unruly Friends: Dervish Groups in the Islamic Later Middle Period, 1200–1550.* Salt Lake City: University of Utah Press, 1994.

Kārnāme-yi Ardashīr-i Bābakān. Edited by Muhammad Javād Mashkūr. Tehran: Dunyā-yi Kitāb, 1990.

———. *Dah Risālah.* Edited by Rasūl Ja'fariān. Isfahan: Imam Ali Public Library, 1992.

Kāshānī, Muhsin-i Fayz. "Muhākama bayn al-mutasawwifa wa ghayrihīm." *Nashriyah-yi Dānishkadah-yi Adabiyāt-i Tabriz* 9, no. 2 (1957): 118–135.

Kashani-Sabet, Firuzeh. *Frontier Fictions: The Shaping of the Iranian Nation, 1904–1946.* Princeton: Princeton University Press, 1999.

Kāshī, Mawlanā Shaykh Hasan. *Tārīkh-i Muhammadī.* Edited by Rasūl Ja'fariān. Qum: Kitābkhānah-yi Takhassusī-yi Tārīkh-i Islam va Irān, 1998.

Kāshifī, Husayn Vā'iz. *Futuvvatnāme-yi Sultānī.* Edited by Muhammad Ja'far Mahjūb. Tehran: Buhyad-i Farhang-i Iran, 1971.

Kasravī, Ahmad. *Musha'sha'īyān.* 3rd ed. Tehran: Intishārāt-i Sahar, 1977.

———. *Shaykh Safī va Tabārash.* Tehran: Nashr va Pakhsh-i Kitāb, 1976.

———. *"Tārīkhchah-i Shīr va Khurshīd."* Armaghan 11, 7 (1930): 542–554.

Katz, Jonathan Glustrom. *Dreams, Sufism, and Sainthood: The Visionary Career of Muhammad al-Zawāwī.* Leiden: Brill, 1996.

Kay Kāvūs b. Iskandar b. Qābūs b. Vashmgīr. *Qābūsnāme.* Edited by Reuben Levy. London: Luzac, 1951.

Kennedy, Hugh. *The Early Abbasid Caliphate: A Political History.* London: Croom Helm, 1981.

Keyvani, Mehdi. *Artisans and Guild Life in the Later Safavid Period: Contributions to the Social-Economic History of Persia.* Vol. 65, Islamkundliche Untersuchungen. Berlin: Klaus Schwarz, 1982.

Khākī-yi Khurāsānī. *Dīvān-i Khākī.* Edited by Ivanov. Bombay: A. A. A. Fryzee, 1933.

Khalidi, Tarif. *Arabic Historical Thought in the Classical Period.* Cambridge Studies in Islamic Civilization. Cambridge: Cambridge Uiversity Press, 1994.

Khānbābā, Mushār. *Fihrist-i Kitābhāh-yi Chāpī-yi Fārsī.* Tehran: Bungāh-i Tarjumah va Nashr-i Kitāb, 1971.

Khatā'ī. *Il Canzoniere di Shah Isma'il.* Edited by Tourkhan Gandjei. Naples: Instituto Universitario Orientale, 1959.

Khoury, Nuha. *Ideologies and Inscriptions: The Epigraphy of the Masjid-i Shah and the Ahmediye in the Context of Safavid-Ottoman Relations. Muqarnas.* Leiden: Brill, forthcoming.

Khunjī-Isfahānī, Fazl Allah b. Rūzbihān. *Tārīkh-i 'Ālam Ārā-yi Amīnī.* Edited by John E. Woods. London: Royal Asiatic Society, 1993.

———. *Persia in A.D. 1487–1490: An Abridged Translation of Fazlullā b. Rūzbihān Khunjī's Tārīkh-i 'Ālam Ārā-yi Amīnī.* Edited by V. Minosky. London: Royal Asiatic Society, 1957.

Khwāndamīr, Ghiyās al-dīn. *Tārīkh-i Habīb al-siyar.* Edited by Jalāl al-dīn Humā'i. Tehran: Khayyām, 1954.

Khwānsāri, Āqā Jamāl. *'Aqā'id al-nisā'*. Edited by Mahmud Katīrā'ī. Tehran: Tāhirī Press, 1970.

Khwānsāri, Muhammad Bāqir. *Rawzāt al-jannāt fī ahwāl al-'ulamā wa al-sādāt*. Edited by Sayyid Muhammad Taqī al-Kāshifī. 8 vols. Tehran: Dār al-Kutūb al-Islāmiyya, 1970.

———. *Rawzāt al-jannāt fī Ahwāl al-'ulamā wa al-sādāt*. Persian translation by Hajj Shaykh Muhammad Bāqir Sā'idī Khurāsānī. 2 vols. Tehran: n.p., 1970.

Kiyā, Sādiq. "Nuqtaviyān yā Pasikhāniyān." *Iran Kudeh* 13 (1941): 1–132.

———. *Vazhahnāme-yi Gurgānī*. Tehran: Dānishgāh-i Tehran, 1951.

Klimkeit, Hans-Joachim. *Manichaean Art and Calligraphy*. Leiden: Brill, 1982.

Kissah-yi Sayyid Junayd ve Reshīd-i Arab. Bibliothèque Nationale de Paris, Supplement Turc, MS 636.

Knysh, Alexander D. *Islamic Mysticism: A Short History*. Vol. 1, Themes in Islamic Studies. Leiden: E. J. Brill, 2000.

Kohlberg, Etan. "From Imāmiyya to Ithnā-'ashariyya." *Bulletin of the School of Oriental and African Studies* 39 (1976): 521–534.

Kollmann, Nancy Shields. *By Honor Bound: State and Society in Early Modern Russia*. Ithaca: Cornell University Press, 1999.

Köprülü, Mehmet Fuat. *Islam in Anatolia after the Turkish Invasion: Prolegomena*. Translated and edited by Gary Leiser. Salt Lake City: University of Utah Press, 1993.

———. *The Origins of the Ottoman Empire*. Translated by Gary Leiser, SUNY Series in the Social and Economic History of the Middle East. Albany: State University of New York Press, 1992.

Kotov, Fedot Afanas'evich. *Khozhenie kuptsa Fedota Kotova v Persiiu*. Moscow: Izd-vo vostochnoi lit-ry, 1958.

Krader, Lawrence. *Social Organization of the Mongol-Turkic Pastoral Nomads*. The Hague: Mouton, 1993.

Krasnowolska, Anne. *Some Key Figures of Iranian Calendar Mythology*. Krakow: Universitas, 1998.

Kulaynī, Muhammad b. Ya'qūb. *al-Kāfī fī 'ilm al-dīn*. Edited by 'Alī Akbar Ghaffārī. Tehran: Maktabah al-Islāmiyah, 1957–1960.

Lassner, Jacob. *Islamic Revolution and Historical Memory: An Inquiry into the Art of 'Abbāsid Apologetics*. Vol. 66, American Oriental Series. New Haven: American Oriental Society, 1986.

Le Gall, Dina. "The Ottoman Naqshbandiyya in the Pre-Mujaddidi Phase: A Study in Islamic Religious Culture and Its Transmission." Ph.D. diss., Princeton University, 1989.

Le Roy Ladurie, Emmanuel. *Le Territoire de l'historien (The Mind and Method of the Historian)*. Translated by Siān Reynolds and Ben Reynolds. Chicago: University of Chicago Press, 1978.

Levy, Reuben. *The Epic of the Kings: Shāhnāme, the National Epic of Persia*. New York: Mazda, 1980.

Lewis, Bernard, and P. M. Holt, eds. *Historians of the Middle East*. Vol. 4, Historical Writing on the Peoples of Asia. London: Oxford University Press, 1962.

L'Orange, Hans Peter. *Studies on the Iconography of Cosmic Kingship in the Ancient World*. Cambridge: Harvard University Press, 1953.

Losensky, Paul. *Welcoming Fighani: Imitation and Poetic Individuality in the Safavid-Mughal Ghazal*. Costa Mesa: Mazda, 1998.

Lotman, Yuri M. *Universe of the Mind: A Semiotic Theory of Culture*. Bloomington: Indiana University Press, 1990.

Lotman, Yuri M., and Boris A. Uspenskii. *The Semiotics of Russian Culture*. Translated by Ann Shukman. Vol. 11, *Michigan Slavic Contributions*. Ann Arbor: University of Michigan Press, 1984.

Ma'sūm 'Alī Shah, Muhammad Ma'sūm Shīrāzī. *Tarīqat al-haqā'iq*. Edited by Muhammad Ja'far Muhjūb. 3 vols. Tehran: Kitābkhānah-yi Bārān, 1960.

Madelung, Wilferd. *Religious Trends in Early Islamic Iran*. Vol. 4, *Columbia Lectures on Iranian Studies*. Albany, NY: Persian Heritage Foundation, 1988.

Mahdavī, Sayyid Muslih al-Dīn. *Tazkirat al-Qubūr yā Dānishmandān va Buzurgān-i Isfahān*. Isfahan, n.p., 1969–1970.

―――. *Zindigīnāmah-yi 'Allamah Majlisī*. 2 vols. Isfahan: n.p., n.d.

Mahjūb, Muhammad Ja'far. "Dāstānhā-yi 'Āmiyānāh-i Fārsī." *Majallah-i Sukhan* 10, nos. 1–3 (1959): 167–386.

―――. "The Evolution of Popular Eulogy of the Imams along the Shi'a." In *Authority and Political Culture in Shi'ism*. Edited by Said

Amir Arjomand. Translated and adapted by John Perry. Albany: State University of New York Press, 1988.

Majlisī, Jr., Muhammad Bāqir b. Muhammad Taqī. *Bihār al-anwār.* 110 vols. Tehran: Dār al-Kutub al-Islāmīyah, 1948–1968.

———. *Raj'a.* Edited by Abū Zarr Bīdār. Tehran: Risālat-i Qalam, 1988.

Majlisī (Sr.), Muhammad Taqī. *Ikhtiyārāt al-ayām.* British Library, MS Egerton 1002.

Makdisi, George. "The Diary in Islamic Historiography: Some Notes." *History and Theory* 25 (1986): 173–185.

Mar'ashī, Mīr Taymūr. *Tārīkh-i Khāndān-i Mar'ashī-yi Māzandarān.* Edited by M. Sutūdah. Tehran: Intisharat-i Itilā'āt, 1977.

Mar'ashī Shūshtarī, 'Alā al-Mulk Husaynī Mar'ashī. *Firdaws dar Tārīkh-i Shūshtar va Barkhī az Mashāhīr-i ān.* Edited by Mīr Jalāl al-Dīn Husaynī Urmavī. Tehran: Intishārāt-i Itilā'āt, 1973.

Mar'ashī, Sayyid Zāhir al-Dīn. *Tārīkh-i Gīlān va Daylamistān.* Edited by M. Sutūdah. Tehran: Intishārāt-i Itilā'at, 1968.

———. *Tārīkh-i Tabaristān va Rūyān va Māzandarān.* Edited by M. H. Tasbīhī. Tehran: Intishārāt-i Itilā'āt, 1966.

Marlow, Louise. *Hierarchy and Egalitarianism in Islamic Thought.* Cambridge Studies in Islamic Civilization. Cambridge: Cambridge University Press, 1997.

Massignon, Louis. *La Passion de Husayn b. Mansūr Hallāj: Martyr Mystique de l'Islam.* Paris: Gallimard, 1975.

Mas'ūdī. Ali b. al-Husayn. *Kitāb al-tanbīh wa al-ishrāf.* Edited by M. J. de Goeje and translated by B. Carra da Vaux as *Livre de l'avertissement et de la Rèvision.* Paris: Imprimerie Nationale, 1896.

———. *Murūj al-zahab (Les Prairies d'or).* Translated by C. Barbier de Meynard. 9 vols. Paris: L'imprimerie Impériale, 1861–1877.

Matthee, Rudolph P. *The Politics of Trade in Safavid Iran: Silk for Silver 1600–1730.* Cambridge: Cambridge University Press, 1999.

———. "The Career of Mohammad Beg, Grand Vizier of Shah Abbas II (r. 1642–1666)." *Iranian Studies* 24 (1991): 17–36.

Mazzaoui, Michel, and Vera B. Moreen, eds. *Intellectual Studies on Islam: Essays Written in Honor of Martin B. Dickson.* Salt Lake City: University of Utah Press, 1990.

Mazzaoui, Michel M. *The Origins of the Safavids: Shi'ism, Sufism, and the Ghulāt.* Vol. 3, Freiburger Islamstudien. Wiesbaden: Steiner, 1972.

McChesney, Robert. "The Four Sources on Shah Abbas's Building of Isfahan," *Muqarnas* 5 (1988): 103–134.

———. "A Note on Iskandar Beg's Chronology." *Journal of Near Eastern Studies* 39 (1980): 53–63.

———. "Waqf and Public Policy: The Qaqf of Shah Abbas, 1011–1023/1602–1616." *Asian and African Studies* 15 (1981): 165–190.

Mélikoff, Iréne. *Abu Muslim: Le "Porte-Hache" de Khorasan dans la tradition epique Turco-Iranienne.* Paris: Adrien Maisonneuve, 1962.

Melville, Charles. P., ed. *Persian and Islamic Studies in Honor of P. W. Avery.* Pembroke Papers 1. Cambridge: University of Cambridge, Center for Middle Eastern Studies, 1990.

———. "Shah Abbas and the Pilgrimage to Mashad." In *Safavid Persia: The History and Politics of an Islamic Society.* London: Tauris, 1996.

Membré, Michele. *Mission to the Lord Sophy of Persia (1539–1542).* Translated by A. H. Morton. London: School of Oriental and African Studies, 1993.

Miller, Barnette. *The Palace School of Muhammad the Conqueror.* New York: Arno Press, 1973.

Minorsky, Vladimir. "The Poetry of Shah Isma'il I." *Bulletin of the School of Oriental and African Studies* 10 (1942): 1006–1053.

———. *Tazkirāt al-mulūk.* London: Gibb Memorial Series, 1989.

al-Miqdādī, Muttahar Muhammad [Mīr Lawhī]. *Salvat al-shī'a wa quvvat al-sharī'a.* Mar'ashī Library, MS 4296 and MS 4014.

Mīrkhwand, Muhammad. *Rawzat al-safā.* Edited by 'Abbās Zaryāb. Tehran: Intishārāt-i īlmī, 1994.

Mīrza Rafī'ā. *Dastūr al-mulūk.* Edited by Muhammad Taqī Dānishpazhū. *Majallah-yi Dānishkadah-yi Adabiyāt va 'Ulūm-i Insānī,* Tehran University 16 (nos. 1–4).

Mobed, Shah (Mushin Fānī). *Dabistān al-mazāhib.* Edited by Rahim Rezāzādah-yi Malik. Tehran: Kitābkhānah-i Tahūrī, 1983–1984.

Modarresi-Tabātabā'ī, Sayyid Husayn. *Crisis and Consolidation in the Formative Period of Shi'ite Islam.* Princeton: Darwin Press, 1993.

————. *An Introduction to Shi'i Law: A Bibliographical Study*. London: Ithaca Press, 1984.

————. *Turbat-i Pākān: Āsār va Banāhā-yi Qadīm-i Mahdūdah-yi Kunūnī-yi Dār al-mu'minīn-i Qum*. 2 vols. Qum: Chāpkhānah-yi Mihr, 1957.

————. *Zamīn dar Fiqh-i Islāmī*. 2 vols. Tehran: Daftar-i Nashr-i Farhang-i Islāmī, 1984.

————. *Bargī az Tārīkh-i Qazvīn*. Qum: Mar'ashī Library Press, 1982.

Molé, Marijan. "Les Kubrawiya entre Sunnisme et Shi'isme aux Huitième Siècle de l'Hégire." *Revue des Etudes Islamiques* 29 (1961): 61–142.

Momen, Moojan. *An Introduction to Shi'i Islam: The History and Doctrines of Twelver Shi'ism*. New Haven: Yale University Press, 1985.

Moosa, Matti. *Extremist Shi'ites: The Ghulāt Sects*. Syracuse, NY: Syracuse University Press, 1987.

Morony, Michael G. *Iraq after the Muslim Conquest*. Princeton: Princeton University Press, 1984.

Morris, James Winston. *The Wisdom of the Throne: An Introduction to the Philosophy of Mulla Sadra*. Princeton Library of Asian Translations. Princeton: Princeton University Press, 1981.

————. "Situating Islamic Mysticism: Between Written Traditions and Popular Spirituality." In *Typologies of Mysticism: The Quest for God in Judaism, Christianity and Islam*. Edited by Robert Herrera. Washington, D.C.: Catholic University Press, 1992.

Morton, A. H. "The Ardabil Shrine in the Reign of Shah Tahmasb I." *Iran: Journal of the British Institute of Persian Studies* 12, 13 (1974, 1975): 31–64, 39–58.

————. "The Chub-i Tarīq and Qizilbash Ritual in Safavid Persia." In *Etudes Safavides*. Edited by Jean Calmard. Paris: L'Institut Français de Recherche en Iran, 1993.

————. "The Date and Attribution of the *Ross Anonymous*: Notes on a Persian History of Shah Ismā'il I." In *Persian and Islamic Studies in Honor of P. W. Avery* Edited by Charles P. Melville. Cambridge: Cambridge University Centre for Middle Eastern Studies, 1990.

————. "The Early Years of Shah Isma'il in the *Afzal al-tavārīkh* and Elsewhere." In *Safavid Persia: The History and Politics of an Islamic Society.* Edited by Charles P. Melville. London: Tauris, 1996.

Mottahedeh, Roy. "Some Islamic Views of the Pre-Islamic Past." *Harvard Middle Eastern and Islamic Review* 1 (1994): 17–26.

————. *Loyalty and Leadership in an Early Islamic Society.* Princeton: Princeton University Press, 1980.

————. *The Mantle of the Prophet: Religion and Politics in Iran.* New York: Simon and Schuster, 1985.

———— "The Shu'ubiyah Controversy and the Social History of Early Islamic Iran." *International Journal of Middle Eastern Studies* 7 (1976): 161–182.

Mu'īn, Muhammad. *Farhang-i Fārsī.* 6 vols. Tehran: Amīr Kabīr, 1963–1973.

Mudarris, Muhammad Ali. *Rayhānat al-adab.* 8 vols. Tehran: Chāpkhānah-yi Shirikat-i Sihāmī, 1948–1955.

Munzavī, Ahmad. *Fihrist-i Nuskhahā-yi Khattī-yi Fārsī.* 6 vols. Tehran: Mu'assasah-yi Farhangi, 1969.

Munzavī, 'Alīnaqī, and M. T. Dānishpazhū. *Fihrist-i Kitābkhānah-yi Madrasah-yi Sipahsālār.* 5 vols. Tehran: Chāpkhānah-yi Shirikat-i Sihāmī 1962.

Muqtadirī, Muhammad Taqī. "Pazīrā'ī-yi Shāhānah." *Nashriyah-yi Vizārat-i Umūr-i Khārija* 2 (1956–1957): 48–56.

Najmabadi, Afsaneh. *Women with Mustaches and Men without Beards: Gender and Sexual Anxieties of Iranian Modernity.* Berkeley: University of California Press, forthcoming.

Nakkash, Yitzhak. "An Attempt to Trace the Origins of the Rituals of 'Ashura." *Die Welt des Islams* 33 (1993): 161–181.

Nāsirī, Muhammad Ibrāhīm b. Zayn al-'Abidīn. *Dastūr-i Shahriyārān.* British Library, MS 2942.

Nasr, Sayyid Husayn. "The School of Isfahan." In *A History of Muslim Philosophy.* 2 vols. Edited by M. M. Sharif. Wiesbaden: Steiner, 1966.

Nasrābādī, Muhammad Tāhir. *Tazkirah-yi Nasrābādī.* Edited by V. Dastgirdī. Tehran: Armaghān, 1973.

Navā'ī, 'Abd al-Husayn. *Asnād va Mukātibāt-i Irān.* Tehran: 1984.

————. *Shah Tahmasb Safavī: Majmū'ah-yi Asnād vā Mukātibāt-i Tārīkhī.* Tehran: Intisharat-i Arghavān, 1989.

Nawbakhtī, al-Hasan b. Musā. *Firaq al-shī'a.* Edited by Muhammad Sādiq Bahr al-Ulūm. al-Najaf: al-Matba'ah al-Haydarīyah, 1936.

Necipoglu, Gülru. *Architecture, Ceremonial and Power: The Topkapi Palace in the Fifteenth and Sixteenth Centuries.* Cambridge: MIT Press, 1991.

————. *The Topkapi Scroll: Geometry and Ornament in Islamic Architecture. Topkapi Palace Museum Library MS H. 1956, Sketchbooks and Albums.* Santa Monica, CA: Getty Center for the History of Art and the Humanities, 1995.

Neusner, Jacob. *Formative Judaism: Religious, Historical, and Literary Studies: Second Series.* Vol. 41, Brown Judaic Studies. Chico, CA: Scholars Press, 1983.

Newman, Andrew. "The Myth of the Clerical Migration to Safavid Iran." *Die Welt des Islams* 33 (1993): 66–112.

————. "Towards a Reconsideration of the Isfahan School of Philosophy: Shaykh Baha'i and the Role of the Safavid Ulama." *Studia Iranica* 15 (1986): 165–199.

Nora, Pierre. *Realms of Memory: Rethinking the French Past.* Translated by Arthur Goldhammer. New York: Columbia University Press, 1996.

North, John David, and Roy Porter. *The Norton History of Astronomy and Cosmology.* New York: Norton, 1994.

O'Connor, Kathleen. "The Alchemical Creation of Life (Takwīn) and Other Concepts of Genesis in Medieval Islam." Ph.D. diss., University of Pennsylvania, 1994.

Olearius, Adam. *The Voyages and Travels of the Ambassadors Sent by Frederick, Duke of Holstein, to the Great Duke of Muscovy and the King of Persia,* 3 vols. London: Printed for John Starkey and Thomas Basset, 1669.

Omidsalar, Mahmoud. "Storytellers in Classical Persian Texts." *Journal of American Folklore* 97, no. 384 (April–June 1984): 204–212.

Page, Mary Ellen. "Professional Storytelling in Iran: Transmission and Practice." *Iranian Studies* 7, no. 3–4 (1979): 195–215.

Pakalin, Mehmet Zaki. *Osmanli Tarihi Deyinleri ve Termileri Sözlügü.* 2nd ed. 3 vols. Istanbul: Millī Egitim Basimevi, 1971.

Pascal, Roy. *Design and Truth in Autobiography.* Cambridge: Harvard University Press, 1960.

Pearson, James. *Index Islamicus, 1906–1955.* London: Bowker-Saur, 1958.

Perikhanian, A. "Iranian Society and Law." *The Cambridge History of Iran.* Edited by Ihsan Yarshater. Vol. 3 (2). Cambridge: Cambridge University Press, 1983.

Petrushevski, I. *Kishāvarzī va Munāsibāt-i Arzī dar Irān-i 'Ahd-i Mughūl.* Translated by Karīm Kishāvarz. Tehran: Bungāh-i Tarjumah va Nashr-i Kitāb 1976–1977.

———. "Nahzat-i Sarbidārān." Translated by Karim Kishāvarz. *Farhang-i Irān Zamīn* 10 (1962): 124–224.

Pierce, Leslie. *The Imperial Harem: Women and Sovereignty in the Ottoman Empire.* London: Oxford University Press, 1993.

Pingree, David Edwin. *The Thousands of Abū Ma'shar.* Vol. 30, Studies of the Warburg Institute. London: Warburg Institute, 1968.

Pirouzdjou, Hassan. *Mithraïsme et Emancipation: Anthropologie Sociale et Culturelle des Mouvements Populaires en Iran au VIIIe, IXe et du XIVe au Début du XVIe siècle: Le Cas du Mouvement Safavide.* Paris: Harmattan, 1999.

Pourshariati, Parvaneh. "Iranian Tradition in Tus and the Arab Presence in Khurasan." Ph.D. diss., Columbia University, 1995.

Pseudo-Ardabīlī, Ahmad b. Muhammad. *Hadīqat al-shī'a.* Tehran: n.p., 1964.

al-Qadi, Wadad. "The Development of the Term *Ghulāt* in Muslim Literature with Special Reference to the Kaysaniyya." In *Akten des VII. Kongresses Für Arabistik und Islamwissenschaft Göttingen.* Edited by Albert Dietrich. Göttingen: Vandenhoeck & Ruprecht, Abhandlungen der Akademie der Wissenschaften in Göttingen, 1976.

Qazīnī, Muhammad Tāhir Vahīd. *'Abbāsnāme.* Edited by I. Dihqān. Arāk: Kitabfurushī-yi Davudī, 1950–1951.

Qazvīnī Rāzī, Abd al-Jalīl. *Kitāb al-naqz.* Edited by Sayyid Jalāl al-dīn Husaynī Urmavī. Tehran: Chapkhānah-yi Sipihr, 1952.

Quinn, Sholeh Alysia. *Historical Writing during the Reign of Shah 'Abbās: Ideology, Imitation, and Legitimacy in Safavid Chronicles.* Salt Lake City: University of Utah Press, 2000.

Qummī, Muhammad Tāhir b. Muhammad Husayn. *Risālah-yi Radd bar Sūfiyān.* Mar'ashī Library, MS 4014.

———. *Tuhfat al-akhyār.* Qum: Intisharat-i Nūr, 1973.

———. *Usūl al-fusūl al-tawzīh.* Mar'ashī Library, MS 4296.

———. *al-fawā'id al-dīniyya.* Tehran University Library, MS 2479.

Qummī, Qāzī Ahmad. *Gulistān-i Hunar.* Edited by Ahmad Suhaylī Khwānsārī. Tehran: Kitabkhanah-yi Manuchehri, 1973.

———. *Khulāsat al-tavārīkh.* 2 vols. Edited by Ihsān Ishrāqī. Tehran: Tehran University Press, 1980 and 1984.

Rabbi Yehudah ben El Azar. *Duties of Judah.* Translated by Amnon Netzer. Jerusalem: Ben Zvi Institute, 1995.

Radtke, Bernd. "Iranian and Gnostic Elements in Early Tasawwuf Observations Concering the Umm al-kitāb." *Proceedings of the First European Conference of Iranian Studies.* Edited by G. Gnoli and A. Panaino. Rome: Istituto Italiano Per il Medio ed Estremo Oriente, 1990.

Rahman, Fazlur. *The Philosophy of Mulla Sadra.* Albany: State University of New York Press, 1975.

Razavī, Mīr Muhammad Zamān b. Ja'far. *Sahīfat al-irshād.* Mar'ashī Library, MS 4014 (Majm'ūah).

al-Rāzī, Abū Bakr Muhamamd b. Zakariya. *Abi Bakr Mohammadi Filii Zachariae Raghensis Opera Philosophica.* Edited by Paul Kraus. Cairo: n.p., 1939.

Rāzī, Muhammad b. Husaynī al-Murtazā. *Tabsīrāt al-'avāmm.* Edited by Abbās Iqbāl. Tehran: Matba'-yi Majlis, 1934.

Redhouse, Sir James. *Turkish-English Lexicon.* Istanbul: Kalem Matbaasi, 1980.

Ricoeur, Paul. *Time and Narrative.* Translated by Kathleen McLaughlin. 3 vols. Chicago: University of Chicago Press, 1984.

Rieu, Charles. *Catalogue of Persian Manuscripts in the British Museum.* London: British Museum, 1879–1883.

———. *Supplement to the Catalogue of Persian Manuscripts in the British Museum.* London: British Museum, 1895.

Rizvi, Kishwar. "Transformation in Early Safavid Architecture: The Shrine of Shaykh Safi al-din Ardabili in Iran." Ph.D. diss., Massachusetts Institute of Technology, 2000.

Roemer, Hans R. "The Safavid Period." In *Cambridge History of Iran,* vol. 6, *The Timurid and Safavid Periods,* ed. Peter Jackson and Laurence Lockhart, 189–350. Cambridge: Cambridge University Press, 1986.

Röhrborn, K. M. *Nizām-i Iyālāt dar Dawrah-yi Safaviyyah (Provinzen und Zentralgewalt Persiens im 16. und 17. Jahrhundert).* Translated by Kaykāvūs Jahāndārī. Tehran: Bungāh-i Tarjumah va Nashr-i Kitāb, 1978.

Rossabi, Morris. "Khublai Khan and the Women in His Family." In *Studia Sino-Mongolica: Festschrift für Herbert Franke.* Edited by W. Bauer. Wiesbaden: Steiner, 1979.

Rūmlū, Hasan Bek. *Ahsān al-tavārīkh.* Edited by 'Abd al-Husayn Navā'ī. Tehran: Bungah-i Tarjumah va Nashr-i Kitāb, 1978.

Russell, James. "Mysticism and Esotericism among Zoroastrians." *Iranian Studies* 26 (1993): 73–94.

Sabzavārī, Muhammad b. Muhammad Lawhī (Mīr Lawhī). *Kifāyat al-muhtadī fī ma'rifat al-mahdī (Arba'īn).* Tehran University, MS 1154.

Sa'dī. *Gulistān-i Sa'dī.* Edited by Ghulām Husayn Yūsufī. Tehran: Khwārazmī, 1989.

Sadighi, Gholam Hossein. *Les Mouvements Religieux Iraniens au IIe et au IIIe siècle de l'hegire.* Paris: Les Presses Modernes, 1938.

Sadiqi Bek. *Majma' al-khawāss.* Edited by 'Abd al-Rasūl Khayyāmpūr. Tabriz: Akhatr-i Shumāl, 1948.

Safavī, Sām Mīrzā. *Tuhfah-yi Sāmī.* Edited by Rukn al-Dīn Humāyūn Farrūkh. Tehran: 'Ilmī, n.d.

Safavī, Shah Tahmasb. *Bayāz-i Mukālimah-yi Shah Tahmasb bā īlchīyān.* St. Petersberg, Dorn MS 302.

———. *Tazkire-yi Shah Tahmasb.* Edited by D. C. Phillott. Calcutta: Asiatic Society, 1912.

Sanuto, Marino. *I diarii di Marino Sanuto (MCCCCXCVI–MDXXXIII) dall'autografo Marciano ital. cl. VII codd. CDXIX–CDLXXVII.* Edited by Federico Stefani, Guglielmo Berchet, et al. Venice: Visentini, 1879–1903.

Schimmel, Annemarie. *The Triumphal Sun: A Study of the Works of Jalāliddin Rumi.* London: East-West Publications, 1980.

Scholem, Gershom Gerhard. *Kabbalah.* New York: Merdian, 1978.

Scott-Meisami, Julie. *Persian Historiography to the End of the Twelfth Century.* Edinburgh: Edinburgh University Press, 1999.

————. "The Past in the Service of the Present: Two Views of History in Medieval Persia." *Poetics Today* 14, no. 2 (1993): 247–275.

Serefeddin, M. "Simavne Kadisi Oglü Shaykh Bedreddin'e Dair Bir Kitāp." *Turkiyat Mecmuasi (Istanbul Universitesi Enstitusu),* 3 (1926–1933): 233–256.

Sewell, William. "Geertz, Cultural Systems, and History: From Synchrony to Transformation. In *The Fate of "Culture": Geertz and Beyond.* Edited by Sherry Ortner. Berkeley: University of California Press, 1999.

Shahīdī, Shaykh Zayn al-dīn b. Muhammad. *al-Sihām al-māriqah fi ighrāz al-zanādiqah.* Mar'ashī Library, MS 1576.

Shahrastānī, Muhammad ibn Abd al-Karīm. *al-Milal wa-al-nihal.* Edited by M. R. Jalālī Nā'īnī. Tehran: n.p., 1971.

Shaked, Shaul. *Esoteric Trends in Zoroastrianism.* Jerusalem: Israel Academy of Sciences and Humanities, 1969.

————. *From Zoroastrian Iran to Islam: Studies in Religious History and Intercultural Contacts.* Aldershot: Variorum, 1995.

————, trans. and ed., *The Wisdom of the Sasanian Sages: Denkard VI.* Boulder: Westview Press, 1979.

Shaki, Mansour. "The Sassanian Matrimonial Relations." *Archīv Orientālnī* 39 (1971): 322–345.

————. "The Social Doctrine of Mazdak in the Light of Middle Persian Evidence." *Archīv Orienālnī* 46 (1978): 289–306.

————. "The Cosmogonical and Cosmological Teachings of Mazdak." *Acta Iranica: Papers in Honour of Professor Mary Boyce.* Leiden: Brill, 1985.

Shāmlū, Valī Qulī. *Qisas al-khāqānī.* Bibliothèque Nationale, MS Suppl. Pers. 227.

Sharif, M. M. *A History of Muslim Philosophy: With Short Accounts of Other Disciplines and the Modern Renaissance in Muslim Lands.* Wiesbaden: Harrassowitz, 1963.

Shaw, Gregory. *Theurgy and the Soul: The Neoplatonism of Iamblichus.* University Park, PA: Pennsylvania State University Press, 1995.

Shaybī, Kāmil Mustafā. *Sufism and Shī'ism.* Surbiton, Surrey, England: Laam, 1991.

Shīrāzī, 'Abdī Bek Khwajah Zayn al-'Abidīn 'Alī. *Takmīlat al-akhbār.* Edited by 'Abd al-Husayn Navā'ī. Tehran: Nashr-i Nay, 1990.

Shīrāzī, Sadr al-Dīn Muhammdad (Mullā Sadrā). *Kasr asnām al-jāhiliyya.* Edited by M. T. Dānishpazhūh. Tehran: Matbalat Jāmilat, 1962.

———. *Risālah-yi Sih Asl.* Edited by S. H. Nasr. Tehran: Tehran University, 1961.

Shūshtarī, Nūr Allah b. Abd Allah. *Majālis al-mu'minīn.* 2 vols. Tehran: Kitābfurūshī-i Islāmīyah, 1986.

Sīstānī, Malik Shah Husayn. *Ihyā al-mulūk.* Edited by Manūchihr Sutūdah. Tehran: Bunqāh-i Tarjumah va Nashr-i Kitāb, 1965.

Smith, John M. *The History of the Sarbadār Dynsty, 1336–81, and Its Sources.* The Hague: Mouton, 1970.

Soucek, Priscilla. "Nizami on Painters and Painting." In *Islamic Art in the Metropolitan Museum of Art.* Edited by Richard Ettinghausen. New York: Metropolitan Museum of Art, 1972.

Soudavar, Abolala. "Between the Safavids and the Mughals: Art and Artists in Transition." *Iran: Journal of the British Institute of Persian Studies* 36 (1999).

Stansfield-Johnson, Rosemary. "Sunni Survival in Safavid Iran: Anti-Sunni Activities during the Reign of Tahmasb I." *Iranian Studies* 27, nos. 1–4 (1994): 123–133.

———. "The Tabarrā' and the Early Safavids." Forthcoming.

Stewart, Devin. "A Biographical Notice on Bahā' al-Dīn al-'Āmilī." *Journal of the Americal Oriental Society* 3 (1991): 563–571.

———. "The First Shaykh al-Islam of the Safavid Capital Qazvin." *Journal of the Americal Oriental Society* 3 (1996): 387–405.

Storey, Charles. *Persian Literature: A Bio-bibliographical Survey.* 2 vols. London: Luzac & Co., 1927. Reprint, 1970.

———. *Persidskaya Literatura: Bio-bibliograficheskiy Obzor.* Translated and edited by Yuri E. Bregel. 3 vols. Moscow: Central Department of Oriental Literature, 1972.

Szuppe, Maria. "La Participation des Femmes de la Famille Royale à l'Exercise du Pouvoir en Iran Safavide au XVIe Siècle." *Studia Iranica* 23 (1994) and 24 (1995): 211–258, 61–122.

Tabarī. *The History of al-Tabarī: The Ancient Kingdoms.* Translated by with annotations Moshe Perlmann. Vol. 4, SUNY Series in Near Eastern Studies. Albany: State University of New York Press, 1987.

———. *The History of al-Tabarī: The First Civil War.* Translated by with annotations G. R. Hawting. Vol. 17, SUNY Series in Near Eastern Studies. Albany: State University of New York Press, 1987.

———. *The History of al-Tabarī: The Victory of the Marwānids.* Translated by with annotations Michael Fishbein. Vol. 21, SUNY Series in Near Eastern Studies. Albany: State University of New York Press, 1990.

———. *The History of al-Tabarī: The Waning of the Umayyad Caliphate.* Translated by with annotations Carole Hillenbrand. Vol. 26, SUNY Series in Near Eastern Studies. Albany: State University of New York Press, 1987.

———. *The History of al-Tabarī: The Abbāsid Revolution.* Translated by with annotations John Alden Williams. Vol. 27, SUNY Series in Near Eastern Studies. Albany: State University of New York Press, 1985.

Tabrīzī, Muhammad Husayn b. Khalaf. *Burhān-i Qāti'.* Edited by Muhammad Mu'īn. Tehran: Ibn-i Sīnā, 1963.

Tadayyun, Mehdi. "Hadīqat al-Shī'a yā Kāshif al-Haqq?" *Ma'ārif* 2, no. 3 (1985): 453–469.

Tafrishī, Mīr Muhammad Husayn. *A Sketch of Shah Safi's Reign from 1038/1629–1041/1631–2.* Flügel I, 281 (1) Chester Beaty Collection, MS 384.

Tafrishī, Razī al-dīn. *Tārīkh-i Safaviyān.* British Library, MS Add. 6587.

Tāliqānī, 'Abd al-Muttalib b. Yahyā. *Khulāsat al-favā'id.* Mar'ashī Library, MS 4014.

Tapper, Richard. *Frontier Nomads of Iran: A Political and Social History of the Shahsevan.* Cambridge: Cambridge University Press, 1997.

Tavakoli-Targhi, Muhammad. "Contested Memories: Narrative Structures and Allegorical Meanings of Iran's Pre-Islamic History." *Iranian Studies* 29, no. 1–2 (1996): 149–175.

―――. "Refashioning Iran: Language and Culture during the Constitutional Revolution." *Iranian Studies* 23, nos. 1–4 (1990): 77–101.

Tavernier, Jean-Baptiste. *Les Six Voyages de Jean Baptise Tavernier*. 2 vols. Amsterdam: Chez Johaness van Someren, 1678.

―――. *Voyages en Perse et Description de ce Royaume*. Chartres: L'Imprimerie Durand, 1930.

Tavernier, Jean-Baptiste, John Phillips, and Edmund Everard. *Collections of Travels through Turkey into Persia, and the East-Indies*. London: George Monke and William Ewney, 1688.

Thackston, Wheeler. "The Dīvān of Khatā'ī: Pictures for the Poetry of Shah Isma'il." *Asian Art* (Fall 1988): 37–63.

al-Tihrānī, Muhammad Muhsin Āqā Buzurg. *al-dharī'a ilā tasānīf al-shī'a*. 25 vols. Tehran: 1936–1978.

Togan, Zeki Velidi. "Sur l'origine des Safavides." *Melanges Massignon III* (1959): 346–348.

Tucker, William. "Rebels and Gnostics: al-Mughīra Ibn Sa'īd and the Mughīriyya." *Arabica* 22 (1975): 33–47.

Tunukābunī, Mīrzā Muhammad. *Qisas al-'ulamā*. 2nd ed. Tehran: Intishārāt-i 'Ilmiyya Islāmiyya, 1985.

Turkmān, Iskandar Bek Munshī. *Tārīkh-i 'Ālam Ārā-yi 'Abbāsī*. 2 vols. Tehran: Amīr Kabīr, 1971.

Turkmān, Iskandar Bek Munshī, and Muhammad Yūsuf Vālī. *Zayl-i Tārīkh-i 'Ālam Ārā-yi 'Abbāsī*. Edited by Suhaylī Khwānsarī. Tehran: Kitabfurūshi-yi Islāmiyya, 1938–1939.

Turner, Victor. *Dramas, Fields, and Metaphors: Symbolic Action in Human Society*. Ithaca: Cornell University Press, 1974.

Tūsī, Abū Tāhir. *Abū Muslimnāme*. Bibliothèque Nationale de Paris. MS 860.

―――. *Abū Muslimnāme*. Bibliothèque Nationale de Paris. Ancien Fond Turc, MS 59.

―――. *Abū Muslimnāme*. Bibliothèque Nationale de Paris. Supplement Turc, MS 1011.

——. *Abū Muslimnāme.* Bibliothèque Nationale de Paris. Supplement Persan, MS 842, 842 bis, 843–844.

——. *Kissa-yi Sayyid Junayd ve Reshīd-i Arab.* Bibliothèque Nationale de Pars. Supplement Turc, MS 636.

——. *Abū Muslimnāme: Hamāsah-yi Abū Muslim-i Khurāsānī.* Edited by Iqbāl Haghmā'ī. Tehran: Intishārāt-i Gutanbirg, 1956.

Tūsī, Muhammad b. al-Hasan. *al-istibsār fī-mā ikhtalafa min al-akhbār.* Edited by Hasan al-Mūsāwī Kharsān. Najaf: Dār al-Kutūb al-Islāmīyah, 1956.

Tūsī, Nizām al-Mulk. *Siyāsatnāme.* Edited by Murtazā Mudarrisī Chahārdahī. Tehran: Tehran University, 1955.

Ustādī, Rizā. *Fihrist-i Nuskhahā-yi Khattī-yi Kitābkhānah-yi Madrasah-yi Fayziyya.* 3 vols. Qum: n.p., n.d.

Vajda, Georges. "Les zindiqs en pays d'Islam au debut de la période Abbaside." *Rivista degli Studi Orientali* 17 (1938): 173–229.

Velasco, Ismael. "Academic Irrelevance or Disciplinary Blind-spot: Middle Eastern Studies and the Baha'i Faith Today." *MESA Bulletin* 35 (Winter 2001): 188–198.

Von Grunebaum, Gustave E., and Roger Caillois. *The Dream and Human Societies.* Berkeley: University of California Press, 1966.

Walzer, Richard. "al-Biruni and Idolatry." In *Commémoration Cyrus: Actes du Congrès de Shiraz 1971.* Leiden: Brill, 1974.

Wasserstrom, Steven. *Between Muslim and Jew: The Problem of Symbiosis under Early Islam.* Princeton: Princeton University Press, 1995.

——. "The Moving Finger Writes: Mughīra b. Sa'īd's Islamic Gnosis and the Myths of Its Rejection." *History of Religions* 25 (1985): 1–29.

Widengren, Geo. "The Sacral Kingship of Iran: *La Regalita Sacra.*" *Contributions to the Central Theme of the Eighth International Congress for the History of Religions* (Rome, April 1955). Leiden: Brill, 1959.

Wilber, Donald. *Reza Shah Pahlavi: The Resurrection and Reconstruction of Iran.* New York: Exposition Press, 1975.

Windfuhr, Gernot. "The Gates of Mithra, the Nocturnal Sun, and the Dates of Zarathustra." Paper presented at the First North American

International Avesta Conference, Framingham, MA, November 1997.

———. "References to Zoroaster and Zoroastrian Time-Reckoning in Rumi's Masnavi." *Proceedings of the Third International Congress.* K. R. Cama Oriental Institute, Bombay, January 6–9, 2000.

Wood, David, ed. *On Paul Ricoeur: Narrative and Interpretation.* London: Routledge, 1991.

Woods, John E. *The Aqquyunlu: Clan, Confederation, Empire.* 2nd ed. Salt Lake City: University of Utah Press, 1999.

———. *The Aqquyunlu Clan, Confederation, Empire: A Study in 15th/9th Century Turko-Iranian Politics.* Vol. 3, Studies in Middle Eastern History. Minneapolis: Bibliotheca Islamica, 1976.

Wüstenfeld, Ferdinand, and Eduard Mahler. *Wüstenfeld-Mahler'sche Vergleichungs-Tabellen zu muslimischen und iranischen Zeitrechnung mit Tafeln zur Umrechnung orient-christlicher Ären.* Wiesbaden: Steiner, 1961.

Ya'qūb, Āzhand. *Hurūfīyah dar Tārīkh.* Tehran: Nashr-i Nay, 1990–91.

Yarshater, Ihsan. "Iranian Common Beliefs and Worldviews." In *Cambridge History of Iran.* Edited by Ihsan Yarshater. Vol. 3(1). Cambridge: Cambridge University Press, 1983.

———. "Mazdakism." In *Cambridge History of Iran.* Edited by Ihsan Yarshater. Vol. 3(2). Cambridge: Cambridge University Press, 1983.

Yazdī, Jalāl al-dīn Munajjim. *Tārīkh-i 'Abbāsī.* Tehran: Intishārāt-i Vahīd, 1987.

Yazdī, Kamāl b. Jalāl Munajjim. *Zubdat al-tavārīkh.* Royal Asiatic Society: MS Morley, 43.

Zaehner, R. C. *Zurvan: A Zoroastrian Dilemma.* Oxford: Clarendon Press, 1955.

Zāhidī, Shaykh Husayn. *Silsilat al-nasab al-Safaviyyah.* Berlin: Chāpkhānah-yi Irānshahr 1964.

Zarrīnkūb, Abd al-Husayn. *Arzish-i Mīrās-i Sūfīyyah.* Tehran: Amīr Kabīr, 1965.

———. *Bāmdād-i Islam.* Tehran: Intishārāt-i Sā'ib, 1967.

———. *Az Khūchah-yi Rindān.* Tehran: Intishārāt-i Sukhan, 1994.

———. *Dunbālah-yi Justijū dar Tasavvuf-i Iran.* Tehran: Amīr Kabīr, 1987.

———. *Justjū dar Tasavvuf-i Irān.* Tehran: Amīr Kabīr, 1978.

Zemon-Davis, Natalie. "Boundaries and the Sense of Self in Sixteenth-Century France." In *Reconstructing Individualism.* Edited by Thomas C. Heller, Morton Sosna, and David Wellbery. Palo Alto: Stanford University Press, 1986.

———. "Anthropology and History in the 1980s: The Possibilities of the Past." *Journal of Interdisciplinary History* 11 (1981): 267–276.

Index of Book Titles

545

Index of Concepts

549

Index of Names, Places, and Terms

HARVARD MIDDLE EASTERN MONOGRAPHS

1. *Syria: Development and Monetary Policy,* by Edmund Y. Asfour. 1959.

2. *The History of Modern Iran: An Interpretation,* by Joseph M. Upton. 1960.

3. *Contributions to Arabic Linguistics,* Charles A. Ferguson, Editor. 1960.

4. *Pan-Arabism and Labor,* by Willard A. Beling. 1960.

5. *The Industrialization of Iraq,* by Kathleen M. Langley. 1961.

6. *Buarij: Portrait of a Lebanese Muslim Village,* by Anne H. Fuller. 1961.

7. *Ottoman Egypt in the Eighteenth Century,* Stanford J. Shaw, Editor and Translator. 1962.

8. *Child Rearing in Lebanon,* by Edwin Terry Prothro. 1961.

9. *North Africa's French Legacy: 1954-1962,* by David C. Gordon. 1962.

10. *Communal Dialects in Baghdad,* by Haim Blanc. 1964.

11. *Ottoman Egypt in the Age of the French Revolution,* Translated with Introduction and Notes by Stanford J. Shaw. 1964.

12. *The Economy of Morocco: 1912-1962,* by Charles F. Stewart. 1964.

13. *The Economy of the Israeli Kibbutz,* by Eliyahu Kanovsky. 1966.

14. *The Syrian Social Nationalist Party: An Ideological Analysis,* by Labib Zuwiyya Yamak. 1966.

15. *The Practical Visions of Ya'qub Sanu',* by Irene L. Gendizier. 1966.